The Collected Works of J. Krishnamurti

Volume V

1948–1949

Choiceless Awareness

COLLECTED WORKS VOLUME 5

Photo: J. Krishnamurti, ca 1945

P.O Box 1560, Ojai, CA 93024

Website: www.kfa.org

Printed in the United States of America

ISBN 13: 9781934989388
ISBN: 193498938X

Contents

Preface

Jiddu Krishnamurti was born in 1895 of Brahmin parents in south India. At the age of fourteen he was proclaimed the coming World Teacher by Annie Besant, then president of the Theosophical Society, an international organization that emphasized the unity of world religions. Mrs. Besant adopted the boy and took him to England, where he was educated and prepared for his coming role. In 1911 a new worldwide organization was formed with Krishnamurti as its head, solely to prepare its members for his advent as World Teacher. In 1929, after many years of questioning himself and the destiny imposed upon him, Krishnamurti disbanded this organization, saying:

Truth is a pathless land, and you cannot approach it by any path whatsoever, by any religion, by any sect. Truth, being limitless, unconditioned, unapproachable by any path whatsoever, cannot be organized; nor should any organization be formed to lead or to coerce people along any particular path. My only concern is to set men absolutely, unconditionally free.

Until the end of his life at the age of ninety, Krishnamurti traveled the world speaking as a private person. The rejection of all spiritual and psychological authority, including his own, is a fundamental theme. A major concern is the social structure and how it conditions the individual. The emphasis in his talks and writings is on the psychological barriers that prevent clarity of perception. In the mirror of relationship, each of us can come to understand the content of his own consciousness, which is common to all humanity. We can do this, not analytically, but directly in a manner Krishnamurti describes at length. In observing this content we discover within ourselves the division of the observer and what is observed. He points out that this division, which prevents direct perception, is the root of human conflict.

His central vision did not waver after 1929, but Krishnamurti strove for the rest of his life to make his language even more simple and clear. There is a development in his exposition. From year to year he used new terms and new approaches to his subject, with different nuances.

Because his subject is all-embracing, the *Collected Works* are of compelling interest. Within his talks in any one year, Krishnamurti was not able to cover the whole range of his vision, but broad amplifications of particular themes are found throughout these volumes. In them he lays the foundations of many of the concepts he used in later years.

The *Collected Works* contain Krishnamurti's previously published talks, discussions, answers to specific questions, and writings for the years 1933 through 1967. They are an authentic record of his teachings, taken from transcripts of verbatim shorthand reports and tape recordings.

The Krishnamurti Foundation of America, a California charitable trust, has among its purposes the publication and distribution of Krishnamurti books, videocassettes, films, and tape recordings. The production of the *Collected Works* is one of these activities.

Bangalore, India, 1948

First Talk in Bangalore

Instead of making a speech, I am going to answer as many questions as possible, and before doing so, I would like to point out something with regard to answering questions. One can ask any question, but to have a right answer, the question must also be right. If it is a serious question put by a serious person, by an earnest person who is seeking out the solution of a very difficult problem, then, obviously, there will be an answer befitting that question. But what generally happens is that lots of questions are sent in, sometimes very absurd ones, and then there is a demand that all those questions be answered. It seems to me such a waste of time to ask superficial questions and expect very serious answers. I have several questions here, and I am going to try to answer them from what I think is the most serious point of view; and if I may suggest, as this is a small audience, perhaps you will interrupt me if the answer is not very clear, so that you and I can discuss the question.

Question: What can the average decent man do to put an end to our communal problem?

KRISHNAMURTI: Obviously, the sense of separatism is spreading throughout the world. Each successive war is creating more separatism, more nationalism, more sovereign governments, and so on. Especially in India this problem of communal dissension is on the increase. Why? First of all, obviously, because people are seeking jobs. The more separate governments there are, the more jobs there will be, but that is a very shortsighted policy, is it not? Because, eventually the world's tendency will be more and more towards federation, towards a coming together, and not a constant breaking up. Surely, any decent person who really thinks about this situation—which is not merely Indian, but a world affair—must first be free from nationalism, not only in matters of state, but in thought, in action, in feeling. After all, communalism is merely a branch of nationalism. Belonging to a particular country, to a particular race or group of people, or to a particular ideology tends more and more to divide people, to create antagonism and hatred between man and man. Obviously, that is not the solution to the world's chaos. So, what each one of us can do is to be non-communal; we can cease to be Brahmins, cease to belong to any caste or to any country. But that is very difficult because by tradition, by occupation, by tendency, we are conditioned to a particular pattern of action, and to break away from it is extremely hard. We may want to break away, but family tradition, religious orthodoxy, and so on, all prevent us. It is only men of goodwill who really seek goodwill, who desire to be friendly, and only such men will free themselves from all these limitations which create chaos.

So, it seems to me that to put an end to this communal contention, one must begin with oneself and not wait for somebody else, for legislation, for government, to act. Because, after all, compulsion or legislation does not solve the problem. The spirit of communalism, separatism, of belonging to a particular class or ideology, to a religion, does ultimately create conflict and antagonism between human beings. Friendliness is not brought about by compulsion, and to look to compulsion, surely, is not the answer. So the way out of this is for each one, for every individual, for you and me to break away from the communal spirit, from nationalism. Is that not the only way out of this difficulty? Because, as long as the mind and the heart are not willing to be open and friendly, mere compulsion or legislation is not going to solve this problem. So, it is obviously the responsibility of each one of us, living as we do in a particular community, in a particular nation or group of people, to break away from the narrow spirit of separatism.

The difficulty is that most of us have grievances. Most of us agree with the ideal that we should break away and create a new world, a new set of ideas, and so on, but when we go back home the compulsion of environmental influences is so strong that we fall back—and that is the greatest difficulty, is it not? Intellectually we agree about the absurdity of communal contention, but very few of us care to sit down and think out the whole issue and discover the contributory causes. Belonging to any particular group, whether of social action or of political action, does create antagonism, separatism; and real revolution is not brought about by following any particular ideology because revolution based on ideology creates antagonisms at different levels and, therefore, is a continuation of the same thing. So this communal dissension, obviously, can come to an end only when we see the whole absurdity of separate action, of a particular ideology, morality, or organized religion—whether Christianity, Hinduism, or any other organized and limited religion.

Comment: All this sounds very convincing, but in action it is very difficult, and as you say, when we go home most of us are entirely different people from what we are here. Although we may listen to you and think about what you say, the result depends on each one of us. There is always this "but."

Comment: This move to do away with organized religion may itself form an organized religion.

KRISHNAMURTI: How, sir?

Comment: For instance, neither Christ nor Ramakrishna Paramahamsa wanted an organized religion, but forgetting the very essence of the teachings, people have built around them an organized religion.

KRISHNAMURTI: Why do we do this? Is it not because we want collective security, we want to feel safe?

Comment: Are all institutions separatist in character?

KRISHNAMURTI: They are bound to be.

Comment: Is even belonging to a family wicked?

KRISHNAMURTI: You are introducing the word *wicked* which I never used.

Comment: We are repudiating our family system. Our family system is ancient.

KRISHNAMURTI: If it is misused, it must obviously be scrapped.

Comment: So an institution by itself need not be separatist?

KRISHNAMURTI: Obviously. The post office is not separatist because all communities use it. It is universal. So, why is it that individual human beings find it important to belong to something—to a religious organization, to a society, to a club, and so on? Why?

Comment: There is no life without relationship.

KRISHNAMURTI: Obviously. But why seek separatism?

Comment: There are natural relationships and unnatural relationships. A family is a natural relationship.

KRISHNAMURTI: I am just asking: Why is there the desire, the urge, to belong to an exclusive group? Let us think it out and not just make statements. Why is it that I belong to a particular caste or nation? Why do I call myself a Hindu? Why have we got this exclusive spirit?

Comment: Selfishness. The ego of power.

KRISHNAMURTI: Throwing in a word or two does not mean an answer. There is some motive power, a drive, an intention that makes us belong to a certain group of people. Why? Is it not important to find out? Why does one call oneself a German, an Englishman, a Hindu, a Russian? Is it not obvious that there is this desire to identify oneself with something because identification with something large makes one feel important? That is the fundamental reason.

Comment: Not always: a Harijan, *for instance, belongs to a very low community. He does not take pride in it.*

KRISHNAMURTI: But we keep him there. Why don't we invite him into our particular caste?

Comment: We are trying to invite him.

KRISHNAMURTI: But why is it that individuals identify themselves with the greater, with the nation, with an idea which is beyond them?

Comment: Because from the moment the individual is born, certain ideas are instilled into him. These ideas develop, and he thinks he is a slave. In other words, he is so conditioned.

KRISHNAMURTI: Exactly. He is so conditioned that he cannot break away from his serfdom. The identification with the greater exists because one wants to be secure, safe, through belonging to a particular group of thought or of action. Sirs, this is obvious, is it not? In ourselves we are nothing, we are timid, afraid to remain alone, and therefore we want to identify ourselves with the larger, and in that identification we become very exclusive. This is a world process. This is not my opinion, it is exactly what is taking place. Identification is religiously or nationalistically inflamed at moments of great crisis, and the problem is vast; it is not just in India, it is everywhere throughout the world—this sense of identification with a particular group which gradually becomes exclusive and thereby creates between people antagonism, hatred. So, that is why, when answering this question, we will have to deal with nationalism as well as communalism, in which is also involved the identification with a particular organized religion.

Comment: Why do we identify ourselves at all?

KRISHNAMURTI: For the very simple reason that if we did not identify ourselves with something, we would be confused, we would be lost, and because of that fear, we identify ourselves in order to be safe.

Comment: Fear of what? Is it not ignorance rather than fear?

KRISHNAMURTI: Call it what you like, fear or ignorance—they are all the same. So the point is really this: Can you and I be free from this fear, can we stand alone and not be exclusive? Aloneness is not exclusive; only loneliness is exclusive. Surely, that is the only way out of the problem because the individual is a world process, not a separate process, and as long as individuals identify themselves with a particular group or a particular section, they must be exclusive, thereby inevitably creating antagonism, hatred, and conflict.

Question: Man must know what God is before he can know God. How are you going to introduce the idea of God to man without bringing God to man's level?

KRISHNAMURTI: You cannot, sir. Now, what is the impetus behind the search for God, and is that search real? For most of us, it is an escape from actuality. So, we must be very clear in ourselves whether this search after God is an escape, or whether it is a search for truth in everything—truth in our relationships, truth in the value of things, truth in ideas. If we are seeking God merely because we are tired of this world and its miseries, then it is an escape. Then we create God, and therefore it is not God. The God of the temples, of the books is not God, obviously—it is a marvelous escape. But if we try to find the truth, not in one exclusive set of actions, but in all our actions, ideas, and relationships, if we seek the right evaluation of food, clothing, and shelter, then because our minds are capable of clarity and understanding, when we seek reality we shall find it. It will not then be an escape. But if we are confused with regard to the things of the world—food, clothing, shelter, relationship, and ideas—how can we find reality? We can only invent reality. So, God, truth, or reality is not to be known by a mind that is confused, conditioned, limited. How can such a mind think of reality or God? It has first to decondition itself. It has to free itself from its own limitations, and only then can it know what God is, obviously not before. Reality is the unknown, and that which is known is not the real. So, a mind that wishes to know reality has to free itself from its own conditioning, and that conditioning is imposed either externally or internally; and as long as the mind creates contention, conflict in relationship, it cannot know reality. So, if one is to know reality, the mind must be tranquil, but if the mind is compelled, disciplined to be tranquil, that tranquillity is in itself a limitation, it is merely self-hypnosis. The mind becomes free and tranquil only when it understands the values with which it is surrounded.

So, to understand that which is the highest, the supreme, the real, we must begin very low, very near; that is, we have to find the value of things, of relationship, and of ideas, with which we are occupied every day. And without understanding them, how can the mind seek reality? It can invent "reality," it can copy, it can imitate because it has read so many books, it can repeat the experience of others. But surely, that is not the real. To experience the real, the mind must cease to create because whatever it creates is still within the bondage of time. The problem is not whether there is or is not God, but how man may discover God, and if in his search he disentangles himself from everything, he will inevitably find that reality. But he must begin with the near and not with the far. Obviously, to go far one must begin near. But most of us want to speculate, which is a very convenient escape. That is why religions offer such a marvelous drug for most people. So, the task of disentangling the mind from all the values which it has created is an extremely arduous one, and because our minds are weary, or we are lazy, we prefer to read religious books and speculate about God; but that, surely, is not the discovery of reality. Realizing is experiencing, not imitating.

Question: Is the mind different from the thinker?

KRISHNAMURTI: Now, is the thinker different from his thoughts? Does the thinker exist without thoughts? Is there a thinker apart from thought? Stop thinking, and where is the thinker? Is the thinker of one thought different from the thinker of another thought? Is the thinker separate from his thought, or does thought create the thinker, who then identifies himself with thought when he finds it convenient and separates himself when it is not convenient? That is, what is the 'I', the thinker? Obviously, the thinker is composed of various thoughts which have become identified as the 'me'. So, the thoughts produce the thinker; not the other way round. If I have no thoughts, then there is no thinker, not that the thinker is different each time, but if there are no thoughts, there is no thinker. So, thoughts produce the thinker, as actions produce the actor. The actor does not produce actions.

Comment: You seem to suggest, sir, that by ceasing to think, the 'I' will be absent.

KRISHNAMURTI: The 'I' is made up of my qualities, my idiosyncracies, my passions, my possessions, my house, my money, my wife, my books. These create the idea of 'me'. I do not create them. Do you agree?

Comment: We find it difficult to agree.

KRISHNAMURTI: If all thoughts were to cease, the thinker would not be there. Therefore, the thoughts produce the thinker.

Comment: All the thoughts and environments are there, but that does not produce the thinker.

KRISHNAMURTI: How does the thinker come into being?

Comment: He is there.

KRISHNAMURTI: You take it for granted that he is there. Why do you say so?

Comment: That we do not know. You must answer that for us.

KRISHNAMURTI: I say the thinker is not there. There is only the action, the thought, and then the thinker comes in.

Comment: How does the 'I', the thinker, come into being?

KRISHNAMURTI: Now, let us go very slowly. Let us all try to approach the problem with the intention of finding the truth, then discussing it will be worthwhile. We are trying to find out how the thinker, the 'I', the 'mine', comes into being. Now, first there is perception, then contact, desire, and identification. Before that, the 'I' is not in existence.

Comment: When my mind is away, I shall not perceive at all. Unless there is first the perceiver, there is no sensation. A dead body cannot perceive though the eyes and the nerves may be there.

KRISHNAMURTI: You take it for granted that there is a superior entity and the object it sees.

Comment: It appears so.

KRISHNAMURTI: You say so. You take it for granted that there is. Why?

Comment: My experience is that without the cooperation of the 'I', there is no perception.

KRISHNAMURTI: We cannot talk of pure perception. Perception is always mixed up with the perceiver—it is a joint phenomenon. If we talk of perception, the perceiver is immediately dragged in. It is beyond our experience to speak of perceiving; we never have such an experience as perceiving. You may fall into a deep sleep when the perceiver does not perceive himself, but in deep sleep there is neither perception nor perceiver. If you know a state in which the perceiver is perceiving himself without bringing in other objects of perception, then only can you validly speak of the perceiver. As long as that state is unknown, we have no right to talk of the perceiver as apart from perception. So, the perceiver and the perception are a joint phenomenon—they are the two sides of the same medal. They are not separate, and we have no right to separate two things which are not separate. We insist on separating the perceiver from the perception when there is no valid ground for it. We know no perceiver without perception, and we know no perception without a perceiver. Therefore, the only valid conclusion is that perception and perceiver, the 'I' and the will, are two sides of the same medal, they are two aspects of the same phenomenon, which is neither perception nor perceiver; but an accurate examination of it requires close attention.

Comment: Where does that take us?

Comment: We must discover a state in which perceiver and perception do not exist apart, but are part and parcel of the same phenomenon. The act of perceiving, feeling, thinking brings in the division of perceiver and perception because that is the basic phenomenon of life. If we can follow up these fleeting moments of perceiving, of knowing, of feeling, of acting, and divorce them from perception on the one side, and the perceiver on the other. . . .

KRISHNAMURTI: Sir, this question arose out of the inquiry about the search for God. Obviously, most of us want to know the experience of reality. Surely, it can be known only when the experiencer stops experiencing because the experiencer is creating the experience. If the experiencer is creating the experience, then he will create God; therefore, it will not be God. Can the experiencer cease? That is the whole point in this question. Now, if the experiencer and the experience are a joint phenomenon, which is so obvious, then the experiencer, the actor, the thinker, has to stop thinking. Is that not obvious? So, can the thinker cease to think? Because, when he thinks, he creates, and what he creates is not the real. Therefore, to find out whether there is or there is not reality, God, or what you will, the thought process has to come to an end, which means that the thinker must cease. Whether he is produced by thoughts is irrelevant for the moment. The whole thought process, which includes the thinker, has to come to an end. It is only then that we will find reality. Now, first of all, in bringing that process to an end, how is it to be done, and who is to do it? If the thinker does it, the thinker is still the product of thought. The thinker putting an end to thought is still the continuity of thought. So, what is the thinker to do? Any exertion on his part is still the thinking process. I hope I am making myself clear.

Comment: It may even mean resistance to thinking.

KRISHNAMURTI: Resistance to thinking, putting down all thinking, is still a form of thinking; therefore, the thinker continues, and therefore he can never find the truth. So, what is one to do? This is very serious and requires sustained attention. Any effort on the part of the thinker projects the thinker on a different level. That is a fact. If the thinker, the experiencer, positively or negatively makes an effort to understand reality, he is still maintaining the thought process. So, what is he to do? All that he can do is to realize that any effort on his part, positively or negatively, is detrimental. He must see the truth of that and not merely verbally understand it. He must see that he cannot act because any action on his part maintains the actor, gives nourishment to the actor; any effort on his part, positively or negatively, gives strength to the 'I', the thinker, the experiencer. So all that he can do is not to do anything. Even to wish positively or negatively is still part of thinking. He must see the fact that any effort he makes is detrimental to the discovery of truth. That is the first requirement. If I want to understand, I must be completely free from prejudice, and I cannot be in that state when I am making an effort, negatively or positively. It is extremely hard. It requires a sense of passive awareness in which there is no effort. It is only then that reality can project itself.

Comment: Concentration upon the projected reality?

KRISHNAMURTI: Concentration is another form of exertion, which is still an act of thinking. Therefore, concentration will obviously not lead to reality.

Comment: You said that, positively or negatively, any action of the part of the thinker is a projection of the thinker.

KRISHNAMURTI: It is a fact, sir.

Comment: In other words, you distinguish between awareness and thought.

KRISHNAMURTI: I am going at it slowly. When we talk of concentration, concentration implies compulsion, exclusion, interest in something exclusive, in which choice is involved. That implies effort on the part of the thinker, which strengthens the thinker. Is that not a fact? So, we will have to go into the problem of thought. What is thought? Thought is reaction to a condition, which means thought is the response of memory, and how can memory, which is the past, create the eternal?

Comment: We do not say memory creates it because memory is a thing without awareness.

KRISHNAMURTI: It is unconscious, subconscious; it comes of its own accord, involuntarily. We are now trying to find out what we mean by thought. To understand this question, don't look into a dictionary, look at yourself, examine yourself. What do you mean by thinking? When you say you are thinking, what are you actually doing? You are reacting. You are reacting through your past memory. Now, what is memory? It is experience, the storing up of yesterday's experience, whether collective or individual. Experience of yesterday is memory. When do we remember an experience? Surely, only when it is not complete. I have an experience, and that experience is incomplete, unfinished, and it leaves a mark. That mark I call memory, and memory responds to a further challenge. This response of memory to a challenge is called thinking.

Comment: On what is the mark left?

KRISHNAMURTI: On the 'me'. After all, the 'me', the 'mine', is the residue of all memories—collective, racial, individual, and so on. That bundle of memories is the 'me', and that 'me' with its memory responds. That response is called thinking.

Comment: Why are these memories bundled together?

KRISHNAMURTI: Through identification. I put everything in a bag, consciously or unconsciously.

Comment: So, there is a bag separate from memory.

KRISHNAMURTI: Memory is the bag.

Comment: Why do the memories stick together?

KRISHNAMURTI: Because they are incomplete.

Comment: But memories are nonexistent, they are in a state of inertia unless somebody is there to remember.

KRISHNAMURTI: In other words, is the rememberer different from memory? The rememberer and the memory are two sides of a coin. Without memory, there is no rememberer, and without the rememberer, there is no memory.

Comment: Why do we insist on separating the perceiver from the perception, the rememberer from the memory? Is this not at the root of our trouble?

KRISHNAMURTI: We separate it because the rememberer, the experiencer, the thinker, becomes permanent by separation. Memories are obviously fleeting, so the rememberer, the experiencer, the mind, separates itself because it wants permanency. The mind that is making an effort, that is striving, that is choosing, that is disciplined, obviously cannot find the real because as we said, through that very effort it projects itself and sustains the thinker. Now, how to free the thinker from his thoughts? This is what we are discussing. Because, whatever he thinks must be the result of the past, and therefore he creates God, truth, out of memory, which is obviously not real. In other words, the mind is constantly moving from the known to the known. When memory functions, the mind can move only in the field of the known, and when it moves within the field of the known, it can never know the unknown. So, our problem is how to free the mind from the known. To free ourselves from the known, any effort is detrimental because effort is still of the known. So, all effort must cease. Have you ever tried to be without effort? If I understand that all effort is futile, that all effort is a further projection of the mind, of the 'I', of the thinker; if I realize the truth of that, what happens? If I see very clearly the label "poison" on a bottle, I leave it alone. There is no effort not to be attracted to it. Similarly—and in this lies the greatest difficulty—if I realize that any effort on my part is detrimental, if I see the truth of that, then I am free of effort. Any effort on our part is detrimental, but we are not sure because we want a result, we want an achievement—and that is our difficulty. Therefore, we go on striving, striving, striving. But God, truth, is not a result, a reward, an end. Surely, it must come to us, we cannot go to it. If we make an effort to go to it, we are seeking a result, an achievement. But for truth to come, a man must be passively aware. Passive awareness is a state in which there is no effort; it is to be aware without judgment, without choice, not in some ultimate sense, but in every way; it is to be aware of your actions, of your thoughts, of your relative responses without choice, without condemnation, without identifying or denying, so that the mind begins to understand every thought and every action without judgment. This evokes the question of whether there can be understanding without thought.

Comment: Surely, if you are indifferent to something.

KRISHNAMURTI: Sir, indifference is a form of judgment. A dull mind, an indifferent mind, is not aware. To see without judgment, to know exactly what is happening, is awareness. So, it is vain to seek God or truth without being aware now, in the immediate present. It is much easier to go to a temple, but that is an escape into the realm of speculation. To understand reality, we must know it directly, and reality is obviously not of time and space; it is in the present, and the present is our own thought and action.

July 4, 1948

Second Talk in Bangalore

In a talk like this it is more important, I think, to experience what is being said rather than to discuss merely on the verbal level. One is apt to remain on the verbal level without deeply experiencing what is said, and experiencing an actual fact is much more important than to discover if the ideas themselves are true or not, because ideas are never going to transform the world. Revolution is not based on mere ideas. Revolution comes only when there is a fundamental conviction, a realization that there must be an inward transformation, not merely an outward one, however significant the outward demand may be. What I would like to discuss here during these five Sunday meetings is how to bring about, not a superficial change, but a radical transformation which is so essential in a world that is rapidly disintegrating.

If we are at all observant, it should be obvious to most of us, whether we travel or remain in one place, that a fundamental change or revolution is necessary. But to perceive the full significance of such a revolution is difficult because though we think we want a change, a modification, a revolution, most of us look to a particular pattern of action, to a system either of the left or of the right, or in between. We see the confusion, the frightful mess, the misery, the starvation, the impending war; and, obviously, the thoughtful demand action. But unfortunately, we look to action according to a particular formula or theory. The left has a system, a pattern of action, and so has the right. But can there be revolution according to any particular pattern of action, according to a line laid down, or does revolution come into being from the awakened individual's interest and awareness? Surely, it is only when the individual is awake and responsible that there can be a revolution. Now, obviously, most of us want an agreed plan of action. We see the mess, not only in India and in our own lives, but throughout the world. In every corner of the world there is confusion, there is misery, there is appalling strife and suffering. There is never a moment when men can be secure because as the arts of war are developed more and more, the destruction becomes greater and greater. We know all that. That is an obvious fact which we need not go into. But is it not important to find out what our relationship is to this whole confusion, chaos, and misery? Because, after all, if we can discover our relationship to the world and understand that relationship, then perhaps we may be able to alter this confusion. So, first, we must clearly see the relationship that exists between the world and ourselves, and then perhaps, if we change our lives, there can be a fundamental and radical change in the world in which we live.

So, what is the relationship between ourselves and the world? Is the world different from us, or is each one of us the result of a total process, not separate from the world, but part of the world? That is, you and I are the result of a world process, of a total process, not of a separate, individualistic process because, after all, you are the result of the past, you are conditioned through environmental influences—political, social, economic, geographical, climatic, and so on. You are the result of a total process; therefore, you are not separate from the world. You are the world, and what you are, the world is. Therefore, the world's problem is your problem, and if you solve your problem, you solve the world's problem. So, the world is not separate from the individual. To try to solve the world's problem without solving your individual problem is futile, utterly empty, because you and I make up the world. Without you and me, there is no world. So, the world problem is your problem—it is an obvious fact. Though we would like to think that we are individualistic in our actions, separate, independent, apart, that narrow individualistic action of each human being is, after all, part of a total process which we call the world. So, to understand the world and to bring about a radical transformation in the world, we must begin with ourselves—with you and me, and not with somebody else. Mere reformation of the world has no meaning without the transformation of you who create the world. Because, after all, the world is not distant from you; it is where you live, the world of your family, of your friends, of your neighbors; and if you and I can fundamentally transform ourselves, then there is a possibility of changing the world, and not otherwise. That is why all great changes and reforms in the world have begun with a few, with individuals, with you and me. So-called mass action is merely the collective action of individuals who are convinced, and mass action has significance only when the individuals in the mass are awake; but if they are hypnotized by words, by an ideology, then mass action must lead to disaster.

So, seeing that the world is in an appalling mess, with impending wars, starvation, the disease of nationalism, with corrupt organized religious ideologies at work—recognizing all this, it is obvious that to bring about a fundamental, radical revolution, we must begin with ourselves. You may say, "I am willing to change myself, but it will take an infinite number of years if each individual is to change." But is that a fact? Let it take a number of years. If you and I are really convinced, really see the truth that revolution must begin with ourselves and not with somebody else, will it take very long to convince, to transform the world? Because you are the world, your actions will affect the world you live in, which is the world of your relationships. But the difficulty is to recognize the importance of individual transformation. We demand world transformation, the transformation of society about us, but we are blind, unwilling to transform ourselves. What is society? Surely, it is the relationship between you and me. What you are and what I am produces relationship and creates society. So, to transform society, whether it calls itself Hindu, communist, capitalist, or what you will, our relationship has to change, and relationship does not depend on legislation, on governments, on outward circumstances, but entirely upon you and me. Though we are a product of the outward environment, we obviously have the power to transform ourselves, which means seeing the importance of the truth that there can be revolution only when you and I understand ourselves, and not merely the structure which we call society. So, that is the first difficulty we have to face in all these talks. The aim is not to bring about a reformation through new legislation because legislation ever demands further legislation, but it is to see the truth that you and I, on whatever social level we may live, wherever we are, must bring about a radical, lasting revolution in ourselves. And as I said, revolution which is not static, which is lasting, revolution which is constant from moment to moment cannot come into being according to any plan, either of the left or of the right. That constant revolution which is self-sustaining can come into being only when you and I realize the importance of individual transformation; and I am going to discuss with you, I am going to talk and answer questions from that point of view during the five Sundays that follow.

Now, if you observe, you will find that in all historical revolutions there is revolt according to a pattern; and when the flame of that revolt comes to an end, there is a falling back into the old pattern, either on a higher or a lower level. Such a revolution is not revolution at all—it is only a change, which means a modified continuity. A modified continuity does not relieve suffering; change does not lead to the cessation of sorrow. What does lead to the cessation of sorrow is to see yourself individually as you are, to be aware of your own thoughts and feelings and to bring about a revolution in your thoughts and feelings. So, as I said, those of you who look to a pattern of action will, I am afraid, be liable to disappointment during these talks. Because, it is very easy to invent a pattern, but it is much more difficult to think out the issues and see the problem clearly. If we merely look for an answer to a problem, whether economic, social, or human, we shall not understand the problem because we shall be concentrated upon the answer and not upon the problem itself. We shall be studying the answer, the solution. Whereas, if we study the question, the problem itself, then we shall find that the answer, the solution, lies in the problem and not away from the problem. So, our problem is the transformation of the individual, of you and me, because the individual's problem is the world's problem, they are not separate. What you are, the world is—which is so obvious.

What is our present society? Our present society, whether Western or Eastern, is the result of man's cunning, deceit, greed, ill will, and so on. You and I have created the structure, and only you and I can destroy it and introduce a new society. But to create the new society, the new culture, you must examine and understand the structure which is disintegrating, which you and I have built together. And to understand that which you have built, you must understand the psychological process of your being. So, without self-knowledge, there can be no revolution, and a revolution is essential—not of the bloody kind, which is comparatively easy, but a revolution through self-knowledge. That is the only lasting and permanent revolution because self-knowledge is a constant movement of thought and feeling in which there is no refuge, it is a constant flow of the understanding of what you are. So, the study of oneself is far more important than the study of how to bring about a reformation in the world because if you understand yourself and thereby change yourself, there will naturally be a revolution. To look to a panacea, to a pattern of action for revolution in outward life may bring about a temporary change, but each temporary change demands further change and further bloodshed. Whereas, if we study very carefully the problem of ourselves, which is so complex, then we shall bring about a far greater revolution of a much more lasting, more valuable kind than the mere economic or social revolution.

So, I hope we see the truth and the importance of this: That, with the world in such confusion, misery, and starvation, to bring order in this chaos we must begin with ourselves. But most of us are too lazy or too dull to begin to transform ourselves. It is so much easier to leave it to others, to wait for new legislation, to speculate and compare. But our issue is to study the problem of suffering intelligently and wisely, to see its causes which lie, not in outward circumstances, but in ourselves, and to bring about a transformation.

To study any problem, there must be the intention to understand it, the intention to go into it, to unravel it, not to avoid it. If the problem is sufficiently great and immediate, the intention also is strong, but if the problem is not great, or if we do not see its urgency, the intention becomes weak. Whereas, if we are fully aware of the problem and have a clear and definite intention to study it, then we shall not look to outward authorities, to a leader, to a guru, to an organized system because the problem is ourselves, it cannot be resolved by a system, a formula, a guru, a leader, or a government. Once the intention is clear, then the understanding of oneself becomes comparatively easy. But to establish this intention is the greatest difficulty because no one can help us in understanding ourselves. Others may verbally paint the picture, but to experience a fact which is in us, to see without judgment a particular thought, action, or feeling, is much more important than verbally to listen to others or to follow a particular rule of conduct, and so on.

So, the first thing is to realize that the world's problem is the individual's problem; it is your problem and my problem, and the world's process is not separate from the individual process. They are a joint phenomenon, and therefore what you do, what you think, what you feel, is far more important than to introduce legislation or to belong to a particular party or group of people. That is the first truth to be realized, which is obvious. A revolution in the world is essential, but revolution according to a particular pattern of action is not a revolution. A revolution can take place only when you, the individual, understand yourself and therefore create a new process of action. Surely, we need a revolution because everything is going to pieces—social structures are disintegrating, there are wars and more wars. We are standing on the edge of a precipice, and obviously there must be some kind of transformation, for we cannot go on as we are. The left offers a kind of revolution, and the right proposes a modification of the left. But such revolutions are not revolutions; they do not solve the problem because the human entity is much too complex to be understood through a mere formula. And as a constant revolution is necessary, it can only begin with you, with your understanding of yourself. That is a fact, that is the truth, and you cannot avoid it from whatever angle you approach it. After seeing the truth of that, you must establish the intention to study the total process of yourself because what you are, the world is. If your mind is bureaucratic, you will create a bureaucratic world, a stupid world, a world of red tape; if you are greedy, envious, narrow, nationalistic, you will create a world in which there is nationalism, which destroys human beings, a social structure based on greed, division, property, and so on. So, what you are, the world is, and without your transformation, there can be no transformation of the world. But to study oneself demands extraordinary care, extraordinarily swift pliability, and a mind burdened with the desire for a result can never follow the swift movement of thought. So then, the first difficulty is to see the truth that the individual is responsible, that you are responsible for the whole mess, and when you see your responsibility, to establish the intention to observe and therefore to bring about a radical transformation in yourself.

Now, if the intention is there, then we can proceed, then we can begin to study ourselves. To study yourself, you must come with an unburdened mind, must you not? But once you assert that you are atma, paramatma, or whatever it is, once you seek a satisfaction of that kind, then you are already caught in a framework of thought, and therefore you are not studying your total process. You are looking at yourself through a screen of ideas, which is not study, which is not observation. If I want to know you, what do I have to do? I have to study you, have I not? I cannot condemn you because you are a Brahmin or belong to some other blinking caste. I must study you, I must watch you, I must observe your moods, your temperament, your speech, your words, your mannerisms, and so on. But if I look at you through a screen of prejudice, of conclusions, then I do not understand you; I am only studying my own conclusions, which have no significance when I am trying to understand you. Similarly, if I want to understand myself, I must discard the whole set of screens, the traditions and beliefs established by other people—it does not matter if it is Buddha, Socrates, or anybody else—because the 'you', the 'I', is an extraordinarily complex entity with a different mask, a different facet depending on time and occasion, circumstance, environmental influence, and so on. The self is not a static entity, and to know and understand oneself is far more important than to study the sayings of others or to look at oneself through the screen of others' experiences.

So, when the intention is there to study ourselves, then the screens, the assertions, the knowledge and experiences of others obviously have no value. Because, if I want to know myself, I must know what I am, and not what I should be. A hypothetical 'me' has no value. If I want to know the truth of something, I must look at it, not shut the door on it. If I am studying a motorcar, I must study it for itself, not compare a Packard with a Rolls Royce. I must study the car as the Rolls Royce, as the Packard, as the Ford. The individual is of the highest importance because he, in his relationships, creates the world. When we see the truth of that, we shall begin to study ourselves irrespective of the assertions of others, however great. Then only shall we be able to follow without condemnation or justification the whole process of every thought and feeling that exists in us, and so begin to understand it.

So, when the intention is there, I can proceed to investigate that which I am. Obviously, I am the product of environment. That is the beginning, the first fact to see. To find out if I am anything more than merely a product of environmental and climatic influences, I must first be free from those influences which exist about me and of which I am the product. I am the result of the conditions, the absurdities, the superstitions, the innumerable factors, good and bad, which form the environment about me; and to find out if I am something more, I must obviously be free of those influences, must I not? To understand something more, I must first understand *what is.* Merely to assert that I am something more has no meaning until I am free from the environmental influences of the society in which I am living. Freedom is the discovery of the true value of the things about me, not merely a denial of them. Surely, freedom comes with the discovery of truth in everything that is about me—the truth of property, the truth of things, the truth of relationship, the truth of ideas. Without discovering the truth of these things, I cannot find what one may call the abstract truth or God. Being caught in the things about me, obviously the mind cannot go further, cannot see or discover what is beyond. A man who is seeking to understand himself must understand his relationship to things, to property, to possessions, to country, to ideas, to the people immediately about him. This discovery of the truth of relationship is not a matter of repeating words, verbally throwing at others ideas about relationship. The discovery of the truth of relationship comes only through experience in relationship with property, with people, with ideas; and it is that truth which liberates, not mere effort to be free from property or from relationship. One can discover the truth of property, of relationship, of ideas only when there is the intention to find out the truth and not be influenced by prejudice, by the demands of a particular society or belief, or by preconceptions concerning God, truth, or what you will, because the name, the word, is not the thing. The word *God* is not God, it is only a word; and to go beyond the verbal level of the mind, of knowledge, one must experience directly, one must be free from those values which the mind creates and clings to. Therefore, to understand this psychological process of oneself is far more important than to understand the process of outward environmental influences. It is important to understand yourself first because in understanding yourself, you will bring about a revolution in your relationships and thereby create a new world.

I have been given several questions, and I shall answer some of them.

Question: How can we solve our present political chaos and the crisis in the world? Is there anything an individual can do to stop the impending war?

KRISHNAMURTI: War is the spectacular and bloody projection of our everyday life, is it not? War is merely an outward expression of our inward state, an enlargement of our daily action. It is more spectacular, more bloody, more destructive, but it is the collective result of our individual activities. So, you and I are responsible for war, and what can we do to stop it? Obviously, the impending war cannot be stopped by you and me because it is already in movement; it is already taking place though still chiefly on the psychological level. It has already begun in the world of ideas, though it may take a little longer for our bodies to be destroyed. As it is already in movement, it cannot be stopped—the issues are too many, too great, and are already committed. But you and I, seeing that the house is on fire, can understand the causes of that fire, can go away from it and build in a new place with different materials that are not combustible, that will not produce other wars. That is all that we can do. You and I can see what creates wars, and if we are interested in stopping wars, then we can begin to transform ourselves, who are the causes of war.

So, what causes war—religious, political, or economic? Obviously, belief, either in nationalism, in an ideology, or in a particular dogma. If we had no belief, but goodwill, love, and consideration between us, then there would be no wars. But we are fed on beliefs, ideas, and dogmas, and therefore we breed discontent. Surely, the present crisis is of an exceptional nature, and we as human beings must either pursue the path of constant conflict and continuous wars, which are the result of our everyday action, or else see the causes of war and turn our back upon them.

Obviously, what causes war is the desire for power, position, prestige, money, and also the disease called nationalism, the worship of a flag, and the disease of organized religion, the worship of a dogma. All these are the causes of war, and if you as an individual belong to any of the organized religions, if you are greedy for power, if you are envious, you are bound to produce a society which will result in destruction. So again, it depends upon you and not on the leaders, not on Stalin, Churchill, and all the rest of them. It depends upon you and me, but we do not seem to realize that. If once we really felt the responsibility of our own actions, how quickly we could bring to an end all these wars, this appalling misery! But you see, we are indifferent. We have three meals a day, we have our jobs, we have our bank accounts, big or little, and we say, "For God's sake, don't disturb us, leave us alone." The higher up we are, the more we want security, permanency, tranquillity, the more we want to be left alone, to maintain things fixed as they are; but they cannot be maintained as they are because there is nothing to maintain. Everything is disintegrating. We do not want to face these things; we do not want to face the fact that you and I are responsible for wars. You and I may talk about peace, have conferences, sit around a table and discuss, but inwardly, psychologically, we want power, position, we are motivated by greed. We intrigue, we are nationalistic, we are bound by beliefs, by dogmas, for which we are willing to die and destroy each other. Do you think such men, you and I, can have peace in the world? To have peace, we must be peaceful; to live peacefully means not to create antagonism. Peace is not an ideal. To me, an ideal is merely an escape, an avoidance of *what is,* a contradiction of *what is.* An ideal prevents direct action upon *what is*—which we will go into presently, in another talk. But to have peace, we will have to love, we will have to begin, not to live an ideal life, but to see things as they are and act upon them, transform them. As long as each one of us is seeking psychological security, the physiological security we need—food, clothing, and shelter—is destroyed. We are seeking psychological security, which does not exist; and we seek it, if we can, through power, through position, through titles, names—all of which is destroying physical security. This is an obvious fact, if you look at it.

So, to bring about peace in the world, to stop all wars, there must be a revolution in the individual, in you and me. Economic revolution without this inward revolution is meaningless, for hunger is the result of the maladjustment of economic conditions produced by our psychological states—greed, envy, ill will, and possessiveness. To put an end to sorrow, to hunger, to war, there must be a psychological revolution, and few of us are willing to face that. We will discuss peace, plan legislation, create new leagues, the United Nations, and so on and on, but we will not win peace because we will not give up our position, our authority, our monies, our properties, our stupid lives. To rely on others is utterly futile; others cannot bring us peace. No leader is going to give us peace, no government, no army, no country. What will bring peace is inward transformation which will lead to outward action. Inward transformation is not isolation, is not a withdrawal from outward action. On the contrary, there can be right action only when there is right thinking, and there is no right thinking when there is no self-knowledge. Without knowing yourself, there is no peace.

To put an end to outward war, you must begin to put an end to war in yourself. Some of you will shake your heads and say, "I agree"—and go outside and do exactly the same as you have been doing for the last ten or twenty years. Your agreement is merely verbal and has no significance, for the world's miseries and wars are not going to be stopped by your casual assent. They will be stopped only when you realize the danger, when you realize your responsibility, when you do not leave it to somebody else. If you realize the suffering, if you see the urgency of immediate action and do not postpone, then you will transform yourself; and peace will come only when you yourself are peaceful, when you yourself are at peace with your neighbor.

Question: Family is the framework of our love and greed, of our selfishness and division. What is its place in your scheme of things?

KRISHNAMURTI: Sirs, I have no scheme of things. See in what an absurd way we are thinking of life! Life is a living thing, a dynamic, active thing, and you cannot put it in a frame. It is the intellectuals who put life in a frame, who have a scheme to systematize it. So, I have no scheme, but let us look at the facts. First, there is the fact of our relationship with another, whether it is with a wife, a husband, or a child—the relationship which we call the family. Let us examine the fact of *what is*, not what we should like it to be. Anyone can have rash ideas about family life, but if we can look at, examine, understand *what is*, then perhaps we shall be able to transform it. But merely to cover up *what is* with a lovely set of words, calling it responsibility, duty, love—all that has no meaning. So, what we are going to do is to examine what we call the family. Because, sirs, to understand something, we must examine *what is*, and not cover it up with sweet-sounding phrases.

Now, what is it that you call the family? Obviously, it is a relationship of intimacy, of communion. Now, in your family, in your relationship with your wife, with your husband, is there communion? Surely, that is what we mean by relationship, do we not? Relationship means communion without fear, freedom to understand each other, to communicate directly. Obviously, relationship means that—to be in communion with another. Are you? Are you in communion with your wife? Perhaps you are physically, but that is not relationship. You and your wife live on opposite sides of a wall of isolation, do you not? You have your own pursuits, your ambitions, and she has hers. You live behind the wall and occasionally look over the top—and that you call relationship. That is a fact, is it not? You may enlarge it, soften it, introduce a new set of words to describe it, but that is the actual fact—that you and another live in isolation, and that life in isolation you call relationship.

Now, if there is real relationship between two people, which means there is communion between them, then the implications are enormous. Then there is no isolation, then there is love, and not responsibility or duty. It is the people who are isolated behind their walls that talk about duty and responsibility. But a man who loves does not talk about responsibility—he loves. Therefore he shares with another his joy, his sorrow, his money. Are our families such? Is there direct communion with your wife, with your children? Obviously not, sirs. Therefore, the family is merely an excuse to continue your name or tradition, to give you what you want, sexually or psychologically. So, the family becomes a means of self-perpetuation, of carrying on your name. That is one kind of immortality, one kind of permanency. Also, the family is used as a means of gratification. I exploit others ruthlessly in the business world, in the political or social world outside, and at home I try to be kind or generous. How absurd! Or the world is too much for me—I want peace, and I go home. I suffer in the world, and I go home and try to find comfort. So I use relationship as a means of gratification, which means I do not want to be disturbed by my relationship.

So, what is happening, sirs, is this, is it not? In our families there is isolation and not communion, and therefore there is no love. Love and sex are two different things, which we will discuss another time. We may develop in our isolation a form of selflessness, a devotion, a kindness, but it is always behind the wall because we are more concerned with ourselves than with others. If you were really in communion with your wife, with your husband, and were therefore open to your neighbor, the world would not be in this misery. That is why families in isolation become a danger to society.

So then, how to break down this isolation? To break down this isolation, we must be aware of it, we must not be detached from it or say that it does not exist. It does exist, that is an obvious fact. Be aware of the way you treat your wife, your husband, your children, be aware of the callousness, the brutality, the traditional assertions, the false education. Do you mean to say, sirs and ladies, that if you loved your wife or your husband, we would have this conflict and misery in the world? It is because you do not know how to love your wife, your husband, that you don't know how to love God. You want God as a further means of isolation, a further means of security. After all, God is the ultimate security, but such a search is not for God, it is merely a refuge, an escape. To find God you must know how to love, not God, but the human beings around you, the trees, the flowers, the birds. Then, when you know how to love them, you will really know what it is to love God. Without loving another, without knowing what it means to be completely in communion with one another, you cannot be in communion with truth. But you see, we are not thinking of love, we are not concerned with being in communion with another. We want security, either in the family, in property, or in ideas, and where the mind is seeking security, it can never know love. For love is the most dangerous thing because when we love somebody, we are vulnerable, we are open, and we do not want to be open. We do not want to be vulnerable. We want to be enclosed, we want to be more at ease within ourselves.

So again, sirs, to bring about transformation in our relationship is not a matter of legislation, of compulsion according to *shastras,* and all that. To bring about radical transformation in relationship, we must begin with ourselves. Watch yourself, how you treat your wife and children. Your wife is a woman, and that is the end of it—she is to be used as a doormat! Don't look at the ladies, look at yourselves. Sirs, I don't think you realize what a catastrophic state the world is in at the present time; otherwise, you wouldn't be so casual about all this. We are at the edge of a precipice—moral, social, and spiritual. You don't see that the house is burning and you are living in it. If you knew that the house was burning, if you knew that you were on the edge of a precipice, you would act. But unfortunately, you are at ease, you are afraid, you are comfortable, you are dull, you are weary, demanding immediate satisfaction. Therefore you let things drift, and therefore the world's catastrophe is approaching. It is not a mere threat, it is an actual fact. In Europe war is already moving—war, war, war, disintegration, insecurity. After all, what affects another affects you. You are responsible for another, and you cannot shut your eyes and say, "I am secure in Bangalore." That is obviously a very shortsighted and stupid thought.

So, the family becomes a danger where there is isolation between husband and wife, between parents and children, because then the family encourages general isolation, but when the walls of isolation are broken down in the family, then you are in communion not only with your wife and children but with your neighbor. Then the family is not enclosed, limited, it is not a refuge, an escape. So the problem is not somebody else's, but our own.

Question: How do you propose to justify your claim of being the World Teacher?

KRISHNAMURTI: I am not really interested in justifying it. The label is not what matters, sirs. The degree, the title does not matter; what matters is what you are. So, scrap the title—put it in the wastebasket, burn, destroy it, get rid of it. We live by words, we don't live by the reality of *what is*. What does it matter what I call myself or don't call myself? What matters is whether what I am saying is truth, and if it is truth, then find out the truth and live by it for yourselves.

Sirs, titles, whether spiritual titles or titles of the world, are a means of exploiting people. And we like to be exploited. Both the exploiter and the exploited enjoy the exploitation. (Laughter) You laugh, you see! And that is all you will do because you don't see that you yourself are exploited and therefore create the exploiter—whether the capitalistic exploiter or the communistic exploiter. We live by titles, words, phrases, which have no meaning; that is why we are inwardly empty, and that is why we suffer. Sirs, do examine what is being said, or what I say, and don't merely live on the verbal level, for on that level there can be no experience. You may read all the books in the world, all the sacred books and psychological books, but merely living on that level will not satisfy you, and I am afraid that is what is happening. We are empty in ourselves, and that is why we fall in with other peoples' ideas, other peoples' experiences, moods, mottos, and thereby we become stagnant; and that is what is happening throughout the world. We look to authority, to the guru, the teacher, which is all on the verbal level. To experience the truth for yourself, to understand and not follow somebody else's understanding, you must leave the verbal level. To understand the truth for yourself, you must be free of all authority, the worship of another, however great, for authority is the most pernicious poison that prevents direct experience. Without direct experience, without understanding, there can be no realization of the truth.

So, I am not introducing new ideas because ideas do not radically transform mankind. They may bring superficial revolutions, but what we are trying to do is something quite different. In all these talks and discussions, if you care to attend them, we are trying to understand what it is to look at things as they are, and in understanding things as they are, there is a transformation. To know that I am greedy without finding excuses for it or condemning it, without idealizing its opposite and saying, "I must not be greedy"—simply to know that I am greedy is already the beginning of transformation. But you see, you don't want to know what you are, but what the guru is, what the teacher is. You worship others because it gives you gratification. It is very much easier to escape by studying somebody else than to look at yourself as you are. Sirs, God or truth is within, not in illusions. But to understand that which is, is very difficult, for that which is, is not static, it is constantly changing, undergoing modifications. To understand *what is,* you need a swift mind, a mind not anchored to a belief, to a conclusion, or to a party. And to follow *what is,* you have to understand the process of authority, why you cling to authority, and not merely discard it. You cannot discard authority without understanding its whole process because then you will create a new authority to free you from the old one. So, this question has no meaning if you are merely looking at the label because I am not interested in labels. But if you care to, we can undertake a journey together to find out *what is,* and in knowing ourselves, we can create a new world, a happy world.

July 11, 1948

Third Talk in Bangalore

As there are only a few of us, instead of my making an introductory speech as I did last time before answering questions, may I suggest that we turn this into a discussion meeting? Perhaps that may be more worthwhile than my making a formal speech, and so on. So, would you mind coming in a little closer?

What subject shall we discuss which will be worthwhile and profitable? What would you suggest, sirs, as a subject to be discussed?

Question: Why are you touring around?

KRISHNAMURTI: Do you really want to discuss why I am touring around?

Question: May we discuss the purpose of life?

KRISHNAMURTI: Does that interest everybody—to discuss what is the purpose of life, reincarnation, and karma?

Comment: Yes.

KRISHNAMURTI: Then let us discuss what is the purpose of life, and perhaps later we shall introduce other subjects.

First of all, in discussing any subject of this kind, we must obviously be earnest and not academic, scholarly, or superficial because that will not lead us anywhere. So, we have to be very serious, and that means we cannot merely accept or reject, but must investigate to find out the truth of any subject. One must be attentive and not academic. One must be open to suggestion, and therefore one must have a desire to investigate and not merely accept the authority, either of the platform or of a book, of the dead past or of the present. So, in discussing what is the purpose of life, we have to find out what we mean by "life" and what we mean by "purpose"—not merely the dictionary meaning, but the significance we give to those words. Surely, life implies everyday action, everyday thought, everyday feeling, does it not? It implies the struggles, the pains, the anxieties, the deceptions, the worries, the routine of the office, of business, of bureaucracy, and so on. All that is life, is it not? By life we mean, not just one department or one layer of consciousness, but the total process of existence which is our relationship to things, to people, to ideas. That is what we mean by life—not an abstract thing.

So, if that is what we mean by life, then has life a purpose? Or is it because we do not understand the ways of life—the everyday pain, anxiety, fear, ambition, greed—because we do not understand the daily activities of existence, that we want a purpose, remote or near, far away or close? We want a purpose so that we can guide our everyday life towards an end. That is obviously what we mean by purpose. But if I understand how to live, then the very living is in itself sufficient, is it not? Do we then want a purpose? If I love you, if I love another, is that not sufficient in itself? Do I then want a purpose? Surely, we want a purpose only when we do not understand or when we want a mode of conduct with an end in view. After all, most of us are seeking a way of life, a way of conduct, and we either look to others, to the past, or we try to find a mode of behavior through our own experience. When we look to our own experience for a pattern of behavior, our experience is always conditioned, is it not? However wide the experiences one may have had, unless these experiences dissolve the past conditioning, any new experiences only further strengthen the past conditioning. That is a fact which we can discuss. And if we look to another, to the past, to a guru, to an ideal, to an example for a pattern of behavior, we are merely forcing the extraordinary vitality of life into a mold, into a particular shape, and thereby we lose the swiftness, the intensity, the richness of life.

So, we must find out very clearly what we mean by purpose, if there is a purpose. You may say there is a purpose: to reach reality, God, or what you will. But to reach that, you must know it, you must be aware of it, you must have the measure, the depth, the significance of it. Do we know reality for ourselves, or do we know it only through the authority of another? So, can you say that the purpose of life is to find reality when you do not know what reality is? Since reality is the unknown, the mind that seeks the unknown must first be free from the known, must it not? If my mind is clouded, burdened with the known, it can only measure according to its own condition, its own limitation, and therefore it can never know the unknown, can it?

So, what we are trying to discuss and find out is whether life has a purpose, and whether that purpose can be measured. It can only be measured in terms of the known, in terms of the past; and when I measure the purpose of life in terms of the known, I will measure it according to my likes and dislikes. Therefore, the purpose will be conditioned by my desires, and therefore it ceases to be the purpose. Surely, that is clear, is it not? I can understand what is the purpose of life only through the screen of my own prejudices, wants, and desires—otherwise I cannot judge, can I? So, the measure, the tape, the yardstick, is a conditioning of my mind, and according to the dictates of my conditioning, I will decide what the purpose is. But is that the purpose of life? It is created by my want, and therefore it is surely not the purpose of life. To find out the purpose of life, the mind must be free of measurement; then only can it find out—otherwise, you are merely projecting your own want. This is not mere intellection, and if you go into it deeply, you will see its significance. After all, it is according to my prejudice, to my want, to my desire, to my predilection, that I decide what the purpose of life is to be. So, my desire creates the purpose. Surely, that is not the purpose of life. Which is more important—to find out the purpose of life, or to free the mind itself from its own conditioning and then inquire? And perhaps when the mind is free from its own conditioning, that very freedom itself is the purpose. Because, after all, it is only in freedom that one can discover any truth.

So, the first requisite is freedom, and not seeking the purpose of life. Without freedom, obviously, one cannot find it; without being liberated from our own petty little wants, pursuits, ambitions, envies, and ill will—without freedom from these things, how can one possibly inquire or discover what is the purpose of life? So, is it not important, for one who is inquiring about the purpose of life, to find out first if the instrument of inquiry is capable of penetrating into the processes of life, into the psychological complexities of one's own being? Because, that is all we have, is it not?—a psychological instrument that is shaped to suit our own needs. And as the instrument is fashioned out of our own petty desires, as it is the outcome of our own experiences, worries, anxieties, and ill will, how can such an instrument find reality? Therefore, is it not important, if you are to inquire into the purpose of life, to find out first if the inquirer is capable of understanding or discovering what that purpose is? I am not turning the tables on you, but that is what is implied when we inquire about the purpose of life. When we ask that question, we have first to find out whether the questioner, the inquirer, is capable of understanding.

Now, when we discuss the purpose of life, we see that we mean by life the extraordinarily complex state of interrelationship without which there would be no life. And if we do not understand the full significance of that life, its varieties, impressions, and so on, what is the good of inquiring about the purpose of life? If I do not understand my relationship with you, my relationship with property and ideas, how can I go further? After all, sir, to find truth or God, or what you will, I must first understand my existence, I must understand the life around me and in me; otherwise, the search for reality becomes merely an escape from everyday action, and as most of us do not understand everyday action, as for most of us life is drudgery, pain, suffering, anxiety, we say, "For God's sake, tell us how to escape from it." That is what most of us want—a drug to put us to sleep so that we don't feel the aches and pains of life. Have I answered your question about the purpose of life?

Question: May one say that the purpose of life is to live rightly?

KRISHNAMURTI: It is suggested that the purpose of life is to live rightly. Sirs, I do not want to quibble, but what do we mean by a "right life"? We have the idea that to live according to a pattern laid down by Shankaracharya, Buddha, X, Y, or Z is to live rightly. Is that living rightly? Surely, that is only a conformity which the mind seeks in order to be secure, in order not to be disturbed.

Comment: There is a Chinese saying that the purpose of life is the pleasure of it, the joy of it. It is not an abstract joy, but it is the joy of living, the pleasures of sleeping, drinking, the joy of meeting people and talking to them, of coming, of going, of working. The joy of living, of everyday happenings, is the purpose of life.

KRISHNAMURTI: Surely, sirs, there is a joy. There is real happiness in understanding something, is there not? If I understand my relationship with my neighbor, my wife, with the property over which we fight, wrangle, and destroy each other—if I understand these things, surely out of that understanding there comes a joy; then life itself is a joy, a richness, and with that richness one can go further, deeper. But without that foundation, you cannot build a great structure, can you? After all, happiness comes naturally, easily, only when there is no friction either in us or about us, and friction ceases only when there is an understanding of things in their right proportion, in their right values. To find out what is right, one must first know the process, the working of one's own mind. Otherwise, if you do not know your own mind, how can you discover the right value of anything?

So, we are confused; our relationships, our ideas, our governments are really confused. It is only a foolish man who does not see the confusion. The world is in an awful mess, and the world is the projection of ourselves. What we are, the world is. We are confused, fearfully entangled in ideas, and we do not know what is true and what is false; and being confused, we say, "Please, what is the purpose of life, what is the need of all this mess, this misery?"

Now, some will naturally give you a verbal explanation of what the purpose of life is, and if you like it, you accept it and mold your life accordingly. But that does not solve the problem of confusion, does it? You have only postponed it, you have not understood *what is*. Surely, the understanding of *what is*—the confusion within me and therefore about me—is more important than to inquire how to behave rightly. If I understand what has caused this confusion, and therefore how to put an end to it, if I understand these things, there comes naturally a true, affectionate behavior. So, being confused, my problem is not to find out what is the end or purpose of life, nor how to get out of confusion, but rather how to understand the confusion because if I understand it, then I can dissolve it. To put an end to confusion requires the understanding of *what is* at any given moment, and that demands enormous attention, interest to find out *what is*, and not merely the dissipation of our energies in the pursuit of our life, of our own methods, of our actions according to a particular pattern—all of which is so much easier because it is not tackling our problems but rather escaping from them.

So, as you are confused, every man who becomes a leader, political or religious, is merely the expression of your own confusion, and because you follow the leader, he becomes the voice of confusion. He may lead you away from a particular confusion, but he will not help you to resolve the cause of confusion, and therefore you will still be confused because you create the confusion, and confusion is where you are. So, the question is not how to get out of confusion but how to understand it, and in understanding it, perhaps you will find the meaning of all these struggles, these pains, these anxieties, this constant battle within and without.

So, is it not important to find out why we are confused? Can anybody, except a very few, say that they are not confused politically, religiously, economically? Sirs, you have only to look around you. Every newspaper is shouting in confusion, reflecting the uncertainties, the pains, the anxieties, the impending wars; and the sane, thoughtful person, the earnest person who is trying to find a way out of this confusion surely has first to tackle himself. So then, our question is this, What causes confusion? Why are we confused? One of the obvious factors is that we have lost confidence in ourselves, and that is why we have so many leaders, so many gurus, so many holy books telling us what to do and what not to do. We have lost self-confidence. Obviously, there are people, the technicians, who are full of confidence because they have achieved results. For example, give a first class mechanic any machine and he will understand it. The more technique we have, the more capable we are of dealing with technical things, but surely, that is not self-confidence. We are not using the word *confidence* as it applies to technical matters. A professor, when he deals with his subject, is full of confidence—at least, when other professors are not listening—or a bureaucrat, a high official, feels confident because he has reached the top of the ladder in the technique of bureaucracy, and he can always exert his authority. Though he may be wrong, he is full of confidence—like a mechanic when you give him a motor he knows all about. But surely, we do not mean that kind of confidence, do we, because we are not technical machines. We are not mere machines ticking according to a certain rhythm, revolving at a certain speed, a certain number of revolutions per minute. We are life, not machines. We would like to make ourselves into machines because then we could deal with ourselves mechanically, repetitiously, and automatically—and that is what most of us want. Therefore, we build walls of resistance, disciplines, controls, tracks along which we run. But even having so conditioned, so placed ourselves, having become so automatic and mechanical, there is still a vitality that pursues different things and creates contradictions. Sirs, our difficulty is that we are pliable, that we are alive, not dead; and because life is so swift, so subtle, so uncertain, we do not know how to understand it, and therefore we have lost confidence. Most of us are trained technically because we have to earn our livelihood, and modern civilization demands higher and higher technique. But with that technical mind, that technical capacity, you cannot follow yourself because you are much too swift, you are more pliable, more complicated than the machine, so you are learning to have more and more confidence in the machine and are losing confidence in yourself and are therefore multiplying leaders. So, as I said, one of the causes of confusion is this lack of confidence in ourselves. The more imitative we are, the less confidence we have, and we have made life into a copy book. From early childhood up, we are told what to do—we must do this, we must not do that. So what do you expect? And must you not have confidence in order to find out? Must you not have that extraordinary inward certainty to know what truth is when you meet it?

So, having made life into a technical process, conforming to a particular pattern of action, which is merely technique, naturally we have lost confidence in ourselves, and therefore we are increasing our inward struggle, our inward pain and confusion. Confusion can be dissolved only through self-confidence, and this confidence cannot be gained through another. You have to undertake, for yourself and by yourself, the journey of discovery into the process of yourself in order to understand it. This does not mean you are withdrawn, aloof. On the contrary, sirs, confidence comes the moment you understand, not what others say, but your own thoughts and feelings, what is happening in yourself and around you. Without that confidence which come from knowing your own thoughts, feelings, and experiences—their truth, their falseness, their significance, their absurdity—without knowing that, how can you clear up the whole field of confusion which is yourself?

Comment: Confusion can be dispelled by being aware.

KRISHNAMURTI: You are saying, sir, that by being aware, by being conscious of the confusion, that confusion can be dissipated. Is that it?

Comment: Yes, sir.

KRISHNAMURTI: For the moment we are not discussing how to dissipate confusion. Having lost self-confidence, our problem is how to get it back—if we ever had it at all. Because, obviously, without that element of confidence we shall be led astray by every person we come across—and that is exactly what is happening. What is right purpose politically, and how are you to know it? Should you not know it? Should you not know what is true in it? Similarly, must you not know what is true in the babble of tongues of religion? And how are you going to find out what is true among all the innumerable sayings—Christian, Hindu, Muslim, and so on? In this frightful confusion, how are you going to find out? To find out, you must obviously be in a great strait, you must be burning to know what you are in yourself. Are you in such a position? Are you burning to find out the truth of anything, whether of communism, fascism, or capitalism? To find out what is true in the various political actions, in the religious assertions and experiences which you so easily accept—to find out the truth of all these things, must you not be burning with the desire to know the truth? Therefore, never accept any authority. Sir, after all, acceptance of authority indicates that the mind wants comfort security. A mind that seeks security, either with a guru or in a party, political or any other, a mind that is seeking safety, comfort can never find truth, even in the smallest things of our existence. So, a man who wants this creative self-confidence must obviously be burning with the desire to know the truth of everything, not about empires or the atomic bomb, which is merely a technical matter, but in our human relationships, our relationship with others, and our relationship to property and to ideas. If I want to know the truth, I begin to inquire, and before I can know the truth of anything, I must have confidence. To have confidence, I must inquire into myself and remove those causes that prevent each experience from giving its full significance.

Question: Our minds are limited. What is the way out of this impasse?

KRISHNAMURTI: Now wait a minute. Before we inquire how to free the mind from its own conditioning, which creates confusion, let us try to find out how to discover the truth of anything—not of technical things, but the truth of ourselves in relation to something, even in relation to the atomic bomb. You understand the problem, sir? We are not self-confident, there is no confidence in us, that creative thing which gives sustenance, life, vitality, understanding. We have lost it, or we have never had it, and because we do not know how to judge anything, we have been led here and pushed there, beaten up driven,—politically, religiously, and socially. We don't know, but it is difficult to say we don't know. Most of us think we do, but actually we know very little except in technical matters—how to run a government, a machine, or how to kick the servant or wife or children, or whatever it is. But we do not know ourselves, we have lost that capacity. I am using the word *lost,* but that is probably the wrong word because we have never had it. Since we do not know ourselves and yet we want to find out what truth is, how are we going to find it? Do you understand the question, sir? I am afraid not.

Someone wanted to discuss reincarnation. Now, I want to know the truth of reincarnation, not what the Bhagavad-Gita, Christ, or my pet guru has said. I want to know the truth of that matter. Therefore, what am I to do to know the truth of it? What is the first requirement? I must not be eager to accept it, must I? I must not be persuaded by the clever arguments or by the personality of another, which means I am not easily satisfied by the reassuring comfort which reincarnation gives. Must I not be in that position? That is, I am not seeking comfort; I am trying to find out what is true. Are you in that position? Surely, when you are seeking comfort, you can be persuaded by anyone, and therefore you lose self-confidence; but when you do not seek comfort but want to know the truth, when you are completely free from the desire to take refuge, then you will experience truth, and that experience will give you confidence. So, that is the first requirement, is it not? To know the truth of anything psychologically, you cannot seek comfort because the moment you want comfort, security, a haven in which you are protected, you will have what you want, but what you have will not be the truth. Therefore, you will be persuaded by another who offers a greater comfort, a greater security, a better refuge, and so you are driven from port to port, and that is why you have lost confidence. You have no confidence because you have been driven from one refuge to another by your own desire to be comfortable, to be secure. So, a man who would seek the truth in relationship must be free of the destructive and limiting desire to be comfortable, to be secure. This fear of losing oneself psychologically must go. Only then can you find the truth of reincarnation or of anything else—because you are seeking truth and not security. Then truth will reveal to you what is right, and therefore you will have confidence. Sir, is it not more important to find out the truth than to believe that there is or is not continuity? That is the question, is it not? If I want to know the truth, I am in a position not to be easily persuaded.

Comment: When we asked the question about reincarnation, we wanted to be reassured that there is reincarnation, we did not want to know about truth and all that.

KRISHNAMURTI: Of course, you want to know if there is reincarnation, if reincarnation is a fact, but you don't want to know the truth of it; and I want to know the truth of reincarnation, not the fact. It may or may not be a fact. I do not know if the distinction is clear.

Comment: It is not clear.

KRISHNAMURTI: All right, sir, let us discuss it.

Comment: When we ask the question about reincarnation, it is in order to be assured that there is reincarnation. In other words, we put the question in a state of anxiety that there should be reincarnation, and being anxious, we listen with a biased mind. We do not want to find out the real truth of it; we only want to be assured that there is such a thing as reincarnation.

Comment: Do you want to know whether there is such a thing as reincarnation, or do you want to know the truth? Are you anxious that there should be reincarnation, or are you seeking to find out the truth, whatever it is?

Comment: Both.

Comment: You cannot do both. Either you want to know the truth about reincarnation, or you want to be assured that there is reincarnation. Which is the case?

KRISHNAMURTI: Let us be very clear on this point. If I am anxious to know whether there is reincarnation or not, what is the motive behind that question?

Comment: The motive is quite clear, I think.

KRISHNAMURTI: What is it, sir?

Comment: The motive is that life begins at a certain stage and ends at a certain stage.

KRISHNAMURTI: Which means what?

Comment: It means that the purpose is understood and the goal is reached or not reached.

Comment: When you say that life is limited, are you anxious?

Comment: I did not say that life is limited.

Comment: You said it begins at a certain point and ends at a certain point.

Comment: I mean by that, birth and death.

Comment: Life is spanned by birth and death. It is limited.

Comment: Yes.

Comment: When you ask whether there is reincarnation, are you in a state of mind which desires it?

Comment: I am in a state of inquiry.

Comment: Are you a believer?

Comment: An inquirer, a seeker.

KRISHNAMURTI: If I seek, what is the state of my mind? What is making me seek?

Comment: I do not understand, sir.

KRISHNAMURTI: What is making me seek?

Comment: We desire to know the truth.

KRISHNAMURTI: Therefore, you are not anxious.

Comment: There is no motive, only anxiety.

KRISHNAMURTI: So you are saying you are anxious?

Comment: Everybody is.

KRISHNAMURTI: Therefore you are not seeking truth. You are not passive.

Comment: I seek out the anxiety to know the truth.

KRISHNAMURTI: Yes, sir?

Comment: What are you anxious about?

Comment: I am not anxious about anything. I am viewing it merely from an academic point of view.

KRISHNAMURTI: Either we are discussing merely academically, superficially, or we are discussing very seriously.

Comment: Certainly.

KRISHNAMURTI: I am not saying you are superficial, but surely, we must know if we are merely discussing out of curiosity. If we are, it will lead us in one direction, and if we are discussing to find out the truth, then it will lead us in another direction. Which is it? As I said right from the beginning this evening, if we are merely discussing as a club for intellectual amusement, then I am afraid I shall not partake in it because that is not my intention, but if we are seeking to find out the truth of anything, that is, the truth of our relationship, then let us discuss.

Now, if I ask about reincarnation because I am anxious, surely that anxiety comes into being because I am afraid of death, of coming to an end, of not fulfilling myself, of not seeing my friends, of not finishing my book, and all the rest of it. That is, my inquiry is based on fear; therefore, fear will dictate the answer, fear will determine what truth shall be. But if I am not afraid and am seeking the truth of *what is,* then reincarnation has a different meaning. So, inwardly, psychologically, we must be very clear what it is that we are seeking. Are we seeking the truth about reincarnation, or are we seeking reincarnation out of anxiety?

Comment: I do not think there is much difference between the two. I am seeking.

Comment: I think he used the word anxiety *to mean* earnestness.

Comment: It is obvious that if you are seeking truth out of anxiety, you are prejudiced in favor of a certain answer which will relieve you of that anxiety, and therefore you cannot find the truth.

Comment: I can honestly tell you that I am neither in favor of this nor of that. I want to know the truth. The question arose in me when we were discussing the subject.

Comment: Why did it arise?

Comment: I cannot explain. That is for you to explain.

Comment: People usually ask questions about reincarnation in order to be assured that there is such a thing as reincarnation.

Comment: Not all.

Comment: It is very rare that somebody asks about reincarnation just to know the truth.

Comment: You can naturally understand that I am very much interested in the subject.

KRISHNAMURTI: All right. I am not answering your question for the moment. We are discussing it generally. Does our approach lie through anxiety, through fear, or, without being afraid, do we want to know? Because, the results of our inquiry will be different in each case. As has been pointed out by one of you, either I am anxious to know, and therefore my anxiety is going to color *what is,* or, I want to know without fear, I want to know the truth about continuity, independent of my likes and dislikes, fears and anxieties. I want to know *what is.* Now, most of us are a mixture of both, are we not? When my son dies, I am anxious, I am burning with pain, with loneliness, and I want to know. Then my inquiries are based on anxiety. But sitting and discussing in this hall and casually saying, "Well, I would like to know," when there is no crisis—can such a mind know? Surely, you can find truth only in a crisis and not away from the crisis. It is then that you will have to inquire, not when you casually say, "Let us discuss whether there is truth or not." Is that not so? When my son dies, I want to know, not whether he lives, but the truth about continuity, which means that I am willing to understand the subject. Does it not imply that? I have lost my son, and I want to know what makes me suffer and if there is an end to suffering. So, it is in that moment of crisis alone, when there is pressure, that I will find the truth, if I want to know the truth. But in the moment of crisis, in the moment of pressure, we want comfort, we want alleviation, we want to put our head on somebody's lap; in moments of anxiety we want to be lulled to sleep. And I say, on the contrary, the moment of anxiety is the right moment to inquire and to find the truth. When I want comfort in the moment of crisis, I am not inquiring. Therefore, I must know the state of my own being, of my psychological or spiritual being, I must know the state I am in before I can inquire and find out what truth is.

Sir, most of us are in a crisis—about the war, about a job, about our wives running away with somebody. We have crises about us and in us all the time, whether we admit it or not, and is that not the moment to inquire, rather than to wait until the ultimate moment when the bomb is thrown? Because, though we may deny it, we are in a crisis from moment to moment, politically, psychologically, economically. There is intense pressure all the time, and is this not the moment to find out? Are we not in this moment? If you say, "I have no crisis, I am only sitting back and looking at life," that is merely avoiding the issue, isn't it? Is any one of us in that position? Surely, that is not true of any person. We have crises one after another, but we have become dull, secure, indifferent; and our difficulty is, is it not, that we do not know how to meet crises? Are we to meet them with anxiety, or to inquire and so find the truth of the matter? Most of us meet a crisis with anxiety; growing weary, we say, "Will you please solve this problem?" When we talk, we are looking for an answer and not for the understanding of the problem. Similarly, in discussing the question of reincarnation, the problem of whether there is or is not continuity, what we mean by continuity, what we mean by death—to understand such a problem, the problem of continuity or no continuity, we must not seek an answer away from the problem. We must understand the problem itself—which we will discuss at another meeting because our time is nearly up.

My point is that there must be self-confidence—and I have sufficiently explained what I mean by self-confidence. It is not the confidence that you have through technical capacity, technical knowledge, technical training. The confidence that comes with self-knowledge is entirely different from the confidence of aggressiveness and of technical skill, and that confidence born of self-knowledge is essential to clear up the confusion in which we live. Obviously, you cannot have this self-knowledge given to you by another because what is given to you by another is mere technique. That creative confidence in which there is the joy of discovering, the bliss of understanding, can come only when I understand myself, the whole total process of myself, and to understand oneself is not such a very complex business, one can begin at any level of consciousness. But, as I said last Sunday, to have that confidence there must be the intention to know oneself. Then I am not easily persuaded—I want to know everything about myself, and so I am open to all the intimations concerning me, whether they come from another or from within myself. I am open to the conscious and the unconscious within me, open to every thought and feeling that is constantly moving, urging, arising and fading away in myself. Surely, that is the way to have this confidence—to know oneself completely, whatever one is, and not pursue an ideal of what one should be or assume that one is this or that, which is really absurd. It is absurd because then you are merely accepting a preconceived idea, whether your own or another's, of what you are or would like to be. But to understand yourself as you are, you must be voluntarily open, spontaneously vulnerable to all the intimations of yourself; and as you begin to understand the flow, the movement, the swiftness of your own mind, you will see that confidence comes from the understanding. It is not the aggressive, brutal, assertive confidence, but the confidence of knowing what is taking place in oneself. Surely, without that confidence, you cannot dispel confusion, and without dispelling the confusion within you and about you, how can you possibly find the truth of any relationship?

So, to find out what is true, or what is the purpose of life, or to discover the truth of reincarnation or of any human problem, the inquirer who is demanding truth, who wants to know truth, must be very clear as regards his intentions. If his intentions are to seek security, comfort, then obviously he does not want truth because truth may be one of the most devastating, discomforting things. The man who is seeking comfort does not want truth; he only wants security, safety, a refuge in which he will not be disturbed. But a man who is seeking truth must invite disturbances, tribulations because it is only in moments of crisis that there is alertness, watchfulness, action. Then only that *which is* is discovered and understood.

July 18, 1948

Fourth Talk in Bangalore

As I was saying the last time we met, the problems of the world are so colossal, so very complex, that to understand and so to resolve them, one must approach them in a very simple and direct manner; and simplicity, directness, do not depend on outward circumstances nor on our particular prejudices and moods. As I was pointing out, the solution is not to be found through conferences, blueprints, or through the substitution of new leaders for old, and so on. The solution obviously lies in the creator of the problem, in the creator of the mischief, of the hate, and of the enormous misunderstanding that exists between human beings. The creator of this mischief, the creator of these problems, is the individual, you and I, not the world as we think of it. The world is your relationship with another. The world is not something separate from you and me; the world, society, is the relationship that we establish or seek to establish between each other.

So, you and I are the problem, and not the world, because the world is the projection of ourselves, and to understand the world, we must understand ourselves. The world is not separate from us; we are the world, and our problems are the world's problems. This cannot be repeated too often because we are so sluggish in our mentality that we think the world's problems are not our business, that they have to be resolved by the United Nations, or by substituting new leaders for the old. It is a very dull mentality that thinks that way because we are responsible for this frightful misery and confusion in the world, this impending war. To transform the world, we must begin with ourselves, and as I said, what is important in beginning with ourselves is the intention. The intention must be to understand ourselves and not to leave it to others to transform themselves or to bring about a modified change through revolution, either of the left or of the right. So, it is important to understand that this is our responsibility, yours and mine, because however small may be the world we live in, if we can transform ourselves, bring about a radically different point of view in our daily existence, then perhaps we shall affect the world at large, the extended relationship with others.

So, as I said, we are going to discuss and find out the process of understanding ourselves, which is not an isolating process. It is not withdrawal from the world because you cannot live in isolation. To be is to be related, and there is no such thing as living in isolation. It is the lack of right relationship that brings about conflicts, misery, and strife; and however small our world may be, if we can transform our relationship in that narrow world, it will be like a wave extending outward all the time. I think it is important to see that point—that the world is our relationship, however narrow—and if we can bring a transformation there, not a superficial but a radical transformation, then we shall begin actively to transform the world. Real revolution is not according to any particular pattern, either of the left or the right, but it is a revolution of values, a revolution from sensate values to the values that are not sensate or created by environmental influences. To find these true values which will bring about a radical revolution, a transformation or a regeneration, it is essential to understand oneself. Self-knowledge is the beginning of wisdom and therefore the beginning of transformation or regeneration. To understand oneself, there must be the intention to understand—and that is where our difficulty comes in. Because, although most of us are discontented, we desire to bring about a sudden change; our discontent is canalized merely to achieve a certain result; being discontented, we either seek a different job or merely succumb to environment. So, discontent, instead of setting us aflame, causing us to question life—the whole process of existence is canalized, and thereby we become mediocre, losing that drive, that intensity to find out the whole significance of existence. Therefore, it is important to discover these things for ourselves because self-knowledge cannot be given to us by another, it is not to be found through any book. We must discover, and to discover there must be the intention, the search, the inquiry. As long as that intention to find out, to inquire deeply, is weak or does not exist, mere assertion or a casual wish to find out about oneself is of very little significance.

So, the transformation of the world is brought about by the transformation of oneself because the self is the product and a part of the total process of human existence. To transform oneself, self-knowledge is essential because without knowing what you are, there is no basis for right thought, and without knowing yourself, there cannot be transformation. One must know oneself as one is, not as one wishes to be, which is merely an ideal and therefore fictitious, unreal; and it is only that which is that can be transformed, not that which you wish to be. So, to know oneself as one is requires an extraordinary alertness of mind because *what is* is constantly undergoing transformation, change, and to follow it swiftly, the mind must not be tethered to any particular dogma or belief, to any particular pattern of action. If you would follow anything, it is no good being tethered. So, to know yourself, there must be the awareness, the alertness of mind in which there is freedom from all beliefs, from all idealization because beliefs and ideals only give you a color, perverting true perception. If you want to know what you are, you cannot imagine or have belief in something which you are not. If I am greedy, envious, violent, merely having an ideal of nonviolence, of nongreed is of little value. But to know that one is greedy or violent, to know and understand it requires an extraordinary perception, does it not? It demands honesty, clarity of thought. Whereas, to pursue an ideal away from *what is* is an escape; it prevents you from discovering and acting directly upon what you are.

So, the understanding of what you are, whatever it be—ugly or beautiful, wicked or mischievous—the understanding of what you are without distortion is the beginning of virtue. Virtue is essential, for it gives freedom. It is only in virtue that you can discover, that you can live—not in the cultivation of a virtue, which merely brings about respectability, and not understanding and freedom. There is a difference between being virtuous and becoming virtuous. Being virtuous comes through the understanding of *what is,* whereas becoming virtuous is postponement, the covering up of *what is* with what you would like to be. Therefore, in becoming virtuous you are avoiding action directly upon *what is.* This process of avoiding *what is* through the cultivation of the ideal is considered virtuous, but if you look at it closely and directly, you will see that it is nothing of the kind. It is merely a postponement of coming face to face with *what is.* Virtue is not the becoming of what is not; virtue is the understanding of *what is* and therefore the freedom from *what is.* And virtue is essential in a society that is rapidly disintegrating. In order to create a new world, a new structure away from the old, there must be freedom to discover; and to be free, there must be virtue, for without virtue there is no freedom. Can the immoral man who is striving to become virtuous ever know virtue? The man who is not moral can never be free, and therefore he can never find out what reality is. Reality can be found only in understanding *what is,* and to understand *what is, there must be freedom, freedom from the fear of what is.*

Is virtue, then, a matter of time? The understanding of *what is,* which is virtue, for it gives freedom, immediate release—is this a matter of time? Are you kind, generous, affectionate through the process of time? That is, will you be kind day after tomorrow? Can kindness be thought of in terms of time? After all, affection, mercy, generosity, are necessities of life, they are the only solvent for all our problems. Goodwill is essential, and we have not got it, have we? Neither the politicians nor the leaders nor the followers have real goodwill, which is not an ideal; and without goodwill, without that extraordinary mellowness of being which gives affection, our problems cannot be solved by mere conferences. So, you, like the politicians and the vast majority of human beings the world over are not kind; you have not got that goodwill which is the only solution, and since you have not got it, is it a mere question of time? Will you have goodwill tomorrow or ten years hence? Is it not fallacious reasoning to think in terms of time, of becoming kind in the future? If you are not kind now, you will never be kind. You may think that by slow practice, discipline, and all the rest of it, you will be kind tomorrow or ten years later, but in the meantime, you are being unkind. And kindness, goodwill, affection is the only solvent for the immediate problems of existence; it is the only remedy that will destroy the poison of nationalism, of communalism, the only cement that can bring us together.

Now, if kindness, mercy, is not a matter of time, then why is it that you and I are not kind immediately, directly? Why is it that we are not kind now? If we can understand why we are not kind, understanding being immediate, we shall be kind immediately; then we shall forget what our caste is, we shall forget our communal, religious, and nationalistic differences and be immediately generous, kind. Therefore, we must understand why we are not kind and not patiently practice goodness or meditate on generosity—which is all absurd. But if I know why I am unkind and I want to be kind, then, because my intention is to be kind, I will be. So again, the intention matters enormously, but the intention is futile if I do not know the cause of unkindness. Therefore, I must know the whole process of my thinking, the whole process of my attitude towards life. So, the study of oneself becomes tremendously important, but self-knowledge is not an end. One must study oneself more and more, but not with an object in view, to achieve a result, because if we seek an object, a result, we put an end to inquiry, to discovery, to freedom. Self-knowledge is the understanding of the process of oneself, the process of the mind; it is to be aware of all the intricacies of the passions and their pursuits, and as one knows oneself more and more deeply and widely, extensively and profoundly, there comes a freedom, a liberation from the entanglements of fear—the fear which brings about beliefs, dogmas, nationalism, castes, and all the hideous inventions of the mind to keep itself isolated in fear. And when there is freedom, there is the discovery of that which is eternal. Without that freedom, merely asking what is the eternal or reading books about the eternal has no value at all. It is like children playing with toys. Eternity, reality, God, or what you will can be discovered only by you. It comes into being only when the mind is free, untrammeled by beliefs, untrammeled by prejudice, not caught in the net of passion, ill will, and worldliness. But a mind that is entangled in nationalism or in beliefs and rituals is caught in its own desires, ambitions, and pursuits, and obviously such a mind cannot possibly understand. It is not prepared to receive.

Only the discovery of truth will bring happiness, and to discover there must be the understanding of oneself. To understand oneself, there must be the intention to understand, and with the intention comes an inquiring mind—a mind that is alertly aware without condemnation, without identification or justification, and such awareness brings an immediate release from the problem. Therefore, our whole search is not for the answer to a problem, but for the understanding of the problem itself. And the problem is not outside you—it is you, the problem is you. To understand the problem, to understand the creator of the problem, which is yourself, you have to discover yourself spontaneously from day to day as you are because it is only at the moment when your responses arise that you can understand them. But if you discipline your responses to a particular pattern, either of the left or of the right, or if you follow a particular rule of conduct, then you cannot discover your own responses. Experiment with it, and you will find that you discover your responses by being aware of each response as it arises, seeing it without condemnation or justification and pursuing the whole implication of that response. Freedom is in release from the response, not in disciplining that response.

So, our whole inquiry into the purpose of existence, our question as to whether there is reality or not has very little meaning if there is no understanding of the mind, which is yourself. The problem, which is so vast, so complex, so immediate, lies in you, and no one can solve it except yourself; no guru can solve it, no teacher, no savior, no organized compulsion. The outward organization can always be overthrown because the inner is much stronger than the outward structure of man's existence. Without understanding the inner, merely to change the pattern of the outer has very little meaning. To bring about a lasting reorganization in outer things, each one of us must begin with himself, and when there is that inner transformation, the outer can then be transformed with intelligence, with compassion, and with care.

There are several questions, and I will try to answer as many of them as possible this afternoon.

Question: Do you have a special message for youth?

KRISHNAMURTI: Sirs, is there a very great difference between the young and the old? Youth, the young people, if they are at all alive, are full of revolutionary ideas, full of discontent, are they not? They must be; otherwise, they are already old. Please, this is very serious, so don't agree or disagree. We are discussing life—I am not making a speech from the platform to please you or to please myself.

As I was saying, if the young have not that revolutionary discontent, they are already old, and the old are those who were once discontented but have settled back. They want security, they want permanency, either in their jobs or in their souls. They want certainty in ideas, in relationship, or in property. If in you, who are young, there is a spirit of inquiry which makes you want the truth of anything, of any political action whether of the left or of the right, and if you are not bound by tradition, then you will be the regenerators of the world, the creators of a new civilization, a new culture. But, like the rest of us, like the past generation, young people also want security, certainty. They want jobs, they want food, clothing, and shelter; they don't want to disagree with their parents because it means going against society. Therefore, they fall in line, they accept the authority of older people. So, what happens? The discontent which is the very flame of inquiry, of search, of understanding—that discontent is made mediocre, it becomes merely a desire for a better job, or a rich marriage, or a degree. So, their discontent is destroyed, it merely becomes the desire for more security. Surely, what is essential for the old and for the young is to live fully, completely. But you see, there are very few people in the world who want to live completely. To live fully and completely, there must be freedom, not an acceptance of authority, and there can be freedom only when there is virtue. Virtue is not imitation; virtue is creative living. That is, creativeness comes through the freedom which virtue brings, and virtue is not to be cultivated, it does not come through practice or at the end of your life. Either you are virtuous and free now, or you are not. And to find out why you are not free, you must have discontent, you must have the intention, the drive, the energy to inquire, but you dissipate that energy sexually or through shouting political slogans, waving flags, or merely imitating, passing examinations for a better job.

So, the world is in such misery because there is not that creativeness. To live creatively there cannot be mere imitation, following either Marx, the Bible, or the Bhagavad-Gita. Creativeness comes through freedom, and there can be freedom only when there is virtue, and virtue is not the result of the process of time. Virtue comes when you begin to understand *what is* in your everyday existence. Therefore, to me the division between the old and the young is rather absurd. Sirs, maturity is not a matter of age. Although most of us are older, we are infantile, we are afraid of what society thinks, we are afraid of the past. Those who are old seek permanency, comforting assurances, and the young also want security. So, there is no essential difference between the old and the young. As I said, maturity does not lie in age. Maturity comes with understanding, and there is no understanding as long as we escape from conflict, from suffering; and we escape from suffering when we seek comfort, when we seek an ideal. But it is when we are young that we can really, ardently, purposefully inquire. As we grow older, life is too much for us, and we become more and more dull. We waste our energies so uselessly. To conserve that energy for purposes of inquiry, to discover reality, requires a great deal of education—not mere conformity to a pattern, which is not education. Merely passing examinations is not education. A fool can pass examinations, it only requires a certain type of mind. But to inquire deeply and find out what life is, to understand the whole basis of existence requires a very alert and keen mind, a mind that is pliable. But the mind is made unpliable when it is forced to conform, and the whole structure of our society is based on compulsion. However subtle compulsion may be, through compulsion there cannot be understanding.

Question: Is your self-confidence born of your own release from fear or does it arise from the conviction that you are solidly backed by great beings like the Buddha and the Christ?

KRISHNAMURTI: Sirs, first of all, how does confidence come into being? Confidence is of two types. There is the confidence that comes through the acquisition of technical knowledge. A mechanic, an engineer, a physicist, a man who masters the violin has confidence because he has studied or practiced for a number of years and has acquired a technique. That gives one type of confidence—a confidence which is merely superficial, technical. But there is another type of confidence which comes from self-knowledge, from knowing oneself entirely, both the conscious and the unconscious, the hidden mind as well as the open. I say it is possible to know yourself completely, and then there comes a confidence which is not aggressive, not self-assertive, not shrewd, not that confidence which comes from achievement; but it is the confidence of seeing things as they are from moment to moment without distortion. Such confidence comes into being naturally when thought is not based on personal achievement, personal aggrandizement, or personal salvation, and when each thing reveals its true significance. Then you are backed by wisdom, whether it is of the Buddha or of the Christ. That wisdom, that confidence, that extraordinarily swift pliability of mind is not for the exclusive few. There is no hierarchy of understanding. When you understand a problem of relationship, whether with physical objects, with ideas, or with your neighbor, that understanding frees you from all sense of time, of position, of authority. Therefore, there is not the Master and the pupil, the guru sitting on a platform and you sitting down below. Sirs, such confidence is love, affection; and when you love somebody, there is no difference, there is neither high nor low. When there is love, this extraordinary flame, then that itself is its own eternity.

Question: Can we come to the real through beauty, or is beauty sterile as far as truth is concerned?

KRISHNAMURTI: Now, what do we mean by beauty and what do we mean by truth? Surely, beauty is not an ornament; mere decoration of the body is not beauty. We all want to be beautiful, we all want to be presentable—but that is not what we mean by beauty. To be neat, to be tidy, to be clean, courteous, considerate, and so on, is part of beauty, is it not? But these are merely expressions of the inward release from ugliness. Now, what is happening in the world? Every day, more and more, we are decorating the outer. The cinema stars, and you who copy them, are keeping beautiful outwardly, but if you have nothing inside, the outward decoration, the ornamentation, is not beauty. Sirs, don't you know that inward state of being, that inward tranquillity in which there is love, kindliness, generosity, mercy? That state of being, obviously, is the very essence of beauty, and without that, merely to decorate oneself is to emphasize the sensate values, the values of the senses; and to cultivate the values of the senses, as we are doing now, must inevitably lead to conflict, to war, to destruction.

The decoration of the outer is the very nature of our present civilization, which is based on industrialization. Not that I am against industrialization—it would be absurd to destroy industries. But merely to cultivate the outer without understanding the inner must inevitably create those values which lead men to destroy each other, and that is exactly what is taking place in the world. Beauty is regarded as an ornament to be bought and sold, to be painted, and so on. Surely, that is not beauty. Beauty is a state of being, and that state of being comes with inward richness—not the inward accumulation of riches which we call virtue, ideals. That is not beauty. Richness, inward beauty with its own imperishable treasures comes into being when the mind is free, and the mind can be free only when there is no fear. The understanding of fear comes through self-knowledge, not through resistance to fear. If you resist fear, that is, any form of ugliness, you merely build a wall against it. Behind the wall there is no freedom, there is only isolation, and what lives in isolation can never be rich, can never be full. So, beauty has a relationship to reality only when reality manifests itself through those virtues which are essential.

Now, what do we mean by truth, or God, or what you will? Obviously, it cannot be formulated, for that which is formulated is not the real, it is the creation of the mind, the result of a thought process, and thought is the response of memory. Memory is the residue of incomplete experiences; therefore, truth, or God, or what you will is the unknown and it cannot be formulated. For the unknown to be, the mind itself must cease to be attached to the known, and then there is relationship between beauty and reality, then reality and beauty are not different, then truth is beauty, whether it is in a smile, the flight of a bird, the cry of a baby, or in the anger of your wife or husband. To know the truth of *what is* is good, but to know the beauty of that truth, the mind must be capable of understanding, and mind is not capable of understanding when it is tethered, when it is afraid, when it is avoiding something. This avoidance takes the form of outward decoration, ornamentation; being inwardly insufficient, poor, we try to become outwardly beautiful. We build lovely houses, buy a great many jewels, accumulate possessions. All these are indications of inward poverty. Not that we should not have nice saris, good houses, but without inner richness, they have no meaning. Because we are not inwardly rich, we cultivate the outer, and therefore the cultivation of the outer is leading us to destruction. That is, when you cultivate sensate values, expansion is necessary, markets are necessary; you must expand through industry, and the competitive expansion of industry means more and more controls, whether of the left or of the right, inevitably leading to war; and we try to solve the problems of war on the basis of sensate values.

The seeker after truth is the seeker after beauty—they are not distinct. Beauty is not merely outward ornamentation but that richness that comes through the freedom of inward understanding, the realization of *what is.*

Question: Why do you decry religion, which obviously contains grains of truth? Why throw out the baby with the bathwater? Need not truth be recognized wherever it is found?

KRISHNAMURTI: Sirs, what do you mean by religion? Organized dogma, belief, rituals, worshipping any person however great, reciting prayers, repeating *shastras,* quoting the Bible—is that religion? Or is religion the search for truth or God? Can you find God through organized belief? By your calling yourself a Hindu and following all the rituals of Hinduism or of any other ism, will you find God or truth? Surely, what I decry is not religion, not the search for reality, but organized belief with its dogmas and separative forces and influences. We are not seeking reality but are caught in the net of organized beliefs, repetitive rituals—you know the whole business of it—which I call nonsense because they are drugs that distract the mind from seeking; they offer escapes, and thereby make the mind dull, ineffective.

So, as our minds are caught in the net of organized beliefs with their whole system of authorities, priests, and gurus, all of which are engendered through fear and the desire for certainty; as we are caught in that net, obviously, we cannot merely accept, we must inquire, we must look directly, experience directly, and see what it is we are caught in and why we are caught. Because my great grandfather did some ritual, or my mother is going to cry if I do not do it, therefore I must do it. Surely, such a man who is psychologically dependent on others and hence fearful is incapable of finding out what truth is. He may talk about it, he may repeat the name of God umpteen times, but he is nowhere, he has no reality. Reality will shun him because he is encased in his own prejudices and fears. And you are responsible for this organized religion, whether of the East or of the West, whether of the left or of the right, which, being based on authority, has separated man from man. Why do you want authority, either of the past or of the present? You want authority because you are confused, you are in pain, in anxiety, there is loneliness and you are suffering. Therefore, you want help from outside, so you create authority, whether political or religious, and having created that authority, you follow its directions, hoping that the confusion, the anxiety, the pain in your heart will be removed. Can another remove your pains, your sorrows? Others may help you to escape from sorrow, but it is always there.

So, it is you who create authority, and having created the authority, you become its slaves. Belief is a product of authority, and because you want to escape from confusion, you are caught in belief and therefore continue in confusion. Your leaders are the outcome of your confusion; therefore, they must be confused. You would never follow anyone if you were clear, unconfused, and directly experiencing. It is because you are confused that there is no direct experience. Out of your confusion you create the leader, organized religion, separative worship, which brings about the strife that is going on in the world at the present time. In India it is taking the form of communal conflicts between the Muslims and Hindus; in Europe it is the communists against the rightists, and so on and on. If you look into it carefully, analyze it, you will see that it is all based on authority; one person says this and another person says that, and authority is created by you and me because we are confused. This may sound oversimplified verbally, but if you go into it, it is not simple, it is extremely complex. Being confused, you want to be led out—which means you are not understanding the problem of confusion, you are only seeking an escape. To understand confusion, you must understand the person who is making the confusion, which is yourself; and without understanding yourself, what is the good of following somebody? Being confused, do you think you will find truth in any practice or organized religion? Though you may study the Upanishads, the Gita, the Bible, or any other book, do you think that you are capable of reading the truth of it when you yourself are confused? You will translate what you read according to your confusion, your likes and dislikes, your prejudices, your conditioning. Your approach, surely, is not to reality. To find the truth, sir, is to understand yourself. Then truth comes to you, you do not have to go to truth—and that is the beauty of it. If you go to truth, that which you approach is projected out of yourself, and therefore it is not truth. Then it becomes merely a process of self-hypnosis, which is organized religion. To find truth, for truth to come to you, you must see very clearly your own prejudices, opinions, ideas, and conclusions; and that clarity comes through freedom which is virtue. For the virtuous mind, there is truth everywhere. Then you do not belong to any organized religion, then you are free.

So, truth comes into being when the mind is capable of receiving it, when the heart is empty of the things of the mind. At present our hearts are full of the things of the mind, and when the heart frees itself of the mind, then it is receptive, sensitive to reality.

Question: Some of us who have listened to you for many years agree, perhaps only verbally, with all that you say. But actually, in daily life, we are dull, and there is not the living from moment to moment that you speak of. Why is there such a huge gap between thought, or rather words, and action?

KRISHNAMURTI: I think we mistake verbal appreciation for real understanding. Verbally we understand each other, we understand the words. I communicate to you verbally certain thoughts that I have, and you remain on the verbal level, and from that verbal level, you hope to act. So, you will have to find out if verbal appreciation brings about understanding, action. For example, when I say that goodwill, affection, love, is the only solution, the only way out of this mess, verbally you understand, and if you are at all thoughtful, you will probably agree. Now, why don't you act? For the very simple reason that the verbal response is identified with the intellectual response. That is, intellectually you think you have grasped the idea, and so there is division between idea and action. That is why the cultivation of ideas creates, not understanding, but mere opposition, counter-ideas; and although this opposition may bring about a revolution, it will not be a real transformation of the individual and therefore of society.

I do not know if I am making myself clear on this point. If we dwell on the verbal level, then we merely produce ideas because words are things of the mind. Words are sensate, and if we dwell on the verbal level, words can only create sensate ideas and values. That is, one set of ideas creates counter-ideas, and these counter-ideas produce an action, but that action is merely reaction, the response to an idea. Most of us live merely verbally, we feed on words; the Bhagavad-Gita says this, the Puranas say that, or Marx says this, Einstein says that. Words can only produce ideas, and ideas will never produce action. Ideas can produce a reaction, but not action—and that is why we have this gap between verbal comprehension and action.

Now, the questioner wants to know how to build the bridge between word and action. I say you cannot, you cannot bridge the gap between word and action. Please see the importance of this. Words can never produce action. They can only produce a response, a counteraction or reaction, and therefore still further reaction, like a wave, and in that wave you are caught. Whereas, action is quite a different thing, it is not reaction. So, you cannot bridge the gap between the word and the action. You have to leave the word—and then you will act. Our difficulty, then, is how to leave the word. That means, how to act without reaction. Do you follow? Because as long as you are fed on words, you are bound to react; therefore, you have to empty yourself of words, which means emptying yourself of imitation. Words are imitation; living on the verbal level is to live in imitation, and since our whole life is based on imitation, on copying, naturally we have made ourselves incapable of action. Therefore you have to investigate the various patterns which make you copy, imitate, live on the verbal level; and as you begin to unravel the various patterns that have made you imitative, you will find that you act without reaction.

Sir, love is not a word, the word is not the thing, is it? God is not the word *God*, love is not the word *love*. But you are satisfied with the word because the word gives you a sensation. When somebody says, "God," you are psychologically or nervously affected, and that response you call the understanding of God. So, the word affects you nervously and sensuously, and that produces certain action. But the word is not the thing, the word *God* is not God; you have merely been fed on words, on nervous, sensuous responses. Please see the significance of this. How can you act if you have been fed on empty words? For words are empty, are they not? They can only produce a nervous response, but that is not action. Action can take place only when there is no imitative response, which means the mind must inquire into the whole process of verbal life. For example, some leader, political or religious, makes a statement, and without thought you say you agree, and then you wave a flag, you fight for India or Germany. But you have not examined what was said, and since you have not examined, what you do is merely a reaction, and between reaction and action there can be no relationship. Most of us are conditioned to reaction, so you have to discover the causes of this conditioning, and as the mind begins to free itself from the conditioning, you will find that there is action. Such action is not reaction, it is its own vitality, it is its own eternity.

So, with most of us the difficulty is that we want to bridge the unbridgeable, we want to serve both God and mammon, we want to live on the verbal plane, and yet act. The two are incompatible. We all know reaction, but very few of us know action because action can come only when we understand that the word is not the thing. When we understand that, then we can go much deeper; we can begin to uncover in ourselves all the fears, the imitations, escapes, and authorities; but that means we have to live very dangerously, and very few of us want to live in a state of perpetual revolution. What we want is a backwater refuge where we can settle down and be comforted, emotionally, physically, or psychologically. As between a lazy man and a very active man there is no relationship, so there is no relationship between word and action; but once we understand that and see the whole significance of it, then there is action. Such action, surely, leads to reality; it is the field in which reality can operate. Then we do not have to seek out reality; it comes directly, mysteriously, silently, stealthily. And a mind that is capable of receiving reality is blessed.

July 25, 1948

Fifth Talk at Bangalore

In the last two talks we were considering the importance of individual action, which is not opposed to collective action. The individual is the world; he is both the root and the outcome of the total process, and without transformation of the individual, there can be no radical transformation in the world. Therefore, the important thing is not individual action as opposed to collective action, but to realize that true collective action can come about only through individual regeneration. It is important to understand the individual action which is not opposed to the collective. Because, after all, the individual, you and your neighbor, are part of a total process; the individual is not a separate, isolated process. You are, after all, the product of the whole of humanity, though you may be climatically, religiously, and socially conditioned. You are the total process of man, and therefore, when you understand yourself as a total process—not as a separate process opposed to the mass or the collective—then through that understanding of yourself there can be a radical transformation. That is what we were talking about the last two times we met.

Now, what do we mean by action? Obviously, action implies behavior in relation to something. Action by itself is nonexistent; it can only be in relation to an idea, to a person, or to a thing. And we have to understand action because the world at the present time is crying for an action of some kind. We all want to act, we all want to know what to do, especially when the world is in such confusion, in such misery and chaos, when there are impending wars, when ideologies are opposing each other with such destructive force and religious organizations are pitting man against man. So, we must know what we mean by action, and in understanding what we mean by action, then perhaps we shall be able to act truly.

To understand what we mean by action—which is behavior, and behavior is righteousness—we must approach it negatively. That is, all positive approach to a problem must of necessity be according to a particular pattern, and action conforming to a pattern ceases to be action—it is merely conformity, and therefore not action. In order to understand action—that is, behavior, which is righteousness—we have to find out how to approach it. We must understand first that any positive approach which is trying to fit action to a pattern, to a conclusion, to an idea is no longer action; it is merely continuity of the pattern, of the mold, and therefore it is not action at all. Therefore, to understand action, we must go to it negatively—that is, we must understand the false process of a positive action. Because, when I know the false as the false, and the truth as the truth, then the false will drop away and I will know how to act. That is, if I know what is false action, unrighteous action, action that is merely a continuation of conformity, then seeing the falseness of that action, I shall know how to act rightly.

It is obvious that we need in everyday existence, in our social structure, in our political and religious life, a radical transformation of values, a complete revolution. Without laboring the point, I think it is obvious that there must be a change—or rather, not a change, which implies a modified continuity, but a transformation. There must be transformation, there must be a complete revolution—politically, socially, economically—in our relationship with each other, in every phase of life. Because, things cannot go on as they are—which is self-evident to any thoughtful person who is alert, watching world events. Now, how is this revolution in action to be brought about?—which is what we are discussing. How can there be action that transforms, not in time, but now? Is that not what we are concerned with? Because, there is so much misery, here in Bangalore as everywhere else throughout the world; there are economic slumps, there is dirt, poverty, unemployment, communal struggle, and so on and on, with the constant threat of a war in Europe. So, there must be a complete change of values, must there not? Not theoretically, because merely to discuss on the verbal level is futile, it has no meaning. It is like discussing food in front of a hungry man. So, we will not discuss merely verbally, and please don't be like spectators at a game. Let us both experience what we are talking about because if there is experiencing, then perhaps we shall understand how to act, and this will affect our lives and therefore bring a radical transformation. So, please do not be like spectators at a football game. You and I are going to take a journey together into the understanding of this thing called action because that is what we are concerned with in our daily life. If we can understand action in the fundamental sense of the word, then that fundamental understanding will affect our superficial activities also but first we must understand the fundamental nature of action.

Now is action brought about by an idea? Do you have an idea first and act afterwards? Or, does action come first and then, because action creates conflict, you build around it an idea? That is, does action create the actor, or does the actor come first? This is not a philosophical speculation, it is not based on the *shastras,* the Bhagavad-Gita, or any other book. They are all irrelevant. Don't let us quote what other people say because as I have read none of the books, you will win. We are trying to find out directly whether action comes first and the idea afterwards, or whether idea comes first and then action follows. It is very important to discover which comes first. If the idea comes first, then action merely conforms to an idea, and therefore it is no longer action but imitation, compulsion according to an idea. It is very important to realize this because as our society is mostly constructed on the intellectual or verbal level, the idea comes first with all of us, and action follows. Action is then the handmaid of an idea, and the mere construction of ideas is obviously detrimental to action. That is, ideas breed further ideas, and when there is merely the breeding of ideas, there is antagonism, and society becomes top-heavy with the intellectual process of ideation. Our social structure is very intellectual; we are cultivating the intellect at the expense of every other factor of our being, and therefore we are suffocated with ideas.

All this may sound rather abstract, academic, professorial, but it is not. Personally, I have a horror of academic discussion, theoretical speculations, because they lead nowhere. But it is very important that we find out what we mean by an idea because the world is dividing itself over the opposing ideas of the left and of the right, the ideas of the communists as opposed to those of the capitalists; and without understanding the whole process of ideation, merely to take sides is infantile, it has no meaning. A mature man does not take sides; he tries to solve directly the problems of human suffering, human starvation, war, and so on. We take sides only when we are molded by the intellect, whose function is to fabricate ideas. So, it is very important, is it not, to find out for ourselves, and not go according to what Marx, the *shastras,* the Bhagavad-Gita, or any of them say. You and I have to find out because it is our problem; it is our daily problem to discover what is the right solution to our aching civilization.

Now, can ideas ever produce action, or do ideas merely mold thought and therefore limit action? When action is compelled by an idea, action can never liberate man. Please, it is extraordinarily important for us to understand this point. If an idea shapes action, then action can never bring about the solution to our miseries because before it can be put into action, we have first to discover how the idea comes into being. The investigation of ideation, of the building up of ideas, whether of the socialists, the capitalists, the communists, or of the various religions, is of the utmost importance, especially when our society is at the edge of a precipice, inviting another catastrophe, another excision; and those who are really serious in their intention to discover the human solution to our many problems must first understand this process of ideation. As I said, this is not academic; it is the most practical approach to human life. It is not philosophical or speculative because that is sheer waste of time. Let us leave it to the undergraduates to discuss theoretical matters in their unions or in their clubs.

So, what do we mean by an idea? How does an idea come into being? And can idea and action be brought together? That is, I have an idea, and I wish to carry it out, so I seek a method of carrying out that idea; and we speculate, waste our time and energies in quarreling over how the idea should be carried out. So, it is really very important to find out how ideas come into being, and after discovering the truth of that, we can discuss the question of action. Without discussing ideas, merely to find out how to act has no meaning.

Now, how do you get an idea?—a very simple idea, it need not be philosophical, religious, or economic. Obviously, it is a process of thought, is it not? Idea is the outcome of a thought process. Without a thought process, there can be no idea. So, I have to understand the thought process itself before I can understand its product, the idea. What do we mean by thought? When do you think? Obviously, thought is the result of a response, neurological or psychological, is it not? It is the immediate response of the senses to a sensation, or it is psychological, the response of stored-up memory. There is the immediate response of the nerves to a sensation, and there is the psychological response of stored-up memory, the influence of race, group, guru, family, tradition, and so on—all of which you call thought. So, the thought process is the response of memory, is it not? You would have no thoughts if you had no memory, and the response of memory to a certain experience brings the thought process into action. Say, for example, I have the stored-up memories of nationalism, calling myself a Hindu. That reservoir of memories of past responses, actions, implications, traditions, customs, responds to the challenge of a Muslim, a Buddhist, or a Christian, and the response of memory to the challenge inevitably brings about a thought process. Watch the thought process operating in yourself, and you can test the truth of this directly. You have been insulted by someone, and that remains in your memory; it forms part of the background, and when you meet the person, which is the challenge, the response is the memory of that insult. So, the response of memory, which is the thought process, creates an idea; therefore, the idea is always conditioned—and this is important to understand. That is, idea is the result of the thought process, the thought process is the response of memory, and memory is always conditioned. Memory is always in the past, and that memory is given life in the present by a challenge. Memory has no life in itself; it comes to life in the present when confronted by a challenge. And all memory, whether dormant or active, is conditioned, is it not?

What, then, is memory? If you observe your own memory and how you gather memory, you will notice that it is either factual, technical—having to do with information, with engineering, mathematics, physics, and all the rest of it—or it is the residue of an unfinished, uncompleted experience, is it not? Watch your own memory and you will see. When you finish an experience, complete it, there is no memory of that experience in the sense of a psychological residue. There is residue only when an experience is not fully understood, and there is no understanding of experience because we look at each experience through past memories, and therefore we never meet the new as the new, but always through the screen of the old. Therefore, it is clear that our response to experience is conditioned, always limited.

So, we see that experiences which are not completely understood leave a residue, which we call memory. That memory, when challenged, produces thought. That thought creates the idea, and the idea molds action. Therefore, action based on an idea can never be free, and therefore there is no release for any of us through an idea. Please, this is very important to understand. I am not building up an argument against ideas, I am painting the picture of how ideas can never bring about a revolution. Ideas can modify the present state or change the present state, but that is not revolution. A substitution, or a modified continuity, is not revolution. As long as I am exploited, it matters very little whether I am exploited by private capitalists or by the state, but exploitation by the state we consider better than exploitation by the few. Is it any better? I am not talking of the top dogs. Is it any better for the man who is exploited? So, mere modification is not revolution; it is merely reaction to a condition. That is, the capitalistic background may produce a reaction in the form of communism, but that is still on the same level. It is the modified continuity of capitalism in a different form. I am not advocating either capitalism or communism. We are trying to find out what we mean by change, what we mean by revolution. So, an idea can never produce revolution in the deepest sense of the word, in the sense of complete transformation. An idea can bring about a modified continuity of *what is*, but that is obviously not revolution. And we need a revolution, not a substitution, but a complete transformation.

So, to bring about revolution, that complete transformation, I must first understand ideas and how they arise; and if I understand ideas, if I see the false as the false, then I can proceed to inquire what we mean by action; if thought creates idea—or, if thought itself, put into verbal form, is what I call idea—and if that thought is always conditioned because it is the response of memory to a challenge which is always new, then an idea can never bring about revolution in the deepest sense of the word; and yet that is what we are trying to do. We are looking to an idea to bring about transformation. I hope I am making myself clear.

So, our problem is this: If I cannot look to an idea, which is a thought process, then how can I act? Please, before I can find out how to act, I must be completely sure that action based on an idea is utterly false; I must see that ideas shape action, and that action which is shaped by ideas will ever be limited.

Therefore, there is no release through action based on an idea on an ideology or on a belief because such action is the outcome of a thought process which is but the response of memory. That thought process must inevitably create an idea which is conditioned, limited, and an action based on a limitation can never free man. Action based on an idea is limited action, conditioned action, and if I look to that action as a means of freedom, obviously I can only continue in a conditioned state. Therefore, I cannot look to an idea as a guide to action. And yet that is what we are doing because we are so addicted to ideas, whether they are other people's ideas or our own.

So, what we have to do now is to find out how to act without the thought process—which sounds quite loony, but is it? Just see our problem, it is quite interesting. When I live and act within the thought process, which gives rise to idea, which in turn molds action, there is no release. Now, can I act without the thought process, which is memory? Please, don't let us be confused—by memory I do not mean factual memory. It would be absurd to talk of throwing away all the technical knowledge—how to build a house, a dynamo, a jet plane, how to break the atom, and so on and so on—that man has acquired through centuries, generation after generation. But can I live, can I act, be in relationship with another without the psychological response of memory which results in ideation, and which in turn controls action? To most of us this may sound very odd, for we are accustomed to having an idea first and then conforming action to the idea. All our disciplines, all our activities are based on this—the idea first, and then conformity to the idea; and when I put the question to you, you have no answer because you have not thought about it in this direction at all. As I say, it will sound crazy to many of you, but if you really examine the whole process of life very closely and seriously because you want to understand and not just throw words at each other, then this question as to what we mean by action is bound to arise.

Now, is action really based on idea, or does action come first and the idea afterwards? If you observe still more closely, you will see that action comes first always, and not the idea. The monkey in the tree feels hungry, and then the urge arises to take a fruit or a nut. Action comes first, and then the idea that you had better store it up. To put it in different words, does action come first, or the actor? Is there an actor without action? Do you understand? This is what we are always asking ourselves: Who is it that sees? Who is the watcher? Is the thinker apart from his thoughts, the observer apart from the observed, the experiencer apart from the experience, the actor apart from the action? Is there an entity always dominating, overseeing, observing action—call it parabrahman, or what you will? When you give a name, you are merely caught in the idea, and that idea compels your thoughts, and therefore you say the actor comes first, and then the action. But if you really examine the process very carefully, closely, and intelligently, you will see that there is always action first, and that action with an end in view creates the actor. Do you follow? If action has an end in view, the gaining of that end brings about the actor. If you think very clearly and without prejudice, without conformity, without trying to convince somebody, without an end in view, in that very thinking there is no thinker—there is only the thinking. It is only when you seek an end in your thinking that you become important, and not thought. Perhaps some of you have observed this. It is really an important thing to find out because from that we shall know how to act. If the thinker comes first, then the thinker is more important than thought, and all the philosophies, customs, and activities of the present civilization are based on this assumption; but if thought comes first, then thought is more important than the thinker. Of course they are related—there is no thought without the thinker, and there is no thinker without the thought. But I do not want to discuss this now because we will get off the point.

So, can there be action without memory? That means, can there be action which is constantly revolutionary? The only thing that is constantly revolutionary is action without the screen of memory. An idea cannot bring about constant revolution because it always modifies action according to the background of its conditioning. Our question is, then, can there be action without the thought process which creates the idea, which in turn controls action? I say there can be, and that it can take place immediately when you see that idea is not a release, but a hindrance to action. If I see that, my action will not be based on any idea, and therefore I am in a state of complete revolution; and therefore there is the possibility of a society which is never static, which never needs to be overthrown and rebuilt. I say you can live with your wife, with your husband, with your neighbor in that state of action which does not conform to an idea; and that is possible only when you understand the significance of idea, how idea is brought about and molds action. The idea that molds action is detrimental to action, and a man who looks to an idea as a means of bringing about a revolution either in the mass or the individual is looking in vain. Revolution is constant, it is never static. Ideas create, not a revolution, but merely a modified continuity. Only that action which is not based on an idea can bring about revolution which is constant and therefore ever renewing.

There are many questions and I shall answer as many of them as possible.

Question: What is the place of power in your scheme of things? Do you think human affairs can be run without compulsion?

KRISHNAMURTI: Now, what do you mean by "your scheme of things"? Obviously, you think I have a pattern in which I am putting life. (Laughter) Please, this is important, don't laugh it off. Most of us have a scheme, a blueprint of how life should be according to Marx, Buddha, Christ, or Shankara, or according to the United Nations, and we force life into that mold. We say, "It is a marvelous scheme, let us fit into it"—which is absurd. Beware of the man who has a scheme of life; anyone who follows him, follows confusion and sorrow. Life is much bigger than any scheme that any human being can invent. So, that is out.

"What is the place of power? Do you think human affairs can be run without compulsion?" Now, what do we mean by power? There is the power that wealth gives, the power that knowledge brings, the power of an idea, the power of the technician. Which power do we mean? Obviously, the power to control, to dominate. That is what we mean by power, isn't it? The power that each one wants is the power which we exercise at home over the wife or the husband—only we want greater power to control, to dominate others. Also, there is the power which you give to the leader. Because you are confused, you hand over to the leader the reins of authority, and he guides and controls you; or you yourself would like to be the leader, and so on and on. And there is the power of love, of understanding, of kindliness, of mercy, the power of reality. Now, we have to be very clear which power we are referring to. There is the power of an army, that enormous power to destroy, to maim, to bring horror to mankind; and there is the power of a strong government, or of a strong personality. Merely to be in power is comparatively easy.

Power implies domination, and the more power you have, the more evil you become—which is shown over and over again throughout history. The power to dominate, to mold, to shape, to control, to force others to think what the authorities want them to think—surely, this is a power which is utterly evil, utterly dark and stupid. So also is the power of the rich man swaggering in his factory, and the power of the ambitious man in government affairs. Obviously, all that is power in its most stupid form because it dominates, controls, shapes, warps human beings.

Now, there is the so-called power of love, the power of understanding. Is love a power? Does love dominate, twist, shape the human heart? If it does, it is not longer love. Love, understanding, truth, has its own quality; it does not compel, therefore it is not on the same level as power. Love, truth, or understanding comes when all these ideas of compulsion, authority, dogmatism, have ceased. Humility is not the opposite of authority or of power. The cultivation of humility is merely the desire for authority, for power, in a different guise.

So, what is happening in the world? The power of governments, of states, the power of leaders, of the clever orators and writers, is used more and more for the shaping of man, compelling man to think along a certain line, teaching him, not how to think, but what to think. That has become the function of governments, with their enormous power of propaganda—which is the ceaseless repetition of an idea, and any repetition of an idea or of truth becomes a lie. Because there is confusion, misery in our minds and hearts, we create leaders who control us, shape us, and so do our governments. All over the world there is conformity to the dictates of the military, the social environment is influencing us to conform; and do you think that understanding or love comes through compulsion? Do you have goodwill through compulsion? If I am the dictator can I compel you to have goodwill? So, the compulsion which comes with placing enormous power in the hands of those who can wield it does not bring men together.

As I was explaining in my talk, compulsion is the outcome of an idea. Surely, a man who is drunk with ideology is intolerant; he creates the torture of compulsion. Obviously, there can never be understanding, love, communion with each other when there is compulsion, and no society can be built on compulsion. Such a society may for a time succeed technically, superficially, but inwardly there is the agony of being compelled, and therefore, like a prisoner kept within four walls, there is always the seeking for a release, for an escape, a way out. So, a government or a society that compels, shapes, forces the individual from the outside, will eventually create disorder, chaos, and violence. That is exactly what is happening in the world.

Then, we compel ourselves to conform to a pattern, calling it discipline, which is suppression, and suppression gives you a certain power. But in either extreme, in either opposite, there is no stability, and human minds go from one to another, evading the quiet stability of understanding. A mind that is compelled, a mind that is caught in power, can never know love, and without love, there is no solution to our problems. You may postpone understanding, intellectually you may avoid it, you may cleverly build bridges, but they are all temporary; and without goodwill, without mercy, without generosity, without kindliness, there is bound to be ever-increasing misery and destruction because compulsion is not the cement that brings human beings together. Compulsion in any form, inward or outward, only creates further confusion, further misery. What we need in world affairs at the present time is not more ideas, more blueprints, bigger and better leaders, but goodwill, affection, love, kindliness. Therefore, what we need is the person who loves, who is kind—and that is you, not somebody else. Love is not the worship of God; you may worship a stone image or your conception of God, and that is a marvelous escape from your brutal husband or your nagging wife, but it does not solve our difficulty. Love is the only solvent, and love is kindness to your wife, to your child, to your neighbor.

Question: Why are we so callous to each other in spite of all the suffering it involves?

KRISHNAMURTI: Why am I or why are you callous to another man's suffering? Why are we indifferent to the coolie who is carrying a heavy load, to the woman who is carrying a baby? Why are we so callous? To understand that, we must understand why suffering makes us dull. Surely, it is suffering that makes us callous; because we don't understand suffering, we become indifferent to it. If I understand suffering, then I become sensitive to suffering, awake to everything, not only to myself, but to the people about me, to my wife, to my children, to an animal, to a beggar. But we don't want to understand suffering, and the escape from suffering makes us dull, and therefore we are callous. Sir, the point is that suffering, when not understood, dulls the mind and heart; and we do not understand suffering because we want to escape from it, through the guru, through a savior, through mantras, through reincarnation, through ideas, through drink and every other kind of addiction—anything to escape *what is*. So, our temples, our churches, our politics, our social reforms are mere escapes from the fact of suffering. We are not concerned with suffering, we are concerned with the idea of how to be released from suffering. We are concerned with ideas, not with suffering; we are constantly looking for a better idea and how to carry it out—which is so infantile. When you are hungry, you don't discuss how to eat; you say, "Give me food"—you are not concerned with who will bring it, whether the left or the right, or which ideology is the best. But when you want to avoid the understanding of *what is*, which is suffering, then you escape into ideologies, and that is why our minds, though superficially very clever, have essentially become dull, rude, callous, brutal. To understand suffering requires seeing the falseness of all the escapes, whether God or drink. All escapes are the same though socially each may have a different significance. When I escape from sorrow, all escapes are on the same level—there is no "better" escape.

Now, the understanding of suffering does not lie in finding out what the cause is. Any man can know the cause of suffering—his own thoughtlessness, his stupidity, his narrowness, his brutality, and so on. But if I look at the suffering itself without wanting an answer, then what happens? Then, as I am not escaping, I begin to understand suffering; my mind is watchfully alert, keen, which means I become sensitive, and being sensitive, I am aware of other people's suffering. Therefore I am not callous, therefore I am kind, not merely to my friends—I am kind to everyone because I am sensitive to suffering. We are callous because we have become dull to suffering; we have dulled our minds through escapes. Escape gives a great deal of power, and we like power, we like to have a radio, a motorcar, an airplane, we like to have money and enjoy immense power. But when you understand suffering, there is no power, there is no escape through power. When you understand suffering, there is kindliness, there is affection. Affection, love, demands the highest intelligence, and without sensitivity there is no great intelligence.

Question: Can you not build up a following and use it rightly? Must you remain a voice in the desert?

KRISHNAMURTI: Now, what do you mean by a following, and what do you mean by a leader? Why do you follow, and why do you create a leader? If you are interested, please consider this closely. When do you follow? You follow only when you are confused; when you are unhappy, when you feel torn down, you want someone—a political, a religious, a military leader—to help you, to take you out of your misery. When you are clear, when you understand, you do not want to be led. You want to be led only when you are yourself in confusion, with all its implications. So, what happens? When you are confused, how can you see clearly? Since you cannot see clearly, you will choose a leader who is also confused. (Laughter) Don't laugh. This is what is happening in the world, and it is disastrous. It may sound very clever, but it is not. How can a blind man choose a leader? He can only choose those around him. Similarly, a confused man can only choose a leader who is as confused as himself. And what happens? Being confused, your leader naturally leads you to further confusion, further disaster, further misery. That is what is taking place all over the world. For God's sake, sirs, look at it—it is your misery. You are being led to the slaughter because you refuse to see and clear away the cause of your own confusion. And because you refuse to see it, you are creating out of your confusion the clever, the cunning leaders who exploit you; because, the leader, like you, is seeking self-fulfillment. Therefore you become a necessity to the leader, and the leader becomes a necessity to you—it is a mutual exploitation.

So, why do you want a leader? And can there ever be a right leadership? You and I can help each other to clear up our own confusion—which does not mean that I become your leader and you become my follower, or I am your guru and you are my pupil. We simply help each other to understand the confusion that exists in our own hearts and minds. It is only when you do not want to understand the confusion that you run away from it, and then you will turn to somebody, to a leader or a guru. But if you want to understand it, then you must look to the common misery, the aches, the burdens, the loneliness; and you can look only when you are not trying to find an answer, a way out of the confusion. You look at it because confusion itself leads to misery; therefore, you want to understand it, and when you understand, clear it up, you will be free as the air, you will love, you will not follow, you will have no leaders; and then will come the society of true equality, without class or caste.

Sirs, you are not seeking truth, you are trying to find a way out of some difficulty; and that is your misery. You want leaders to direct you, to pull you along, to force you, to make you conform—and that inevitably leads to destruction, to greater suffering. Suffering is what is happening directly in front of us, yet we refuse to see it and we want "right" leaders—which is so immature. To me, all leadership indicates a deterioration of society. A leader in society is a destructive element. (Laughter) Don't laugh it off, don't pass it by—look at it. It is very serious, especially now. The world is on the verge of a catastrophe, it is rapidly disintegrating, and merely to find another leader, a new Churchill, a greater Stalin, a different God, is utterly futile because the man who is confused can choose only according to the dictates of his own mind, which is confusion. Therefore, it is no good seeking a leader, right or wrong. There is no "right" leader—all leaders are wrong. What you have to do is to clear your own confusion. And confusion is set aside only when you understand yourself; with the beginning of self-knowledge, there comes clarity. Without self-knowledge, there is no release from confusion; without self-knowledge, confusion is like a wave eternally catching you up. So, it is very important for those who are really serious and in earnest to begin with themselves and not seek release or escape from confusion. The moment you understand confusion, you are free of it.

Question: Grains of truth are to be found in religions, theories, ideas, and beliefs. What is the right way of separating them?

KRISHNAMURTI: The false is the false, and by seeking you cannot separate the false from the truth. You have to see the false as the false, and then only is there the cessation of the false. You cannot seek the truth in the false, but you can see the false as the false, and then there is a release from the false. Sir, how can the false contain the truth? How can ignorance, darkness, contain understanding, light? I know we would like to have it so; we would like to think that somewhere in us there is eternity, light, truth, piety, all covered over with ignorance. Where there is light, there is no darkness; where there is ignorance, there is always ignorance, but never understanding. So, there is release only when you and I see the false as the false, that is, when we see the truth about the false, which means not dwelling in the false as the false. Our seeing the false as the false is prevented by our prejudice, by our conditioning. With that understanding, let us proceed.

Now, the question is, Is there not truth in religions, in theories, in ideals, in beliefs? Let us examine. What do we mean by religion? Surely, not organized religion, not Hinduism, Buddhism, or Christianity—which are all organized beliefs with their propaganda, conversion, proselytism, compulsion, and so on. Is there any truth in organized religion? It may engulf, enmesh truth, but the organized religion itself is not true. Therefore, organized religion is false—it separates man from man. You are a Muslim, I am a Hindu, another is a Christian or a Buddhist—and we are wrangling, butchering each other. Is there any truth in that? We are not discussing religion as the pursuit of truth, but we are considering if there is any truth in organized religion. We are so conditioned by organized religion to think there is truth in it that we have come to believe that by calling oneself a Hindu, one is somebody, or one will find God. How absurd, sir; to find God, to find reality, there must be virtue. Virtue is freedom, and only through freedom can truth be discovered—not when you are caught in the hands of organized religion, with its beliefs. And is there any truth in theories, in ideals, in beliefs? Why do you have beliefs? Obviously, because beliefs give you security, comfort, safety, a guide. In yourself you are frightened, you want to be protected, you want to lean on somebody, and therefore you create the ideal, which prevents you from understanding that which is; therefore, an ideal becomes a hindrance to action. Sir, when I am violent, why do I want to pursue the ideal of nonviolence? For the obvious reason that I want to avoid violence, escape from violence. I cultivate the ideal in order not to have to face and understand violence. Why do I want the ideal at all? It is an impediment. If I want to understand violence, I must try to understand what it is directly, not through the screen of an ideal. The ideal is false, fictitious, preventing me from understanding that which I am. Look at it more closely and you will see. If I am violent, to understand violence I do not want an ideal; to look at violence, I do not need a guide. But I like to be violent; it gives me a certain sense of power, and I will go on being violent though I cover it up with the ideal of nonviolence. So, the ideal is fictitious, it is simply not there. It exists only in the mind; it is an idea to be achieved, and in the meantime I can be violent. Therefore, an ideal, like a belief, is unreal, false.

Now, why do I want to believe? Surely, a man who is understanding life does not want beliefs. A man who loves has no beliefs—he loves. It is the man who is consumed by the intellect that has beliefs because intellect is always seeking security, protection; it is always avoiding danger, and therefore it builds ideas, beliefs, ideals, behind which it can take shelter. What would happen if you dealt with violence directly, now? You would be a danger to society; and because the mind foresees the danger, it says, "I will achieve the ideal of nonviolence ten years later"—which is such a fictitious, false process. So, theories—we are not dealing with mathematical theories, and all the rest of it, but with the theories that arise in connection with our human, psychological problems—theories, beliefs, ideals, are false because they prevent us from seeing things as they are. To understand *what is* is more important than to create and follow ideals because ideals are false, and *what is* is the real. To understand *what is* requires an enormous capacity, a swift and unprejudiced mind. It is because we don't want to face and understand *what is* that we invent the many ways of escape and give them lovely names as the ideal, the belief, God. Surely, it is only when I see the false as the false that my mind is capable of perceiving what is true. A mind that is confused in the false can never find the truth. Therefore, I must understand what is false in my relationships, in my ideas, in the things about me because to perceive the truth requires the understanding of the false. Without removing the causes of ignorance, there cannot be enlightenment, and to seek enlightenment when the mind is unenlightened is utterly empty, meaningless. Therefore, I must begin to see the false in my relationships with ideas, with people, with things. When the mind sees that which is false, then that which is true comes into being, and then there is ecstasy, there is happiness.

August 1, 1948

Sixth Talk in Bangalore

We have been discussing, the several times that we have met, the problem of transformation, which alone can bring about the revolution which is so necessary in the world's affairs. And, as we have seen, the world is not different from you and me—the world is what we make it. We are the result of the world, and we are the world; so the transformation must begin with us, not with the world, not with outward legislation, blueprints, and so on. It is essential that each one should realize the importance of this inner transformation, which will bring about an outward revolution. Mere change in the outward circumstances of life is of very little significance without the inner transformation; and, as we said, this inner transformation cannot take place without self-knowledge. Self-knowledge is to know the total process of oneself, the ways of one's own thinking, feeling, and action; and without knowing oneself, there is no basis for broader action. So, self-knowledge is of primary importance. One must obviously begin to understand oneself in all one's actions, thoughts, and feelings because the self, the mind, the 'me' is so very complex and subtle. So many impositions have been placed upon the mind, the 'me', so many influences—racial, religious, national, social, environmental—have shaped it, that to follow each step, to analyze each imprint, is extremely difficult; and if we miss one, if we do not analyze properly and miss one step, then the whole process of analysis miscarries. So, our problem is to understand the self, the 'me'—not just one part of the 'me' but the whole field of thought, which is the response of the 'me'. We have to understand the whole field of memory from which all thought arises, both the conscious and the unconscious; and all that is the self—the hidden as well as the open, the dreamer and what he dreams.

Now, to understand the self, which alone can bring about a radical revolution, a regeneration, there must be the intention to understand its whole process. The process of the individual is not opposed to the world, to the mass, whatever that term may mean, because there is no mass apart from you—you are the mass. So, to understand that process, there must be the intention to know *what is,* to follow every thought, feeling, and action; and to understand *what is* is extremely difficult because *what is* is never still, never static, it is always in movement. The *what is* is what you are, not what you would like to be; it is not the ideal because the ideal is fictitious, but it is actually what you are doing, thinking, and feeling from moment to moment. *What is* is the actual, and to understand the actual requires awareness, a very alert, swift mind. But if we begin to condemn *what is,* if we begin to blame or resist it, then we shall not understand its movement. If I want to understand somebody, I cannot condemn him—I must observe, study him. I must love the very thing I am studying. If you want to understand a child, you must love and not condemn him. You must play with him, watch his movements, his idiosyncrasies, his ways of behavior; but if you merely condemn, resist, or blame him, there is no comprehension of the child. Similarly, to understand *what is,* one must observe what one thinks, feels, and does from moment to moment. That is the actual. Any other action, any ideal or ideological action is not the actual—it is merely a wish, a fictitious desire to be something other than *what is.*

So, to understand *what is* requires a state of mind in which there is no identification or condemnation, which means a mind that is alert and yet passive. We are in that state when we really desire to understand something; when the intensity of interest is there, that state of mind comes into being. When one is interested in understanding *what is,* the actual state of the mind, one does not need to force, discipline, or control it; on the contrary, there is passive alertness, watchfulness. If I want to understand a picture or a person, I must put aside all my prejudices, my preconceptions, my classical or other training, and study the picture or the person directly. This state of awareness comes when there is interest, the intention to understand.

Now, the next question is whether transformation is a matter of time. Most of us are accustomed to think that time is necessary for transformation—I am something, and to change what I am into what I should be requires time. I am greedy, with its results of confusion, antagonism, conflict, and misery; and to bring about the transformation, which is nongreed, we think time is necessary. That is, time is considered as a means for evolving something greater, for becoming something. Do you understand the problem? The problem is this: One is violent, greedy, envious, angry, vicious, or passionate. Now, to transform *what is,* is time necessary? First of all, why do we want to change *what is,* or bring about a transformation? Why? Because what we are dissatisfies us; it creates conflict, disturbance; and disliking that state, we want something better, something nobler, more idealistic. So, we desire transformation because there is pain, discomfort, conflict. Now, is conflict overcome by time? If you say it will be overcome by time, you are still in conflict. That is, you may say it will take 20 days or 20 years to get rid of conflict, to change what you are, but during that time you are still in conflict, and therefore time does not bring about transformation. When we use time as a means of acquiring a quality, a virtue, or a state of being, we are merely postponing or avoiding *what is;* and I think it is important to understand this point. Greed or violence causes pain, disturbance, in the world of our relationship with another, which is society; and being conscious of this state of disturbance, which we term greed or violence, we say to ourselves, "I will get out of it in time. I will practice nonviolence, I will practice nonenvy, I will practice peace." Now, you want to practice nonviolence because violence is a state of disturbance, conflict, and you think that in time you will gain nonviolence and overcome the conflict. So, what is actually happening? Being in a state of conflict, you want to achieve a state in which there is no conflict. Now, is that state of no conflict the result of time, of a duration? Obviously not. Because, while you are achieving a state of nonviolence, you are still being violent and are therefore still in conflict.

So, our problem is: Can a conflict, a disturbance, be overcome in a period of time, whether it be days, years, or lives? What happens when you say, "I am going to practice nonviolence during a certain period of time"? The very practice indicates that you are in conflict, does it not? You would not practice if you were not resisting conflict, and you say the resistance to conflict is necessary in order to overcome conflict and for that resistance you must have time. But the very resistance to conflict is itself a form of conflict. You are spending your energy in resisting conflict in the form of what you call greed, envy, or violence, but your mind is still in conflict. So, it is important to see the falseness of the process of depending on time as a means of overcoming violence, and thereby being free of that process. Then you are able to be what you are—a psychological disturbance which is violence itself.

Now, to understand anything, any human or scientific problem, what is important, what is essential? A quiet mind, is it not? A mind that is intent on understanding. It is not a mind that is exclusive, that is trying to concentrate—which again is an effort of resistance. If I really want to understand something, there is immediately a quiet state of mind. That is, when you want to listen to music or look at a picture which you love, which you have a feeling for, what is the state of your mind? Immediately there is a quietness, is there not? When you are listening to music, your mind does not wander all over the place; you are listening. Similarly, when you want to understand conflict, you are no longer depending on time at all; you are simply confronted with *what is,* which is conflict. Then immediately there comes a quietness, a stillness of mind. So, when you no longer depend on time as a means of transforming *what is* because you see the falseness of that process, then you are confronted with *what is;* and as you are interested to understand *what is,* naturally you have a quiet mind. In that alert yet passive state of mind, there is understanding. As long as the mind is in conflict—blaming, resisting, condemning—there can be no understanding. If I want to understand you, I must not condemn you, obviously. So, it is that quiet mind, that still mind, which brings about transformation. When the mind is no longer resisting, no longer avoiding, no longer discarding or blaming *what is,* but is simply passively aware, then in that passivity of the mind you will find, if you really go into the problem, that there comes a transformation.

So, transformation is not the result of time—it is the result of a quiet mind, a steady mind, a mind that is still, tranquil, passive. The mind is not passive when it is seeking a result, and the mind will seek a result as long as it wishes to transform, change, or modify *what is.* But if the mind simply has the intention to understand *what is* and is therefore still, in that stillness you will find there is an understanding of *what is,* and therefore a transformation. We actually do this when we are confronted with anything in which we are interested. Observe yourself, and you will see this extraordinary process going on. When you are interested in something, your mind is quiet. It has not gone to sleep, it is extremely alert and sensitive, and is therefore capable of receiving hints, intimations; and it is this stillness, this alert passivity, that brings a transformation. This does not involve using time as a means of transformation, modification, or change.

Revolution is only possible now, not in the future; regeneration is today, not tomorrow. If you will experiment with what I have been saying, you will find that there is immediate regeneration, a newness, a quality of freshness, because the mind is always still when it is interested, when it desires or has the intention to understand. The difficulty with most of us is that we have not the intention to understand because we are afraid that if we understood it might bring about a revolutionary action in our life, and therefore we resist. It is the defense mechanism that is at work when we use time or an ideal as a means of gradual transformation.

So, regeneration is only possible in the present, not in the future, not tomorrow. A man who relies on time as a means through which he can gain happiness, or realize truth or God, is merely deceiving himself; he is living in ignorance and, therefore, in conflict. But a man who sees that time is not the way out of our difficulty, and who is therefore free from the false—such a man naturally has the intention to understand; therefore, his mind is quiet spontaneously, without compulsion, without practice. When the mind is still, tranquil, not seeking any answer or any solution, neither resisting nor avoiding—it is only then that there can be a regeneration because then the mind is capable of perceiving what is true; and it is truth that liberates, not your effort to be free.

I will answer some of the questions that have been given to me.

Question: You speak so much about the need for ceaseless alertness. I find my work dulls me so irresistibly that to talk of alertness after a day's work is merely putting salt on the wound.

KRISHNAMURTI: Sir, this is an important question. Please let us examine it together carefully and see what it involves. Now, most of us are dulled by what we call our work, the job, the routine. Those who love work and those who are forced to work out of necessity and who see that work makes them dull—they are both dull. Both those who love their work and those who resist it are made dull, are they not? A man who loves his work—what does he do? He thinks about it from morning to night, he is constantly occupied with it. He is so identified with his work that he cannot look at it—he is himself the action, the work; and to such a person, what happens? He lives in a cage, he lives in isolation with his work. In that isolation he may be very clever, very inventive, very subtle, but still he is isolated; and he is made dull because he is resisting all other work, all other approaches. His work is therefore a form of escape from life—from his wife, from his social duties, from innumerable demands, and so on. And there is the man in the other category, the man who, like most of you, is compelled to do something he dislikes and who resists it. He is the factory worker, the bank clerk, the lawyer, or whatever our various jobs are.

Now, what is it that makes us dull? Is it the work itself? Or is it our resistance to work, or our avoidance of other impacts upon us? Do you follow the point? I hope I am making it clear. That is, the man who loves his work is so enclosed in it, so enmeshed that it becomes an addiction. Therefore his love of work is an escape from life. And the man who resists work, who wishes he were doing something else—for him there is the ceaseless conflict of resistance to what he is doing. So, our problem is: Does work make the mind dull? Or is dullness brought about by resistance to work on the one hand, and by the use of work to avoid the impacts of life, on the other? That is, does action, work, make the mind dull? Or is the mind made dull by avoidance, by conflict, by resistance? Obviously, it is not work, but resistance, that dulls the mind. If you have no resistance and accept work, what happens? The work does not make you dull because only a part of your mind is working with the job that you have to do. The rest of your being, the unconscious, the hidden, is occupied with those thoughts in which you are really interested. So there is no conflict. This may sound rather complex, but if you will carefully follow it, you will see that the mind is made dull, not by work, but by resistance to work, or by resistance to life. Say, for example, you have to do a certain piece of work which may take five or six hours. If you say, "What a bore, what an awful thing, I wish I could be doing something else," obviously your mind is resisting that work. Part of your mind is wishing you were doing something else. This division, brought about through resistance, creates dullness because you are using your effort wastefully, wishing you were doing something else. Now if you do not resist it, but do what is actually necessary, then you say, "I have to earn my livelihood and I will earn that livelihood rightly." But right livelihood does not mean the army, the police, or being a lawyer because they thrive on contention, disturbance, cunning, subterfuge and so on. This is quite a difficult problem in itself, which we will perhaps discuss later if we have time.

So, if you are occupied in doing something which you have to do to earn your livelihood, and if you resist it, obviously the mind becomes dull because that very resistance is like running an engine with the brake on. What happens to the poor engine? Its performance becomes dull, does it not? If you have driven a car, you know what will happen if you keep putting on the brake—you will not only wear out the brake but you will wear out the engine. That is exactly what you are doing when you resist work. Whereas, if you accept what you have to do and do it as intelligently and as fully as possible, then what happens? Because you are no longer resisting, the other layers of your consciousness are active irrespective of what you are doing; you are giving only the conscious mind to your work, and the unconscious, the hidden part of your mind is occupied with other things in which there is much more vitality, much more depth. Though you face the work, the unconscious takes over and functions.

Now, if you observe, what actually happens in your daily life? You are interested, say, in finding God, in having peace. That is your real interest, with which your conscious as well as your unconscious mind is occupied—to find happiness, to find reality, to live rightly, beautifully, clearly. But you have to earn a livelihood because there is no such thing as living in isolation—that which is, is in relationship. So, being interested in peace, and since your work in daily life interferes with that, you resist work. You say, "I wish I had more time to think, to meditate, to practice the violin"—or whatever it be. When you do that, when you merely resist the work you have to do, that very resistance is a waste of effort, which makes the mind dull; whereas, if you realize that we all do various things which have got to be done—

writing letters, talking, clearing away the cow dung, or what you will—and therefore don't resist, but say, "I have got to do that work," then you will do it willingly and without boredom. If there is no resistance, the moment that work is over, you will find that the mind is peaceful; because the unconscious, the deeper layers of the mind, are interested in peace, you will find that peace begins to come. So, there is no division between action which may be routine, which may be uninteresting, and your pursuit of reality; they are compatible when the mind is no longer resisting, when the mind is no longer made dull through resistance. It is the resistance that creates the division between peace and action. Resistance is based on an idea, and resistance cannot bring about action. It is only action that liberates, not the resistance to work.

So, it is important to understand that the mind is made dull through resistance, through condemnation, blame, and avoidance. The mind is not dull when there is no resistance. When there is no blame, no condemnation, then it is alive, active. Resistance is merely isolation, and the mind of man who, consciously or unconsciously, is continually isolating himself is made dull by this resistance.

Question: Do you love the people you talk to? Do you love the dull and ugly crowd, the shapeless faces, the stinking atmosphere of stale desires, of putrid memories, the decaying of many needless lives? No one can love them. What is it that makes you slave away in spite of your repugnance, which is both obvious and understandable?

KRISHNAMURTI: No, sirs, there is no repugnance, which is apparently obvious and understandable to you. I am not repelled. I only see it like I see a fact. A fact is never ugly. When you are talking seriously, a man may be scratching his ear, or playing with his legs, or looking about. As for you, you just observe it—which does not mean that you are revolted, that you want to avoid it, or that you hate the fact. A smell is a smell—you just take it, and it is very important to understand that point. To see a fact as a fact is an important reality. But the moment you regret or avoid it, call it a name, give it an emotional content, obviously there is repugnance, avoidance, and then resistance comes into being. Now, that is not my attitude at all, and I am afraid the questioner has me wrongly there. It is like seeing that a person has a red sari or a white coat, but if you give emotional content to the red and the white, saying this is beautiful or that is ugly, then you are repelled or attracted.

Now, the point in this question is: Why do I talk? Why do I wear myself out if I don't love the people who have "shapeless faces, stale desires, putrid memories," and so on? And the questioner says that no one can love them. Now, does one love people, or is there love? Is love independent of people, and therefore you love people, or is one in a state of love? Do you follow what I mean? If I say, "I love people," and slave away, wear myself out talking, then the people become very important, and not love. That is, if I have the intention to convert you to a particular belief, and slave away at it from the morning until night because I think I can make you happy if you believe in my particular formula, then it is the formula, the belief that I love, not you. Then I put up with all the ugliness, "the stale desires, the putrid memories, the stinking atmosphere," and I say it is part of the whole routine; I become a martyr to my belief, which I think will help you. So, I am in love with my belief, and as my belief is my own projection, therefore I am in love with myself. After all, a man who loves a belief, an idea, a scheme, identifies himself with that formula, and that formula is a projection of himself. Obviously, he never identifies himself with something of which he does not approve. If he likes me, that very liking is his own projection.

Now, if I may say it without being personal, to me it is quite different. I am not trying to convert you, to proselytize you or to do propaganda against any particular religion. I am just stating the facts because I feel the very understanding of these facts will help man to live more happily. When you love something, when you love a person, what is the actual state? Are you in love with the person, or are you in a state of love? Surely, the person attracts or repels you only when you are not in that state. When you are in that state of love, there is no repugnance. It is like a flower giving perfume; next to it a cow may have left its mark, but the flower is still a flower giving forth its perfume. But a man comes along and, seeing the cow dung beside the flower, regards it differently. Sir, in this question is involved the whole problem of attraction and repulsion. We want to be attracted, that is, to identify ourselves with that which is pleasant, and avoid that which is ugly. But if you merely look at things as they are, the fact itself is never ugly or repellent—it is simply a fact. A man who loves is consumed by his love, he is not concerned with whether people have "shapeless faces, stale desires and putrid memories." Don't you know, sirs? When you are in love with someone, actually you are not very much concerned with what that person looks like, whether it is a shapeless face or a beautiful face. When there is love, you are not concerned; though you observe the facts, the facts do not repel you. It is not love, but the empty heart, the arid mind, the stale intellect, that is repelled or attracted. And when one loves, there is no "slaving away." There is ever a renewal, a freshness, a joy—not in talking, not in putting out a lot of words, but in that state itself. It is when one does not love that all these things matter—whether you are attractive or repellent, whether the face is shapeless or beautiful, and so on and on.

So, why I "slave away" is not important. Our problem is that we have no love. Because our hearts are empty, our minds dull, weary, exhausted, we seek to fill the empty heart with the things made by the mind or by the hand; or we repeat words, mantras, do pujas. Those things will not fill the heart; on the contrary, they will empty the heart of whatever it has. The heart can be filled only when the mind is quiet. When the mind is not creating, fabricating, caught up in ideas—only then is the heart alive. Then one knows what it is to have that warmth, the richness in holding the hand of another.

Question: Is not all caress sexual? Is not all sex a form of revitalization, through interpretation and exchange? The mere exchange of loving glances is also an act of sex. Why do you castigate sex by linking it up with the emptiness of our lives? Do empty people know sex? They know only evacuation.

KRISHNAMURTI: I am afraid it is only the empty people who know sex because sex then is an escape, a mere release. I call him empty who has no love, and for him sex becomes a problem, an issue, a thing to be avoided or to be indulged. The heart is empty when the mind is full of its own ideas, fabrications and mechanization. Because the mind is full, the heart is empty, and it is only the empty heart that knows sex. Sirs, have you not noticed? An affectionate man, a man full of tenderness, kindliness, consideration, is not sexual. It is the man who is intellectual, full of knowledge, knowledge being different from wisdom, the man who has schemes, who wants to save the world, who is full of intellection, full of mentation—it is he who is caught up in sex. Because his life is shallow, his heart empty, sex becomes important—and that is what is happening in the present civilization. We have overcultivated our intellect, and the mind is caught in its own creations as the radio, the motorcar, the mechanized amusements, the technical knowledge, and the various addictions the mind indulges in. When such a mind is caught, there is only one release for it, which is sex. Sirs, look at what is happening within each one of us, don't look at somebody else. Examine your own life and you will see how you are caught in this problem, how extraordinarily empty your life is. What is your life, sirs? Bright, arid, empty, dull, weary, is it not? You go to your offices, do your jobs, repeat your mantras, perform your pujas. When you are in the office, you are subjugated, dull, you have to follow a routine; you have become mechanical in your religion; it is mere acceptance of authority. So, religiously, in the world of business, in your education, in your daily life, what is actually happening? There is no creative state of being, is there? You are not happy, you are not vital, you are not joyous. Intellectually, religiously, economically, socially, politically, you are dull, regimented, are you not? This regimentation is the result of your own fears, your own hopes, your own frustrations; and since for a human being so caught there is no release, naturally he looks to sex for a release—there he can indulge himself, there he can seek happiness. So, sex becomes automatic, habitual, routine, and that also becomes a dulling, a vicious process. That is your life, actually, if you look at it, if you don't try to dodge it, if you don't try to excuse it. The actual fact is, you are not creative. You may have babies, innumerable babies, but that is not creative action, that is an accidental action of existence.

So, a mind that is not alert, vital, a heart that is not affectionate, full, how can it be creative? And not being creative, you seek stimulation through sex, through amusement, cinemas, theaters, through watching others play while you remain a spectator; others paint the scene or dance, and you yourself are but an observer. That is not creation. Similarly, so many books are printed in the world because you merely read. You are not the creator. Where there is no creation, the only release is through sex, and then you make your wife or husband the prostitute. Sirs, you have no idea of the implications, the wickedness, the cruelty of all this. I know you are uncomfortable. You are not thinking it out. You are shutting your mind, and therefore sex has become an immense problem in modern civilization—either promiscuity, or the mechanical habit of sexual release in marriage. Sex will remain a problem as long as there is no creative state of being. You may use birth control, you may adopt various practices, but you are not free of sex. Sublimation is not freedom, suppression is not freedom, control is not freedom. There is freedom only when there is affection, when there is love. Love is pure, and when that is missing, your trying to become pure through the sublimation of sex is mere stupidity. The factor that purifies is love, not your desire to be pure. A man who loves is pure though he may be sexual, and without love, sex is what it is now in your lives—a routine, an ugly process, a thing to be avoided, ignored, done away with, or indulged in.

So, this problem of sex will exist as long as there is no creative release. There can be no creative release, religiously, if you accept authority, whether of tradition, the sacred books, or the priest; for authority compels, distorts, perverts. Where there is authority there is compulsion, and you accept authority because you hope through religion to have security; and while the mind is seeking security, intellectually or religiously, there can be no creative understanding, there can be no creative release. It is the mind, the mechanism of the mind that is always seeking security, always wanting certainty. The mind is ever moving from the known to the known, and mere cultivation of the mind, of the intellect, is not a release. On the contrary, the intellect can grasp only the known, never the unknown. Therefore the mere cultivation of the mind through more and more knowledge, more and more technique, is not creative. A mind that wishes to be creative must set aside the desire to be secure, which means the desire to find authority. Truth can come into being only when the mind is free from the known, when the mind is free from security, the desire to be certain. But look at our education—mere passing of examinations to get a job, adding a few letters after your name. It has become so mechanical, it is but the cultivation of the mind, which is memory. In that way there is no release either.

So, socially, religiously, in every way, you are caught and held. Therefore a man who wishes to solve this problem of sex must disentangle himself from the thoughts of his own making, and when he is in that state of freedom, there is creativeness which is understanding of the heart. When one loves, there is chastity; it is the lack of love that is unchaste, and without love no human problem can be solved. But instead of understanding the hindrances that prevent love, we merely try to sublimate, suppress, or find a substitute for the sexual appetite; and substitution, sublimation, or suppression is called the attainment of reality. On the contrary, where there is oppression, there is no comprehension; where there is substitution, there is ignorance. Our difficulty is that we are caught in this habit of withholding, suppressing, sublimating. Surely, one has to look at this habit to be aware of its full significance, not just for one or two moments, but all through life. One has to see how one is caught in the machine of routine, and to break away from that needs understanding, self-knowledge. Therefore, it is important to understand oneself, but that understanding becomes extremely difficult if there is no intention to study and to understand oneself. The problem of sex, which is now so important, so vast in our lives, loses its meaning when there is the tenderness, the warmth, the kindliness, the mercy of love.

Question: Are you sure that it is not the myth of world teachership that keeps you going? To put it differently, are you not loyal to your past? Is there not a desire in you to fulfill the many expectations put in you? Are they not a hindrance to you? How can you go on unless you destroy the myth?

KRISHNAMURTI: The myth gives life, a spurious life, a life of impotence. The myth becomes necessary when there is no understanding of truth every minute. Most people's lives are guided by myths, which means that they believe in something, and the belief is a myth. Either they believe themselves to be the world teacher or they follow an ideal, or they have a message for the world, or they believe in God, or they hold to the left formula for the government of the world, or to the right. Most people are caught in a myth, and if the myth is taken away, their life is empty. Sirs, if all your beliefs, all your titles, all your possessions, all your memories are removed, what are you? You are empty, are you not? Therefore your possessions, your ideas, your beliefs are myths which you must hold to, or you are lost.

Now, the questioner wants to know if it is not the myth of world teachership that keeps me going. I am really not interested in whether I am or I am not; I am not particularly concerned because I am interested to find out *what is* and to see the truth of *what is* from moment to moment. Truth is not a continuity. That which continues has an end, that which continues knows death. But that which is from moment to moment is eternal, it is timeless, and to be aware of that which is true from moment to moment is to be in the state of eternity. To know the eternal there must be the moment to moment life, not the continuous life, for that which continues has an end, it knows death; whereas, that which is living from moment to moment, without the residue of yesterday, is timeless—and that is not myth. That state can be only when one is not loyal to the past because it is the past, yesterday, that corrupts, destroys, and prevents the present, which is now, today. Yesterday uses today as a passage to tomorrow, so the past molds the present and projects the future; and that process, that continuity of mind knows death, and such a mind can never discover reality.

So, it is neither the myth nor loyalty to the past, nor the desire to fulfill those expectations that have been placed in me that makes me go on. On the contrary, they are all a hindrance. The expectations, the past and loyalty to the past, the attachment to a label—they are a perverting influence, they give a fictitious life. That is why those people who believe in a myth are very active and enthusiastic. Don't you know people who believe in myths? How they work, work, work; and the moment they don't work, they come to an end. Sir, the man who works making money, that is his myth. Just watch him when he retires at the age of 50 or 60—he declines very rapidly because his myth is taken away. Similarly with the political leader; remove his myth and you will see how soon he sinks, he disintegrates. It is the same with the man who believes in something. Doubt, question, condemn, remove his belief, and he is done for. Therefore, belief, loyalty, or adherence to the past, or living up to an expectation is a hindrance.

So, you want to know why I keep going? Obviously, sir, I feel I have something to say. And also there is the natural affection for something, the love of truth. When one loves, one keeps going—and love is not a myth. You can build a myth about love, but to the man who knows love, love is not a myth. He may be alone in a room or sitting on a platform or digging in the garden—to him it is the same because his heart is full. It is like having a well in your garden that is always filled with fresh waters—the waters that quench the thirst, the waters that purify, the waters that put away corruption—and when there is such love, it is not mere mechanical routine to go from meeting to meeting, from discussion to discussion, from interview to interview. That would be a bore, and I could not do it. To do something which becomes a routine thing would be to destroy oneself.

Sirs, when you love, when your heart is full, you will know what it is to strive without effort, to live without conflict. It is the mind that does not love that is taken up with flattery, that enjoys adulation and avoids insult, that needs a crowd, a platform, that needs confusion; but such a mind, such a heart, will not know love. The man whose heart is filled with the things of the mind, his world is a world of myth, and on myths he lives; but he who is free of myths knows love.

August 8, 1948

Seventh Talk in Bangalore

I think by understanding relationship we shall understand what we mean by independence. Life is a process of constant movement in relationship, and without understanding relationship we shall bring about confusion and struggle and fruitless effort. So, it is important to understand what we mean by relationship because out of relationship society is built, and there can be no isolation. There is no such thing as living in isolation. That which is isolated soon dies.

So, our problem is not what is independence but what we mean by relationship. In understanding relationship, which is the conduct between human beings whether intimate or foreign, whether close or far away, we shall begin to understand the whole process of existence and the conflict between bondage and independence. So, we must very carefully examine what we mean by relationship. Is not relationship at present a process of isolation and, therefore, a constant conflict? The relationship between you and another, between you and your wife, between you and society, is the product of this isolation. By isolation I mean that we are all the time seeking security, gratification, and power. After all, each one of us in our relationship with another is seeking gratification, and where there is search for comfort, for security—whether it be a nation or an individual—there must be isolation, and that which is in isolation invites conflict. Anything that resists is bound to produce conflict between itself and that which it is resisting; and since most of our relationship is a form of resistance, we create a society which inevitably breeds isolation and hence conflict within and without that isolation. So, we must examine relationship as it actually works in our lives. After all, what I am—my actions, my thoughts, my feelings, my motives, my intentions—brings about that relationship between myself and another which we call society. There is no society without this relationship between two people, and before we can talk about independence, wave the flag, and all the rest of it, we have to understand relationship, which means we must examine ourselves in our relationship with another.

Now, if we examine our life, our relationship with another, we will see that it is a process of isolation. We are really not concerned with another; though we talk a great deal about it, actually we are not concerned. We are related to someone only as long as that relationship gratifies us, as long as it gives us a refuge, as long as it satisfies us. But the moment there is a disturbance in the relationship which produces discomfort in ourselves, we discard that relationship. In other words, there is relationship only as long as we are gratified. This may sound harsh, but if you really examine your life very closely, you will see it is a fact; and to avoid a fact is to live in ignorance, which can never produce right relationship. So, if we look into our lives and observe relationship, we see it is a process of building resistance against another, a wall over which we look and observe the other; but we always retain the wall and remain behind it, whether it be a psychological wall, a material wall, an economic wall, or a national wall. As long as we live in isolation, behind a wall, there is no relationship with another, and we live enclosed because it is much more gratifying, we think it is much more secure. The world is so disruptive, there is so much sorrow, so much pain, war, destruction, misery, that we want to escape and live within the walls of security of our own psychological being. So, relationship with most of us is actually a process of isolation, and obviously such relationship builds a society which is also isolating. That is exactly what is happening throughout the world—you remain in your isolation and stretch your hand over the wall, calling it nationalism, brotherhood, or what you will, but actually, sovereign governments, armies, continue. That is, clinging to your own limitations, you think you can create world unity, world peace—which is impossible. As long as you have a frontier, whether national, economic, religious, or social, it is an obvious fact that there cannot be peace in the world.

Now, the process of isolation is a process of the search for power, and whether one is seeking power individually or for a racial or national group, there must be isolation because the very desire for power, for position, is separatism. After all, that is what each one wants, is it not? He wants a powerful position in which he can dominate, whether at home, in the office, or in a bureaucratic regime. Each one is seeking power, and in seeking power he will establish a society which is based on power, military, industrial, economic, and so on—which again is obvious. Is not the desire for power in its very nature isolating? I think it is very important to understand this because the man who wants a peaceful world, a world in which there are no wars, no appalling destruction, no catastrophic misery on an immeasurable scale, must understand this fundamental question, must he not? As long as the individual seeks power, however much or however little, whether as a prime minster, as a governor, a lawyer, or merely as a husband or a wife in the home—that is, as long as you desire the sense of domination, the sense of compulsion, the sense of building power, influence, surely you are bound to create a society which is the result of an isolating process because power in its very nature is isolating, is separating. A man who is affectionate, who is kindly, has no sense of power, and therefore such a man is not bound to any nationality, to any flag. He has no flag. But the man who is seeking power in any form, whether derived from bureaucracy or from the self-projection which he calls God, is still caught in an isolating process. If you examine it very carefully, you will see that the desire for power in its very nature is a process of enclosure. Each one is seeking his own position, his own security, and as long as that motive exists, society must be built on an isolating process. Where there is the search for power, there is a process of isolation, and that which is isolated is bound to create conflict. That is exactly what is happening throughout the world: each group is seeking power and thereby isolating itself, and this is the process of nationalism, of patriotism, ultimately leading to war and destruction.

Now, without relationship, there is no possibility of existence in life, and as long as relationship is based on power, on domination, there must be the process of isolation, which inevitably invites conflict. There is no such thing as living in isolation—no country, no people, no individual, can live in isolation, yet because you are seeking power in so many different ways, you breed isolation. The nationalist is a curse because through his very nationalistic, patriotic spirit, he is creating a wall of isolation. He is so identified with his country that he builds a wall against another. And what happens, sirs, when you build a wall against something? That something is constantly beating against your wall. When you resist something, the very resistance indicates that you are in conflict with the other. So nationalism, which is a process of isolation, which is the outcome of the search for power, cannot bring about peace in the world. The man who is a nationalist and talks of brotherhood is telling a lie, he is living in a state of contradiction.

So, peace in the world is essential, otherwise we will be destroyed; a few may escape, but there will be greater destruction than ever before unless we solve the problem of peace. Peace is not an ideal; an ideal, as we discussed, is fictitious. What is actual must be understood, and that understanding of the actual is prevented by the fiction which we call an ideal. The actual is that each one is seeking power, titles, positions of authority, and so on—all of which is covered up in various forms by well-meaning words.

This is a vital problem, it is not a theoretical problem nor one that can be postponed—it demands action now because the catastrophe is obviously coming. If it does not come tomorrow, it will come next year, or soon after, because the momentum of the isolating process is already here; and he who really thinks about it must tackle the root of the problem, which is the individual's search for power, creating the power-seeking group, race, and nation.

Now, can one live in the world without the desire for power, for position, for authority? Obviously one can. One does it when one does not identify oneself with something greater. This identification with something greater—the party, the country, the race, the religion, God—is the search for power. Because you in yourself are empty, dull, weak, you like to identify yourself with something greater. That desire to identify yourself with something greater is the desire for power. That is why nationalism or any communal spirit is such a curse in the world; it is still the desire for power. So, the important thing in understanding life, and therefore relationship, is to discover the motive that is driving each one of us because what that motive is, the environment is. That motive brings either peace or destruction in the world. And so it is very important for each one of us to be aware that the world is in a state of misery and destruction and to realize that if we are seeking power, consciously or unconsciously, we are contributing to that destruction, and therefore our relationship with society will be a constant process of conflict. There are multiple forms of power, it is not merely the acquisition of position and wealth. The very desire to be something is a form of power, which brings isolation and therefore conflict; and unless each one understands the motive, the intention of his actions, mere government legislation is of very little importance because the inner is always overcoming the outer. You may outwardly build a peaceful structure but the men who run it will alter it according to their intention. That is why it is very important for those who wish to create a new culture, a new society, a new state, first to understand themselves. In becoming aware of oneself, of the various inward movements and fluctuations, one will understand the motives, the intentions, the perils that are hidden; and only in that awareness is there transformation. Regeneration can come about only when there is cessation of this search for power; and then only can we create a new culture, a society which will not be based on conflict, but on understanding. Relationship is a process of self-revelation, and without knowing oneself, the ways of one's own mind and heart, merely to establish an outward order, a system, a cunning formula, has very little meaning. So, what is important is to understand oneself in relationship with another. Then relationship becomes, not a process of isolation, but a movement in which you discover your own motives, your own thoughts, your own pursuits; and that very discovery is the beginning of liberation, the beginning of transformation. It is only this immediate transformation that can bring about the fundamental, radical revolution in the world which is so essential. Revolution within the walls of isolation is not a revolution. Revolution comes only when the walls of isolation are destroyed, and that can take place only when you are no longer seeking power.

I have several questions, and I will try to answer as many of them as possible.

Question: Can I remain a government official if I want to follow your teachings? The same question would arise with regard to so many professions. What is the right solution to the problem of livelihood?

KRISHNAMURTI: Sirs, what do we mean by livelihood? It is the earning of one's needs, food, clothing, and shelter, is it not? The difficulty of livelihood arises only when we use the essentials of life—food, clothing, and shelter—as a means of psychological aggression. That is, when I use the needs, the necessities, as a means of self-aggrandizement, then the problem of livelihood arises; and our society is essentially based, not on supplying the essentials, but on psychological aggrandizement, using the essentials as a psychological expansion of oneself. Sirs, you have to think it out a little bit. Obviously, food, clothing, and shelter could be produced abundantly; there is enough scientific knowledge to supply the demand, but the demand for war is greater, not merely by the warmongers, but by each of us, because each one of us is violent. There is sufficient scientific knowledge to give man all the necessities; it has been worked out, and they could be produced so that no man would be in need. Why does it not happen? Because, no one is satisfied with food, clothing, and shelter; each one wants something more, and, put in different words, the 'more' is power. But it would be brutish merely to be satisfied with needs. We will be satisfied with needs in the true sense, which is freedom from the desire for power, only when we have found the inner treasure which is imperishable, which you call God, truth, or what you will. If you can find those imperishable riches within yourself, then you are satisfied with few things—which few things can be supplied.

But, unfortunately, we are carried away by sensate values. The values of the senses have become more important than the values of the real. After all, our whole social structure, our present civilization, is essentially based on sensate values. Sensate values are not merely the values of the senses but the values of thought because thought is also the result of the senses; and when the mechanism of thought, which is the intellect, is cultivated, then there is in us a predominance of thought, which is also a sensory value. So, as long as we are seeking sensate value—whether of touch, of taste, of smell, of perception, or of thought—the outer becomes far more significant than the inner, and the mere denial of the outer is not the way to the inner. You may deny the outer and withdraw from the world into a jungle or a cave and there think of God; but that very denial of the outer, that thinking of God, is still sensate because thought is sensate; and any value based on the sensate is bound to create confusion—which is what is happening in the world at the present time. The sensate is dominant, and as long as the social structure is built on that, the means of livelihood becomes extraordinarily difficult.

So, what is the right means of livelihood? This question can be answered only when there is a complete revolution in the present social structure, not according to the formula of the right or of the left, but a complete revolution in values which are not based on the sensate. Now, those who have leisure—like the older people who are drawing their pensions, who have spent their earlier years seeking God or else various forms of destruction—if they really gave their time, their energy, to finding out the right solution, then they would act as a medium, as an instrument for bringing about revolution in the world. But they are not interested. They want security. They have worked so many years for their pensions, and they would like to live comfortably for the rest of their lives. They have time, but they are indifferent; they are only concerned with some abstraction which they call God, and which has no reference to the actual; but their abstraction is not God, it is a form of escape. And those who fill their lives with ceaseless activity are caught in the middle, they have not the time to find the answers to the various problems of life. So, those who are concerned with these things, with bringing about a radical transformation in the world through the understanding of themselves, in them alone is there hope.

Sirs, surely we can see what is a wrong profession. To be a soldier, a policeman, a lawyer, is obviously a wrong profession because they thrive on conflict, on dissension; and the big businessman, the capitalist, thrives on exploitation. The big businessman may be an individual, or it may be the state—if the state takes over big business it does not cease to exploit you and me. And as society is based on the army, the police, the law, the big businessman—that is, on the principle of dissension, exploitation, and violence—how can you and I, who want a decent, right profession, survive? There is increasing unemployment, greater armies, larger police forces with their secret service; and big business is becoming bigger and bigger, forming vast corporations which are eventually taken over by the state, for the state has become a great corporation in certain countries. Given this situation of exploitation, of a society built on dissension, how are you going to find a right livelihood? It is almost impossible, is it not? Either you will have to go away and form, with a few people, a community—a self-supporting, cooperative community—or merely succumb to the vast machine. But you see, most of us are not interested in really finding the right livelihood. Most of us are concerned with getting a job and sticking to it in the hope of advancement with more and more pay. Because each one of us wants safety, security, a permanent position, there is no radical revolution. It is not those who are self-satisfied, contented, but only the adventurous, those who want to experiment with their lives, with their existence, who discover the real things, a new way of living.

So, before there can be a right livelihood, the obviously false means of earning a livelihood must first be seen—the army, the law, the police, the big business corporations that are sucking people in and exploiting them, whether in the name of the state, of capital, or of religion. When you see the false and eradicate the false, there is transformation, there is revolution; and it is that revolution alone that can create a new society. To seek, as an individual, a right livelihood is good, is excellent, but that does not solve the vast problem. The vast problem is solved only when you and I are not seeking security. There is no such thing as security. When you seek security, what happens? What is happening in the world at the present time? All Europe wants security, is crying for it, and what is happening? They want security through their nationalism. After all, you are a nationalist because you want security, and you think that through nationalism you are going to have security. It has been proved over and over again that you cannot have security through nationalism because nationalism is a process of isolation, inviting wars, misery, and destruction. So, right livelihood on a vast scale must begin with those who understand what is false. When you are battling against the false, then you are creating the right means of livelihood. When you are battling against the whole structure of dissension, of exploitation, whether by the left or by the right, or the authority of religion and the priests, that is the right profession at the present time because that will create a new society, a new culture. But to battle, you must see very clearly and very definitely that which is false so that the false drops away. To discover what is false, you must be aware of it; you must observe everything that you are doing, thinking, and feeling, and out of that you will not only discover what is false, but out of that there will come a new vitality, a new energy, and that energy will dictate what kind of work to do or not to do.

Question: Can you state briefly the basic principles on which a new society should be built?

KRISHNAMURTI: I can state the principles—that is very simple—but it would be of no value. What has value is that you and I should discover together the basic principles on which a new society can be built because the moment we discover together what are the basic principles, there is a new basis of relationship between us. Do you understand? Then I am no longer the teacher and you the pupil, or you the audience and I the lecturer—we start on a different footing altogether. That means no authority, does it not? We are partners in discovering, and therefore we are in cooperation; therefore, you do not dominate or influence me, nor I you. We are both discovering, and when there is the intention on your part as well as on mine to discover what are the basic principles of a new culture, obviously there cannot be an authoritative spirit, can there? Therefore, we have established a new principle already, have we not? As long as there is authority in relationship, there is compulsion; and nothing can be created through compulsion. A government that compels, a teacher that compels, an environment that compels, does not bring about relationship but merely a state of slavery. So, we have discovered one thing together, for we know that we both want to create a new society in which there can be no authority; and that has an enormous significance because the structure of our present social order is based on authority. The specialist in education, the specialist in medicine, the military specialist, the specialist in law, the bureaucrat—they all dominate us. The *shastras* say so, therefore it must be true; my guru says so, therefore it must be right—and I am going to follow it. In other words, in a society where there is the search for the real, the search for understanding, the search for the establishment of right relationship between two human beings, there can be no authority. The moment you discard authority, you are in partnership; therefore, there is cooperation, there is affection—which is contrary to the present social structure.

At present, you leave your children to the educator, while the educator himself needs educating. Religiously, you are merely imitative, copying machines. In every direction you are dominated, influenced, compelled, forced; and how can there be a relationship between the exploiter and the exploited, between those who are in power and those who are subject to power, unless you yourself want the same kind of power? If you do, then you are in relationship with that power. But if you see that any desire for power is in itself destructive, then there is no relationship with those who seek power. So, we begin to discover the basic principles upon which a new society can be built. Obviously, a relationship based on domination is no longer a relationship. When there is no domination, no authority, no compulsion, what does it mean? Obviously, there is affection, there is tenderness, there is love, there is understanding. For that to take place, domination must disappear. But we can discuss this presently, if you will listen to me. You seem irritated—perhaps I am upsetting your apple cart a little bit, but you will go out and do exactly the same thing that you did before because you are not really concerned with the finding of a new basic order. You want to be secure, you want your positions, or such positions as you have, and you want to use them for your own purpose, which you call noble; but it is still a form of self-expansion, exploitation.

So, our difficulty in these discussions and talks is that we are not very serious about all this. We would like things to be altered, but slowly, gradually, and at our convenience. We don't want to be disturbed too much, so we are not really basically concerned with a new culture. The man who is concerned sees as false the obviously pernicious things such as authority, belief, nationalism, the whole hierarchical spirit. When all that is put aside, what happens? You are merely a citizen, a human being without authority; and when you have no authority, then perhaps you will have love, and therefore you will have understanding. That is what is required—a group of people who understand, who have affection, whose hearts are not filled with empty words and empty phrases, the things of the mind. It is they who will create a new culture, not the spinner of words. Therefore, it is very important for each one of us to see himself in the mirror of relationship, for out of that alone can there be a new culture.

Question: What must we do to have really good government, and not merely self-government?

KRISHNAMURTI: Sirs, to have a good government, you must first understand what you mean by government. Don't let us use words without a referent, words without meaning, without something behind them. The word *watch* has a referent, but *good government* has no referent. To find the referent, we will have to discuss what we mean by *government* and what we mean by *good;* but merely to say what is good government has no meaning.

So, first, let us find out what we mean by good. I am not splitting hairs, I am not being schoolboyish discussing at a union because it is very important to find out what we are talking about, and not merely use words that have little meaning. I know we are fed on words; it creates an impression for us to talk of having self-government and wave the flag—you know the whole business of being enchanted with words when our hearts and minds are empty. So, let us find out what we mean by good government.

What do we mean by good? Good obviously has a referent based on pleasure and pain. Good is that which gives you pleasure; bad that which gives you pain, whether outwardly or inwardly, whether inside or outside the skin. That is a fact, is it not? We are discussing the fact, not what you would like it to be. The fact is, as long as you seek pleasure in various forms—as security, as comfort, as power, as money—that pleasure is what you call good; and anything that disturbs the state of pleasure, you call not good. I am not discussing philosophically, but actually. Pleasure is what you want; so obviously you call good that which gives you security, comfort, position, power, safety. Do you follow? That is, good government is that body which can supply what you want; and if the government does not give you what you want, you say, "Throw it out"—unless it is a totalitarian government. Even totalitarian governments can be destroyed if the people say, "We don't want this." But nowadays it is almost impossible to bring about physical revolution because the airplanes and other war machines, without which there cannot be modern revolution, are in the hands of the government. So, the good is what you want, is it not, sirs; don't let us fool ourselves and spin a lot of words about abstract good and abstract evil. Actually in your daily life, the fact is that those who give you what you want, you call good, noble, efficient, and so on, using various terms. What you want is gratification in different forms, and that which can give it to you, you call beneficient.

So, the government is the body which you create out of your want, is it not? That is, the government is you. What you are, the government is, which is an obvious fact in the world. You hate a particular country, and elect those people who will support your hate. You are communalistically inclined and you create a government that has your communalistic outlook—which is again an obvious fact, we need not elaborate it. Since what you are, your government is, how can you have *good* government? You can have good government only when you have transformed yourselves. Otherwise, the government is merely a bureau, a group of people whom you have elected to supply you with what you want. You say you don't want war, but you encourage all the causes that breed war, like nationalism, communalism, and so on. That being your condition, you create a government, as you create a society, after your own likeness; and having created that government, the government in turn exploits you. So, it is a vicious circle. There can be good—I won't call it good—there can be sane government only when you yourself are sane. Sirs, don't smile. It is a fact; we are insane, we are not rational, clean human beings. We are unbalanced; therefore, our governments are unbalanced. Do you mean to say, sirs, that, seeing the whole world caught up in the appalling catastrophe of war and the production of war machines, a sane human being does not want to break it up? Therefore, he will find out what are the causes of war and not say, "Well, it is my country, I must protect it"—which is too immature and silly.

Now, one of the causes of war is greed—greed to be something greater—which causes you to identify yourself with the country. You say, "I am a Hindu," "I am a Buddhist," "I am a Christian," "I am a Russian," or what you will. That is one of the causes of war. And a man who is sane says, "I am going to get rid of that insane imitation which ultimately produces destruction." Therefore, we must first create sanity, not a plan for a new government, or a so-called good government; and in order to be sane, you must know what you are, you must be aware of yourself. But again, you see, you are not interested. You are interested in waving flags, you are interested in listening to speeches which have no meaning, you are interested in stimulation. All these are indications of insanity. And how can you expect a sane government when the citizens are not fully awake, when they are half-alert and unbalanced?

Sirs, when you yourselves are in confusion, you create the leader who is confused, and you will hear the voice of him who is confused. If you are not confused, if you are clear, tranquil, you will have no leader; if you are clear, you will not wait for the government to tell you what to do. Why does a man want a government? Sirs, some of you smile, and you will push it out. Because you don't know how to love rationally, humanly, you want somebody to tell you what to do; therefore, there is the multiplication of laws, laws, and more laws, what you must and must not do. So, it is your fault, sirs. You are responsible for the government that you have, or are going to have, because unless you radically transform yourselves, what you are your government is. If you are communalistically minded, you will create a government that is like you. And what does it mean? More disturbance, more destruction.

So, there can be a sane society, a sane world, only when you, as part of that society, that world, are breaking away, that is, becoming sane; and there can be sanity only when you spurn authority, when you are not caught in the nationalistic, patriotic spirit, when you treat human beings as human beings, not as Brahmins or as of any other caste or country. And it is impossible to treat human beings as human beings if you label them, if you term them, if you give them a name as Hindus, Russians, or what you will. It is so much easier to label people, for then you can pass by and kick them, drop a bomb on India or Japan. But if you have no labels, but merely meet people as human beings, then what happens? You have to be very alert, you have to be very wise in your relationship with another. But as you don't want to do that, you create a government befitting yourself.

Question: What is eternal—love or death? What happens to love when death breaks its thread? What happens to death when love asserts it claim?

KRISHNAMURTI: Now again, let us find out what we mean by death and what we mean by love. Sorry, some of you get bored with all this. Are you bored?

Comment: No, sir.

KRISHNAMURTI: I am surprised because we have taken up very serious things. Life is serious, life is very earnest. It is only the empty-headed and the dull at heart who are trivial, and if you are bored with the serious things of life, it indicates your own immaturity. This is a question with which everyone is concerned, whether it be the totalitarian, the politician, or you, because death awaits each one of us, whether we like it or not. You may be a high government official with titles, wealth, position, and a red carpet, but there is this inevitable thing at the end of it. So, what do we mean by death? By death we obviously mean putting an end to continuity, do we not? There is a physical death, and we are a little bit anxious about it, but that does not matter if we can overcome it by continuing in some other form. So when we ask about death, we are concerned with whether there is continuity or not. And what is the thing that continues? Obviously, not your body because every day we see that people who die are burned or buried. Therefore, we mean, do we not, a supersensory continuity, a psychological continuity, a thought continuity, a continuity of character, which is termed the soul, or what you will. We want to know if thought continues. That is, I have meditated, I have practiced so many things, I have not finished writing my book, I have not completed my career, I am weak and need time to grow strong, I want to continue my pleasure, and so on—and I am afraid that death will put an end to all that. So, death is a form of frustration, is it not? I am doing something, and I don't want to end it; I want continuity in order to fulfill myself. Now, is there fulfillment through continuity? Obviously, there is fulfillment of a sort through continuity. If I am writing a book, I don't want to die until I have finished it; I want time to develop a certain character, and so on. So, there is fear of death only when there is the desire to fulfill oneself because to fulfill oneself, there must be time, longevity, continuity. But if you can fulfill yourself from moment to moment, you are not afraid of death.

Now, our problem is how to have continuity in spite of death, is it not? And you want an assurance from me, or, if I don't assure you of that, you go to somebody else, to your gurus, to your books, or to various other forms of distraction and escape. So, you listening to me and I talking to you, we are going to find out together what we actually mean by continuity, what it is that continues, and what we want to continue. That which continues is obviously a wish, a desire, is it not? I am not powerful but I would like to be; I have not built my house but I would like to build it; I have not got that title but I would like to get it; I have not amassed enough money but I will do so presently; I would like to find God in this life—and so on and on. So, continuity is the process of want. When this is put an end to, you call it death, do you not? You want to continue desire as a means of achievement, as a process through which to fulfill yourself. Surely, this is fairly simple, is it not? Now, obviously thought continues in spite of your physical death. This has been proved. Thought is a continuity because, after all, what are you? You are merely a thought, are you not? You are the thought of a name, the thought of a position, the thought of money; you are merely an idea. Remove the idea, remove the thought, and where are you? So, you are an embodiment of thought as the 'me'. Now, you say thought must continue because thought is going to enable me to fulfill myself, that thought will ultimately find the real. Is that not so? That is why you want thought to continue. You want thought to continue because you think thought is going to find the real, which you call happiness, God, or what you will.

Now, through the continuity of thought, do you find the real? To put it differently, does the thought process discover the real? Do you understand what I mean? I want happiness, and I search for it through various means—property, position, wealth, women, men, or whatever it be. All that is the demand of a thought for happiness, is it not? Now, can thought find happiness? If it can, then thought must have a continuity. But what is thought? Thought is merely the response of memory, is it not? If you had no memory, there would be no thought. You would be in a state of amnesia, of complete blankness—as most people want to be. Thinking mesmerizes itself and remains in a certain state, which is a state of blankness. But we are not trying to discuss the state of amnesia, we want to find out what thought is. Thought, if you will look at it a little closely, is obviously the response of memory, and memory is the result of an uncompleted experience. So, through an incomplete experience you think you are going to find the complete, the whole, the real. How can it be done? Do you follow what I mean? Sirs, probably you are not thinking this out. You want to know if there is or if there is not continuity, that is all; you want an assurance. When you are seeking an assurance you are seeking authority, gratification—you don't want to know the real. It is only the real that will liberate, not an assurance or my giving you that assurance. We are trying to find out what is true in all this.

Since thought is the outcome of an incomplete experience—because you don't remember, in the psychological sense, a complete experience—how can thought, through its own conditioned, incomplete state, find that which is complete? Do you follow? So, our question is: Can there be a renewal, a regeneration, a freshness, a newness, through the continuity of the thought process? After all, if there is renewal, then we are not afraid of death. If for you there is renewal from moment to moment, there is no death. But there is death, and the fear of death, if you demand a continuity of the thought process. It is only thought that can continue, obviously, an idea about yourself. That idea is the outcome of thought, the outcome of a conditioned mind, because thought is the outcome of the past, it is founded on the past. And through time, through continuing the past, will you find the timeless?

So, we look to continuity as a means of renewal, as a means of bringing about a new state. Otherwise we don't want continuity, do we? That is, I want continuity only if it promises the new state; otherwise, I don't want it because my present state is miserable. If through continuity I can find happiness, then I want continuity. But can I find happiness through continuity? There is only the continuity of thought—thought being the response of memory, and memory is always conditioned, always in the past. Memory is always dead, it comes to life only through the present. Therefore, thought as a continuity cannot be the means of renewal. So, to continue thought is merely to continue the past in a modified form, and therefore it is not a renewal; therefore, through that passage there is no hope. There is hope only when I see the truth that through continuity there is no renewal. And when I see that, what happens? Then I am only concerned with the ending of the thought process from moment to moment—which is not insanity! The thought process ceases only when I understand the falseness of the thought process as a means of achieving a desirable end or of avoiding a painful one. When I see the false as the false, the false drops away. When the false drops away, what then is the state of mind? Then the mind is in a state of high sensitivity, of high receptivity, of great tranquillity, because there is no fear. What happens when there is no fear? There is love, is there not? It is only in the negative state that love can be, not in the positive state. The positive state is the continuity of thought towards an end, and as long as that exists, there cannot be love.

The questioner also wants to know what happens to love when death breaks its thread. Love is not a continuity. If you watch yourself, if you observe your own love, you will see that love is from moment to moment, you are not thinking that it must continue. That which continues is a hindrance to love. It is only thought that can continue, not love. You can think about love, and that thought can continue, but the thought about love is not love—and that is your difficulty. You think about love, and you want that thought to continue; therefore, you ask, "What happens to love when death comes?" But you are not concerned with love; you are concerned with the thought of love, which is not love. When you love, there is no continuity. It is only the thought that wishes love to continue, but the thought is not love. Sirs, this is very important. When you love, when you really love somebody, you are not thinking, you are not calculating—your whole heart, your whole being is open. But when you merely think about love, or about the person whom you love, your heart is dry—and therefore you are already dead. When there is love, there is no fear of death. Fear of death is merely the fear of not continuing, and when there is love there is no sense of continuity. It is a state of being.

The questioner also asks, "What happens to death when love asserts its claim?" Sirs, love has no claim—and that is the beauty of love. That which is the highest state of negation does not claim, does not demand; it is a state of being. And when there is love, there is no death; there is death only when the thought process arises. When there is love, there is no death, because there is no fear; and love is not a continuous state—which is again the thought process. Love is merely being from moment to moment. Therefore, love is its own eternity.

August 15, 1948

Poona, India, 1948

First Talk in Poona

As we are to have several talks during the coming weeks, I think it is important to understand the relationship between the speaker and yourself. First of all, we are not dealing with ideas nor with opinions. I am not trying to convince you of any particular point of view, nor am I trying to convey any idea because I do not believe that ideas, opinions, can bring about a fundamental change in action. What brings about a radical change is understanding the truth of *what is*. So, we are not dealing with opinions or with ideas. Ideas always meet with resistance; one idea can be opposed by another idea, and an opinion can create a contradiction. Therefore, to seek the solution to a problem through an idea is utterly futile. As I say, ideas do not bring about a radical transformation, and at the present time in world affairs and in our individual lives, a radical transformation, a revolution of values, is essential. Such a change of values is not brought about by merely changing ideas or by substituting systems. So, I am not trying to persuade you or dissuade you on any particular point of view. Nor am I acting as a guru to anybody because I do not think that a guru is necessary in the discovery of truth. On the contrary, a guru is an impediment to the discovery of the real. Nor am I acting as a leader, creating an opinion, an organization, for a leader is a deteriorating factor in society.

So, we must be very clear, both you and I, as to the nature of our relationship, and you must know what is the attitude of the speaker before you can reject or accept what he says. If I may suggest, before you reject any of the things I say, first very carefully examine them without any bias. It is very difficult to examine a thing without bias, without prejudice; but if we are to understand something, there must be no prejudice, and we cannot merely relegate what is being said to some ancient authority. That is merely another form of escape. What I want to try to do during these discussions and talks is to point out certain things; and while I point them out, please do not become mere observers, spectators, listeners. Because, you and I are going to undertake a journey to see if we can discover the whole sequence of modern civilization, its splendor and its catastrophe, in which both the East and the West are involved. It is a voyage of discovery which you and I are going to undertake together in order to see very clearly and directly what is taking place. For that, you do not want a leader, you do not want a guru, you do not need an organization, or any opinions. What you do need is clarity of perception to see things as they are, and when you see things thus clearly, truth comes into being. To see clearly you must give not sporadic attention but sustained, direct, positive attention without any distraction—and that is going to be our difficulty.

We have so many problems—political, economic, social, and religious—all demanding action, but before we can act, we must know what the problem is. It would be really absurd merely to act without knowing the whole sequence of a problem. But most of us are concerned with action; we want to do something. There are communal problems, national problems, problems of war, problems of starvation, of linguistic differences, and innumerable other problems; and being confronted with them, we want to know what to do. Our whole impulse, our motive, is not to study the question or the problem but to do something about it. After all, a problem like starvation requires a great deal of study, a great deal of understanding. In understanding, there is action. Merely to act on some superficial response is utterly futile, leading to greater confusion.

Now, if you will, what you and I are going to do is to examine very clearly, sanely, and rationally the whole problem of our existence. I am not going to tell you what to think—which is what the propagandists do; but in examining *what is,* we are going to learn how to think about a problem, which is far more important than to be told what to think. The world problem at the present time is so grave, the catastrophe so imminent, the disaster so rapidly spreading, that to think merely according to a formula, whether of the left or of the right, is utterly futile. A formula cannot produce an answer; it can only produce action according to its own limited standard. So, what is important in these discussions and talks is first of all to realize that we are confronted with problems which need very careful study, not according to any premeditated plan or preconceived idea. I am not giving you a plan, nor am I telling you what to do, but you and I together are going to find out what the problem is. In understanding the problem, we shall understand the truth with regard to the problem—which is the only rational approach. If you are looking for a formula, for a system, I am afraid you will be disappointed because I do not propose to give you a formula. Life has no formula. It is the intellectual people who have a formula which they want to superimpose on life. We must be very clear about this. If you have come to this meeting out of curiosity because you have read something about my supposed position, you may be either satisfied or dissatisfied; but without serious intention, you will never understand the whole problem of existence. The problem is not merely Indian, Maharashtra or Gujarat, which is all childish; the problem is universal. Your problem is my problem, it is the problem of every individual, whether in Europe, America, or Russia.

So, I am going to help you to think rightly; you and I are going to undertake a journey into the problems of the present world crisis. To do that, I must invite your cooperation. Cooperation in this case consists in right listening; that is, you must experience what is being said as we go along together, and not merely listen to the lecture and then go away with certain set ideas of acceptance or denial. You and I together are to undertake a journey, and to undertake the journey you must be prepared to experience, to observe, to watch, and to be aware of the implications of that journey. So, if I may say so, to understand you must not merely listen objectively to what is being discussed but inwardly experience it. I am not being dogmatic—it is stupid to be dogmatic, and people who are dogmatic are intolerable. The man who says he knows does not know—one should beware of such people. In undertaking the journey, we must be very clear about what is necessary. The first essential is that we should not be tethered to any past experience, whether national, religious, or personal. If we undertake a journey of real investigation, we must set aside all those bondages that are holding us. That is difficult, especially for the older people who are more firmly rooted in tradition, in family, and for people with a bank account; and the young will come forward if there is any reward, if they are guaranteed a joy, a position, an immediate answer. So, we are beset with many difficulties.

Now, what is our problem? The common daily problem of existence is obviously one of suffering, is it not? Suffering in different forms is the common lot of all of us, whether it be economic, social, the suffering that death brings, and so on. There is naturally a desire to be secure in the midst of the insecurity, the uncertainty about us. We want to have security with regard to food, clothing, and shelter; we want security in our relationships, in our ideas. Is that not what we are seeking? We want to be certain in our possessions, whether those possessions be things, people, or ideas; and for our possessions we are willing to battle, maim, destroy. In order to be secure in our relationships, secure in our possessions, secure in our ideas, we have created national frontiers, beliefs, Gods, leaders, and so on. When each one of us is thus seeking security, naturally there must be opposition, and this opposition creates conflict in our life. When we are seeking security, existence is one constant battle, one constant conflict; and being in conflict, being in misery, we want to find the truth. Put succinctly, that is our position, and we will work out the details as we go along. The important thing in our life is how to avoid conflict, how to have no resistance—surely, that is our problem, is it not?

Throughout the world there are wars, starvation, strife, conflict between peoples, between families, in the family and outside the family; there is division between Brahmins and non-Brahmins, between Indians and Europeans, between Japanese and Americans, and so on and on. Our immediate problem is that of food, clothing, and shelter, and whether these necessities can be produced for everybody so that there is no starvation in the world. Each party, each system, whether of the left or of the right, offers a conflicting solution, and you and I are equally in the strife, politically, economically, and socially. Our life is one of constant struggle to maintain our position, to accumulate money and to hold on to it; and we are beset with innumerable other problems—the problem of death and what happens after death, the problem of whether there is God, what truth is, and so on. How are you and I to approach these complex problems? All the intellectual people of the world who have gone into these problems and have tried to show us the way have failed. That is the calamity of modern civilization, is it not? The intellectual people have collapsed, their formulas are unworkable, and we are directly confronted with the problem of starvation and of right relationship. So, our concern is with action, with relationship, with finding out how you and I can approach anew all these problems. We have seen that approaching them along the old and routine lines has not produced any fundamental change but has only increased the confusion. So, how can you and I approach these problems anew? Obviously, we cannot wait for somebody else, a guru or a leader, to resolve our difficulties. That is infantile, it is immature thinking. The responsibility is yours and mine, and since leaders have failed, since systems and formulas have no meaning, we cannot sit back as onlookers and expect to be told what to do. So, how are you and I going to act with regard to these problems?

Before we can act, we must know how to think. There is no action without thought.

Most of us do act without thought, and acting without thought has led us to this confusion. So, we must find out how to think before we can know how to act. You and I must find out the right way to think, must we not? If we merely quote the Bhagavad-Gita, the Bible, or the Koran, it has no meaning—quoting what somebody else has said is of no value. Repeating a truth is to repeat a lie. By repeating, we think we have solved the problem. How absurd! Authority, whether modern or ancient, has no relation to right thinking. Only when you and I find out how to think rightly can we solve the colossal problems that confront us. If we wait for other people to do the work, they will become leaders, and leaders inevitably lead us to catastrophe.

Now, how do you set about thinking rightly? To think rightly, you must know yourself, must you not? If you do not know yourself, you have no basis for right thinking, and therefore what you think has no value. You are not different from the world; the world problem is your problem, and the process of yourself is the total process of the world. That is, you have created the problem, which is both individual and universal, and to bring about the right action which will solve it, you must be able to think rightly; and to think rightly, you must obviously know yourself. So, our chief concern is not mere personal salvation, but to know how to think rightly through self-knowledge. Individuals, you and I, create the world; therefore, the individual is of the highest importance. You and I are responsible for the brutal confusion in the world—the patriotism, the conflicting nationalisms, the absurd divisions of people. We will go into all this later. But obviously, you and I are responsible for the world's misery, not some mysterious force. It is our direct responsibility, and to bring about the right action, there must be right thinking. Therefore, you and I are of the utmost importance. As I said, as long as you do not know what you are, you have no basis for right thinking, and that is why it is essential to know yourself before you do something. The clever people who are here may say, "We know all about the world's problem." When they say that, it is because they do not want to act. To offer a solution for the world's problem without knowing oneself is merely a postponement of the inevitable because the world's problem is one's own problem, and the individual is not apart from the world.

In understanding yourself, you are not withdrawing from the world. There is no such thing as existence in isolation. Nothing lives in isolation, and I am not proposing an escape from life, an avoidance or a withdrawal from life. On the contrary, you can understand yourself only in relationship with things, with people, and with ideas, and that relationship is always in existence, it is never absent. Relationship is a process of self-revelation. You cannot deny relationship; if you deny it, you cease to be. So, what I am saying is practical, it is not something vague. But you must first see the problem and then find out how to approach it, and in approaching it rightly, you will be able to solve the problem. That is why you are of the highest importance.

I am going to talk to you during the next six weeks on how to understand oneself in order to have right thinking, and therefore right action, with regard to the problems that confront us. There is a difference between right thinking and right thought. Right thought is static whereas right thinking is pliable and in constant movement. Right thinking leads to discovery, to direct knowledge, and it comes through the observation of oneself. The individual is constantly varying, and therefore you require a mind that is extraordinarily swift. That is the only way to right thinking and hence to the right action which alone can solve this present confusion.

Three or four questions have been given to me, and I shall try to answer them.

Question: In view of the impending war and the atomic devastation of humanity, is it not futile to concentrate on mere individual transformation?

KRISHNAMURTI: It is a very complicated question and needs very careful study; I hope you will have the patience to go step by step with me, and not leave off halfway. We know what are the causes of war; they are fairly obvious, and even a schoolboy can see them—greed, nationalism, the search for power, geographical and national divisions, economic conflicts, sovereign states, patriotism, one ideology, whether of the left or of the right, trying to impose itself upon another, and so on. These causes of war are created by you and me. War is the spectacular expression of our daily existence, is it not? We identify ourselves with a particular group—national, religious, or racial—because it gives us a sense of power, and power inevitably brings about catastrophe. You and I are responsible for war, not Hitler, Stalin, or some other super-leader. It is a convenient expression to say that capitalists or insane leaders are responsible for war. At heart, each one wants to be wealthy, each one wants power. These are the causes of war, for which you and I are responsible. I think it is fairly clear that war is the result of our daily existence, only more spectacularly, more bloodily so. Since we are all trying to accumulate possessions, pile up money, naturally we create a society with frontiers, boundaries, tariff walls; and when one isolated nationality comes into conflict with another, inevitably war results—which is a fact. I do not know if you have thought of this problem at all. We are confronted with war, and must we not find who is responsible for it? Surely, a sane man will see that he is responsible and will say, "Look, I am creating this war; therefore, I shall cease to be national, I shall have no patriotism, no nationality, I shall not be Hindu, Muslim, or Christian, but a human being." That requires a certain clarity of thought and perception, which most of us are unwilling to face. If you personally are opposed to war—but not for the sake of an ideal because ideals are an impediment to direct action—what are you to do? What is a sane man to do who is opposed to war? First, he must cleanse his own mind, must he not?—free himself from the causes of war, such as greed. Therefore, since you are responsible for war, it is important to free yourself from the causes of war. That means, among other things, that you must cease to be national. Are you willing to do that? Obviously not, because you like to be called a Hindu, a Brahmin, or whatever your label is. That means that you worship the label and prefer it to living sanely and rationally, so you are going to be destroyed, whether you like it or not.

What is a person to do if he wants to free himself from the causes of war? How is he to stop war? Can the coming war be stopped? The momentum of greed, the power of nationalism, which every human being has set in motion—can they be stopped? Obviously they cannot be stopped. War can be stopped only when Russia, America, and all of us transform ourselves immediately and say that we will have no nationalism, we will not be Russians, Americans, Hindus, Muslims, Germans, or Englishmen, but human beings; we will be human beings in relationship, trying to live happily together. If the causes of war are eradicated from the heart and mind, then there is no war. But the momentum of power is still going on. I will give you an example. If a house is burning, what do we do? We try to save as much of the house as possible and study the causes of the fire; then we find the right kind of brick, the proper fire-resisting material, improved construction, and so on, and we build anew. In other words, we leave the house that is burning. Similarly, when a civilization is crumbling, is destroying itself, sane men who see they cannot do anything about it build a new one that will not burn. Surely, that is the only way to act, that is the only rational method—not merely to reform the old, to patch up the burning house.

Now, if I were to collect together, at this meeting and elsewhere, all who feel they are really free from the causes of war, then what would happen? That is, can peace be organized? Look at the implications of it, see what is involved in organizing peace. One of the causes of war is the desire for power—individual, group, and national. What happens if we form an organization for peace? We become a focal point of power, and the pursuit of power is one of the causes of war. There are continued wars, and yet when we organize for peace, we are creating an organization for power, which is one of the causes of war. The moment we organize for peace, we inevitably invite power; and when we have power, we are again creating the causes of war. So, what am I to do? Seeing that one of the causes of war is power, am I to oppose war, which means further power? In the very process of opposition, am I not creating power? Therefore, my problem is quite different. It is not an organizational problem. I cannot talk to a group but only to you as an individual, showing you the causes of war. You and I as individuals must give our thought to it and not leave it to somebody else. Surely, as in a family, when there is affection, when there is mercy, we need no organization for peace, what we need is mutual understanding, mutual cooperation. When there is no love, inevitably there is war. To understand the complex problem of war, one must approach it very simply. To approach it simply is to understand one's own relationship to the world. If in that relationship there is a sense of power, a sense of domination, that relationship inevitably creates a society based on power, on domination, which in turn brings about war. I may see that very clearly, but if I tell ten people about it and organize them, what have I done? I have created power, have I not? Because I have the support of ten people who are in opposition to the warmonger, I also am responsible for creating war. No organization is necessary. The organization is the power element that brings about war. There must be individuals who are opposed to war, but when you gather them into an organization, or represent a creed, the moment you do it you are in the same position as the warmonger. Most of us are satisfied with words, we live on words without meaning, but if we examine the problem very closely, very clearly, then the problem itself yields the answer, you do not have to seek it. So, each one of us must be aware of the causes of war, and each one must be free of them.

Question: Instead of having hairsplitting discussions on the question of being and becoming, why do you not apply yourself to some of the burning questions of the country and show us a way out? What is your position, for instance, on the questions of Hindu-Muslim unity, Pakistan-India amity, Brahmin and non-Brahmin rivalry, and whether Bombay should be a free city or part of Maharashtra? You will do a great service if you can suggest an effective solution to these difficult problems.

KRISHNAMURTI: Whether Bombay should be a free city or not, whether there should be unity among Hindus and Muslims, are problems like those which human beings throughout the world are having. Are they difficult problems or are they childish, immature problems? Surely, we ought to have outgrown this childish kind of business; and do you call these the burning problems of the day? When you call yourself a Hindu and say you belong to a particular religion, are you not quarreling over words? What do you mean by Hinduism? A group of beliefs, dogmas, traditions, and superstitions. Is religion a matter of belief? Surely, religion is the search for truth, and religious people are not those who have these stupid ideas. The man who is searching for truth is a religious man, and he has no need for labels—Hindu, Muslim, or Christian. Why do we call ourselves Hindus, Muslims, or Christians? Because, we are not really religious people at all. If we had love, mercy in our hearts, we would not care two pins what we called ourselves—and that is religion. It is because our hearts are empty that they are filled with things which are childish—and which you call the burning questions! Surely, that is very immature. Whether Bombay should be a free city, whether there should be Brahmins and non-Brahmins—are these the burning problems, or are they a front behind which you are hiding? After all, who is a Brahmin? Surely, not he who wears the sacred thread. A Brahmin is a person who understands, who has no authority in society, who is independent of society, who is not greedy, who is not seeking power, who is outside all power—such a person is a Brahmin. Are you and I such people? Obviously we are not. Then why call ourselves by a label which has no meaning? You call yourself by that label because it is profitable, it gives you a position in society. A sane man does not belong to any group, he does not seek position in a society, which only breeds war. If you were really sane, it would not matter what you are called; you would not worship a label. But labels, words, become important when the heart is empty. Because your heart is empty, you are frightened and are willing to kill others. It is really an absurd problem, this matter of Hindus and Muslims. Surely, sirs, it is childish, unworthy of mature people, is it not? When you see immature people making a mess of things, what do you do? It is no use hitting them on the head. You either try to help them or you withdraw and leave them entirely free to make their mess. They like their toys, so you withdraw and build a new culture, a new society. Nationalism is a poison, patriotism is a drug, and the world conflicts are a distraction from direct relationship with people. If you know that, can you indulge in them any more? If you see that clearly, there will be no division between Hindu and Muslim. Our problem then is much vaster than the question of whether Bombay should be a free city, and we will not therefore lose ourselves in stupid problems in the face of the real issues of life. Sirs, the real issues of life are near at hand, in the battle between you and me, between husband and wife, between you and your neighbor. Out of our personal lives we have created this mess, these quarrels between Brahmin and non-Brahmin, between Hindu and Muslim; you and I have contributed to this mess, and we are directly responsible, not some leaders. Since it is our responsibility, we have to act; and to act, we must think rightly; and to think rightly, we have to put away childish things, all that we know to be utterly false and without meaning. To be mature human beings, we must put away the absurd toys of nationalism, of organized religion, of following somebody politically or religiously. That is our problem. If you are really earnest, serious about all this, then you will naturally free yourself from infantile acts, from calling yourself by particular labels, whether national, political, or religious; and only then shall we have a peaceful world. But if you merely listen, you will go out and do exactly the same thing that you have done before. (Laughter) I know you laugh—and that is where the tragedy lies. You are not interested in stopping war, you are not really interested in having peace in the world. In Poona, perhaps, you are for the moment living peacefully, and you think you will somehow survive. You are not going to survive. You are talking of war between Hyderabad and New India, of communal problems, and so on. We are all on the brink of a precipice. This whole civilization which man has believed in may be destroyed; the things which we have produced, tenderly cultivated—everything is now at stake. For man to save himself from the precipice, there must be a real revolution—not a bloody revolution, but a revolution of inward regeneration. There cannot be regeneration without self-knowledge. Without knowing yourself, there is nothing you can do. We have to think out every problem anew; and to do that, we must free ourselves from the past, which means that the thought process must come to an end. Our problem is to understand the present in its enormity, with its inevitable catastrophes and miseries—we must face it all anew. There can be no newness if we merely carry on with the past, if we analyze the present through the thought process. That is why to understand a problem, the thought process must cease. When the mind is still, quiet, tranquil—only then is the problem resolved. Therefore it is important to understand oneself. You and I must be the salt of the earth, professing a new thought, a new happiness.

September 1, 1948

Second Talk in Poona

It is especially difficult to understand the intricacies and the complexities of human relationship, is it not? Even when one is very familiar with a person, it is often very arduous and almost impossible to find out what his feelings and thoughts are. This becomes comparatively easy when there is affection, love between two people, for then there is immediate communion at the same time and on the same level; but that communion is denied when we are merely discussing or listening on the verbal level. To establish that communion between you and me is extremely difficult because there is no communion, there is no real understanding. Communion ceases to exist when there is fear or prejudice because then the defense mechanism is at work. Perhaps I see things in a way different from that to which you are accustomed, and I want to be in communion with you, I want to communicate to you what I see. I may not see truly or completely, but if you want to examine what I am communicating, you on your side must be open, receptive.

I am not dealing with ideas. To me, ideas have no meaning at all. Ideas do not produce revolution, ideas do not produce regeneration, and it is regeneration that is essential. The communication of ideas is comparatively easy, but to commune with each other beyond the verbal level is extremely arduous. What we have to establish between us is not some imaginative, mystic communion, but a communion that is possible only when both of us are intent on discovering the truth which will solve our problems. For myself, I feel that there is a reality which is from moment to moment, which is not in the realm of time at all. That reality is the only solution to the innumerable problems of our life. When one perceives that reality, or when that reality comes, it is a liberating factor; but no amount of intellectual argumentation, of disputation, of conflict, whether economic, social, or religious, will resolve the problems that the mind itself creates.

We have met to commune with each other, and to do that one must be open and receptive, not accepting or denying, but inquiring. You and I are related, we are not living in isolation. Truth is not something apart from relationship. Relationship is society, and in understanding the relationship between yourself and your wife, between yourself and society, you will find truth, or rather, truth will come to you, and it will bring liberation from all problems. You cannot find truth, you must let it come to you; and for that there must be a mind that is no longer haunted by ignorance. Ignorance is not the lack of technical knowledge, the lack of having read many philosophical books; ignorance is lack of self-knowledge. Though one may have read many philosophical and sacred books and be able to quote them, mere quotations, which are the accumulated words and experiences of others, do not free the mind from ignorance. Self-knowledge arises only when there is the searching out and experiencing of the ways of one's own thoughts, feelings, and actions, which is to be aware of the total process of oneself in relationship, from moment to moment. Self-knowledge, which we will discuss presently, gives the right perspective in approaching any of our problems, the right perspective being the understanding of the truth of the problem; and that understanding will inevitably bring about action in relationship. So, self-knowledge is not opposed to, nor does it deny, action. Self-knowledge reveals the right perspective or the truth of the problem, from which action arises—these three are always interrelated, they are not separate. There is no true action without self-knowledge. If I do not know myself, obviously I have no basis for action; what I do is mere activity, it is the response of a conditioned mind and therefore has no meaning. A conditioned response can never liberate or produce order out of this chaos.

Now, the world and the individual are one process, they are not opposed; and a man who is trying to solve his own problems, which are the problems of the world, must obviously have a basis for his thought. I think this is fairly clear. If I do not know myself, I have no basis for thinking; if I do not know myself and merely act, such action is bound to produce misery and confusion—which is exactly what is taking place in the world at the present time. So, an inquiry into self-knowledge is not a process of isolation, it is not the fancy or luxury of an ascetic. On the contrary, it is an obvious necessity for the man of the world, for the poor and for the rich, and for him who wants to solve the problems of the world because man is the world, he is not apart from the world. I think it is very important to realize that this world is the product of our everyday existence, and that the environment which we have created is not independent of us. The environment is there and you cannot change it without changing yourself; and to change yourself, you must understand your own thoughts, feelings, and actions in relationship. Economists and revolutionary people seek to alter the environment without altering the individual, but mere alteration of environment without understanding oneself has no meaning. Environment is the product of the individual's effort; the two are interrelated, and you cannot alter the one without altering the other. You and I are not isolated; we are the result of the total process, the outcome of the whole human struggle, whether we live in India, Japan, or America. The sum total of humanity is you and me. Either we are conscious of that or we are unconscious of it. To bring about a revolutionary change in the structure of society, each one must understand himself as a total process, not as a separate, isolated entity. If this is very clear, we can proceed with the investigation into the nature of man's mind and what he is. But it must be very clear to the earnest man that there cannot be a complete revolution in the world merely on one level, either economic or spiritual. A total, an enriching revolution cannot take place unless you and I understand ourselves as a total process. You and I are not isolated individuals but are the result of the whole human struggle with its illusions, fancies, pursuits, ignorance, strife, conflict, and misery. One cannot begin to alter the condition of the world without understanding oneself. If you see that, there is immediately within you a complete revolution, is there not? Then no guru is necessary because knowledge of oneself is from moment to moment, it is not the accumulation of hearsay, nor is it contained in the precepts of religious teachers. Because you are discovering yourself in relationship with another from moment to moment, relationship has a completely different meaning. Relationship then is a revelation, a constant process of the discovery of oneself, and from this self-discovery, action takes place.

So, self-knowledge can come only through relationship, not through isolation. Relationship is action, and self-knowledge is the result of awareness in action. It is like this: Suppose you had never read any books, and you were the first person to seek the meaning of existence. There is nobody to tell you how to start; there is no guru, no book, no teacher, and you have to discover the whole process for yourself. How would you set about it? You would have to begin with yourself, would you not? That is our problem. Merely to quote authority is not self-knowledge; it is not the discovery of the process of the self; therefore, it has no value. You have to start as though you knew nothing, and only then is there a discovery which is creative, releasing, and only then does your discovery bring happiness and joy. But most of us are living on words, and words, like memory, are the outcome of the past. A man who lives in the past cannot understand the present. So, you have to discover the process of yourself from moment to moment, which means you have to be aware, conscious of your thoughts, feelings, and actions. Be aware, and then you will see how your thoughts, feelings, and actions are not only based on the pattern created by society, or by the religious teachers, but are the outcome of your own inclinations. To be aware of your thoughts, feelings, and actions is the process of self-knowledge. All of us are aware in the sense that we are conscious that we are doing or thinking something, but we are not conscious of the motive or the urge that lies behind what we think and do. We try to alter the framework of thought, but we never understand the creator of the framework.

So, it is essential to understand ourselves, for without understanding ourselves, without the process of self-discovery, there is no creative revolution. To understand oneself is to be aware of every thought and feeling without condemnation. When you condemn, you put a stop to your feelings and thoughts; but if you do not condemn, justify, or resist, then the content of your thought will reveal itself. Experiment, and you will see. This is very important because to bring about a creative revolution or regeneration, the first essential is to understand oneself. Without understanding oneself, merely to bring about an economic change or introduce new patterns of action has very little value. If we do not understand ourselves, we will merely proceed from conflict to conflict. Nothing can be created in conflict; creation can take place only with the cessation of conflict. For a man constantly in battle with himself and his neighbor, there can never be regeneration—he can only go from reaction to reaction. Regeneration can come only when there is freedom from all reaction, and that freedom takes place only when there is self-knowledge. The individual is not an isolated process, apart from the whole, but is the total process of mankind; therefore, those who are in earnest and who desire to bring about a radical and fundamental revolution of values have to begin with themselves.

I have several questions, and I will try to answer as many as possible.

Question: Image worship, puja, and meditation are natural and obviously useful to man. Why are you denying them and taking away the consolation in suffering which they offer?

KRISHNAMURTI: Let us understand what we mean by meditation. As it is a complex subject, you will have to pay continued attention; otherwise, you will miss the point. Let us first get the main points clear to ourselves. First of all, I am not saying that meditation is not necessary. But before we say whether it is necessary or not, we must understand what it means. My guru, my traditions, say "meditate," so I sit in a room and meditate. Surely, that has no meaning. I must understand what is meant by meditation.

What do we mean by meditation? In meditation, several things are involved: prayer, concentration, the search for truth, or what we call understanding, the desire to seek consolation, and so on. Let us take prayer. What do we mean by it? Prayer is a form of supplication. One is in difficulty, and one looks to somebody to help one out. You and I may not pray, but millions do, and when they pray, obviously they receive an answer; otherwise, they wouldn't do it. They receive a certain consolation. In prayer, does the answer come from God, a superior entity, or does the answer come from somewhere else? What is involved in prayer? First, you repeat certain words; you are a Hindu and you repeat certain words, mantras. By repeating words over and over again, you induce quietness in the mind. If you endlessly repeat something, obviously the mind is made dull, quiet; and when the conscious mind is quiet, then it receives an answer. Where does the answer come from? Does it come from what you call God, or does it come from somewhere else? Why do you pray? Obviously, you pray because you are in some sort of difficulty; there is a state of pain and suffering, and you want an answer. That is, you have created a problem, and by praying, which is a repetition of words, you quiet the mind, and then the mind receives an answer. When you do that, what is actually taking place? The superficial mind is in a quiet, inactive state; then the unconscious projects itself, and you have an answer. Or, to put it differently, you have a problem which you worry and puzzle over for a long time, but you do not find an answer. Then you say, "I will sleep on it." When you wake up the next morning, you have the solution. How does it take place? The conscious mind, after worrying over a problem, puts the problem aside and says, "I will leave it alone"; and when the conscious mind is quiet with regard to the problem, the unconscious is able to project itself into the conscious, and the answer is there. You may call it the still, small voice, the voice of God, or what you will—the name does not matter. It is the unconscious that gives the intimation, that gives an answer to the problem; and prayer is merely a trick to make the conscious mind quiet so that it can receive the answer. But the conscious mind receives an answer according to its conscious desire. As long as the mind is conditioned, its answer will inevitably be conditioned. That is, if I am nationalistic and through prayer I reduce the conscious mind to stillness, I receive an answer according to my nationalistic conditioning. Therefore a Hitler can say, "I hear God's voice." That is one part of this question of meditation.

Then there is the problem of concentration, which is a little more difficult; it requires more application of thought and attention. What do you mean by concentration?

By concentration you mean exclusion. To concentrate upon an object, an idea, an image, means to resist and exclude all other thoughts encroaching upon your mind. To resist the flow of other ideas, to try to force your mind to dwell upon one idea is a constant battle, is it not? You choose an idea, and you try to focus your mind on that idea and resist all other thoughts; and when you are able to concentrate on that idea to the exclusion of all others, you think you have learned complete concentration. When you do this, what is actually taking place? Concentration becomes a constant conflict of resistance. Why do you choose one thought and deny all other thoughts? Because, you think that one particular thought is more important than all the others, which you consider to be lesser ones. So, there is a conflict, a constant battle between the lesser thoughts and the more important thought. But if you follow and understand each thought as it arises, whether important or unimportant—all thoughts are important—then there is no necessity for focusing your thought on one idea. Then concentration is no longer narrowing, but strengthening, creative. Look at a child. Give him a toy, a plaything, something in which he is interested. The child will be completely absorbed in it; you do not have to tell him to concentrate. It is the grown-up people who are not interested and who force themselves to concentrate. The man who makes an effort to concentrate has no interest in what he is doing. If he is interested, concentration is no effort at all. Most of you indulge in meditation because you are not interested in what you are doing everyday. So meditation carries you away from life; it is not a part of your daily existence. Therefore, concentration, which you call meditation, is merely an escape from life; and if you can escape from life completely, you think you have gained something. But if you examine every thought, every feeling as it arises, without condemnation, justification, or resistance, then out of that constant understanding, constant rediscovery, the mind becomes very quiet, still and free. So, meditation is not concentration, meditation is not prayer.

Then there is the performance of rituals. Why do you perform a ritual? What is the truth behind it? My mother dies and I do it for no valid reason. Sirs, this introduces the question of sanity. To do something without thinking is insanity; to use words without a referent, without meaning, is a state of unbalance. Why do you perform rituals for the dead? If it gives you comfort, you are seeking comfort and not understanding. If you know that, why are you doing it? Do you know the full significance, the whole implication of performing rituals? If you do not, obviously you should not do it. Why do you do it, sirs? Some people do it because they have nothing else to do, especially women, and it indicates the state of unbalance in which we are living. The performance of rituals is a marvelous escape from the brutality of life, from a brutal husband, the constant bearing of children, and you condemn those who do not do it. To some it is an escape, to others it is a matter of tradition, of authority. Surely, to perform a ritual for the father or mother who has died, because it is the tradition to do so, is a state of unbalance. You do not know what it means, but it will please the mother, or the father, or the neighbor. He who does something he does not understand is an unbalanced person. Surely, to quote authority, to do something you do not understand because it gives you comfort is not the action of a balanced person.

Finally, there is the worshipping of an image, sitting in front of a picture and losing yourself. Why do you worship dead things? Why don't you worship your wives, your children, and neighbors? You worship dead things because they cannot respond, and you can attribute to them what you want. It is a marvelous escape. You do not worship the living because they can respond and tell you how silly you are.

Now, if meditation is not prayer, is not concentration, is not rituals and the repetition of words, is not the worship of images, then what is meditation? To understand anything, obviously, a quiet mind is necessary. What do we mean by meditation? If you see that meditation is not the mere repetition of words, is not sitting and looking at a picture and getting hypnotized—if you see the truth of this, what happens to your mind? If you see the truth about prayer, about image worship, if you see the truth about rituals and their fallacies, what then is the state of your mind? Obviously, if you have seen the truth about all these things, you are free of them, are you not? Being free of them, your mind becomes much more clear, more tranquil, very quiet; and in that tranquillity, reality comes into being. Meditation, then, is not a disciplining of the mind and heart according to any particular pattern, but meditation is a constant process of understanding from moment to moment. Understanding comes only when there is perception of the truth—not some abstract truth, but the truth of what is actual. If I mistake a rope for a snake, there is a state of falsification; but when I see the rope as a rope, there is truth. There is truth only when I see things as they are in their right perspective; and this whole process of seeing things as they are, clearly and without distortion, is meditation. But it is extremely difficult to see *what is*, not to mistake the rope for the snake, because most of us are incapable of perceiving without distortion. Therefore, meditation is the process of deconditioning the mind; it means being aware without condemnation, justification, or resistance of every thought, every feeling, every fancy that arises according to one's idiosyncracies and particular tendencies. So, meditation means freedom from the past. It is memory of the past that conditions your response, and meditation is the process of freeing the mind from the past.

But here a difficulty arises. It is necessary for the mind to free itself from the past in order not to distort *what is*, in order to see things clearly as they are; and how can the mind, which is the result of the past, free itself from the past? Mind can free itself from the past only when you recognize that every thought is the product of the past and you are fully aware that thought cannot solve any problem. The problem is a challenge, and a challenge is always new; and to translate the new according to the terms of the old is to deny the new. When the mind sees itself as the center of distortion and is free, clear, and unfettered by the past, when it is no longer separating itself as the 'you', the 'I', then it is still; and in that stillness there is understanding, recognition, reality. It is an experience which must be felt by each one; it cannot be repeated. If you repeat it, it is the old. But if you are interested in solving human problems, there must be meditation of this kind; and when the mind becomes naturally quiet, as a pool becomes quiet when the winds cease, then reality comes into being.

Question: Men are born unequal, and any intelligence test will prove it. Our shastras *recognize this fact by dividing men into three types,* satva, rajas, *and* tamas. *Why then do you say that your message is for all, irrespective of differences in temperament and intelligence? Are you not shirking your duty by presuming that all are equal? Is it not a bit of demagogy?*

KRISHNAMURTI: Sir, it is an obvious fact that we are all unequal. There is an extraordinary difference between man and man, between woman and woman. But is there a difference when you love somebody? Is there any inequality? Is there any nationality? When the heart is empty, then types become very important; then we divide human beings into classes, colors, races. But when you love, is there any difference? When there is generosity in your heart, do you distinguish? You give yourself. It is the man who is not generous, who is concerned with his bank account, that wants to keep these differences and divisions. To a man who is seeking the truth, there are no divisions; to seek the truth is to be active, to have wisdom, to know love. The man who is pursuing a particular path can never know the truth because to him that path is exclusive. When I say this is applicable to all, it is not to flatter democracy—which is nonexistent in the world. To appeal to the common man is a cheap trick, the work of the politician. What I am saying is applicable to everyone irrespective of his station in life, whether he be rich or poor and whatever his temperament may be. We are all suffering, we all have our problems, we are burdened by worries and in ceaseless conflicts; death, sorrow, and pain are our constant companions. The hierarchical principle is clearly detrimental to spiritual thought. To divide man as the high and the low indicates ignorance. Since we are all suffering on different levels of consciousness, what I say is applicable to all. We all want to be free from suffering, whether rich, poor, or in between. Suffering is our common lot, and as we are all seeking a way out of suffering, what I say is applicable to all.

Now, as we are suffering, it is no good merely escaping from it. Suffering cannot be understood through escape, but through loving and understanding it. You understand something when you love it. You understand your wife when you love her, you understand your neighbor when you love him—which is not merely being carried away by the word *love.* Most of us run away from suffering through the innumerable clever tricks of the mind. Suffering is understood only when we are face to face with suffering, not when we are ceaselessly trying to avoid it. Through the desire to avoid suffering we have developed a culture of distraction, of organized religion with its ceremonies and pujas, and we accumulate wealth by exploiting people. All these are indicative of the avoidance of suffering. Surely, you and I, the man in the street, anyone, can understand suffering, only we must give our attention to it. But, unfortunately, modern civilization merely helps us to escape through amusements, through distractions, or through illusions, the repetition of words, and so on. All this helps us to avoid *what is,* and therefore we have to be aware of these innumerable escapes. It is only when man is free from escapes that he will dissolve the cause of suffering. To a happy man, a man who loves, there are no divisions; he is neither a Brahmin nor an Englishman, neither a German nor a Hindu. To such a man there is no division of high and low. It is because we do not love that we have all these invidious divisions. When you love, there is a sense of richness, that perfume of life, and you are willing to share your heart with another. When the heart is full, the things of the mind fall away.

Question: Maharashtra is the land of saints. Dyaneswari, Tukaram, *and a host of others belonging to Maharashtra have striven through* Bakthi Marga *to proclaim the truth and give assistance to millions of common men and women, who still visit* Pandharpur *temple year after year in devout faith. These saints have given mantras. Why do you not simplify your message and bring it to the level of the common man?*

KRISHNAMURTI: Most of us are devout and want to worship something, and as the mantras have simplified life and helped the millions, why do I not make my teaching simple? That is the gist of the question. Sir, by repeating words, by repeating a name, do you think you can give sustenance to the soul? Or do you merely dull the mind? Surely, anything that is repeated over and over again makes the mind insensitive. Is this constant repetition of words not a trick to make the mind dull so that all revolution, all inquiry and sensitive response are destroyed? It has become one of the functions of governments to make the mind dull by constant repetition: "We are right, and other parties are wrong." By your endless repetition of a name, by your constant performance of a ritual, surely the mind, which should be sensitive and pliable, becomes dull. Most of us have an inclination to live a kind of devout life; but unfortunately, these repetitive exercises destroy it. It is important to understand that the path of devotion and the path of wisdom are not separate. Relationship, which is a process of self-revelation, is not understood through any one path. If I want to understand life, I must live it, I must be active, I must be full of wisdom concerning life. To follow one path at the expense of the other is distortion, a state of contradiction within oneself.

The questioner wants to know why I cannot make my teaching simple enough for the common man. This is an extraordinary thing. Why are you concerned about the common man? Are you really concerned about the common man? I doubt it very much. If you were concerned about the common man, then you would not worship any system, there would be no political party, either left or right. A system becomes important when you do not love the common man but only love the system, an ideology for which you are willing to kill and destroy the common man. After all, the common man is you and I. What is the difficulty in understanding what I say? The first difficulty is that you do not want to understand. If you understood, you would have a revolution, and this would disturb you; it would upset your father, your mother, or your wife, so you say, "Your teachings are too complex." In other words, sir, when you do not want to understand a thing, you make the thing complex. When you want to understand something, you love it, and when you love, life becomes simple. It is because you have no love for your wife or for anything that this becomes a complicated philosophy which you are finding extremely difficult. When you love one person you love others, the heart is warm towards everyone. Then you are in a sensitive, pliable state. Because we have not that pliable, warm affection, we live on words, we are sustained by words. We worship a system, with its appalling class and racial divisions, with its economic frontiers, because our hearts are empty. To understand, you must have love in your hearts. Love is not a thing to be cultivated; it comes into being swiftly and directly when it is not hindered by the things of the mind. Our hearts are empty, and that is why there is no communion between you and me. We listen, we have words, we have argumentation, but there is no communion between us because between us there is no love. When there is love—that warmth, that generosity, that kindliness, that mercy—there is no need for philosophy, there is no need for teachers, for love is its own truth.

September 5, 1948

Third Talk in Poona

Since all of us are concerned with action, and without action we cannot live, we ought to go into this question fully and try to understand it comprehensively. It is a difficult question, and we will have to follow it at its different levels because most of us live unintegrated lives; we live in departments, our life is compartmental. Philosophies, actions, and activities exist at different levels, unconnected with each other; and such living inevitably leads to confusion and disorder. So, in trying to understand the complex problem of action, we must find out what is activity and what is action. There is a vast difference between activity and action. We live an unintegrated life at different levels and try to solve the many problems each on its own level. The economist tries to solve the whole problem of existence on the economic level, the religious person on the psychological or so-called spiritual level, and the man who believes in social reform is concerned with outward transformation, with change, the modification of social standards, and so on.

So, we see that most of us are acting departmentally, isolating the problem and trying to solve it as if it were wholly an economic problem, or wholly a psychological or spiritual problem, wholly inside the skin or outside the skin. Surely, this unrelated action is unintegrated action, and such departmental action is mere activity. That is, when we try to solve a problem on its own level as if it were unrelated to other issues of life, then such treatment is mere activity. Activity is action unrelated to the whole. When we say, "Change the environment first, and everything will follow," surely such an idea reveals compartmental thinking, leading to mere activity. Man does not live on one level alone, he lives at different levels of consciousness, and to separate his life into compartments, into different unrelated levels, is obviously detrimental to action. It is important to understand the distinction between activity and action. I would call activity the conduct of life based on unrelated or unintegrated levels—trying to live as though life were merely on one level and not be concerned with other levels, with other fields of consciousness. If we examine such activities, we will find that they are based on idea, and idea is a process of isolation; therefore, activity is always a process of isolation, not unification. If you look into activity, you will find that it is the outcome of an idea; that is, the idea is considered the most important thing, and such an idea is always separative. An idea which brings forth activity, or activity based on the pattern of an idea, must inevitably be the cause of conflict—and that is what is happening in our life. We have an idea and then conform to that idea; but if you will examine it closely, you will find that the idea is separative. An idea can never be integrating; idea is always separative, dividing. He who indulges in mere activities based on an idea is obviously creating mischief, causing misery, bringing about disorder. Integrated action is not born of an idea; it comes into being only when we understand life as a total process, not broken up into separate departments, separate activities apart from the whole of existence. Integrated action is action not based on idea. It is comprehension of the whole, of the total process; and what is a total process has not the limitation of an idea. So, he who wants to act seriously, earnestly, and fully without bringing about disorder must comprehend action as a whole, not based on idea. When action is based on idea, it is mere activity, and all activity is separative, exclusive.

Our problem, then, is how to act integrally, as a whole, not on different unrelated levels. To act as a whole, to act integrally, the obvious necessity is self-knowledge. Self-knowledge is not an idea—it is a movement. An idea is always static, and without self-knowledge, mere action based on an idea obviously leads to disorder, suffering, and pain. So, for action, there must be self-knowledge. Self-knowledge is not a technique; it is not to be learned from a book. One discovers the process of self-knowledge through relationship, relationship with one or with society. Society is the relationship of myself with another. There can be integrated action only when there is self-knowledge, and self-knowledge is the outcome, not of an idea, but of relationship, which is in constant movement. If you observe, you will see that relationship can never be fixed, can never be bound by an idea; relationship is in constant movement, it is never static. Therefore, to understand relationship is arduous, extremely difficult, and that is why we turn to mere activity, ideation, as a pattern of action. So, the earnest man obviously must not be caught in activity, but understand relationship through the process of self-knowledge. Understanding the process of the 'me', of the 'mine' in its entire field brings about integrated action; and such action is complete, such action will not create conflict.

Now, I have several questions, and I will try to answer as many of them as I can. I have looked over these questions, but I have not thought about them. I have had to choose a few questions out of many, and the rest we will deal with another week. So, I am answering without premeditated response, and if you also will think out each problem, we can proceed together and find the truth of the question. If you merely listen to the response and wait for a solution from me, this gathering will mean very little, but if we can think out the problems and find the truth together, then the meeting will have great significance. It is the truth that you want to find, and for truth to come into being, your mind must be prepared. To receive the truth, the mind must be swift, pliable, and alert. If you merely wait for an answer from me, obviously your mind is dull, insensitive; and it is essential that the mind be swift and sensitive. The mind is not sensitive when you are merely in a state of receiving. Let us think out the problems, the manner of approach to each question, and try to find the true answer together.

Question: What are the duties of a wife?

KRISHNAMURTI: I wonder who has put this question, the wife or the husband? If the wife has put it, it demands a certain response, and if the husband has put it, it demands a certain other response. In this country, a husband is the boss; he is the law, the master, because he is economically dominant, and it is he who says what the duties of a wife are. Since the wife is not dominant and is economically dependent, what she says are not duties. We can approach the problem from the point of view of the husband, or of the wife. If we approach the problem of the wife, we see that because she is not free economically, her education is limited, or her thinking capacities may be inferior; and society has imposed upon her regulations and modes of conduct determined by the men. Therefore, she accepts what are called the rights of the husband; and as he is dominant, being economically free, and has the capacity to earn, he lays down the law. Naturally, where marriage is a matter of contract, there is no limit to its complications. Then there is *duty*—a bureaucratic word that has no significance in relationship. When one establishes regulations and begins to inquire into the duties and rights of husband and wife, there is no end to it. Surely, such a relationship is an appalling affair, is it not? When the husband demands his rights and insists on having a dutiful wife, whatever that may mean, their relationship is obviously merely a business contract. It is very important to understand this question, for surely, there must be a different approach to it. As long as relationship is based on contract, on money, on possession, authority, or domination, then inevitably relationship becomes a matter of rights and duties. One can see the extreme complexity of relationship when it is the result of a contract—determining what is right, what is wrong, what is duty. If I am the wife and you insist on certain actions, not being independent, naturally I have to succumb to your wishes, your holding the reins. You impose on the wife certain regulations, rights, and duties, and therefore relationship becomes merely a matter of contract, with all its complexities.

Now, is there not a different approach to this problem? That is, when there is love, there is no duty. When you love your wife, you share everything with her—your property, your trouble, your anxiety, your joy. You do not dominate. You are not the man and she the woman to be used and thrown aside, a sort of breeding machine to carry on your name. When there is love, the word *duty* disappears. It is the man with no love in his heart who talks of rights and duties, and in this country duties and rights have taken the place of love. Regulations have become more important than the warmth of affection. When there is love, the problem is simple; when there is no love, the problem becomes complex. When a man loves his wife and his children, he can never possibly think in terms of *duty* and *rights*. Sirs, examine your own hearts and minds. I know you laugh it off—that is one of the tricks of the thoughtless, to laugh at something and push it aside. Your wife does not share your responsibility, your wife does not share your property, she does not have the half of everything that you have because you consider the woman less than yourself, something to be kept and to be used sexually at your convenience when your appetite demands it. So you have invented the words *rights* and *duty;* and when the woman rebels, you throw at her these words. It is a static society, a deteriorating society, that talks of duty and rights. If you really examine your hearts and minds, you will find that you have no love. If you had love, you would not have put this question. Without love, I do not see the point of having children. Without love, we produce ugly, immature, thoughtless children; and they will be immature, thoughtless, all their lives because they never had affection and were merely used as toys and amusements, as something to carry on your name. For a new society, a new culture to come into being, obviously there cannot be domination either by the man or by the woman. Domination exists because of inward poverty. Being psychologically poor, we want to dominate, to swear at the servant, at the wife or husband. Surely, it is the sense of affection, that warmth of love, which alone can bring about a new state, a new culture. The cultivation of the heart is not a process of the mind. The mind cannot cultivate the heart, but when the process of the mind is understood, then love comes into being. Love is not a mere word. The word is not the thing. The word *love* is not love. When we use that word and try to cultivate love, it is merely a process of the mind. Love cannot be cultivated, but when we realize that the word is not the thing, then the mind, with its laws and regulations, with its rights and duties, ceases to interfere, and then only is there a possibility of creating a new culture, a new hope, and a new world.

Question: What is that quality which gives us the perception of the whole?

KRISHNAMURTI: Let us first understand the question. Most of us act without integration. We perceive only a part of any problem and then act; and when our activity is based on the perception of only a part and not the whole of a problem, obviously there must be confusion and misery. So, the question is, how to perceive in its entirety any human problem? Because, when we perceive a problem in its entirety and act upon it as a whole, the problem is solved. Such action does not create further problems. If I can see as a whole, and not merely partially, the problem of greed, of violence, of nationalism, of war, then my action will not produce further catastrophe, further misery. So, the question is, "What is that quality which gives us the perception of the whole?"

Now, how do you approach a problem? When you approach a problem seeking an answer, or trying to find the cause of the problem, or trying to resolve it, you approach it with a very agitated mind, don't you? You have a problem and you want to find an answer; therefore, you are concerned with the solution, and your mind is already occupied with finding that solution. That is, you are not interested in the problem, you are only concerned to find an answer to the problem. So, what happens? Because you want an answer to the problem, you are not aware of the significance of the problem itself. Since your mind is agitated, you cannot possibly see the problem in its entirety, for you can see a problem in its entirety only when the mind is still. There is perception of the whole only when the mind is utterly silent. But this silence, this stillness, is not induced, is not brought about through discipline or control. Stillness comes only when distractions cease, that is, when the mind is aware of all distractions. The mind is interested in many things, in multifarious problems, and if it chooses one interest and excludes other interests, then it is not aware of the entire problem, and therefore there is distraction; but if the mind is aware of every interest as it arises and sees its meaning, there is no distraction. There is distraction only when you choose a central interest, for then anything away from the central interest is a distraction. When you choose a central interest, is the mind consumed, absorbed in that interest? Obviously it is not. You may choose a central interest, but if you examine your mind you will see that it is not consumed in any one thing. If it were consumed in one thing, there would be no distraction; but your mind is not consumed in one thing, it has many interests. The implication of a distraction is that there is a central interest, and therefore anything that competes with the central interest is a distraction. A mind which has a central interest and is resisting the so-called distractions is not a still mind. Such a mind is merely fixed in an idea, in an image or a formula, and a fixed mind is not a quiet mind—it is merely held in bondage.

So, a still mind is essential for the perception of the whole, and the mind is still only as it understands each thought and each feeling as it arises. That is, the mind becomes still when the thought process stops. Merely to resist, to build a wall of isolation and live in that isolation is not stillness, is not tranquillity. Stillness that is cultivated, disciplined, or enforced, tranquillity that is compelled, is spurious, and such a mind can never perceive the problem as a whole. Sir, living is an art and art is not learned in a day. The art of living cannot be found in books; no guru can give it to you, but since you have bought books and followed gurus, your mind is full of false ideas, full of discipline, regulations, and restrictions. Because your mind is never quiet, never still, it is incapable of perceiving any issue as a whole. To see anything fully, completely, there must be freedom, and freedom does not come through compulsion, a process of discipline, of suppression, but only when the mind understands itself, which is self-knowledge. That higher form of intelligence which is negative thinking comes only when the thought process has stopped and the mind is fully aware, alert; and in that alert stillness, the whole of the problem is perceived. Then only is there integrated action—action which is full, right, and complete.

Question: You say that repeating mantras and performing rituals makes the mind dull. Psychologists tell us that when the mind is concentrated on one thing, or on an idea, it becomes sharp. A mantra is supposed to purify the mind. Is not your statement contradictory to the findings of modern psychologists?

KRISHNAMURTI: If you are going to depend on authorities, you are lost. A specialist is an unintegrated person, and what he says about his specialty cannot lead to integrated action. Besides, if you quote one psychologist and somebody else quotes another contradicting him, where are you? What you and I think is much more important than all the psychologists put together. Let us, you and I, find out for ourselves and not quote what the psychologists or experts say. That way leads to complete confusion and ignorant strife. The question is: Does the repetition of a mantra, or the performance of a ritual, dull the mind? And the other question is: Does concentration on an idea sharpen the mind? Let us find out the truth about it.

The repetition of a word, however well-sounding, is obviously a mechanical process, is it not? Look at your own mind. When you take the word *om* and keep on repeating it, what happens to your mind? When you keep on repeating that word day after day, you have a certain stimulation, a certain sensation which is the outcome of repetition. It is a mechanical response; and do you think a mind that keeps on repeating a word or a phrase is capable of sharpness or swift thought? You have repeated mantras, and is your mind sharp, pliable, swift? You can see whether your mind is swift or not only in your relationship with another. If you observe yourself in your relationship with your wife, your children, your neighbor, you will see that your mind is dull. You just imagine that your mind is *sharp*—a word that has no referent in your action, in your relationship, which is never clear, complete, full. Such an imaginative mind is an unbalanced mind. The mere repetition of words obviously gives a certain stimulation, a certain sensation, but that is bound to make the mind dull.

Similarly, when you perform rituals, ceremonies, day after day, what is happening? The regular performance of a ritual obviously gives a certain stimulation, like going to the cinema, and you are satisfied with that stimulation. When a man takes a drink, a cocktail, for the moment he may feel uninhibited; but let him keep on drinking and he gets more and more dull. It is the same when you keep on repeating rituals—you pour into your rituals an enormous significance which they do not have. Sir, it is your mind that is responsible for making itself dull, thereby making your life a mechanical process. You do not know what it means. If you thought it out, if you started all over again, you would not go on repeating words. You do so because somebody has said that repeating these words, these mantras, will help you. To find truth you need no guru, no book; to have a clear mind you have to think out every issue, every movement of thought, every flutter of feeling. Since you do not want to find truth, you have this convenient dope, and the dope is the mantra, the word. I know you will go on doing these rituals because to break away from this practice would create disturbance in the family, it would upset the wife or the husband. There would be trouble in the family, so you carry on. A man who carries on, not knowing what he does, is obviously an unbalanced person; and I am not at all sure that those who perform rituals are not unbalanced. If these rituals have any meaning, they must have a response in daily life. If you are a factory manager or owner and do not share your profits with the workmen, do you think you will get peace by repeating that word umpteen times? Men who are using people, monstrously exploiting their servants and employees, perform rituals and repeat the word *peace, peace*—it is a marvelous escape. Such a man is an ugly, unbalanced entity, and no amount of talking about purity of life, performing rituals, repeating the word *om,* changing the clothes of his God, is going to alter it. What is the good of your mantras and rituals? You are talking of peace on the one hand and causing misery on the other. Do you think such action is balanced? You will do innumerable rituals, but you will not act with generosity because there is no spark of life in you. Most of us want to be dull because we do not want to face life, and a dull mind can go to sleep and live happily in a semicomatose condition. Mantras, the performance of rituals, help to produce that sleeping condition—and that is what you want. You are listening to words, but you are not going to do a thing. That is what I am objecting to. You do not drop your rituals, you won't stop exploiting, you will never share your profits with others, you have no interest in raising the standard of the underprivileged. It is all right for you to live in a big house, but it is all wrong for them. Since you are not going to do a thing, I do not see why you listen so raptly.

The second problem is whether concentration on an idea can produce clarity or sharpness of the mind. It is a complex problem and many things are involved in it, so let us think it out. What do you mean by concentration? A child does not talk about concentration when he has an interest. Give him a watch, a toy, anything in which he takes interest—he will be completely absorbed in it, nothing else exists for him. You are not interested; therefore, you make an effort to concentrate. That is, you choose a pleasurable or gratifying idea which you call truth, a quality which gives you a sense of well-being, and try to fix your mind on it. Other thoughts creep in and you push them aside, and you spend your time battling against them in an effort to concentrate. If you can concentrate and fix your mind on one idea, if you are able to exclude other thoughts and isolate yourself with that one idea, you think you have achieved something. In other words, your concentration is merely exclusion. Life is too much for you; therefore, you concentrate on an idea, and then you think your mind will be sharp. Will it? Can the mind ever be sharp if it lives in insolation, in exclusion? The mind is sharp, clear, swift, only when it is inclusive, when it does not live in isolation, when it is capable of following every thought completely through and seeing its consequences. Then only is the mind capable of being sharp—not when concentrating on an idea, which is an exclusive process.

There is another question involved in this: What do you mean by *idea?* What is an idea? Obviously, a fixed thought. What is thought? Thought is the response of memory. There is no thought without memory, there is no thought without the past, so thought comes into being as the response of memory. And what is memory? Memory is the residue of incomplete experience, of experience which is not completely understood; so memory is the product of incomplete action. Naturally I cannot go into it fully, as it would take a great deal of time, but briefly, memory is incomplete experience, and that incomplete experience which you call memory produces thought, from which there is an idea. So, idea is incomplete, and when you concentrate, your mind is incomplete, and a mind that is incomplete must always be dull. The mind becomes sensitive only when it is swift, clear, when it is aware of its own response and is free of the response. When you want to understand something, you love it; you watch that something very intently, without condemnation, without justification, without blame, without response. Then your mind is swift, then your action is not based on an idea—which is merely the continuation of memory and therefore incomplete. A mind that is forced to concentrate, that is immolated to an idea, identified with an idea, is a dull mind because an idea can never be complete; and as most of us live on ideas, our minds are dull. Only when the mind is free, capable of extraordinary pliability, can there be the understanding of truth.

Question: Does a man go to sleep when his body is asleep?

KRISHNAMURTI: This is an extraordinarily complex problem. If you have the inclination and the interest and are not too tired, we can go into it. What do you mean by sleep? Do you mean the body going to sleep? Are we asleep when we think we are sleeping? Are not most of us living in a state of dreams in which we do things automatically? When environmental influences compel you to certain forms of action, are you not asleep? Surely, merely going to bed is not the only form of sleep that most people aim at. Most of us want to forget, we want to be dull, undisturbed, we want an easy, comfortable life, so we put ourselves to sleep mentally and emotionally while we are actively doing things.

To understand this problem, we have to understand the question of consciousness. What do we mean by consciousness? Do not quote what somebody has said about it, either a Shankara or a Buddha. Think it out for yourselves. I have not read any sacred books, the Bhagavad-Gita or the Upanishads, nor any books on psychology. One has to think anew when one wants to find the truth, one cannot find the truth through another. What you repeat is a lie. It may be true for another, but when you repeat it, it becomes a lie. Truth cannot be repeated, it must be experienced, and you cannot experience it if you are caught in the net of words. We will have to find what we mean by consciousness. Surely, consciousness is a process of response to challenge, which you call experience. That is, there is a challenge, which is always new, but the response is always old. The response to the new, the response to a challenge, is experience. That experience is termed, named, given a label as good or bad, pleasurable or painful, and then recorded, put away. So, consciousness at different levels is the total process of experiencing—responding to a challenge, naming, and recording. That is actually what is going on at different levels of our being, a constant process, not a periodic process—response to a challenge, naming or terming it, and storing it up in order to communicate or to hold it. That total process at different levels is called consciousness. I am not inventing—if you observe yourselves, you will see that this is actually what is taking place. Memory is the storehouse, the record, and it is memory that interferes, responds to a challenge—and this process we call consciousness. This is exactly what is taking place.

Now, when the body goes to sleep, when you are asleep, what happens? The process is going on, the mind is still active, is it not? You can often see that the mind is active in sleep when you have a problem. During the day you think about it, worry about it, but you cannot find an answer. When you wake up, you have a new way of looking at the problem. How does that happen? Obviously, when the conscious mind, after having worried over the problem, becomes relaxed, into that quiet superficial mind the unconscious is able to project itself, and when you wake up, you have the answer. The conscious mind is never still; it is everlastingly active in all its different layers. It is not possible during the waking hours to still the mind; but when in sleep the superficial layer of consciousness is quiet, the unconscious projects itself and gives the right answer.

It is only when the mind, consciousness, is not naming, not storing, but merely experiencing—only then is there freedom, liberation. Sleep has a different meaning. We have no time now to go into that question, but we will deal with it on another occasion. The question is, What happens when the body is asleep? Obviously, the superficial mind is quiet, but the whole consciousness goes on. The vastness, the deeper significance of sleep is not understood if we are not fully aware during the waking hours of the process of consciousness. The process of consciousness is experiencing, naming, and storing or recording, and as long as that full process is kept up, there is no freedom. Freedom, liberation can come only when thought ceases—thought being the product of memory, which in turn is experiencing, naming, and recording. Freedom is possible only when there is full, peaceful awareness of everything about you and in yourself. Again, this brings up the question, what is awareness? We will have to discuss it another time.

Question: Belief in God has been a powerful incentive to better living. Why do you deny God? Why do you not try to revive man's faith in the idea of God?

KRISHNAMURTI: Let us look at the problem widely and intelligently. I am not denying God—it would be foolish to do so. Only the man who does not know reality indulges in meaningless words. The man who says he knows does not know; the man who is experiencing reality from moment to moment has no means of communicating that reality. Let us go into this question. The men who dropped the atomic bomb on Hiroshima said that God was with them; those who flew from England to destroy Germany said that God was their copilot. The Hitlers, the Churchills, the generals all talk of God; they have immense faith in God. Are they doing service, making a better life for man? The people who say they believe in God have destroyed half the world, and the world is in complete misery. Through religious intolerance, there are divisions of people as believers and nonbelievers, leading to religious wars. It indicates how extraordinarily politically minded you are. And the capitalist has his fat bank account, his dull heart, and empty mind. (Laughter) Don't laugh, because you do exactly the same thing. The empty of heart also talk of God. Is belief in God "a powerful incentive to better living"? Why do you want an incentive to better living? Surely, your incentive must be your own desire to live cleanly and simply, must it not? If you look to an incentive, you are not interested in making life possible for all, you are merely interested in your incentive, which is different from mine—and we will quarrel over the incentive. But if we live happily together, not because we believe in God, but because we are human beings, then we will share the entire means of production in order to produce things for all. Through lack of intelligence we accept the idea of a super-intelligence which we call "God"; but this "God," this super-intelligence, is not going to give us a better life. What leads to a better life is intelligence; and there cannot be intelligence if there is belief, if there are class divisions, if the means of production are in the hands of a few, if there are isolated nationalities and sovereign governments. All this obviously indicates lack of intelligence, and it is the lack of intelligence that is preventing a better living, not nonbelief in God.

Now, the other point is, what do you mean by God? First of all, the word is not God, the word is not the thing. When you say the word *God*, it is not God. When you repeat that word, naturally it produces a certain sensation, a pleasurable response. Or if you say you do not believe in God, this rejection also has a psychological significance. That is, the word *God* creates in you a nervous response, which is also emotional and intellectual, according to your conditioning; but such responses are obviously not God. Now, how are you going to find the truth? Not by isolation, not by withdrawing from life. To find truth, sir, the mind must be free from the response of the past, for truth is not seen when the mind is fixed, it has to see anew from moment to moment. A mind that is the product of memory, of time, cannot follow truth. For reality to be seen the thought process must cease. Every thought is the product of time, the outcome of yesterday, and the mind that is caught in the field of time cannot perceive something beyond itself. What it perceives is still within the field of time, and that which is in the field of time is not reality. Reality can be only when the mind which is the product of time ceases; and then there is the experiencing of that reality, which is not fictitious, which is not self-hypnosis. The thought process ceases only when you understand yourself; and you can understand yourself completely, fully, not in isolation, not in withdrawal from life, but only in your relationship with your wife, your children, your mother, your neighbor. So, reality is not far away, regeneration is not a matter of time. Regeneration, that inward revolution of clarity, comes into being only when you perceive *what is*. It does not need time, it needs understanding, it needs clarity of attention. Only when the mind is tranquil does regeneration come. The experiencing of reality is not a matter of belief; he who believes it does not know it, and when he talks about it, he is merely indulging in words. Words are not experience, they are not reality. Reality is immeasurable, it cannot be caught in the garland of words, as life cannot be contained within the walls of possession. Only when the mind is free can creation come into being.

September 12, 1948

Fourth Talk in Poona

It is fairly obvious that most of us are confused intellectually. We see that the so-called leaders in all departments of life have no complete answer to our various questions and problems. The many conflicting political parties, whether of the left or of the right, seem not to have found the right solution for our national and international strife, and we also see that socially there is an utter destruction of moral values. Everything about us seems to be disintegrating; moral and ethical values have become merely a matter of tradition, without much significance. War, the conflict between the right and the left, seems to be a constantly recurring factor in our lives; everywhere there is destruction, everywhere there is confusion. In ourselves we are utterly confused, though we do not like to acknowledge it; we see confusion in all things, and we do not know exactly what to do. Most of us who recognize this confusion, this uncertainty, want to do something, and the more confused we are, the more anxious we are to act. So, for those people who have realized that there is confusion in themselves and about them, action becomes all-important. But when a person is confused, how can he act? Whatever he does, whatever his course of action may be, it is bound to be confused, and naturally such action will inevitably create greater confusion. To whatever party, institution, or organization he may belong, until he clears up his own sphere of confusion, obviously, whatever he does is bound to produce further chaos. So, what is he to do? What is a man to do who is earnest and desirous of clearing up the confusion about him and in himself? What is his first responsibility—to act, or to clear up the confusion in himself and therefore outside of himself? I think this is an important question that most of us are unwilling to face. We see so much social disorder which we feel needs immediate reform that action becomes an engulfing process. Being anxious to do something, we proceed to act, we try to bring about reforms, we join political parties, either of the left or of the right; but we soon find out that reforms need further reform, leaders need regrouping, organizations demand more organizing, and so on. Whenever we try to act, we find that the actor himself is the source of confusion; so what is he to do? Is he to act when he is confused, or remain inactive? That is really the problem most of us face.

Now, we are afraid to be inactive, and to withdraw for a period to consider the whole problem requires extraordinary intelligence. If you were to withdraw for a time to reconsider, to revaluate the problem, then your friends, your associates, would consider you an escapist. You would become a nonentity, socially you would be nowhere. If when there is flag-waving you do not wave a flag, if when everyone puts on a particular cap you do not have that cap, you feel left out; and as most of us do not like to remain in the background, we plunge into action. So, the problem of action and inaction is quite important to understand. Is it not necessary to be inactive to consider the whole issue? Obviously, we must carry on with our daily responsibility of earning bread; all the necessities must be carried on. But the political, religious, social organizations, the groups, committees, and so on—need we belong to them? If we are very serious about it, must we not reconsider, revalue the whole problem of existence? And to do that, must we not for the time being withdraw in order to consider, ponder, meditate? Is that withdrawal inaction? Is not that withdrawal really action? In that so-called inaction there is the extraordinary action of reconsidering the whole question, revaluing, thinking over the confusion in which one lives. Why are we so afraid to be inactive? Is it inaction to reconsider? Obviously not. Surely, the man who is avoiding action is he who is active without reconsidering the issue. He is the real escapist. He is confused, and in order to escape from his confusion, from his insufficiency, he plunges into action, he joins a society, a party, an organization. He is really escaping from the fundamental issue, which is confusion. So, we are misapplying words. The man who plunges into action without reconsidering the problem, thinking that he is reforming the world by joining a society or a party—it is he who is creating greater confusion and greater misery; whereas, the so-called inactive man who withdraws and is seriously considering the whole question—surely, such a man is much more active.

In these times especially, when the whole world is on the edge of a precipice and catastrophic events are taking place, is it not necessary for a few at least to be inactive, deliberately not to allow themselves to be caught in this machine, this atomic machine of action, which does not produce anything except further confusion, further chaos? Surely, those who are in earnest will withdraw, not from life, not from daily activities, but withdraw in order to discover, study, explore, investigate, the cause of confusion; and to find out, to discover, to explore, one need not go into the innumerable plans and blueprints of what a new society should or should not be. Obviously, such blueprints are utterly useless because a man who is confused and who is merely carrying out blueprints will bring about further confusion. Therefore, as I have repeatedly said, the important thing, if we are to understand the cause of confusion, is self-knowledge. Without understanding oneself there cannot be order in the world; without exploring the whole process of thought, feeling, and action in oneself, there cannot possibly be world peace, order, and security. Therefore, the study of oneself is of primary importance, and it is not a process of escape. This study of oneself is not mere inaction. On the contrary, it requires an extraordinary awareness in everything that one does, awareness in which there is no judgment, no condemnation, nor blame. This awareness of the total process of oneself as one lives in daily life is not narrowing but ever expanding, ever clarifying; and out of this awareness comes order, first in oneself, and then externally in one's relationships.

So, the problem is one of relationship. Without relationship, there is no existence; to be is to be related. If I merely use relationship without understanding myself, I increase the mess and contribute to further confusion. Most of us do not seem to realize this—that the world is my relationship with others, whether one or many. My problem is that of relationship. What I am, that I project; and obviously, if I do not understand myself, the whole of relationship is one of confusion in ever-widening circles. So, relationship becomes of extraordinary importance, not with the so-called mass, the crowd, but in the world of my family and friends, however small that may be—my relationship with my wife, my children, my neighbor. In a world of vast organizations, vast mobilizations of people, mass movements, we are afraid to act on a small scale; we are afraid to be little people clearing up our own patch. We say to ourselves, "What can I personally do? I must join a mass movement in order to reform." On the contrary, real revolution takes place not through mass movements but through the inward revaluation of relationship—that alone is real reformation, a radical, continuous revolution. We are afraid to begin on a small scale. Because the problem is so vast, we think we must meet it with large numbers of people, with a great organization, with mass movements, Surely, we must begin to tackle the problem on a small scale, and the small scale is the 'me' and the 'you'. When I understand myself, I understand you, and out of that understanding comes love. Love is the missing factor; there is a lack of affection, of warmth in relationship; and because we lack that love, that tenderness, that generosity, that mercy in relationship, we escape into mass action which produces further confusion, further misery. We fill our hearts with blueprints for world reform and do not look to that one resolving factor which is love. Do what you will, without the regenerating factor of love, whatever you do will produce further chaos. The action of the intellect is not going to produce a solution. Our problem is relationship, and not which system, which blueprint to follow, what kind of United Nations Organization to form; it is the utter lack of goodwill in relationship, not with humanity, whatever that may mean, but the utter lack of goodwill and love in the relationship between two people. Have you not found how extraordinarily difficult it is to work with another, to think out a problem together with two or three? If we cannot think out problems with two or three, how can we think them out with a mass of people? We can think out problems together only when there is that generosity, that kindliness, that warmth of love in relationship; but we deny love and try to find the solution in the arid fields of the mind.

So, relationship is our problem; and without understanding relationship, merely to be active is to produce further confusion, further misery. Action is relationship; to be is to be related. Do what you will, withdraw to the mountains, sit in a forest, you cannot live in isolation. You can live only in relationship, and as long as relationship is not understood, there can be no right action. Right action comes in understanding relationship, which reveals the process of oneself. Self-knowledge is the beginning of wisdom, it is a field of affection, warmth, and love, therefore a field rich with flowers.

Question: The institution of marriage is one of the chief causes of social conflict. It creates a seeming order at the cost of terrible repression and suffering. Is there another way of solving the problem of sex?

KRISHNAMURTI: Every human problem requires great consideration, and to understand the problem there must be no response, no rejection, no acceptance. That which you condemn, you do not understand. So, we must go into the problem of sex very closely, fully and carefully, step by step—which is what I propose to do. I am not going to lay down what should or should not be done, which is silly, which is immature thinking. You cannot lay down a pattern for life, you cannot put life into the framework of ideas; and because society inevitably puts life into the framework of moral order, society is always breeding disorder. So, to understand this problem, we must neither condemn nor justify, but we will have to think it out anew.

Now, what is the problem? Is sex a problem? Let us think it out together; do not wait for me to answer. If it is a problem, why is it a problem? Have we made hunger into a problem? Has starvation become a problem? The obvious causes of starvation are nationalism, class differences, economic frontiers, sovereign governments, the means of production in the hands of a few, separative religious factors, and so on. If we try to eliminate the symptoms without eradicating the causes, if instead of tackling the root we merely trim the branches because it is so much easier, the same old problem continues. Similarly, why has sex become a problem? To curb the sexual urge, to hold it within bounds, the institution of marriage has been created; and in marriage, behind the door, behind the wall, you can do anything you like and show a respectable front outside. By using her for your sexual gratification you can convert your wife into a prostitute, and it is perfectly respectable. Under the guise of marriage, you can be worse than an animal; and without marriage, without restraint, you know no bounds. So, in order to set a limit, society lays down certain moral laws which become tradition, and within that limit you can be as immoral, as ugly as you like; and that unrepressed indulgence, that habitual sexual action is considered perfectly normal, healthy, and moral. So, why is sex a problem? To a married couple, is sex a problem? Not at all. The woman and the man have an assured source of constant pleasure. When you have a source of constant pleasure, when you have a guaranteed income, what happens? You become dull, weary, empty, exhausted. Have you not noticed that people who before marriage were full of vital energy become dull the moment they are married? All the springs of life have gone out of them. Have you not noticed it in your own sons and daughters? Why has sex become a problem? Obviously, the more intellectual you are, the more sexual you are. Have you not noticed that? And the more there is of emotion, of kindliness, of affection, the less there is of sex. Because our whole social, moral, and educational culture is based on the cultivation of the intellect, sex has become a problem full of confusion and conflict. So, the solution of the problem of sex lies in understanding the cultivation of the intellect. The intellect is not the means of creation, and creation does not take place through the functioning of the intellect; on the contrary, there is creation when the intellect is silent. Only when there is creation does the functioning of intellect have a meaning; but without creation, without that creative affection, the mere functioning of the intellect obviously creates the problem of sex. As most of us live in the brain, as most of us live on words, and words are of the mind, most of us are not creative. We are caught in words, in spinning new words and rearranging old ones. Surely, that is not creation. Since we are not creative, the only expression of creativeness left to us is sex. In the sexual act there is forgetfulness, and in forgetfulness alone there is creation. The sexual act for a split second gives you freedom from that self which is of the mind, and therefore it has become a problem. Surely, creativeness comes into being only when there is absence of thought which is of the 'me', of the 'mine'. I do not know if you have noticed that in moments of great crisis, in moments of great joy, the consciousness of 'me' and 'mine' which is the product of the mind, disappears. In that moment of expansive appreciation of life, of intense joy, there is creativeness. To put it simply, when self is absent there is creation; and since all of us are caught in the arid intellect, naturally there is no absence of self. On the contrary, in that field, in that striving to be, there is an exaggerated expansion of the self and therefore no creativeness. Therefore, sex is the only means of being creative, of experiencing the absence of the self; and since the mere sexual act becomes habitual, that too is wearisome and gives strength to the continuity of the self, so sex becomes a problem.

In order to solve the problem of sex, we will have to approach it, not on any one level of thought, but from every direction, from every side—the educational, religious, and moral. When we are young, we have a strong feeling of sex attraction, and we marry—or are married off by our parents, as happens here in the East. Parents are often concerned only with getting rid of their boys and girls, and the pair, the boy and the girl, have no knowledge of sexual matters. Within the sacred law of society, the man can suppress his wife, destroy her, give her children year after year—and it is perfectly all right. Under the guise of respectability, he can become a completely immoral person. One has to understand and educate the boy and the girl—and that requires extraordinary intelligence on the part of the educator. Unfortunately, our fathers, mothers, and teachers all need this same education; they are as dull as dishwater, they only know the do's, don'ts, and taboos, they have no intelligence for this problem. To help the boy and girl we will have to have a new teacher who is really educated. But through the cinema and the advertisements with their half-naked girls, their luscious women, and lavish houses, and through various other means, society is giving stimulation to sensate values, and what do you expect? If he is married, the man takes it out on his wife; if he is not married, he goes to someone under cover. It is a difficult problem to bring intelligence to the boy and the girl. On every side human beings are exploiting each other through sex, through property, through relationship; and religiously, there is no creativeness at all. On the contrary, the constant meditation, the rituals or pujas, the repetition of words are all merely mechanical acts with certain responses; but that is not creative thinking, creative living. Religiously, you are merely traditional therefore, there is no creative inquiry into the discovery of reality. Religiously, you are regimented, and where there is regimentation, whether it is in the military or the religious sense, obviously there cannot be creativeness; therefore, you seek creativeness through sex. Free the mind from orthodoxy, from ritual, from regimentation and dogmatism so that it can be creative, and then the problem of sex will not be so great or so dominant.

There is another side to this problem: in the sexual relationship between man and woman, there is no love. The woman is merely used as a means of sexual gratification. Surely, sirs, love is not the product of the mind; love is not the result of thought; love is not the outcome of a contract. Here in this country the boy and the girl hardly know each other, yet they are married and have sexual relations. The boy and girl accept each other and say, "You give me this, and I give you that," or "You give me your body, and I give you security, I give you my calculated affection." When the husband says, "I love you," it is merely a response of the mind; because he gives his wife a certain protection, he expects of her and she gives him her favor. This relationship of calculation is called love. It is an obvious fact—you may not like me to put it so brutally, but it is the actual fact. Such marriage is said to be for love, but it is a mere matter of exchange; it is a *bania* marriage, it reveals the mentality of the market place. Surely, in such marriage there cannot be love, can there? Love is not of the mind, but since we have cultivated the mind, we use that word *love* to cover the field of the mind. Surely, love has nothing to do with the mind, it is not the product of the mind; love is entirely independent of calculation, of thought. When there is no love, then the framework of marriage as an institution becomes a necessity. When there is love, then sex is not a problem—it is the lack of love that makes it into a problem. Don't you know? When you love somebody really deeply—not with the love of the mind, but really from the heart—you share with him or her everything that you have, not your body only, but everything. In your trouble, you ask her help and she helps you. There is no division between man and woman when you love somebody, but there is a sexual problem when you do not know that love. We know only the love of the brain; thought has produced it, and a product of thought is still thought, it is not love.

So, this problem of sex is not simple and it cannot be solved on its own level. To try to solve it purely biologically is absurd; and to approach it through religion or to try to solve it as though it were a mere matter of physical adjustment, of glandular action, or to hedge it in with taboos and condemnations is all too immature, childish, and stupid. It requires intelligence of the highest order. To understand ourselves in our relationship with another requires intelligence far more swift and subtle than to understand nature. But we seek to understand without intelligence; we want immediate action, an immediate solution, and the problem becomes more and more important. Have you noticed a man whose heart is empty, how his face becomes ugly and how the children he produces are ugly and immature? And because they have had no affection, they remain immature for the rest of their lives. Look at your faces sometime in the mirror—how unformed, how undefined they are! You have brains to find out, and you are caught in the brain. Love is not mere thought; thoughts are only the external action of the brain. Love is much deeper, much more profound, and the profundity of life can be discovered only in love. Without love, life has no meaning—and that is the sad part of our existence. We grow old while still immature; our bodies become old, fat, and ugly, and we remain thoughtless. Though we read and talk about it, we have never known the perfume of life. Mere reading and verbalizing indicates an utter lack of the warmth of heart that enriches life; and without that quality of love, do what you will, join any society, bring about any law, you will not solve this problem. To love is to be chaste. Mere intellect is not chastity. The man who tries to be chaste in thought is unchaste because he has no love. Only the man who loves is chaste, pure, incorruptible.

Question: In the modern institution of society, it is impossible to live without organization. To shun all organizations as you seem to do is merely escapism. Do you call the postal system a nucleus of power? What should be the basis of organization in the new society?

KRISHNAMURTI: Again, sir, it is a complex question. Surely, all organizations exist for efficiency. The post office is an organization for the efficiency of communication; but when the postmaster becomes a quasi-tyrant over his clerks, the post office becomes a means of power, does it not? The postmaster general is interested in the efficiency of communication, or he should be; his position is obviously not intended to be a means of power, authority, self-aggrandizement—which in fact it is. So, every institution or organization is used by human beings, not simply for efficiency of communication, distribution, and so on, but as a means of power—and that is what I am objecting to. Surely, the post office, the tramway, and various other public services are a necessity in modern society, and they must be organized. The power house which creates electricity needs careful organization; but when that organization is used for political purposes as a means of self-aggrandizement, as a means of exploitation, obviously the organization becomes the tool of extraordinary brutality.

Now, the religious organizations as Hinduism, as Catholicism, as Buddhism, and so on are not for efficiency and are wholly unnecessary. They become pernicious; the priest, the bishop, the church, the temple are an extraordinary means of exploiting men. They exploit you through fear, through tradition, through ceremony. Religion is obviously and truly the search for reality, and such organizations are unnecessary because the search for reality is not carried on through an organized group of people. On the contrary, an organized group of people becomes a hindrance to reality; therefore, Hinduism, Christianity, or any other organized belief is a hindrance to truth. Why do we need such organizations? They are not efficient because the search for truth lies in your own hands; it cannot be realized through an organization, not through a guru or his disciples when they are organized for power. We obviously need technical organizations, such as the post office, the tramway, and so on; but surely, when man is intelligent every other organization is unnecessary. Because we ourselves are not intelligent, we turn over to those people who call themselves intelligent the power to rule us. An intelligent man does not want to be ruled; he does not want any organization other than that which is necessary for the efficiency of existence.

The necessities of life cannot be truly organized when they are in the hands of a few, of a class, or a group; and when the few act as representing the many, surely there is the same problem of power. Exploitation arises when organizations are used as a means of power, whether by the individual, by the group, by the party, or the state. It is this self-expansion through organization that is pernicious, such as a state identifying itself as a sovereign government, with which goes nationalism and in which the individual is also involved. It is this expansive, aggressive, self-defending power that is objectionable. Surely, in order for me to come here, there must be an organization. I must write a letter, and that letter can reach you only if there is a properly organized system of postal distribution. All this is right organization. But when organizations are used by the clever, by the cunning, as a means of exploiting men, such organizations must be eradicated; and they can be eradicated only when you yourself, in your little circle, are not seeking power, dominance. As long as the search for power exists, there must be a hierarchical process from the government's minister to the clerk, from the bishop to the priest, from the general to the common soldier.

Surely, we can have a decent society only when individuals, you and I, are not seeking power in any direction, whether through wealth, through relationship, or through an idea. It is the search for power that is the cause of this disaster, this disintegration of society. Our existence at present is all power politics, dominance in the family by the man or by the woman, dominance through an idea. Action based on an idea is always separative, it can never be inclusive; and the search for power, whether by the individual or by the state, indicates the expansion, the cultivation of the intellect in which there is no love. When you love someone, you are very careful, you organize spontaneously, don't you? You are watchful, you are efficient in helping that one or this one. It is when there is no love that organization as a means of power comes into being. When you love others, when you are full of affection and generosity, then organizations have a different meaning; they are kept on their own level. But when the individual's position becomes all-important, when there is craving for power, then organizations are used as the means to that power—and power and love cannot exist together. Love is its own power, its own beauty, and it is because our hearts are empty that we fill them with the things of the mind; and the things of the mind are not things of the heart. Because our hearts are filled with the things of the mind, we look to organizations as a means of bringing order, of bringing peace to the world. It is not organizations, but only love that can bring order and peace to the world; it is not blueprints of any utopia, but only goodwill that can achieve conciliation between people. Because we have no warmth of love, we depend upon organizations; and the moment we have organizations without love, the clever and the cunning come to the top and use them. We start an organization for the welfare of man, and before we know where we are, somebody is using it for his own ends. We create revolutions, bloody, disastrous revolutions to bring about world order, and before we know it, the power is in the hands of a few maniacs after power, and they become a powerful new class, a new dominating group of commissars with their secret police, and love is driven out.

Sirs, how can man live without love? We can only exist, and existence without love is control, confusion, and pain—and that is what most of us are creating. We organize for existence and we accept conflict as inevitable because our existence is a ceaseless demand for power. Surely, when we love, organization has its own place, its right place; but without love, organization becomes a nightmare, merely mechanical and efficient, like the army. When there is love, there will be no army; but as modern society is based on mere efficiency, we have to have armies—and the purpose of an army is to create war. Even in so-called peace, the more intellectually efficient we are, the more ruthless, the more brutal, the more callous we become. That is why there is confusion in the world, why bureaucracy is more and more powerful, why more and more governments are becoming totalitarian. We submit to all this as being inevitable because we live in our brains and not in our hearts, and therefore love does not exist. Love is the most dangerous and uncertain element in life; and because we do not want to be uncertain, because we do not want to be in danger, we live in the mind. A man who loves is dangerous, and we do not want to live dangerously; we want to live efficiently, we want to live merely in the framework of organization because we think organizations are going to bring order and peace in the world. Organizations have never brought order and peace. Only love, only goodwill, only mercy can bring order and peace, ultimately and therefore now.

Question: Why is woman prone to permit herself to be dominated by man? Why do communities and nations permit themselves to be bossed by a leader or a Fuehrer?

KRISHNAMURTI: Now, sir, why do you ask this question? Why don't you look into your own mind to find out why you want to be dominated, why you dominate, and why you seek a leader? Why do you dominate the woman or the man? And this domination is also called love, is it not? When the man dominates, the woman likes it and considers it as affection, and when a woman bosses the man, he also likes it. Why? It is an indication that the domination gives you a certain sense of closeness of relationship. If my wife dominates me, I feel very close to her, and if she does not dominate, I feel she is indifferent. You are afraid of indifference from your wife or your husband, from the woman or the man. You will accept anything as long as you do not feel someone is indifferent. You know how closely you want to keep to your guru; you will do anything—sacrifice your wife, honesty, everything—to be close to him because you want to feel that he is not indifferent to you. That is, we use relationship as a means of self-forgetfulness, and as long as relationship does not show us what we actually are, we are satisfied. That is why we accept the domination of another. When my wife or husband dominates me, it does not reveal what I am but is a source of gratification. If my wife does not dominate me, if she is indifferent and I discover what I really am, it is very disturbing. What am I? I am an empty, dour, sloppy being with certain appetites—and I am afraid to face all that emptiness. Therefore I accept the domination of my wife or husband because it makes me feel very close to him or to her, and I do not want to see myself as I am. And this domination gives a sense of relationship; this domination brings jealousy—the moment you do not dominate me, you are looking at somebody else. Therefore I am jealous because I have lost you, and I do not know how to get rid of jealousy, which is still on the plane of the brain. Sir, a man who loves is not jealous. Jealousy is of the brain, but love is not of the brain; and where there is love, there is no domination. When you love somebody, you are not dominating, you are a part of that person. There is no separation, but complete integration. It is the brain that separates and creates the problem of domination.

"Why do communities and nations permit themselves to be bossed by a leader?" What are communities and nations? A group of people living together. To put it differently, society, the community, the nation, is you, the individual, in your relationship with another; and this is an obvious fact. Why do you seek a leader? Obviously, you do it because you are confused, do you not? A man who is very clear, who is integrated, does not want a leader. To him a leader is a nuisance, a factor of disintegration in society. You seek a leader because you are confused; you do not know what to do, and you want to be told what to do, so you seek modes of conduct, socially, politically, and religiously. Being confused, you seek a leader—follow the implications of this, sir. If when you are confused you seek a leader who will lead you out of the confusion, it means that you are not seeking clarity, you are not interested in the cause of confusion, you merely want to be led out of it. But being confused, you will choose a leader who is also confused. (Laughter) Do not laugh, but please see the importance of this. You won't seek a leader who is clear because he will tell you to look to your own confusion, not to escape from it;

he will say that the cause of confusion is in yourself. But you do not want that, you want a leader who will lead you out of confusion, and because your mind is confused, you will seek one who is also confused. How can one confused mind lead another out of confusion? A mind that is confused must have a leader who is also confused; therefore, all leaders are inevitably confused because you create the leader out of your own confusion—and this is very important to understand. When you realize this fact, you will not seek a leader, you will become responsible for the clearing up of your own confusion. It is only a confused man that, not knowing how to act, seeks a leader to help him to act; but the leader is also confused, and that is why leaders are a disintegrating factor in your life. The leader is projected out of your own confusion; therefore, he is but yourself in a different form, as your governments are. It is self-projection that creates the leader; a national hero is yourself exemplified externally. What you are, or what you want to be—such is your leader; therefore, such a leader cannot bring you out of your chaos. The resolution of the chaos lies in your own hands, not in the hands of another. Regeneration comes through understanding yourself, not through following somebody, for that somebody is yourself with a greater power of words, but equally confused, equally tyrannical, equally traditional.

So, then, the problem is not the leader but how to eradicate confusion. Can another help you in removing confusion? If you look to another to remove your confusion, he can only help you to increase it because a confused mind can never choose that which is clear; since it is in confusion, it can only choose that which is confused. If you wish radically to get rid of confusion, you will set your own mind and heart in order, you will consider the causes that bring about confusion. Confusion arises only when there is no self-knowledge. When I do not know myself and do not know what to do or what to think, naturally I am caught in the whirlwind of confusion. But when I know myself, the whole total process of myself—which is extraordinarily simple if one has the intention to know oneself—then out of that understanding comes clarity, out of that understanding comes conduct and right behavior. So, it is of the highest importance not to follow a leader but to understand oneself. The understanding of oneself brings love, brings order. Chaos exists only in relationship to something, and as long as I do not understand that relationship, there must be confusion. To understand relationship is to understand myself, and to understand myself is to bring about that quality of love in which there is well-being. If I know how to love my wife, my children, or my neighbor, I know how to love everyone. Since I do not love the one, I am merely remaining on the intellectual or verbal level with humanity. The idealist is a bore—he loves humanity with his brain, he does not love with his heart. When you love, no leader is necessary. It is the empty of heart who seek a leader to fill that emptiness with words, with an ideology, with a utopia of the future. Love is only in the present, not in time, not in the future. For him who loves, eternity is now, for love is its own eternity.

September 19, 1948

Fifth Talk in Poona

This evening instead of making a long introductory speech, I will make a brief one and answer as many questions as possible. This meeting is meant for teachers and their problems, so I will answer questions only on the subject of education; and as there are twenty of them, I will have to answer briefly and succinctly.

It is difficult in modern civilization to bring about, by means of education, an integrated individual. We have divided life into so many departments and our lives are so unintegrated that education has very little meaning except merely when learning a particular technique, a particular profession. Throughout the world, education has obviously failed—as the first function of education is to create a human being who is intelligent. To attempt to solve the problems of existence merely at their respective levels, separated into different departments, indicates an utter lack of intelligence. Our problem, then, is how to create an individual who is integrated through intelligence, so that he would be able to grapple with life from moment to moment, to face life as it comes with its complexities, with its conflicts, with its miseries, with its inequalities—an individual who can meet life, not according to a particular system either of the left or of the right, but intelligently, without seeking an answer or a pattern of action. Since education has not produced such an individual, and since there have been successive wars, one after the other, each more devastating and destructive, bringing greater sorrow and misery to man, obviously the educational systems throughout the world have completely failed. So, there is something radically wrong with the way we bring up our children. We all acknowledge that there is something wrong, we are all aware of it, but we do not know how to tackle that problem. The problem is not the child but the parent and the teacher, and what is necessary is to educate the educator. Without educating the educator, merely to stuff the child with a lot of information, making him pass examinations, is the most unintelligent form of education. The really important thing is to educate the educator, and that is one of the most difficult undertakings. The educator is already crystallized in a system of thought or a pattern of action; he is already a nationalist, he has already given himself over to a particular ideology, to a particular religion, to a particular standard of thought. So the difficulty is, is it not, that modern education teaches the child what to think and not how to think. Surely, it is only when one has the capacity to think intelligently that one can meet life. Life cannot be made to conform to a system or be fitted into a framework, and the mentality that has merely been trained in factual knowledge is incapable of meeting life with its variety, its complexities, its subtleties, its depths, and great heights. So, when our children are trained in a particular system of thought, according to a particular discipline, obviously they are incapable of meeting life as a whole because they are taught to think in terms of departments; they are not integrated. For the teacher who is interested, the question is how to bring out an integrated individual. To do that, obviously the teacher himself must also be integrated. One cannot bring up a child to be an integrated individual if one does not understand integration in oneself. That is, what you are in yourself is much more important than the traditional question of what to teach the child. The important thing is not what you think but how you think, whether thought is merely an unintegrated process or a complete, total process. Thought as an integrated process can be understood only when there is self-knowledge—and into this we will go during the later talks and discussions.

As there are numerous questions, I will try to answer briefly, quickly, and definitely as many of the representative ones as possible. You may ask innumerable questions, but please bear in mind that to find the right answer you must have the capacity to listen; otherwise, you will merely be carried away by words without much content. The art of listening is extremely arduous because it consists in being interested and giving your full attention, but most of us are not interested in this question of education. We send our children to school, and that is the end of it; we consider that it is good riddance, and that it is the function of the teacher to educate them. Since most of us are not interested, it is extremely difficult to listen carefully and to understand. One may use the wrong word, the wrong phrase, an incorrect term; but the person who is very attentive goes through the inaccuracies of terminology and gets the gist of the meaning. So, I hope you will be able to follow swiftly and wisely.

Question: Do you approve of the Montessori and other systems of education? Have you any to recommend?

KRISHNAMURTI: What is implied in a system of education? A framework into which you are fitting the child; and the questioner wants to know which framework will best help the child. Will any system of education really help to bring about integration? Or must there be not a particular system but intelligence on the part of the teacher to understand the child, to see what kind of child he is? There must be very few children for each teacher. It is very easy to have a system for a large number of people—that is why systems are popular. You can force a great number of boys and girls into a particular system, and then you, the teacher, need not spend your thought on them. You practice your system on the poor children. Whereas, when you have no system, you must study each child, and that requires a great deal of intelligence, alertness, and affection on the part of the teacher, does it not? It means classes limited to five or six. Such a school would be extraordinarily expensive; therefore, we resort to a system. Systems obviously do not bring about an integrated individual. Systems may help you to understand the child, but surely the primary necessity is that you, who are the teacher, should have the intelligence to use a system when necessary and to drop it when it is not necessary. But when we turn to a system in place of affection, understanding, and intelligence, then the teacher becomes merely a machine, and therefore the child grows up an unintegrated individual. Systems have a use only in the hands of an intelligent teacher; your own intelligence is the factor that will help. But most of us who are teachers have very little intelligence; therefore, we turn to systems. It is so much easier to learn a system and to apply it, whether Montessori or any other, for then the teacher can sit back and watch. Surely, that is not education. Mere dependence on a particular system, however worthy, has very little significance. If the teacher himself is not really intelligent, when we adopt systems we are hindering intelligence. Systems do not make for intelligence. Intelligence comes only through integration, a complete understanding of the total process of oneself and of the child. Therefore, it is necessary for a teacher to study the child directly and not merely to follow a particular system, either of the left or of the right, either Montessori or any other. To study the child implies a swift mind, a quick response, and that can take place only when there is affection. But in a class of sixty children, how can you have such affection? Modern society demands that boys and girls should learn certain professions, and for that there must be efficiency in education. When your object is to produce, not intelligent, alert human beings, but efficient machines, obviously you must have a system. Such a system cannot produce whole, integrated individuals who understand the importance of life but only machines with certain responses; and that is why the present civilization is destroying itself.

Question: As communalism is so rampant in India, how shall we guide the child away from it?

KRISHNAMURTI: Is the child communalistically minded? It is the home and the social environment that is making him communalistically or separatively minded. By himself he does not care whether he plays with a Brahmin or a non-Brahmin, a Negro or an English boy. It is the influence of older people, of the social structure, that impinges on his mind, and naturally he is affected by it. The problem is not the child but the older people with their false, communalistic, separative tendencies. To "guide the child away from it," you will have to break the environment, which means breaking down the structure of modern society. Until you do that, obviously the child will be communalistic. Very few of you want complete revolution; you want patchwork reform, you want to keep things as they are. If you really want to break down the communalistic spirit, your attitude has to change completely, has it not? Look at what happens. At home you may discuss with the child how absurd it is to have a sense of class division, and he will probably agree with you; but when he goes to school and plays with other boys, there is this insane communalistic, separative spirit. So, there is a constant battle between the home and the social environments. Or it may be the other way round—the home may be traditional, narrow, bitter, and the social influence may be broader. Again, the child is caught between the two. Surely, to raise a sane child, to make him intelligent, to help him understand so that he sees through all these stupidities, you have to understand and discuss with him all the faults of traditional acceptance and authority. That means, sir, that you have to encourage discontent whereas most of us want to discourage, to put away discontent. It is only through discontent that we see the falseness of all these things, but as we grow older, we begin to crystallize. Most young men are discontented, but unfortunately their discontent is canalized, standardized: they become class governors, priests, bank clerks, factory managers, and there it ends. They get a job and their discontent soon withers away. To keep this discontent alert, awake, is extremely arduous; but it is discontent, this constant inquiry, this dissatisfaction with things as they are—with government, with the influence of parents, wife or husband, with everything about us—that brings creative intelligence. But we do not want such a child because it is very uncomfortable to live with someone who is all the time questioning, looking into the accepted values. We would rather have people who are fat, contented, lazy.

It is you grown-up people who are responsible for the future, but you are not interested in the future. God knows what you are interested in or why you have so many children because you do not know how to bring them up. If you really loved them instead of merely wanting them to carry on your property and your name, then obviously you would tackle this problem anew. You might have to start new schools; it might mean that you yourself would have to become the teacher. But unfortunately you are not very earnest about anything in life except making money, having food, and sex. In those things you are fairly integrated, but you do not want to face or approach the rest of the complexities and difficulties of life; and therefore, when you produce children and they grow up, they are as immature, unintegrated, unintelligent as yourself, in constant battle with themselves and with the world.

So, it is the older people who are responsible for this communalistic spirit. After all, sirs, why should there be divisions between man and man? You are very like another. You may have a different body, your face may be unlike mine, but inwardly, inside the skin, we are very much alike—proud, ambitious, angry, violent, sexual, seeking power, position, authority, and so on. Remove the label and we are very naked, but we do not want to face our nakedness or transform ourselves, and that is why we worship labels—which is too immature, utterly childish. With the world crashing about our ears, we are discussing what caste one should belong to, or whether one should wear the sacred thread, or what kind of ceremony one should perform—which all indicates utter thoughtlessness, does it not? I know you are listening, sirs and ladies, and some of you nod your heads, but the moment you go home you will do exactly the same thing—and that is the sadness of existence. If, when you hear a truth you do not act upon it, it acts as a poison. You are being poisoned by me because you are not acting upon it. That poison naturally spreads; it brings ill health, psychological unbalance, and disturbance. Most of us are used to listening to talks—it is one of the pastimes of India. You listen, go home, and carry on, but such people have very little significance in life. Life demands extraordinary, creative, revolutionary action. Only when that creative intelligence is awakened is there a possibility of living in a peaceful and happy world.

Question: Obviously there must be some kind of discipline in schools, but how is it to be carried out?

KRISHNAMURTI: Surely, sir, there have been experiments in England and in other places in which schools have had no discipline of any kind at all; the children were allowed to do what they liked and never interfered with. Those schools obviously feel that children need some kind of discipline in the sense of guidance—no rigid do's and don'ts, but some kind of warning, some kind of hint or intimation by way of showing the difficulties. Such a form of discipline, which is really guidance, is necessary. The difficulty arises when discipline is merely forcing the child into a particular pattern of action through compulsion, through fear. The character of such a child is obviously distorted, his mind is made crooked through discipline, through the many taboos of do and don't; so he grows up, as most of us have done, with fear and a sense of inferiority. When discipline forces the child into a particular framework, surely he cannot become intelligent; he is merely the product of discipline, and how can such a child be alert, creative, and therefore grow into an integrated, intelligent man? He is merely a machine functioning very smoothly and efficiently, a machine without human intelligence.

So, the question of discipline is quite a complex problem because we think that without discipline in life, we shall spill over, we shall become too lustful. That is the only problem with which we really concern ourselves: how not to become too lustful. You may spill over in any other direction—seek position, be greedy, violent, do anything—as long as you are within limits regarding sexuality. It is very strange, is it not, that no religion really attacks exploitation, greed, envy, but they are all interested in the sexual act, frightfully concerned about sexual morality. It is very odd that organized religions should be so concerned about that particular morality and let the other things rip. One can see why organized religions place their emphasis on sexual morality. They do not look into the problem of exploitation because organized religions depend on society and live on it, and therefore they dare not attack the root and foundation of that society, so they play with sexual morality.

Though most of us talk of discipline, what do we mean by that word? When you have a hundred boys in a class, you will have to have discipline; otherwise, there will be complete chaos. But if you had five or six in a class and an intelligent teacher with a warm heart, with understanding, I am sure there would be no need for discipline; she would understand each child and help him in the way required. Discipline in schools becomes necessary when there is one teacher to a hundred boys and girls—then you jolly well have to be very strict—but such discipline will not produce an intelligent human being. And most of us are interested in mass movements—large schools with a great many boys and girls—we are not interested in creative intelligence; therefore, we put up huge schools with enormous attendances. At one of the universities I believe there are 45,000 students. What are you going to do, sirs, when we are educating everybody on such a vast scale? Under such circumstances, naturally there must be discipline. I am not against educating everybody, it would be too stupid of me to say so. I am for right education, which is the creation of intelligence, and this can come about, not through mass education, but only through consideration of each child—studying his difficulties, his idiosyncrasies, his tendencies, his capacities, taking care of him with affection, with intelligence. Only then is there a possibility of creating a new culture.

There is a lovely story, an actual fact, about a bishop who read the Bible to the illiterate people of the South Seas, and they were delighted to listen to these stories. He thought to himself that it was marvelous, and that it would be a good thing if he went back to America, collected money, and founded schools all over the South Sea Islands. So he collected a great deal of money in America, returned to the islands, founded schools, and taught the people how to read. At the end of it they were reading the comic papers, the *Saturday Evening Post*, *Look*, and other exciting, suggestive magazines! That is exactly what we are doing. Also, it is an extraordinary thing that the more people read, the less revolt there is. Sirs, have you ever considered how we worship the printed word? If the government issues an order or gives information in print, we accept it, we never doubt it. The printed word has become sacred. The more you teach people, the less there is a possibility of revolution—which does not mean that I am against teaching people to read, but just see the danger involved in it. Governments control people, dominate their minds and hearts, through cunning propaganda. That is happening not only in totalitarian countries, but all over the world. The newspaper has taken the place of thought, the headline has taken the place of real knowledge and understanding.

So, the difficulty is that in the present social structure, discipline has become an important factor because we want large numbers of children to be educated together and as quickly as possible. Educated to be what? To be bank clerks or super-salesmen, capitalists or commissars. When you are a superman of some kind, a super-governor or a subtle parliamentary debater, what have you done? You are probably very clever, full of facts. Anybody can pick up facts, but we are human beings, not factual machines, not beastly routine automatons. But again, sirs, you are not interested. You are listening to me and smiling at each other, and you are not going to do a thing about radically changing the educational system; so it will drag on until there is a monstrous revolution, which will merely be another substitution—there will be much more control because the totalitarian governments know how to shape the minds and hearts of the people, they have learned the trick. That is the misery, that is the unfortunate weakness in us; we want somebody else to alter, to reform, to build. We listen and remain inactive, and when the revolution is successful and others have built a new structure and there are guarantees, then we step in. Surely, that is not an intelligent, creative mind; such a mind is only seeking security in a different form. To seek security is a stupid process. To be secure psychologically you must have discipline, and the discipline guarantees the result—the making of human beings into routine office-holders, whether bank clerks, commissars, kings, or prime ministers. Surely, that is the greatest form of stupidity, for then human beings are merely machines. See the danger of discipline—the danger is that the discipline becomes more important than the human being, the pattern of thought, the pattern of action, far more important than the people who fit into them. Discipline will inevitably exist as long as the heart is empty, for then it is a substitute for affection. As most of us are dry, empty, we want discipline. A warm heart, a rich, integrated human being is free—he has no discipline. Freedom does not come through discipline; you do not have to go through discipline to be free. Freedom and intelligence begin near, not far away, and that is why to go far one must begin intelligently with oneself.

Question: Since until now a foreign government has prevented the right kind of education among our beloved people, what should be the right kind of education in a free India?

KRISHNAMURTI: What do you mean by a "free" India? You have succeeded in substituting one government for another, one bureaucracy for another, but are you free? The exploiter exists as before, only now he is brown, and you are exploited by him as you were by the other. The usurer exists as before, only now he is brown, and you are exploited by him as you were by the other. The user exists as before, the communalism, the class divisions, the quarrels over separate provinces, over which province shall have more or less, over which group in that province shall have the jobs—all these factors still exist. So the same conditions continue as before, only now there is a difference which is psychological. You have got rid of a group of people, and this acts on you psychologically. You can stand up again now—now, at least you are a man whereas, before, somebody was treading on your neck. The white man may not be treading on your neck, but a brown man is, who is your own brother and much more ruthless. Don't you know he is much more ruthless, having no morality? What do you mean by a "free" India? You will probably have your own army and navy—you are following after the rest of the world with their armies, navies, air forces, and regimentation. To see an old people like you playing with things that children should play with is a sad sight, is it not? It is just like an old man flirting with a young girl, it is an ugly thing. That is what you call "free," and you ask what kind of education you should have in a "free" India! First, to have education of the right kind, you must become intelligent. You cannot be intelligent by merely substituting one government for another, one exploiter for another, one class for another. To bring about a new kind of education, all these must go, must they not? You must start anew. That means radical revolution, not of the bloody kind, which does not solve a thing, but a radical revolution of thought, of feeling, of values. That radical revolution can be brought about only by you and me; a revolution that will create a new, integrated individual must begin with you and me. Since you are not putting a stop to racism, organized dogmatism in your religion, how can you produce a new culture, a new education? You can speculate about it, you can write volumes about what the new education should be, but that is an infantile process, another escape. There can be no creation until you throw down the barriers and are free, and then you will be able to build a new culture, a new order, which means you have to revolt against the present conditions, against present values—revolt in the sense of seeing their true significance, understanding them intelligently, and thinking things out anew. It is comparatively easy to dream of a utopia, a brave new world, but that is sacrificing the present for the future—and the future is so uncertain. No man can know what the future will be; there are so many elements intervening between now and the future. We hope that by creating a conceptual utopia, a mental idealization and working for it, we shall have solved the problem, but we shall certainly not solve the problem that way. What we can do, if we are intelligent people, is to tackle the problem ourselves in the present. Now is the only eternity, not the future. I must give full attention to the problem now. Merely to discuss what should be the right kind of education for people in a free India is quite obviously stupid. India is not free; there is no free India. You have a flag and a new anthem, but surely that is not freedom. You speak in your mother tongue and think you are awfully patriotic, nationalistic, and that you have solved the problem. Sir, solving this problem requires thinking anew, not looking through the spectacles of the old formula. That is why it is imperative for those who are serious to create a revolution by regenerating themselves, and there cannot be regeneration unless you break away from the old values, examining them and seeing their significance and their worth, not blindly accepting any one of them as good. That is why it is important to look into ourselves and to see the manner, the ways of our own thinking and feeling. It is only then that we are free, only then that we can produce a new culture and a new education.

Question: How far should government interfere in education, and should children be given military training?

KRISHNAMURTI: This raises a most important question. What do you mean by government? People in authority, a few bureaucrats, cabinet members, the prime minister, and so on? Is that government? Who elects them? You do, don't you? You are responsible for them, are you not? You have the government that you want, so why do you object? If your government, which is yourself, wants military training, why do you object to it? Because you are racial, class-ridden, have economic frontiers, you must have a military government. You are responsible and not the government because the government is the projection, the extension of yourself—its values are your values. Since you want a nationalist India, you must inevitably have the machinery that will protect a national sovereign government, with its pride of power, pomp, and possession; therefore, you must have a military machine whose function is to prepare for war—which means you want war. You may shake your head, but everything that you are doing is preparing for war. The very existence of a sovereign government, with its nationalistic outlook, must cause preparation for war; every general must plan for a future war because that is his duty, his function, his métier. Naturally, if you have such a government, which is yourself, it must protect your nationalism, your economic frontiers, there must be a military machine. Therefore, if you accept all that, military training is inevitable. That is exactly what is happening throughout the world. England, which fought for centuries against conscription, is now conscripting. Fortunately, in this country which is so vast, you cannot for the time being conscript everybody. You are disorganized. But given a few years, you will be able to organize, and then you will probably have the largest army in the world—because that is what you want. You want an army because you want a separate sovereign government, a separate race, a separate religion, a separate class with its own exploiters; I assure you, you want to become the exploiter in turn, and so you keep up this game. And then you ask if government should interfere in education!

Sirs, there should be a class of people who are apart from government, who do not belong to society, who are outside it, so that they can act as guides. They are the chastisers, they are the prophets who can tell you how wrong you are. But there is no such group because the government in the modern world will not support such a group, a group that has no authority, a group that does not belong to the government, a group that does not belong to any religion, caste, or country. It is only such a group that can act as a restraint on governments. Because, governments are becoming more and more powerful, employing a majority of human beings; therefore, more and more citizens are incapable of thinking for themselves. They are being regimented and told what to do. So, it is only when there is such a group, a vital, intelligent, active group—only then is there hope and salvation. Otherwise, each one of us is going to become an employee of the government, and more and more the government will tell us what to do and what to think—not how to think. Obviously, such a government with its nationalism, its pride, envy, and hatred, leading inevitably to war, must have a military machine, so in every school there must be the worship of the flag. If you are proud of your nationalism, of your economic frontiers, of your sovereign government, of your preparedness for war, you must have a government interfering with education, inferring with your lives, regimenting you, controlling your actions. That is exactly what you want. If not, you will break away intelligently from it, free yourself from nationalism, from greed, from envy, from the power that authority gives; and then, being intelligent, you will be able to look at the world situation and contribute to the establishment of a new education and a new culture.

Question: What is the place of art and religion in education?

KRISHNAMURTI: What do you mean by art and what do you mean by religion? Is art the hanging up of a few pictures in a classroom, drawing a few lines? What do you mean by art? What do you mean by religion? Is religion the spreading of organized belief? Is art merely imitating or copying a tree? Surely, art is something more than that. Art implies appreciation of beauty; while it may express itself in writing a poem, painting a picture, composing, it is the appreciation of beauty, that creative richness, the feeling of joy which comes from looking at a tree, at the stars, at the moonlight on still waters. Surely, art does not consist in the mere purchase of a few pictures and hanging them in a room. If you happen to have money and feel that it is safer to invest your money in pictures than in stocks, you do not become an artist, do you? Because you happen to have money and you invest your money in jewels, it obviously does not mean that you appreciate beauty. Surely, beauty is something different from mere security, is it not? Have you ever sat down to look at the waters as they run by; have you ever sat still and watched the moon? Have you ever noticed the smile on a face? Have you ever observed a child laughing or a man crying? Obviously you have not. You are too busy thinking about action, repeating your mantras, making money, being carried away by lustful desires. Not having the appreciation of beauty, we surround ourselves with so-called beautiful things. Don't you know how the rich man surrounds himself with such things? There is an atmosphere of outward beauty, but inwardly it is empty as a drum. (Laughter) Do not laugh at the rich man, sirs; he is a reflection of life as a whole, and you want to be in that position too. So, the appreciation of beauty does not come through mere attachment to the outward expression of beauty. You may put on a lovely sari, powder your face, paint your lips, but that obviously is not beauty, is it? That is merely a part of it. Beauty comes, surely, when there is inward beauty; and there is inward beauty only when there is no conflict, when there is love, when there is mercy, when there is generosity. Then your eyes have meaning, your lips have riches, and your words have significance. Because we lack these things, we merely indulge in an outward show of beauty, we buy jewelry, pictures. Surely, those are not the actions of beauty. As most of our lives are hideous, ugly, dull, and empty beyond words, we surround ourselves with things that we call beautiful. We collect things when the heart is empty; we create a world of ugliness about us because to us things matter enormously. And as most of us are in that state, how can we have art, beauty in the school or in education? When there is no art or beauty in your heart, how can you educate your children? What happens today is that the teacher is hampered with a hundred boys and girls—naughty and mischievous, as they should be. So you put up a picture and talk about art. Your schools indicate an empty mind, an empty heart. Surely, in such a school, in such education, there is no beauty. The light of a smile, the expression of a face—art is to see that these are beautiful, it is not merely the admiring of a picture painted by somebody else. Since we have forgotten how to be kindly, how to look at the stars, the trees, the reflections in the water, we require pictures; therefore, art has no meaning in our lives except as a topic of discussion in the club.

Similarly, religion has very little importance in our lives. You may go to the temple, do puja, wear the sacred thread, repeat words and mantras ad nauseam, but that does not mean you are a religious person. That is merely the expression of a mechanical mind of very little content. Surely, religion consists in seeking truth, reality, not in surrounding yourself with substitutes and false values. The search for reality does not lie far off; it lies very near, in what you are doing, in what you are thinking, what you are feeling. Therefore, truth must be found, not beyond your horizon, but in you, in your words, actions, relationships, and ideas. But we do not want such a religion. We want belief, we want dogma, we want security. As a rich man seeks security in pictures and diamonds, so you seek security in organized religion, with its dogmas, with its superstitions, with its exploiting priests and all the rest of it. There is not much difference between the so-called religious person and a man of the world—both are seeking security, only at different levels. Surely, that is not religion, that is not beauty. Appreciation of beauty, of life, comes only when there is enormous uncertainty, when you are paying attention to every movement of truth, when you see the movement of every shadow, of every thought and feeling, when you are awake to every movement of your child. It comes only when the mind is extremely pliable, and the mind can be pliable only when it is not tethered to a particular form of belief, whether belief in money or belief in an idea. When the mind is free to observe, to give full attention—only then is there creative realization. How extraordinary that most of us have become spectators in life, and not players. Most of us read books, and when we read, it is such twaddle, such piffle. We have lost the art of beauty, we have lost religion. It is the rediscovery of beauty and of reality that is important. Rediscovery comes only when we acknowledge the emptiness of our own mind and heart, when we are aware not only of that emptiness but of its depth, and when we are not trying to run away from it. We seek to run away through pictures, money, diamonds, saris, mantras, innumerable outward expressions. It is only creative intelligence, creative understanding, that can bring to you a new culture, a new world, and a new happiness.

Question: Have diet and regularity any significance in the growth of a child?

KRISHNAMURTI: Obviously they have. Have you the proper food to give the child today? But those who have the food are so unintelligent about their diet; they merely eat to satisfy the palate, they love to eat. Look at your body. Do not smile and pass it by. You just eat what you have been accustomed to. If you are accustomed to highly condimented food and if you are deprived of it, you are lost. You have actually given no consideration to diet. If you did, you would soon find out how simple it is to know what to eat. I cannot tell you what to eat, obviously, because each person has to think out and organize what is most suitable for him. Therefore, one must experiment for a week, for a month. You do not want to experiment because you want to continue with what you have been eating for the past ten or twenty years.

Most obviously, children need a regular life; at their tender age when they are growing up bodily, they must have the right amount of sleep, the right diet, right care. These are obvious necessities in the life of a child. But you do not love the child; you quarrel with your wife and you take it out on the child, or your wife takes it out on the child. When you come home late, you expect the child to keep awake for your amusement. The child becomes a toy to play with and a means to pass on your name. You are not interested in the child; you are interested in yourself. Sir, if you were interested, you would have a revolution tomorrow; if you really loved the child, you would break up this educational system, this social environment. Then you would consider what he eats, whether he leads a regular life, and what is going to happen to him, whether he is going to be fodder for cannon. Then you would investigate the causes of wars, not merely quote others, and have a pattern of action. If you really loved the child, you would have no sovereign governments, no isolated nationalities, no separate religions with their ceremonies and organized dogmatism. If you really loved the child, all these things would change overnight, you would avoid them because they lead to chaos, they lead to destruction, they lead to sorrow and suffering. But you do not love the child, you do not care what happens to him as he grows up and looks after you when you are old, or carries on your name. That is what you are interested in, and you are not interested in the child. If you were, you would not have so many children; you would have one or two, and see to it that your child develops intelligence and the right culture. The pity of it is, sirs, that it is not the fault of the educational system, but of ourselves—our hearts are so empty, so dull. We do not know love. When we say to a person, "I love you," that love is purely gratification—sexual pleasure, or the pride of possession, ownership. Mere pleasure and pride of possession are clearly not love. But it is only those two things that we care about; we are not concerned about our children, we are not concerned about our neighbor. The beggar as we go down the street gets no help, but we talk loudly about how we should help the unfortunate people. You join groups, you join systems, but the man in need goes empty-handed. If you were really interested, your hearts would be rich with feeling and you would be ready to act, and you would change the system overnight.

So, diet and regularity are necessary not only for the child but for each one of us. To find out what is necessary, we must investigate, we must experiment with ourselves first and not with the child. At least we can give him clean food, see that he has a regular time for sleep and rest. It is because we have never thought about it that most children are so small, stunted, and hungry. I am sure you are listening very attentively, and you will go home and make a noise, shout to see if the child is asleep and stuff his mouth with sugar to show how much you love him! I do not think you know what you are doing, that is the pity and the misery of it. We are not aware of our actions, we are not aware of the words we use, we are not aware of the significance of our means of livelihood—we just live, drift, breed, and die. When we have one foot in the grave, we talk about God because we want to be secure when we land on the other side; living a wretched, monstrous, ugly life here, we expect a beautiful life at the end of it. Beauty consists in living a rich life, living reality from the beginning to the end. There is no beauty in a life of exploitation, of greed and hatred, in seeking titles and possessions, and it is odd that you add one more object to your accumulations—God. What you are doing is too ugly for words, it has no meaning, no depth. Most of you live on words, and naturally your child is the same, he also grows up like you. There can be regeneration only when there is transformation of the mind and heart.

Question: As modern civilization is mostly technological, should we not train every child in some vocational profession?

KRISHNAMURTI: Obviously, and then what? He becomes an engineer, a physician, a mathematician, a scientist, or a bureaucrat; he keeps accounts for himself or for his boss. What have you done, sir? You have taught him a profession. Is that the end of life? With most of you, it is the end of life. Having a profession is all right in its place, but there are more vital things in life, are there not? I may want to be an engineer or a musician, and being my parent, you shove me on to become a banker. So for the rest of my life I feel frustrated, and because I feel frustrated I chase every woman I can think of, or turn to God. But I am still frustrated, empty. So, mere technological training or having a vocational aptitude does not solve all the problems of life. It does obviously solve problems at one level, but merely to live at that one level, as most of you do, is destruction. Sir, to make an integrated individual is extremely difficult. I must not only have a technological profession, but I must also have a clear mind, a warm heart. You cannot have a clear mind when it is rattling with a lot of noise which it calls knowledge. There can be integration only when there is warmth, when there is affection, when you love someone entirely, wholly; then affection, warmth, and a clear mind will bring about integration. Such a human being is rare, and it is obviously the function of education to create such human beings. Life is not to be lived at one level, it must be lived all the time at different levels; then only is there harmony, is there beauty, is there warmth in relationship, in feeling; then only is there happiness.

Question: Are not international schools for the cultivation of goodwill necessary?

KRISHNAMURTI: Sir, is goodwill cultivated through internationalism? That is, different nations meet at a round table, but each nation holds on to its own sovereignty, to its own power, to its own prestige. So how can there be a meeting of people for the cultivation of goodwill? You hold on to your armies, I hold on to mine. Is there goodwill between two robbers? There is cooperation to share the spoils. Surely, goodwill is something wholly different; it does not belong to any group, to any nation, to any sovereign government. When the sovereign government becomes all-important, then goodwill disappears. Most of our lives are spent in waving a flag, in being a nationalist, in worshiping the state, which is the new religion, so how can there be goodwill? There is only envy, hatred, and enmity. Goodwill comes only when these labels are put aside, when there is no division between you and me, either of class, of money, of power, or position. When we have goodwill we will not belong to any nation; you and I will live happily together; therefore, there will be no talk of internationalism or one world. To say that through nationalism we shall eventually become international, eventually have brotherhood, is a very wrong process of thought, is it not? It is false reasoning. Through narrowness, how can you go beyond all limits? It is only when you break down the narrow limits of the mind and the heart that you can proceed, and when the walls are thrown down, the vastness of the horizon of life is there. You cannot carry any narrowness when you invite the vast expanse of the eternal. Goodwill does not come through organization. Consider the fallacy of the idea that you can join a society for brotherhood—it is only when you have no brotherhood in your heart that you join such a society. When you have brotherhood in your heart, you do not have to join any society, any organization. The importance you give to organization and to societies shows that you are not brotherly; you want to escape from the actual fact that you are not brotherly; therefore, organizations become important and you belong to them. The difficulty is to be brotherly, to be good, to be kind, to be generous; and that is not possible as long as you are thinking about yourself. You are thinking about yourself when your child becomes all-important as a means to your happiness, when he becomes a means of carrying on your name, your religion, your outlook, your authority, your bank account, your jewelry. When a man is concerned with himself and the extension of himself, how can he have love in his heart, how can he have goodwill? Is goodwill merely a matter of words? This is what happens in the world when all these eminent, clever, and erudite politicians meet—they have no goodwill, far from it. They represent their country, which is themselves and you. Like them, we seek power, position, and authority. Sir, a man of goodwill has no authority, he does not belong to any society—he does not belong to organized religion, he does not worship wealth, titles. The man who does not think about himself will obviously create a new world, a new order, and it is towards this man we must look for happiness, for a new state of culture, and not towards the rich or those who worship riches. Goodwill, happiness, and bliss come only when there is search for the real. The real is near, not far. We are blind, blinded by things which prevent us from seeing that which is near. Truth is life, truth is in your relationship with your wife, truth is to be found in understanding the falseness of belief. You must begin near to go far. Action must be without motive, without seeking an end, and action which is not seeking an end can come only when there is love. Love is not a difficult thing. There is love only when the brain understands itself, when the thought process with its cunning manipulations, with its adjustments, with its search for security, comes to an end; then you will find that the heart is rich, full, blissful, for it has discovered that which is eternal.

September 26, 1948

Sixth Talk in Poona

Perhaps in understanding the question of creativeness, we shall be able to understand what we mean by effort. Is creativeness the outcome of effort, and are we aware in those moments when we are creative? Or, is creativeness a sense of total self-forgetfulness, that sense when there is no turmoil, when one is wholly unaware of the movement of thought, when there is only a complete, full, rich being? Is that state the result of travail, of struggle, of conflict, of effort? I do not know if you have ever noticed that when you do something easily, swiftly, there is no effort, there is complete absence of struggle; but as our lives are mostly a series of battles, conflicts, and struggles, we cannot imagine a life, a state of being, in which strife has fully ceased.

Now, to understand the state of being without strife, that state of creative existence, surely one must inquire into the problem of effort. That is, at present we live with effort, our whole existence is a series of struggles—struggles with our intimate friends, with our neighbors, with people across the mountains and across the seas. Until we understand this question of effort and its consequences, surely we shall not be able to fathom that creative state which is obviously not the product of effort. The painter, the poet, may make an effort in painting or writing, but the impact of the beautiful comes to him only when the struggle has fully ceased. So, we have to inquire into this question of effort, what we mean by effort, by strife, the struggle to become. We mean by effort, the striving to fulfill oneself, to become something, don't we? I am this, and I want to become that; I am not that, and I must become that. In becoming "that," there is strife, there is battle, conflict, struggle. In this struggle we are concerned inevitably with fulfillment through the gaining of an end; we seek self-fulfillment in an object, in a person, in an idea, and that demands constant battle, struggle, the effort to become, to fulfill. So, we have taken this effort as inevitable; and I wonder if it is inevitable—this struggle to become something? Why is there this struggle? Where there is the desire for fulfillment, in whatever degree and at whatever level, there must be struggle. Fulfillment is the motive, the drive behind the effort; whether it is in the big executive, the housewife, or a poor man, there is this battle to become, to fulfill, going on.

Now, why is there the desire to fulfill oneself? Obviously, the desire to fulfill, to become something, arises when there is awareness of being nothing. Because I am nothing, because I am insufficient, empty, inwardly poor, I struggle to become something, outwardly or inwardly, I struggle to fulfill myself in a person, in a thing, in an idea. So, this struggle to become arises only when there is insufficiency, when there is awareness of a void, of that emptiness within oneself. That is, effort comes into being only when there is awareness of emptiness. To fill that void is the whole process of our existence. Being aware that we are empty, inwardly poor, we struggle either to collect things outwardly or to cultivate inward riches. This striving, this struggling, arises from the awareness of insufficiency, and so there is a constant battle to become—which is entirely different from being. There is effort only when there is an escape from that inward void through action, through contemplation, through acquisition, through achievement, through power, and so on. That is our daily existence. I am aware of my insufficiency, my inward poverty, and I struggle to run away from it, or to fill it. This running away, avoiding, or trying to cover up the void entails struggle, strife, effort.

Now, if one does not make an effort to run away, what happens? One lives with that loneliness, that emptiness; and in accepting that emptiness one will find that there comes a creative state which has nothing to do with strife, with effort. Effort exists only as long as we are trying to avoid that inward loneliness, emptiness; but when we look at it, observe it, when we accept *what is* without avoidance, we will find there comes a state of being in which all strife ceases. That state of being is creativeness, and it is not the result of strife—though many of us think that struggle is inevitable and that we must struggle to be creative. It is only when we are creative that there is full, rich happiness; but creativeness does not come into being through effort of any kind, effort being avoidance of *what is.* But when there is understanding of *what is,* which is emptiness, inward insufficiency, when one lives with that insufficiency and understands it fully, there comes creative reality, creative intelligence, which alone brings happiness.

So, action as we know it is really reaction, it is a ceaseless becoming, which is the denial, the avoidance of *what is;* but when there is awareness of emptiness without choice, without condemnation or justification, then in that understanding of *what is* there is action, and this action is creative being. You will understand this if you are aware of yourself in action. Observe yourself as you are acting, not only outwardly, but see also the movement of your thought and feeling. When you are aware of this movement, you will see that the thought process, which is also feeling and action, is based on an idea of becoming. The idea of becoming arises only when there is a sense of insecurity, and that sense of insecurity comes when one is aware of the inward void. So, if you are aware of that process of thought and feeling, you will see that there is a constant battle going on, an effort to change, to modify, to alter *what is.* This is the effort to become, and becoming is a direct avoidance of *what is.* Through self-knowledge, through constant awareness, you will find that strife, battle, the conflict of becoming leads to pain, to sorrow and ignorance. It is only if you are aware of inward insufficiency and live with it without escape, accepting it wholly, that you will discover an extraordinary tranquillity, a tranquillity which is not put together, made up, but a tranquillity which comes with understanding of *what is.* Only in that state of tranquillity is there creative being.

Question: Memory, you say, is incomplete experience. I have a memory and a vivid impression of your previous talks. In what sense is it an incomplete experience? Please explain this idea in all its details.

KRISHNAMURTI: What do we mean by memory? You go to school and are full of facts, technical knowledge. If you are an engineer, you use the memory of technical knowledge to build a bridge. That is factual memory. There is also psychological memory. You have said something to me, pleasant or unpleasant, and I retain it; and when I next meet you, I meet you with that memory, the memory of what you have said or have not said. So, there are two facets to memory, the psychological and the factual. They are always interrelated, therefore not clear cut. We know that factual memory is essential as a means of livelihood. But is psychological memory essential? And what is the factor which retains the psychological memory? What makes one psychologically remember insult or praise? Why does one retain certain memories and reject others? Obviously, one retains memories which are pleasant and avoids memories which are unpleasant. If you observe, you will see that painful memories are put aside more quickly than the pleasurable ones. And mind is memory, at whatever level, by whatever name you call it; mind is the product of the past, it is founded on the past, which is memory, a conditioned state. Now, with that memory we meet life, we meet a new challenge. The challenge is always new, and our response is always old because it is the outcome of the past. So, experiencing without memory is one state, and experiencing with memory is another. That is, there is a challenge, which is always new. I meet it with the response, with the condition of the old. So, what happens? I absorb the new, I do not understand it, and the experiencing of the new is conditioned by the past. Therefore, there is a partial understanding of the new, there is never complete understanding. It is only when there is complete understanding of anything that it does not leave the scar of memory.

When there is a challenge, which is ever new, you meet it with the response of the old. The old response conditions the new, and therefore twists it, gives it a bias, and therefore there is no complete understanding of the new; hence the new is absorbed into the old, and therefore strengthens the old. This may seem abstract, but it is not difficult if you go into it a little closely and carefully. The situation in the world at the present time demands a new approach, a new way of tackling the world problem, which is ever new. We are incapable of approaching it anew because we approach it with our conditioned minds, with national, local, family, and religious prejudices. That is, our previous experiences are acting as a barrier to the understanding of the new challenge, so we go on cultivating and strengthening memory, and therefore we never understand the new, we never meet the challenge fully, completely. It is only when one is able to meet the challenge anew, afresh, without the past, only then does it yield its fruits, its riches.

The questioner says, "I have a memory and a vivid impression of your previous talks. In what sense is it an incomplete experience?" Obviously, it is an incomplete experience if it is merely an impression, a memory. If you understand what has been said, see the truth of it, that truth is not a memory. Truth is not a memory because truth is ever new, constantly transforming itself. You have a memory of the previous talk. Why? Because you are using the previous talk as a guide, you have not fully understood it. You want to go into it, and unconsciously or consciously it is being maintained. But if you understand something completely, that is, see the truth of something wholly, you will find there is no memory whatsoever. Our education is the cultivation of memory, the strengthening of memory. Your religious practices and rituals, your reading and knowledge are all the strengthening of memory. What do we mean by that? Why do we hold to memory? I do not know if you have noticed that as you grow older, you look back to the past, to its joys, to its pains, to its pleasures; and if one is young, one looks to the future. Why are we doing this? Why has memory become so important? For the simple and obvious reasons that we do not know how to live wholly, completely in the present. We are using the present as a means to the future, and therefore the present has no significance. We cannot live in the present because we are using the present as a passage to the future. Because I am going to become something, there is never a complete understanding of myself, and to understand myself, what I am exactly now, does not require the cultivation of memory. On the contrary, memory is a hindrance to the understanding of *what is*. I do not know if you have noticed that a new thought, a new feeling comes only when the mind is not caught in the net of memory. When there is an interval between two thoughts, between two memories, when that interval can be maintained, then out of that interval a new state of being comes which is no longer memory. We have memories and we cultivate memory as a means of continuance. That is, the 'me' and the 'mine' become very important as long as the cultivation of memory exists; and as most of us are made up of 'me' and 'mine', memory plays a very important part in our lives. If you had no memory, your property, your family, your ideas would not be important as such; so, to give strength to 'me' and 'mine', you cultivate memory. But if you observe, you will see that there is an interval between two thoughts, between two emotions. In that interval, which is not the product of memory, there is an extraordinary freedom from the 'me' and the 'mine', and that interval is timeless.

Let us look at the problem differently. Surely, memory is time, is it not? That is, memory creates yesterday, today, and tomorrow. Memory of yesterday conditions today and therefore shapes tomorrow. That is, the past through the present creates the future. There is a time process going on, which is the will to become. Memory is time, and through time we hope to achieve a result. I am a clerk today, and given time and opportunity, I will become the manager or the owner. So, I must have time; and with the same mentality we say, "I shall achieve reality, I shall approach God." Therefore I must have time to realize, which means I must cultivate memory, strengthen memory by practice, by discipline, to be something, to achieve, to gain, which means continuation in time. So, through time we hope to achieve the timeless, through time we hope to gain the eternal. Can you do that? Can you catch the eternal in the net of time, through memory, which is of time? The timeless can be only when memory, which is the 'me' and the 'mine', ceases. If you see the truth of that—that through time the timeless cannot be understood or received—then we go into the problem of memory. The memory of technical things is essential; but the psychological memory that maintains the self, the 'me' and the 'mine', that gives identification and self-continuance, is wholly detrimental to life and to reality. When one sees the truth of that, the false drops away; therefore, there is no psychological retention of yesterday's experience.

Look, sirs, you see a lovely sunset, a beautiful tree in a field, and when you first look at it, you enjoy it completely, wholly; but you go back to it with the desire to enjoy it again. What happens when you go back with the desire to enjoy it? There is no enjoyment because it is the memory of yesterday's sunset that is now making you return, that is pushing, urging you to enjoy. Yesterday there was no memory, only a spontaneous appreciation, a direct response, but today you are desirous of recapturing the experience of yesterday. That is, memory is intervening between you and the sunset; therefore, there is no enjoyment, there is no richness, fullness of beauty. Again, you have a friend who said something to you yesterday, an insult or a compliment, and you retain that memory, and with that memory you meet your friend today. You do not really meet your friend—you carry with you the memory of yesterday which intervenes, and so we go on, surrounding ourselves and our actions with memory, and therefore there is no newness, no freshness. That is why memory makes life weary, dull, and empty. We live in antagonism with each other because the 'me' and the 'mine' are strengthened through memory. Memory comes to life through action in the present; we give life to memory through the present, but when we do not give life to memory, it fades away. So, memory of facts, of technical things, is an obvious necessity, but memory as psychological retention is detrimental to the understanding of life, the communion with each other.

Question: You said that when the conscious mind is still, the subconscious projects itself. Is the subconscious a superior entity? Is it not necessary to pour out all that is hidden in the labyrinths of the subconscious in order to decondition oneself? How can one go about it?

KRISHNAMURTI: I wonder how many of us are aware that there is a subconscious and that there are different layers in our consciousness? I think most of us are aware only of the superficial mind, of the daily activities, the rattling superficial consciousness. We are not aware of the depth, the significance and meaning of the hidden layers; and occasionally, through a dream, through a hint, through an intimation, one is aware that there are other states of being. Most of us are too busy, too occupied with our lives, with amusements, with lustful desires, with our vanities, to be aware of anything but the superficial. Most of us spend our lives in the struggle for power, political or personal, for position, for achievement.

Now, the questioner asks, "Is the subconscious a superior entity?" That is the first point. Is there a superior entity apart from the thought process? Surely, as long as the thought process exists, though it may divide itself up into inferior and superior, there can be no superior entity, no permanent entity apart from that which is transitory. So, we will have to look into this question very carefully and understand the whole significance of consciousness. I have said that when you have a problem and have thought about it until your mind is weary without finding the answer, it often happens that when you sleep on it the answer is found the next morning. While the conscious mind is still, the hidden layers of the unconscious mind are at work on the problem, and when you wake up, you find the answer. Surely, that means that the hidden layers of the mind do not sleep when you go to sleep, but are working all the time. Though the conscious mind may be asleep, the unconscious in its different layers is grappling with that problem, and naturally it projects itself onto the conscious. Now the question is, is that a superior entity? Obviously not. What do you mean by "superior entity"? You mean, do you not, a spiritual entity, an entity that is beyond time. You are full of thoughts, and an entity that you can think about is surely not a spiritual entity—it is part of thought; therefore, it is a child of thought, still within the field of thought. Call it what you will, it is still a product of thought; therefore, it is a product of time, and therefore it is not a spiritual entity.

The next point is, "Is it not necessary to pour out all that is hidden in the labyrinths of the subconscious in order to decondition oneself? How can one go about it?" As I said, consciousness has different layers. First, there is the superficial layer, and below that there is memory, because without memory there is no action. Underneath that there is the desire to be, to become, the desire to fulfill. If you go still deeper, you will find a state of complete negation, of uncertainty, of void. This whole totality is consciousness. Now, as long as there is the desire to be, to become, to achieve, to gain, there must be the strengthening of the many layers of consciousness as the 'me' and the 'mine'; and the emptying of those many layers can come about only when one understands the process of becoming. That is, as long as there is the desire to be, to become, to achieve, memory is strengthened, and from that memory there is action, which only further conditions the mind. I hope you are interested in all this. If not, it does not matter, but I will go on because some of you may be aware of this problem.

Sir, life is not just one layer of consciousness, it is not just one leaf, one branch; life is the whole total process. We must understand the whole total process before we can understand the beauty of life—its greatness, it pains, its sorrows, and its joys. Now, to empty the subconscious, which is to understand the whole state of being of consciousness, we must see what it is made up of, we must be aware of the various forms of conditioning which are the memories of race, family, group, and so on, the various experiences which are not complete. Now, one can analyze these memories, take each response, each memory and unravel it, go into it fully and dissolve it; but for that one would need infinite time, patience, and care. Surely there must be a different approach to the problem. Anyone who has thought about it at all is familiar with the process of taking up a response, analyzing it, following and dissolving it, and doing that with every response; and if one does not analyze a response fully, or misses something in that analysis, then one goes back and spends long days in this unfruitful process. There must be a different approach to deconditioning the whole being of memories so that the mind may be new every moment. How is it to be done? Do you understand the problem? It is this: We are accustomed to meeting life with the old memories, old traditions, old habits; we meet today with yesterday. Now, can one meet today, the present, without the thought of yesterday? Surely, that is a new question, is it not? We know the old method of going step by step, analyzing each response, dissolving it through practice, through discipline, and so on. We see that such a method involves time, and when you use time as a means of deconditioning, obviously it only strengthens the condition. If I use time as a means of freeing myself, in that very process I am becoming conditioned. So, what am I to do? Since it is a new question, I must approach it anew. That is, can one be free immediately, instantaneously? Can there be regeneration without the element of time, which is but memory? I say that regeneration, transformation is now, not tomorrow, and that transformation can come only when there is complete freedom from yesterday. How is one to be free from yesterday? Now, when I put that question, what is happening to your mind?—all those who are really following. What is happening to your mind when you see that your mind must be new, that your yesterday must go? When you see the truth of that, what is the state of your mind? Do you understand the question, sir? That is, if you want to understand a modern painting, you must obviously not approach it with your classical training. If you recognize that as a fact, what happens to your classical training? Your classical training is absent when there is the intention to understand a modern painting—the challenge is new, and you recognize that you cannot understand it through the screen of yesterday. When you see the truth of that, then yesterday is gone, there is complete purgation of yesterday. You must see the truth that yesterday cannot translate the present. It is only truth that deconditions completely, and to see the truth of *what is* requires an enormous attention. Since there is no complete attention as long as there is distraction, what do we mean by distraction? You are distracted when there are several interests from among which you choose one interest and fix your mind on it, for then any interest that takes your mind away from the central interest you call distraction. Now, can you choose an interest and concentrate on that one interest? Why do you choose one interest and discard others? You choose one interest because it is more profitable; therefore, your choice is based on profit, the desire to gain; and the moment you have a desire to gain, you must resist as a distraction everything that takes your thoughts away from the central interest. Apart from your biological appetites, have you a central interest? I really question that you have a central interest. Therefore, you are not distracted—you are merely living in a state without interest. A man who would understand the truth must give to it his undivided attention, and that undivided attention comes only when there is no choice and therefore no idea of distraction. There is no such thing as distraction because life is a movement, and one has to understand this whole movement, not divide it into interests and distractions. Therefore, one has to look at everything to see the truth or falseness of it. When you see the truth of this, it liberates consciousness from yesterday. You can test it out for yourself. To see the truth about nationalism and not be caught up in the arguments, pro and con, you will have to go into it and be open to all the intimations of that problem. In being aware of the problem of nationalism without condemnation or justification, in seeing the truth that it is false, you will find there comes a complete freedom from the whole issue. So, it is only the perception of truth that liberates; and to see, to receive truth, there must be the focusing of attention, which means that you must give your heart and mind to see and to understand.

Question: In spite of your emphatic denial of the need of a guru, are you not yourself a guru? What is the difference?

KRISHNAMURTI: Sir, what do you mean by a guru? Why do you need a guru? Whether you make me one or not, I am not making myself a guru to you. That is why a follower is a curse. The follower is the destroyer, the follower is the exploiter. (Laughter) Do not laugh it away, think about it very earnestly and see the consequence of it. Let us examine this question. Now, what do you mean by a guru? You generally mean, do you not, one who will lead you to reality. Your guru is not the man of whom you can ask the direction to the station. You would not call the professor a guru, the man who teaches you the piano. Obviously, you mean by the guru one who will lead you to truth, give you a mode of conduct, one who will provide a key or open the door, give you nourishment, sustenance, and encouragement—that is, one who will gratify you profoundly. You already know the superficial gratifications, and you want a deeper gratification, a deeper satisfaction, so you turn to someone who will assist you; you seek a guru because you yourself are confused and you want direction, you want to be told how to act and what to do. So, all these things are involved in this; but by a guru we mean primarily one who will help us to unravel life's problems—not the technical problems, but the more subtle, the hidden, psychological problems.

Now, has truth an abiding place? Has truth a fixed point? Has truth an abode, or is truth a dynamic, living thing, and therefore without a resting place? Truth is in constant movement; but if you say it is a fixed point, then you will have to find a guru who will lead you to it, and the guru becomes necessary as a pointer. That means that both you and the guru must know that truth is there, in a fixed place, like the station. Then you can ask the way, then you can approach the fixed point, and in order to achieve that, you need a guru who will direct and lead you to that fixed thing. But is truth a fixed thing? And if it is fixed, is it true? Also, if you want truth and you go to a guru, you must know what truth is, must you not? When you go to a guru, you do not say, "I want to discover reality"; on the contrary, you say, "Help me to realize truth." Therefore, you already have an idea of what it is, you already know its content, its beauty, its loveliness, its fragrance. Do you know what it is? How can a confused man know clarity? He can only know confusion or think of clarity as the opposite of *what is.* Is truth the opposite of *what is,* the opposite of confusion? If you think about truth, surely it is the product of thought, and therefore it is not true; and if the guru can tell you what it is, then he is still within the field of thought; therefore, what he tells you is not true. So, when you go to the guru, obviously you are going for gratification, are you not?—even though you may not like that word. You have tried several things—you have tried position, women, money, and they do not satisfy you, they do not give an assured pleasure, a guaranteed permanency; so you say, "I will find God." That is, you think reality will give you the ultimate peace, the ultimate satisfaction, the ultimate security. You would like truth to be all this, but it may be the most dangerous, devastating thing, it may destroy all your previous values. You are really seeking security, gratification, but you do not call it that—you cover it up by calling it God. Having tried many obvious forms of gratification and grown old, disillusioned, cynical, frustrated, you hope to find fulfillment or satisfaction in God. So, you go to the guru who will give you this satisfaction, and the more he assures you of that satisfaction, the more you worship him. In other words, when you go to the guru, you are not seeking the truth, you are seeking security at a different level, permanency at a different point. But is truth permanency? You do not know, do you? But you dare not say that because to acknowledge, not merely verbally, but actually that one does not know is a very devastating experience. But surely, you must be devastated before you can find truth; you must be in that state of uncertainty, complete frustration, without escape; you must be confronted with the void, the emptiness, without an avenue through which you can run away. Then only, you will find what is truth. But to speculate, to think about truth is to deny truth. Your speculations, your thoughts about truth have no validity. What you think is the product of thought, and thought is memory, and memory is mere identification of oneself with a desired result. So, for the man who is seeking truth, a guru is entirely unnecessary. Truth is not in the distance; truth is near, in what you are thinking and feeling, in your relationship with your family, with your neighbor, with your property, and with ideas. To discover truth in some abstract realm is mere ideation, and most of us seek truth this way as a means of escape from life. Life is too much for us, too taxing, too painful, so we want truth away from life. Therefore we seek a guru who will help us to escape, and the more he helps us to escape, the more we are attached to that guru.

The questioner asks me, "Are you not yourself a guru?" You can make me one, but I am not a guru. I do not want to be one for the simple reason that there is no path to truth. You cannot discover the path because there is no path. Truth is a thing that is living, and to a living thing there is no path—it is only to dead things that there can be a path. Truth being pathless, to discover it you must be adventurous, ready for danger, and do you think a guru will help you to be adventurous, to live in danger? To seek a guru obviously indicates that you are not adventurous, that you are merely seeking a path to reality as a means of security. So, you can make me into a guru if you wish, but it will be your misery because there is no guru to truth, there is no leader to reality. That reality is an eternal being in the present, not in the future; it is in the immediate now, not in the ultimate tomorrow. To understand that now, that eternity, the mind must be free from time, thought must cease; yet everything that you are doing now is cultivating that thought, thereby conditioning the mind so that there is never a freshness, a newness, there is never a moment that is still, quiet. As long as the thought process exists, truth cannot be—which does not mean that you must be in a state of complete forgetfulness. You cannot enforce stillness, you cannot make the mind still, you cannot force thought to stop. You must understand the process of thought and go beyond all thought; only then will truth liberate thought from its own process.

So, truth is not for those who are respectable, nor for those who desire self-extension, self-fulfillment. Truth is not for those who are seeking security, permanency; for the permanency they seek is merely the opposite of impermanency. Being caught in the net of time, they seek that which is permanent, but the permanent they seek is not the real because what they seek is the product of their thought. Therefore, a man who would discover reality must cease to seek—which does not mean that he must be contented with *what is.* On the contrary, a man who is intent upon the discovery of truth must be inwardly a complete revolutionary. He cannot belong to any class, to any nation, to any group or ideology, to any organized religion; for truth is not in the temple or the church, truth is not to be found in the things made by the hand or by the mind. Truth comes into being only when the things of the mind and of the hand are put aside, and that putting aside of the things of the mind and of the hand is not a matter of time. Truth comes to him who is free of time, who is not using time as a means of self-extension. Time means memory of yesterday, memory of your family, of your race, of your particular character, of the accumulation of your experience which makes up the 'me' and the 'mine'. As long as the ego exists, the 'me' and the 'mine', at whatever level it may be, high or low, the atma or not-atma, it is still within the field of thought. Where thought is, there is the opposite because thought creates the opposite, and as long as the opposite exists, there cannot be truth. To understand *what is,* there must be no condemning, no justifying, no blaming; and since our whole structure of being is built upon denial and acceptance, one must become aware of the whole background. Just be aware as I am speaking, for choiceless awareness reveals the truth, and it is the truth that liberates, not your gurus or your systems, not all the pujas and rituals and practices. Through time, through discipline, through denial and acceptance you cannot find truth. Truth comes into being when the mind is utterly and completely still, and that stillness is not made up, put together; that stillness arises only when there is understanding; and this understanding is not difficult, only it demands your whole attention. Attention is denied when you are merely living in the brain, and not with your whole being.

Question: Is not belief in the theory of reincarnation a help to get over the fear of death?

KRISHNAMURTI: It is seven-thirty—I hope you are not tired. Shall I go on with the question? If you are merely spectators and not the players, if you are merely listening and not experiencing, you are losing an awful lot. It is like going to the well with a glass, a small lota; and if you do not come here with your whole heart, you will go away empty handed. But a man who goes to the well wishing to drink deeply of its waters will find in all I have been saying that truth which refreshes, which helps to renew.

What do you mean by fear and what do you mean by death? I am not quibbling. Why are you afraid of death? Obviously you are afraid of death because you have not fulfilled yourself. You love somebody, and you may lose that person; you are writing a book, and you may die without having finished it; you are building your house, and you may die without completing the job; you want to do something, and death may strike you. What are you afraid of? Obviously you are afraid of going off suddenly, of not fulfilling yourself, of being put an end to. Is it not ending that you are afraid of? We are not discussing death for the moment—we will discuss it presently. We are discussing what we mean by fear. Surely, fear exists in relationship to something. There is fear in relation to your fulfillment. So, the question is, is there fulfillment? You may say that this is a roundabout way of answering the question, a long-winded explanation. But it is not, sir; life is not a thing to which you can give answers like yes and no. Life is far more complex, more beautiful, far more subtle than that. The man who wants a quick answer had better take a drug, either the drug of belief or the drug of amusement, and then he will have no problems. To understand life, one must explore, must discover; and that exploration, that discovery is denied if the mind is tethered to any belief. Then it is impossible to understand this whole problem.

What do we mean by fear? There is fear in relation to something, and that something is self-fulfillment, however little or big. Is there such a thing as self-fulfillment? What do we mean by "self"? Let us follow it carefully and you will see what the self is. Obviously the self, the 'me', is a bundle of memories—a bundle of memories which includes the thing I call eternal, permanent. That nonphysical part of the 'me', though I may call it the atma, is still memory, still within the field of thought. You cannot deny that, can you? If you can think about something, it is still within the field of thought. What thought produces is still the product of itself, therefore it is of time. Surely, the whole of that is the 'me', the self, the ego—whether higher or lower, all the divisions are still within the field of thought. Therefore, memory, at whatever level you may like to fix your thought, is still memory. So, the self is a bundle of memories and nothing more. There is no spiritual entity as the 'me' or apart from the 'me' because when you say there is a spiritual entity apart from the 'me', it is still the product of thought; therefore, it is still within the field of thought, and thought is memory. So, the 'you', the 'me', the self—higher or lower, at whatever point it may be fixed—is memory.

Now, as long as there is memory, which is the desire to be, to become, there is always an object of fulfillment, so there is continuation of memory, the 'me' and the 'mine'. That is, as long as there is self-fulfillment, there is continuation of the 'me' and the 'mine'; therefore, there will always be fear. Fear ceases only when there is no continuance of the 'me'—the 'me' being memory. That is, sir, to put it differently, as long as I am seeking fulfillment, that very search entails the fear of uncertainty. Therefore I am afraid of death. When I have no desire to fulfill myself, there is no fear. The desire for self-fulfillment ceases when I understand the process of fulfillment. I cannot merely assert that I have no desire to fulfill myself—that is merely repetition of a truth, which is a lie. As long as there is the activity of the self, there must be fear of death, fear of nonfulfillment, fear of coming to an end, fear of not continuing.

What do we mean by death? Surely, a thing that is used constantly comes to an end; any machine that is constantly used wears out. Similarly, a body, being in constant use, comes to an end through disease, through accident, through age. That is inevitable—it may last a hundred years or ten, but being used, it must wear out. We recognize and accept that because we see it happening continually. But there is the 'me' which is not the body, the 'me' which is my accumulated understanding, the things I have done in this life, the things for which I have labored, the experiences I have gathered, the riches I have stored up—it is not the physical 'me' but the psychological 'me', which is memory, and which I want to have continued; I do not want it to come to an end. It is really not death but this coming to an end that we are afraid of. We want continuity. That is, you want your memories to continue with all their riches, their disturbances, their ugliness, their beauty, and so on—the whole of that you want to have continued. So, anyone who assures you of its continuance you bless, you look up to, and you run away from anyone who says you must understand it. In death it is the psychological ending one is afraid of, is it not? You really do not know what death is. You see bodies being carried away, you see a lifeless thing that was once full of life and activity, and you do not know what is beyond. You see the empty, naked, decaying thing, and you want to know what happens beyond—which means, you want a guarantee of the continuity of your memories. So, you are really not interested in knowing what is beyond, you are not interested in discovering the unknown; what you want is to be assured of the continuity of your memories. You are not interested in death; you are concerned only with the continuity of yourself as memory. It is only when you are interested that you will know what death is, but you are not interested in discovering the significance, the beauty of what lies beyond, you are not interested in the unknown because you are concerned with the known and the continuity of the known. Surely, the unknown is seen only when there is no fear of it—which means that as long as you cling to the known and desire the known to continue, you can never know the unknown. It is a very significant thing, is it not, that you have given your life to the known and not to the unknown. You have written books about death, not about life, because you are concerned with continuity.

Now, have you ever noticed that which continues has no rebirth, no renewal? A thing that is constantly repeated, that is caught in an endless chain of cause and effect, surely has no regeneration. It merely continues; it is somewhat modified, changed, altered, but it remains essentially the same. That which is continually the same can never be new. That is, sirs, I want yesterday to continue through today to tomorrow, and that process of yesterday through today to tomorrow is the 'me'. That 'me' I want to have continued, and such continuance obviously has no renewal, for that which continues knows the fear of ending. Therefore, he who desires to continue will ever be caught in fear. It is only in the unknown that there is renewal; it is in the unknown that there is creativeness, not in continuity. So, you must inquire into the unknown, but to do that you cannot cling to the continuity of the known, for the 'me' and the constant repetition of the 'me' falls within the field of time, with its struggles, with its achievements, with its memories. The self, which is a bundle of memories identified as 'me', wants to continue; and that which is a permanent continuity in time is obviously a deteriorating factor. Only in the unknown is there a renewal, a newness, so you must inquire into the unknown. That is, you must inquire into death as you inquire into life with its relationships, its variety, its depths, its sorrows, its joys. The known is memory and its continuance; and can the known establish a relationship with the unknown? Obviously not. To inquire into the unknown, the mind must become the unknown. You are very familiar with the 'me' and the 'mine', with your companions, your memory, your religious bodies, your vanities and passions—all these things make up your life. You are superficially well aware of these things, and with that mentality of the known you approach the unknown, you try to establish a relationship between the known and the unknown. So, you have no direct relationship with the unknown, and therefore you are afraid of death.

What do you know of life? Very little. You do not know your relationship to property, to your neighbor, to your wife, to ideas. You know only the superficial things, and you want to continue the superficial things. For God's sake, what a miserable life! Is not continuity a stupid thing? It is a stupid person that wants to continue—no man who understood the rich feelings of life would want continuity. When you understand life, you will find the unknown, for life is the unknown, and death and life are one. There is no division between life and death; it is the foolish and the ignorant who make the division, those who are concerned with their body and with their petty continuity. Such people use the theory of reincarnation as a means of covering up their fear, as a guarantee of their stupid little continuity. It is obvious that thought continues; but surely, a man who is seeking truth is not concerned with thought, for thought does not lead to truth. The theory of the 'me' continuing through reincarnation towards truth is a false idea, it is untrue. The 'me' is a bundle of memories, which is time, and the mere continuation of time does not lead you to the eternal, which is beyond time. The fear of death ceases only when the unknown enters your heart. Life is the unknown, as death is the unknown, as truth is the unknown. Life is the unknown, sir; but we cling to one small expression of that life, and that which we cling to is merely memory, which is an incomplete thought; therefore, that which we cling to is unreal, it has no validity. The mind clings to that empty thing called memory, and memory is the mind, the self, at whatever level you like to fix it. So, mind, which is in the field of the known, can never invite the unknown. It is only when there is the unknown, a state of complete uncertainty, that there comes the cessation of fear and with it the perception of reality.

October 3, 1948

Seventh Talk in Poona

We have been saying that without self-knowledge no human problem can permanently be solved. Few of us are prepared to go into a problem completely and see the movement of our own thought, feeling, and action as a comprehensive, integrated whole; most of us want an immediate answer without understanding the whole process of ourselves. In considering this matter, we will have to go into the question of progress and specialization. We believe and we have been carefully nurtured, regimented in the idea that there is progress, there is evolution, there is growth. Now, let us examine that question. There is obviously technological progress—from the bullock cart to the jet airplane. Then there is growth—the acorn becoming an oak. And finally, we think that we ourselves shall become something—we shall achieve a result, an end. So, these three things—technological progress, growth, and becoming—are all considered a kind of evolution. It would be obviously absurd to deny progress in terms of technological advancement. We see the crude internal combustion engine eventually giving place to the turbo-jet, making possible airplanes of enormous speeds, doing 1500 miles per hour and more. It would be equally absurd to deny the growth of a seed into a plant, into a flower, and from that into a fruit. But with that same mentality we approach our own consciousness. We think there is progress, evolution, that through time we shall achieve a result;

and I want to go into the question of whether there is progress at all for man, whether there is evolutionary growth, whether it is possible for you and me to achieve a result in terms of time—the result being the achievement of reality. We talk about the evolutionary advancement of man, that you become something eventually—if not in this life, then in future life. That is, through time you evolve into something greater, more beautiful, more worthy, and so on.

Now, is there such a thing as your becoming more wise, more beautiful, more virtuous, approaching nearer reality through the process of time? That is what we mean when we talk about evolution. There is obviously a physiological evolution, growth; but is there a psychological growth, evolution; or is it merely a fantasy of the mind which, in its desire to transform itself, falls into the erroneous thought of becoming something? Now, to become something, you must specialize, must you not, and anything that specializes soon dies, decays, because all specialization implies lack of adaptability. Only that thing which is capable of adaptation or pliability can survive. So, as long as we are thinking of becoming, there must be specialization, and specialization obviously implies a process of narrowing down in which all pliability is impossible, and therefore there is death, decay, and destruction. You can see that any animal that specializes soon destroys itself. That is a biological fact. And are human beings meant to specialize? You will have to specialize to have a profession—to be a doctor, to be a lawyer, to be the commander of an army, or to get a boat through the stormy seas—but is psychological specialization necessary? That means, is self-knowledge a process of specialization? If it is, then that process of specialization destroys man—which is what is happening in the world. Technological advancement through specialization is extremely rapid, and man is incapable of quick adaptability in the psychological sense because we approach life with the same mentality of specialization. In other words, specialization in the technological field has given us the bias that we must specialize in self-knowledge, become experts, specialists in the understanding of ourselves. So, our mentality, our approach to this problem is that of specialization, in which is implied becoming. To specialize, you must discipline yourself, control yourself, narrow down your capacity, focus your attention on a particular object, and so on. All this is implied in specialization.

Now surely, man is a complex entity, and to understand himself he cannot specialize. As you are complex, subtle, made up of many entities, you must understand them as a whole and not specialize in any one direction. So, to understand the process of the self, which is self-knowledge, specialization is detrimental, specialization prevents quick adaptability, and anything that specializes soon decays and withers away. So, to understand oneself, one needs enormous pliability, and that pliability is denied when we specialize in devotion, in action, in knowledge. There are no paths such as devotion, as action, as knowledge, and he who follows any of these paths separately as a specialist brings about his own destruction. That is, a man who is committed to a particular path, to a particular approach, is incapable of pliability, and that which is not pliable is broken. As a tree that is not pliable breaks in the storm, so a man who has specialized breaks down in moments of crisis. To understand oneself is imperative because self-knowledge alone can solve the innumerable problems that confront us, and you cannot approach self-knowledge through any particular path. The path implies specialization, becoming an expert, and in that process you are broken. Haven't you noticed that an expert is not an integrated person? He is specialized in one direction. To understand the process of life, you need an integrated action, an integrated understanding all the time, and not specialized attention. To think in terms of evolution—that I shall become something in time—implies specialization because to become means achieving a result, and to achieve a result you must control, discipline, and all discipline is obviously a process of narrowing down. Though you may achieve the result, in the process of achieving that result you are broken. That is what is happening with all of us. We have become incapable of quick adaptability to the environment that is constantly changing. Our response to a challenge is always conditioned, and therefore the challenge can never be understood.

So, when you think in terms of evolution, in terms of becoming something psychologically, that becoming implies the achievement of a result, and to achieve a result you must discipline yourself; and for discipline, specialization is necessary, which in turn narrows down your thought; therefore, you become unpliable, incapable of quick adaptability, and that which is not adaptable is broken. A man who would have self-knowledge must put aside this idea of becoming and understand himself from moment to moment without the residual effect of the moment. Surely, if you will observe it, you will see that understanding comes, not through the accumulation of memory, but when memory is not functioning. You understand somebody only when you have no previous record of that person. If you have a previous record, you are merely remembering the past activities and inclinations of that person, but you are not understanding him. To understand, all idea of becoming must cease, which means that each experience must be understood immediately, directly; and you can understand experience immediately only when you do not bring up the old conditioning, the old background, to translate that experience or that challenge.

To understand oneself is of primary importance because I cannot understand any human problem without understanding the instrument that regards, the instrument that perceives, that examines. If I do not know myself, I have no foundation for thought; and to know myself is not the result of specialization, of becoming an expert in knowing myself, which prevents me from knowing myself. Because, the self is desire, it is alive, always moving, it has no resting place, it is constantly undergoing a change; and to understand desire, you cannot have a pattern of action. You must understand desire as it arises from moment to moment; and because our minds are not capable of quick following, instant adaptability, immediate perception of desire, we translate that desire in terms of a pattern to which we are accustomed; and that pattern becomes a conditioned response to the challenge. That is, we never understand desire because we are translating that desire in terms of memory. To understand desire, do not think in terms of changing that desire or of achieving a result. Look at each desire as it arises; do not translate it; let the content of that desire convey its significance. In other words, as I was explaining yesterday, listen to desire as you listen to a song, as you listen to the wind in the trees; listen to the whole process of desire without trying to alter it, without trying to control or transform it. Then you will see that desire gives its full meaning, and it is only when you understand the content of desire that you have freedom.

In short, then, specialization of the psyche is death. If you desire to understand yourself, you cannot go to any expert, to any book, because you are your own master and pupil. If you go to another, he can only help you to specialize; but if you are desirous of understanding yourself, that understanding comes only from moment to moment, when there is no accumulation of yesterday, no accumulation of a previous moment; and when the mind understands itself and its activities completely, fully, only then is there reality.

Question: Will you please explain what is meant by giving full attention?

KRISHNAMURTI: To understand the significance of full attention, you must understand first what you mean by distraction because if a man is not distracted, there is full attention. To merely inquire and be told what is full attention—so-called positive, directed attention—destroys your own capacity to find out what is full attention. Surely, that is clear, is it not? If I were to tell you what is full attention, you would merely copy that, would you not?—which would not be full attention. Following a particular pattern of thought or meditation or keeping the mind focused on a particular idea is not full attention; but if you and I inquire into the question of what is distraction and understand that, then through this negative approach to the question you will find that there is complete attention. I hope I am making myself clear because this is very important. Any positive approach to a problem prevents understanding of the problem, but if we approach this problem negatively—and negative thought is the highest form of thinking—then we will find a complete answer to the question of what is full attention.

Now, what do you mean by distraction? You mean, do you not, that you have chosen an idea from among several ideas, you have chosen an interest from among many interests, and you try to fix your mind on that particular thing; and any other interests that invade your mind you call distraction. That is, I have several interests, and from among these interests I choose one and try to focus my attention on it. But my other interests come between and impede attention, and this is what I call distraction. So if I can understand distraction and put an end to it, then naturally, suddenly, there will be full attention. Our problem is to understand each interest without choice and not choose one interest and attempt to discard others, calling that distraction. If the mind can understand each interest as it arises and therefore free itself from each interest, in that freedom you will have full attention. Sir, most of us are made up of many masks, many entities, and it is no good choosing one entity and saying, "I am going to concentrate on this," because then you are inviting conflict with other entities; and the other entities which are fighting your chosen entity are also yourself. Whereas, if you look at all the entities and revalue them, see their true significance—and you can do that only when you do not condemn, when you do not justify, when you do not compare—then there is a quickening of intelligence. There is attention only when you examine, when you revalue each entity, and that is the highest form of intelligence. A stupid man trying to concentrate on an idea will still remain stupid; but if that stupid man regards all his interests to find their true significance, that very inquiry is the beginning of intelligence.

So, you see that through a negative approach to this problem, you discover a great deal; you become sensitive, alert to the significance of the innumerable problems about you. Then you do not resist them, you do not put them away, but as they arise you understand them, which means that you have the capacity, the swiftness, the vitality to discover. After that discovery you will give full attention. To have full attention, your mind must not be distracted, and since your mind is distracted, why not pursue the various distractions and find out? If you do that, you will see how extraordinarily quickly the mind becomes subtle, vivid, clarified, and vital. It is only when the mind is alert that you can give that full attention in which there is complete understanding.

Question: You talk of seeing a thought through and getting rid of it. Will you please explain this in greater detail?

KRISHNAMURTI: To think a thought through is quite an arduous task and very few of us are willing to do so. We like to transform a thought, to put it in a different frame or mold; we do not want to think it through. There must be no desire to transform a thought, there must be no desire to get rid of it or to put it in a different frame. I am going to take a thought and examine it, and we will see together.

Most of us think we are very intelligent, most of think that we have a bright spot. Now, are we intelligent? On the contrary, we are dull, but we would never admit to ourselves that we are dull, that we lack sensitivity; and if we completely analyzed this, we would not be so sorrowfully stupid. We are not intelligent, we have no bright spot, but we think we are partly bright and partly dull. I am going to think this thought through, so please follow it. When you say, "I am partly dull and partly bright," which is the part that is saying, "I am bright," and which is the part that is saying, "I am dull"? If the bright part is saying that the other part is dull, then obviously the bright part knows itself as being bright. That is, when you say, "I am bright," you are conscious of yourself being very intelligent. Is intelligence self-conscious? The moment I say, "I am intelligent," obviously I am dull. (Laughter) That is not a clever response—you can watch it. When a man says he is clever, he is obviously a stupid man. So that part of the mind which is conscious of itself as being bright is really dull, and a dull mind thinking that a part of itself is bright is still dull. It is very important to follow this because most of us think that somewhere in us there is a bright spot. Obviously, when a dull mind thinks that somewhere it has a bright spot, that thought is still dull, is it not? Sir, we are thinking a thought through. When a dull mind thinks it has a bright spot, that is still the action of a dull mind. When a dull man performs puja, the action is also dull; and if there is a dull mind which thinks that a part of itself is bright, eternal, that part is equally dull.

So, most of us do not like to acknowledge that we are dull; we like to think that somehow, somewhere in us there is a bright spot—God, reality, atma, paramatma, and all the rest of it. But if a dull man thinks about atma, that atma is still dull. How can a dull man think about something which is really intelligent? That which is intelligent is not self-conscious; and the moment I say to myself, "I am intelligent," I reduce myself to the level of stupidity—and that is what most of you are doing. So, you never acknowledge that the whole of you is dull—which it is, if you really look at it. You like to play about with bright things and call yourselves intelligent. Actually, a dull man playing with bright things reduces the bright things to his own level. When a mind is thinking itself to be bright, either it is self-conscious, and therefore dull, or it is dull and thinks of itself as being bright—and is therefore still dull. But when a mind recognizes that it is dull, what is the next response? First, to acknowledge that one is dull is already a tremendous fact; to say that I am a liar is already the beginning of telling the truth. So, when we think out this thought of dullness and brightness, we see that almost all of us are dull right through, and we are afraid to acknowledge it. Don't you know how dull you are? Because we are dull we try to solve our problems partially and unintegratedly, and therefore we still remain dull. But when we do acknowledge it—not mentally or verbally, but actually see that we are dull—what happens? When a dull mind recognizes itself as being dull, when the mind sees it, there is no escape. We are thinking a thought through—just see what happens when you acknowledge and face the reality that you are dull. The moment you acknowledge that fact, that you are entirely dull, what happens? You see that a dull mind thinking of God is still dull—the idea of God may be bright, but a dull mind reduces the idea to its own level. If you can face the fact that you are dull, then already there is the beginning of clarification. Stupidity which is trying to become intelligence will never be intelligence; it will always remain what it is. A dull mind trying to become bright will always remain dull, whatever it does. But the moment you acknowledge the fact that you are dull, there is an immediate transformation.

It is the same with every thought. Take anger. Anger may be the result of a physiological or neurological response, or you are angry because you want to conceal something. Think it out, face it without trying to find an excuse for it. The moment you face the fact, there is the beginning of transformation. You cannot translate a fact; you can mistranslate it, but a fact remains a fact. So, to think a thought through is to see *what is* without distortion; and when I perceive the fact directly, then only is it transformed. It is not possible to bring about transformation as long as I am evading, running away from *what is,* or as long as I am trying to change *what is* into something else, for then I am incapable of direct action.

Then, sir, take violence. Again, let us think that thought through. First, I do not like to acknowledge that I am violent because socially and morally I am told that to be violent is a very bad thing. But the fact is, I am violent. So I meditate, I compel, I try to become something else, but I never face what I actually am, which is violent. I spend my time trying to transform *what is* into something else. To transform, I must look at *what is,* and I am not looking at it as long as I have an ideal. If I see that, I set aside the ideal, which is nonviolence, and look at violence, and then I am fully aware that I am violent; and the very fact that I am directly conscious of it brings about transformation. Experiment with it and you will see. This refusal to see *what is*—that is the problem with all of us. I never want to look at *what is,* I never want to acknowledge that I am ugly, I always give reasons for my ugliness; but if I look at my ugliness as it is, without explanation or excuse, then there is a possibility of transformation.

So, to think a thought through is to see how thought is deceiving itself, running away from *what is.* You can think a thought out fully, completely, only when you stop all avenues of escape and then look at it, which requires an extraordinary honesty; and most of us are dishonest in our thinking, we never want to see any thought through. It is the discovery of how thought is deceiving itself that is important, and when you discover its deceitfulness, then you can face *what is.* Then, only, *what is* reveals its full significance, its meaning.

Question: Instead of addressing heterogeneous crowds in many places and dazzling and confounding them with your brilliance and subtlety, why do you not start a community or colony and create a reference for your way of thinking? Are you afraid that this could never be done?

KRISHNAMURTI: Sir, brilliance and subtlety should always be kept undercover, because too much exposure of brilliance only blinds. It is not my intention to blind or show cleverness, that is too stupid; but when one sees things very clearly, one cannot help setting them out very clearly. This you may think brilliant and subtle. To me, what I am saying is not brilliant—it is obvious. That is one fact. The other is, you want me to found an ashram or a community. Now, why? Why do you want me to found a community? You say that it will act as a reference, that is, something which can be pointed out as a successful experiment. That is what a reference implies, does it not?—a community where all these things are being carried out. That is what you want. I do not want to found an ashram or a community, but you want it. Now, why do you want such a community? I will tell you why. It is very interesting, is it not? You want it because you would like to join with others and create a community, but you do not want to start a community with yourself; you want somebody else to do it, and when it is done you will join it. In other words, sir, you are afraid of starting on your own; therefore, you want a reference. That is, you want something which will give you authority of a kind that can be carried out. In other words, you yourself are not confident, and therefore you say, "Found a community and I will join it." Sir, where you are you can found a community, but you can found that community only when you have confidence. The trouble is that you have no confidence. Why are you not confident? What do I mean by confidence? The man who wants to achieve a result, who gets what he wants, is full of confidence—the business man, the lawyer, the policeman, the general, are all full of confidence. Now, here you have no confidence. Why? For the simple reason you have not experimented. The moment you experiment with this, you will have confidence. Nobody else can give you confidence; no book, no teacher can give you confidence. Encouragement is not confidence; encouragement is merely superficial, childish, immature. Confidence comes as you experiment; and when you experiment with nationalism, with even the smallest thing, then as you experiment you will have confidence because your mind will be swift, pliable; and then where you are there will be an ashram, you yourself will found the community. That is clear, is it not? You are more important than any community. If you join a community, you will be as you are—you will have somebody to boss you, you will have laws, regulations, and discipline, you will be another Mr. Smith or Mr. Rao in that beastly community. You want a community only when you want to be directed, to be told what to do. A man who wants to be directed is aware of his lack of confidence in himself. You can have confidence, not by talking about self-confidence, but only when you experiment, when you try. Sir, the reference is you, so experiment wherever you are, at whatever level of thought. You are the only reference, not the community; and when the community becomes the reference, you are lost. I hope there will be lots of people joining together and experimenting, having full confidence and therefore coming together; but for you to sit outside and say, "Why don't you form a community for me to join?" is obviously a foolish question. I do not want an ashram for the simple reason that you are more important than the ashram; I really feel it. The ashram becomes a nightmare. Sir, what happens in the ashram? The teacher becomes important; it is not the seeker, but the guru who is important. The guru is all authority, and you have given him that authority because the moment you support a guru, you make him into an authority. Therefore, when you join these ashrams you are destroying yourself. (Laughter) Please do not laugh it off. Look at people who have come out of ashrams. They are dull, weary, their blood has been sucked away, and they are thrown out as shadows. Self-immolation to an idea is not finding truth—it is only another form of gratification. Where there is search for gratification, there is no search for reality. So, you are the only reference, not another, not an ashram, not a community. If you want to form a community for experimenting, it should not become your reference, for the moment it becomes your reference, your authority, you are no longer seeking truth—you are basking in the sunshine of another's action. That is what you want. You all want reflected glory. That is why you join ashrams, pursue gurus, form communities; and inevitably they will fail because the teacher becomes all-important and not you. If you are searching for truth, you will never join an ashram, you will never have the reference of another. You will have your own reference, and you can have your own reference only when you are very honest, and that honesty comes only when you experiment. A man who experiments and wants a result is obviously not experimenting. A man who experiments does not know what is going to come out. That is the beauty of experimentation. If you know what is going to come out of it, you are not experimenting. So, the difficulty in having a teacher, a community, an ashram, lies in this: that you make it your reference, you make it your shelter. The guru is not so much at fault as the follower. You make your guru your reference, you hand your life over to him to be told what to do. No man can tell you what to do. If he tells you what to do, he does not know; a man who knows does not know. Do not seek a reference, do not seek shelters, but experiment, become confident; then you will have your own reference, which is truth. Then you will be aware that you are the community, you are your own ashram. Where you are is very important, for truth is very near you if you only look.

Question: Modern man has been a dazzling success in the field of technological development and organization, but he has been a dismal failure in building up harmonious human relationships. How can we resolve this tragic contradiction? Can we conceive of a cumulative increase in the means of grace at the disposal of each person in the world?

KRISHNAMURTI: Let us think out this question and see what it means. The questioner points out that there is contradiction in our life—technologically we are very far advanced, and as psychological entities we are far behind—and he asks: Can each one who is spiritually so far behind overtake that technological advance? Can there be a miracle which will immediately transform me so that the psychological entity catches up with technological progress? I think that is what is implied in this question: Can each person be quickly transformed by accumulated grace so that there is no contradiction? That is, if I understand the question rightly, and to put it simply and directly: Through some miracle can you be transformed? Can the cumulative grace of God act so rapidly that there is not this division, this contradiction? Because technological advance is going faster and faster, and psychologically we are following very slowly, we must have a miracle in order to catch up, otherwise we will be destroyed. I wonder if you follow all this. To put it differently, the turbojet airplane is said to fly at a speed of 1500 miles an hour—and there is the atomic bomb. You can see what that means. With instruments of such power in the hands of a stupid man calling himself a general, a national hero, or what you will, can I, who am an imbecile psychologically, catch up with all that so that I can alter it? The question, in other words, is this: Can I be transformed now? Please follow this. Can a miracle take place so that I may change immediately? I say yes. (Laughter) Do not laugh it off. What I am saying is very serious. I say a miracle can take place now, but you and I must be receptive for that miracle to happen, and you must also be part of that miracle. A blind man who is suffering in his blindness, desires to be cured, he wants to see. If you are in that position you will have a miracle, and I say transformation is not in time, but now. Regeneration is immediate, it is not tomorrow or in the distant future. A miracle can take place if you know how to look at the problem, and that is what I have been trying to show during the past four or five weeks. The miracle takes place if you look at things directly. Sir, if you mistake the rope for a snake and are afraid to look, a miracle is not possible, is it? That is, you will always be afraid. The miracle happens only when you look. To look, you must have the desire, you must be in pain and must want to be cured. That means you must have honesty to solve this problem. But you are not honest, you are not anxious, you want something to happen so that you will be changed, and yet you won't look at the problem, search it out, you won't inquire into it or go into it. So, you remain dull, and technological progress goes much faster than you can keep pace with.

So, there can be a miracle only when you are willing to receive that miracle; and I assure you that a miracle can take place when you are willing to receive it, when you are willing to look at things really as they are. Do not deceive yourself by giving explanations, by justifying yourself, but see yourself as you are—and discover what an extraordinary thing takes place. I assure you regeneration comes when you are not looking to time as a means of transforming yourself. Only then is there transformation, and the miracle is not far. But you are so sluggish, so unwilling, so empty-handed even in your suffering! Sir, the rain falls and gives nourishment to the earth, the trees, the flowers; but if that rain falls on a rock, does it do any good? You are like the rock, your hearts and minds are dull, you are empty and hard, and no amount of rain can wash that away. What will change your hard heart is to see things as they are; do not condemn, do not find an excuse for them, but recognize, look at them—and you will see a miracle. When you see and acknowledge that your heart is hard, your mind full of childish toys—when you recognize it, you will see a transformation take place. But, to look, to see, to observe, you must have the intention. Sirs, look at you—some are yawning, some are twiddling their thumbs, some are cleaning their glasses. Do you think a miracle can happen to you? Do you think a miracle can happen when you are secure, when you have money? When your hands are full of money, it cannot happen. You must let go, you must be willing to let go, then the miracle can happen. You must be aware of yourself as you are—simply, constantly, and directly, with all your ugliness, your cheerfulness, your brutality, joy, and suffering. As you become aware, you will see a miracle happening that you would never have suspected, a miracle that is truth, that transforms, that liberates.

Question: You seem to suggest that concentration and the willful focusing of one's attention is exclusive and therefore a dulling process. Will you please explain what is meditation and how the mind can be stilled and got rid of?

KRISHNAMURTI: I do not know what is meant by "got rid of," but that does not matter. I have carefully explained that concentration is not meditation, for concentration is mere exclusive choice, and therefore there is a narrowing down of the mind. A mind that is narrowed down can never understand that which is limitless, immeasurable. I have explained that. You can read about it in the books that have been published. Also, I have said that meditation is not prayer. Prayer is another trick of the mind to quiet itself. Through the repetition of words and sentences you can make the mind still, and in that stillness receive a response, but that response is not the response of reality because such prayer is merely a repetition, a begging, a supplication. In prayer there is duality, one who begs and the other who grants. I have said that meditation is not concentration, meditation is not prayer. Now, most of you who practice meditation belong to either of these two categories. That is, you are concentrating to achieve a result, or you pray for something you want, either a refrigerator or a virtue. You can inquire into what meditation is only when you do not want anything. You can not go into the significance of meditation if you approach if from either of those two points of view. I have explained all that, and I won't go into it now.

What do we mean by meditation? Obviously it means, does it not, a mind that is capable of swift pliability so that it is aware extensively and widely, so that every problem as it arises is dissolved instantaneously, every challenge is understood, and there is no response of yesterday. Sir, a meditative mind is a mind that knows itself, which means that meditation is the beginning of self-knowledge. You cannot meditate without knowing yourself. Without knowing yourself, your meditation is vain, it has no meaning. To meditate rightly, you must first know yourself. Therefore, meditation is self-knowledge. To know yourself is to see all the content of the mind, both the conscious and the unconscious activities, when it is awake and when it is in its so-called sleep. That is not difficult, and I am going to show how to do it; but experiment with it now, do not wait until you go home. When you experiment, you do not know what you are going to discover. Each time you approach any problem, there is something new—that is the beauty of reality. It is always creative, it is always new. That newness cannot come through memory. So, meditation is the beginning of self-knowledge, which is to know the conscious activities and also the whole content of the hidden layers of the mind. Please follow this. Meditate with me as I go along step by step. I am not mesmerizing you, I am not using words for their neurological value. I am going to find out what it means to meditate, to discover reality through meditation. We are experimenting to find out, not tomorrow, but now. You can question me tomorrow. Please follow this, sirs. First, I recognize the fact that without knowing myself I cannot meditate; meditation has no meaning without self-knowledge. Self-knowledge is not high or low—it is the whole process of thought, the open thought with which you are familiar and all the concealed thought that is hidden in the unconscious. I am going to meditate and uncover the whole process—which can be done immediately. Truth can be perceived directly.

Now, what is the self? Obviously, it is memory; at whatever level, high or low, it is still memory, which means thought. You may call the self atma, or merely the response to environment; when you call it atma, you place it at a high level, but it is still part of thought, which is memory. Therefore, to understand this whole process of 'myself' is to understand memory—memory which is not only acquired the previous minute, but also the memory of centuries, the memory which is the result of accumulated racial experience, national, geographical, climatic influences, and so on. All this is memory, whether superficial or very deep, and we are going to be aware of the whole of memory in all its details. As most of us can see, when we say that the self is memory—not a particular memory, but the total memory of all entities—the implication is that to uncover its various layers needs time. To investigate the conscious and the unconscious memory, one must have time; and to use time to discover truth, reality, is to deny it. I hope you are following all this. So, I must use the right means for the right end. That is, sirs, if I take time to analyze all the layers, conscious and unconscious, I am using time as a means of achieving the timeless. Therefore, I am using the wrong means to approach the right end. Surely, I must approach the right end with the right means. That is, I must not use time. But I am in the habit of using time as a means of achieving the timeless. Discipline, meditation, control, suppression all imply time, and memory is time. So, I see something—that I must use the right means to find the right end. Therefore, I have a problem which I must dissolve without time. To analyze all the layers of memory and go into their value involves time. If I use time, then I am introducing the wrong means to a right end because I am using time in order to find the timeless. I can find the timeless only if I use the right means. Therefore, my problem is how thought, which is the result of memory, which is memory, can be dissolved instantaneously. Any other approach is an approach through time. Watch it, sir, please follow it. A problem is put in front of you: it is that the self, the 'you', is memory, a bundle of memories, and it must be dissolved because the continuance of memory is time, and through time you can never find that which is eternal, immeasurable, spaceless, beyond time. How is it to be done? It can be done only when memory completely ceases. Now, how is that memory to cease? Please follow this. I see that as long as memory functions, reality cannot be—that is a fact, is it not? I have explained it enough. That is, sir, I see that mind is the product, the result of memory, and when that mind tries to think out how to be free, memory is still functioning. When the mind asks, "How am I to be free from memory?" the very question implies an answer which is the outcome of memory. Perhaps I am putting it too concisely.

The mind, both conscious and unconscious, is a bundle of memories, and when the mind says to itself, "I must be free of memory in order to understand reality," that very wish to be free is part of memory. That is a fact. Therefore, the mind no longer wishes to be anything—it merely faces the fact that it itself is memory; it does not wish to transform, it does not wish to become something else. When the mind sees that any action on its own part is still the functioning of memory, and therefore that it is incapable of finding truth, what then is the state of the mind? It becomes still. When the mind perceives that any activity of its own is futile, is all part of memory and therefore of time, seeing that fact, it stops, does it not? If your mind sees the reality of what I am saying, that whatever it does is still part of memory, and therefore it cannot act to be free of memory, it does not act. When mind sees that it cannot proceed that way, it stops. Therefore, the mind, the whole content of the mind, the conscious and the unconscious, becomes still. Now the mind is without action, it has seen that whatever it does is on a horizontal line, which is memory; therefore, seeing the fallacy of that, it becomes quiet. It has no object in view, it has no desire for a result, it is absolutely tranquil, without movement in any direction. Therefore, what has happened? The mind is tranquil, it has not been made tranquil. See the difference between a mind that is put to sleep, and a mind that is quiet. In that state you will find an enormous movement, extreme vitality, a newness, peaceful and alert. All positive action has ceased, and the mind is in a state of the highest intelligence because it has approached the problem of memory through negative thinking, which is the highest form of thinking. So, the mind is peaceful, swift and yet still; it is not exclusive, it is not concentrating or focusing, but is extensively aware. Now what happens? In that awareness there is no choice but merely seeing things as they are—red as red, blue as blue, without any distortion. In that state which is peaceful, choicelessly aware, and alert, you will find that all verbalization, all mentation, or intellection has completely stopped. There is a stillness which is not induced, a stillness in which the mind is no longer using thought to revive itself; therefore, there is neither the thinker nor the thought. There is neither the experiencer nor the experienced because the experiencer and the experienced come into being through the thought process, and the thought process has entirely stopped. There is only a state of experiencing. In that state of experiencing, there is no time; all time as yesterday, today, and tomorrow has completely stopped. If you can go further into it, you will see that the mind which was the product of time has completely transformed itself and is now without time; and that which is without time is eternal, that which is without time is immeasurable, it has no beginning and no end, it is without cause and therefore without effect—and that which is without cause is the real. You can experience that now, but not through centuries of practice, discipline, or control. It must be now or never.

So, the mind that wishes to understand meditation must begin to understand itself—understand itself in its relationships, not in isolation. A mind that is the product of time can be free of time, not eventually, but immediately; and that freedom comes into being only when there is the right approach—and meditation is the right approach—to all human problems. The positive approach is conditioned by a pattern of action. Meditation is the negative approach, and therefore it is the highest form of thinking—which is not thinking. All thinking is of time. If you want to understand a human problem, there must be no thought process, and to free the mind from the thought process is to meditate, and you cannot meditate without self-knowledge. Only when there is self-knowledge, of which meditation is the beginning, does reality come into being; and it is reality that liberates.

October 10, 1948

Eighth Talk in Poona

We have touched upon many things during the course of these Sunday talks, but it seems to me that one of the most important questions to discuss and find out the significance of is that of time. The lives of most of us are rather sluggish—like still waters, they are dull, dreary, ugly, and insipid—and some of us, realizing this, bury ourselves in political, social, or religious activities, and thereby we think we can enrich our lives. But surely, such action is not enrichment because our lives are still empty; though we may talk about political reform, yet our minds and hearts continue to be dull. We may be very active socially or may dedicate our lives to religion, yet the meaning of virtue is still a matter of ideas, of mere ideation. So, do what we may, we find our lives to be dull; they are without much significance, for mere action without understanding does not bring about enrichment or freedom. So, if I may, I would like to talk a little about what is time because I think the enrichment, the beauty and significance of that which is timeless, of that which is true, can be experienced only when we understand the whole process of time. After all, we are seeking, each in his own way, a sense of happiness, of enrichment. Surely, a life that has significance, the riches of true happiness, is not of time. Like love, such a life is timeless; and to understand that which is timeless, we must not approach it through time but rather understand time. We must not utilize time as a means of attaining, realizing, apprehending the timeless. But that is what we are doing most of our lives—spending time in trying to grasp that which is timeless. So, it is important to understand what we mean by time because I think it is possible to be free of time. It is very important to understand time as a whole, and not partially; but I will have to deal with it as rapidly and as briefly as possible because I have many questions to answer and this is the last evening of these talks. So, I hope you will not mind if I am very brief and to the point.

It is interesting to realize that our lives are mostly spent in time—time, not in the sense of chronological sequence, of minutes, hours, days, and years, but in the sense of psychological memory. We live by time, we are the result of time. Our minds are the product of many yesterdays, and the present is merely the passage of the past to the future. So, our minds, our activities, our beings, are founded on time; without time we cannot think because thought is the result of time, thought is the product of many yesterdays, and there is no thought without memory. Memory is time, for there are two kinds of time—the chronological and the psychological. There is time as yesterday by the watch and as yesterday by memory. You cannot reject chronological time, which would be absurd—then you would miss your train. But is there really any time at all apart from chronological time? Obviously, there is time as yesterday, but is there time as the mind thinks of it? That is, is there time apart from the mind? Surely, time, psychological time, is the product of the mind. Without the foundation of thought there is no time—time merely being memory as yesterday in conjunction with today, which molds tomorrow. That is, memory of yesterday's experience in response to the present is creating the future—which is still the process of thought, a path of the mind. So, the thought process brings about psychological progress in time, but is it real, as real as chronological time? And can we use that time which is of the mind as a means of understanding the eternal, the timeless? Because, as I said, happiness is not of yesterday, happiness is not the product of time, happiness is always in the present, a timeless state. I do not know if you have noticed that when you have ecstasy, a creative joy, a series of bright clouds surrounded by dark clouds, in that moment there is no time—there is only the immediate present. But the mind, coming in after the experiencing in the present, remembers and wishes to continue it, gathering more and more of itself, thereby creating time. So, time is created by the 'more'; time is acquisition, and time is also detachment, which is still an acquisition of the mind. Therefore, merely disciplining the mind in time, conditioning thought within the framework of time, which is memory, surely does not reveal that which is timeless.

So, there is chronological time, and there is the time of the mind, the time which is mind itself, and we are always confusing these two issues. Obviously, chronological time is confused with the psychological, with the psyche of one's being; and with that chronological mentality we try to become, we try to achieve. So, this whole process of becoming is of time, and one must surely inquire if there really is such a thing as becoming—becoming in the sense of finding reality, God, happiness. Can you use time as a means to the timeless? That is, through a wrong means can the right end be achieved? Surely, the right means must be employed for the right end because the means and the end are one. When we try to find the timeless in terms of becoming—which implies disciplining, conditioning, rejecting, accepting, acquiring, and denying, all of which involves time—we are using the wrong means for the right end; therefore, our means will produce a wrong end. As long as you are using the wrong means, which is time, to find the timeless, the timeless is not; for time is not the means to the timeless. Therefore, to find the timeless, to realize that which is eternal, time must stop—which means the whole process of thinking must come to an end; and, if you examine it really closely, widely, and intelligently, it is not as difficult as it appears. Because, there are moments when the mind is absolutely still, not put together, but still of itself. Surely, there is a difference between a mind that is made still and a mind that is still. But those moments of stillness are mere remembrances, and remembrances become the time element which prevents the further experiencing of those moments.

So, as I said, for thought to come to an end and for the timeless to be, you must understand memory—for without memory, there is no thought, without memory, there is no time. Memory is merely incomplete experience—for that which you experience fully, completely, is without any response, and in that state there is no memory. At the moment when you are experiencing something, there is no memory, there is no experiencer apart from the experienced, there is neither the observer nor the observed—there is only a state of experiencing in which time is not. Time comes in only when experiencing has become a memory, and most of you are living on the memory of yesterday's experiencing, either your own or that of your guru, and so on and on. Therefore, if we understand this psychological functioning of memory, which springs from chronological action, we cannot confuse the two. We must see the whole problem of time without apprehension and without a desire to continue, because most of us desire to continue, and it is this continuity that must come to an end. Continuity is merely time, and continuity cannot lead to the timeless. To understand time is to understand memory, and to understand memory is to become aware of our relationship to all things—to nature, to people, to property, and to ideas. Relationship reveals the process of memory, and the understanding of that process is self-knowledge. Without understanding the process of the self, at whatever level that self is placed, you cannot be free of memory, and therefore you are not free of time, and hence the timeless is not.

Question: Have dreams any meaning? If so, how should one interpret them?

KRISHNAMURTI: What do we mean by "dream"? When we are asleep, when the body is asleep, the mind is functioning, and when we wake up, we remember certain impressions, symbols, word expressions, or pictures. That is what we mean by dreams, is it not?—those impressions that are recollected upon waking, those symbols, intimations, hints to the conscious mind concerning things not fully understood. That is, during our waking consciousness the mind is completely occupied with earning a livelihood, with immediate relationships, with amusements, and so on. So, the conscious mind leads a very superficial life. But our life is not merely the superficial layer—it is going on at different levels all the time. These different levels are constantly trying to convey their meaning, their significance, to the conscious mind; and when the conscious mind is quiet, as during sleep, the hints and the intimations of the hidden are communicated in the form of symbols, and on waking, these symbols are remembered as dreams. Then, having dreams, you try to interpret those dreams, or you go to a psychoanalyst to have them interpreted for you. That is what actually takes place. Perhaps you do not go to the interpreter because it is too expensive, and it does not lead you to hope; but still you depend on interpretation, you want your dreams to be explained, you look to their meaning, you search out their significance, you try to analyze them; and in that process of interpretation, of analysis, there is always hope, doubt, and uncertainty.

Now, need we dream at all? There are dreams which are very superficial. When you overeat at night, naturally you have violent dreams. There are dreams which are the result of the suppression of sexual and other cravings. When they are suppressed, they assert themselves while you are asleep, and you remember them as dreams when you awake. There are many forms of dreams, but my point is this: Need one dream at all? If it is possible not to dream, then there is nothing that needs to be interpreted. Psychologists—not that I have read them, but I know several—have told me that it is impossible not to dream. I think it is possible not to dream, and you can experiment with it for yourself and therefore put aside the fear of interpretation, with its anxieties, with its uncertainties. As I said, you dream because the conscious mind is not aware of what is actually taking place every minute, is not aware of all the intimations, hints, impressions, and responses that are constantly coming on. And is it not possible to be passively aware so that everything is immediately perceived and understood? Surely, it can be done. It is only when there is passive awareness of each problem that it is immediately resolved and not carried over to the next day. Now, when you have a problem and that problem causes considerable worry, what happens? You go to bed and you say, "I will sleep on it." Next morning when you look at the problem, you see it can be solved, and you are free. What actually happens is that the conscious mind, having searched and worried, becomes quiet; and then the unconscious mind, which goes on working on the problem, gives its hints, its intimations, and when you wake up the problem is solved.

So, it is possible to meet every problem afresh, anew, and not carry it over. You can meet every problem anew, with quickness, with rapidity, only when you do not condemn, when you do not justify, because only then can the problem tell you its whole significance; and it is possible to live so alertly, so passively aware, that each problem gives its full significance as it arises. You can test this out for yourselves, you do not have to accept another's word for it. But the whole conscious mind must be alert, watchful, so that there is no part of it that is sluggish and that has therefore to be quickened through dreams, through symbols. Only when the conscious mind is aware, not merely at one depth or in one layer, but fully and entirely, is it possible not to dream.

Dreams are also self-projections, the interpretation through symbols of different experiences. Also the conversation one has with people in a dream is obviously still self-projection—which does not mean that it is impossible for thought to meet thought, for one identified thought to meet another identified thought. This is too vast a subject to go completely into now; but one can see that as long as we deal with problems partially and not fully, as long as there is conditioned response to challenge, there must be these intimations, these hints from that part of the mind which is alert, either through dreams or through rude shocks. As long as problems are not fully understood, you will dream, and those dreams need interpretation. Interpretations are never complete, for they always arise out of fear, anxiety; there is in them an element of the unknown, and the conscious mind always rejects that which is unknown. Whereas, if one can experience each challenge completely, fully, then there is no necessity for dreams nor for an interpreter of dreams.

Question: What is the meaning of right relationship with nature?

KRISHNAMURTI: Sir, I do not know if you have discovered your relationship with nature. There is no "right" relationship, there is only the understanding of relationship. Right relationship implies the mere acceptance of a formula, as does right thought. Right thought and right thinking are two different things. Right thought is merely conforming to what is right, what is respectable, whereas right thinking is movement, it is the product of understanding, and understanding is constantly undergoing modification, change. Similarly, there is a difference between right relationship and understanding our relationship with nature. What is your relationship with nature?—nature being the rivers, the trees, the swift-flying birds, the fish in the water, the minerals under the earth, the waterfalls and shallow pools. What is your relationship to them? Most of us are not aware of that relationship. We never look at a tree, or if we do, it is with a view of using that tree—either to sit in its shade or to cut it down for lumber. In other words, we look at trees with a utilitarian purpose; we never look at a tree without projecting ourselves and utilizing it for our own convenience. We treat the earth and its products in the same way. There is no love of earth, there is only usage of earth. If one really loved the earth, there would be frugality in using the things of the earth. That is, sir, if we were to understand our relationship with the earth, we should be very careful in the use we made of the things of the earth. The understanding of one's relationship with nature is as difficult as understanding one's relationship with one's neighbor, wife, and children. But we have not given a thought to it, we have never sat down to look at the stars, the moon, or the trees. We are too busy with social or political activities. Obviously, these activities are escapes from ourselves, and to worship nature is also an escape from ourselves. We are always using nature, either as an escape or for utilitarian ends—we never actually stop and love the earth or the things of the earth. We never enjoy the rich fields, though we utilize them to feed and clothe ourselves. We never like to till the earth with our hands—we are ashamed to work with our hands. There is an extraordinary thing that takes place when you work the earth with your hands. But this work is done only by the lower castes; we upper classes are much too important apparently to use our own hands! So, we have lost our relationship with nature. If once we understood that relationship, its real significance, then we would not divide property into yours and mine; though one might own a piece of land and build a house on it, it would cease to be "mine" or "yours" in the exclusive sense—it would be more a means of taking shelter. Because we do not love the earth and the things of the earth but merely utilize them, we are insensitive to the beauty of a waterfall, we have lost the touch of life, we have never sat with our backs against the trunk of a tree; and since we do not love nature, we do not know how to love human beings and animals. Go down the street and watch how the bullocks are treated, their tails all out of shape. You shake your head and say, "Very sad." But we have lost the sense of tenderness, that sensitivity, that response to things of beauty; and it is only in the renewal of that sensitivity that we can have understanding of what is true relationship. That sensitivity does not come in the mere hanging of a few pictures, or in painting a tree, or putting a few flowers in your hair; sensitivity comes only when this utilitarian outlook is put aside. It does not mean that you cannot use the earth, but you must use the earth as it is to be used. Earth is there to be loved, to be cared for, not to be divided as "yours" and "mine." It is foolish to plant a tree in a compound and call it "mine." It is only when one is free of exclusiveness that there is a possibility of having sensitivity, not only to nature, but to human beings and to the ceaseless challenges of life.

Question: While talking about right means of livelihood, you said that the profession of the army, of the lawyer, and of government service were obviously not right means of livelihood. Are you not advocating sannyasism, withdrawal from society, and is that not running away from social conflicts and supporting the injustice and exploitation around us?

KRISHNAMURTI: To transform anything or to understand anything you must first examine *what is;* then only is there a possibility of a renewal, a regeneration, a transformation. Merely to transform *what is* without understanding it is a waste of time, a retrogression. Reform without understanding is retrogression because we do not face *what is;* but if we begin to understand exactly *what is,* then we shall know how to act. You cannot act without first observing, discussing, and understanding *what is.* We must examine society as it is with its weaknesses, its foibles; and to examine it we must see directly our connection, our relationship with it, not through a supposedly intellectual or theoretical explanation.

Now, as society exists at present, there is no choice between right livelihood and wrong livelihood. You take any job you can get, if you are lucky enough to get one at all. So, to the man who is pressed for an immediate job, there is no problem. He takes what he can get because he must eat. But to those of you who are not so immediately pressed, it should be a problem, and that is what we are discussing—what is the right means of livelihood in a society which is based on acquisition and class differences, on nationalism, greed, violence, and so on? Given these things, can there be right livelihood? Obviously not. And there are obviously wrong professions, wrong means of livelihood, such as the army, the lawyer, the police, and the government.

The army exists not for peace but for war. It is the function of the army to create war, it is the function of the general to plan for war. If he does not, you will throw him out, won't you? You will get rid of him. The function of the general staff is to plan and prepare for future wars, and a general staff that does not plan for future wars is obviously inefficient. So the army is not a profession for peace; therefore, it is not a right means of livelihood. I know the implications as well as you do. Armies will exist as long as sovereign governments exist with their nationalism and frontiers; and since you support sovereign governments, you must support nationalism and war. Therefore, as long as you are a nationalist, you have no choice about right livelihood.

Similarly, the police. The function of the police is to protect and to maintain things as they are. It also becomes the instrument of investigation, of inquisition, not only in the hands of totalitarian governments, but in the hands of any government. The function of the police is to snoop around, to investigate into the private lives of people. The more revolutionary you become, outwardly or inwardly, the more dangerous you are to government. That is why governments, and especially totalitarian governments, liquidate those who are outwardly or inwardly creating a revolution. So, obviously, the profession of police is not a right means of livelihood.

Similarly, the lawyer. He thrives on contention; it is essential for his livelihood that you and I should fight and wrangle. (Laughter) You laugh it off. Probably many of you are lawyers, and your laugh indicates a mere nervous response to a fact, and through avoidance of that fact, you will still go on being lawyers. You may say that you are a victim of society, but you are victimized because you accept society as it is. So, law is not a right means of livelihood. There can be right means of livelihood only when you do not accept the present state of things, and the moment you do not accept it, you do not accept law as a profession.

Similarly, you cannot expect to find a right means of livelihood in the big corporations of business men who are amassing wealth, nor in the bureaucratic routine of government with its officials and red tape. Governments are only interested in maintaining things as they are, and if you become an engineer for the government, you are directly or indirectly helping war.

So, as long as you accept society as it is, any profession, whether the army, the police, the law, or the government, is obviously not a right means of livelihood. Seeing that, what is an earnest man to do? Is he to run away and bury himself in some village? Even there, he has to live somehow. He can beg, but the very food that is given to him comes indirectly from the lawyer, the policeman, the soldier, the government. And he cannot live in isolation because that again is impossible; to live in isolation is to lie, both psychologically and physiologically. So, what is one to do? All that one can do, if one is earnest, if one is intelligent about this whole process, is to reject the present state of things and give to society all that one is capable of. That is, sir, you accept food, clothing, and shelter from society, and you must give something to society in return. As long as you use the army, the police, the law, the government as your means of livelihood, you maintain things as they are, you support dissension, inquisition, and war. But if you reject the things of society and accept only the essentials, you must give something in return. It is more important to find out what you are giving to society than to ask what is the right means of livelihood.

Now, what are you giving to society? What is society? Society is relationship with one or with many; it is your relationship with another. What are you giving to another? Are you giving anything to another in the real sense of the word, or merely taking payment for something? As long as you do not find out what you are giving, whatever you take from society is bound to be a wrong means of livelihood. This is not a clever answer, and therefore you have to ponder, inquire into the whole question of your relationship to society. You may ask me in return, "What are you giving to society in order that you be clothed, given shelter and food?" I am giving to society that of which I am talking today—which is not merely the verbal service any fool can give. I am giving to society what to me is true. You may reject it and say, "Nonsense, it is not true." But I am giving what to me is true, and I am far more concerned with that than with what society gives me. Sir, when you do not use society or your neighbor as a means of self-extension, you are completely content with the things that society gives you in the way of food, clothing, and shelter. Therefore, you are not greedy, and not being greedy, your relationship with society is entirely different. The moment you do not use society as a means of self-extension, you reject the things of society, and therefore there is a revolution in your relationship. You are not depending on another for your psychological needs—and it is only then that you can have a right means of livelihood.

You may say this is all a very complicated answer, but it is not. Life has no simple answer. The man who looks for a simple answer to life has obviously a dull mind, a stupid mind. Life has no conclusion, life has no definite pattern; life is living, altering, changing. There is no positive, definite answer to life, but we can understand its whole significance and meaning. To understand, we must first see that we are using life as a means of self-extension, as a means of self-fulfillment; and because we are using life as a means of self-fulfillment, we create a society which is corrupt, which must begin to decay the very moment it comes into existence. So, an organized society has inherent in it the seed of decay.

It is very important for each one of us to find out what his relationship is with society, whether it is based on greed—which means self-extension, self-fulfillment, in which is implied power, position, authority—or if one merely accepts from society such essentials as food, clothing, and shelter. If your relationship is one of need and not of greed, then you will find the right means of livelihood wherever you are, even when society is corrupt. So, as the present society is disintegrating very rapidly, one has to find out; and those whose relationship is one of need only will create a new culture, they will be the nucleus of society in which the necessities of life are equitably distributed and are not used as a means of self-extension. As long as society remains for you as a means of self-extension, there must be a craving for power, and it is power that creates a society of classes divided as the high and the low, the rich and the poor, the man who has and the man who has not, the literate and the illiterate, each struggling with the other, all based on acquisitiveness and not on need. It is acquisitiveness which gives power, position, and prestige, and as long as that exists, your relationship with society must be a wrong means of livelihood. There can be right means of livelihood when you look to society only for your needs—and then your relationship with society is very simple. Simplicity is not the 'more', nor is it the putting on of a loincloth and renouncing the world. Merely limiting yourself to a few things is not simplicity. Simplicity of the mind is essential, and that simplicity of the mind cannot exist if the mind is used for self-extension, self-fulfillment, whether that self-fulfillment comes through the pursuit of God, of knowledge, of money, property, or position. The mind that is seeking God is not a simple mind, for its God is its own projection. The simple man is he who sees exactly *what is* and understands it—he does not demand anything more. Such a mind is content, it understands *what is*—which does not mean accepting society as it is, with its exploitation, classes, wars, and so on. But a mind that sees and understands *what is* and therefore acts—such a mind has few needs, it is very simple, quiet; and it is only when the mind is quiet that it can receive the eternal.

Question: Every art has a technique of its own, and it takes effort to master the technique. How can one reconcile creativeness with technical achievement?

KRISHNAMURTI: You cannot reconcile creativeness with technical achievement. You may be perfect in playing the piano and not be creative; you may play the piano most brilliantly and not be a musician. You may be able to handle color, to put paint on canvas most cleverly, and not be a creative painter. You may create a face, an image out of a stone because you have learned the technique, and not be a master creator. Creation comes first, not technique, and that is why we are miserable all our lives. We have technique—how to put up a house, how to build a bridge, how to assemble a motor, how to educate our children through a system—we have learned all these techniques, but our hearts and minds are empty. We are first-class machines; we know how to operate most beautifully, but we do not love a living thing. You may be a good engineer, you may be a pianist, you may write in a good style in English or Marathi or whatever your language is, but creativeness is not found through technique. If you have something to say, you create your own style; but when you have nothing to say, even if you have a beautiful style, what you write is only the traditional routine, a repetition in new words of the same old thing. So, if you watch yourself very critically, you will see that technique does not lead to creativeness, but when you have creativeness, you can have technique within a week. To express something there must be something to express; you must have a song in your heart to sing. You must have sensitivity to receive in order to express, and the expression is of very little importance. The expression is important only when you want to convey it to another, but it has very little importance when you write for your own amusement.

So, having lost the song, we pursue the singer. We learn from the singer the technique of song, but there is no song; and I say the song is essential, the joy of singing is essential. When the joy is there, the technique can be built up from nothing; you will invent your own technique, you won't have to study elocution or style. When you have, you see, and the very seeing of beauty is an art. The expression of that seeing becomes beautiful, technically perfect when you have something to say. To have a song in your heart, that is the important thing, not the technique—though technique is essential. What is important is to be creative. It is really an important problem because you are not creative; you may produce children galore, but that is merely accidental, that is not creative. You may be able to write about creative thinkers, but that is not being creative. You may watch, you may be spectators at a play, but you are not the actors. Since the mere learning of a technique is more and more emphasized, you have to find what it is to be creative.

How is one to be creative? Creativeness is not imitation. Our whole life is imitative, not only on the verbal level, but inwardly and psychologically also; it is nothing but imitation, conformity, and regimentation. Do you think there can be creativeness when you are thinking according to a pattern, a technique? There is creativeness only when there is freedom from imitation, from regimentation, which means freedom from authority, not only external authority, but the inward authority of experience which has become memory. Again, there cannot be creativeness if there is fear, for fear produces imitation, fear creates copy, fear engenders the desire to be secure, to be certain, which in turn creates authority; and there cannot be creativeness as long as the mind moves from the known to the known. As long as the mind is held by technique, as long as the mind is engaged in knowledge, there cannot be creativeness. Knowledge is of the past, of the known, and as long as the mind moves from the known to the known, there cannot be creativeness. As long as the mind is moving in a series of changes, there cannot be creativeness because change is merely modified continuity. There can be creativeness only in ending, not in continuity. Most of us do not want to end; we all want to continue, and our continuance is merely the continuance of memory. Memory can be placed at the level of the atma or at a lower level, but still it is memory. As long as all these things exist, there cannot be creativeness. It is not difficult to be free of these things, but one needs attention, observation, intention to understand; then, I assure you, creativeness comes into being.

When a man wishes to create, he must ask himself and see what it is he wants to create. Is it motor cars, war machines, gadgets? The mere pursuit of things distracts the mind and interferes with generosity, with the instinctive response to beauty. That is what we are all doing with our minds. As long as the mind is active, formulating, fabricating, criticizing, there cannot be creativeness; and, I assure you, that creativeness comes silently, with extraordinary swiftness, without any enforcement when you understand the truth that the mind must be empty for creativeness to take place. When you see the truth of that, then instantaneously there is creativeness. You do not have to paint a picture, you do not have to sit on the platform, you do not have to invent new mathematical theorems, for creativeness does not necessarily demand expression. The very expression of it begins to destroy it. That does not mean that you must not express it, but if the expression becomes more important than creativeness, then creativeness recedes. For you, expression is so important—to paint a picture and put your name at the bottom! Then you want to see who is criticizing it, who is going to buy it, how many critics have written about it, and what they say; and when you are knighted, you think you have achieved something! That is not creativeness; that is decay, disintegration. Creativeness comes into being only when the mind with its prompting and corruption ceases; and for the mind to come to an end is not a difficult task, nor is it the ultimate task that you should undertake. On the contrary, it is the immediate task. Our lives are in the present with its miseries, with its confusion, its extraordinarily mounting sorrow and strife. So, the only thing is for the mind, which is thought, to come to an end, and then, I assure you, you will know creativeness. There is creativeness only when the mind, understanding its own insufficiency, its own poverty, its own loneliness, comes to an end. Being aware of itself, it puts an end to itself; then that which is creative, that which is immeasurable, comes subtly and swiftly. To put an end to the process of thought is to be passively aware of one's own insufficiency, one's own poverty, one's own void, emptiness, without struggling against it; only then there comes that thing which is not the product of the mind, and that which is not the product of the mind is creativeness.

Question: You are telling us every day that the root cause of our trouble and ugliness in life is the absence of love. How is one to find the pearl of real love?

KRISHNAMURTI: To answer this question fully, one must think negatively because negative thinking is the highest form of thinking. Mere positive thinking is conformity to a pattern; therefore, it is not thinking at all—it is adjustment to an idea, and an idea is merely the product of the mind, therefore unreal. So, to think this problem through completely, fully, we must approach it negatively—which does not mean denial of life. Do not jump to conclusions but follow step by step, if you kindly will. If you will follow this experience deeply and not merely verbally, then as we proceed you will find out what love is. We are going to inquire into love. Mere conclusions are not love; the word *love* is not love. Let us begin very near in order to go very far.

Now, do you call it love when in your relationship with your wife there is possessiveness, jealousy, fear, constant nagging, dominating, and asserting? Can that be called love? When you possess a person and thereby create a society which helps you to possess the person, do you call that love? When you use somebody for your sexual convenience or in any other way, do you call that love? Obviously it is not. That is, where there is jealousy, where there is fear, where there is possessiveness, there is no love. You may call it love, but it is not love. Surely, love does not admit of contention, of jealousy. When you possess, there is fear and though you may call it love, it is far from love. Experience it, sirs and ladies, as we go along. You are married and have children; you have wives or husbands whom you possess, whom you use, of whom you are afraid or jealous. Be aware of that and see if it is love. You may see a beggar in the street; you give him a coin and express a word of sympathy. Is that love? Is sympathy love? What does that mean? By giving a coin to the beggar, sympathizing with his state, have you solved the problem? I am not saying that you should not be sympathetic—we are inquiring into the question of love. Is it love when you give a coin to the beggar? You have something to give, and when you give it, is that love? That is, when you are conscious of giving, is that love? Obviously, when you give consciously, it is you who are important, not the beggar. So, when you give and you express sympathy, you are important, are you not? Why should you have something to give? You give a coin to the beggar; the multimillionaire also gives and is always sympathetic to poor humanity. What is the difference between you and him? You have ten coins, and you give one; he has umpteen coins, and he gives a few more. He has got that money through acquiring, multiplying, revolutionizing, exploiting. When he gives, you call it charity, philanthropy; you say, "How noble." Is that noble? (Laughter) Do not laugh, sirs, you also want to do the same thing. When you have and you give something, is that love? Why is it that you have and others have not? You say it is the fault of society. Who has created society? You and I. Therefore, to attack society, we have to begin with ourselves.

So, your sympathy is not love. Is forgiveness love? Let us go into it and you will see. I hope you are experiencing as I am talking, not merely listening to words. Is forgiveness love? What is implied in forgiveness? You insult me and I resent it, remember it; and then, either through compulsion or through repentance, I say, "I forgive you." First I retain, and then I reject. Which means what? I am still the central figure. I am still important; it is I who am forgiving somebody. Surely, as long as there is the attitude of forgiving, it is I who am important, not the man who is supposed to have insulted me. So, when I accumulate resentment and then deny that resentment, which you call forgiveness, it is not love. A man who loves obviously has no enmity, and to all these things he is indifferent. So, sympathy, forgiveness, the relationship of possessiveness, jealousy, and fear—all these things are not love. They are all of the mind, are they not? As long as the mind is the arbiter, there is no love, for the mind arbitrates only through possessiveness, and its arbitration is merely possessiveness in different forms. The mind can only corrupt love, it cannot give birth to love, it cannot give beauty. You can write a poem about love, but that is not love.

So, the mind is the product of time, and time exists when love is denied; therefore, love is not of time. Love is not a coin to be distributed. Giving you something, giving you satisfaction, giving you courage to fight with—all these belong to the field of time, which is of the mind. Therefore, mind destroys love. It is because we as so-called civilized people are cultivating the mind, the intellect, the verbal expression, the technique, that there is no love; and that is why there is this confusion, why our troubles, our miseries multiply. It is because we are seeking an answer through the mind that there is no answer to any of our problems, that wars succeed wars, disasters follow disasters. The mind has created these problems, and we are trying to solve them on their own level, which is that of the mind. So, it is only when the mind ceases that there is love, and it is only love that will solve all our problems, like sunshine and darkness. There is no relationship between the mind and love. Mind is of time, love is not of time. You can think about a person whom you love, but you cannot think about love. Love cannot be thought about; though you may identify yourself with a person, a country, a church, the moment you think about love, it is not love—it is merely mentation. What is thought about is not love, and there is emptiness in the heart only when the mind is supremely active. Because the mind is active, it fills the empty heart with the things of the mind; and with these things of the mind we play, we create problems. The playing with problems is what we call activity, and our solution of the problems is still of the mind. Do what you will, build churches, invent new parties, follow new leaders, adopt political slogans, they will never solve our problems. The problems are the product of the mind, and for the mind to solve its own problem it has to stop, for only when the mind stops is there love. Love cannot be thought about, love cannot be cultivated, love cannot be practiced. The practice of love, the practice of brtherhood, is still within the field of the mind; therefore, it is not love. When all this has stopped, then love comes into being, then you will know what it is to love. Then love is not quantitative, but qualitative. You do not say, "I love the whole world," but when you know how to love one, you know how to love the whole. Because we do not know how to love one, our love of humanity is fictitious. When you love, there is neither one nor many—there is only love. It is only when there is love that all our problems can be solved, and then we shall known its bliss and its happiness.

October 17, 1948

New Delhi, India, 1948

A Radio Talk

The world is in confusion and misery, and every nation, including India, is looking for a way out of this conflict, this mounting sorrow. Though India has gained so-called freedom, she is caught in the turmoil of exploitation like every other people; communal and caste antagonisms are rife, and though she is not as advanced as the West in technological matters, yet she is faced like the rest of the world with problems that no politician, no economist, or reformer, however great, is able to solve. She seems to be so completely overwhelmed by the unexpected problems confronting her that she is willing to sacrifice, for immediate ends, the essential values and the cumulative understanding of man's struggle. India is giving her heart over to the glittering and glamorous pomp of a modern state. Surely this is not freedom.

India's problem is the world problem, and merely to look to the world for the solution of her problem is to avoid the understanding of the problem itself. Though India has been, in ancient times, a source of great action, merely to look to that past, to breathe the dead air of things that have been, does not bring about creative understanding of the present. Until we understand this aching present, there can be no resolution of any human problem, and merely to escape into the past or into the future is utterly vain.

The present crisis, which is obviously unprecedented, demands an entirely new approach to the problem of our existence. Throughout the world, man is frustrated and in sorrow, for all the avenues through which he has sought fulfillment have failed him. So far, the diagnosis and the remedy of this problem have been left to the specialists, and all specialization denies integrated action. We have divided life into departments, and each department has its own expert; and to these experts we have handed over our life to be shaped according to the pattern of their choice. We have therefore lost all sense of individual responsibility, and this irresponsibility denies self-confidence. The lack of confidence in oneself is the outcome of fear, and we try to cover up this fear through so-called collective action, through the search for immediate results, or through the sacrifice of the present for a future utopia. Confidence comes with action which is fully thought out and felt out.

Because we have allowed ourselves to become irresponsible, we have bred confusion, and out of our confusion we have chosen leaders who are themselves confused. This has led us to despair, to a deep and aching frustration; it has emptied our hearts, which do not respond eagerly and swiftly, and therefore we never find a new approach to our problems. All that we seem able to do, unfortunately, is to follow some leader, old or new, who promises to take us to another world of hope. Instead of understanding our own irresponsibility, we turn to some ideology or to some easily recognizable social activity. It requires intelligence to perceive clearly that the problem of existence is relationship, which must be approached directly and simply. Because we do not understand relationship, whether with the one or with the many, we look to the expert for the solution of our problems; but it is vain to rely on the specialists, for they can only think within the pattern of their conditioning. For the solution of this crisis, you and I must look to ourselves—not as of the East or of the West with a special culture of our own, but as human beings.

Now, we are challenged by war, by race and class, and by technology; and if our response to this challenge is not creatively adequate, we shall have to face greater disaster and greater sorrow. Our real difficulty is that we are so conditioned by our Eastern or Western outlook, or by some cunning ideology, that it has become almost impossible for us to think of the problem anew. You are either an Englishman, an Indian, a Russian, or an American, and you try to answer this challenge according to the pattern in which you have been brought up. But these problems cannot be adequately met as long as you are not free from your national, social, and political background or ideology; they can never be solved according to any system, whether of the left or of the right. The many human problems can be solved only when you and I understand our relationship to each other and to the collective—which is society. Nothing can live in isolation. To be is to be related, and because we refuse to see the truth of this, our relationship is fraught with conflict and pain. We have avoided the challenge by escaping into the abstraction called the mass. This escape has no true significance, for the mass is you and I. It is a fallacy to think in terms of the mass, for the mass is yourself in relationship with another; and if you do not understand this relationship, you become an amorphous entity exploited by the politician, the priest, and the expert.

The ideological warfare that is going on at the present time has its roots in the confusion which exists in your relationship with another. War is obviously the spectacular and bloody expression of your daily life. You create a society that represents you, and your governments are the reflection of your own confusion and lack of integration. Being unaware of this, you try to solve the problem of war merely on the economic or the ideological level. War will exist as long as there are nationalistic states with their sovereign governments and frontiers. The gathering round a table of the various national representatives will in no way end war, for how can there be goodwill as long as you cling to organized dogmas called religion, as long as you remain nationalistic, with particular ideologies backed up by fully armed sovereign governments? Until you see these things as a hindrance to peace and realize their cultivated falsehood, there can be no freedom from conflict, confusion, and antagonism; on the contrary, whatever you say or do will contribute directly to war.

The class and racial divisions which are destroying man are the outcome of the desire to be secure. Now, any kind of security, except the physiological, is really insecurity. That is, the pursuit of psychological security destroys physical security, and as long as we seek psychological security, which creates an acquisitive society, the needs of man can never be sanely and effectively organized. The effective organization of man's needs is the real function of technology, but when used for our psychological security, technology becomes a curse. Technological knowledge is intended for the use of man, but when the means have lost their true significance and are misapplied, then they ride the man—the machine becomes the master.

In this present civilization, man's happiness is lost because technological knowledge is being used for the psychological glorification of power. Power is the new religion, with its national and political ideologies; and this new religion, the worship of the state, has its own dogmas, priests, and inquisitions. In this process the freedom and the happiness of man are completely denied, for the means have become a way of postponing the end. But the means are the end; the two cannot be separated, and because we have separated them, we inevitably create a contradiction between the means and the end.

As long as we use technological knowledge for the advancement and glorification of the individual or of the group, the needs of man can never be sanely and effectively organized. It is this desire for psychological security through technological advancement that is destroying the physical security of man. There is sufficient scientific knowledge to feed, clothe, and shelter man, but the proper use of this knowledge is denied as long as there are separative nationalities with their sovereign governments and frontiers—which in turn give rise to class and racial strife. So, you are responsible for the continuance of this conflict between man and man. As long as you, the individual, are nationalistic and patriotic, as long as you hold to political and social ideologies, you are responsible for war because your relationship with another can only breed confusion and antagonism. Seeing the false as the false is the beginning of wisdom, and it is this truth alone that can bring happiness to you and so to the world.

As you are responsible for war, you must be responsible for peace. Those who creatively feel this responsibility must first free themselves psychologically from the causes of war and not merely plunge into organizing political peace groups—which will only breed further division and opposition.

Peace is not an idea opposed to war. Peace is a way of life, for there can be peace only when everyday living is understood. It is only this way of life that can effectively meet the challenge of war, of class, and of ever-increasing technological advancement. This way of life is not the way of the intellect. The worship of the intellect in opposition to life has led us all to our present frustration with its innumerable escapes. These escapes have become far more important than the understanding of the problem itself. The present crisis has come into being because of the worship of the intellect, and it is the intellect that has divided life into a series of opposing and contradictory actions; it is the intellect that has denied the unifying factor which is love. The intellect has filled the empty heart with the things of the mind, and it is only when the mind is aware of its own reasoning and is able to go beyond itself that there can be the enrichment of the heart. Only the incorruptible enrichment of the heart can bring peace to this mad and battling world.

Broadcast from All-India Radio in New Delhi, November 6, 1948

First Talk in New Delhi

Action is relationship, and we cannot live or exist without action. Action seems to produce constant friction, constant misunderstanding, and anxiety; and we see in the world that all organized action has most unfortunately led to a series of disasters. We see in the world about us confusion, misery, and conflicting desires; and realizing this world chaos, most thoughtful and earnest people—not the people who are playing at make-believe, but people who are really concerned—will naturally see the importance of thinking out the problem of action. There is mass action and individual action; and mass action has become an abstraction, a convenient escape for the individual. By thinking that this chaos, this misery, this disaster that is constantly arising, can somehow be transformed or brought to order by mass action, the individual becomes irresponsible. The mass is surely a fictitious entity; the mass is you and I. It is only when you and I do not understand the relationship of true action that we turn to the abstraction called the mass—and thereby become irresponsible in our action. For reform in action, we look either to a leader or to organized, collective action, which again is mass action. When we turn to a leader for direction in action, we invariably choose a person we think will help us to go beyond our own problems, our own misery. But, because we choose a leader out of our confusion, the leader himself is also confused. We do not choose a leader unlike ourselves; we cannot. We can only choose a leader who, like ourselves, is confused; therefore, such leaders, such guides, and so-called spiritual gurus invariably lead us to further confusion, to further misery. Since what we choose must be out of our own confusion, when we follow a leader we are only following our own confused self-projection. Therefore, such action, though it may produce an immediate result, invariably leads to further disaster.

So, we see that mass action, though in certain cases it may be worthwhile, is bound to lead to disaster, to confusion, and bring about irresponsibility on the part of the individual and that the following of a leader must also increase confusion. And yet we have to live. To live is to act; to be is to be related. There is no action without relationship, and we cannot live in isolation. There is no such thing as isolation. Life is to act and to be related. So, to understand the action which does not create further misery, further confusion, we have to understand ourselves with all our contradictions, our opposing elements, our many facets that are constantly in battle with each other. Until we understand ourselves, action must inevitably lead to further conflict, to further misery.

So, our problem is to act with understanding, and that understanding can come about only through self-knowledge. After all, the world is the projection of myself. What I am, the world is; the world is not different from me; the world is not opposed to me. The world and I are not separate entities. Society is myself; there are not two different processes. The world is my own extension, and to understand the world I have to understand myself. The individual is not in opposition to the mass, to society, because society is the individual. Society is the relationship between you and me and another. There is opposition between the individual and society only when the individual becomes irresponsible. So, our problem is considerable. There is an extraordinary crisis which faces every country, every person, every group. What relationship have we, you and I, to that crisis, and how shall we act? Where shall we begin so as to bring about a transformation? As I said, if we look to the mass, there is no way out because the mass implies a leader, and the mass is always exploited by the politician, the priest, and the expert. And since you and I make up the mass, we have to assume the responsibility for our own action; that is, we have to understand our own nature, we have to understand ourselves. To understand ourselves is not to withdraw from the world because to withdraw implies isolation, and we cannot live in isolation. So, we have to understand action in relationship, and that understanding depends on awareness of our own conflicting and contradictory nature.

I think it is foolish to conceive of a state in which there is peace and to which we can look. There can be peace and tranquillity only when we understand the nature of ourselves and not presuppose a state which we do not know. There may be a state of peace, but mere speculation about it is useless.

So, in order to act rightly, there must be right thinking; to think rightly there must be self-knowledge, and self-knowledge can come about only through relationship, not through isolation. Right thinking can come only in understanding ourselves, from which there springs right action. So, right action is that which comes out of the understanding of ourselves, not one part of ourselves, but the whole content of ourselves, our contradictory natures, all that we are. As we understand ourselves, there is right action, and from that action there is happiness. After all, it is happiness that we want, that most of us are seeking through various forms, through various escapes—escapes of social activity, of the bureaucratic world, of amusement, of worship and the repetition of phrases, of sex, and innumerable other escapes. But we see these escapes do not bring lasting happiness, they give only a temporary alleviation. Fundamentally, there is nothing true in them, no lasting delight, and I think we will find that delight, that ecstasy, that real joy of creative being, only when we understand ourselves. This understanding of ourselves is not easy; it needs a certain alertness, awareness. That alertness, that awareness, can come only when we do not condemn, when we do not justify, because the moment there is condemnation or justification, there is a putting an end to the process of understanding. When we condemn someone, we cease to understand that person, and when we identify ourselves with that person, we again cease to understand him. It is the same with ourselves. To observe, to be passively aware of what you are is most difficult, but out of that passive awareness there comes an understanding, there comes a transformation of *what is,* and it is only that transformation which opens the door to reality.

Our problem, then, is action, understanding, and happiness. There is no foundation for true thinking unless we know ourselves. Without knowing myself, I have no foundation for thought—I can only live in a state of contradiction, as most of us do. To bring about a transformation in the world, which is the world of my relationship, I must begin with myself. You may say, "To bring about transformation in the world that way will take an infinitely long time." If we are seeking immediate results, naturally we will think it takes too long. The immediate results are promised by the politicians, but I am afraid for the man seeking truth there is no immediate result. It is truth that transforms, not the immediate action; it is only the discovery of truth by each one that will bring about happiness and peace in the world. To live in the world and yet not be of the world is our problem, and it is a problem of earnest pursuit because we cannot withdraw, we cannot renounce, but we have to understand ourselves. The understanding of oneself is the beginning of wisdom. To understand oneself is to understand one's relationship with things, people, and ideas. Until we understand the full significance and meaning of our relationship with things, people, and ideas, action—which is relationship—will inevitably bring about conflict and strife. So, a man who is really earnest must begin with himself, he must be passively aware of all his thoughts, feelings, and actions. Again, this is not a matter of time. There is no end to self-knowledge. Self-knowledge is only from moment to moment, and therefore there is a creative happiness from moment to moment.

So, as all of us are concerned with right action, with peace and happiness, these things can come about only through the understanding of our own complex natures. That understanding is not of great difficulty, but it demands a certain earnestness, certain pliability of mind. When there is constant, passive awareness of our speech, of our thoughts and feelings, without condemnation or justification, that very awareness brings its own action and therefore its own transformation—which is not a result of our efforts to transform ourselves. But for that truth to be, there must be a quality of receptivity in which there is no demand, no fear, no desire; and that can come into being only when there is passive awareness.

We will discuss all these things during the next few weeks, but now I will answer some questions. To have the right answer, there must be a right question. Anybody can put a question. But to find the answer to a question, we must study the problem itself and not the answer because the answer is contained in the problem. There is an art in looking into a problem and understanding it. So, when I deal with your questions, please do not wait for an answer because you and I are going to think out the problem together and find the answer in the problem. But if you merely wait for an answer, I am afraid you will be disappointed. Life has no categorical yes or no, although that is what we would like. Life is more complex than that, more subtle. So, to find the answer we must study the problem, which means we must have the patience and intelligence to go into it.

Question: What place has organized religion in modern society?

KRISHNAMURTI: Let us find out what we mean by religion and what we mean by modern society? What do we mean by religion? What does religion mean to you? It means, does it not, a set of beliefs, rituals, dogmas, many superstitions, puja, the repetition of words, vague, unfulfilled, frustrated hopes, reading certain books, pursuing gurus, going to the temple occasionally, and so on. Surely, all that is religion to most of our people. But is that religion? Is religion a custom, a habit, a tradition? Surely, religion is something far beyond all that, is it not? Religion implies the search for reality, which has nothing whatever to do with organized belief, temples, dogmas, or rituals; and yet our thinking, the very fabric of our being, is enmeshed, caught up in beliefs, superstitions, and so on. So, obviously, modern man is not religious; therefore, his society is not a sane, balanced society. We may follow certain doctrines, worship certain pictures, or create a new religion of the state, but obviously, all these things are not religion. I said that religion is the search for reality, but that reality is unknown; it is not the reality of the books, it is not the experience of others. To find that reality, to uncover it, to invite it, the known must stop; the significance of all the traditions and beliefs must be gone into, understood, and discarded. For this, the repetition of rituals has no meaning. So, a man who is religious obviously does not belong to any religion, to any organization; he is neither Hindu nor Muslim, he does not belong to any class.

Now, what is the modern world? The modern world is made up of technique and efficiency in mass organizations. There is an extraordinary advancement in technology and a maldistribution of mass needs; the means of production are in the hands of a few, there are conflicting nationalities, constantly recurring wars because of sovereign governments, and so on. That is the modern world, is it not? There is technical advancement without an equally vital psychological advancement, and so there is a state of unbalance; there are extraordinary scientific achievements, and at the same time human misery, empty hearts, and empty minds. Many of the techniques we have learned have to do with building airplanes, killing each other, and so on. So, that is the modern world, which is yourself. The world is not different from you. Your world, which is yourself, is a world of the cultivated intellect and the empty heart. If you look into yourselves, you will see that you are the very product of modern civilization. You know how to do a few tricks, technical, physical tricks, but you are not creative human beings. You produce children, but that is not creative. To be able to create, one needs extraordinary inward richness, and that richness can come about only when we understand truth, when we are capable of receiving truth.

So, organized religion and the modern world go together—they both cultivate the empty heart, and that is the unfortunate part of our existence. We are superficial, intellectually brilliant, capable of great inventions, producing the most destructive means of liquidating each other, and creating more and more division between ourselves. But we do not know what it means to love; we have no song in our hearts. We play the gramophone, listen to the radio, but there is no singing because our hearts are empty. We have created a world that is utterly confused, miserable; and our relationships are flimsy, superficial. Yes, organized religion and the modern world go together because both lead to confusion, and this confusion of organized religion and the modern world is the outcome of ourselves. They are the self-projected expressions of ourselves. So, there can be no transformation in the world outside unless there is a transformation within the skin of each one of us; and to bring about that transformation is not the problem of the expert, of the specialist, of the leader, or the priest. It is the problem of each one of us. If we leave it to others, we become irresponsible, and therefore our hearts become empty. An empty heart with a technical mind is not a creative human being; and because we have lost that creative state, we have produced a world that is utterly miserable, confused, broken by wars, torn by class and racial distinctions. So, it is our responsibility to bring about a radical transformation within ourselves.

Question: I am in conflict and suffering. For thousands of years we have been told of the causes of suffering and the way of its cessation, and yet we are where we are today. Is it possible to end this suffering?

KRISHNAMURTI: I wonder how many of us are aware that we are suffering. Are you aware, not theoretically but actually, that you are in conflict? And if you are, what do you do? You try to escape from it, don't you? The moment one is aware of this conflict and suffering, one tries to forget it in intellectual pursuits, in work, or in seeking enjoyment, pleasure. One seeks an escape from suffering, and all escapes are the same, are they not, whether they are cultured or crude. What do we mean by conflict? When are you aware that you are in conflict? Conflict arises, surely, when there is the consciousness of the 'me'. There is awareness of the conflict only when the 'me' suddenly becomes conscious of itself; otherwise, you lead a monotonous, superficial, dull, routine life, don't you? You are aware of yourself only when there is conflict, and as long as everything is moving smoothly without a contradiction, without a frustration, there is no consciousness of yourself in action. As long as I am not pushed around, as long as I am getting what I want, I am not in conflict, but the moment I am blocked, I am aware of myself and become miserable. In other words, conflict arises only when there is a sense of 'myself' facing a frustration in action. So, what do we want? We want to have an action which is constantly self-fulfilling, without frustration; that is, we want to live without being blocked. In other words, we want our desires fulfilled, and as long as those desires are not fulfilled, there is conflict, there is contradiction. So, our problem is how to fulfill, how to achieve self-fulfillment without frustration. I want to possess something—property, a person, a title, or what you will—and if I can get it and go on getting what I want, then I am happy, there is no contradiction. So, what we are seeking is self-fulfillment, and as long as we can achieve that fulfillment, there is no friction.

Now, the question is, is there such a thing as self-fulfillment? That is, can I achieve something, become something, realize something? And in that desire, is there not a constant battle? That is, as long as I crave to become something, to achieve something, to fulfill myself, there must be frustration, there must be fear, there must be conflict; and therefore, is there such a thing as self-fulfillment? What do we mean by self-fulfillment? By self-fulfillment we mean self-expansion—the 'me' becoming wider, greater, more important; the 'me' becoming the governor, the executive, the bank manager, and so on. Now, if you go into it a little more deeply, you will see that as long as there is this action of the self, that is, as long as there is self-consciousness in action, there must be frustration; therefore, there must be suffering. Hence our problem is not how to overcome suffering, how to put aside conflict, but to understand the nature of the self, the 'me'. I hope I am not making this too complicated. If we merely try to overcome conflict, try to put sorrow aside, we do not understand the nature of the creator of sorrow.

As long as thought is concerned with its own improvement, its own transformation, its own advancement, there must be conflict and contradiction. So, we come back to the obvious fact that conflict, suffering, will exist as long as I do not understand myself. Therefore, to understand oneself is more important than to know how to overcome sorrow and conflict. We can go further into all this later. But to escape from sorrow through rituals, through amusements, through beliefs, or any other form of distraction is to take your thought further and further away from the central issue, which is to understand yourself. To understand suffering, there must be cessation of all escapes, for only then are you able to face yourself in action; and in understanding yourself in action—which is relationship—you will find a way of completely freeing thought from all conflict and living in a state of happiness, of reality.

Question: We live, but we know not why. To so many of us, life seems to have no meaning. Can you tell us the meaning and purpose of our living?

KRISHNAMURTI: Now, why do you ask this question? Why are you asking me to tell you the meaning of life, the purpose of life? What do we mean by life? Does life have a meaning, a purpose? Is not living in itself its own purpose, its own meaning? Why do we want more? Because, we are so dissatisfied with our life, our life is so empty, so tawdry, so monotonous; doing the same thing over and over again, we want something more, something beyond what we are doing. Since our everyday life is so empty, so dull, so meaningless, so boring, so intolerably stupid, we say life must have a fuller meaning; and that is why you ask this question. Surely, sir, a man who is living richly, a man who sees things as they are and is content with what he has is not confused; he is clear, therefore, he does not ask what is the purpose of life. For him the very living is the beginning and the end. So, our difficulty is that since our life is empty, we want to find a purpose of life and strive for it. Such a purpose of life can only be mere intellection without any reality, and when the purpose of life is pursued by a stupid, dull mind, by an empty heart, that purpose will also be empty. Therefore, our problem is how to make our life rich, not with money and all the rest of it, but inwardly rich—which is not something cryptical. When you say that the purpose of life is to be happy, the purpose of life is to find God, surely that desire to find God is an escape from life, and your God is merely a thing that is known. You can only make your way towards an object that you know, and if you build a staircase to the thing that you call God, surely that is not God. Reality can be understood only in living, not in escape. When you seek a purpose of life, you are really escaping and not understanding what life is. Life is relationship, life is action in relationship, and when I do not understand relationship, or when relationship is confused, then I seek a fuller meaning. Why are our lives so empty? Why are we so lonely, frustrated? Because, we have never looked into ourselves. We never admit to ourselves that this life is all we know, and that it should therefore be understood fully and completely. We prefer to run away from ourselves, and that is why we seek the purpose of life away from relationship. But if we begin to understand action, which is our relationship with people, with property, with beliefs and ideas, then we will find that relationship itself brings its own reward. You do not have to seek. It is like seeking love. Can you find love by seeking it? Love cannot be cultivated. You will find love only in relationship, not outside of relationship, and it is because we have no love that we want a purpose of life. When there is love, which is its own eternity, then there is no search for God, because love is God.

It is because our minds are full of technicalities and superstitious mutterings that our lives are so empty, and that is why we seek a purpose beyond ourselves. To find life's purpose we must go through the door of ourselves, but consciously or unconsciously we avoid facing things as they are in themselves, and so we want God to open for us a door which is beyond. This question about the purpose of life is put only by him who does not love, and love can be found only in action, which is relationship.

Question: The only thing that gives zest to life is the desire to do something worthwhile. You tell us that this is a false step. If this incentive to work is removed, what is left?

KRISHNAMURTI: Sir, why do we want an incentive to work, why do we want an incentive to do anything? What do we mean by "incentive"? We want a reward for our action, do we not? We may not seek money, an objective reward, but we want a psychological reward, a psychological incentive for what we do. That is why we go to a guru. It is incentive that makes us act; otherwise, psychologically we would not live at all. That is, psychologically, inwardly, we want rewards—reward for our search, reward for our thinking, for our feeling. That is a fact, is it not? And what is the reward that we want? Inevitably, it is gratification. As long as we can find psychological gratification, we will do something. So, what we are seeking is constant gratification, constant satisfaction, and when that is denied, we feel frustrated.

Now, is there gratification, is there ever a lasting gratification? Or is there only temporary gratification that inevitably brings conflict, pain? So, we have to find out for ourselves if there is a permanent gratification. We may put aside the obviously temporary gratifications because we see that they bring misfortunes, frustrations, anxieties, fear, and so on; but we think we can find a lasting, an enduring gratification which we call truth, God, and for that we want to work. But is there such a thing as permanent gratification? That is, is there permanent psychological security? You have invented the permanent psychological security as God, as a continuous living after death, and so on. But is there such complete gratification, security? Or is it that the mind, not knowing what is in the future—the future being uncertain—projects its own creation as a certainty? That is, the mind moves from the unknown to the known; it cannot move to the unknown; therefore, it wants an assurance of the next known, and when the next known is questioned, we become anxious.

So, while physical security is necessary, there is no such thing as permanent psychological security, and the moment you have that security, which is self-projected, you become lazy, contented, and stagnant. But when there is no security, then you must have a mind that is living from moment to moment, therefore living in uncertainty; and the mind that is uncertain, the mind that does not know, that is not seeking gratification, is creative. That creative state of being comes about only when the mind is completely silent, when it is not seeking, when it is not looking for a reward. Then there is abiding peace, and because we do not know how to arrive at that state, we seek gratification and hold it, and that gratification becomes the incentive for action. But gratification, however refined, entails endless fear, anxiety, doubt, violence, and all the rest. But if the mind understands itself and thereby finds that state in which there is complete tranquillity, then creation takes place, and that creation is itself the total end of all existence.

November 14, 1948

Second Talk in New Delhi

To continue what we were talking about last Sunday, it seems to me that it is important to understand that conflict of any kind does not produce creative thinking. Until we understand conflict and the nature of conflict and what it is that one is in conflict with, merely to struggle with a problem or with a particular background or environment is utterly useless. Just as all wars create deterioration and inevitably produce further wars, further misery, so to struggle with conflict leads to further confusion. So, conflict within oneself, projected outwardly, creates confusion in the world. It is therefore necessary, is it not, to understand conflict and to see that conflict of any kind is not productive of creative thinking, of sane human beings. And yet all our life is spent in struggle, and we think that struggle is a necessary part of existence. There is conflict within oneself and with the environment—environment being society—which in turn is our relationship with people, with things, and with ideas. This struggle is considered as inevitable, and we think that struggle is essential for the process of existence. Now, is that so? Is there any way of living which excludes struggle, in which there is a possibility of understanding without the usual conflict? I do not know whether you have noticed that the more you struggle with a psychological problem, the more confused and entangled you get; and that it is only when there is cessation of struggle, of all thought process, that understanding comes. So, we will have to inquire if conflict is essential and if conflict is productive.

Now, we are talking about conflict in ourselves and with the environment. The environment is what one is in oneself. You and the environment are not two different processes; you are the environment, and the environment is you—which is an obvious fact. You are born into a particular group of people, whether in India, America, Russia, or England, and that very environment with its influences of climate, tradition, social and religious custom creates you—and you are that environment. To find out if there is something more than merely the result of environment, you have to be free of the environment, free of its conditioning. That is obvious, is it not? If you look carefully into yourself, you will see that, being born in this country, you are climatically, socially, religiously, and economically its product or result. That is, you are conditioned, and to find out if there is something more, something greater than the mere result of a condition, you have to be free of that condition. Being conditioned, merely to inquire if there is something more, something greater than the mere product of environment, has no meaning. Obviously, one must be free of the condition, of the environment, and then only can we find out if there is something more. To assert that there is or is not something more is surely a wrong way of thinking. One has to discover, and to discover one has to experiment.

So, to understand this environment and be free of it in ourselves, not only is it necessary to know all the hidden, stored-up influences in the unconscious, but to know what we are in conflict with. As we have seen, each one of us is the result of environment, and we are not separate from environment. So, what is it that we are in conflict with? What is it that responds to environment? What is the thing we call struggle? We are in constant battle—but with what? We are struggling with the environment, and yet, since we are part of the environment, our struggle is only a process separating us from the environment. Therefore, there is no understanding of the environment, but merely a conflict. That is, to put it differently, if there is understanding of the environment without struggle, there is no self-consciousness. After all, you are self-conscious only when there is conflict. If there is no conflict, you are not conscious of yourself in action. You are conscious of yourself in action only when there is a conclusion, when there is frustration, when you want to do something but are prevented. When you want to achieve something and are blocked, there is frustration, and then only there is awareness of conflict or self-consciousness.

Now, what is it that we are struggling with? With our problems, are we not? What are the problems? The problems arise only in relationship; they do not exist independently of relationship. So, as long as I do not understand myself in relation to environment, which is my relationship with things, with property, with ideas, and with human beings—whether my wife, my neighbor, or my particular group—as long as I do not understand my relationship with environment, there must be conflict. Environment is relationship, which is action with regard to things, people, and ideas. As long as I do not understand relationship, there must be conflict, and this conflict separates me as an entity different from the environment. I do not know if this is a little too abstract, and in any case we will discuss it further on Tuesdays, Thursdays, and Saturdays. But I think it is important to understand this point because if we can understand the significance of conflict, perhaps we shall approach the problem differently.

So, we do not understand environment—environment being relationship in action—and relationship exists only between yourself and things, people, and ideas. Since we do not understand environment, there is conflict, that is, self-consciousness, and therefore there is a process of separation between you and the environment. It is this conflict that creates separation; the individual as the 'I' is born out of the conflict, and then the 'I' wants to achieve, positively or negatively. So, conflict inevitably creates a separative process, creates the individual as apart from the group, from the community, and so on. This separative process of the 'I' only emphasizes and strengthens the conflict which we see in daily life.

Now, is it possible to live without conflict? Because, conflict invariably increases the separative process, and therefore there is no way out of it. There is a way out only when conflict ceases. Is it possible to live without conflict? To find out if it is possible to live without conflict, we must understand what we mean by living. What do we mean by living? Surely, we mean the process of relationship because there is no living in isolation. Nothing can live in isolation. By living we mean, do we not, the extensive process of relationship—relationship in action. Now, is it possible to understand relationship and not create out of relationship a conflict? Is it possible for relationship to be without conflict? Please see the importance of this—that as long as there is conflict, there is no creative thinking and living. Conflict only accentuates separation and further strengthens the conflict. Is it possible to live, to be in relationship, without conflict? I say it is possible only if you understand relationship and do not resist it. That is, I have to understand my psychological relationship with things, with people, and with ideas. Is it possible to understand that conflict, and is conflict necessary for understanding? That is, do I have to struggle with the problem to understand the problem? Or is there a different approach?

I say there is a different approach to the problem of conflict, with which you can experiment for yourself, and that is to understand the significance of conflict. That is, when I struggle with a problem, a human problem or even an abstract problem of mathematics or physics, the mind is kept in agitation—it is worried. Surely an agitated, worried mind is incapable of understanding. Understanding comes when the mind is nonviolent, not when it is in battle with a problem. We have problems with regard to property, with regard to people, and with regard to ideas—and I shall deal with these on the following Sundays—but the first thing to realize, it seems to me, is that no form of conflict produces right understanding. It is only when I understand a problem that it ceases, and to understand a problem I must not only think about it but be capable of leaving it alone. I do not know whether you have noticed that when you have a problem you worry over it like a dog over a bone. You think about it all day long, and at the end of the day you are exhausted and you put it aside, you sleep on it, and then suddenly you find the answer. This happens to most people. Why? Surely, it is very simple. The conscious mind, worrying over the problem, is not capable of looking at it completely without seeking an answer. The conscious mind wants an answer to that problem; therefore, it is not concerned with the problem but with the answer. The conscious mind not only wants an answer, but it does not want to go into the whole problem itself. Therefore, the conscious mind is avoiding the problem and looking for an answer. But the answer is in the problem, not away from it. So, there must be the investigation of the problem completely, without seeking an answer, so that the mind can be quiet, still. I will presently take this up with regard to our relationship with people, with things, and with ideas and see if we cannot be free of our problems immediately without going through the conflict which only confuses the problem.

Now I am going to answer the questions given to me. The repetition of truth prevents the understanding of truth, which means that repetition of truth is a hindrance. Truth cannot be repeated. You can read a book about truth, but mere repetition of a statement from the book is not truth. The word *truth* is not truth, the word is not the thing. To find that which is truth is to experience directly, independently of the word. So, in considering these questions, please let us bear in mind that we are undertaking a journey together to discover things together; therefore, there is no danger of the relationship of pupil and teacher. You are not here as the spectator to watch me play; we are both playing; therefore, neither of us is exploiting the other.

Question: What is meditation, and how to do it?

KRISHNAMURTI: As it is an enormous and very complex problem, let us go very carefully into the whole question. First of all, let us approach it negatively because to think positively about something we do not know is to continue the problem, and we do not know what meditation is. We have been told the way we should meditate, how we should concentrate, what we should do and not do, and all that—but that cannot be meditation. So, we must approach the problem of meditation negatively to find out what it is. To approach it positively and say this or that is meditation is obviously repetition because you have been told what meditation is, and you are merely repeating what you have been told. Therefore it is not meditation but mere repetition. I do not know if you follow what I am talking about. Perhaps it will be clearer as we go along. If we can see what meditation is not, then there is a possibility of finding out what meditation is. Surely, that is the way of investigation and rational approach. So, let us find out.

Now, concentration is not meditation. We shall see what that means. Concentration implies exclusiveness. I hope you are interested in all this because to discuss with somebody who is not interested is rather a trial for me as well as for you who are not interested. I shall tell you why you should be interested in this question: because it opens up an enormous field in human consciousness. Without understanding that consciousness, you have no basis for action. To me, to join parties, repeat slogans, and so on, has no meaning. In understanding this problem of meditation, I am understanding the whole problem of living. Meditation is not apart from living, as I shall show presently.

I said that concentration is not meditation. What do we mean by concentration? I do not know if you have ever tried to concentrate. When you try to concentrate, what are you doing? You are choosing one interest among a great many and trying to focus your attention on that particular interest. It is not an interest really, but you think you ought to be interested in it. That is, you think you ought to meditate about higher things, and that is one interest among a great many, so you choose to concentrate on it and exclude all other interests. That is what actually takes place when you concentrate. Therefore, such concentration is an exclusive process. Now, what happens when you are trying to concentrate on a picture, an image, or an idea? What is happening? Other thoughts come in, and you try to brush them aside, and the more you brush them aside, the more they come in. So, you spend your time in resisting and in trying to develop a particular idea. This process is called concentration—the effort to fix your mind on one interest which you have chosen and exclude all other interests. That is what we mean by concentration.

Now, to understand something you must give your full attention to it—full attention being attention that has no obstruction. You must give your whole being, and then you understand something. But what happens when you try to concentrate and at the same time resist? You are trying to follow along a certain track, but your mind is continually going off in another direction, and you are not giving your full attention. You are giving only partial attention, and therefore there is no understanding. Therefore, concentration does not help towards understanding, and it is very important to understand this point. Where there is exclusiveness of attention, there must be distraction. If I try to force my attention to focus on one thing, then the mind is resisting something else. That resistance is distraction. Therefore, where there is conflict between attention and distraction, there is no concentration at all. It is a battle, and that battle goes on until the mind, weary of the struggle, settles upon the chosen interest. Surely, to settle upon the chosen interest is not meditation. It is merely craving, the resistance and exclusiveness of choice. Such a mind is a dull mind. Such a mind is insensitive; it is incapable of response because it has spent itself in resisting, excluding, wasted its energy in the conflict between distraction and attention. It has lost its elasticity, the power to reveal glory; therefore it is a decadent mind and is incapable of quickness and pliability. So, meditation is not concentration.

Now, meditation is not prayer. Let us examine what we are doing when we pray. What actually takes place, psychologically, when we pray? What do we mean by prayer? The repetition of certain phrases, supplication, and petition. When I pray, I petition a higher entity, a higher intelligence, to clear up my vision, to free me from a difficulty, to help me to understand a problem, or to grant me comfort or happiness. So, prayer generally implies supplication or petition, either to be helped out of one's difficulty or to receive a response—which I shall explain presently. Now, I do not know if you have prayed. Probably some have. What happens when you pray? Don't deny it by saying it is nonsense, because millions pray, and they must receive a response; otherwise, they would not do it. Whether or not that response is truth, we are going to find out. Now, what happens when you pray? By repeating certain phrases or words, by repeating certain charms, the mind becomes quiet. So, part of the function of prayer is to drug the mind into quietness, because when the mind is quiet, it is able to receive. That is, by sitting down or kneeling, by clasping one's hands and repeating certain phrases, the mind naturally subsides; and in that quiet state, it is capable of receiving. Now, what does it receive? It receives the answer it is seeking, and then I say that God has spoken to me, that my prayers have been answered and I have found a way out of my difficulties. Therefore I say that in prayer I find reality. But what has actually happened? The superficial conscious mind, which has been agitated, becomes quiet; and in that quiet state it is capable of receiving the intimations of the hidden, of the unconscious mind, and those intimations are the things which I want. Can these answers be from God or reality? Surely, it is a most extraordinary idea we have—that God is so awfully interested in us that when we have by our greed, envy, and violence created a mess in the world, we have only to pray and he will answer. That is the way a Hitler prays, the Catholics pray, the Allies pray—and this country also prays to God. Where is the difference? We all want an answer that will be gratifying, and since prayer is a means of gratification, the answer will be gratifying. Whether you call it the inner voice or the voice of reality, it is always gratifying. Therefore, prayer is a means of quieting the mind in order to find or receive gratification. As long as the mind is seeking gratification, it is not in search of reality. As long as the mind is seeking comfort, refuge, it is not capable of receiving the unknown; it is capable of receiving only that which is known, which is its own self-projection. That is why prayer is gratifying and why it finds a gratifying answer.

So, concentration is not meditation, and prayer is not meditation. Nor is devotion meditation, obviously. What are you devoted to? When you say, "I am of a devotional nature, I am devoted to something," what do you mean by devotion? You are devoted to something which in return gratifies you; you are not devoted to something which creates trouble. You are devoted to something that pleases you, that brings satisfaction, a sense of security, of well-being, that makes you sentimental; and that thing which you are devoted to is a projection of yourself. What you are devoted to gives you subtle satisfaction, positively or negatively, and therefore your devotion is not meditation.

Then what is meditation? If concentration, prayer, and devotion are not meditation, then what is meditation? Obviously, meditation begins with the understanding of oneself. To understand yourself is to be aware of yourself in action, which is to see what is actually taking place when you concentrate, when you pray, when you are devoted. It is a process in which you are discovering yourself. You can discover yourself only in relationship, which is action. After all, if you see what is happening when you concentrate, then you are discovering the ways of your own thinking; when you look into concentration, you begin to discover yourself in operation, and therefore through concentration you are beginning to understand yourself. Similarly, you begin to see yourself in operation when you are praying or when you are feeling devotion. As you discover all the implications of prayer and devotion, you begin to understand yourself. So, when you trace the process of thought with regard to concentration, with regard to prayer, with regard to devotion, you are discovering yourself in relation to those things—and all this is a process of meditation.

So, meditation is the beginning of self-knowledge—knowledge of oneself as one is and not as one should be. The desire to be something else is a barrier to seeing yourself as you are. Meditation is awareness without condemnation of every thought, every feeling, every word. The moment you condemn, you put into motion another thought process, and self-discovery ceases. After all, as I said, meditation is a process of self-discovery, and that self-discovery is without an end. Therefore, meditation is an eternal, timeless process. To understand that which is timeless, which is unknown, which is real, which cannot be put into words—to realize that, the thought processes must be completely understood; and it can be understood, not in abstraction, not in isolation, but only in relationship. There is no such thing as isolation. A man who sits in an enclosed room or withdraws to a jungle or a mountain is still related; he cannot escape relationship. And it is only through relationship that I am capable of knowing myself and, therefore, knowing how to meditate.

Meditation, then, is the beginning of understanding, meditation is the beginning of self-knowledge. Without meditation, there is no self-knowledge; without self-knowledge, there is no meditation. So, you must begin to know what you are. You cannot go far without beginning near, without understanding your daily process of thought, feeling, and action. In other words, thought must understand its own working, and when you see yourself in operation, you will observe that thought moves from the known to the known. You cannot think about the unknown. That which you know is not real because what you know is only in time. To be free from the net of time is the important concern, not to think about the unknown, because you cannot think about the unknown. The answers to your prayers are of the known. To receive the unknown, the mind itself must become the unknown. The mind is the result of the thought process, the result of time, and this thought process must come to an end. The mind cannot think of that which is eternal, timeless; therefore, the mind must be free of time, the time process of the mind must be dissolved. Only when the mind is completely free from yesterday, and is therefore not using the present as a means to the future, is it capable of receiving the eternal. That which is known has no relationship with the unknown. Therefore you cannot pray to the unknown, you cannot concentrate on the unknown, you cannot be devoted to the unknown. All that has no meaning. What has meaning is to find out how the mind operates, it is to see yourself in action. Therefore, our concern in meditation is to know oneself, not only superficially, but the whole content of the inner, hidden consciousness. Without knowing all that and being free of its conditioning, you cannot possibly go beyond the mind's limits. That is why the thought process must cease, and for this cessation there must be knowledge of oneself. Therefore meditation is the beginning of wisdom, which is the understanding of one's own mind and heart.

This is a matter of life and death because if you understand what I have been saying, it will produce a revolution in your life, a devastating experience. But if it is merely verbal, a casual amusement instead of going to the cinema, then you can go on merely listening without disturbance. But if you know how to listen, you will be tremendously moved, and therefore a revolution is possible. So, sir, please do not merely listen to the words, for words have very little meaning. But most of us are fed on words without any substance; we cannot think without words, and to think without words is negative thinking, which is the highest form of thinking. That is not possible when words are important, when the word is the end. Take the word *God*. When the word God is used, you get very excited, you get psychologically thrilled, which means that the word is important and not the thing the word represents. So, you are caught in the net of words. The man who is seeking the real does not confuse the word, the language, with that which it represents.

I hope you don't mind if I answer another question.

Question: Does not interest in a thing, a person, or an idea bring about an effortless but nonetheless exclusive concentration on the object of interest?

KRISHNAMURTI: I have not seen the question before, so I am going to think it out with you. The questioner wants to know, if I interpret him rightly, when one is interested in something, is there not effortlessness and at the same time exclusive attention? That is, when I am interested in understanding a problem and pay attention to it, is that attention not exclusive? The second point is, if one has interest, is there not effortlessness?

Now, what do we mean by interest? Can we honestly say that we are interested in only one thing? Obviously, that would not be a true statement. We are interested in many things. Our attention is focused sometimes on one thing, sometimes on another. Whenever a particular interest attracts our attention, it creates a disturbance, and then we pay attention. That is what actually takes place. That is, I have many interests, I am an entity of many masks. From among these entities with many interests, I choose one, thinking that it will help me. What happens when I do so? When I am concentrating my attention, I am really excluding other interests. Surely, when I focus my attention on one interest, my attention is exclusive; therefore, though I am interested in other things, I try to shut them out. That is, I have many interests, and I choose one interest and try to fix my attention on it, and when I do that, I create resistance, which means a state of struggle, of pain. There is effortlessness only when there is an understanding of all the interests, and not the exclusive choice of one interest because, after all, you are not made up of one interest. You are the total of many variable and multiple interests, and these are being modified all the time, and to choose one interest and focus your mind upon it is to make the mind narrow, petty, and exclusive. Such a mind cannot understand. Whereas, a mind that sees the significance of each interest as it arises from moment to moment is capable of extensive awareness, extensive feeling. Look at what is happening in this hall right now. You are paying attention to what I am saying. You are not exclusive, are you? You are listening to the truth of *what is,* which is an obvious fact, so your awareness is extensive and not limited. You are just allowing yourself to see and enjoy. There is no effort, but your attention is fully focused without any resistance or exclusion. It is an extraordinary thing if you go into it. We are extensive, and yet we can pay attention to the particular. Concentration on the particular destroys extensive awareness, whereas if you are capable of being extensively aware, then you can give attention to the particular without resistance. I do not know if you see the beauty of it. Sir, that is love, isn't it? Love is extensive; therefore, you can give love to the particular. But most of us have not this extensive love, and therefore we go to the particular, and the particular destroys us.

So, there is attention which is effortless, which alone brings about understanding when the multiple and variable interests are taken together and understood. But when the attention is focused on one interest to the exclusion of other interests, such attention is exclusive and destructive; it makes the mind narrow and is therefore a deteriorating factor. The narrow mind may produce immediate results, but it cannot understand extensively; but when the mind is extensive, it can include the particular also. This elasticity, pliability, swiftness of the mind, cannot come about if there is resistance; therefore, one has to be aware of and understand the many interests and not resist them. As each interest comes up, look at it; don't condemn or justify it, but go into it, absorb it fully and completely. It does not matter whether it is a sexual interest, the desire to be somebody, or any other interest. Go into each interest and feel its implications, think it out; and then you will find that the mind is capable of being extensively aware of every interest, seeing the implications of it immediately without going into it step by step. Surely, such a mind is essential for understanding the real because the real, that which is true, is not exclusive. The mind is exclusive because we have trained it to deal only with the particular, forced it to focus on one interest and exclude other interests. Therefore, it is incapable of receiving that which is limitless. Though you may read about the limitless and repeat what you read, by doing so you are merely hypnotizing yourself. Whereas, if you can look at each interest without condemnation or justification, without identifying yourself, if you can be aware of its whole content, then you will see that the mind, being free, is both swift and very slow. It is like a high-powered and perfectly balanced engine—though it can run at great speed, it can go very slowly also. It is only then that the mind is capable of receiving the intimations of the real. Whereas, a mind that is exclusive, limited, conditioned, can never understand that which is eternal. To understand the eternal is to understand oneself. When there are multiple interests, we have to understand each interest as it arises, and only then can there be that freedom in which the real is discovered.

November 28, 1948

Third Talk in New Delhi

As this is the last talk, perhaps it might be just as well if I made a brief summary of what we have been discussing for the last six weeks. Our life is beset with so many problems at different levels. We have not only the physical problems, but the much more subtle and more intricate psychological problems; and without solving the psychological problems or even trying to understand their subtleness, we seek merely to rearrange their effects. We try to reconcile the effects without really understanding the causes which produce these effects. Therefore, it seems to me much more important to understand the psychological conflicts and sorrows than merely to rearrange the pattern of effects because the mere reconciliation of effects cannot profoundly and ultimately solve the problems that are produced. If we merely rearrange the effects without understanding the psychological struggles that produce these effects, we will naturally produce further confusion, further antagonism, further conflict. So, in understanding the psychological factors that bring about our well-being, there may be a possibility—and I think there is a definite possibility—of creating a new culture and a new civilization; but it must begin with every one of us because, after all, society is my relationship with you and your relationship with another. Society is the outcome of our relationship, and without understanding relationship, which is action, there can be no cessation of conflict. So, relationship and its effect and cause must be thoroughly understood before I can transform or bring about a radical revolution in the ways of my life.

We are concerned, then, with the individual problem and our own psychological sufferings. In understanding the individual problem we will naturally bring about a different arrangement in its effects, but we should not begin with the effects because, after all, we do not live by the effects alone but by the deeper causes. So, our problem is how to understand suffering and conflict in the individual. Mere verbal explanation of suffering, mere intellection, the perception of the causes of suffering, does not resolve suffering. That is an obvious fact, but as most of us are fed on words, and as words have become of such immense importance, we are easily satisfied by explanations. We read the Bhagavad-Gita, the Bible, or any other religious book which explains the cause of suffering, and we are satisfied; we take the explanation for the resolution of suffering. Words have become much more significant than the understanding of suffering itself, but the word is not the thing. Any amount of explanation, any amount of reasoning, will not feed a hungry man. What he wants is food, not the explanation of food or the smell of food. He is hungry, and he must have the substance that nourishes. Most of us are satisfied by the explanation of the cause of suffering. Therefore, we don't take suffering as a thing to be radically resolved, a contradiction in ourselves that must be understood. How is one to understand suffering? One can understand suffering only when explanation subsides and all kinds of escapes are understood and put aside, that is, when one sees the actual in suffering. But you see, you don't want to understand suffering; you run away to the club, you read the newspaper, you do puja, go to the temple, plunge into politics, or social service—anything rather than to face that which is. So, the cultivation of escapes has become much more important than the understanding of sorrow; and it requires a very intelligent mind, a mind that is very alert, to see that it is escaping and to put an end to escapes.

Now, I have explained that conflict is not productive of creative thinking. To be creative, to produce what you will, the mind must be at peace, the heart full. If you want to write, to have great thoughts, to inquire into truth, conflict must cease; but in our civilization, escapes have become much more significant than the understanding of conflict. Modern things help us to escape, and to escape is to be utterly uncreative—it is self-projection. That does not solve our problem. What does solve our problem is to cease to escape and to live with suffering because, after all, to understand something one must give full attention to it, and distractions are mere escapes. To understand escapes, which is to put an end to them by seeing their falseness, and to perceive the whole significance of suffering is a process of self-knowledge; and without self-knowledge, without knowing yourself fundamentally—not the mere superficial effects of your actions, but the whole total process of yourself, both the thinker and the thought, the actor and the action—without that self-knowledge, there is no basis for thought. You can repeat like a gramophone, but you will not be the music maker, there will be no song in your heart.

So, through self-knowledge alone can suffering come to an end. After all, what does suffering mean—not as a verbal explanation, but as a fact? How does suffering arise, not merely as a scientific observation, but actually? In order to know, to find out, surely discontent is essential. One must be thoroughly discontented in order to find out. But when there is discontent—and most of us are discontented—we find an easy way of smothering that discontent. We become something—clerks, governors, ministers, or what you will—anything to smother that flame, that spark, that dissatisfaction. Materially as well as psychologically we want to be sure, we want to be secure, we do not want to be disturbed. We want certainty, and where the mind is looking for certainty, security, there is no discontent, and most of us spend our lives doing this; we are all seeking security. Obviously there must be physical security—food, clothing, and shelter—but that is denied when we seek psychological security—psychological security being self-expansion through physical necessities. A house in itself is not important except as shelter, but we use the house as a means of self-aggrandizement. That is why property becomes very important, and hence we create a social system which denies the right distribution of food, clothing, and shelter.

So, it is discontent that drives, that creates, that urges us on; and if we can understand discontent without smothering it by the search for certainty, psychological security, if we can keep that discontent and its flame alive, then our problem is simple because that very discontent is creative, and from that we can move on. But the moment we smother discontent, put it away, resist it, hide it, then the mind is concerned merely with the reconciliation of effects, and discontent is no longer a means of going forward, plunging into something unknown. That is why it is so important for each one really to understand oneself. The study of oneself is not an end but a beginning, because there is no end in understanding oneself—it is a constant movement. If you observe yourself very carefully, you will see that there is no fixed moment when you can say, "I understand the whole totality of myself"; it is like reading many volumes. The more one studies oneself, the more there is to be studied. Therefore, the movement of the self is timeless; and that self is not the high or the low, but the self which is from moment to moment, with its actions, its thoughts, its words. That self-knowledge is the beginning of wisdom, and in that self-knowledge one discovers a state of utter tranquillity in which the mind is not made still, but is still; and only when the mind is still, when it is not caught up in the thought process or occupied with its own creations—only then is there creativeness, is there reality. It is this creativeness, this perception of reality which will free us from our problem, not the search for an answer to the problem.

So, self-knowledge is the technique of meditation, and without self-knowledge there is no meditation. Self-knowledge is not something acquired from a book or from a guru or teacher. Self-knowledge begins in understanding oneself from moment to moment, and that understanding requires one's full attention to be given to each thought at any particular moment without an end in view, because there cannot be complete attention when there is condemnation or justification. When the mind condemns or justifies, it does so either to deny or to escape what it perceives. It is much easier to condemn a child than to understand a child. Similarly, when a thought arises, it is easier to put it away or discipline it than to give it your undivided attention and thereby discover its full significance. Therefore, the problem is to understand oneself, and one can approach it rightly only where there is no justification, condemnation, or resistance—and then you will find that the problem unfolds like a map.

To discover what is eternal, the process of the mind must be understood. You cannot think about the unknown; you can think only about the known, and what is known is not the real. Reality cannot be thought about, meditated upon, pictured, or formulated; if it is, it is not real because it is merely the projection of the mind. It is only when the thought process ceases, when the mind is literally and utterly still—and stillness can come about only through self-knowledge—that reality is understood; and it is the real that resolves our problems, not our cunning distractions and formulated escapes.

I have several questions here, and I shall try to answer them as briefly and clearly as possible.

Question: I have parents who are orthodox and who depend on me, but I myself have ceased to believe in their orthodoxy. How am I to deal with such a situation? This is a real problem to me.

KRISHNAMURTI: Now, why has one ceased to be orthodox? Before you say, "I have ceased to be orthodox," must you not find out why, for what reason? Is it because you see that orthodoxy is mere repetition without much meaning, a framework in which man lives because he is afraid to go beyond and discover? Or, have you abandoned orthodoxy as a mere reaction because it is the modern thing to do to reject the ancient, the old? Have you rejected the old without understanding it?—which is merely a reaction. If that is the case, it is quite different, it brings about quite a different issue. But if you have ceased to be orthodox because you see that a mind caught in tradition, in habit, is without understanding, then you know the full significance of orthodoxy. I do not know which you have done: Either you have left it in protest or you have abandoned it, or rather, it has fallen away from you naturally, because you understand it. Now, if it is the latter, then what is your responsibility to those people around you who are orthodox? Should you yield to their orthodoxy because they are your mother and father, and they can cry and give you trouble at home, calling you an undutiful son? Should you yield to them because they create trouble? What is your responsibility? If you yield, then your understanding of orthodoxy has no meaning; then you are placatory, you don't want trouble, you want to let sleeping dogs lie. But surely, you must have trouble, a revolution is essential—not the bloody kind of revolution, but a psychological revolution, which is far more important than mere revolution in outward effects. Most of us are afraid to have a fundamental revolution; we yield to the parents, saying, "There is enough trouble as it is in the world, why should I add more?" But surely, that is not the answer, is it? When one has trouble, it must be exposed, opened up and looked into. Merely to accept an attitude, to concede to the parents because they are going to give you trouble, kick you out of the house, does not bring out clarity; it merely hides, suppresses conflict, and a conflict which is suppressed acts as a poison in the system, in the psychological being.

If there is tension between you and your parents, this contradiction has to be faced if you want to live creatively, happily; but as most of us do not want to lead a creative life and are satisfied to be dull, we say, "It is all right, I will yield." After all, relationship with another, especially with a father, mother, or child is a very difficult thing because relationship with most of us is a matter of gratification. We do not want any trouble in relationship. Surely, a person who is looking for gratification, satisfaction, comfort, security in relationship, ceases to have a relationship that is alive; he makes that relationship into a dead thing. After all, what is relationship? What is the function of relationship? Surely, it is a means by which I discover myself. Relationship is a process of self-revelation, but if the self-revelation is unpleasant, unsatisfactory, disturbing, we do not want to look any further into it. So, relationship becomes merely a means of communication and, therefore, a dead thing. But if relationship is an active process in which there is self-revelation, in which I discover myself as in a mirror, then that relationship not only brings about conflict, disturbance, but out of it comes clarity and joy.

The question then is: When you are not orthodox, what is your responsibility to the person who is dependent on you? Now, the older you grow, the more orthodox you become; that is, because you know you are soon coming to the end of your life and you don't know what awaits you on the other side, you seek safety, security, on both sides. But a man who believes without understanding is obviously stupid, and should you encourage stupidity? Belief creates antagonism, the very nature of belief is to divide: You believe in one thing, I believe in another; you are a communist, I am a capitalist, which is merely a matter of belief; you call yourself a Hindu, I call myself a Muslim, and we slaughter each other. So, belief is obviously a device which sets man against man, and recognizing all these factors, what is your responsibility? Can one advise another as to what to do? You and I can discuss, but it is for you to act, after looking into it. To look into it you must pay attention, and you must face the consequences of your decision, you cannot leave it to me or to anybody else. That means you understand and are quite willing to face trouble, to be thrown out, to be called an ungrateful son, and all the rest of it; it means that for you orthodoxy does not matter, but that truth, which is the understanding of the problem, matters immensely, and therefore you are prepared to face trouble. But most of us do not want the clear happiness that truth brings; we want mere gratification, and therefore we concede and say, "All right, I will do what you want me to do, but for God's sake, leave me alone." That way you will never create a new society, a new culture.

Question: It is the universally accepted conclusion of modern intellectuals that educators have failed. What is, then, the task of those whose function it is to teach the young?

KRISHNAMURTI: There are several problems involved in this, and to understand them, one must go very carefully into them. First of all, why do you have children? Is it mere accident, an unwanted event? Do you have children to carry on your name, title, or estate? Or do you love, and therefore you have children? Which is it? If you have children merely as toys, something to play with, or if you are lonely and a child helps you to cover up that loneliness—then children become important because they are your own self-projection. But if children are not a mere means of amusement or a result of accidents, if you really love them in the profound sense of the word—and to love somebody means to be in complete communion with them—then education has quite a different significance. If as a parent you really love your children, you will see that they have the right kind of education. In other words, children must be helped to be intelligent, sensitive, to have a mind and heart that are pliable, able to deal with any situation. Surely, if you really love your child, you as a parent will not be a nationalist, you will not belong to any country, you will not belong to any organized religion because, obviously, if you are a nationalist, if you worship the state, then you inevitably destroy your son because you are creating war. If you really love your son, you will find out what is your right relationship with property, because it is the possessive instinct which has given property such enormous significance and which is destroying the world. Again, if you really love your children, you will not belong to any particular religion because belief creates antagonism between man and man. If you love your children, you will do all these things. So, that is one aspect.

Then the other aspect is that the educator needs educating. What are you educating the children for? To become clerks or glorified clerks, governors, engineers, technicians? Is that all life is—merely a matter of glorified clerks, technicians, mechanics, human beings made into cannon fodder? What is the purpose and intention of education? Is it to turn out soldiers, lawyers, and policemen? Surely, the occupations of soldier, lawyer, and policeman are not right professions for decent human beings. (Laughter) Don't laugh it off. By laughing it off, you are pushing it aside. You can see that these professions do not contribute to the total well-being of man, though they may be necessary in a society that has already become corrupt. Therefore, first of all, you have to find out why it is that you have children, and what it is that you are educating them for. If you are merely educating them to be technicians, naturally you will find the best technician to educate your child, and he will be made into a machine, he will discipline himself to conform to a pattern. Is that all there is to our existence, our struggle, and our happiness—merely to become mechanics, tank or airplane experts, scientists, physicists inventing new ways of destruction? Therefore, education is your responsibility, is it not? What is it you want your children to be, or not to be? What is the purpose of existence? If it is merely to adjust to a system, to efface oneself for a party, then it is very simple; then all that you have to do is to conform and fit in. But if life is meant to be lived rightly, fully, joyously, sensitively, then there must be quite a different process of education in which there is the cultivation of sensitivity, of intelligence, and not mere technique—though technique is necessary.

So, as a parent—and God knows why you are parents—you have to find out what your responsibility is. Sirs, you love so easily; you say you love, but really you don't love your children. You have no feeling. You accept social events and conditions as inevitable; you don't want to transform them, to create a revolution and bring about a new culture, a new society. Surely, it depends on you what kind of education your children will have. As the questioner says, education throughout the world has failed, it has produced catastrophe after catastrophe, destruction and more destruction, bloodshed, rape, and murder. Obviously, education has failed, and if you look to the experts, the specialists, to educate your children, the disaster must continue because the specialists, being concerned only with the part and not with the whole, are themselves inhuman. Surely, the first thing is to have love, for if there is love, it will find the way to educate the children rightly. But you see, we are all brains and no heart; we have cultivated the intellect, and in ourselves we are so absurdly lopsided—and then the problem arises of what to do with the children. Surely, it is obvious that the educator himself needs educating—and the educator is you, for the home environment is as important as the school environment. So, you have to transform yourself first to give the right environment to the child, for the environment can make him either a brute, an unfeeling technician, or a very sensitive, intelligent human being. The environment is yourself and your action, and unless you transform yourself, the environment, the present society in which we live, must inevitably harm the child, make him rude, rough, unintelligent.

Surely, sirs, those who are deeply interested in this problem will begin to transform themselves and thereby transform society, which will in turn bring about a new means of education. But you are really not interested. You will listen to all this and say, "Yes, I agree, but it is too impracticable." You don't treat it as a direct responsibility; you are not really, fundamentally, concerned. If you really loved your son and knew the war was coming, as it inevitably is, do you mean to say you would not act, you would not find a way of stopping war? You see, we don't love; we use the word *love,* but the content of that word has no meaning anymore. We just use the word without a referent, without substance, and we live merely on the word, so the complex problem is there still, and we have to face it. And don't say I have not shown you a way out of it. The way is yourself and your relationship with your children, your wife, your society. You are the gleam, you are the hope; otherwise, there is no way out of this at all.

Look at what is happening. More and more governments are taking charge of education, which means they want to produce efficient beings, either as technicians or for war, and therefore, the children must be regimented, they must be told not how to think but what to think. They are taught to live on propaganda, slogans. Because those who are in power don't want to be disturbed, they want to keep the power; it has become the function of government to maintain the status quo with little alterations here and there. So, taking all these factors into consideration, you have to find out what is the meaning of existence, why you are living, why you are producing children; and you have to find out how to create a new environment—for, what the environment is, your child is. He listens to your talk, he repeats what the older people think and do. So, you have to create a right environment, not only at home, but outside, which is society; and you have to create a new kind of government which is radically different, which is not based on nationalism, on the sovereign state with its armies and efficient ways of murdering people. That implies seeing your responsibility in relationship, and you actually see that responsibility in relationship only when you love somebody. When your heart is full, then you find a way. This is urgent, it is imminent—you cannot wait for the experts to come and tell you how to educate your child. Only you who love will find the way, for those hearts are empty that look to the experts.

You have listened to all this, and what is your reaction? You will say, "Yes, very nice, very good, it should be done, but let somebody else begin"—which means, really, you don't love your child, you have no relationship with your child, so you don't see the difficulty. The more irresponsible you become, the more the state takes over all responsibility—the state being the few, the party, left or right. You yourself have to work it out because we are facing a great crisis—not a verbal crisis, not a political or an economic crisis, but a crisis of human degradation, of human disintegration. Therefore, it is your responsibility as the father, as the mother; you have got to transform yourself. These are not just words I am indulging in. One sees this calamity approaching so closely and dangerously, and we sit here and do not do a thing about it, or if we do, we look to some leader and turn our hearts over to him. It is an obvious fact that when you pursue a leader, you choose that leader out of your own confusion, and therefore the leader himself is confused. (Laughter) Don't laugh it off as a clever remark—please look at it, see what you are doing. It is you who are responsible for the appalling horror which we have come to, and you are not facing it. You go out and do exactly the same thing that you did yesterday, and you feel your responsibility is over when you ask that question about education and pass your child on to a teacher who teaches and beats him. Don't you see? Unless you love your wife, your children, and not merely use them as a tool or means for your own gratification, unless you are really touched by this, you will not find a right way of education. To educate your children means to be interested in the whole process of life. What you think, what you do, and what you say matters infinitely because that creates the environment, and it is the environment which creates the child.

Question: Marriage is a necessary part of any organized society, but you seem to be against the institution of marriage. What do you say? Please also explain the problem of sex. Why has it become, next to war, the most urgent problem of our day?

KRISHNAMURTI: To ask a question is easy, but the difficulty is to look very carefully into the problem itself, which contains the answer. To understand this problem, we must see its enormous implications. That is difficult because our time is very limited and I shall have to be brief, and if you don't follow very closely, you may not be able to understand. Let us investigate the problem, not the answer, because the answer is in the problem, not away from it. The more I understand the problem, the clearer I see the answer. If you merely look for an answer, you will not find one because you will be seeking an answer away from the problem. Let us look at marriage, but not theoretically or as an ideal, which is rather absurd; don't let us idealize marriage, let us look at it as it is, for then we do something about it. If you make it rosy, then you can't act, but if you look at it and see it exactly as it is, then perhaps you will be able to act.

Now, what actually takes place? When one is young, the biological, sexual urge is very strong, and in order to set a limit to it you have the institution called marriage. There is the biological urge on both sides, so you marry and have children. You tie yourself to a man or to a woman for the rest of your life, and in doing so you have a permanent source of pleasure, a guaranteed security, with the result that you begin to disintegrate; you live in a cycle of habit, and habit is disintegration. To understand this biological, this sexual urge, requires a great deal of intelligence, but we are not educated to be intelligent. We merely get on with a man or a woman with whom we have to live. I marry at 20 or 25, and I have to live for the rest of my life with a woman whom I have not known. I have not known a thing about her, and yet you ask me to live with her for the rest of my life. Do you call that marriage? As I grow and observe, I find her to be completely different from me, her interests are different from mine; she is interested in clubs, I am interested in being very serious, or vice versa. And yet we have children—that is the most extraordinary thing. Sirs, don't look at the ladies and smile; it is your problem. So, I have established a relationship the significance of which I do not know; I have neither discovered it nor understood it.

It is only for the very, very few who love that the married relationship has significance, and then it is unbreakable, then it is not mere habit or convenience, nor is it based on biological, sexual need. In that love, which is unconditional, the identities are fused, and in such a relationship there is a remedy, there is hope. But for most of you, the married relationship is not fused. To fuse the separate identities, you have to know yourself, and she has to know herself. That means to love. But there is no love, which is an obvious fact. Love is fresh, new, not mere gratification, not mere habit. It is unconditional. You don't treat your husband or wife that way, do you? You live in your isolation, and she lives in her isolation, and you have established your habits of assured sexual pleasure. What happens to a man who has an assured income? Surely, he deteriorates. Have you not noticed it? Watch a man who has an assured income and you will soon see how rapidly his mind is withering away. He may have a big position, a reputation for cunning, but the full joy of life is gone out of him.

Similarly, you have a marriage in which you have a permanent source of pleasure, a habit without understanding, without love, and you are forced to live in that state. I am not saying what you should do, but look at the problem first. Do you think that is right? It does not mean that you must throw off your wife and pursue someone else. What does this relationship mean? Surely, to love is to be in communion with somebody, but are you in communion with your wife, except physically? Do you know her, except physically? Does she know you? Are you not both isolated, each pursuing his or her own interests, ambitions, and needs, each seeking from the other gratification, economic or psychological security? Such a relationship is not a relationship at all—it is a mutually self-enclosing process of psychological, biological, and economic necessity—and the obvious result is conflict, misery, nagging, possessive fear, jealousy, and so on. Do you think such a relationship is productive of anything except ugly babies and an ugly civilization? Therefore, the important thing is to see the whole process, not as something ugly, but as an actual fact which is taking place under your very nose, and realizing that, what are you going to do? You cannot leave it at that, but because you do not want to look into it, you take to drink, to politics, to a lady around the corner, to anything that takes you away from the house and from that nagging wife or husband—and you think you have solved the problem. That is your life, is it not? Therefore, you have to do something about it, which means you have to face it, and that means, if necessary, breaking up; because, when a father and mother are constantly nagging and quarreling with each other, do you think that has not an effect on the children? And we have already considered, in the previous question, the education of children.

So, marriage as a habit, as a cultivation of habitual pleasure, is a deteriorating factor because there is no love in habit. Love is not habitual; love is something joyous, creative, new. Therefore, habit is the contrary of love, but you are caught in habit, and naturally your habitual relationship with another is dead. So, we come back again to the fundamental issue, which is that the reformation of society depends on you, not on legislation. Legislation can only make for further habit or conformity. Therefore, you as a responsible individual in relationship have to do something—you have to act, and you can act only when there is an awakening of your mind and heart. I see some of you nodding your heads in agreement with me, but the obvious fact is that you don't want to take the responsibility for transformation, for change; you don't want to face the upheaval of finding out how to live rightly. And so the problem continues; you quarrel and carry on, and finally you die, and when you die somebody weeps, not for the other fellow, but for his or her own loneliness. You carry on unchanged, and you think you are human beings capable of legislation, of occupying high positions, talking about God, finding a way to stop wars, and so on. None of these things means anything because you have not solved any of the fundamental issues.

Then, the other part of the problem is sex and why sex has become so important. Why has this urge taken such a hold on you? Have you ever thought it out? You have not thought it out because you have just indulged; you have not searched out why there is this problem. Sirs, why is there this problem? And what happens when you deal with it by suppressing it completely—you know, the ideal of *bramacharya*, and so on? What happens? It is still there. You resent anybody who talks about a woman, and you think that you can succeed in completely suppressing the sexual urge in yourself and solve your problem that way, but you are haunted by it. It is like living in a house and putting all your ugly things in one room, but they are still there. So, discipline is not going to solve this problem—discipline being sublimation, suppression, substitution—because you have tried it, and that is not the way out. So, what is the way out? The way out is to understand the problem, and to understand is not to condemn or justify. Let us look at it, then, in that way.

Why has sex become so important a problem in your life? Is not the sexual act, the feeling, a way of self-forgetfulness? Do you understand what I mean? In that act there is complete fusion; at that moment there is complete cessation of all conflict; you feel supremely happy because you no longer feel the need as a separate entity, and you are not consumed with fear. That is, for a moment there is an ending of self-consciousness, and you feel the clarity of self-forgetfulness, the joy of self-abnegation. So, sex has become important because in every other direction you are living a life of conflict, of self-aggrandizement, and frustration. Sirs, look at your lives—political, social, religious—you are striving to become something. Politically you want to be somebody powerful, to have position, prestige. Don't look at somebody else, don't look at the ministers. If you were given all that, you would do the same thing. So, politically you are striving to become somebody, you are expanding yourself, are you not? Therefore, you are creating conflict; there is no denial, there is no abnegation of the 'me'. On the contrary, there is accentuation of the 'me'. The same process goes on in your relationship with things, which is ownership of property, and again in the religion that you follow. There is no meaning in what you are doing, in your religious practices. You just believe, you cling to labels, words. If you observe you will see that there, too, there is no freedom from the consciousness of the 'me' as the center. Though your religion says, "Forget yourself," your very process is the assertion of yourself, you are still the important entity. You may read the Gita or the Bible, but you are still the minister, you are still the exploiter, sucking the people and building temples.

So, in every field, in every activity, you are indulging and emphasizing yourself, your importance, your prestige, your security. Therefore, there is only one source of self-forgetfulness, which is sex, and that is why the woman or the man becomes all-important to you and why you must possess. So, you build a society which enforces that possession, guarantees you that possession, and naturally sex becomes the all-important problem when everywhere else the self is the important thing. And do you think, sirs, that one can live in that state without contradiction, without misery, without frustration? But when there is honestly and sincerely no self-emphasis, whether in religion or in social activity, then sex has very little meaning. It is because you are afraid to be as nothing—politically, socially, religiously—that sex becomes a problem, but if in all these things you allowed yourself to diminish, to be the less, you would see that sex becomes no problem at all.

There is chastity only when there is love. When there is love, the problem of sex ceases; and without love, to pursue the ideal of *bramacharya* is an absurdity because the ideal is unreal. The real is that which you are, and if you don't understand your own mind, the workings of your own mind, you will not understand sex because sex is a thing of the mind. The problem is not simple. It needs, not mere habit-forming practices, but tremendous thought and inquiry into your relationship with people, with property, and with ideas. Sir, it means you have to undergo strenuous searching of your heart and mind, thereby bringing a transformation within yourself. Love is chaste, and when there is love, and not the mere idea of chastity created by the mind, then sex has lost its problem and has quite a different meaning.

Question: In my view, the guru is one who awakens me to the truth, to reality. What is wrong with my taking to such a guru?

KRISHNAMURTI: This question arises because I have said that gurus are an impediment to truth. Don't say you are wrong and I am right, or I am wrong and you are right, but let us examine the problem and find out. Let us inquire like mature, thoughtful people, without denying and without justifying.

Which is more important, the guru or you? And why do you go to a guru? You say, "To be awakened to truth." Are you really going to a guru to be awakened to the truth? Let us think this out very clearly. Surely, when you go to a guru you are actually seeking gratification. That is, you have a problem and your life is a mess; it is in confusion, and because you want to escape from it, you go to somebody whom you call a guru to find consolation verbally or to escape an ideation. That is the actual process, and that process you call seeking truth. That is, you want comfort, you want gratification, you want your confusion cleared away by somebody, and the person who helps you to find escapes you call a guru. Actually, not theoretically, you look to a guru who will assure you of what you want. You go guru-hunting as you go window-shopping: You see what suits you best and then buy it. In India, that is the position: You go around hunting for gurus, and when you find one you hold on to his feet or neck or hand until he gratifies you. To touch a man's feet—that is one of the most extraordinary things. You touch the guru's feet and kick your servants, and thereby you destroy human beings, you lose human significance. So, you go to a guru to find gratification, not truth. The idea may be that he should awaken you to truth, but the actual fact is that you find comfort. Why? Because you say, "I can't solve my problem, somebody must help me." Can anybody help you solve the confusion which you have created? What is confusion? Confusion with regard to what? Suffering with regard to what? Confusion and suffering exist in your relationship with things, people, and ideas; and if you cannot understand that confusion which you have created, how can another help you? He can tell you what to do, but you have to do it yourself, it is your own responsibility; and because you are unwilling to take that responsibility, you sneak off to the guru—that is the right expression to use, "sneak off"—and you think you have solved the problem. On the contrary, you have not solved it at all; you have escaped, but the problem is still there. And, strangely, you always choose a guru who will assure you of what you want; therefore, you are not seeking truth, and therefore the guru is not important. You are actually seeking someone who will satisfy you in your desires; that is why you create a leader, religious or political, and give yourself over to him, and that is why you accept his authority. Authority is evil, whether religious or political, because it is the leader and his position that are all-important, and you are unimportant. You are a human being with sorrow, pain, suffering, joy, and when you deny yourself and give yourself over to somebody, you are denying reality because it is only through yourself that you can find reality, not through somebody else.

Now, you say that you accept a guru as one who awakens you to reality. Let us find out if it is possible for another to awaken you to reality. I hope you are following all this because it is your problem, not mine. Let us find out the truth about whether another can awaken you to reality. Can I, who have been talking for an hour and a half, awaken you to reality, to that which is real? The term *guru* implies, does it not, a man who leads you to truth, to happiness, to bliss eternal. Is truth a static thing that someone can lead you to? Someone can direct you to the station. Is truth like that—static, something permanent to which you can be led? It is static only when you create it out of your desire for comfort. But truth is not static; nobody can lead you to truth. Beware of the person who says he can lead you to truth because it is not true. Truth is something unknown from moment to moment; it cannot be captured by the mind, it cannot be formulated, it has no resting place. Therefore, no one can lead you to truth. You may ask me, "Why are you talking here?" All that I am doing is pointing out to you *what is* and how to understand *what is* as it is, not as it should be. I am not talking about the ideal but about a thing that is actually right in front of you, and it is for you to look and see it. Therefore, you are more important than I, more important than any teacher, any savior, any slogan, any belief, because you can find truth only through yourself, not through another. When you repeat the truth of another, it is a lie. Truth cannot be repeated. All that you can do is to see the problem as it is and not escape. When you see the thing as it actually is, then you begin to awaken, but not when you are compelled by another. There is no savior but yourself. When you have the intention and the attention to look directly at *what is,* then your very attention awakens you because in attention everything is implied. To give attention, you must be devoted to *what is,* and to understand *what is,* you must have knowledge of it. Therefore, you must look, observe, give it your undivided attention, for all things are contained in that full attention you give to *what is.*

So, the guru cannot awaken you; all that he can do is to point out *what is.* Truth is not a thing that can be caught by the mind. The guru can give you words; he can give you an explanation, the symbols of the mind, but the symbol is not the real, and if you are caught in the symbol, you will never find the way. Therefore, that which is important is not the teacher, it is not the symbol, it is not the explanation, but it is you who are seeking truth. To seek rightly is to give attention, not to

God, not to truth, because you don't know it, but attention to the problem of your relationship with your wife, your children, your neighbor. When you establish right relationship then you love truth, for truth is not a thing that can be bought, truth does not come into being through self-immolation or through the repetition of mantras. Truth comes into being only when there is self-knowledge. Self-knowledge brings understanding, and when there is understanding, there are no problems. When there are no problems, then the mind is quiet, it is no longer caught up in its own creations. When the mind is not creating problems, when it understands each problem immediately as it arises, then it is utterly still, not made still. This total process is awareness, and it brings about a state of undisturbed tranquillity which is not the outcome of any discipline, of any practice or control, but is the natural outcome of understanding every problem as it arises. Problems arise only in relationship, and when there is understanding of one's relationship with things, with people, and with ideas, then there is no disturbance of any kind in the mind, and the thought process is silent. In that state there is neither the thinker nor the thought, the observer nor the observed. Therefore, the thinker ceases, and then the mind is no longer caught in time, and when there is no time, the timeless comes into being. But the timeless cannot be thought of. The mind, which is the product of time, cannot think of that which is timeless. Thought cannot conceive or formulate that which is beyond thought. When it does, its formulation is still part of thought. Therefore, eternity is not a thing of the mind; eternity comes into being only when there is love, for love in itself is eternal. Love is not something abstract to be thought about; love is to be found only in relationship with your wife, your children, your neighbor. When you know that love which is unconditional, which is not the product of the mind, then reality comes into being, and that state is utter bliss.

December 19, 1948

Banaras, India, 1949

First Talk at Rajghat

As during the next few weeks there will be a series of talks every Sunday and discussions Tuesdays, Thursdays, and Saturdays, it is important, it seems to me, first to learn the art of listening. Most of us listen in order to confirm our beliefs or strengthen our opinions, or we listen merely to refute or to sharpen our intellect or to learn some new technique. But it seems to me that it is a false way of listening if it is only to strengthen one's beliefs or to learn a new jargon or a new way of examination. But, surely, there is a true way of listening, especially to something that may perhaps be foreign, something that may be new, that one may hear for the first time. When one listens to something new, one is apt to brush it aside as not understandable, or one is apt to be too quick in one's judgment. Whereas, if one were able to listen very attentively, perhaps one would gather much more than by merely listening through the screen of one's own prejudices and impressions.

That is, if I want to understand something you are saying, I must listen not only to the verbal expression but also to what you intend to convey. Words do not matter so immensely, so greatly; what matters is what you intend to convey. So, communication is more important than the verbal expression, and there can be communion between two people only when there is the intent to understand; if you do not want to understand, if you are here merely to criticize, to verbalize, to intellectualize, there can be no communion. But there will be communion between us, deeply, wisely, extensively, if there is the intent to understand. And I think that intent is far more important than the facility to philosophize, to criticize, or to learn a new way of expressing a thought. Throughout these talks during the next six weeks, you and I must be in communion so that we can understand each other, understand each other's problems, each other's difficulties, how we approach the conflict in our life, and so on. So, the basis of our relationship must be that communion.

I am not here merely to give a series of talks, to expound my ideas, because I do not believe in "ideas." Ideas do not transform; ideas will not produce the true revolution. Ideas merely give irritation to further ideas, but ideas will never produce a lasting, fundamental, radical revolution which is necessary—we will go into this presently, during all these talks.

So, we must, if we would, try to establish a relationship of communion—but not as between a lecturer and an audience or as between a teacher and a disciple, which would be absurd. Because we have to deal with our own problems of life and understand those problems, we have to examine them very closely and attentively, and that is what we are going to do. To understand is to pay full attention. With most of us the difficulty is that we are trying to find an answer to the problem. Perhaps this needs further explanation. When we have a problem, whether sociological, psychological, or so-called spiritual, we are always trying to find, are we not, an answer, a way out, away from the problem. You look at your own problem and you will see that the tendency is to find a solution to the problem, isn't it? Whereas, if we know how to look at the problem, then the solution is in the problem, not away from the problem. So, if I may emphasize it, that is what we are going to do during all these talks. I am not offering a solution for you to accept or adopt as a new pattern of action. But, if we two can look at the problem together, see its implications, see its significance, then perhaps, seeing it together, we shall find the right answer—not an answer away from the problem, but in the problem itself.

Sirs, what is our problem? What is the problem with which we are confronted at the present time? Is it an individual problem or a mass problem? Is it the problem of a particular country or a particular people, or is it a problem which affects the whole world, independent of race, of nationality? Surely, it is a problem that is not only affecting the individual, the 'you' and the 'me', but it is a problem that is confronting the whole world; it is the problem of disintegration, the problem of collapse. All the experiments, sociological and psychological, are rapidly losing their value; wars are ever threatening, and there is class or communal strife; though one may talk of peace, there is ever the preparation for war, with which we are daily familiar; one ideology coming into conflict with another ideology, the left against the right, and so on.

Now, is this vast problem of the world your problem and my problem, or is it independent of us? Is war independent of you? Is the national strife independent of you, the communal strife independent of you? The corruption, the degradation, the moral disintegration—are they independent of each one of us? This disintegration is directly related to us, and therefore the responsibility rests with each one of us. Surely, that is the main problem, isn't it? That is, to put it differently: Is the problem to be left to the few leaders, either of the left or the right, to the party, to the discipline, to an ideology, to the United Nations, to the expert, to the specialist? Or is it a problem that directly involves us, which means: Are we directly responsible for these problems, or are we not? Surely, that is the issue, is it not? Perhaps, many of you may not have thought about this; therefore, it may be quite strange to you, but the question is, is it not, whether the individual problem is the world problem, whether you can do anything about it?—the religious collapse, the moral collapse, the political corruption, the so-called independence that has produced nothing but decay. Is it your problem, or do you leave it all to chance or wait for some miracle to happen so that it will produce a revolution? Or do you leave it to some authority, to a political party of the left or of the right? What is your response? Don't you have to solve it, don't you have to attack it, don't you have to respond vitally to a challenge of this kind? I am not being rhetorical but merely factual; this is no place for rhetoric, that would be absurd. There is a challenge given to us all the time; life is a challenge. And do we respond, and according to what conditioning do we respond? And when we do respond, is that response capable of meeting the challenge?

So, to meet this world catastrophe, this world crisis, this enormous unprecedented challenge, have we not to discover how we, individually, respond? Because, after all, a society is the relationship between you and me and another. There is no society which is not founded on relationship. What you and I and another are, is the society, surely. And have we not to understand that relationship between you and me and another in order to transform society, in order to bring about a revolution—a complete, radical transformation? Because, obviously, that is what is needed—a revolution, not of the bloody kind, not of mere ideas, not based on ideas, but a revolution of fundamental value, not according to any pattern or ideology, but a revolution born out of the understanding of the relationship between you and me and another, which is society. So in order to bring about a fundamental, radical transformation in society, is it not our responsibility, our individual responsibility, to discover what is our direct response to this challenge? Do we respond as a Hindu or a Muslim or a Christian or a communist or a socialist? And is such a response a valid response, a response which will bring about a fundamental change? I hope I am making the problem clear. If you respond to this world crisis, which is a new challenge, as a Hindu, surely you are not understanding the challenge. You are merely responding to the challenge, which is always new, according to an old pattern, and therefore, your response has no corresponding validity, newness, freshness. If you respond as a Catholic or a communist, again you are responding, are you not, according to a patterned thought. Therefore your response has no significance. And has not the Hindu, the Muslim, the Buddhist, the Christian, created this problem? As the new religion is the worship of the state, the old religion was the worship of an idea. So if you respond to a challenge according to an old conditioning, your response will not enable you to understand the new challenge. Therefore, what one has to do in order to meet the challenge is to strip oneself completely, denude oneself entirely of the background and meet the challenge anew. Surely, a state, a country, a civilization, and a people endure, last, or survive only when they can meet the challenge anew; otherwise, they succumb, they are destroyed. And that is exactly what is happening. Technologically we are tremendously advanced, but morally, spiritually, we are very far behind. And with this lack of moral stamina, we meet this extraordinary technological progress, and therefore there is always a friction, a contradiction.

So, surely, our problem is, is it not, that there is this new challenge. And all leaders have failed—spiritual, moral, political—and leaders will always fail because we choose leaders out of our confusion, and any leader whom we choose will inevitably lead us to confusion. Sir, see the importance of it; don't brush it aside as a clever statement. See the danger of a leader, not only politically, but religiously. Because, the one whom we choose for a leader is chosen out of our confusion. Because I am confused, I do not know what to do, how to act, I come to you, and because I am confused I choose you. If I am clear, I will not choose you; I do not want a leader because I am a light unto myself—I can think out my problems for myself. It is only when I am confused that I go to another. I may call him a guru, a mahatma, a political leader, and so on, but I go to him because of my confusion. I only see through the darkness of my own confusion.

A man who earnestly wishes to investigate the whole catastrophic problem of sorrow must begin with himself. It is only through creative understanding of ourselves that there can be a creative world, a happy world, a world in which ideas do not exist.

Question: You are preaching the idea of one world, of a classless society, which is the basis of communism. But what are your sanctions, what is your technique for the new revolution?

KRISHNAMURTI: Now, what do you mean by sanctions? You mean, "What is my authority?" don't you? Who has given me authority to speak? Or, what is my label? In other words, you are interested, are you not, in the label, in the name, to find out who has given me authority, the sanction. Which means that you are more interested in knowing my label than in finding out what truth there is in what I am saying, aren't you? Are you listening, sirs, or paying attention to something else? Sir, this is rather an important question, and we will go into it fairly thoroughly, shall we?

Most of us appreciate a thing, or follow a thing, because it has been sanctioned by authority. So-and-so has painted a picture; therefore, it must be a beautiful picture. So-and-so has written a poem, and he is well-known; therefore, that poem must be good. He has a large following; therefore, what he says must be true. In other words, your sanction depends on popularity, on success, on the richness of language, on outward show. Doesn't it? So, when you ask me what my sanction is, you want to know if I am the World Teacher. And I say, don't let us be stupid. Whether I am or I am not is irrelevant; it is utterly unimportant what my sanction is. But what is fundamentally important is to examine what I am saying, to find out for yourself without the comfort of authority. That is why I am against organizations; that is one of the reasons—because organizations, spiritually, create a background of authority—but a man who is seeking truth is not concerned with authority, neither of a book, the Bhagavad-Gita, the Bible, nor of a person. He is seeking truth, not the authority of a person. So, as long as you are looking at my label to find out if that label is worth worshipping, listening to, I am afraid that you and I are wasting our time. Because, I have no authority, I have no sanction. I am saying something which to me is true by direct experience, not through reading some books and following somebody. Because, I have not read any of the so-called psychological, religious books; and as it is my direct experience, if you wish to look at it, you are perfectly welcome; but if you look around the corner for the label, you won't find it; and I'm afraid most of us are doing that. That is why this question is asked, "What is your sanction?" Since I have no sanction, since I have no authority, I am not acting as a guru or as an authority for you or for any other person. So, if you are interested, you will listen to what I am saying directly and find out the truth of what is being said, which means you must strip your mind of all authority and be capable of looking at things directly and simply.

Now, the questioner wants to know also, what is the new technique that I propose. Now, sir, let us again understand that word *technique*. Is revolution a matter of technique? A political revolution, a sociological revolution, may need a certain technique because you can pursue a certain ideology to produce a certain result; and to produce that result, you must know that ideology and the way to work out that ideology—whether the communistic ideology or the fascist or the capitalist, you must learn a technique to produce a result; but is that the fundamental revolution? Will a technique produce the true revolution? There must be a radical, fundamental revolution sociologically. The whole thing has to be transformed. Now, will a technique transform it, technique being a method, a way? Or, must there be individuals, you and I, who understand the problem, and who in themselves are in a state of revolution? Therefore their action upon society is revolutionary; they are not merely learning a technique of revolution; they themselves are in revolution. Am I making myself clear?

So when you ask what is my method or technique of revolution, I say let us look first at what you mean by that word *technique*. Is it not more important, more essential, that you be revolutionary and not merely try to find a technique of revolution? Now, why aren't you revolutionary? Why isn't there the new process of life in you? A new way of looking at life, a flame, a tremendous discontent? Why? Because, a person that is completely discontented, not merely discontented with certain things, but inherently discontented, need have no technique to be revolutionary. He is a revolution, and he is a danger to society, and such a man you call revolutionary. Now, why aren't you such a person? And for me, what is important is not the technique, but to make you be revolutionary, to help you to awaken to the importance of complete transformation. And when you are transformed, then you will be able to act, then there is the constant flow of newness, which is, after all, revolution.

Therefore, to me, the importance of inward revolution, of psychological transformation, is far greater than the outward revolution. The outward revolution is merely change, which is modified continuity, but inward revolution has no resting place; there is no stopping, it is constantly renewing itself. And that is what we need at the present time—a people who are completely discontented and therefore ready to perceive the truth of things. A man who is complacent, a man who is satisfied with money, with position, with an idea, can never see truth. It is only the man who is discontented, who is investigating, who is asking, questioning, looking, that discovers truth, and such a person is a revolution in himself and therefore in his relationships. Therefore that which is his world—which is his relationship with people—he begins to transform. Then he affects the world within his own relationship. So, merely to look for a technique or to inquire what is my technique for the new revolution seems to me beside the point—or rather, that you miss the importance of being revolutionary in yourself; and to be a revolution in yourself, you must awaken to the environment, to that in which you live.

Sirs, any new culture, any new society, must begin with you. How did Christianity, Buddhism, or any other vital thing begin? With a few who really were aflame with the idea, with that feeling. They had their hearts open to a new life. They were a nucleus, not believing in something, but in themselves they had the experience of reality—reality of what they saw. And what you and I have to do, if I may suggest, is to see things for ourselves directly, not through a technique. Sir, you may read a love poem; you may read what love is, but if you have not experienced what love is, no amount of your reading or learning the technique will give you the perfume of love. And because we have not that love, we are looking for the technique. We are jaded, we are famished, so we are superficially looking for a technique. A hungry man doesn't look for technique. He just goes after food, he doesn't stand outside the restaurant and smell the food. So when you ask for a technique it indicates that you are really not hungry. The "how" is not important, but why you ask the "how" is important.

So, there can be a revolution, the inward, continuous renewal, only when you understand yourself. You understand yourself in relationship, not in isolation. As nothing can live in isolation, to understand yourself, to have that knowledge of yourself at whatever level can only be learned in relationship. And as relationship is painful, is constantly in motion, we want to escape from it and find a reality outside of relationship. There is no reality outside of relationship. When I understand relationship, then that very understanding is reality. Therefore, one has to be extraordinarily alert, awake, all the time watching, open to every challenge and to every suggestion and hint. But that demands a certain alertness of mind and heart, but most of us are asleep, most of us are frustrated, most of us have one foot in the grave, though we are young. Because we think in terms of achievement, we think in terms of gain; therefore, we are never living; we are always concerned with the end; we are end-seekers, not people with life. Therefore, we are never revolutionary. If you are concerned directly with life, with living, and not with the idea about living, then you cannot help but be a revolution in yourself; you will be a revolution because you are meeting life directly, not through the screen of words, prejudices, intentions, and ends. And the man who meets life directly is a man who is in a state of discontent, and you must be in a state of discontent to find reality. And it is reality that releases, that frees; it is reality that frees the mind from its illusions and its creations. But to find reality, to be open to reality, is to be discontented. You cannot seek reality, it must come to you, but it can only come to you when the mind is completely discontented and ready. But most of us are afraid to be discontented because God knows where that discontent will lead us to. Therefore our discontent is hedged about with security, with safety, with carefully planned-out action. And such a state of mind cannot understand truth. Truth is not static, for truth is timeless, and the mind cannot follow truth because the mind is the product of time; and that which is of time cannot experience that which is timeless. Truth comes to him who is in that state of discontent, but who does not seek an end, for the seeker of an end is the person who is seeking gratification, and gratification, satisfaction, is not truth.

January 16, 1949

Second Talk at Rajghat

One has to differentiate between the experiences caused by belief, and experiencing. Belief obviously is detrimental to experiencing, and it is only through direct experiencing, not through belief, that one can find the reality of anything. Belief is unnecessary, whereas experiencing is essential, especially in a world where there are so many contradictions and so many specialists, each offering its own solution. We, the ordinary people, have to find out the truth of all this confusion and of all this misery. And so we have to inquire whether belief is essential and if belief helps in experiencing reality.

Now, as we see, the world is torn between two camps: those who believe that material life is of primary importance—the material life of society, the alteration of the environment, the reconditioning of man to environment—and those who believe that spiritual life is primary. The extreme left believes in the modification and the transformation of the environment, and there are those who believe that the spiritual life of man is alone of primary importance.

Now, you and I have to find out the truth of this matter. According to it our life shall be right. The specialists say that environment comes first, and there are those who say that spirit comes first; and you and I have to find out what is the truth of this matter. It is not a question of belief because belief has no validity with regard to experience. On which shall we lay emphasis: the environment or the spiritual life? And how are you and I going to find the truth of this matter? Not by endless reading, not by following the experts of the left or of the right, not by following those who believe that the material life of society is of primary importance, and not by studying all their books, all their expert knowledge, nor by following those who believe that spiritual life comes first, with all their literature. Merely to believe the one or the other is, surely, not to find the truth of the matter.

And yet most of us are caught in belief, most of us are uncertain. Sometimes we think this, and sometimes we think that. We are not sure; we are as confused as the experts in their certainty. We cannot take anything for granted; we cannot follow the one or the other because they both lead to confusion, because any acceptance of authority in these matters is obviously detrimental to society. Leadership in a society is a factor of deterioration of society, and yet you and I, being caught between the two and not knowing what to do, have to find out what the truth of this matter is—and not according to any specialist.

So, how do you set about it? Sir, that is one of the primary questions at the present time: We have those who put all their energy, all their capacities, all their power and thought into the alteration of the environment, which they hope will ultimately transform the individual; and there are those who more and more would turn to belief, to orthodoxy, to organized religion, and so on. These two are at war with each other, and you and I must decide—not decide which side we should take, because it is not a question of taking sides. But we must be sure of the truth of these.

Also, we cannot, obviously, depend on our particular prejudices because our prejudices will not show us the truth of the matter. If you have been conditioned in a religious environment, you will say spirit comes first. Another, brought up differently, will say the material life of society is of primary importance.

Now, how are you and I, ordinary people, not dependent on the accumulation of knowledge, theory, proofs, historical proofs—how are we, you and I, going to find out the truth of all this? Is it not a vital question? Because, on that discovery our future responsibility of action depends. So it is not a question of belief; belief again is a form of conditioning, and belief will not help us to find the truth of this matter.

So, first, to find the truth of this, must we not be free from our religious background as well as our materialistic background? Which means that we cannot merely accept; we must be free from the conditioning which makes us think that the materialistic life of society is of primary importance, as well as from the conditioning which makes us believe that the spiritual life, the life of the spirit, is of primary importance. We must be free of both in order to find the truth of both. Surely, that is an obvious thing, is it not? To find the truth of something, you must approach it afresh, anew, without any prejudice.

So, to find the truth of this, you and I must liberate ourselves from our background, from our environment; is it possible? That is, do we live by bread alone? Or, is there some other factor that shapes the outward end, the environment, according to our inner psychology? And to find the truth of this matter is obviously of primary importance to each responsible and earnest person because on this his action will depend; and to find the truth of that, one has to study oneself, and one has to be aware of oneself in action. Does the material aspect of society play the primary part in your life? Does environment play the principal role in your life? With most of us it obviously does. Does environment shape our thoughts, feelings? And where does the so-called spiritual life begin, and where does the environmental influence cease? Surely, to find out, one must study one's own actions, thoughts, and feelings. In other words, there must be self-knowledge—not the knowledge found in a book, gathered from various sources, but as you live from day to day, from moment to moment, that knowledge of the self at whatever level you find it.

So, the truth of the matter lies in the understanding of yourself in relationship to environment, in relationship to an idea called the spirit. Surely, as we discussed yesterday and the last few days, life is a question of relationship. Living, existence, implies relationship; and it is only in relationship, in understanding relationship, that we shall begin to discover the truth of this matter: whether material life is of primary importance or not. Therefore, we have to experience it in understanding relationship and not merely cling to belief. Then experiencing will give us the reality of these two.

So, self-knowledge, then, is of primary importance in the discovery of truth, which means that one has to be aware of every thought and feeling and see from whence these responses come; and one can be aware so clearly, so extensively, only if there is no condemnation or justification. That is, if we are aware of a thought, of a feeling, and follow it through without any condemnation, then we shall be able to see whether it is a response to the environment or merely a reaction to a materialistic demand, or if that thought has a different source.

So, through awareness without condemnation, without justification, we shall begin to understand ourselves—ourselves being the various responses to various stimuli, responses to the environment, which is relationship. Therefore relationship, or rather the understanding of relationship, becomes very important—the relationship of ourselves to property, of ourselves to people, of ourselves to ideas; and that movement of relationship cannot be understood if there is any sense of condemnation or justification. If you want to understand a thing, obviously you must not condemn it. If you want to understand your child, your son, you have to study him, you have to observe him, you have to study his various moods, when he is at play, and so on. So likewise, we must study ourselves all the time, not just at a given time; and we can study ourselves only when there is no condemnation, and it is extremely difficult not to condemn because condemnation or comparison is an escape from *what is;* and to study *what is* requires an extraordinary alertness of mind, and that alertness is dulled when it is merely caught in comparison, when there is condemnation. To condemn is not to understand, surely. It is so much easier to condemn a child, a person, rather than to understand that person. To understand that person requires attention, interest.

So, our problem is the comprehension of ourselves, as ourselves, for each one of us is both the environment and something more. The something more is not the result of a belief. We have to discover it, we have to experience it, and belief is an impediment to experiencing. So, we must take ourselves as we are and study ourselves as we are, and this study can be done only in relationship, and not in isolation.

I have been given several questions. Now, it is very easy to ask a question. Anybody can ask a question. But a right question, when asked seriously, will find a right response. Now you have asked me several questions here, and, if I may suggest, there is a way of listening which will help in understanding the problem. You have a problem, you have put to me a question and you want an answer. Surely there is a way of listening which is receptive. It is like sitting in front of a picture and absorbing the content of that picture without struggling to understand the picture. I do not know if it has happened to you that when you see some of the modern surrealist, abstract pictures, the first inclination is to condemn them, to say, "What nonsense, what is it all about?"—because you are trained to appreciate classical art. But there is another way of looking at those pictures, that is, without condemnation, but with receptivity so that the pictures may tell you their story. Surely, that is the only way to understand anything—to be receptive, not of course to every absurd thing, but so receptive that your particular question receives the answer which will be true if you listen to it rightly.

Surely, the subconscious is much more eager to understand than the conscious because the conscious is agitated, worried, pulled about, torn, has innumerable problems. But there is, surely, a part of the mind which is not agitated, which is eager to find out. Now, if we can give an opportunity for that part of the mind to listen, to be receptive, then, I am sure, you will find that your questions will be answered without your struggling to understand them. That is, to put it differently, understanding is not a matter of effort. The understanding of any problem that one has does not come through your constantly worrying over that problem. Similarly, if I may suggest, listen to understand rather than to refute or to confirm your own particular vanities and prejudices.

Question: Can the past dissolve all at once, or does it invariably need time?

KRISHNAMURTI: We are the result of the past. Our thought is founded upon yesterday, and many thousand yesterdays. We are the result of time, and our responses, our present attitudes, are the cumulative effect of many thousand moments, incidents, and experiences. So the past is, for the majority of us, the present—which is a fact, which cannot be denied. You, your thoughts, your actions, your responses, are the result of the past. Now the questioner wants to know if that past can be wiped out immediately, which means not in time, but immediately wiped out; or does this cumulative past require time for the mind to be freed in the present? It is important to understand the question. That is, as each one of us is the result of the past, with a background of innumerable influences, constantly varying, constantly changing, is it possible to wipe out that background without going through the process of time? Is that clear? The question is clear, surely.

Now, what is the past? What do we mean by the past? Surely we do not mean the chronological past, the second that was before—we don't mean that, that is just over. We mean, surely, the accumulated experiences, the accumulated responses, memories, traditions, knowledge, the subconscious storehouse of innumerable thoughts, feelings, influences, and responses. With that background, it is not possible to understand reality because reality must be of no time—it is timeless. So, one cannot understand the timeless with a mind which is the outcome of time. The questioner wants to know if it is possible to free the mind, or for the mind, which is the result of time, to cease to be immediately, or must one go through a long series of examinations and analyses and so free the mind from its background. You see the difficulty in the question.

Now, the mind is the background; the mind is the result of time; the mind is the past; the mind is not the future. It can project itself into the future, and the mind uses the present as a passage to the future, so it is still—whatever it does, whatever its activity, its future activity, its present activity, its past activity—in the net of time. And is it possible for the mind to cease completely, which means, for the thought process to come to an end? Now, there are obviously many layers to the mind; what we call consciousness has many layers, each layer interrelated with the other layer, each layer dependent on the other, interacting; and our whole consciousness is not only experiencing but also naming or terming, and also storing up as memory. That is the whole process of consciousness, is it not? Or is this all too difficult?

When we talk about consciousness, do we not mean the experiencing, the naming or the terming of that experience, and thereby storing up that experience in memory? Surely, all this, at different levels, is consciousness. And, can the mind, which is the result of time, go through the process of analysis, step by step, in order to free itself from the background; or is it possible to be free entirely from time and look at reality directly?

Now, let us see. Are you interested in this? Because you know, this is really quite an important question because it is possible, as I will presently explain, to be free of the background, therefore to renew life immediately without dependence on time—to recreate ourselves immediately and not depend on time. If you are interested, I will proceed, and you will see.

To be free of the background, many of the analysts say that you must examine every response, every complex, every hindrance, every blockage, which implies a process of time, obviously, which means the analyzer must understand what he is analyzing, and he must not misinterpret what he analyzes. Because, if he mistranslates what he analyzes, it will lead him to wrong conclusions, and therefore establish another background. Do you follow? Therefore the analyzer must be capable of analyzing his thoughts, feelings, without the slightest deviation; and he must not miss one step in his analysis because to take a wrong step, to draw a wrong conclusion, is to reestablish a background along a different line, on a different level. And this problem also arises: Is the analyzer different from what he analyzes? Are not the analyzer and the thing that is analyzed a joint phenomenon? Sir, I am not sure you are interested in this, but I will go on.

Surely the experiencer and the experience are a joint phenomenon; they are not two separate processes. So, first of all, let us see the difficulty of analyzing. It is almost impossible to analyze the whole content of our consciousness and thereby be free through that process. Because, after all, who is the analyzer? The analyzer is not different, though he may think he is different, from that which he is analyzing. He may separate himself from that which he analyzes, but the analyzer is part of that which he analyzes. I have a thought, I have a feeling—say, for example, I am angry. The person who analyzes anger is still part of anger, and therefore the analyzer as well as the analyzed are a joint phenomenon; they are not two separate forces or processes, and so the difficulty of analyzing ourselves, unfolding, looking at ourselves page after page, watching every reaction, every response, is incalculably difficult and long. Surely, therefore, that is not the way to free ourselves from the background. Is it? So there must be a much simpler, a more direct way, and that is what you and I are going to find out. But to find out we must discard that which is false and not hold on to it. So analysis is not the way, and we must be free of the process of analysis. As you would not take a path which you know does not lead anywhere, similarly the process of analysis will not lead anywhere; therefore, you do not take that path; therefore, it is out of your system.

Then what have you left? You are only used to analysis, are you not? The observer observing—the observer and the observed being a joint phenomenon—the observer trying to analyze that which he observes will not free him from his background. If that is so, and it is, you abandon that process, do you not? I do not know if you follow all this. If you see that it is a false way, if you realize, not merely verbally, but actually that it is a false process, then what happens to your analysis? You stop analyzing, do you not? Then what have you left? Watch it, sir, follow it, if you will, kindly, and you will see how rapidly and swiftly one can be free from the background. If that is not the way, what else have you left? What is the state of the mind which is accustomed to analysis, to probing, looking into, dissecting, drawing conclusions, and so on? If that process has stopped, what is the state of your mind?

You say that the mind is blank. Now, proceed further into that blank mind. In other words, when you discard what is known as being false, what has happened to your mind? After all, what have you discarded? You have discarded the false process which is the outcome of a background. Is that not so? With one blow, as it were, you have discarded the whole thing. Therefore your mind, when you discard the analytical process with all its implications and see it as false, is freed from yesterday and therefore is capable of looking directly, without going through the process of time, and thereby discarding the background immediately.

Sir, to put the whole question differently, thought is the result of time, is it not? Thought is the result of environment, of social and religious influences, which is all part of time. Now, can thought be free of time? That is, thought which is the result of time, can it stop and be free from the process of time? Thought can be controlled, shaped, but the control of thought is still within the field of time, and so our difficulty is: How can a mind that is the result of time, of many thousand yesterdays, be instantaneously free of this complex background? And you can be free of it, not tomorrow, but in the present, in the now. That can be done only when you realize that which is false, and the false is obviously the analytical process, and that is the only thing we have, and when the analytical process completely stops, not through enforcement, but through understanding the inevitable falseness of that process, then you will find that your mind is completely dissociated from the past—which does not mean that you do not recognize the past, but your mind has no direct communion with the past. So it can free itself from the past immediately, now, and this dissociation from the past, this complete freedom from yesterday—psychologically, not chronologically, but psychologically—is possible and that is the only way to understand reality.

Now, to put it very simply, when you want to understand something, what is the state of your mind? When you want to understand your child, when you want to understand somebody, something that someone is saying, what is the state of your mind? You are not analyzing, criticizing, judging what the other is saying; you are listening, are you not? Your mind is in a state where the thought process is not active, but is very alert. Yes? And that alertness is not of time, is it? You are merely being alert, passively receptive, and yet fully aware; and it is only in this state that there is understanding. Surely, when the mind is agitated, questioning, worrying, dissecting, analyzing, there is no understanding. And when there is the intensity to understand, the mind is obviously tranquil. This, of course, you have to experiment with, not take my word for it. But you can see that the more and more you analyze, the less and less you understand. You may understand certain events, certain experiences, but the whole content of consciousness cannot be emptied through the analytical process. It can be emptied only when you see the falseness of the approach through analysis. When you see the false as the false, then you begin to see what is true, and it is truth that is going to liberate you from the background. To receive that truth, the mind must cease to be analytical, must not be caught in the thought process, which obviously is analysis, which brings us to quite a different question, which is: "What is right meditation?"—which we will discuss at another time.

Question: I need the sunshine of the teacher's love to enable me to flower. Is such a psychological need not of the same order as the need for food, clothing, and shelter? You seem to condemn all psychological needs. What is the truth of this matter?

KRISHNAMURTI: Presumably, most of you have some kind of a teacher, have you not? Some kind of guru, either in the Himalayas, or here, round the corner. Do you not? Some kind of guide. Now why do you need him? You do not, obviously, need him for material purposes unless he promises you a good job the day-after-tomorrow. So, presumably, you need him for psychological purposes, do you not? Now, why do you need him? Basically, obviously, you need him because you say, "I am confused, I do not know how to live in this world; things are too contradictory. There is confusion, there is misery, there is death, decay, degradation, disintegration; and I need somebody to advise me what to do." Is that not the reason why you need a guru, why you go to a guru? You say, "Being confused, I need a teacher who will help me to clear up the confusion, or rather, help me to resolve the confusion." Is that not it? So your need is psychological. You do not treat your prime minister as your guru because he merely deals with the material life of society. You look to him for your physical needs; whereas, here you look to a teacher for your psychological needs.

Now, what do you mean by the word *need?* I need sunshine, I need food, clothes, and shelter; and in the same way, do I need a teacher? To answer that question, I must find out who has created this awful mess around me and in me. If I am responsible for the confusion, I am the only person that can clear up the confusion, which means that I must understand the confusion myself; but you generally go to a teacher in order that he may extricate you from the confusion or show you the way, give you directions on how to act with regard to the confusion. Or you say, "Well, this world is false; I must find truth." And the guru or the teacher says, "I have found truth," so you go to him to partake of that truth.

Can confusion be cleared by another, however great? Surely this confusion exists in our relationship; therefore, we have to understand our relationship with each other, with society, with property, with ideas, and so on; and can someone give us the understanding of that relationship? Someone may point out, may show, but I have to understand my relationship, where I am. Sir, are you interested in this? My difficulty is that I feel you are not interested because you are watching somebody else doing something. When you ask a question, you do not feel the importance of listening to the answer. Therefore, you are really treating your guru and your confusion very lightly. Really it does not matter to you two pins what your guru says, but it is just a habit—let us go to the guru. Therefore, life to you is not important, is not vital, creative, something which must be understood. And I can see it in your face; you are not vitally interested in this question. You listen either to be confirmed in your search for gurus or to strengthen your own conviction that gurus are essential. But that way we do not find the truth of the matter. You can find the truth of the matter by searching out your heart, why you need a guru.

So, sir, many things are involved in this question. You seem to think that truth is static, and therefore a guru can lead you to it. As a man can direct you to the station, so you think a guru can direct you to truth. That means truth is static, but is truth static? You would like it to be, for that which is static is very gratifying; at least you know what it is and you can hold on to it. So, you are really seeking gratification. You want security, you want the assurance of a guru, you want him to say to you, "You are doing very well, carry on"; you want him to give you mental comfort, an emotional pat on the back. So you go to a guru that really gratifies you, invariably. That is why there are so many gurus, as there are so many pupils, which means that you are not really seeking truth; you want gratification, and the person who gives you the greatest satisfaction, you call him your guru. That satisfaction is either neurological, that is, physical or psychological, and you think in his presence you feel great peace, great quietness, a sense of being understood. In other words, you want a glorified father or mother who will help you overcome the difficulty. Sir, have you ever sat quietly under a tree? There also you will find great peace. You will also feel that you are being understood. In other words, in the presence of a very quiet person, you also become quiet, and this quietness you attribute to the teacher, and then you put a garland around him and kick your servant. So, when you say you need a guru, surely all these things are implied in it, are they not? And the guru that assures you an escape—that guru becomes your need.

Now, confusion exists only in relationship, and why do we need somebody else to help us to understand this confusion? And you might say now, "What are you doing? Are you not acting as our guru?" Surely I am not acting as your guru because, first of all, I am not giving you any gratification; I am not telling you what you should do from moment to moment or from day to day, but I am just pointing something out to you; you can take it or leave it, depending on you, not on me. I do not demand a thing from you—neither your worship nor your flattery, nor your insults, nor your gods. I say this is a fact; take it or leave it. But most of you will leave it for the obvious reason that you will not find gratification in it. But the man who is really in earnest, who is really serious in his intention to find out, he will have sufficient food in what is being said, which is, that confusion exists only in your relationship, and therefore, let us understand that relationship.

To understand that relationship is to be aware, not to avoid it, to see the whole content of relationship. The truth is not in the distance, truth is near—truth is under every leaf, in every smile, in every tear, in the words, in the feelings, thoughts, that one has. But it is so covered up that we have to uncover it and see. To uncover is to discover what is false, and the moment you know what is false—and when that drops away—the truth is there.

So truth is a thing that is living from moment to moment to be discovered, not to be believed in, not to be quoted, not to be formulated. But to see that truth, your mind, your heart must be extremely pliable, alert. But most of us, unfortunately, do not want an alert, pliable mind, a swift mind; we want to be put to sleep by mantras, pujas—good God, in how many ways we put ourselves to sleep! Obviously we need a certain environment, a certain atmosphere, solitude, not the pursuit nor the avoidance of loneliness, but a certain aloneness in which there is full attention; and that aloneness, that certain complete attention, is there only when you are in trouble, when your problems are really intense; and, if you have a friend, if you have somebody who can help you, you go to him; but surely, to treat him as your guru is obviously immature, obviously childish. It is like seeking the mother's apron-strings.

I know all our instinct is, when we are in difficulty, to turn to somebody, to the mother, to the father, or to a glorified father whom you call the Master or the guru. But if the guru is worth his salt, he will obviously tell you to understand yourself in action, which is relationship. Surely, sir, you are far more important than the guru; you are far more important than I because it is your life, your misery, your strife, your struggle. The guru or I or someone else may be free, but what value has it to you? Therefore, the worship of the guru is detrimental to your understanding of yourself. And there is a peculiar factor in this: The more you show respect to the one, the less you show respect to others. You salute your guru most profoundly and kick your servant. Therefore, your respect has very little significance. I know these are all facts, and I know probably most of you do not like all that has been said because your mind wants to be comforted, because it has been bruised so much. It is caught up in such troubles and miseries, and it says, "For God's sake give me some hope, some refuge." Sir, only the mind that is in despair can find reality. A mind that is completely discontented can jump into reality—not a mind that is content, not a mind that is respectable, hedged about by beliefs.

So you flower only in relationship; you flower only in love, not in contention. But our hearts are withered; we have filled our hearts with the things of the mind, and so we look to others to fill our minds with their creations. Since we have no love, we try to find it with the teacher, with someone else. Love is a thing that cannot be found. You cannot buy it, you cannot immolate yourself to it. Love comes into being only when the self is absent; and as long as you are seeking gratification, escapes, refusing to understand your confusion in relationship, you are merely emphasizing the self and therefore denying love.

Shall I answer some more questions, or is that enough? Are you not tired? No? Sirs, are you being mesmerized by my voice and words? Surely, sirs, what we have discussed, what I said before answering the questions, and these two questions, must be very disturbing to you? It must be very disturbing; if it is not disturbing, something is wrong with you. Because, one is attacking the whole structure of your thought process, your comfortable ways, and that disturbance must be very fatiguing. And if you are not tired, if you are not disturbed, then what is the point of your sitting here? Sirs, let us be very clear about what we are trying to do, you and I. Probably, most of you will say, "I know all this; Shankara, Buddha, somebody else has said this." Your very statement indicates that, having read so much, superficially, you relegate what is being said to one of the pigeonholes in your mind, and thereby discard it. It is a convenient way of disposing of what you have heard, which means you are listening merely on the verbal level, and not taking in the full content of what is being said and which creates a disturbance. Sirs, peace cannot be had without a great deal of searching; and what you and I are doing is searching out our minds and hearts in order to find out what is true and what is false; and to search out is to expend energy, vitality; it is as physically exhausting—it should be as exhausting—as digging. But you see, unfortunately, you are used to listening; you are merely the spectators enjoying, observing what another is playing; therefore, you are not tired. The spectators are never tired, which indicates that they are really not partaking in the game. And as I have said over and over again, you are not the spectator, and I am not the player for you. You are not here to listen to a song. What you and I are trying to do is to find a song in our own hearts and not listen to the song of another. You are accustomed to listening to the song of another, and so your hearts are empty, and they will always be empty because you fill your hearts with the song of another. That is not your song; then you are merely gramophones, changing the records according to the moods, but you are not musicians. And especially in times of great travail and trouble we have to be the musicians, each one of us; we have to recreate ourselves with song, which means to free, to empty the heart of those things which are filled by the mind. Therefore, we have to understand the creations of the mind and see the falseness of those creations. Then we will not fill our hearts with those creations. Then, when the heart is empty—not, as in your case, filled with ashes—when the heart is empty and the mind is quiet, then there is a song, the song that cannot be destroyed or perverted because it is not put together by the mind.

January 23, 1949

Third Talk at Rajghat

Seeing that there are so few of us, should we turn this into a discussion first and answer questions afterwards? Perhaps it might be worthwhile to consider the question of revolution, of change and reform—their implications and their enduring significance in life—and whether revolution is not the only permanent solution, and not reform and change.

Reform in a given social order is merely retrogression—don't look surprised—is it not? Is not reform merely maintaining an existing social condition and giving it a certain modification but fundamentally maintaining the same structure? Reformation is, is it not, a modified continuity of a social pattern which gives a certain stability to society; and change also is of the same character, is it not? Change also is a modified continuity because change implies a formula which you are trying to follow or a standard which you are establishing—approximating the present to that standard. So, reformation and change are more or less the same thing, basically. Both imply the continuance of the present in a modified form. Both imply, do they not, that the reformer or the one who wishes to bring about the change has a measure or a pattern according to which he is approximating his action; therefore, his change, his reformation, is the reaction to the background in which he has been conditioned. So his reformation or change is the response of the background or the conditioning, which is merely approximating to a self-projected standard. I hope you are following all this. I am thinking aloud. I haven't thought of this before, so let us proceed.

So, a man who wishes to reform, to bring about certain reformation and change, is really a person who is acting as a detriment to revolution. A reformer or a man who wishes to bring about a change is really retrogressive because either there is constant revolution or merely change—a reforming modification. That modification, being the response of the background or of the conditioning in which he has been brought up, merely continues the background in another form. The reformer wishes to bring about a change in a given society, but his reformation is only the reaction to a certain background; the approximation to a certain standard he wishes to establish is still the projection of his background. So, the reformer, the one who wishes to bring about a change, acts in society as a retrogressive factor. Please think about it; don't deny, don't brush it aside.

Now, what is the relationship between the reformer and the revolutionary, and what do we mean by the revolutionary? Is a man who has a definite pattern or a formula and wishes to work out that formula—is he a revolutionary? Whether the technique is pacific or bloody is irrelevant; that is not the point. Is a man who has a formula, a standard, a pattern to which he is approximating his action, a revolutionary in the fundamental sense of the word? It is very important to find this out because everybody is concerned—or at least many people are concerned—about the question of revolution, about the left, the right, the center, and so on.

Now, when we talk about revolution, it is about the revolution according to a pattern either of the left or of the right or from the center; and when a person calls himself a revolutionary, is he not really a factor of retrogression in society, as is the reformer, as is the man who wishes to bring about a change? So, the man who has a formula and tries to approximate society to that is really a person who acts as a retrogressive factor in society.

Who, then, is a real revolutionary? We can see that the revolutionary who has a formula, and the man who wishes to bring about a change, and the reformer, are alike. They are not dissimilar because they have basically the same attitude towards action. Action to them is the approximation to an idea; the idealist, the reformer, and the revolutionary have a pattern. So, their actions are basically, are they not, the reaction to their background and therefore a factor of retrogression.

And that is why such a revolution ultimately fails—because it is merely an approximation to the left or to the right, a reaction to an opposite. You follow? And reform is similar. The reformer wants to alter a certain maladjustment in society, and his reformation has its source in the response to his background, to his conditioning; so they all have a similarity, have they not? The bloody one, the reformer, and the continued modifier. They obviously are not really revolutionary.

Now, we are going to find out what we mean by revolution. Is not revolution a series of intervals between two conditioned responses? Is revolution the outcome of a static state, of action which is dynamic, or is revolution the constant breaking away of the background and therefore leaving nothing static at any given moment? That is, is revolution a sudden break in the modified continuity and therefore in the response of the background, or is revolution a constant movement which is never at any given moment static?

Therefore, can revolution ever imply change or reform? Reform and change indicate a state in which there has been no true action and which must be transformed, changed, a static state which needs to be altered; and, as we said, the reformer or the one who wishes a change, and even the so-called revolutionary, are similar in their aims. Reform or revolution to them is only a gradual process of becoming static. I think that's clear. We allow ourselves—that is, the society, the community, the group—to become static, static in the sense of continuing the same pattern of action; though we may seem to move, live and act, produce children and build houses, it is always within the same static pattern.

Now, is what I suggest possible, and is that not the only true revolution—that is, of never allowing oneself to become static? Society, which is the relationship between you and me, must never become static; only then can there be constant revolution in our relationship. Now, what is it that makes us static, that makes us act without depth, without meaning, without purpose, without beauty—which is what most of our lives are? We live, we produce, we build, but it is a static state, surely; it is not a creative state. And what is it that makes us static, what is it that makes society—which is really our relationship, your relationship with me and my relationship with another—static? What are the factors which produce action that has no significance, a life that has no meaning?

What is it that produces in our relationship a sense of death? Though I may live with you, though I may work with you, there is something that is always destructive, that is always dead, that is always darkness, which is static. If we can understand and remove that, then, in our relationship there will be constant revolution, constant dynamism, constant change—no, I don't want to use the word change—constant transformation.

Now what makes for transformation, what makes for true revolution and not the modified continuity, what brings about the destruction of this static state? What is it that brings about death in our relationship? Why do we grow stale, weary, exhaust ourselves sexually, physically, and in various ways decay, why? If we can understand that, then we will be in a constant state of transformation. Now, what makes for death in relationship? What makes us stale, spoiled, corrupted, and what makes us seek modification, change, and all the rest of it? Surely, our thinking, which is the outcome of the past. There is no thought without memory, and memory is always the dead entity; it is over, only it revives itself in action, in the present, but it is an action of decay, of death. Though it seems so active, so alive, so full of speed and energy, thought is really, is it not, the outcome of a fixed pattern of memory. Memory is fixed and therefore what comes out of it must also be limited; and so does not the process of thinking itself bring about staleness, death, weariness, that static state? Therefore a revolution based on an idea, on thought, must sooner or later result in death. Thought, which is ideation, or the groping towards an ideal, is the sacrifice of the present to a utopia, the future. Sir, do you see something in this?

A relationship based on thought which is usage, habit, must produce a society which is static, and the action of the reformer who wishes to change that society is still the action of death, darkness, or the response of a static mind. If you observe, what makes us stale in our relationship is thinking, thinking, thinking, calculating, judging, weighing, adjusting ourselves; and the one thing which frees us from that is love, which is not a process of thought. You cannot think about love. You can think about the person whom you love, but you cannot think about love.

So, the man who loves is the real revolutionary, and he is truly the religious person because what is truly religion is not based on thought or on beliefs or dogmas. A person who is a net of beliefs and dogmas is not a religious person, he is a stupid person; whereas the man who really loves is the real revolutionary—in him is the real transformation. So, love is not a thought process; you cannot think about love. You may imagine what it should be; that is merely a thought process, but it is not love, and the man who loves is the real religious person, whether he loves the one or the many. Love is not personal or impersonal; it is love, it has no frontiers, it has no class, race. A man who loves is revolutionary—he alone is revolutionary. Love is not the product of thought, for thought is the outcome of memory, the outcome of conditioning, and can only produce death, decay.

So, there can be true revolution, a fundamental transformation, only when there is love, and that is the highest religion. That state comes into being when the thought process ceases, when there is the abnegation of that process. There can be abnegation of something only when it is understood, not denied. A community, a society, a group, can be really revolutionary, continuously transforming itself only when in that state, and not according to a formula because a formula is merely the product of a thought process, and therefore inherently the cause of a static state. We can also see that hate cannot produce a radical revolution, for inevitably, that which is the product of conflict, antagonism, confusion, cannot be real, cannot be creatively revolutionary. Hate is the outcome of this thought process; hate is thought, and that transformation which love brings can only be when the thought process ceases; therefore, thought can never produce a living revolution.

Question: Do you believe in the soul?

KRISHNAMURTI: Now, let us examine those two words, *believe* and the word *soul*. Has the word belief a referent? You know what the word *referent* means? Something to which you refer. When you say you believe that there is God, what is it, what is the referent behind that belief or behind that word *God?* I am not discussing God for the moment, but what is the referent behind that belief?

Surely, to believe is to project one's own intention, isn't it? Say you believe in God, you believe in nationalism. What does that mean? You clothe yourself with the idea; you use the idea of self-protection through nationalism, and you come to believe in nationalism. A belief is surely the outcome of a desire to be secure subjectively or outwardly, or it is an experience based on memory which dictates your belief. When you say you believe in the soul, what makes you believe in it, put your faith in it, trust it, what you will? It's your conditioning, surely? But the leftist, the nonbeliever, says there is no such thing because he too has been conditioned in his way; the believer is conditioned, as the nonbeliever is conditioned.

Now, is there such a thing as the soul?—that's what you want to know from me. Soul, implying a spiritual entity, no?—or character? Sirs, what do you mean by the soul when you talk about the soul? You mean the psyche? We are asking ourselves, are we not, if the soul, the psychological entity, exists. Obviously it exists, but surely we mean much more than that. Soul as character exists, but surely, we mean more than character when we talk about the soul. And character can be modified, changed, according to environment. There is nothing permanent about character; it can be modified, changed, according to environmental influences. But we mean much more—there is the plus quality—when we talk about the soul, don't we? Something which we posit as spiritual, as the 'more'. The difficulty is this, sirs. When you ask a question of this kind, one must go into it very carefully.

As far as one can see, there is only character modified, controlled, shaped by the environment. One can find out if there is something more only when the environmental influences and their limitations are understood and broken. The limited mind, which is the mind conditioned by environment, cannot find out if there is the plus quality, which is what you are asking. It is not a question of belief; either it is or it is not, and that can only be experienced, not believed in; and you can experience it only when there is no conditioning factor which is the thought process.

We can see very well what is happening in the world. The plus quality can never be controlled, shaped, caught in the net of time, but character can be changed. You are born in a certain country; there you have certain influences, certain molds of character, certain factors which are shaping the mind, but in another country the same shaping is going on in a different way. So, the so-called character of a person can be changed, modified, controlled, enlarged, what you will. Surely, that character is not the plus quality; therefore, to understand the plus quality, the character or the conditioning must cease. Which does not mean that you must become vague and loose; all we can do is to make the character fluid, not static, capable of immediate adjustments. After all, virtue is the capacity for swift adjustment; it is not the cultivation of an idea; cultivation of an idea is not virtue. Virtue is not the denial of vice; it is a state of being, and being is not an idea. The man who cultivates virtue is not virtuous. To experience that which is not an idea, ideation, which is thought process, must cease.

So, we see that character can be modified, changed, molded, and that is going on consciously or unconsciously all the time. But, the plus quality is what you are after. You cannot believe in it. The moment you use the word *believe,* you will never find it because believing is a process of thought. Thought can never find what is beyond, what is the plus. With the instrument of discovery that you have, which is the mind, you have never found it. You can invent, you can talk, you can describe, you can fool around with it. But, thought can never find it; the plus quality is obviously not of time, and the only instrument that we have is of time, as character, so we come back to the same question in a different way.

As long as we use the mind as a means of understanding, there can be no understanding. Thought does not produce understanding; on the contrary, you understand only with the cessation of thought—don't call it intuition, for God's sake! By intuition you mean perception and not action, but such a division is not real. This implies a great deal; we will go into it another time.

Question: In the light of the new approach, what is the content of education?

KRISHNAMURTI: Now, what do you mean by the new approach? Presumably, all that has been said during the last ten discussions—all that has been said, unfortunately, by me. Sorry to introduce myself into it. Now, the questioner wants to know what is the content of education in the light of all that.

Sir, what do you mean by education? Why are we educating ourselves? Why do you send your children to school? You would say, wouldn't you, to learn a technique by which to earn a livelihood. That's all you are interested in, isn't it? As long as he becomes a B.A., an M.A., and God knows what else, you will give him a certain instrument, a certain faculty by which he will be able to earn his livelihood; isn't that it? You are only interested, the majority of you, in giving the child a technique, aren't you?

Now, is the cultivation of technique education? I know it is necessary to be able to read and write, to learn engineering or something else, because in our society that is essential. But will technique give the faculty, give the capacity, rather, to experience? Because, after all, what we mean by education is to be able to experience life and not merely learn a technique which, surely, is only a part of life; we want to be able to experience life as a whole, don't we? Can I learn to experience as a whole through merely learning a technique? We admit technique is necessary, but to meet life as a whole, as an integrated whole, I need to experience, don't I? To experience pain, suffering, joy, everything, beauty, ugliness, love—I have to experience life, I have to taste life, haven't I?—at whatever level. Now, will technique help me to face life? I know, we admit technique is necessary, don't let us minimize it, but if that is the only thing which we are striving for, are we not denying the whole experiencing of life? But if you can help one to experience life as a whole, then that very experience will create its technique, and not the other way round.

Is this difficult, is this a little bit complicated? Now, sir, let me put it another way. We create the instrument to experience, isn't that so? After all, you educate your son to experience life, marriage, sex, worship, fear, government, which is all life. We create the instrument to experience, but can the instrument, which is technique, experience? You give him the tools and say, "Go and experience!" What? Can the tool, or the thing that holds the tools, experience?

If we approach it differently, that is, help the student to experience, then the very experiencing will create the instrument and not, as mere technique does now, act as a hindrance to experience. Is this a little bit abstract?

Again, let me put it differently. You teach me to be an engineer, give me the technique of livelihood, and my whole life is that of an engineer. I think, dream, compete; I am an engineer; I treat my wife, my children, my neighbors as an engineer. The profession, the technique, the faculty, the function has become important, but the function cannot experience life; I mean the whole of life, not just the mere building of a bridge or the building of a road or an ugly house.

Now, what are we doing? We are emphasizing the making of the instrument. So, we hope through the instrument to experience life, and that is why modern education is a complete failure—because you have got only the technique; you have marvelous scientists, marvelous physicists, mathematicians, bridge builders, space conquerors, and then what? Are you experiencing life? Only as specialists, and can a specialist experience life? Only when he ceases to be a specialist. So, first we make him the specialist and then hope he will experience. You see how wrong an approach it is? Whereas, is it not possible to create an environment in a school or in a community where the experiencing can go on, as a child, as a boy or girl, directly through the capacity for experiencing? Do you see what is meant?

Surely, that is real revolution—to experience integrally, as a whole human being, and as he experiences he will create, obviously; that is, if he experiences art, beauty, he will inevitably create the technique of painting, writing. He will want to express it, but now, you stop him by telling him how to write essays and teaching him styles and all the rest of it. But, if he is capable of experiencing a feeling, then the feeling will find its expression, then he will find his own style; when he writes a love poem it will be a love poem, not a carefully calculated rhyme.

So, now what are we doing? We create the instrument but destroy the man. The function has become all-important and not the man, but if the man is experiencing integrally all the time, he will create his own instrument. Sir, this is not an outrageous dream. This is what we do when we are real people, when we are not stuffed with stupid facts which we call education. When you have something to say, you say it, and it is style; but now we have nothing to say because we have destroyed ourselves through technique and have made that the final aim of life because we treat life as merely a matter of earning bread and butter, a job; life is a job for us.

So if we see this, cannot those who are experiencing express through teaching? If the person who is a teacher is really experiencing, then his expression will be teaching according to his temperament, faculties, capacities, and so on. Then that teaching will be the instrument of help to another human being to experience and not to be caught in a technique.

Sir, to put it differently: As long as we don't understand life, we use the instrument hoping to understand life; but the instrument cannot understand life; life has to be lived, understood by life, by action, by experience. You see, another factor is that the cultivation of technique gives one a sense of security, not only economic, but psychological, because you think you have the capacity to do something. And the capacity to do something gives you an extraordinary strength. You say,

"I can do this, or that; I can play the piano; any time I can go out and build a house." That gives you a sense of independence, vitality. But we deny life and its experience by strengthening the capacity because life is dangerous; it is unexpected, extraordinarily fluid; we don't know the content of it; it must be experienced constantly, continually renewed. Being afraid of that unknown quantity we say, "Let's cultivate technique because that will give us a certain sense of security, inwardly or outwardly." So, as long as we use technique as a means of inward security, life cannot be understood, and without experiencing life, technique has no meaning and we are only destroying ourselves.

We have marvelously capable technicians, and what's happening? Techniques are being used by experts to destroy each other. That's what governments want. They want technicians; they don't want human beings because human beings become dangerous to governments. Therefore, governments are going to control all education because they want more and more technicians.

So, the new approach is not the mere cultivation of a technique—which does not mean you deny technique—but it is the helping to create an integrated human being who will come by the technique through experiencing. Surely, sir, that is very simple, I mean, it is simple in words. But you can see the extraordinary effect it will have in society. We shall not be washed out at the age of 50 or 45 by a technique. Now, when I am 45 or 50, I am finished, having given my life to a rotten society or to a government that has no meaning at all except for the few who boss it; I have slaved my life away and I am exhausted. Whereas, life should become richer and richer, but that can happen only when technique is not used in the place of experiencing. Sir, if one really thinks of it, it is a complete revolution. As long as there is the cultivation of technique without experiencing the integrated action of life, there must be destruction, there must be competition, there must be confusion, ruthless antagonism. You are becoming entities with perfect capacities, and the more you emphasize technique, the more destruction there will be. If there were people who were experiencing and therefore teaching, they would be real teachers and they would create their own technique.

Therefore, experiencing comes first, life comes first, and not technique. Sir, when you have the creative impulse to paint, you take a brush and paint, you don't bother about the technique; you may learn the technique, but that impulse creates its own technique and that's the greatest art.

There is something very interesting happening in the world, especially in America. The engineers are frantically designing engines which do not need a single human being to run them. Life will be run entirely by machines, by various kinds of machines, and what is going to happen to human beings? Because they are all fast becoming technicians, they are going to destroy one another, for they will have nothing else to do. They won't know how to utilize their leisure, so they will seek escape through magazines or verbose ideations, through the radio, the cinema, and enfeebling amusements. What else will they have to do? The solution is in the capacity, the integrated capacity to experience life as a whole. Therefore, it means educating the educator to experience as a whole, helping him to be a human being and not a technician, a specialist.

That is quite difficult as we have all learned some technique or other. Some of you know how to meditate; you learned the technique, but you are not meditators. Some of you have learned the technique of playing the piano, but you are not musicians. You know how to read, but you cannot write because there is nothing in you crying for expression; you have filled your hearts and minds with technique. You are full of quotations, and you think you are marvelous because you can talk about what others have thought or said. What is there behind your technique? Words, words, mere verbalization, which is the technique. This is what we are doing with ourselves—so don't laugh it off.

So, experiencing comes first, living comes first, not technique. Love comes first, not how to express love. You read books about love, but your hearts are dry; that is why you read—to stimulate yourself. That is what you are all doing, because you have cultivated thought, and thought is death; and as you are dying slowly, you want stimulation and think technique will give you that stimulation; but stimulation always brings decay, making you more and more dull and weary.

Question: You have been leading a crusade against blind belief, superstition, and organized religion. Would I be wrong if I say that in spite of your verbal denunciation of the Theosophical tenets, you are fulfilling the central fact in Theosophy? You are preaching real Theosophy. There is no real contradiction between your position and the position of the Theosophical Society, whose great president first introduced you to the world. (Laughter)

KRISHNAMURTI: Now, don't let us discuss personalities, Dr. Besant and myself, for then we are lost.

Let us find out if I am leading a crusade against blind belief, superstition, and organized religion. I am merely trying to state a fact. A fact can be interpreted by anyone according to his conditioning, but the fact will remain a fact. I may translate it according to my like and dislike, but that fact is not altered—it is there.

Similarly, a belief, a superstition, an organized dogma of religion cannot help you to understand truth. Truth must be looked at without the screen of these, and only then is there understanding, and not according to my wishes; and organized beliefs, religions which are organized dogmas, cannot help me to understand life. They can help me to translate life according to my conditioning, but that is not understanding life, which again means that I am translating life according to my instrument, faculty, or conditioning. But that is not experiencing life, and religion is not the experiencing of life through a belief; religion is experiencing life directly without the conditioning. Therefore, there must be freedom from organized religion, and so on and on.

Now what is the Theosophical view? When the questioner says I am fulfilling the central fact in Theosophy, you and I must find out what the central fact in Theosophy is, and what the Theosophical Society is, according to the questioner. Now what is the central fact in Theosophy? I really do not know, but let us go at it. What are the certain facts of Theosophy—divine wisdom? That is what the word means. (Interruption) "No religion higher than truth." Is that the central fact?

Theosophy and the Theosophical Society are two different things. Now, which are you talking about? Please, sir, first let me assure you, I am not attacking or defending. We want to find the truth of the matter, at least I do. You may not; at least the adherents, those who have committed themselves, those who have vested interests in it, insist that this is Theosophy—but those people are not truth seekers; they are merely depending on their vested interest, hoping to be rewarded; therefore, they are not truth seekers.

Now, we must find out if there is a difference between Theosophy and the Theosophical Society. Surely the teachings of Christ are different from the Church. The teachings of Buddha are different from Buddhism, the organized religion. Obviously. The teaching is one thing, and organized society, organized religion, organized teaching, is another, is it not?

So, Theosophy and the Theosophical Society are two different things, are they not? Now, which do you want to find: the central fact of Theosophy, or the Theosophical Society? If you are interested in the central fact of Theosophy, which is divine wisdom, how are you going to find it out? That is, the central fact in Theosophy is wisdom, isn't it? Isn't that so, sir? Call it divine or human wisdom, it doesn't matter which. Now, is wisdom sought in a book, is wisdom given by another, is wisdom to be described, put into words, verbalized, learned, and repeated—is that wisdom? When I repeat the verbalization of the experience of a Buddha, is that wisdom? And is not that repetition a lie? Is not wisdom to be directly experienced? And I cannot experience wisdom when I have only the information about the wisdom of another.

Sirs, those of you who want to find the central fact in Theosophy, please listen carefully, do not close your ears. Is wisdom to be organized, to be spread around as you spread political propaganda or political views? Can wisdom be organized and spread around for the benefit of others? Is wisdom to be caught through authority, and is not wisdom come at through direct experience, and not through the technique of knowing what another has said about wisdom? Now, when you say that there is no religion higher than truth, it means that the central fact of Theosophy is to find truth, is it not? To discover truth, to understand it, to love it? And is truth a thing to be repeated and learned? Can you learn a truth as you can learn a technique? Again, is it not to be directly experienced, directly felt, directly known? I am not saying that Theosophy does not imply all this. We are discussing what the central fact is. I have not read Theosophical books any more than I have read other religious books . . . probably that is why one can think a little more freely about all these things.

So, can the central fact of Theosophy, which is wisdom and truth, be expressed through an organized society; or can an organized society help another to reach that? So let us leave that now—the central fact of Theosophy.

Now, the Theosophical Society. How you take notice, I don't know why you are interested in all this!

Now, what is an organized society, what is the function of an organized society—not as you would like it, but actually, factually? What is the function of an organized society, especially of this kind: to spread this wisdom, is it not? Then what? To translate this wisdom, to found a platform for people to come together in search of it? You would say yes, wouldn't you? That is, an organized society for the gathering together of those who will seek truth and wisdom? Surely! No? (Interruption) Sir, I am not trying to catch you, for, after all, an organized body exists for something. We at once become protagonists—he on one side, I on the other (Laughter); he, the ruler of a society or a section of the society, and I the opponent. Sir, let me please say here I am not your opponent, but I feel, on the contrary, that such societies are an impediment to understanding.

Why does your society exist? To propagate ideas? Or to help people to seek the central fact of Theosophy? Or, to act as a platform of tolerance so that people of different views can translate truth according to their conditioning? You are either a group of people who feel congenial to each other and say, "We are in this society because we have common views together," or you have come together as a means of seeking truth and helping each other to find it. These are four possibilities, and to these we can add. Now, all these resolve essentially into two: that we come together as a society to find truth, and to propagate truth. Now, can you propagate truth, and can you seek truth? Let us examine.

Can you propagate truth? What do you mean by propaganda? You think, for instance, that reincarnation is a fact. I am taking that as an example; you say let us go and propagate that; it will help people, alleviate their suffering, and so on—which means that you know the truth of reincarnation. Do you know the truth of reincarnation, or do you know only the verbal expression of an idea that there is continuity? You have read it in a book, and you propagate that, the words; you follow, sir? Is that spreading the truth? Can you propagate truth? Then you might turn around and say to me, "What are you doing?" I tell you I am not propagating truth; we are helping each other to be free, so the truth may come to us. I am not propagating, I am not giving you an "idea." What I am doing is helping you to see what are the impediments that prevent you from directly experiencing the truth. Is the person who propagates truth a truth speaker? Please, this is a very serious question. You can propagandize, but your propaganda is not truth, is it? The word *truth* is not the truth, is it? You are merely spreading the word *truth*, *reincarnation*, or you are explaining it, but the word *truth* is not the truth. It must be experienced; therefore, your propagandizing is merely verbal, untrue.

The other point is: People come together to seek truth, that is part of it. Now, can you seek truth, or does truth come to you? There is an enormous difference there. If you seek truth, you are wanting to utilize truth. You are using truth as a safeguard or to reach comfort, security, this or that; you are using it as a means of your own gratification, or what you will. When I seek something, that is my objective; don't let us deceive ourselves by a lot of words. When I seek power I go after it, I use it. And when you go after truth, it means you must already know it, for you cannot go after something unknown. When you know it, you are going to use it. What you know is self-protective, and therefore it is not truth. Can truth be found, or can you receive truth through belief?

Now, in discussing the Theosophical Society—of course, you understand, I am not concerned with it, I am out of it completely. You want to know if what I am saying, teaching, and the central fact of Theosophy and the Theosophical Society are the same. I say obviously they are not. You would like to patch it up and say we have produced you, and therefore you are a part of us, as a baby is part of the father and mother. That is a very convenient argument, but actually the boy is entirely different from the father when he grows a little older.

Surely, sir, when you are becoming more and more, spiritually climbing the ladder, you are denying truth, are you not? Truth is not at the top of the ladder; truth is where you are, in what you are doing, thinking, feeling, when you kiss and hug, when you exploit—you must see the truth of all that, not a truth at the end of innumerable cycles of life. To think that you may be a Buddha someday is but another self-projected aggrandizement. It is immature thinking, unworthy of people who are alive, deeply thoughtful, affectionate. If you think that you will be something in the future, you are not it now. What matters is now, not tomorrow. If you are not brotherly now, you will never be brotherly tomorrow because tomorrow is also the now.

You have come together as a society, and you ask me if you and I meet. I say we do not. You can make us "meet," you can twist anything to suit your convenience. You can pretend that white is black; but a mind that is not straight, that is incapable of direct perception of things as they are, merely thinks in terms of vested interest, whether in belief, in property, or in so-called spiritual status. I am not saying you should leave your society. I am not at all concerned whether you leave it or don't leave it, but if you think you are truth seekers and have come together to find reality, I am afraid you are going about it very wrongly. You may say, "That is your opinion." I would say that you are perfectly right. If you say, "We are trying to be brotherly," I would say again that you are going the wrong way because brotherhood is not at the end of the passage; and if you say you are cultivating tolerance, brotherhood, I would say that brotherhood and tolerance do not exist. They are not to be cultivated; you do not cultivate tolerance. When you love someone, you do not cultivate tolerance. It is only the man who has no love in his heart that cultivates tolerance. It is again an intellectual feat. If you say your society is not based on belief at all, inwardly or outwardly, then I would say that from your outward as well as your inward actions, you are a factor of separation, not of unity. You have your secret rituals, secret teachings, secret Masters, all indicating separation. It is the very function of an organized society to be separate in that sense.

So, I am afraid that when you go very deeply into the matter, you, the Theosophical Society, and I do not meet. You might like to make us meet, but that is quite a different matter—which does not mean you must leave yours and come over to this camp. There is no "this camp," there are no sides to truth. Truth is truth, one, alone; it has no sides, no paths; all paths do not lead to truth. There is no path to truth; it must come to you.

Truth can come to you only when your mind and heart are simple, clear, and there is love in your heart, not if your heart is filled with the things of the mind. When there is love in your heart, you do not talk about organizing for brotherhood, you do not talk about belief, you do not talk about division or the powers that create division, you need not seek reconciliation. Then you are a simple human being without a label, without a country. This means that you must strip yourself of all those things and allow truth to come into being, and it can come only when the mind is empty, when the mind ceases to create. Then it will come without your invitation. Then it will come as swiftly as the wind and unbeknown. It comes obscurely, not when you are watching, wanting. It is there as sudden as sunlight, as pure as the night, but to receive it, the heart must be full and the mind empty. Now you have the mind full and your heart empty.

February 6, 1949

Fourth Talk at Rajghat

I wonder what action means to most of us? Is action the outcome of an idea or the approximation to an idea or conformity to a pattern or ideation? Is action independent of relationship? Is not action, relationship? And if we base it on an idea, on a principle, on a conclusion, is it action? Is an action based on belief, which is a form of ideation, creative? Has such action the power of releasing not only vitality but creative energy, creative understanding?

Surely, it is important to find out, is it not, how far our action is dependent on an idea and whether the idea comes first or action comes first, whether mentation is the step preceding action or whether action is independent of mentation, of thought process. We have to discuss this and find out because if action is merely conforming to a particular pattern, to an idea or ideation, then the idea becomes all-important, and not action. Action then is merely the carrying out of that idea. Then, the problem arises of how to approach action with the idea, how to put the idea into practice in order to complete the idea, how to fulfill the idea through action, and so on. Is idea the primary incentive to action, or does action take place first, and then the ideation come into being? Surely, if we observe very closely, action comes first: first we do something, pleasurable or nonpleasurable, and then the idea is born out of that action. The idea then further controls the action, so the idea becomes all-important, and not action. Action then is merely the continuation of an idea. So, with most of us, the difficulty is, is it not, that ideas, which are the recording of previous experiences, of the past, are controlling, guiding, and shaping action.

Now, as I said, action is relationship, and what happens when action, when relationship, is based on an idea? Action born of an idea must continue to condition thought because an idea is the outcome of one's background, and the background shapes the action and therefore controls relationship. Therefore, action born of an idea can never be releasing; it must always be conditioned because the idea is a conditioned response, and an action born of an idea is necessarily conditioned. There is no freedom, no creative release through action which is based on an idea, and yet all our systems of action are based on ideation.

So, to look to an idea as a means of revolution, as a means of releasing creative energy, is obviously erroneous. Then, what is action without ideation? I hope you are interested because this is our problem. Our life is action; action is relationship, and if that action is merely the outcome of an idea, which is but the residue of previous experience, then that action can never be releasing; it is merely the continuation of the past, only modified. So, we cannot look for freedom, for liberation, for the understanding of reality through action which is the outcome of an idea. An experience, a previous experience, cannot be the way to truth. Experience which leaves a scar, as memory, cannot be the way to the understanding of truth. Therefore, experience as an idea, as a memory of yesterday shaping action, surely cannot be the way to truth. Memory is not the way to understanding. That is, if action is based on an idea which is the result of previous experience, then that action, being the outcome of the past, can never understand the living present.

So, what is the way of true action—action which is not the outcome of an idea? There is an action which is not merely the repetition of an idea. Experience is not the way to truth, but to most of us, experience is of the highest importance. We experience through the screen of memories, which again conditions the experience. That is, the idea, the background, has met the challenge, and out of that response, there is experience. That experience is conditioned; therefore, action is conditioned; therefore action, as experience, cannot lead to truth, cannot lead us to understanding. Please see the importance of this: that experience is a hindrance to the state of experiencing, for experience is a conditioned action, and being limited, can never be complete. Therefore, an experience is always a hindrance to the understanding of reality. This is contrary to what we have believed—that we must have more and more experience, knowledge, technique, in order to understand.

So, there has to be quite a different approach. You have to find out for yourself, inwardly, whether you are acting on an idea and if there can be action without ideation. We see that action based on an idea does not lead to truth, that action based on experience is limited action. That which is measurable cannot understand the immeasurable, and experience is always measurable. So, experience is not what we have made it out to be. Therefore, action based on experience is an impediment to understanding reality or to understanding anything new. So, there must be a different approach. Let us find out what that is—action which is not based on an idea.

When do you act without ideation? When is there an action which is not the result of experience? Because, an action based on experience is, as we said, limiting and therefore a hindrance. Action which is not the outcome of an idea is spontaneous when the thought process, which is based on experience, is not controlling action—which means, there is action independent of experience when the mind is not controlling action. That is the only state in which there is understanding: when the mind, based on experience, is not guiding action; when thought, based on experience, is not shaping action. What is action when there is no thought process? Can there be action without thought process? That is, I want to build a bridge, a house. I know the technique, and the technique tells me how to build it. We call that action. There is the action of writing a poem, of painting, of governmental responsibilities, of social, environmental responses. All are based on an idea or previous experience shaping action. But is there an action when there is no ideation?

Surely, there is such action when the idea ceases, and the idea ceases only when there is love. Love is not memory. Love is not experience. Love is not the thinking about the person that one loves, for then it is merely thought. Surely, you cannot think of love. You can think of the person you love or are devoted to—your guru, your image, your wife, your husband—but the thought, the symbol, is not the real which is loved. Therefore, love is not an experience.

Now, when there is love, there is action, is there not? And is that action not liberating? It is not the result of mentation, and there is no gap between love and action as there is between idea and action. Idea is always old, casting its shadow on the present and trying to build a bridge between action and idea. When there is love—which is not mentation, which is not ideation, which is not memory, which is not the outcome of an experience, of a practiced discipline—then that very love is action. That is the only thing that frees. As long as there is mentation, as long as there is the shaping of action by an idea which is experience, there can be no release; and as long as that process continues, all action is limited. When the truth of this is seen, the quality of love which is not mentation, which you cannot think about, comes into being.

This is what actually happens when you love somebody with all your being; this is exactly what takes place. You may think of that person, but that is not the actual, and unfortunately, what happens is that thought takes the place of love. Thought can then adjust itself to the environment, but love can never adjust itself. Adjustment is essentially of the mind, and the mind can invent "love." When I say, "I love you," I am adjusting myself to you, but there can be no adjustment where there is love—it is alone, it has no second. Therefore it cannot adjust itself to anything. When there is love, this idea of adjustment, of conformity of action based on idea, completely ceases. When there is love, there is action which is relationship, and where there is adjustment in relationship, there is no love. When I adjust myself to you because I love you, it is merely conforming to your desires, and the adjustment is always to the lower. How can you adjust yourself to the higher, to that which is noble, pure? You cannot. So, adjustment exists only when there is no love. Love is second to none; it is alone, but not isolated. Such love is action, which is relationship; it has not the possibility of corruption, as mentation has, because there is no adjustment. As long as action is based on an idea, action is mere adjustment, a reformed, modified continuity;

and a society which is the outcome of an approximation to an idea is a society of conflict, misery, and strife. There is freedom in the action which is not the result of mentation, and love is not devotion to something which is ideation. A devotee is not a lover of truth. Devotion is not love. In love, there is not the you and the other. There is complete fusion of the two, whether of the man with the woman or the devotee with his idea. Such love is not the gift of the few; it is not reserved for the mighty ones.

But you have not understood the implications of action based on experience. When one really sees that profoundly, when one is aware of all the implications, there is the cessation of mentation. Then there is that state of being which is the outcome of discontent. Discontent is not pacified through self-fulfillment, but as long as there is no self-fulfillment, discontent is the springboard from which there is a jump into the unknown. It is this quality of the unknown which is love. The man who is aware that he is in a state of love is not loving. Love is not of time. Therefore, you cannot think about it; what you can think about is of time. What you can think about is merely the projection of itself; it is already the known. When you know love, when you practice love, surely it ceases to be love because it is merely an adjustment of experience to the present and where there is adjustment, there can be no love.

Question: What is the best method of stilling the mind? Meditation and repetition of God's name are known to be the only method. Why do you condemn them? Can intellect by itself ever achieve this?

KRISHNAMURTI: Let us go into this question of meditation, which is really a very complex problem and needs careful thinking. Let us see its whole implication. Let us unroll the map of what we call meditation.

What do we mean by meditation? By meditation, we mean, don't we, the stilling of the mind, as it is generally understood; and let us see how we approach it, because the means matter, for the means create the end. If you employ wrong means, you will create a wrong end. If you discipline your mind to be quiet, then your mind should be quiet, but it is not. It is merely a disciplined mind, a mind that is held within the room, and such a mind is not quiet—it is only tethered, held in control. So, we have to go into this question carefully.

What is the purpose of meditation? Is it to still the mind? Is the stilling of the mind necessary for the discovery of truth or the experiencing of reality? Is the process of exclusion, meditation? Let us approach it negatively, because we do not know what right meditation is. People have said this and that, and you do not know what is real meditation. Is it through a series of denials of thought, or through resistance, that you come to the quietness of mind? That is, the mind is vagrant; it wanders ceaselessly, and you proceed to choose one course and resist all others, which is a process of exclusion, denial. You build a wall of resistance by concentration on a thought which you have chosen, and you try to ward off all the others. That is what you are doing all the time, struggling to learn concentration. Concentration then is an exclusion. You choose to rest your thinking on a word or an image, on a phrase or a symbol, and you resist every other thought that comes and interferes. So, what we call meditation is the cultivation of resistance, of exclusive concentration on an idea of our choice.

What makes you choose? What makes you say this is good, true, noble, and the rest is not? Obviously, the choice is based on pleasure, reward, or achievement; or it is merely a reaction of one's conditioning or tradition. Why do you choose at all? Why not examine every thought? When you are interested in the many, why choose one? Why not examine every interest? Instead of creating resistance, why not go into each interest as it arises and not merely concentrate on one idea, on one interest? After all, you are made up of many interests; you have many masks, consciously and unconsciously. Why choose one and discard the others—in controlling which you spend all your energies—thereby creating resistance, conflict and friction? Whereas, if you examine every thought as it arises—every thought, not just a few thoughts—then there is no exclusion, but it is an arduous thing to examine every thought. Because, as you are looking at one thought, another thought slips in, but if you are aware without domination or justification you will see that by merely looking at that thought, no other thought intrudes. It is only when you condemn, compare, approximate, that other thoughts come in. Is that clear?

So, concentration is not meditation. We are going to find out what meditation is, but first we must see what it is not. Concentration implies discipline, various forms of denial and resistance. A mind that is caught up in exclusive concentration can never find truth. But a mind that understands every interest, every movement of thought, a mind that is aware of every feeling, every response, and sees the truth in every response—such a mind, being extremely pliable, swift, is capable of understanding *what is,* which is truth. But a mind that is concentrated is not a swift mind; a mind that is disciplined is not a pliable mind. How can the mind be subtle, swift, and pliable when it has learned merely to concentrate?

Then, meditation cannot be supplication, supplication being prayer. Have you ever prayed? What actually happens when you pray? Why do you pray? You pray, don't you, only when you are in difficulty, only when you are troubled. You do not pray when you are happy, joyous, clear; you pray only when there is confusion, when there is fear of a certain event, in order to ward it off, or you pray to gain what you want. You pray because there is fear in you. I do not say prayer is only fear, but all supplication arises from fear. A petition, a prayer, may give you joy; the supplicatory prayer to the so-called unknown may bring you the answer you seek, but that answer to your petition may come from your unconscious or from the general reservoir, the storehouse of all your demands. The answer is not the still voice of God.

What happens when you pray? By the constant repetition of certain phrases and by controlling your thoughts, the mind becomes quiet, doesn't it? At least, the conscious mind becomes quiet. You kneel as the Christians do, or sit as the Hindus do, and you repeat and repeat; and through that repetition, the mind becomes quiet. In that quietness, there is an intimation of something. That intimation of something for which you have prayed may be from your unconscious or it may be the response of your memories. But, surely, it is not the voice of reality, for the voice of reality must come to you; it cannot be appealed to, you cannot pray to it. You cannot entice it into your little cage by doing puja, bhajan, and all the rest of it, by offering it flowers, by placating it, by suppressing yourself, or emulating others. Those are all forms of self-hypnosis; but once you have learned the trick of quieting the mind through the repetition of words and of receiving hints in that quietness, the danger is—unless you are fully alert as to whence these hints come—that you will be caught; and then prayer becomes a substitute for the search for truth. So, a mind that is made quiet through prayer is not a still mind, for it is a thing that is put together and so can be undone. All that happens is that the conscious layer of your mind, made quiet through pacification, made dull through repetition, receives some response to your petition; and that which you ask for, you get—but it is not the truth. If you want and if you petition, you receive, but you will pay for it in the end.

We see, therefore, that prayer as petition, supplication, helps to make the mind still, but there is also another form of prayer, which is to be completely receptive, not asking a thing, at least not consciously. This sensitive receptivity, induced through prayer, is also a form of stillness. It is merely your desire that is calling the response out of the unconscious, and that open receptivity of the conscious mind that is made still is not capable of understanding because the mind is made still, but is not still. A mind that is made still can never be still; it can receive an answer only from within the confines of its own limitation. A stupid mind can be made still, but its answer will be stupid. A stupid mind may think that the answer it has received is directly from God, but it is not. A mind that is made still can only receive an answer in accordance with its own conditioning. So, we see that prayer is not meditation.

Neither is devotion, meditation. Meditation is not self-immolation to an idea. What is your devotion? You are devoted to something that will give you gratification. If it does not give you gratification, you will not be devoted. You are a devotee as long as that to which you are devoted gives you gratification; when it ceases, you go elsewhere. You change your guru, you change the idea. The teacher, the guru, the image, is the self-projection of the devotee, and that self-projection is based on gratification. So, you are really being devoted to yourself, externalized as a deity, as an idea, or as a Master, or a picture. You are devoted only to that which gives you gratification, and so a devotee with all his puja, his garlands, his chants, is worshipping his own image, glorified, enlarged. Surely, that is not meditation.

Meditation is not discipline. Merely to discipline the mind is to limit the mind, to build a wall around it so that it cannot escape. That is why a mind that is disciplined, a mind that has found substitutes, that has found sublimation, a mind that is shaped, controlled, suppressed—that is still a mind that is incapable of freedom. Does freedom come into being through discipline? Can you discipline yourself to be free? If you use wrong means, the end will also be wrong, for the end is not different from the means. So, when a mind is disciplined in order to achieve a result, the result is only the projection of the disciplined mind. Therefore, there is no freedom, there is only a disciplined state. So meditation is not discipline.

Meditation is not concentration, meditation is not prayer, meditation is not devotion, meditation is not a process of discipline. Then, what is it? We are going to find out. Now, when you discover that concentration, prayer, devotion, discipline, are not meditation, then what happens? You are discovering yourself in action, are you not? The understanding of these things is the discovery of your own process of thinking, which is self-knowledge, is it not? The uncovering of this process is the uncovering of yourself in action; to understand this is to understand yourself. Therefore, meditation is the process of understanding yourself. There is no meditation without self-knowledge, and that is what you have discovered just now. Therefore, you are watching yourself in action through concentration, through prayer, through discipline, through devotion.

What we are doing now is discovering ourselves as we are without deception, without illusion. Then what happens? Self-knowledge is not an end in itself; self-knowledge is the movement of becoming. In examining these four aspects of myself in action, I have found that there is only one process—and that is that I am interested in becoming, in continuing. So then, the more knowledge of the self there is, of the self at any level—which is seeing the truth of every moment, the truth which is not the outcome of experience, but immediate perception—the more is there tranquillity of the mind. For example, seeing the truth of prayer and all its implications surely frees the mind from prayer, from fear, from supplication. Similarly, in seeing the truth of discipline, with all its implications, there is freedom from discipline. So, there is that much more knowledge, intelligence, and awareness. The mind is made free from its becoming; therefore, there is the awareness of truth.

Now, we have to experience this; we cannot go further without experiencing. If you are still caught in prayer, then your going further has no meaning; if you are still caught in discipline, what we proceed into has no meaning—so, too, if you are still concerned about the control of thought. But a mind that is quiet—not made quiet, not put together—a mind that is quiet because it has real interest, because it has seen truth, because truth has come to it, is a mind that is intelligent, that is free of conflict. Conflict has been resolved through the perception of every movement of thought and feeling, and by seeing the truth of that movement. Truth can be perceived, or truth can come into being only when condemnation, justification, and comparison cease; only then is the mind quiet, only then is there the cessation of memory.

Now, what happens when the mind is tranquil, when it is still, when it is no longer becoming, no longer seeking an end, when it is extraordinarily alert, passive? In that silence there is a movement, there is an experiencing, in which time is not. It is a state of being in which neither the past nor the present nor the future exists.

Meditation is the living from moment to moment every day. It is not isolating oneself in a room or in a cave, for that way one can never know reality. Reality is to be found in relationship, not in the distant relationship, but in the relationship of our daily existence. If there is no understanding of truth in relationship, you will not understand what it is to have a mind that is still. It is the truth that makes the mind still, not your desire to be still; and truth is to be found in relationship, which is action, which is as a mirror in which to see yourself.

So, self-knowledge is the beginning of wisdom, and without wisdom there can be no tranquillity. Wisdom is not knowledge. Knowledge is a hindrance to wisdom, to the uncovering of the self from moment to moment. A mind that is still shall know being, shall know what it is to love. Love is neither personal nor impersonal. Love is love, not to be defined or described by the mind as exclusive or inclusive. Love is its own eternity; it is the real, the supreme, the immeasurable.

February 13, 1949

Fifth Talk at Rajghat

As this is the last talk, I would like, if I may, to make a brief résumé of what we have been discussing during the last five weeks. It is the lack of capacity to understand that creates problems. The incapacity to understand a problem brings about conflict, and if we have the capacity to understand a problem, then the problem itself ceases to exist. It is the incapacity to understand a challenge that brings about a problem.

Life is, and must be, a series of challenges and responses. The challenge is not according to our likes and dislikes, nor according to our particular desires, but assumes different forms at different times. And if we have the capacity to meet that challenge adequately, fully, directly, then there is no problem. But because we do not meet that challenge fully, adequately, a problem arises. How is it possible to have that capacity? Life's challenge is not at any one particular level of existence. Life is not at one level only, neither the economic nor the spiritual. Life is, as we discussed, a relationship at different levels; it is all the time in flux, all the time expressing itself in different ways; and he is a happy man who is able to meet life completely and fully at different levels all the time.

So, the man who regards life as being merely the conditioning by environment, either economic or intellectual, and who meets life only from that point of view is obviously an unintegrated person, and his conflicts are innumerable because surely life isn't at one level of existence. Life is relationship with things, people, and ideas; and if we do not meet these relationships rightly, fully, then conflicts arise from the impact of the challenge.

So, our problem is, is it not, how to bring about, how to cultivate deliberately—if one can deliberately cultivate—that capacity to meet the challenge all the time. Because, there is not a moment when there is no challenge, and if there is not a response, there is death, there is decay. It is only when we know how to meet the challenge all the time, continuously, freely, fully, that there is life, that there is depth, the height of thought and feeling.

Now, how is one to have that capacity, how does one come by it? Surely, no information can give it. Though you may study all the books written about how to meet life, that very factual understanding is really an impediment because, having the facts, you try to meet the challenge with that framework of information. And, obviously, facts do not create or bring about that capacity. Without the capacity to meet life fully, life becomes a constant source of pain. So, it is not facts, it is not knowledge—you may read the Bhagavad-Gita, you may read all the sacred books, listen to the talks given by all the saints, practice innumerable disciplines—that will help you to have that capacity with which to meet life.

So, if it is not facts, if it is not knowledge, what is it that is required? Before we can find out, we have to discover, have we not, what is life itself, what is living. If we can understand that, perhaps we shall have the capacity to meet the challenge, which is life itself. Life is, is it not, both challenge and response. It is not challenge alone nor response alone. Life is experience, experience in relationship. One cannot live in isolation, so life is relationship, and relationship is action. And how can one have that capacity for understanding relationship, which is life? Does not relationship mean not only communion with people but intimacy with things and ideas? Life is relationship, which is expressed through contact with things, with people, and with ideas. In understanding relationship, we shall have the capacity to meet life fully, adequately. So, our problem is not capacity—for capacity is not independent of relationship—but rather the understanding of relationship, which will naturally produce the capacity for quick pliability, for quick adjustment, for quick response.

Relationship, surely, is the mirror in which you discover yourself. Without relationship you are not; to be is to be related; to be related is existence. And you exist only in relationship; otherwise, you do not exist, existence has no meaning. It is not because you think you are that you come into existence. You exist because you are related, and it is the lack of understanding of relationship that causes conflict.

Now, there is no understanding of relationship because we use relationship merely as a means of furthering achievement, furthering transformation, furthering becoming. But, relationship is a means of self-discovery because relationship is to be; it is existence. Without relationship, I am not. To understand myself, I must understand relationship. So, relationship is a mirror in which I can see myself. That mirror can either be distorted, or it can be "as is," reflecting that which is. But most of us see in relationship, in that mirror, things we would rather see; we do not see *what is.* We would rather idealize, escape; we would rather live in the future than understand that relationship in the immediate present.

So, the present is merely used by the past as a passage to the future. And so, relationship, which is always in the present, and not in the future or in the past, has no meaning, and therefore conflict arises. Conflict arises because we use the present as a passage to the future or the past. The mind is the result of the past; without the past, there is no thought. Without the background, without the conditioning, there is no thought. But thought, which is the result of the past, cannot understand the present as it only uses the present as a passage to the future. The future is always a becoming, so the present, in which alone there can be understanding, is never grasped. While there is a becoming, there is conflict, and the becoming is always the past using the present to be, to achieve. In the process of that becoming, thought is caught in the net of time. And time is not a solution to our problems. You understand only in the immediate, not tomorrow or yesterday—always in the now, though that now may be tomorrow. So, understanding is timeless. You cannot understand next life or next year.

So, that capacity to understand life comes into being only when one understands relationship. Relationship is a mirror. It must reflect, not as one wishes oneself to be, ideally or romantically, but what one actually is, and it is very difficult to perceive oneself as one actually is because one is so accustomed to escaping from *what is;* it is arduous to perceive, to observe silently *what is,* because one is so used to condemning, justifying, comparing, identifying. And in that process of justification, condemnation, that which is, is not understood. Only in the understanding of *what is* is there freedom from *what is.*

So, life has problems and conflicts and miseries only when you use relationship as a means of becoming, that is, when you gratify yourself through relationship. When I use another, or when I use property or an idea as a means of self-expansion, which is the perpetuation of gratification, then life becomes a series of ceaseless conflicts and miseries. It is only when I understand relationship—which is the beginning of self-knowledge—that self-knowledge brings about right thinking with regard to *what is;* and it is right thinking that dissolves our problems—not the gurus, not the heroes, not the mahatmas, not the literature, but the capacity to see *what is* and not escape from *what is.*

To acknowledge *what is* is to understand *what is.* But to acknowledge *what is* is most difficult, as the mind refuses to see, to observe, to accept *what is.* To see *what is,* to observe *what is,* demands action; and an ideal, the process of becoming, is an escape from action, is the avoidance of action. Since we surround ourselves with inaction, with escape, with ideals, we are running away from *what is,* which is relationship; but it is only in that relationship that we see ourselves clearly as we are. The more you go into *what is,* the more you see the deeper layers of consciousness, that is, life at different levels. In that there is freedom—not of discipline, not of cultivated, enclosed thought, but the freedom that truth, as virtue, brings; for without virtue there is no freedom. But the man who is becoming virtuous is not free. Virtue is only in the present, not in the future. So, we see that the whole significance of existence is not the avoidance of the present, but the comprehension of the present in relationship, and there is no relationship except in the present, and therein is the beauty of relationship.

After all, that is love, is it not? Love is not in the tomorrow. You cannot say that you will love tomorrow. Either you love now, or never. And that tremendous thing, that significance and beauty of love, can be understood only in relationship, but the mere cultivation of love through discipline is the denial of love. Then love is merely intellection. A man who loves with the mind is empty of heart. Mind can adjust itself, thought can adjust itself, but love never "adjusts." It is a state of being. What is pure is pure always, though it be divided. And it is that love, it is that truth which liberates.

Question: You say the mind, memory, and the thought process have to cease before there can be understanding, and yet you are communicating to us. Is what you say the experience of something in the past, or are you experiencing as you communicate?

KRISHNAMURTI: When do you communicate? When do you tell another your experience? When you have had the experience, not in the moment of experiencing. It is only an after-result, this communication. You must have memory, words, gestures, to communicate an experience which you have had. So your communication is the expression of an experience which is over.

Now, when do you understand, when is there understanding? I do not know if you have noticed that there is understanding when the mind is very quiet, even for a second; there is the flash of understanding when the verbalization of thought is not. Just experiment with it and you will see for yourself that you have the flash of understanding, that extraordinary rapidity of insight, when the mind is very still, when thought is absent, when the mind is not burdened with its own noise. So, the understanding of anything—of a modern picture, of a child, of your wife, of your neighbor, or the understanding of truth which is in all things—can only come when the mind is very still. But such stillness cannot be cultivated because if you cultivate a still mind, it is not a still mind, it is a dead mind.

It is essential to have a still mind, a quiet mind, in order to understand, which is fairly obvious to those who have experimented with all this. The more you are interested in something, the more your intention to understand, the more simple, clear, free the mind is. Then verbalization ceases. After all, thought is word, and it is the word that interferes. It is the screen of words, which is memory, that intervenes between the challenge and the response. It is the word that is responding to the challenge, which we call intellection. So, the mind that is chattering, that is verbalizing, cannot understand truth—truth in relationship, not an abstract truth. There is no abstract truth. But truth is very subtle. It is the subtlety that is difficult to follow. It is not abstract. It comes so swiftly, so darkly, it cannot be held by the mind. Like a thief in the night, it comes darkly, not when you are prepared to receive it. Your reception is merely an invitation of greed. So, a mind that is caught in the net of words cannot understand truth.

The next question is: Is it not possible to communicate as one is experiencing? For communication there must be factual memory. As I am talking to you, I use words which you and I understand. Memory is a result of the cultivation of the faculty of learning, of storing words. The questioner wants to know how to have a mind that does not merely express or communicate after the event, after the experience, but a mind that is experiencing and at the same time communicating. That is, a new mind, a fresh mind, a mind that is experiencing without the interference of memory, the memory of the past. So, first let us see the difficulty in this.

As I said, most of us communicate after the experience; therefore, communication becomes a hindrance to further experience because communication, the verbalization of an experience, merely strengthens the memory of that experience. And strengthening the memory of one experience prevents the free experiencing of the next. We communicate either to strengthen an experience or to hold onto it. We verbalize it in order to fix it as memory or to communicate it. The very fixing, through verbalization, of an experience is the strengthening of an experience that is over. Therefore, you are strengthening memory, and so it is memory that is meeting the challenge. In that state, when the response to challenge is merely verbal, experience of the past becomes a hindrance. So, our difficulty is to be experiencing and, in communicating it, not to make verbalization a hindrance to further experience.

In all these discussions and talks, if I merely repeated the experience of the past, it would not only be extremely boring to you and to me but it would also strengthen the past and therefore prevent experiencing in the present. What is actually taking place is that the experience is going on, and at the same time there is communication. The communication is not verbalization; it is not clothing the experience. If we clothe the experience, give it a garment, shape it, the perfume and depth of that experiencing will be lost. So, there can be a fresh mind, a new mind, only when experiencing is not clothed by words. And in expressing it verbally, there is the danger of clothing it, giving it a shape, a form, and therefore burdening the mind with the image, with the symbol. It is possible to have a new mind, a fresh mind, only when it is not the word which is important, but the experiencing. That experiencing is from moment to moment. There cannot be experiencing if it becomes accumulative, for then it is accumulation that experiences, and there is no experiencing. There is experiencing from moment to moment only when there is no accumulation. Verbalization is accumulation. It is extremely difficult and arduous to express and still not be caught in the net of words.

Mind is, after all, the result of the past, of yesterday. And that which is not of time cannot be followed by time. The mind cannot follow that which is exceedingly swift, not of space, not of time; but in that state of the mind which is experiencing, which is not becoming, everything is new. It is the word that makes *what is* old. It is the memory of yesterday that clothes the present. And to understand the present, there must be experiencing, but experiencing is prevented when the word becomes all-important. So, there is a new mind—the mind that is experiencing continuously without shaping or being shaped by the experience—only when the word, the past, is not used as a means of becoming.

Question: Is marriage compatible with chastity?

KRISHNAMURTI: Let us together explore this question. Many things are involved in it. Chastity is not the product of the mind.

Chastity doesn't come through discipline. Chastity is not an ideal to be achieved. That which is the product of the mind, which is created by the mind, is not chaste because the mind, when it creates the ideal of chastity, is escaping from *what is;* and a mind which is attempting to become chaste is unchaste. That is one thing. We will explore it presently.

Then, in this question there is involved the problem of our sexual appetites, the whole problem of sex. Let us find out why for most of us sex has become a problem. And also, how is it possible to meet the sexual demand intelligently and not turn it into a problem?

Now, what do we mean by sex? The purely physical act, or the thought that excites, stimulates, furthers that act? Surely, sex is of the mind, and because it is of the mind, it must seek fulfillment or there is frustration. Do not be nervous about the subject. You have all become very tense, I see. Let us talk it over as though it were any other subject. Don't look so grave and lost! Let us deal with this subject very simply and directly. The more complex a subject is, the more it demands clear thinking, the more must it be approached simply and directly.

Why is it that sex has become such a problem in our lives? Let us go into it, not with constraint, not with anxiety, fear, condemnation. Why has it become a problem? Surely, for most of you it is a problem. Why? Probably, you have never asked yourself why it is a problem. Let us find out.

Sex is a problem because it would seem that in that act there is complete absence of the self. In that moment you are happy because there is the cessation of self-consciousness, of the 'me'; and desiring more of it—more of the abnegation of the self in which there is complete happiness, without the past or the future, demanding that complete happiness through full fusion, integration—naturally it becomes all-important. Isn't that so? Because it is something that gives me unadulterated joy, complete self-forgetfulness, I want more and more of it. Now, why do I want more of it? Because, everywhere else I am in conflict, everywhere else, at all the different levels of existence, there is the strengthening of the self. Economically, socially, religiously, there is the constant thickening of self-consciousness, which is conflict. After all, you are self-conscious only when there is conflict. Self-consciousness is in its very nature the result of conflict. So, everywhere else we are in conflict. In all our relationships with property, with people, and with ideas there is conflict, pain, struggle, misery; but in this one act there is complete cessation of all that. Naturally you want more of it because it gives you happiness, while all the rest leads you to misery, turmoil, conflict, confusion, antagonism, worry, destruction; therefore, the sexual act becomes all-significant, all-important.

So, the problem is not sex, surely, but how to be free from the self. You have tasted that state of being in which the self is not, if only for a few seconds, if only for a day, or what you will; and where the self is, there is conflict, there is misery, there is strife. So, there is the constant longing for more of that self-free state. But the central problem is the conflict at different levels and how to abnegate the self. You are seeking happiness, that state in which the self, with all its conflicts, is not, which you find momentarily in that act. Or, you discipline yourself, you struggle, you control, you even destroy yourself through suppression—which means you are seeking to be free of conflict because with the cessation of conflict there is joy. If there can be freedom from conflict, then there is happiness at all the different levels of existence.

What makes for conflict? How does this conflict arise in your work, in your relationships, in teaching, in everything? Even when you write a poem, even when you sing, when you paint, there is conflict.

How does this conflict come into being? Does it not come into being through the desire to become? You paint, you want to express yourself through color, you want to be the best painter. You study, worry, hope that the world will acclaim your painting. But, wherever there is the desire to become the 'more', there must be conflict. It is the psychological urge that demands the 'more'. The need for more is psychological, the urge for the 'more' exists when the psyche, the mind is becoming, seeking, pursuing an end, a result. When you want to be a mahatma, when you want to be a saint, when you want to understand, when you are practicing virtue, when you are class-conscious as a "superior" entity, when you subserve function to heighten yourself—all these are indications, obviously, of a mind that is becoming. The 'more', therefore, is conflict. A mind which is seeking the 'more', is never conscious of *what is* because it is always living in the 'more'—in what it would like to be, never in *what is*. Until you resolve the whole content of that conflict, this one release of the self, through sex, will remain a hideous problem.

Sirs, the self is not an objective entity that can be studied under the microscope or learned through books or understood through quotations, however weighty those quotations may be. It can be understood only in relationship. After all, conflict is in relationship, whether with property, with an idea, with your wife, or with your neighbor; and without solving that fundamental conflict, merely to hold onto that one release through sex is obviously to be unbalanced. And that is exactly what we are. We are unbalanced because we have made sex the one avenue of escape; and society, so-called modern culture, helps us to do it. Look at the advertisements, the cinemas, the suggestive gestures, postures, appearances.

Most of you married when you were quite young, when the biological urge was very strong. You took a wife or a husband, and with that wife or husband you jolly well have to live for the rest of your life. Your relationship is merely physical, and everything else has to be adjusted to that. So what happens? You are intellectual, perhaps, and she is very emotional. Where is your communion with her? Or she is very practical, and you are dreamy, vague, rather indifferent. Where is the contact between you and her? You are oversexed and she is not, but you use her because you have rights. How can there be communion between you and her when you use her? Our marriages are now based on that idea, on that urge; but more and more there are contradictions and great conflicts in marriage, and so divorces.

So, this problem requires intelligent handling, which means that we have to alter the whole basis of our education; and that demands understanding not only the facts of life but also our everyday existence, not only knowing and understanding the biological urge, the sexual urge, but also seeing how to deal with it intelligently. But now, we don't do that, do we? It is a hushed subject, it is a secret thing, only talked about behind walls. When the urge is very strong, irrespective of anything else, we get mated for the rest of our life. See what one has done to oneself and to another.

How can the intellectual meet, commune, with the sentimental, the dull, or with the one who is not educated? And what communion is there then, except the sexual? The difficulty in all this is, is it not, that the fulfillment of the sexual urge, the biological urge, necessitates certain social regulations; therefore, you have marriage laws. You have all the ways of possessing that which gives you pleasure, security, comfort; but that which gives constant pleasure dulls the mind. As constant pain dulls the mind, so constant pleasure withers the mind and heart.

And how can you have love? Surely, love is not a thing of the mind, is it? Love is not merely the sexual act, is it? Love is something which the mind cannot possibly conceive. Love is something which cannot be formulated. And, without love you become related; without love, you marry. Then, in that marriage, you "adjust yourselves" to each other. Lovely phrase! You adjust yourselves to each other, which is again an intellectual process, is it not? She has married you, but you are an ugly lump of flesh, carried away by your passions. She has got to live with you. She does not like the house, the surroundings, the hideousness of it, your brutality. But she says, "Yes, I am married, I have got to put up with it." So, as a means of self-protection she yields, she presently begins to say, "I love you." You know, when, through the desire for security, we put up with something ugly, that ugly thing seems to become beautiful because it is a form of self-protection; otherwise, we might be hurt, we might be utterly destroyed. So we see that which was ugly, hideous, has become gradually beautiful.

This adjustment is obviously a mental process. All adjustments are. But, surely, love is incapable of adjustment. You know, sirs, don't you, that if you love another, there is no "adjustment." There is only complete fusion. Only when there is no love, do we begin to adjust. And this adjustment is called marriage. Hence, marriage fails because it is the very source of conflict, a battle between two people. It is an extraordinarily complex problem, like all problems, but more so because the appetites, the urges, are so strong.

So, a mind which is merely adjusting itself can never be chaste. A mind which is seeking happiness through sex can never be chaste. Though you may momentarily have, in that act, self-abnegation, self-forgetfulness, the very pursuit of that happiness, which is of the mind, makes the mind unchaste. Chastity comes into being only where there is love. Without love, there is no chastity. And love is not a thing to be cultivated. There is love only when there is complete self-forgetfulness, and to have the blessing of that love, one must be free through understanding relationship. Then, when there is love, the sexual act has quite a different significance. Then that act is not an escape, is not habit. Love is not an ideal; love is a state of being. Love cannot be where there is becoming. Only where love is, is there chastity, purity; but a mind that is becoming, or attempting to become chaste, has no love.

Question: We have been told that thought must be controlled to bring about that state of tranquillity necessary to understand reality. Could you please tell us how to control thought?

KRISHNAMURTI: First, sir, don't follow any authority. Authority is evil. Authority destroys, authority perverts, authority corrupts; and a man who follows authority is destroying himself and destroying also that which he has placed in a position of authority. The follower destroys the master as the master destroys the follower. The guru destroys the pupil as the pupil destroys the guru. Through authority you will never find anything. You must be free of authority to find reality. It is one of the most difficult things to be free of authority, both the outer and the inner. Inner authority is the consciousness of experience, consciousness of knowledge. And outward authority is the state, the party, the group, the community. A man who would find reality must shun all authority, external and inward. So, don't be told what to think. That is the curse of reading—the word of another becomes all-important.

The questioner begins by saying, "We have been told." Who is there to tell you? Sir, don't you see that leaders and saints and great teachers have failed, because you are what you are? So leave them alone. You have made them failures because you are not seeking truth; you want gratification. Don't follow anyone, including myself; don't make of another your authority. You yourself have to be the master and the pupil. The moment you acknowledge another as a master and yourself as a pupil, you are denying truth. There is no master, no pupil, in the search for truth. The search for truth is important, not you or the master who is going to help you to find the truth. You see, modern education, and also the previous education, have taught you what to think, not how to think. They have put you within a frame, and that frame has destroyed you, because you seek out a guru, a teacher, a leader, political or other, only when you are confused. Otherwise you never follow anybody. If you are very clear, if you are inwardly a light unto yourself, you will never follow anyone. But because you are not, you follow; you follow out of your confusion, and what you follow must also be confused. Your leaders as well as yourself are confused, politically and religiously. Therefore, first clear up your own confusion, become a light unto yourself, and then the problem will cease. The division between the master and the pupil is unspiritual.

Now, the questioner wants to know how to control thought. First of all, to control it you must know what thought is and who is the controller. Are they two separate processes or a joint phenomenon? You must first understand what thought is, must you not, before you say, "I will control thought"; and also you must know what the controller is. Is there a controller without thought? If you have no thoughts, is there a thinker? The thinker is the thought; the thought is not separate from the thinker; they form a single process.

So, you have only thoughts left, not the thinker. Though you use the words *I think*, it is only a form of communication; there is actually only a state in which thought is. And thought creates the thinker who then communicates his thought. The thinker is merely the verbalization of the thought.

So, we have to find out what is thought. Then we shall know whether it is possible to control it or not and why you want to control it. There may be quite a different approach to putting an end to the thought process, but it is not by control. Because, the moment you exert control, making an effort through an act of will, you do not understand thought. You are then merely condemning one thought and justifying another. That which you have justified, you want to hold onto. That which you condemn, you want to push aside. So, let us find out what we mean by thought.

What is thought? Without memory there is no thought, is there? Thought is the result of accumulated experience, is it not, which is the past. Without the past, there can be no thought in the present, can there? So thought is a response of the past to the present challenge. That is, thought surely is the reaction of memory. But, what is memory? Memory, the continuance of remembering, is the verbalization of experience, isn't it? There is challenge, response—which is experience—and that experience is verbalized. That verbalization creates memory, and the response of memory to challenge is thought. So thought is verbalization, isn't it?

I do not know if you have ever tried to think without words. The moment you think, you must use words. I am not saying that there is not a state in which there is no verbalization. We are not discussing that. The thought is the word. Without verbalization, without the word, thought—the thought that we know—is not. So, if you see that the word—the verbalization—is the thought process, then it is not a question of controlling thought, but of the cessation of thinking as verbalization. Where there is verbalization of an experience, there must be thought. To think is to verbalize. So, our problem is not how to control thought, but whether it is possible not to verbalize, not to put everything into words. Why do we put our responses, our reactions, into words? Why do we do that? For one obvious reason—to communicate, to tell another our feeling. Also, we verbalize in order to strengthen that feeling, don't we, in order to fix it, in order to look at it, in order to recapture that feeling which is gone. The word has taken the place of the feeling which has gone. So the word becomes all-important, and not the feeling, not the response, not the experience. The word has taken the place of experiencing. So, the word becomes the thought, which prevents experiencing.

Our problem, then, is this: Is it possible not to verbalize, not to name, not to give a term? Obviously it is possible. You do this often, only unconsciously. When you are faced with a crisis, with a sudden challenge, there is no verbalization. You meet it fully. So, it is possible, but only when the word is not important, which means when thought is not important, when the idea is not important. When an idea assumes importance, then the pattern becomes important, the ideology becomes important, and the revolution based on an idea becomes important; but a revolution based on an idea is not a revolution, it is merely the continuation, the modified continuity of an old idea, an idea of yesterday.

So, the word becomes important only when experiencing is not important, when there is not the state of experiencing, which is to meet the challenge without verbalization, without the screen of words. You give life to the word, which is memory, when it is that memory which meets the challenge, because memory has no life in itself, has it? The word has no meaning in itself. It gains vitality, strength, impetus, fullness, only when the past, the memory, meets the challenge. Therefore, out of the living, the dead comes to life. And as it gains more life from that which in itself is dead, then thought becomes all-important. Thought by itself has no meaning except in relation to the past, which is verbal. And it is not a question of controlling thought. On the contrary, a controlled mind is incapable of receiving truth. A controlled mind is an anxious mind, a mind that is resisting, suppressing, substituting, and such a mind is afraid, and how can a mind that is anxious be still? How can a mind that is afraid be tranquil? There can be tranquillity only when the mind is no longer caught in the net of words. When the mind is no longer verbalizing every experience, then naturally it is in a state of experiencing.

Where there is experiencing, there is neither the experiencer nor the experienced. In that state of experiencing, which is always new, which is always being—though one can communicate that being by using words—one knows that the word is not the experience, the word is not the thing, the word has no content; only the experience itself is full of content. Then, experiencing is not verbalization. Experiencing is the highest form of understanding because it is the negation of thinking. The negative form of thinking is the highest form of comprehension, and there can be no negative thinking when there is verbalization of thought. So, it is not a question of controlling thought at all but of being free from thought. It is only when the mind is free from thought that there is a perception of that which is, of that which is eternal, which is truth.

Question: What do you mean by transformation?

KRISHNAMURTI: Obviously, there must be a radical revolution. The world crisis demands it. Our lives demand it. Our everyday incidents, pursuits, anxieties, demand it. Our problems demand it. There must be a fundamental, radical revolution because everything about us has collapsed. Though seemingly there is order, in fact there is slow decay, destruction—the wave of destruction is constantly overtaking the wave of life. So there must be a revolution—but not a revolution based on an idea. Such a revolution is merely the continuation of the idea, not a radical transformation. And a revolution based on an idea brings bloodshed, disruption, chaos. Out of chaos you cannot create order; you cannot deliberately bring about chaos and hope to create order out of that chaos. You are not the God-chosen who are to create order out of confusion. That is such a false way of thinking on the part of those people who wish to create more and more confusion in order to bring about order. Because the moment they have power, they assume they know all the ways of producing order. But seeing the whole of this catastrophe—the constant repetition of wars, the ceaseless conflict between classes, between peoples, the awful economic and social inequality, the inequality of capacity and gifts, the gulf between those who are extraordinarily happy, unruffled, and those who are caught in hate, conflict, and misery—seeing all this, there must be a revolution, there must be complete transformation, must there not?

Now, is this transformation, is this radical revolution an ultimate thing, or is it from moment to moment? I know we would like it to be the ultimate thing because it is so much easier to think in terms of far away. Ultimately we shall be transformed, ultimately we shall be happy, ultimately we shall find truth, but in the meantime, let us carry on. Surely, such a mind, thinking in terms of the future, is incapable of acting in the present, and therefore such a mind is not seeking transformation, it is merely avoiding transformation. And what do we mean by transformation?

Transformation is not in the future, can never be in the future. It can only be now, from moment to moment. So, what do we mean by transformation? Surely, it is very simple—seeing the false as the false and the true as the true. Seeing the truth in the false, and seeing the false in that which has been accepted as the truth. Seeing the false as the false and the true as the true is transformation. Because, when you see something very clearly as the truth, that truth liberates. When you see that something is false, that false thing drops away. Sir, when you see that ceremonies are mere vain repetitions, when you see the truth of it and do not justify it, there is transformation, is there not, because another bondage is gone. When you see that class distinction is false, that it creates conflict, creates misery, division between people—when you see the truth of it, that very truth liberates. The very perception of that truth is transformation, is it not? And as we are surrounded by so much that is false, perceiving the falseness from moment to moment is transformation. Truth is not cumulative. It is from moment to moment. That which is cumulative, accumulated, is memory, and through memory you can never find truth, for memory is of time—time being the past, the present, and the future. Time, which is continuity, can never find that which is eternal; eternity is not continuity. That which endures is not eternal. Eternity is in the moment. Eternity is in the now. The now is not the reflection of the past nor the continuance of the past through the present to the future.

A mind which is desirous of a future transformation, or looks to transformation as an ultimate end, can never find truth. For truth is a thing that must come from moment to moment, must be discovered anew, and surely, there can be no discovery through accumulation. How can you discover the new if you have the burden of the old? It is only with the cessation of that burden that you discover the new. So, to discover the new, the eternal, in the present, from moment to moment, one needs an extraordinarily alert mind, a mind that is not becoming. A mind that is becoming can never know the full bliss of contentment—not the contentment of smug satisfaction, not the contentment of an achieved result, but the contentment that comes when the mind sees the truth in *what is* and the false in *what is.* The perception of that truth is from moment to moment, and that perception is delayed through verbalization of the moment.

So, transformation is not an end result. Transformation is not a result. Result implies residue, a cause and an effect. Where there is causation, there is bound to be effect. The effect is merely the result of your desire to be transformed. When you desire to be transformed, you are still thinking in terms of becoming, and that which is becoming can never know that which is being. Truth is being from moment to moment, and happiness that continues is not happiness. Happiness is that state of being which is timeless. That timeless state can come only when there is a tremendous discontent—not the discontent that has found a channel through which it escapes, but the discontent that has no outlet, that has no escape, that is no longer seeking fulfillment. Only then, in that state of supreme discontent, can reality come into being. That reality is not to be bought, to be sold, to be repeated; it cannot be caught in books. It has to be found from moment to moment, in the smile, in the tear, under the dead leaf, in the vagrant thoughts, in the fullness of love—for love is not different from truth. Love is that state in which thought process as time has completely ceased. And where love is, there is transformation. Without love, revolution has no meaning, for then revolution is merely destruction, decay, a greater and greater, ever-mounting misery. Where there is love, there is revolution, because love is transformation from moment to moment.

February 20, 1949

Ojai, California, 1949

First Talk in The Oak Grove

I think it is very important that we should be most earnest. Those who come to these gatherings, those who go to various meetings of this kind, think they are very earnest and serious. But I would like to find out what we mean by being earnest, by being serious. Is it earnestness, does it show seriousness, if we go from one lecturer or talker to another, from one leader to another, from one teacher to another, if we go to different groups or pass through different organizations in search of something? So, before we begin to find out what it is to be earnest, surely we must find out what it is that we are seeking.

What is it that most of us are seeking? What is it that each one of us wants? Especially in this restless world where everybody is trying to find some kind of peace, some kind of happiness, a refuge, surely it is important to find out, isn't it, what it is that we are trying to seek, what it is that we are trying to discover. Probably most of us are seeking some kind of happiness, some kind of peace; in a world that is ridden with turmoil, wars, contention, strife, we want a refuge where there can be some peace. I think that is what most of us want. And so we pursue, go from one leader to another, from one religious organization to another, from one teacher to another.

Now, is it that we are seeking happiness, or is it that we are seeking gratification of some kind from which we hope to derive happiness? Surely, there is a difference between happiness and gratification. Can you seek happiness? Perhaps you can find gratification, but surely, you cannot find happiness. Happiness is derivative, surely; it is a byproduct of something else. So, before we give our minds and hearts to something which demands a great deal of earnestness, attention, thought, care, we must find out, must we not, what it is that we are seeking—whether it is happiness, or gratification. I am afraid most of us are seeking gratification. We want to be gratified, we want to find a sense of fullness at the end of our search.

Now, can you seek anything? Why do you come to these meetings? Why are you all sitting here and listening to me? It would be very interesting to find out why you are listening, why you take the trouble to come from long distances on a hot day and listen. And, to what are you listening? Are you trying to find a solution for your troubles, and is that why you go from one lecturer to another, and through various religious organizations, and read books, and so on and on; or, are you trying to find out the cause of all the trouble, the misery, contention, and strife? Surely, that does not demand that you should read a great deal, that you should attend innumerable meetings, or search out teachers? What it demands is clarity of intention, doesn't it?

After all, if one is seeking peace, one can find it very easily. One can devote oneself blindly to some kind of a cause, to an idea, and take shelter there. Surely, that does not solve the problem. Mere isolation in an enclosing idea is not a release from conflict. So, we must find, must we not, what it is, inwardly as well as outwardly, that each one of us wants. If we are clear on that matter, then we don't have to go anywhere, to any teacher, to any church, to any organization. So, our difficulty is, is it not, to be clear in ourselves regarding our intention. Can we be clear? And does that clarity come through searching, through trying to find out what others say, from the highest teacher to the ordinary preacher in a church round the corner? Have you got to go to somebody to find out? And yet, that is what we are doing, is it not? We read innumerable books, we attend many meetings and discuss, we join various organizations—trying thereby to find a remedy to the conflict, to the miseries in our lives. Or, if we don't do all that, we think we have found; that is, we say that a particular organization, a particular teacher, a particular book satisfies us; we have found everything we want in that, and we remain in that, crystallized and enclosed.

So, we have to come to the point when we ask ourselves really earnestly and profoundly if peace, happiness, reality, God, or what you will can be given to us by someone else. Can this incessant search, this longing, give us that extraordinary sense of reality, that creative being which comes when we really understand ourselves? Does self-knowledge come through search, through following someone else, through belonging to any particular organization, through reading books, and so on? After all, that is the main issue, is it not?—that as long as I do not understand myself, I have no basis for thought, and all my search will be in vain. I can escape into illusions; I can run away from contention, strife, struggle; I can worship another; I can look for my salvation through somebody else. But as long as I am ignorant of myself, as long as I am unaware of the total process of myself, I have no basis for thought, for affection, for action.

But that is the last thing we want—to know ourselves. Surely, that is the only foundation on which we can build. But, before we can build, before we can transform, before we can condemn or destroy, we must know that which we are. So, to go out seeking, changing teachers, gurus, practicing yoga, breathing, performing rituals, following Masters, and all the rest of it, is utterly useless, is it not? It has no meaning even though the very people whom we follow may say, "Study yourself." Because, what we are, the world is. If we are petty, jealous, vain, greedy—that is what we create about us, that is the society in which we live.

So, it seems to me that before we set out on a journey to find reality, to find God, before we can act, before we can have any relationship with another, which is society, surely it is essential that we begin to understand ourselves first. And I consider the earnest person to be one who is completely concerned with this first, and not with how to arrive at a particular goal. Because, if you and I do not understand ourselves, how can we, in action, bring about a transformation in society, in relationship, in anything that we do? And it does not mean, obviously, that self-knowledge is opposed to, or isolated from, relationship. It does not mean, obviously, emphasis on the individual, the 'me', as opposed to the mass, as opposed to another. I do not know if some of you have seriously undertaken to study yourselves, watching every word and its responses, watching every movement of thought and feeling—just watching it, being conscious of your bodily responses, whether you act from your physical centers, or whether you act from an idea, how you respond to the world condition. I do not know if you have ever seriously gone into this question at all. Perhaps sporadically, as a last resort, when everything else has failed and you are bored, some of you have tried it.

Now, without knowing yourself, without knowing your own way of thinking and why you think certain things, without knowing the background of your conditioning and why you have certain beliefs about art and religion, about your country and your neighbor and about yourself, how can you think truly about anything? Without knowing your background, without knowing the substance of your thought and whence it comes, surely, your search is utterly futile, your action has no meaning, has it? Whether you are an American or a Hindu or whatever your religion is has no meaning either.

So, before we can find out what the end-purpose of life is, what it all means—wars, national antagonisms, conflicts, the whole mess—surely, we must begin with ourselves, must we not? It sounds so simple, but it is extremely difficult. Because, to follow oneself, to see how one's thought operates, one has to be extraordinarily alert so that as one begins to be more and more alert to the intricacies of one's own thinking and responses and feelings, one begins to have a greater awareness, not only of oneself, but of another with whom one is in relationship. To know oneself is to study oneself in action, which is relationship. But, the difficulty is that we are so impatient; we want to get on, we want to reach an end. And so we have neither the time nor the occasion to give ourselves the opportunity to study, to observe. Or we have committed ourselves to various activities—to earning a livelihood, to rearing children—or have taken on certain responsibilities of various organizations; we have so committed ourselves in different ways that we have hardly any time for self-reflection, to observe, to study. So, really, the responsibility of the reaction depends on oneself, not on another. And the pursuit, as in America and all the world over, of gurus and their systems, reading the latest books on this and that, and so on, seems to me so utterly empty, so utterly futile; for you may wander all over the earth, but you have to come back to yourself. And, as most of us are totally unaware of ourselves, it is extremely difficult to begin to see clearly the process of our thinking and feeling and acting. And that is the thing I am going to deal with during the weeks that are to follow in which I am to talk.

The more you know yourself, the more clarity there is. Self-knowledge has no end—you don't come to an achievement, you don't come to a conclusion. It is an endless river. And as one studies it, as one goes into it more and more, one finds peace. Only when the mind is tranquil—through self-knowledge and not through imposed self-discipline—only then, in that tranquillity, in that silence, can reality come into being. It is only then that there can be bliss, that there can be creative action. And it seems to me that without this understanding, without this experience, merely to read books, to attend talks, to do propaganda is so infantile—just an activity without much meaning. Whereas, if one is able to understand oneself and thereby bring about that creative happiness, that experiencing of something that is not of the mind, then perhaps there can be a transformation in the immediate relationship about us, and so in the world in which we live.

Question: Do I have to be at any special level of consciousness to understand you?

KRISHNAMURTI: To understand anything—not only what I am saying, but to understand anything—what is required? To understand yourself, to understand your husband, your wife, to understand a picture, to understand the scenery, the trees, what is required? Right attention, isn't it? Because, to understand something, you must give your whole being to it, your undivided, full, deep attention, must you not? And how can there be deep, full attention when you are distracted?—for example, when you are taking down notes as I am talking, you catch a good phrase, probably, and you say, "By Jove, I am going to take that down, I am going to use it in my talk." How can there be full attention when you are merely concerned with words? That is, you are concentrated on the verbal level and so are incapable of going beyond that verbal level. Words are only a means of communication. But, if you are not capable of communicating and merely stick to words, obviously there cannot be full attention; therefore, there is no right understanding.

So, listening is an art, is it not? To understand something, you must give full attention, and that is not possible when there is any kind of distraction—taking notes or when you are sitting uncomfortably or when you are struggling to understand by making an effort. Making an effort to understand is obviously a hindrance to understanding because your whole attention has gone into making the effort. I do not know if you have ever noticed that when you are interested in something that another is saying, you are not making an effort, you are not building up a wall of resistance against distraction. There are no distractions when you are interested; you are giving your full attention eagerly, spontaneously, to something that is being said. When there is vital interest, there is spontaneous attention. But most of us find such attention very difficult because consciously, on the upper level of the mind, you may want to understand, but inwardly there is resistance, or inwardly there may be a desire to understand, but outwardly, superficially, there is resistance.

So, to give full attention to something, there must be integration of your whole being. Because, at one level of consciousness you may want to find out, you may want to know, but at another level, that very knowing may mean destruction because it may make you change your whole life. So, there is an inward contention, an inward struggle, of which you are perhaps unaware. Though you think you are paying attention, there is really a distraction going on inwardly or outwardly, and that is the difficulty.

So, to understand anything, one must give complete attention; and that is why I have been suggesting at various meetings that no notes should be taken, that you are not here to do propaganda for me or for yourself, that you should listen only in order to understand. Our difficulty in understanding is that our mind is never quiet. We never look at anything quietly, in a receptive mood. A lot of rubbish is thrown at us by newspapers, magazines, politicians, tub-thumpers; every preacher around the corner tells us what to do and what not to do. All that is constantly pouring in, and naturally there is also an inward resistance to it all. There can be no understanding as long as the mind is disturbed. As long as the mind is not very quiet, silent, tranquil, receptive, sensitive, it is not possible to understand; and this sensitivity of the mind is not merely at the upper level of consciousness, in the superficial mind. There must be tranquillity right through, an integrated tranquillity. When you are in the presence of something very beautiful, if you begin to chatter you will not sense its meaning. But the moment you are quiet, the moment you are sensitive, its beauty comes to you. Similarly, if we would understand anything, not only must we be physically still, but our minds must be extremely alert, yet tranquil. That alert passivity of the mind does not come about through compulsion. You cannot train the mind to be silent; then it is merely like a trained monkey, outwardly quiet, but inwardly boiling. So, listening is an art, and you must give your time, your thought, your whole being to that which you want to understand.

Question: Can I understand easier what you are saying by teaching it to others?

KRISHNAMURTI: You may learn, by telling it to others, a new way of putting things, a clever way of transmitting what you want to say, but surely, that is not understanding. If you don't understand yourself, how in the name of names can you tell it to somebody else? Surely, that is merely propaganda, isn't it? You don't understand something, but you tell others about it, and you think a truth can be repeated. Do you think, if you have an experience, you can tell it to others? You may be able to communicate verbally, but can you tell others of your experience—that is, can you convey the experiencing of a thing? You may describe the experience, but you cannot convey the state of experiencing. So, a truth that is repeated ceases to be a truth. It is only the lie that can be repeated, but the moment you "repeat" a truth, it loses its meaning. And most of us are concerned with repeating, but are not experiencing. A man who is experiencing something is not concerned with mere repetition, with trying to convert others, with propaganda. But unfortunately, most of us are concerned with propaganda because through propaganda, we try not only to convince others but also gain a living by exploiting others; it gradually becomes a racket.

So, if you are not caught up in mere verbalization but are really occupied with experiencing, then you and I are in communion. But, if you want to do propaganda—and I say truth cannot be propagandized—then there is no relationship between us. And I am afraid that is our difficulty at the present time. You want to tell others without experiencing, and in telling, you hope to experience. That is mere sensation, mere gratification; it has no significance. It has no validity, no reality behind it. But, a reality experienced, if communicated, creates no bondage. So, experiencing is much more important, has greater significance, than communication on the verbal level.

Question: It seems to me that the movement of life is experienced in relationship with people and ideas. To detach oneself from such stimulation is to live in a depressing vacuum. I need distractions to feel alive.

KRISHNAMURTI: In this question is involved the whole problem of detachment and relationship. Now, why do we want to be detached? What is this instinct in most of us that wants to push away, that wants to be detached? It may be that for most of us this idea of detachment has come into being because so many religious teachers have talked about it—"You must be detached in order to find reality; you must renounce, you must give up, and then only will you find reality." And can we be detached in relationship? What do we mean by relationship? So, we will have to go into this question a little carefully.

Now, why have we this instinctive response, this constant looking to detachment? The various religious teachers have said you must be detached. Why? First of all the problem is, Why are we attached? Not how to be detached, but *why* is it that you are attached? Surely, if you can find the answer to that, then there is no question of detachment, is there? Why are we attached to attractions, to sensations, to things of the mind or of the heart? If we can discover why we are attached, then perhaps we will find the right answer—not how to be detached.

Why are you attached? And what would happen if you were not attached? If you were not attached to your particular name, property, position—you know, the whole mass of things that makes up you: your furniture, your car, your characteristics, your idiosyncrasies, your virtues, your beliefs, your ideas—what would happen? If you were not attached, you would find yourself to be as nothing, would you not? If you were not attached to your comforts, to your position, to your vanity, you would be suddenly lost, would you not? So, the fear of emptiness, the fear of being nothing makes you attached to something, whether it is to your family, to your husband, wife, to a chair, to a car, to your country—it doesn't matter what. The fear of being nothing makes some cling to something, and in the process of holding on, there is conflict, there is pain. Because, what you hold onto soon disintegrates, dies—your car, your position, your property, your husband. So, in the process of holding, there is pain, and in order to avoid pain, we say we must be detached. You look into yourself and you will see that this is so. Fear of loneliness, fear of being nothing, fear of emptiness makes us attach ourselves to something—to a country, to an idea, to a God, to some organization, to a Master, to a discipline, what you will. In the process of attachment, there is pain, and to avoid that pain, we try to cultivate detachment, and so we keep up this circle which is always painful, in which there is always a struggle.

Now, why can't we be as nothing, a nonentity? Not merely on the verbal level, but inwardly? Then there is no problem of attachment or detachment, is there? And, in that state, can there be relationship? Because, that is what this questioner wants to know. He says that without relationship to people and to ideas, one lives in a depressing vacuum. Is that so? Is relationship a process of attachment? When you are attached to somebody, are you related to that person? When I am attached to you, hold on to you, possess you, am I related to you? You become a necessity to me because without you I am lost, I am made uncomfortable, I feel miserable, I feel lonely. So, you become a necessity, a useful thing, a thing to fill my emptiness. You are not important; what is important is that you fill my need. And is there any relationship between us when to me you are a need, a necessity, like a piece of furniture?

To put it differently, can one live without relationship? And is relationship merely a stimulation? Because, without that, which you call distraction, you feel lost, you do not feel alive. That is, you treat relationship as a distraction, which makes you feel alive. That is what the questioner says.

So, can one live in the world without relationship? Obviously not. There is nothing that can live in isolation. Some of us, perhaps, would like to live in isolation, but one cannot do it. Therefore, relationship becomes merely a distraction, which makes you feel as though you were alive; quarreling with each other, having struggles, contention, and so on give one a sense of aliveness. So, relationship becomes merely a distraction. And, as the questioner says, without distractions, you feel you are dead. Therefore, you use relationship merely as a means of distraction; and distraction, whether drink, going to cinemas, accumulating knowledge—any form of distraction—obviously dulls the mind and heart, does it not? A dull mind, a dull heart—how can it have any relationship with another? It is only a sensitive mind, a heart that is awakened to affection, that can be related to something.

So, as long as you treat relationship as a distraction, you are obviously living in a vacuum because you are frightened to go out of that state of distraction. Hence you are afraid of any kind of detachment, any kind of separation. Relationship then is a distraction which makes you feel alive. Whereas, true relationship, which is not a distraction, is really a state in which you are constantly in a process of understanding yourself in relation to something. That is, relationship is a process of self-revelation, not of distraction, and that self-revelation is very painful because in relationship you soon find yourself out, if you are open to discover it. But as most of us do not want to discover ourselves, as most of us would rather hide ourselves in relationship, relationship becomes blindly painful, and we try to detach ourselves from it. Relationship is not a stimulation. Why do you want to be stimulated through relationship? And if you are, then relationship, like stimulation, becomes dull. I do not know if you have noticed that any kind of stimulation eventually dulls the mind and the sensitivity of the heart.

So, the question of detachment should never arise because only the man who possesses thinks of renouncing, but he never questions why he possesses, what is the background that has made him possessive. When he understands the process of possessing, then there is naturally freedom from possession—not the cultivation of an opposite as detachment. And relationship is merely a stimulation, a distraction, as long as we are using another as a means of self-gratification or as a necessity in order to escape from ourselves. You become very important to me because in myself I am very poor; in myself I am nothing; therefore, you are everything. Such a relationship is bound to be a conflict, a pain; and a thing that gives pain is no longer a distraction. Therefore, we want to escape from that relationship, which we call detachment.

So, as long as we use the mind in relationship, there can be no understanding of relationship. Because, after all, it is the mind that makes us be detached. When there is love, there is no question of attachment or detachment. The moment there is the cessation of that love, then the question of attachment and detachment begins. Love is not the product of thought; you cannot think about love. It is a state of being. And, when the mind interferes by its calculation, by its jealousies, by its various cunning deceptions, then the problem of relationship arises. Relationship has significance only when it is a process of revealing oneself to oneself; and if in that process one proceeds deeply, widely, and extensively, then in relationship there is peace—not the contention, not the antagonism between two people. Only in that quietness, in that relationship in which there is the fruition of self-knowledge, is there peace.

July 16, 1949

Second Talk in The Oak Grove

As I was suggesting yesterday, we should be able to listen to what is being said without rejection or acceptance. We should be able to listen so that if something new is being said, we do not immediately reject it—which does not mean either that we must accept everything that is being said. That would be really absurd because then we would merely be building up authority, and where there is authority, there can be no thinking, feeling; there can be no discovery of the new. And, as most of us are inclined to accept something eagerly, without true understanding there is a danger, is there not, that we may accept without thought or investigation, without looking deeply into it. This morning I may perhaps say something new, or put something differently, which you may pass by if you do not listen with that ease, with that quietness which brings understanding.

I want to discuss this morning a subject which may be rather difficult—the question of action, activity, and relationship. Then I will answer questions. But before I do that, we have to understand first what we mean by activity, what we mean by action. Because, our whole life seems based on action, or rather, activity—I want to differentiate between activity and action. We seem to be so engrossed in doing things; we are so restless, so consumed with movement, doing something at any cost, getting on, achieving, trying for success. And what is the place of activity in relationship? Because, as we were discussing yesterday, life is a question of relationship. Nothing can exist in isolation, and if relationship is merely an activity, then relationship has not much significance. I do not know if you have noticed that the moment you cease to be active, there is immediately a feeling of nervous apprehension; you feel as though you are not alive, not alert, so you must keep going. And there is the fear of being alone—of going out for a walk alone, of being by yourself without a book, without a radio, without talking, the fear of sitting quietly without doing something all the time with your hands or with your mind or with your heart.

So, to understand activity, surely we must understand relationship, must we not? If we treat relationship as a distraction, as an escape from something else, relationship then is merely an activity. And is not most of our relationship merely a distraction and therefore but a series of activities involved in relationship? As I said, relationship has true significance only when it is a process of self-revelation, when it is the revealing to oneself in the very action of relationship. But most of us do not want to be revealed in relationship. On the contrary, we use relationship as a means of covering up our own insufficiency, our own troubles, our own uncertainty. So, relationship becomes mere movement, mere activity. I do not know if you have noticed that relationship is very painful and that as long as it is not a revealing process in which you are discovering yourself, relationship is merely a means of escape from yourself.

I think it is important to understand this because, as we were discussing yesterday, the question of self-knowledge lies in the unfolding of relationship, whether to things, to people, or to ideas. Can relationship be based on an idea? And, surely, any act based on an idea must be merely the continuation of that idea, which is activity. Action is not based on an idea. Action is immediate, spontaneous, direct, without the process of thought involved. But when we base action on an idea, then it becomes an activity; and if we base our relationship on an idea, then surely such a relationship is merely an activity, without comprehension. It is merely carrying out a formula, a pattern, an idea. Because we want something out of relationship, such relationship is always restricting, limiting, confining.

Idea is, is it not, the outcome of a want, of a desire, of a purpose. If I am related to you because I need you, physiologically or psychologically, then that relationship is obviously based on idea, is it not, because I want something from you. And such a relationship, based on an idea, cannot be a self-revealing process. It is merely a momentum, an activity, a monotony, in which habit is established. Hence, such relationship is always a strain, a pain, a contention, a struggle, causing us agony.

Is it possible to be related without idea, without demand, without ownership, possession? Can we commune with each other—which is real relationship on all the different levels of consciousness—if we are related to each other through a desire, a physical or psychological need? And can there be relationship without these conditioning causes arising from want? As I said, this is quite a difficult problem. One has to go very deeply and very quietly into it. It is not a question of accepting or rejecting.

We know what our relationship is at present—a contention, a struggle, a pain, or, mere habit. If we can understand fully, completely, relationship with the one, then perhaps there is a possibility of understanding relationship with the many, that is, with society. If I do not understand my relationship with the one, I certainly shall not understand my relationship with the whole, with society, with the many. And if my relationship with the one is based on a need, on gratification, then my relationship with society must be the same. Therefore, there must follow contention with the one and with the many. And is it possible to live with the one and with the many without demand? Surely, that is the problem, is it not? Not only between you and me, but between me and society. And to understand that problem, to inquire into it very deeply, you have to go into the question of self-knowledge because without knowing yourself as you are, without knowing exactly *what is,* obviously you cannot have right relationship with another. Do what you will—escape, worship, read, go to cinemas, turn on radios—as long as there is no understanding of yourself, you cannot have right relationship. Hence the contention, battle, antagonism, confusion, not only in you, but outside of you and about you. As long as we use relationship merely as a means of gratification, of escape, as a distraction which is mere activity, there can be no self-knowledge. But self-knowledge is understood, is uncovered, its process is revealed, through relationship—that is, if you are willing to go into the question of relationship and expose yourself to it. Because, after all, you cannot live without relationship. But we want to use that relationship to be comfortable, to be gratified, to be something. That is, we use relationship based on an idea, which means the mind plays the important part in relationship. And as mind is concerned always with protecting itself, with remaining always within the known, it reduces all relationship to the level of habit, or of security, and therefore, relationship becomes merely an activity.

So, you see that relationship, if we allow it, can be a process of self-revelation, but since we do not allow it, relationship becomes merely a gratifying activity. As long as the mind merely uses relationship for its own security, that relationship is bound to create confusion and antagonism. And is it possible to live in relationship without the idea of demand, of want, of gratification? Which means, is it possible to love without the interference of the mind? We love with the mind, our hearts are filled with the things of the mind, but surely, the fabrications of the mind cannot be love. You cannot think about love. You can think about the person whom you love, but that thought is not love, and so, gradually, thought takes the place of love. And, when the mind becomes supreme, the all-important, then obviously there can be no affection. Surely, that is our problem, is it not? We have filled our hearts with the things of the mind. And the things of the mind are essentially ideas—what should be, and what should not be. Can relationship be based on an idea? And if it is, is it not a self-enclosing activity and therefore inevitable that there should be contention, strife, and misery? But if the mind does not interfere, then it is not erecting a barrier, it is not disciplining, suppressing, or sublimating itself. This is extremely difficult because it is not through determination, practice, or discipline that the mind can cease to interfere; the mind will cease to interfere only when there is full comprehension of its own process. Then only is it possible to have right relationship with the one and with the many, free of contention and discord.

Question: I gather definitely from you that learning and knowledge are impediments. To what are they impediments?

KRISHNAMURTI: Obviously, knowledge and learning are an impediment to the understanding of the new, the timeless, the eternal. Surely, developing a perfect technique does not make you creative. You may know how to paint marvelously; you may have the technique, but you may not be a creative painter. You may know how to write poems, technically most perfect, but you may not be a poet. To be a poet implies, does it not, being capable of receiving the new—to be sensitive enough to respond to something new, fresh. But, with most of us, knowledge, or learning, has become an addiction, and we think that through knowing we shall be creative. A mind that is crowded, encased in facts, in knowledge—is it capable of receiving something new, sudden, spontaneous? If your mind is crowded with the known, is there any space in it to receive something that is of the unknown? Surely, knowledge is always of the known, and with the known, we are trying to understand the unknown, something which is beyond measure.

Take, for example, a very ordinary thing that happens to most of us: those who are religious—whatever that word may mean for the moment—try to imagine what God is or try to think about what God is. They have read innumerable books, they have read about the experiences of the various saints, the Masters, the mahatmas, and all the rest, and they try to imagine, or try to feel, what the experience of another is. That is, with the known, you try to approach the unknown. Can you do it? Can you think of something that is not knowable? You can only think of something that you know. But there is this extraordinary perversion taking place in the world at the present time—we think we shall understand if we have more information, more books, more facts, more printed matter.

Surely, to be aware of something that is not the projection of the known, there must be the elimination through the understanding of the process of the known. Why is it that the mind clings always to the known? Is it not because the mind is constantly seeking certainty, security? Its very nature is fixed in the known, in time, and how can such a mind whose very foundation is based on the past, on time, experience the timeless? It may conceive, formulate, picture the unknown, but that is all absurd. The unknown can come into being only when the known is understood, dissolved, put aside. And that is extremely difficult because the moment you have an experience of anything, the mind translates it into the terms of the known and reduces it to the past. I do not know if you have noticed that every experience is immediately translated into the known, given a name, tabulated, and recorded. So, the movement of the known is knowledge. And, obviously, such knowledge, learning, is a hindrance.

Suppose you had never read a book, religious or psychological, and you had to find the meaning, the significance, of life. How would you set about it? Suppose there were no Masters, no religious organizations, no Buddha, no Christ, and you had to begin from the beginning. How would you set about it? First, you would have to understand your process of thinking, would you not, and not project yourself, your thoughts, into the future and create a God which pleases you—that would be too childish. So, first you would have to understand the process of your thinking. Surely, that is the only way to discover anything new, is it not?

When we say that learning or knowledge is an impediment, is a hindrance, surely we are not including technical knowledge—how to drive a car, how to run machinery, or the efficiency which such knowledge brings. We have in mind quite a different thing—that sense of creative happiness which no amount of knowledge or learning will bring. And, to be creative in the truest sense of that word is to be free of the past from moment to moment. Because, it is the past that is continually shadowing the present. Merely to cling to information, to the experiences of others, to what someone has said, however great, and try to approximate your action to that—all that is knowledge, is it not? But, to discover anything new you must start on your own; you must start on a journey completely denuded, especially of knowledge. Because, it is very easy through knowledge and belief to have experiences, but those experiences are merely the products of self-protection and therefore utterly unreal, false. And if you are to discover for yourself what is the new, it is no good carrying the burden of the old, especially knowledge—the knowledge of another, however great. Now, you use knowledge as a means of self-protection, security, and you want to be quite sure that you have the same experiences as the Buddha, or the Christ, or X. But a man who is protecting himself constantly through knowledge is obviously not a truth-seeker.

For the discovery of truth, there is no path. You must enter the uncharted sea—which is not depressing, which is not being adventurous. Surely, when you want to find something new, when you are experimenting with anything, your mind has to be very quiet, has it not? But if your mind is crowded, filled with facts, knowledge, they act as an impediment to the new; and our difficulty is, for most of us, the mind has become so important, so predominantly significant, that it interferes constantly with anything that may be new, with anything that may exist simultaneously with the known. So, knowledge and learning are impediments for those who would seek, for those who would try to understand that which is timeless.

Question: I gather from your various talks that thought must cease before there can be understanding. What is that thinking which must come to an end? What do you mean by thinking and thought?

KRISHNAMURTI: I hope you are interested in all this. After all, you should be because that is what you are doing. The only instrument we have is the mind, thought; and what do we mean by thinking? What do we mean by thought? How does it arise? What is its function? So, let us investigate it together. Though I may answer it, you too, please, think it out; let us think it out together.

What is thought? Surely, thought is the result of the past, isn't it? Thought is founded upon the reaction of the past, of yesterday, and of many, many, many yesterdays. You would not be capable of thinking if there were no yesterdays. So, thought is the result of the conditioned responses established in the mind as the past. The mind is the result of the past. That is, thinking is the response of memory. If you had no memory, there would be no thinking. If you had no memory of the way to your house, you could not get there. So, thinking is the response of memory. Memory is a process, a residue of experiences—whether immediate or of the past. Contact, sensation, and desire, create experience. That is, through contact, sensation, and desire, there is experience; that experience leaves a residue which we call memory, whether pleasant or unpleasant, profitable or unprofitable. From that residue there is a response, which we call thinking, conditioned according to different environmental influences, and so on and so on. That is, the mind—not only the upper levels of consciousness, but the whole process—is the residue of the past. After all, you and I are the result of the past. Our whole conscious process of living, thinking, feeling, is based on the past, and most of us live in the upper levels of consciousness, the superficial mind. There we are active, there we have our problems, innumerable contentions, everyday questions—and with that we are satisfied. But surely, what is on the surface, the little that shows, is not the whole content of consciousness. To understand the whole content of consciousness, the superficial mind must be quiet, if only for a few seconds, a few minutes. Then it is possible, is it not, to receive what is the unknown.

Now, if thought is merely the response of the past, then the thought process must cease for something new, must it not? If thought is the result of time, which it is, then to have the intimation of the timeless, of something which you do not know, the thought process must come to an end, must it not? To receive something new, the old must cease. If you have a modern picture, and if you don't understand it, you cannot approach it with your classical training; at least for the time being you must put it aside to understand the new. Similarly, if you are to understand that which is new, timeless, then the mind, which is the instrument of thought, which is the residue of the past, must come to an end; and the process of ending thought—though that may sound rather crazy—does not come through discipline, through so-called meditation. We will discuss presently, in the following weeks, what is right meditation, and so on. But we can see that any action on the part of the mind to make itself come to an end is still a process of thought.

So, this problem is really quite arduous to go into, and quite subtle. Because, there can be no happiness, there can be no joy, no bliss, unless there is creative renewal; and this creative renewal cannot take place if the mind is constantly projecting itself into the future, into the tomorrow, into the next second. And, as it does that all the time, we are uncreative. We may produce babies, but to be inwardly creative, to have that extraordinary sense of renewal in which there is constant newness, freshness, in which the mind is totally absent—that sense of creativeness cannot take place if the mind is constantly projecting itself into the future, into the tomorrow. That is why it is important to understand the whole thought process. Without understanding the thought process—all its subtleties, its varieties, its depth—you cannot come to the other. You may talk about it, but you have to stop thinking—though it sounds crazy. To have that renewal, that freshness, that extraordinary sense of otherness, the mind must understand itself. And that is why it is important that there should be deeper and wider awareness of self-knowledge.

Question: I agree with you that knowledge has not brought happiness. I have been trying to be receptive, to be intuitive and eager for hints from within. Am I on the right track?

KRISHNAMURTI: To understand this question, we must understand what we mean by consciousness because what you call intuition may be the projection of your own desire. There are so many people who say, "I believe in reincarnation. I feel it is so. My intuition tells me." It is obviously their desire to prolong, to continue themselves. Because they are so scared of death, they want to be assured that there is a next life, another opportunity, and so on, and so on. Therefore, "intuitively" they feel it is correct. So, to understand this question, we must understand what you mean by within and without. Is it possible to receive intimations of that which is within when you are continually seeking an end—when you want to attain, when you want to cultivate, when you want to be happy? Surely, to receive intimations from within, the mind, the upper mind, must be completely free from all entanglements and prejudices, from all want, from all nationalism; otherwise, your "intimations" will make you into the greatest nationalist and a terror to the rest of the world.

So, our question is, How is it possible to receive the intimation of the unknown without warping it, without translating it into our conditioned thought pattern? To understand that, we must go into the question of what is consciousness. What do we mean by being conscious? What is the process of consciousness? When do you say you are conscious? Surely, you say, "I am conscious," when you are experiencing, do you not? When there is an experience—whether pleasurable or not pleasurable is irrelevant—then, there is an awareness of your being conscious of that experience. Then, from that experiencing, the next step is you name it, you term it, do you not? You say, "It is pleasure, it is not pleasure; this I remember, that I do not remember." So you give it a name. Then you record it, do you not? By the very process of giving it a name, you are recording it. Are you following all this, or is it too Sunday-morningish? (Laughter)

So, there is consciousness only when there is experiencing, terming, and recording. Don't accept what I am saying—watch it yourself, and you will see this is how it operates. This is going on at all the levels, all the time, consciously or unconsciously. And, at the deeper levels of consciousness the process is almost instantaneous, as on the upper level; but the difference is, is it not, that on the upper level there is choice, there is choosing; at the wider, deeper level, there is instant recognition without choice. And, the upper mind or the superficial mind can receive the intimation only when this terming or naming or recording process comes to an end—which happens when the problem is much too great, or much too difficult. You try to solve a problem, and there is no answer. Then you let it go. The moment you let it go, there is a response, there is an intimation, because the mind, the conscious mind, is no longer struggling, trying to find an answer. It is quiet. The very exhaustion is a process of quietness, and therefore, the mind is capable of receiving the intimation. But the so-called intuition that the majority of people have is really their own wish-fulfillment. That is why there are so many wars, organized beliefs, antagonisms, so much contention—because each one thinks his intuition is so true that for it he is willing to die or ill-treat others.

I am afraid the person who thinks he is following intuition is obviously on the wrong track because to understand all this, one must transcend reason. To transcend reason, you must first know what the reasoning process is. You cannot go beyond something which you do not know; to go beyond it, you must know what it is; you must understand the whole meaning of reason—how to reason, how to go into it—you cannot jump beyond it. That does not mean that you must have a very clever brain, that you must be a great student, someone erudite. It needs honesty of thinking, clarity, the desire to be open, to invite *what is* without fear of suffering. Then the barrier between the inner and the outer is nonexistent. The inner then is the outer, and the outer is the inner. But to have that integration there must be a comprehension of the process of the mind.

Question: Please explain clearly what part memory has in our life. You seem to distinguish between two forms of memory. Actually, is there not only memory, which is our only means of consciousness, and that which makes us aware of time and space? Therefore, can we dispense with memory, as you seem to suggest?

KRISHNAMURTI: Let us investigate the question anew. Let us forget what has been said, and let us try to find out what we mean. We said this morning that thought is a result of the past, which is an obvious fact—whether you like it or not, it is so. Thought is founded on the past. There can be no thought without being conscious, and as I said, consciousness is a process of experiencing, terming, which is recording. That is what you do all the time: If you see that, (pointing to a tree) you call it a tree and name it, and you think you have had an experience. This process of naming is part of memory, is it not? And it is a very convenient way of experiencing. You think you have experienced a thing by naming it. You call me a Hindu, and you think you have understood all Hindus; I call you an American, and it is over. So we think we understand something by giving it a name. We give it a name in order to recognize it, as a species, or this or that, but that is not understanding, experiencing a thing. And we do it out of slackness—it is so much easier to dispense with people by giving them a name.

So, this process of experiencing, which is contact, sensation, desire, consciousness, identification, and experience—this process, with naming, is considered consciousness, isn't it? Part of that consciousness is awake, and the other part is dormant. The conscious mind, our everyday mind, the upper level of our mind, is awake. The rest is sleeping. Now, when we sleep, the conscious, upper mind is silent, and therefore it is able to receive hints, intimations, translated as dreams, but which need further interpretation. Now, the questioner wants to know what we mean by memory—what is its function, and whether we can dispense with it. So, the question really is, What is the function of thought? Memory has no function apart from thinking. So, the question is, What is the function of thought? Can thought be divided at all? Is it to be dispensed with?

So, what is the function of thought? We say thought is the response of memory, which it is; and memory is incomplete experience, termed and thought out for self-protection, and so on, and so on. Now, if thought is the result of memory, what function has thought in life? When do you use thought? I wonder if you have ever considered this? You use your thought when you want to go to your home, do you not? You think how to get to your place. This is one kind of thought. When does your thought function? When you are protecting yourself, isn't it? When you are seeking security—economic, social, psychological. Isn't that so? When you want to safeguard yourself. That is, thought functions when there is the urge for self-protection. When you are kind to another, is that a thought process? When you love another, is that a thought process? When you love another and use that love as a means of self-enrichment, then obviously, it is a thought process; then, it is no longer love. So, thought process comes into being when there is fear, when there is the desire to possess, when there is conflict—in other words, thought process comes into being when the self, the 'me', becomes important, surely? Because, after all, thought is concerned with me; when the 'I', the 'me', predominates, then the thought process as self-protection begins. Otherwise you don't think; you are unaware of your thought process, are you not? It is only when there is conflict that you are aware of the thought process—either to protect or to discard, to accept or to deny.

Now, the questioner wants to know what part memory plays in our life. If we understand that the thought process begins only when the 'me' becomes important, and that the 'me' is important only when there is the desire to safeguard itself, then we see that most of our life is spent in safeguarding ourselves. Therefore, thought has a very important part in our life because most of us are concerned with ourselves. Most of us are concerned with how to protect ourselves, how to gain, how to arrive, how to achieve, how to become more perfect, how to have this virtue and that virtue, how to discard, how to deny, how to be detached, how to find happiness, how to be more beautiful, how to love, how to be loved—you know how we are concerned with ourselves.

So, we are consumed in the thought process. We are the thought process. We are not separate from the thought. And thought is memory—how to be more of something. That is, when there is the urge to be the 'more' or the 'less', the 'positive' or the 'negative', then thought process comes into being. The thought process does not come into being when there is the recognition of *what is*. A fact does not demand a thought process, but if you want to avoid a fact, then the thought process begins. If I accept that I am what I am, then thought is not, but something else takes place when I accept *what is*. Quite a different process, which is not the process of thought, comes into being. So, as long as there is the desire for the 'more', or the 'less', there must be thought, there must be the process of memory. After all, if you want to be a very rich man, a powerful man, a popular man, or a man of God, if you want to become something, you must have memory. That is, you must think about it; the mind must constantly sharpen itself to become something.

Now, what part has that 'becoming' in life? Surely, as long as we want to be something, there must be contention; as long as our desire, our urge, our pursuit, is to be the 'more', or to be the 'less'—the 'positive' or the 'negative'—there must be strife, antagonism. But it is extremely arduous, extremely difficult, not to be the 'more' or the 'less'. Verbally you may throw it off and say, "I am nobody," but that is merely living on the verbal level, without much significance—it is empty-headedness. That is why one has to understand the thought process, which is consciousness—which means, the whole problem of time, of yesterday, of tomorrow. And a man who is caught in yesterday can never understand that which is timeless. And most of us are caught in the net of time. Our thought is basically entangled in the net of time—it is the net of time. Our thought is the net of time, and with that thought process—educated, cultivated, sharpened, made keen, subtle—we want to find something that is beyond.

We go to one teacher after another, one hero after another, one Master after another. Our mind is sharpening itself on all these, and thereby hopes to find that which is beyond. But, thought can never find that which is beyond because thought is the result of time, and that which is of the known cannot receive the unknown. Therefore, the man who is entangled in the known is never creative; he may have moments of creativeness, as some painters do, some musicians, some writers; but they get entangled in the known—popularity, money, a hundred other things, and then they are lost. And that is why those who are trying to understand themselves—not to find, because that is a wrong process, you cannot find—must cease to search. All that you can do is understand yourself, understand the intricacies, the extraordinary subtlety of your thought and your being. And that can be understood only in relationship, which is action; and that action is denied when relationship is based on an idea; then relationship is mere activity, it is not action, and activity merely dulls the mind and the heart. It is only action that makes the mind alert and the heart subtle so that it is capable of receiving, of being sensitive. That is why it is important that there be self-knowledge before you seek. If you seek, you will find, but it will not be the truth. Therefore, this craze, this fear, this anxiety to arrive, to search out, to find, must end; then, with self-knowledge, ever wide and deep, there comes that sense of reality which cannot be invited. It comes into being, and only then is there creative happiness.

July 17, 1949

Third Talk in The Oak Grove

Last Saturday and Sunday we were discussing the importance of self-knowledge, because, as I explained, I do not see how we can have any foundation for right thinking without self-knowledge, how any action, however inclusive, however collective or individualistic, can possibly be a harmonious and true action without fully knowing oneself. Without knowing oneself, there is no possibility of really searching out what is true, what is significant, what are the right values in life. Without self-knowledge, we cannot go beyond the self-projected illusions of the mind. Self-knowledge, as we explained, implies not only the action of relationship between one individual and another, but also the action of relationship with society; and there can be no complete, harmonious society without this knowledge. So, it is really very important and significant that one should know oneself as completely and fully as possible. And, is this knowledge possible? Can one know integrally, not partially, the total process of oneself? Because, as I said, without knowing oneself, one has no basis for thinking. One gets caught in illusions: political, religious, social illusions—they are limitless, endless. Is it possible to know oneself? And, how is it possible to know oneself—what are the means, what are the ways, what are the processes?

I think to find out what are the ways, one must find out first, must one not, what are the impediments; and by studying what we consider important in life, those things which we have accepted—the values, the standards, the beliefs, the innumerable things that we hold—by examining them, perhaps we shall find out the ways of our own thinking and thereby know ourselves. That is, by understanding the things that we accept, by questioning them, going into them—by that very process we shall know the ways of our own thinking, our responses, our reactions; and through them, we shall know ourselves as we are. Surely, that is the only way we can find out the manner of our thinking, our responses—by studying, by going fully into the values, the standards, the beliefs that we have accepted for generations. And, seeing behind these values, we shall know how we respond, what our reactions are to them; and thereby, perhaps, we shall be able to uncover the ways of our own thinking. In other words, to know oneself, surely, is to study the responses, the reactions that one has in relation to something. One cannot know oneself through isolation. That is an obvious fact. You may withdraw to a mountain, into a cave, or pursue some illusion on the banks of a river, but if one isolates oneself, there can be no relationship, and isolation is death. It is only in relationship that one can know oneself as one is. So, by studying the things that we have accepted, by going into them fully, not superficially, perhaps we shall be able to understand ourselves.

Now, one of the things, it seems to me, that most of us eagerly accept and take for granted is the question of beliefs. I am not attacking beliefs. What we are trying to do this evening is to find out why we accept beliefs; and if we can understand the motives, the causation of acceptance, then perhaps we may be able not only to understand why we do it but also be free of it. Because, one can see how political and religious beliefs, national and various other types of beliefs do separate people, do create conflict, confusion, and antagonism—which is an obvious fact; and yet we are unwilling to give them up. There is the Hindu belief, the Christian belief, the Buddhist, innumerable sectarian and national beliefs, various political ideologies—all contending with each other, trying to convert each other. One can see, obviously, that belief is separating people, creating intolerance; and is it possible to live without belief? One can find that out only if one can study oneself in relationship to a belief. Is it possible to live in this world without a belief—not change beliefs, not substitute one belief for another, but be entirely free from all beliefs so that one meets life anew each minute? This, after all, is the truth—to have the capacity of meeting everything anew, from moment to moment, without the conditioning reaction of the past, so that there is not the cumulative effect which acts as a barrier between oneself and that which is.

Obviously, most of us accept or take on beliefs because, first of all, there is fear. We feel that without a belief we shall be lost. Then we use belief as a means of conduct, as a pattern, according to which we direct our lives. And also we think that through belief there can be collective action. So, in other words, we think that belief is necessary for action. And is that so? Is belief necessary for action? That is, belief being an idea, is ideation necessary for action? Which comes first—idea or action? Surely, first there is action, which is either pleasurable or painful, and according to that we build up various theories. Action invariably comes first, does it not? And, when there is fear, when there is the desire to believe in order to act, then ideation comes in.

Now, if you consider, you will see that one of the reasons for the desire to accept a belief is fear. Because, if we had no belief, what would happen to us? Wouldn't we be very frightened of what might happen? If we had no pattern of action based on a belief—either in God or in communism, or in socialism, or in imperialism, or in some kind of religious formula, some dogma in which we are conditioned—we would feel utterly lost, wouldn't we? And is not this acceptance of a belief the covering up of that fear—the fear of being really nothing, of being empty? After all, a cup is useful only when it is empty; and a mind that is filled with beliefs, with dogmas, with assertions, with quotations, is really an uncreative mind, it is merely a repetitive mind. And, to escape from that fear—that fear of emptiness, that fear of loneliness, that fear of stagnation, of not arriving, not succeeding, not achieving, not being something, not becoming something—is surely one of the reasons, is it not, why we accept beliefs so eagerly and greedily. And, through acceptance of belief, do we understand ourselves? On the contrary. A belief, religious or political, obviously hinders the understanding of ourselves. It acts as a screen through which we are looking at ourselves. And, can we look at ourselves without beliefs? If we remove those beliefs, the many beliefs that one has, is there anything left to look at? If we have no beliefs with which the mind has identified itself, then the mind, without identification, is capable of looking at itself as it is—and then, surely, there is the beginning of the understanding of oneself. If one is afraid, if there is fear which is covered over by a belief, and if, in understanding beliefs, one comes face to face with fear, without the screen of beliefs—is it not possible then to be free from that reaction of fear? That is, to know one is afraid and to stay there without any escape? To be with *what is* is surely much more significant, much more worthwhile than to escape from *what is* through a belief.

So, one begins to see that there are various forms of escape from oneself, from one's own emptiness, from one's own poverty of being—escapes such as knowledge, such as amusement, various forms of addictions and distractions, both learned and stupid, clever or not worthwhile. We are surrounded by these; we are them; and if the mind can see the significance of the things to which it is held, then, perhaps, we shall be face to face with what we are, whatever it be; and I think the moment we are capable of doing that, then there is a real transformation. Because then, there is no question of fear, for fear exists only in relationship to something. When there is you and something else to which you are related, and when you dislike that thing to which you are related and try to avoid it—then there is fear. But when you are that very thing, then there is no question of avoidance. A fact gives fear only when you bring an emotional reaction to it, but when a fact is faced as it is, there is no fear. And when what we call fear is no longer named, but only looked at without it being given a term, then, surely, there takes place a revolution; there is no longer that sense either of avoidance or acceptance.

So, to understand belief, not superficially, but profoundly, one must find out why the mind attaches itself to various forms of beliefs, why beliefs have become so significant in our lives: belief about death, about life, about what happens after death, beliefs asserting that there is God or there is no God, that there is reality or there is no reality, and various political beliefs. Are these beliefs not all indicative of our own sense of inward poverty, and, do they not reveal a process of escape or act as a defense? And in studying our beliefs, do we not begin to know ourselves as we are, not only at the upper levels of our mind, of our consciousness, but deeper down? So, the more one studies oneself in relationship to something else, such as beliefs, the more the mind becomes quiet, without false regimentation, without compulsion. The more the mind knows itself, the more quiet it is, obviously. The more you know something, the more you are familiar with it, the more the mind becomes quiet. And the mind must be really quiet, not made quiet. Surely, there is a vast difference between a mind that is made quiet and a mind that is quiet. You can compel a mind by circumstances, by various disciplines, tricks, and so on, to be quiet. But that is not quietude, that is not peace—that is death. But a mind that is quiet because it understands the various forms of fear, and because it understands itself—such a mind is creative, such a mind is renewing itself constantly. It is only the mind that is self-enclosed by its own fears and beliefs that stagnates. But a mind that understands its relationship to the values about it—not imposing a standard of values, but understanding *what is*—surely, such a mind becomes quiet, is quiet. It is not a question of becoming. It is only then, surely, that the mind is capable of perceiving what is real from moment to moment. Reality is, surely, not something at the end—an end result of accumulative action. Reality is to be perceived only from moment to moment, and it can be perceived only when there is not the accumulative effect of the past on the moment, the now.

There are many questions, and I will answer some of them.

Question: Why do you talk?

KRISHNAMURTI: I think this question is quite interesting—for me to answer and also for you to answer. Not only why do I talk, but why do you listen? No, seriously, if I talked for self-expression, then I would be exploiting you. If my talking is a necessity for me in order to feel myself flattered, egotistic, self-aggressive, and all the rest of it, then I must use you; then you and I have no relationship because you are a necessity for my egotism. I need you then to bolster myself up, to feel myself rich, free, applauded, having so many people listening to me. Then I am using you; then one uses another. Then, surely, there is no relationship between you and me because you are useful to me. When I use you, what relationship have I with you? None. And, if I speak because I have various sets of ideas which I want to convey to you, then ideas become very important; and I do not believe that ideas ever bring about a fundamental, radical change, a revolution in life. Ideas can never be new; ideas can never bring about a transformation, a creative surge, because ideas are merely the response of a continued past, modified or altered, but still of the past. If I talk because I want you to change, or I want you to accept my particular way of thinking, belong to my particular society, become my particular disciple, then you as an individual are a nonentity because then I am only concerned with transforming you according to a particular view. Then you are not important; then the pattern is important.

So, why am I talking? If it is none of these things, why am I talking? We will answer that presently. Then the question is, Why are you listening? Isn't that equally important? Perhaps more. If you are listening to get some new ideas or a new way of looking at life, then you will be disappointed because I am not going to give you new ideas. If you are listening to experience something you think I have experienced, then you are merely imitating, hoping to capture something which you think I have. Surely, the real things of life cannot be vicariously experienced. Or, because you are in trouble, sorrow, pain, have innumerable conflicts, you come here to find out how to get out of them. Again, I am afraid I cannot help you. All that I can do is to point out your own difficulty, and we can then talk it over with each other, but it is for you yourself to see. Therefore, it is very important to find out for yourself why you come here and listen. Because, if you have one purpose, one intention, and I another, we shall never meet. Then, there is no relationship between you and me, there is no communion between you and me. You want to go north, and I am going south. We will pass each other by. But, surely, that is not the intention of these gatherings. What we are trying to do is to undertake a journey together and experience together as we go along—not that I am teaching you or you are listening to me, but together we are exploring, if that is possible, so that you are not only the Master but also the disciple in discovering and understanding. There is not then this division of the high and low, the one that is learned and the one that is ignorant, the one that has achieved and the one that is still on the way to achievement. Such divisions, surely, distort relationship, and without understanding relationship, there can be no understanding of reality.

I have told you why I speak. Perhaps you will think then that I need you in order to discover. Surely not. I have something to say—you can take it or leave it. And, if you take it, it is not that you are taking it from me. I merely act as a mirror in which you see yourself. You might not like that mirror and so discard it, but when you do look into the mirror, look at it very clearly, unemotionally, without the blur of sentimentality. And surely it is important, is it not, to find out why you come and listen. If it is merely an afternoon's amusement, if instead of going to a cinema you come here, then it is utterly valueless. If it is merely for the sake of argumentation, or to catch new sets of ideas so that you can use them when you lecture or write a book or discuss—again, that is valueless. But if you come really to discover yourself in relationship, which might help in your relationship with others, then it has significance, then it is worthwhile, then it will not be like so many other meetings which you attend. Surely, these gatherings are intended, not for you to listen to me, but to see yourself reflected in the mirror which I am trying to describe. You don't have to accept what you see—that would be foolish. But, if you look at the mirror dispassionately, as you would listen to music, as you would sit under a tree and watch the shadows of an evening, without condemnation, without any kind of justification—merely look at it—that very awareness of *what is* does a most extraordinary thing if there is no resistance. Surely, that is what we are trying to do in all these talks. So, real freedom comes, but not through effort; effort can never bring about freedom. Effort can only bring about substitution, suppression, or sublimation; but none of those things is freedom. Freedom comes only when there is no longer effort to be something. Then, the truth of *what is* acts, and that is freedom.

Question: Is there a distinction between my intention in listening to you and in going from one teacher to another?

KRISHNAMURTI: Surely, it is for you to find out, isn't it? Why do you go from one teacher to another, from one organization to another, from one belief to another? Or, why are you so closed in by one belief—Christian, or what you will? Why? Why do we do this? This is happening not in America only, but right through the world—this appalling restlessness, this desire to find. Why? Do you think by searching, you will find? But, before you can search, you must have the instrument for search, must you not? You must be capable of searching—not merely start out to search. To search, to have the capacity to search, you must understand yourself, surely. How can you search without first knowing yourself, without knowing what it is you are searching for, and what it is that is searching? The Hindus come over here and give their stuff—the yogis, the swamis, you know—and you go over there and preach and convert. Why? It will be a happy world when there are neither teachers nor pupils.

What is it really that we are seeking? Is it that we are bored with life, bored with one set of ceremonies, one set of dogmas, church rituals, and so we go to another because it is something new, more exciting—Sanskrit words, men with beards, togas, and all the rest of it? Is that the reason? Or, do we want to find a refuge, an escape, in Buddhism, in Hinduism, or in some other organized religious belief? Or, are we seeking gratification? It is very difficult to distinguish and be aware of what we are really seeking. Because, from period to period we vary; when we are bored, when we are tired, when we are miserable, we want something ultimate, lasting, final, absolute. It is only a very few who are consistent in their search—in their inquiry, rather. Most of us want distraction. If we are intellectual, we want intellectual distraction, and so on, and so on.

So, can one genuinely, authentically, for oneself, find out what it is that one wants? Not what one should have, or what one thinks one ought to have, but to find out for oneself, inwardly, what it is that one wants, what it is that one is searching after so ceaselessly. And, can one find when one seeks? Surely, we will find that which we are seeking, but when we get what we want, it soon fades away, it turns to ashes. So, before we start out searching, gathering what we want, surely it is important, isn't it, to find out who the searcher is and what he is seeking because if the seeker does not understand himself, then what he finds will be merely a self-projected illusion. And, you may live in that illusion happily for the rest of your life, but it will still be illusion.

So, before you seek, before you go from teacher to teacher, from organization to organization, from belief to belief, surely it is important to find out who is the person that is seeking and what he is seeking—not just vaguely go from shop to shop, hoping to find the right dress. So, surely, the thing of primary importance is to know yourself, not to go out and search—which does not mean that you should become an introvert and avoid all action, which is impossible. You can know yourself only in relationship, not in isolation. So, what is the distinction between one's intention in coming here and listening, and in going to another teacher? Surely, there is no distinction if one merely comes here to get something—to be pacified, to be comforted, to be given new ideas, to be persuaded to join or to leave some organization, or God knows what else. Surely, here there is no refuge, no organization. Here, you and I are trying to see exactly *what is,* if we can—see ourselves as we are—which is extremely difficult because we are so cunning; you know the innumerable tricks that we play upon ourselves. Here, we are trying to strip ourselves naked and see ourselves, for in that stripping, there comes wisdom, and it is that wisdom which gives happiness. But, if your intention is to find comfort, something which will hide you from yourself, something which will offer an escape, then, obviously, there are many ways of doing it—through religion, politics, amusement, knowledge—you know, the whole gamut of it. And, I do not see how any form of addiction, any form of distraction, any escape—however pleasant or however uncomfortable, to which one so eagerly adjusts oneself because it promises a reward at the end—can bring about that self-knowledge which is so essential and which alone can give creative peace.

Question: Our mind knows only the known. What is it in us that drives us to find the unknown, reality, God?

KRISHNAMURTI: Does your mind urge towards the unknown? Is there an urge in us for the unknown, for reality, for God? Please think seriously about it. This is not a rhetorical question, but actually let us find out. Is there an inward urge in each one of us to find the unknown? Is there? How can you find the unknown? If you do not know it, how can you find it? Please, I am not being clever. Don't brush it off that way. So, is it an urge for reality? Or, is it merely a desire for the known, expanded? Do you understand what I mean? I have known many things; they have not given me happiness, satisfaction, joy. So, now I want something else that will give me greater joy, greater happiness, greater hope, greater vitality—what you will. And, can the known, which is my mind—because, my mind is the known, the result of the known, the result of the past—can that mind seek the unknown? If I do not know reality, the unknown, how can I search for it? Surely, it must come. I cannot go after it. If I go after it, I am going after something which is the known, projected from me.

So, our problem is not what is in us that drives us to find the unknown—that is clear enough. It is our own desire to be more secure, more permanent, more established, more happy, to escape from turmoil, from pain, confusion. Surely, that is our obvious drive. And, when there is that drive, that urge, you will find a marvelous escape, a marvelous refuge—in the Buddha, in the Christ, or in political slogans, and all the rest of it. But, surely, that is not reality; that is not the unknowable, the unknown. Therefore, the urge for the unknown must come to an end, the search for the unknown must stop; which means, there must be the understanding of the cumulative known, which is the mind. The mind must understand itself as the known because that is all it knows. You cannot think about something that you do not know. You can only think about something that you know.

Our difficulty is for the mind not to proceed in the known, and that can only happen when the mind understands itself and how all its movement is from the past, projecting itself through the present to the future. It is one continuous movement of the known, and can that movement come to an end? It can come to an end only when the mechanism of its own process is understood, only when the mind understands itself and its workings, its ways, its purposes, its pursuits, its demands—not only the superficial demands, but the deep inward urges and motives. This is quite an arduous task; it isn't just in a meeting or at a lecture or by reading a book that you are going to find out. On the contrary, it needs constant watchfulness, constant awareness of every movement of thought—not only when you are waking, but also when you are asleep. It must be a total process, not a sporadic, partial process.

And also, the intention must be right. That is, there must be a cessation of the superstition that inwardly we all want the unknown. It is an illusion to think that we are all seeking God—we are not. We don't have to search for light. There will be light when there is no darkness, and through darkness, we cannot find the light. All that we can do is to remove those barriers that create darkness, and the removal depends on the intention. If you are removing them in order to see light, then you are not removing anything—you are only substituting the word light for darkness. Even to look beyond the darkness is an escape from darkness.

So, we have to consider not what it is that is driving us but why there is in us such confusion, such turmoil, such strife and antagonism—all the stupid things of our existence. When these are not, then there is light; we don't have to look for it. When stupidity is gone, there is intelligence. But the man who is stupid and tries to become intelligent is still stupid. Surely, stupidity can never be made wisdom; only when stupidity ceases is there wisdom, intelligence. But the man who is stupid and tries to become intelligent, wise, obviously can never be. To know what is stupidity, one must go into it, not superficially, but fully, completely, deeply, profoundly; one must go into all the different layers of stupidity, and when there is the cessation of that stupidity, there is wisdom.

So, it is important to find out, not if there is something more, something greater than the known, which is urging us to the unknown, but to see what it is in us that is creating confusion—the wars, the class differences, the snobbishness, the pursuit of the famous, the accumulation of knowledge, the escape through music, through art, through so many ways. It is important, surely, to see them as they are and to come back to ourselves as we are. And, from there we can proceed. Then the throwing off of the known is comparatively easy. When the mind is silent, when it is no longer projecting itself into the future, into the tomorrow, wishing for something, when the mind is really quiet, profoundly peaceful, the unknown comes into being. You don't have to search for it. You cannot invite it. That which you can invite is only that which you know. You cannot invite an unknown guest. You can only invite one whom you know. But you do not know the unknown, God, reality, or what you will. It must come. It can only come when the field is right, when the soil is tilled. But, if you till in order for it to come, then you will not have it.

So, our problem is not to seek the unknowable but to understand the accumulative processes of the mind, which is ever with the known. And that is an arduous task: that demands attention, that demands a constant awareness in which there is no sense of distraction, of identification, of condemnation; it is being with *what is*. Then only can the mind be still. No amount of meditation, discipline, can make the mind still in the real sense of that word. Only when the breezes stop does the lake become quiet. You cannot make the lake quiet. So, our job is not to pursue the unknowable but to understand the confusion, the turmoil, the misery in ourselves, and then that thing darkly comes into being in which there is joy.

July 23, 1949

Fourth Talk in The Oak Grove

I would like this morning to discuss what is simplicity and perhaps from that arrive at the discovery of sensitivity. We seem to think that simplicity is merely an outward expression, a withdrawal—having few possessions, wearing a loincloth, having no home, putting on few clothes, having a small bank account. Surely, that is not simplicity. That is merely an outward show. And it seems to me that simplicity is essential, but simplicity can come into being only when we begin to understand the significance of self-knowledge, which we have discussed previously, and which we will be discussing here until the end of August.

Simplicity is not merely adjustment to a pattern. It requires a great deal of intelligence to be simple and not merely conform to a particular pattern, however worthy outwardly. Unfortunately, most of us begin by being simple externally, in outward things. It is comparatively easy to have few things and to be satisfied with few things, to be content with little, and perhaps to share that little with others. But, a mere outward expression of simplicity in things, in possessions, surely does not imply the simplicity of inward being. Because, as the world is at present, more and more things are being urged upon us, outwardly, externally. Life is becoming more and more complex. And, in order to escape from that, we try to renounce or be detached from things—from cars, from houses, from organizations, from cinemas, and from the innumerable circumstances outwardly thrust upon us. We think we shall be simple by withdrawing. A great many saints, a great many teachers, have renounced the world, and it seems to me that such a renunciation on the part of any of us does not solve the problem. Simplicity which is fundamental, real, can only come into being inwardly, and from that there is an outward expression. How to be simple, then, is the problem because that simplicity makes one more and more sensitive. A sensitive mind, a sensitive heart, is essential, for then it is capable of quick perception, quick reception.

So, one can be inwardly simple, surely, only by understanding the innumerable impediments, attachments, fears, in which one is held. But most of us like to be held—by people, by possessions, or by ideas. We like to be prisoners. Inwardly we are prisoners, though outwardly we seem very simple. Inwardly we are prisoners to our desires, to our wants, to our ideals, to the innumerable motivations. And simplicity cannot be found unless one is free inwardly. Therefore, it must begin first inwardly, not outwardly.

We were discussing yesterday afternoon the freedom from beliefs. Surely, there is an extraordinary freedom when one understands the whole process of belief, why the mind is attached to a belief. And, when there is freedom from beliefs, there is simplicity. But that simplicity requires intelligence, and to be intelligent, one must be aware of one's own impediments. To be aware, one must be constantly on the watch, not established in any particular groove, in any particular pattern of thought or action. Because, after all, what one is inwardly does affect the outer. Society, or any form of action, is the projection of ourselves, and without transforming inwardly, mere legislation has very little significance outwardly; it may bring about certain reforms, certain adjustments, but what one is inwardly always overcomes the outer. If one is inwardly greedy, ambitious, pursuing certain ideals, that inward complexity does eventually upset, overthrow outward society, however carefully planned it may be.

So, surely, one must begin within—not exclusively, not rejecting the outer. You come to the inner, surely, by understanding the outer, by finding out how the conflict, the struggle, the pain, exists outwardly; and as one investigates it more and more, naturally one comes into the psychological states which produce the outward conflicts and miseries. The outward expression is only an indication of our inward state, but to understand the inward state one must approach through the outer. Most of us do that. And, in understanding the inner—not exclusively, not by rejecting the outer, but by understanding the outer and so coming upon the inner—we will find that as we proceed to investigate the inward complexities of our being, we become more and more sensitive, free. It is this inward simplicity that is so essential. Because, that simplicity creates sensitivity. A mind that is not sensitive, not alert, not aware, is incapable of any receptivity, any creative action. That is why I said that conformity as a means of making ourselves simple really makes the mind and heart dull, insensitive. Any form of authoritarian compulsion imposed by the government, by oneself, by the ideal of achievement, and so on—any form of conformity must make for insensitivity, for not being simple inwardly. Outwardly you may conform and give the appearance of simplicity, like so many religious people do. They practice various disciplines, join various organizations, meditate in a particular fashion, and so on—all giving an appearance of simplicity. But, such conformity does not make for simplicity. Compulsion of any kind can never lead to simplicity. On the contrary, the more you suppress, the more you substitute, the more you sublimate, the less there is simplicity; but the more you understand the process of sublimation, suppression, substitution, the greater the possibility of being simple.

Our problems—social, environmental, political, religious—are so complex that we can solve them only by being simple, not by becoming extraordinarily erudite and clever. Because, a simple person sees much more directly, has a more direct experience, than the complex person. And, our minds are so crowded with an infinite knowledge of facts of what others have said that we have become incapable of being simple and having direct experience ourselves. These problems demand a new approach, and they can be so approached only when we are simple, inwardly really simple. That simplicity comes only through self-knowledge, through understanding ourselves: the ways of our thinking and feeling, the movements of our thoughts, our responses, how we conform through fear to public opinion, to what others say, what the Buddha, the Christ, the great saints have said—all of which indicates our nature to conform, to be safe, to be secure. And, when one is seeking security, one is obviously in a state of fear, and therefore there is no simplicity.

Without being simple, one cannot be sensitive to the trees, to the birds, to the mountains, to the wind, to all the things that are going on about us in the world. And, if one is not simple, one cannot be sensitive to the inward intimation of things. Most of us live so superficially, on the upper level of our consciousness; there we try to be thoughtful or intelligent, which is synonymous with being religious; there we try to make our minds simple through compulsion, through discipline. But that is not simplicity. When we force the upper mind to be simple, such compulsion only hardens the mind, does not make the mind supple, clear, quick. To be simple in the whole, total process of our consciousness is extremely arduous. Because, there must be no inward reservation, there must be an eagerness to find out, to inquire into the process of our being, which means to be awake to every intimation, to every hint, to be aware of our fears, of our hopes, and to investigate and be free of them more and more and more. Only then, when the mind and the heart are really simple, not encrusted, are we able to solve the many problems that confront us.

Knowledge is not going to solve our problems. You may know, for example, that there is reincarnation, that there is a continuity after death. You may know—I don't say you do—or you may be convinced of it. But that does not solve the problem. Death cannot be shelved by your theory or by information or by conviction. It is much more mysterious, much deeper, much more creative than that.

So, one must have the capacity to investigate all these things anew because it is only through direct experience that our problems are solved; and to have direct experience, there must be simplicity, which means there must be sensitivity. A mind is made dull by the weight of knowledge. A mind is made dull by the past, by the future. But, only a mind that is capable of adjusting itself to the present, continually, from moment to moment, can meet the powerful influences and pressures constantly put upon us by our environment.

So, a religious man is not really one who puts on a robe, or a loincloth, or lives on one meal a day, or one who has taken innumerable vows to be this and not to be that; but it is he who is inwardly simple, who is not becoming anything. Such a mind is capable of extraordinary receptivity because there is no barrier, there is no fear, there is no going toward something; therefore, it is capable of receiving grace, God, truth, or what you will. But a mind that is pursuing reality is not a simple mind. A mind that is seeking out, searching, groping, agitated, is not a simple mind. A mind that conforms to any pattern of authority, inward or outward, cannot be sensitive. And it is only when a mind is really sensitive, alert, aware of all its own happenings, responses, thoughts, when it is no longer becoming, is no longer shaping itself to be something—only then is it capable of receiving that which is truth. It is only then that there can be happiness, for happiness is not an end, it is the result of reality. And, when the mind and the heart have become simple, and therefore sensitive—not through any form of compulsion, direction, or imposition—then we will see that our problems can be tackled very simply. However complex our problems, we shall be able to approach them anew and see them differently. And that is what is wanted, is it not, at the present time: people who are capable of meeting this outward confusion, turmoil, antagonism, anew, creatively, simply—not with theories, not with formulas, whether of the left or of the right. And you cannot meet it anew if you are not simple.

You know, a problem can be solved only when we approach it anew. But we cannot approach it anew if we are thinking in terms of certain patterns of thought—religious, political, or otherwise. So, we must be free of all these things to be simple. That is why it is so important to be aware, to have the capacity to understand the process of our own thinking, to be cognizant of ourselves totally; and from that there comes a simplicity, there comes a humility which is not a virtue or a practice. Humility that is gained ceases to be humility. A mind that makes itself humble is no longer a humble mind. And it is only when one has humility, not a cultivated humility, that one is able to meet the things of life that are so pressing; because, then one is not important, one doesn't look through one's own pressures and sense of importance, one looks at the problem for itself, and then one is able to solve it.

Question: I have been a member of various religious organizations, but you have destroyed them all. I am utterly bored and work because hunger forces me to it. It is difficult to get up in the morning, and I have no interest in life. I realize I am merely existing from day to day without any human sense of value, but I can feel no spark of enthusiasm for anything. I am afraid to commit suicide. What on earth am I to do? (Laughter)

KRISHNAMURTI: Though you laugh, are not most of us in that position? Though you may still belong to many organizations—religious, political, and otherwise—or you may have given them all up, is there not in you the same inward despair? You may go to analysts or to confession and so feel pacified for the time being, but isn't there the same ache of loneliness, a sense of loss, a despair without end? Joining organizations, indulging in various forms of amusement, being addicted to knowledge, performing daily rituals, and all the rest of it does offer an escape from ourselves, but when those have ceased, when those have been pushed away intelligently and not replaced by other forms of escape, one comes to this, doesn't one? You may have read many books; you may be surrounded by your family, children, wealth—a new car every year, the latest literature, the newest phonograph, and all the rest of it. But, when you intelligently discard distraction, you are inevitably faced with this, aren't you—the sense of inward frustration, the sense of hopeless despair without an end. Perhaps most of you are not aware of it, or if you are, you run away from it. But it is there. So, what is one to do?

First of all, it seems to me, it is very difficult to come to that position—to be so aware that you are directly confronted with that thing. Very few of us are capable of facing that thing directly as it is because it is extremely painful, and when you do face it, you are so anxious to leave it that you might do anything, even commit suicide—or run far away into any illusion, any distraction. So, the first difficulty is to be fully aware that you are confronted with it. Surely, one must be in despair to find something. When you have tried everything about you, every door through which you can possibly escape, and none of them offers an escape, you are bound to come to this point.

Now, if you are at this point, really, actually—not fancifully, not wishing to be there in order to do something else—if you are actually faced with it, then we can proceed and discuss what to do. Then it is worthwhile to proceed. If you have ceased substituting one escape for another, leaving one organization and joining something else, pursuing one thing after another; if all that has stopped—and it must eventually stop for every intelligent man—then what? Now, if you are in that position, what is the next response? When you are no longer escaping, when you are no longer seeking an outlet, a way to avoid it—then what happens? If you observe, what we do is this—because of a sense of fear with regard to it or the desire to understand it, we give it a name. Don't we? We say, "I am lonely, I am in despair, I am this, I want to understand it.'' That is, we establish a relationship between ourselves and that thing which we call loneliness, emptiness, by giving it a name. I hope you understand what I am talking about. By verbalizing our relationship to it, we give it a neurological as well as a psychological significance. But, if we do not name it, but merely regard it, look at it, then we shall have a different relationship to it; then it is not away from us—it is us. We say, for example, ''I am afraid of it.'' Fear exists only in relationship to something; that something comes into being when we curb it, when we give it a name, as being lonely. Therefore, there is the feeling that you and that loneliness are two separate things. But is that so? You, the observer, are observing the fact, which you term as being lonely. Is the observer different from the thing which he observes? It is different only as long as he gives it a name, but if you do not give it a name, the observer is the observed. The name, the term, acts only to divide, and then you have to battle with that thing. But, if there is no division, if there is an integration between the observer and the observed, which exists only when there is no naming—you can try this out and you will see—then the sense of fear is entirely gone. It is fear that is preventing you from looking at this when you say you are empty, you are this, you are that, you are in despair. And fear exists only as memory, which comes when you term; but when you are capable of looking at it without terming, then, surely, that thing is yourself.

So, when you come to that point, when you are no longer naming the thing of which you are afraid, then you are that thing. When you are that thing, there is no problem, is there? It is only when you do not want to be that thing, or when you want to make that thing different from what it is, that the problem arises. But, if you are that thing, then the observer is the observed—they are a joint phenomenon, not separate phenomena—then there is no problem, is there?

Please, experiment with this, and you will see how quickly that thing is resolved and transcended and something else takes place. Our difficulty is to come to that point when we can look at it without fear, and fear arises only when we begin to recognize it, when we begin to give it a name, when we want to do something about it. But, when the observer sees that he is not different from the thing which he calls emptiness, despair, then the word has no longer a meaning. The word has ceased to be; it is no longer despair. When the word is removed with all its implications, then there is no sense of fear or despair. Then, if you proceed further, when there is no fear, no despair, when the word is no longer important, then, surely, there is a tremendous release, a freedom; and in that freedom there is creative being which gives a newness to life.

To put it differently—we approach this problem of despair through habitual channels. That is, we bring our past memories to translate that problem; and thought, which is the result of memory, which is founded upon the past, can never solve that problem because it is a new problem. Every problem is a new problem, and when you approach it, burdened with the past, it cannot be solved. You cannot approach it through the screen of words, which is the thinking process; but when the verbalization stops—because you understand the whole process of it, you leave it—then you are able to meet the problem anew; then the problem is not what you think it is.

So, you might say at the end of this question, ''What am I to do? Here I am in despair, in confusion, in pain; you haven't given me a method to follow, to become free.'' But, surely, if you have understood what I have said, the key is there—a key which opens much more than you realize if you are capable of using it. You can see then how words play an extraordinarily important part in our lives—words like God, like nation, like political leader, like communism, like Catholicism—words, words, words. What extraordinary significance they have in our life! And it is these words that are preventing our understanding the problems anew. To be really simple is to be uncluttered with all these impressions, words and their significance, and to approach the problem anew. And I assure you, you can do it; it is quite an amusement, if you will do it, for it reveals so much. And I feel this is the only way to tackle any fundamental problem. You must tackle a problem which is very deep, profoundly, not at the superficial level. And this problem of loneliness, of despair, with which most of us are somewhat, in our rare moments, acquainted, is not a thing to be dissolved by merely running off into some kind of distraction or worship. It is always there until you are capable of dealing with it directly and experiencing it directly, without any verbalization, without any screen between yourself and it.

Question: What have you to say to a person who, in quiet moments, sees the truth of what you say, who has a longing to keep awake, but who finds himself repeatedly lost in a sea of impulse and small desires?

KRISHNAMURTI: This is what happens to most of us, isn't it? We are awake at moments; at other moments we are asleep. At moments we see everything clearly, with significance; at other moments all is confused, dark, misty. Sometimes there are extraordinary heights of joy, unrelated to any kind of action; at other moments, we struggle for that. Now, what is one to do? Should one memorize, keep awake to those things that we have caught a glimpse of and hang on to them grimly? Or, should we deal with the little desires, impulses, the dark things of our life, as they arise from moment to moment? I know most of us prefer to cling to that joy; we make effort, discipline ourselves to resist, to overcome the petty little things, and try to keep our eyes fixed on the horizon. That is what most of us want, isn't it? Because, that is so much easier—at least, we think so. We prefer to look to an experience that is over, that has given us a great delight, a joy, and hold on to it, like some old people who look to their youth, or like some other people who look to the future, to the next life, to some greatness which they are going to achieve next time, tomorrow, or a hundred years hence. That is, there are those who sacrifice the present to the past, enriching the past, and those who enrich the future. They are both the same. Different sets of words are employed, but the same phenomenon is there.

Now, what is one to do? First of all, let us find out why we want to cling to a pleasurable experience or avoid something which is not pleasurable. Why do we go through this process of holding on, clinging to something which has given us a great joy physically or psychologically? Why do we do this? Why has an experience that is over so much more importance? Because, don't we feel that without that extraordinary experience, there is nothing in the present? The present is an awful bore, a trial; therefore, let us think of the past. The present is irksome, nagging, bothersome; therefore, let us at least be something in the future—a Buddha, a Christ, or God knows what.

So, the past and the future become useful, or pleasurable, only when we do not understand the present. And against the present, we discipline; the present, we resist. Because, take away the past, all your experiences, your knowledge, your accumulations, your enrichments—and what are you? With that past, you meet the present. Therefore, you are really never meeting the present; you are merely overshadowing the present by the past or by the future. And, we discipline ourselves to understand the present. We say, "I must not think of the past; I must not think of the future; I am going to be concentrated in the present." You see the fallacy, the absurdity, the infantilism of thinking of yourself as some marvelous entity tomorrow or in the past, and you say, "Now I must understand it." Can you understand anything through discipline, through compulsion? You may force a boy to be quiet outwardly by disciplining him, but inwardly, he is seething, isn't he? Likewise, when we force ourselves to understand, is there any understanding? But, if we can see the real futility, see the significance of our attachment to the past or to our becoming something in the future—if we really understand it—then that gives sensitivity to the mind to meet the present.

So, our difficulty is not the understanding of the present. Our difficulty is our attachment to the past or to the future. So, we have to investigate why it is that we are attached. Why is the past so important to old people, as the future is to others? Why are we so attached to it? Because we think, do we not, that the experiences have enriched us, so the past has significance. When one was young, one caught a light on the sea, a glimmer; there was a freshness which has faded now. But, at least one can remember that glimmer, that extraordinary sense of élan, that feeling of otherness, of youth. So, one goes back and lives there. That is, one lives in a dead experience. It is over, it is dead, it is gone—yet one gives it life by thinking about it, living in it. But it is a dead thing. So, when one does that, one is also dead in the present—like so many people are—or in the future. In other words, one is afraid to be nothing in the present, to be simple, to be sensitive to the present, so one wants to be enriched by one's experiences of yesterday. Is that enrichment? Are the experiences of yesterday enriching? Surely, you have the memory of them. Is memory enriching? Or, is it merely words with very little content? Surely, you can see that for yourself if you will experiment. When we look to the past for enrichment, we are living on words. We give life to the past; the past has no life in itself; it has life only in relationship to the present. And when the present is disagreeable, we give life to the past, and that, surely, is not enrichment. When you are aware that you are rich, you are surely poor. To be aware of yourself as being something obviously denies that which you are. If you are aware that you are virtuous, surely, you are no longer virtuous; if you aware that you are happy, where is happiness? Happiness comes only when there is self-forgetfulness, when there is no sense of the 'me' as important. But, the 'me' becomes important, the self becomes important, when the past or the future is all-significant. So, mere disciplining of oneself to be something can never bring about that state in which there is no self-consciousness as the 'me'.

Question: I am not interested in anything, but most people are busy with many interests. I don't have to work, so I don't. Should I undertake some useful work?

KRISHNAMURTI: Become a social worker, or a political worker, or a religious worker—is that it? Because you have nothing else to do, therefore you become a reformer! (Laughter) Sir, if you have nothing to do, if you are bored, why not be bored? Why not be that? If you are in sorrow, be sorrowful. Don't try to find a way out of it. Because, your being bored has an immense significance, if you can understand it, live with it. But if you say, "I am bored; therefore, I will do something else," you are merely trying to escape from boredom. And, as most of our activities are escapes, you do much more harm socially and in every other way. The mischief is much greater when you escape than when you are what you are and remain with it. The difficulty is how to remain with it and not run away, and as most of our activities are a process of escape, it is immensely difficult for you to stop escaping and face it. So, I am glad if you are really bored, and I say: Full stop, let's stay there, let's look at it. Why should you do anything? How do you know that in that state, when you are escaping, you are not causing much more harm to people? Your escape into something is an illusion, and when you go into an illusion and propagate that illusion, you are doing much more harm, aren't you, than by merely remaining bored. Sir, if you are bored and remain so, what can you do? This person says he has enough money to live, so he has not that problem for the time being.

If you are bored, why are you bored? What is the thing called boredom? Why is it that you are not interested in anything? There must be reasons and causes which have made you dull: suffering, escapes, beliefs, incessant activity, have made the mind dull, the heart unpliable. To find out what are the causes that have made you dull is not to analyze. That is quite a different problem which we will discuss another time. But, if you could find out why you are bored, why there is no interest, then surely you would solve the problem, wouldn't you? Then the awakened interest will function. But, if you are not interested in why you are bored, you cannot force yourself to be interested in an activity merely to be doing something—like a squirrel going around in a cage. I know that this is the kind of activity most of us indulge in. But, we can find out inwardly, psychologically, why we are in this state of utter boredom; we can see why most of us are in this state—we have exhausted ourselves emotionally and mentally, we have tried so many things, so many sensations, so many amusements, so many experiments, that we have become dull, weary. We join one group, do everything wanted of us, and then leave it; we then go to something else and try that. If we fail with one psychologist, we go to somebody else, or to the priest; if we fail there, we go to another teacher, and so on; we always keep going. This process of constantly stretching and letting go is exhausting, isn't it? Like all sensations, it soon dulls the mind.

So, we have done that; we have gone from sensation to sensation, from excitement to excitement, until we come to a point when we are really exhausted. Now, realizing that, don't proceed any further—take a rest. Be quiet. Let the mind gather strength by itself, don't force it. As the soil renews itself during the wintertime, so, when the mind is allowed to be quiet, it renews itself. But it is very difficult to allow the mind to be quiet, to let it lie fallow after all this, for the mind wants to be doing something all the time. And when you come to that point where you are really allowing yourself to be as you are—bored, ugly, hideous, or whatever it is—then there is a possibility of dealing with it.

What happens when you accept something, when you accept what you are? When you accept that you are what you are, where is the problem? There is a problem only when we do not accept a thing as it is and wish to transform it—which does not mean that I am advocating contentment; on the contrary. So, if we accept what we are, then we see that the thing which we dreaded, the thing which we called boredom, the thing which we called despair, the thing which we called fear, has undergone a complete change. There is a complete transformation of the thing of which we were afraid.

That is why it is important, as I said, to understand the process, the ways of our own thinking. Self-knowledge cannot be gathered through anybody, through any book, through any confession, psychology, or psychoanalyst. It has to be found by yourself because it is your life, and without the widening and deepening of that knowledge of the self—do what you will, alter any outward or inward circumstances, influences—it will ever be a breeding ground of despair, pain, sorrow. To go beyond the self-enclosing activities of the mind, you must understand them; and to understand them is to be aware of action in relationship, relationship to things, to people, and to ideas. In that relationship, which is the mirror, we begin to see ourselves without any justification or condemnation, and from that wider and deeper knowledge of the ways of our own mind, it is possible to proceed further; then it is possible for the mind to be quiet, to receive that which is real.

July 24, 1949

Fifth Talk in The Oak Grove

During the last four talks or discussions we have been considering the question of self-knowledge. Because, as we said, without being aware of one's own process of thought and feeling, it is obviously not possible to act rightly or think rightly. So, the essential purpose of these gatherings or discussions or meetings is really to see if one can, for oneself, directly experience the process of one's own thinking and be aware of it integrally. Most of us are aware of it superficially, on the upper or superficial level of the mind, but not as a total process. It is this total process that gives freedom, that gives comprehension, that gives understanding, and not the partial process. Some of us may know ourselves partially, at least we think we know ourselves a little, but that little is not sufficient because if one knows oneself slightly, it acts as a hindrance rather than a help. And it is only in knowing oneself as a total process—physiologically and psychologically, the hidden, unconscious, deeper layers as well as the superficial layers—it is only when we know the total process that we are able to deal with the problems that inevitably arise, not partially, but as a whole.

Now, this ability to deal with the total process is what I would like to discuss this evening, also whether it is a question of the cultivation of a particular capacity, which implies a certain kind of specialization. Does understanding, happiness, the realization of something beyond the mere physical sensations come through any specialization? Because, capacity implies specialization. In a world of ever-increasing specialization, we depend on the specialists. If anything goes wrong with a car, we turn to the mechanic; if anything goes wrong physically, we go to a doctor. If there is a psychological maladjustment, we run, if we have the money and the means, to a psychologist, or to a priest, and so on. That is, we look to the specialist for help in our failures and miseries.

Now, does the understanding of ourselves demand specialization? The specialist knows only his specialty at whatever level. And does the knowledge of ourselves demand specialization? I do not think so; on the contrary. Specialization implies, does it not, a narrowing-down of the whole, total process of our being to a particular point and specializing on that point. Since we have to understand ourselves as a total process, we cannot specialize. Because, specialization implies exclusion, obviously, whereas to know ourselves does not demand any kind of exclusion. On the contrary, it demands a complete awareness of ourselves as an integral process, and for that, specialization is a hindrance.

After all, what is it that we have to do? Know ourselves, which means to know our relationship with the world, surely—not only with the world of ideas and people, but also with nature, with the things we possess. That is our life—life being relationship to the whole. And does the understanding of that relationship demand specialization? Obviously not. What it demands is awareness to meet life as a whole. How is one to be aware? That is our problem. How is one to have that awareness—if I may use this word without making it mean specialization? How is one to be capable of meeting life as a whole?—which means not only personal relationship with your neighbor but also with nature, with the things that you possess, with ideas, and with the things that the mind manufactures as illusion, desire, and so on. How is one to be aware of this whole process of relationship? Surely, that is our life, is it not? There is no life without relationship, and to understand this relationship does not mean isolation, as I have been insisting, constantly explaining. On the contrary, it demands a full recognition or awareness of the total process of relationship.

Now, how is one to be aware? How are we aware of anything? How are you aware of your relationship with a person? How are you aware of these trees, the calling of that cow? How are you aware of your reactions when you read a newspaper, if you read a newspaper? And, are we aware of the superficial responses of the mind as well as the inner responses? How are we aware of anything? Surely, first we are aware, are we not, of a response to a stimulus, which is an obvious fact; I see the trees, and there is a response, then sensation, contact, identification, and desire. That is the ordinary process, isn't it? We can observe what actually takes place without studying any books.

So, through identification, you have pleasure and pain. And our "capacity" is this concern with pleasure and the avoidance of pain, is it not? If you are interested in something, if it gives you pleasure, there is "capacity" immediately; there is an awareness of that fact immediately, and if it is painful, the "capacity" is developed to avoid it. So, as long as we are looking to "capacity" to understand ourselves, I think we shall fail because the understanding of ourselves does not depend on "capacity." It is not a technique that you develop, cultivate and increase through time, through constantly sharpening. This awareness of oneself can be tested, surely, in the action of relationship; it can be tested in the way we talk, the way we behave. Watch yourself after the meeting is over, watch yourself at the table—just observe, without any identification, without any comparison, without any condemnation; just watch, and you will see an extraordinary thing taking place. You not only put an end to an activity which is unconscious—because most of our activities are unconscious—you not only bring that to an end, but, further, you are aware of the motives of that action without inquiry, without digging into it.

Now, when you are aware, you see the whole process of your thinking and action, but it can happen only when there is no condemnation. That is, when I condemn something, I do not understand it, and it is one way of avoiding any kind of understanding. I think most of us do that purposely; we condemn immediately, and we think we have understood. If we do not condemn but regard it, are aware of it, then the content, the significance of that action begins to open up. Experiment with this and you will see for yourself. Just be aware—without any sense of justification—which may appear rather negative, but is not negative. On the contrary, it has the quality of passivity which is direct action, and you will discover this if you experiment with it.

After all, if you want to understand something, you have to be in a passive mood, do you not? You cannot keep on thinking about it, speculating about it, or questioning it. You have to be sensitive enough to receive the content of it. It is like being a sensitive photographic plate. If I want to understand you, I have to be passively aware; then you begin to tell me all of your story. Surely, that is not a question of capacity or specialization. In that process, we begin to understand ourselves—not only the superficial layers of our consciousness, but the deeper, which is much more important because there are all of our motives or intentions, our hidden, confused demands, anxieties, fears, appetites. Outwardly we may have them all under control, but inwardly they are boiling. Until those have been completely understood through awareness, obviously there cannot be freedom, there cannot be happiness, there is no intelligence.

So, is intelligence a matter of specialization?—intelligence being the total awareness of our process. And is that intelligence to be cultivated through any form of specialization? Because, that is what is happening, is it not? You are listening to me, probably thinking that I am a specialist—I hope not. The priest, the doctor, the engineer, the industrialist, the businessman, the professor—we have the mentality of all that specialization. And we think that to realize the highest form of intelligence—which is truth, which is God, which cannot be described—to realize that, we have to make ourselves specialists. We study, we grope, we search out; and with the mentality of the specialist, or looking to the specialist, we study ourselves in order to develop a capacity which will help to unravel our conflicts, our miseries.

So, our problem is, if we are at all aware, whether the conflicts and the miseries and the sorrows of our daily existence can be solved by another; and if they cannot, how is it possible for us to tackle them? To understand a problem obviously requires a certain intelligence, and that intelligence cannot be derived from or cultivated through specialization. It comes into being only when we are passively aware of the whole process of our consciousness, which is to be aware of ourselves without choice, without choosing what is right and what is wrong. Because, when you are passively aware, you will see that out of that passivity—which is not idleness, which is not sleep, but extreme alertness—the problem has quite a different significance, which means there is no longer identification with the problem, and therefore there is no judgment, and hence the problem begins to reveal its content. If you are able to do that constantly, continuously, then every problem can be solved fundamentally, not superficially. And that is the difficulty because most of us are incapable of being passively aware, letting the problem tell the story without our interpreting it. We do not know how to look at a problem dispassionately—if you like to use that word. Unfortunately, we are not capable of doing that because we want a result from the problem, we want an answer, we are looking to an end; or we try to translate the problem according to our pleasure or pain; or we have an answer already, how to deal with the problem. Therefore, we approach a problem, which is always new, with the old pattern. The challenge is always the new, but our response is always the old, and our difficulty is to meet the challenge adequately, that is, fully. The problem is always a problem of relationship, there is no other problem; and to meet the problem of relationship, with its constantly varying demands—to meet it rightly, to meet it adequately—one has to be aware, passively; and this passivity is not a question of determination, of will, of discipline; to be aware that we are not passive is the beginning. To be aware that we want a particular answer to a particular problem—surely, that is the beginning: to know ourselves in relationship to the problem and how we deal with the problem. Then, as we begin to know ourselves in relationship to the problem—how we respond, what are our various prejudices, demands, pursuits, in meeting that problem—this awareness will reveal the process of our own thinking, of our own inward nature, and in that there is a release.

So, life is a matter of relationship, and to understand that relationship, which is not static, there must be an awareness which is pliable, an awareness which is alertly passive, not aggressively active. And as I said, this passive awareness does not come through any form of discipline, through any practice. It is to be just aware, from moment to moment, of our thinking and feeling, not only when we are awake, for we will see, as we go into it deeper, that we begin to dream, that we begin to throw up all kinds of symbols which we translate as dreams. So, we open the door into the hidden, which becomes the known; but to find the unknown, we must go beyond the door—surely, that is our difficulty. Reality is not a thing that is knowable by the mind because the mind is the result of the known, of the past; therefore, the mind must understand itself and its functioning, its truth, and only then is it possible for the unknown to be.

Question: All religions have insisted on some kind of self-discipline to moderate the instincts of the brute in man. Through self-discipline the saints and mystics have asserted that they have attained godhood. Now, you seem to imply that such disciplines are a hindrance to the realization of God. I am confused. Who is right in this matter?

KRISHNAMURTI: Surely, it is not a question of who is right in this matter. What is important is to find out the truth of the matter for ourselves—not according to a particular saint or to a person who comes from India or from some other place, the more exotic the better. So let us examine it together.

Now, you are caught between these two: someone says discipline, another says no discipline. Generally what happens is, you choose what is more convenient, what is more satisfying: you like the man, his looks, his personal idiosyncrasies, his personal favoritism, and all the rest of it. So, putting all that aside, let us examine this question directly and find out the truth of the matter for ourselves. Because, in this question a great deal is implied, and we have to approach it very cautiously and tentatively.

Most of us want someone in authority to tell us what to do. We look for a direction in conduct because our instinct is to be safe, not to suffer more. Someone is said to have realized happiness, bliss, or what you will, and we hope that he will tell us what to do to arrive there. That is what we want; we want that same happiness, that same inward quietness, joy; and in this mad world of confusion, we want someone to tell us what to do. That is really the basic instinct with most of us, and according to that instinct, we pattern our action. Is God, is that highest thing, unnameable and not to be measured by words—is that come by through discipline, through following a particular pattern of action? Please, we are thinking it out together—don't bother about the rain for the time being. If you are interested, let us go into it. We want to arrive at a particular goal, particular end, and we think that by practice, by discipline, by suppressing or releasing, subliminating or substituting, we shall be able to find that which we are seeking.

What is implied in discipline? Why do we discipline ourselves, if we do? I doubt if we do—but why do we do it? No, seriously, why do we do it? Can discipline and intelligence go together? Let us inquire into it fully and see how far—if the rain allows us—we can go into this matter. Because, most people feel that we must, through some kind of discipline, subjugate, or control the brute, the ugly thing in us. And is that brute, that ugly thing, controllable through discipline? What do we mean by discipline? A course of action which promises a reward, a course of action which, if pursued, will give us what we want—it may be positive or negative. A pattern of conduct which if practiced diligently, sedulously, very, very ardently, will give me in the end what I want. It may be painful, but I am willing to go through it to get that. That is, the self, which is aggressive, selfish, hypocritical, anxious, fearful—you know, all of it, that self which is the cause of the brute in us, we want to transform, subjugate, destroy. And how is this to be done? Is it to be done through discipline or through an intelligent understanding of the past of the self, what the self is, how it comes into being, and so on? That is, shall we destroy the brute in man through compulsion, or through intelligence? And is intelligence a matter of discipline? Let us for the time being forget what the saints and all the rest of the people have said—and I do not know if they have said it, not that I am an expert on saints. But let us go into the matter for ourselves as though we were for the first time looking at this problem; then we may have something creative at the end of it, not just quotations of what other people have said, which is all so vain and useless.

We first say that in us there is conflict—the black against the white, greed against nongreed, and so on. I am greedy, which creates pain, and to be rid of that greed, I must discipline myself. That is, I must resist any form of conflict which gives me pain, which in this case I call greed. I then say it is antisocial, it is unethical, it is not saintly, and so on, and so on—the various social-religious reasons we give for resisting it. Is greed destroyed or put away from us through compulsion? First, let us examine the process involved in suppression, in compulsion, in putting it away, resisting. What happens when you do that, when you resist greed? What is the thing that is resisting greed? That is the first question, isn't it? Why do you resist greed, and who is the entity that says, "I must be free of greed"? The entity that says, "I must be free" is also greed, is he not? Because, up to now, greed has paid him, but now it is painful; therefore, he says, "I must get rid of it." The motive to get rid of it is still a process of greed because he is wanting to be something which he is not. Nongreed is now profitable, so I am pursuing nongreed; but the motive, the intention, is still to be something, to be nongreedy—which is still greed, surely, which is again a negative form of the emphasis on the 'me'.

So, we find that being greedy is painful for various reasons which are obvious. As long as we enjoy it, as long as it pays us to be greedy, there is no problem. Society encourages us in different ways to be greedy; so do religions encourage us in different ways. As long as it is profitable, as long as it is not painful, we pursue it. But the moment it becomes painful, we want to resist it. That resistance is what we call discipline against greed, but are we free from greed through resistance, through sublimation, through suppression? Any act on the part of the 'me' who wants to be free from greed is still greed. Therefore, any action, any response on my part with regard to greed is obviously not the solution.

First of all, there must be a quiet mind, an undisturbed mind, to understand anything, especially something which I do not know, something which my mind cannot fathom—which, this questioner says, is God. To understand anything, any intricate problem—of life or relationship, in fact any problem—there must be a certain quiet depth to the mind. And is that quiet depth come by through any form of compulsion? The superficial mind may compel itself, make itself quiet; but surely, such quietness is the quietness of decay, death. It is not capable of adaptability, pliability, sensitivity. So, resistance is not the way.

Now, to see that requires intelligence, doesn't it? To see that the mind is made dull by compulsion is already the beginning of intelligence, isn't it—to see that discipline is merely conformity to a pattern of action through fear. Because, that is what is implied in disciplining ourselves—we are afraid of not getting what we want. And what happens when you discipline the mind, when you discipline your being? Surely, it becomes very hard, doesn't it, unpliable, not quick, not adjustable. Don't you know people who have disciplined themselves—if there are such people? The result is obviously a process of decay. There is an inward conflict which is put away, hidden away, but it is there, burning.

So, we see that discipline, which is resistance, merely creates a habit, and habit obviously cannot be productive of intelligence: habit never is, practice never is. You may become very clever with your fingers by practicing the piano all day, making something with your hands, but intelligence is demanded to direct the hands, and we are now inquiring into that intelligence.

You see somebody whom you consider happy or as having realized, and he does certain things, and you, wanting that happiness, imitate him. This imitation is called discipline, isn't it? We imitate in order to receive what another has; we copy in order to be happy, which you think he is. Is happiness found through discipline? And, by practicing a certain rule, by practicing a certain discipline, a mode of conduct, are you ever free? Surely, there must be freedom for discovery, must there not? If you would discover anything, you must be free inwardly, which is obvious. Are you free by shaping your mind in a particular way which you call discipline? Obviously, you are not. You are merely a repetitive machine, resisting according to a certain conclusion, according to a certain mode of conduct. So, freedom cannot come through discipline. Freedom can only come into being with intelligence, and that intelligence is awakened, or you have that intelligence, the moment you see that any form of compulsion denies freedom, inwardly or outwardly.

So, the first requirement, not as a discipline, is obviously freedom; and only virtue gives that freedom. Greed is confusion; anger is confusion; bitterness is confusion. When you see that, obviously you are free of them—not that you are going to resist them, but you see that only in freedom can you discover, and that any form of compulsion is not freedom, and therefore there is no discovery. Surely, what virtue does is to give you freedom. The unvirtuous person is a confused person, and in confusion, how can you discover anything? How can you? So, virtue is not the end product of a discipline, but virtue is freedom, and freedom cannot come through any action which is not virtuous, which is not true in itself. Our difficulty is that most of us have read so much, most of us have superficially followed so many disciplines—getting up every morning at a certain hour, sitting in a certain posture, trying to hold our minds in a certain way—you know, practice, practice, discipline. Because, you have been told that if you do these things you will get there; if you do these things for a number of years, you will have God at the end of it. I may put it crudely, but that is the basis of our thinking. Surely, God doesn't come so easily as all that. God is not a mere marketable thing—I do this, and you give me that.

Most of us are so conditioned by external influences, by religious doctrines, beliefs, and by our own inward demand to arrive at something, to gain something, that it is very difficult for us to think of this problem anew, without thinking in terms of discipline. So, first we must see very clearly the implications of discipline—how it narrows down the mind, limits the mind, compels the mind to a particular action through our desire, through influence, and all the rest of it, and a conditioned mind, however ''virtuous'' that conditioning, cannot possibly be free and therefore cannot understand reality. And, God, reality, or what you will—the name doesn't matter—can come into being only when there is freedom; and there is no freedom where there is compulsion, positive or negative, through fear. There is no freedom if you are seeking an end, for you are tied to that end. You may be free from the past, but the future holds you, and that is not freedom. And it is only in freedom that one can discover anything: a new idea, a new feeling, a new perception. And surely, any form of discipline which is based on compulsion denies that freedom, whether political or religious. And since discipline, which is conformity to an action with an end in view, is binding, the mind can never be free. It can function only within that groove, like a gramophone record.

So, through practice, through habit, through cultivation of a pattern, the mind only achieves what it has in view. Therefore, it is not free; therefore, it cannot realize that which is immeasurable. To be aware of that whole process—why you are constantly disciplining yourself to public opinion, to certain saints, you know, the whole business of conforming to opinion, whether of a saint or of the neighbor, it is all the same—to be aware of this whole conformity through practice, through subtle ways of submitting yourself, of denying, asserting, suppressing, sublimating, all implying conformity to a pattern: to be aware of that is already the beginning of freedom, from which there is virtue. Virtue, surely, is not the cultivation of a particular idea. Nongreed, for instance, if pursued as an end is no longer virtue, is it? That is, if you are conscious that you are nongreedy, are you virtuous? And yet that is what we are doing through discipline.

So, discipline, conformity, practice, only gives emphasis to self-consciousness as being something. The mind practices nongreed, and therefore it is not free from its own consciousness as being nongreedy; therefore, it is not really nongreedy. It has merely taken on a new cloak which it calls nongreed. We can see the total process of all this: the motivation, the desire for an end, the conformity to a pattern, the desire to be secure in pursuing a pattern—all this is merely the moving from the known to the known, always within the limits of the mind's own self-enclosing process. To see all this, to be aware of it, is the beginning of intelligence; and intelligence is neither virtuous nor nonvirtuous; it cannot be fitted into a pattern as virtue or nonvirtue. Intelligence brings freedom, which is not licentiousness, not disorder. Without this intelligence there can be no virtue, and virtue gives freedom, and in freedom there comes into being, reality. If you see the whole process totally in its entirety, then you will find there is no conflict. It is because we are in conflict, and because we want to escape from that conflict that we resort to various forms of disciplines, denials, and adjustments. But, when we see what is the process of conflict, then there is no question of discipline because then we understand from moment to moment the ways of conflict. That requires great alertness, watching yourself all the time; and the curious part of it is that although you may not be watchful all the time, there is a recording process going on inwardly, once the intention is there—the sensitivity, the inner sensitivity, is taking the picture all the time so that the inner will project that picture the moment you are quiet.

So, again, it is not a question of discipline. Sensitivity can never come into being through compulsion. You may compel a child to do something—put him in a corner, and he may be quiet, but inwardly he is probably seething, looking out of the window, doing something to get away. That is what we are still doing. So, the question of discipline and who is right and who is wrong can be solved only by yourself. Because, there is much more involved in this than what I have just said.

Also, you see, we are afraid to go wrong because we want to be a success. Fear is at the bottom of the desire to be disciplined, but the unknown cannot be caught in the net of discipline. On the contrary, the unknown must have freedom and not the pattern of your mind. That is why the tranquillity of the mind is essential. When the mind is conscious that it is tranquil, it is no longer tranquil; when the mind is conscious that it is nongreedy, free from greed, it recognizes itself in the new robe of nongreed, but that is not tranquillity. That is why one must also understand the problem in this question of the person who controls and that which is controlled. Surely, they are not separate phenomena, but a joint phenomenon—the controller and the controlled are one. It is a deception to think that they are two different processes, but we will discuss this at another time.

Question: How on earth can we tame the tiger in us, and in our children, without a pattern of clear purpose and cause sustained by vigorous practice?

KRISHNAMURTI: This implies that you know your purpose, and you know the cause, too; doesn't it? Do you know the purpose? Do you know the purpose of life, the end of life, and the way to achieve it? Is that why you must have a vigorous course of action through discipline, through practice, to attain what you want? Isn't it very difficult to find out what you want, the purpose you have in view? Political parties may have a purpose, but even then they are finding it extremely difficult. But can you say, "I know the purpose"? And is there such a thing as a purpose? Please, one has to go into this very carefully—not that I am casting doubt on your purposes. We must understand it. At a certain period of our life, we have a purpose—to be an engine driver, to be a streetcar driver, to be a fireman, this or that—and later on we come to have a different purpose. As we grow much older, again we have a different purpose. The purpose varies all the time, doesn't it, according to our pains and pleasures. You may have a purpose to be a very rich man, a very powerful man; but surely, that is not what we are discussing here for the time being. The ambitious man may have a purpose, but he is antisocial; he can never find reality. An ambitious man is merely one who is projecting himself into the future and wanting to be something, spiritually or secularly. Such a man, obviously, is not capable of finding reality because his mind is only concerned with success, with achieving, with becoming something. He is concerned about himself in relation to what he wants. But most of us, though we are somewhat ambitious—wanting a little more money, a little more friendship, a little more love, a little more beauty, a little more this and that, and so on, many things—do we know what we want ultimately, not just through passing moods? Most religious people say yes, they do; they want reality, they want God, they want the highest. But to desire the highest, you must know what it is; it may be quite different from what you think, and probably it is. Therefore, you cannot want that. If you want it, it is another form of ambition, another form of security. Therefore, it is not reality that you want. So, when you ask, "How can we tame the tiger in us, and in our children, without a pattern of clear purpose and cause sustained by practice?" you mean, do you not, how can we live in relationship with others and not be antisocial, selfish, bound by our own prejudices, and so on. To tame the tiger, we must first know what kind of an animal it is, not just give it a name and try to tame it. You must know what it is made up of. So, if you call it a tiger, it is already a tiger because you have the image, the picture of what the tiger is, or what greed is; but if you do not name it but look at it, then surely, it has quite a different significance. I don't know if you are following all this. We will discuss the same problem at various times because there is only one problem put in different ways.

So, without calling it a tiger, without saying, "I have a purpose, and to fulfill it there must be discipline," let us inquire into the whole process. Don't approach it with a conclusion because, as I said, the problem is always new, and it requires a new mind to look at it, a mind that is not verbalizing, which is extremely difficult. Because, we can only think in terms of words—our thought is word. Try to think without words and see how difficult it is.

So, our point is, how to tame the tiger without discipline, whether in ourselves or in our children, if we are parents. To tame something, you must understand it, know it. The moment you do not know something, you are frightened of it. You say, "I feel there is a conflict in me, an opposing desire, which I call the tiger; and how is that to be tamed, to be calmed down?" Only by understanding it, and I can understand it only when I look at it. I cannot look at it if I condemn it or give it a name or justify it or identify myself with it. I can understand it only when I am passively aware of what it is, and there is no passive awareness as long as I am condemning it. So, my problem is to understand it, not to call the thing by a name. I must understand why I condemn. Because, it is so much easier, isn't it, to condemn something first. It is one of the ways to get rid of it, push it away—call it a German, a Japanese, a Hindu, a Christian, a Communist, or God knows what else, and push it away. And we think we have understood it by giving it a name. So the name, the naming, prevents understanding. That is one fact.

Also, what prevents understanding is judging because we look at a thing already with a bias, with a prejudice, with a want, with a demand. We look at a thing because we want a result from it. We have a purpose, we want to tame it, we want to control it in order that it may be something else. The moment you see that, surely, your mind is passively quiet, watching the thing. It is no longer naming the tiger as the tiger; it has no name, and therefore your relationship to it is direct, not through words. It is because we have no relationship to it directly that there is fear. The moment you are related to something, experience something directly, immediately, fully, there is no fear, is there? So, you have removed the cause of fear, and therefore you are able to understand it, and hence you are able to resolve it. That which you have understood is resolved; that which is not understood continues to be a problem. This is a fact. And our difficulty is to see always *what is* without interpretation because the function of the mind is to communicate, to store up, to translate, according to its fancies and desires—not to understand. To understand, none of these things must take place. To understand, there must be quiet, and a mind that is occupied with judging, with condemning, with translating, is not a quiet mind.

Question: I cannot control my thoughts. Must I control them? Does this not imply choice, and how can I trust my judgment unless I have a standard based on the teachings of the Great Ones?

KRISHNAMURTI: Now, to understand how to control your thoughts, you must first know what your thoughts are, must you not? That is the problem, isn't it? You say, "I cannot control my thoughts." To find out why you cannot control thoughts, you must be aware of what thinking is, must you not? What is thinking? And who is the thinker? Surely, that is the question, isn't it? Who is the thinker, and are the thoughts different from the thinker? Then the problem arises for the thinker to control his thoughts. If the thinker and the thought are one, and not separate processes, then the question of the thinker controlling thought does not arise. So, you have to find out first if the thinker is separate from his thought. Is there a thinker without thought? If you have no thought, is there a thinker? So, the thinker is nonexistent apart from thought; we have only thought. The thoughts have created the thinker; and the thinker, to make himself permanent, secure, and all the rest of it, then says, "I am apart from the thoughts which must be controlled." So, until you solve this problem, until you have a direct experience of this problem—whether the thinker is separate from thought—the question of control will exist; but the moment you see, experience directly, that the thinker is the thought, then you have quite a different problem.

Then, the next question is: When you control thoughts—one set of thoughts as opposed to another—there is choice. You choose certain thoughts and wish to concentrate on those, and not on others; why? We are concerned with thinking, not with a particular set of thoughts. If you say, "I prefer this thought to that," then choice arises; but why do you prefer? And what is the thing that prefers? Sirs, this is not very complicated, this is not metaphysics or big words; just look at it and you will see the difficulty. First, we must see the difficulty before we can solve it. When you choose, who is it that chooses? And, if the chooser has a standard according to the teachings of the Great Ones, as stated in the question, then the chooser becomes very important, doesn't he? Because, if he chooses according to the standards of the teachers, then he is cultivating, emphasizing the chooser, is he not?

Sir, let us put the problem a little more simply. My thoughts wander all over the place. I want to think quietly upon a particular subject, but my thoughts go off in different directions. Now why do they go off? Because, my thoughts are also interested in other things, not only in that particular thing. That is a fact, isn't it; otherwise, they would not wander off. My mind isn't wandering off now because I am interested in what I am talking about. There is no question of effort, there is no question of discipline, there is no question of controlling; nothing else interests me.

So, we must find out the significance of each interest and not exclude other interests for the sake of one. If I can find out the significance of each interest, and its value, then my mind won't wander, will it? But it will wander if I resist the various interests and try to concentrate on the one. So, I say, "All right, let it wander." I look at all the interests that arise, one after the other, so that my mind is made pliable by the whole sweep of interest and not narrowed down by one specific interest. Then what happens? I see that my mind is merely a bundle of interests opposing other interests; it chooses to emphasize one interest and exclude all other interests.

When the mind recognizes that it is a bundle of interests, then every interest has significance; therefore, there is no excluding; therefore, there is no question of choosing; therefore, the mind begins to understand the whole, total process of itself. But if you have a standard of choice in accordance with the Great Ones by which you are trying to live—then what happens? You emphasize the thinker, the chooser, don't you? Obviously. Now, who is the chooser, apart from the choice? As I said, there is no thinker apart from the thought, and it is a trick of the mind to separate itself into the thinker and the thought. When we really understand it, see the real significance of it, experience it—not verbally assert it, for then it has no meaning—then we will see that there is complete transformation in us. Then, we will never put this question. The standard of the great teachers, the teachings of the Great Ones, or whatever else—you are the result of all that, aren't you? You are the result of the whole, total process of man—not just of America but of the world. And you are not separate from the standard. You are the standard, and it is a trick of the mind ever to separate itself.

Because you see that everything is transient, impermanent, you want to feel that at least there is the permanency of the 'me'. You say, "I am different." In that separate action of the mind, there is conflict; it creates for itself an isolation and then says, "I am different from my thought. I must control my thought. How am I to control it?" Such a question is not a valid question. If you think it out, you will see that you are a bundle of interests, a bundle of thoughts; and to choose one thought and discard the others, to choose one interest and resist another, is still to play the trick of separating yourself from the thought. Whereas, if you recognize that the mind is interest, the mind is thought—that there is not a thinker and a thought—then you will approach this problem entirely anew. Then you will see that there is no conflict between the thinker and the thought; then every interest has significance and is worked out, thought out, fully, completely. Then there is no question of a central interest from which there is distraction.

July 30, 1949

Sixth Talk in The Oak Grove

This morning I would like to discuss what is true religion, but in order to find out what it is, we must first examine our life, and not superimpose on it something we think is spiritual, romantic, sentimental. So, let us examine our life to find out what we mean by religion, and if there is a way of discovering what is true religion.

First of all, for most of us, life is full of conflict; we are in pain, we are in sorrow. Our life is boring, empty, and there is always death, and there are the innumerable explanations. Life is mostly a constant repetition of habit. Taken as a whole, it is painful and tiresome, wearisome and sorrowful, and that is the lot of most of us. To escape from that, we turn to beliefs, to rituals, to knowledge, to amusements, to politics, to activity: we welcome any form of escape from our daily, tiresome, boring routine. These escapes, whether political or religious, must, by their very nature, likewise become tiresome, routine, habitual. We move from sensation to sensation, and ultimately, all sensation must become boring, tiresome. As our life is mostly a response from our physical centers, and as it causes disturbance, pain, we try to escape into what we call religion, into spiritual realms.

Now, as long as we are seeking sensation in any form, it must eventually lead to boredom because one is surfeited, one gets tired of it—which is, again, an obvious fact. The more sensations you have, the more tiresome they become at the end, the more boring, the more habitual. And is religion a matter of sensation?—religion being the search for reality, and the discovery, the understanding, or the experiencing of the highest. Is that a matter of sensation, a matter of sentiment, a matter of appeal? To most of us, religion is a set of beliefs, dogmas, rituals, a constant repetition of organized formulas, and so on. If you examine these things you will see that they also are the outcome of the desire for sensation. You go to churches, temples, or to mosques, and you repeat certain phrases, you indulge in certain ceremonies. They are all stimulations, they give you a certain kind of sensation, and you are satisfied with that sensation, giving it a high-sounding name, but it is essentially sensation. You are caught in sensation, you like the impressions, the feeling of being good, the repetition of certain prayers, and so on. But, if one goes into it deeply and intelligently, one finds that basically they are only sensation; and although they may vary in expression and give you a certain feeling of newness, they are essentially sensation and therefore ultimately boring, tiresome, habit-forming.

So, obviously, religion is not ceremony. Religion is not dogma. Religion is not the continuation of certain tenets or beliefs inculcated from childhood. Whether you believe in God or don't believe in God does not make you a religious person. Belief does not make you a religious person, surely. The man who drops an atomic bomb and destroys in a few minutes thousands upon thousands of people may believe in God, and the person who leads a dull life and also believes in God, or the person who does not believe in God—surely, they are not religious. Belief or nonbelief has nothing to do with the search for reality or with the discovery and the experiencing of that reality, which is religion. It is the experiencing of reality that is religion, and it does not lie through any organized belief, through any church, through any knowledge, either Eastern or Western. Religion is the capacity of experiencing directly that which is immeasurable, that which cannot be put into words; but that cannot be experienced so long as we are escaping from life, from life which we have made so dull, so empty, so much a matter of routine. Life, which is relationship, has become a matter of routine because inwardly there is no creative intensity, because inwardly we are poor and therefore outwardly we try to fill that emptiness with belief, with amusement, with knowledge, with various forms of excitement.

That emptiness, that inward poverty, can come to an end only when we cease to escape, and we cease to escape when we are no longer seeking sensation. Then we are able to face that emptiness. That emptiness is not different from us: we are that emptiness. As we were discussing yesterday, thought is not different from the thinker. The emptiness is not different from the observer who feels that emptiness. The observer and the observed are a joint phenomenon, and when you experience that directly, then you will find that the thing which you have dreaded as emptiness—which makes you seek escape into various forms of sensation, including religion—ceases, and you are able to face it and be it. Because we have not understood the significance of escapes, how escapes have come into being; because we have not examined them, gone into them fully, these escapes have become much more significant, much more meaningful than that *which is*. The escapes have conditioned us, and because we have escaped, we are not creative in ourselves. There is creativeness in us when we are experiencing reality constantly, but not continuously—because there is a difference between continuity and experiencing from moment to moment. That which continues decays. That which is being experienced from moment to moment has no death, no decay. If we can experience something from moment to moment, it has a vitality, life; if we can meet life anew all the time, then in that there is creativeness. But to have an experience which you desire to continue—in that there is decay.

So many people have had some kind of pleasurable experience, and they want that experience to continue. So they go back to it, they revive it, they look to it, they long for it, they are miserable because it doesn't continue; and therefore there is a constant decaying process taking place. Whereas, if there is experiencing from moment to moment, there is a renewal. It is that renewal that is creative, and you cannot have that renewal, that creative élan, if your mind is occupied with escapes and caught in those things that we have taken for granted. That is why we have to reexamine all of the values that we have gathered, and one of the main values in our life is religion, which is so organized. We belong to one or another of the various organized religions, groups, sects, or societies because it gives us a certain sense of security. To be identified with the largest organization or with the smallest or the most exclusive gives us satisfaction. It is only when we are capable of reexamining all these influences which are conditioning us, which help us to escape from our own boredom, from our own emptiness, from our own lack of creative responsibility and creative joy; it is only when we have examined them and come back, having put them aside and faced that which is—only then, surely, are we capable of really going into the whole problem of what is truth. Because, in doing that, there is a possibility of self-knowledge. The whole process is self-knowledge, and it is only when there is the knowledge of this process that there is a possibility of thinking, feeling, acting rightly. We cannot practice right thinking in order to be free from the process of thought; to be free, one must know oneself. Self-knowledge is the beginning of wisdom, and without self-knowledge, there can be no wisdom. There can be knowledge, sensation, but sensation is wearisome, boring, whereas that wisdom which is eternal can never decay, can never come to an end.

Question: I find that, by effort, I can concentrate. I can suppress or put aside thoughts that come uninvited. I do not find that suppression is a hindrance to my well-being. Of course, I dream, but I can interpret the dreams and resolve the conflict. A friend tells me that I am becoming smug; do you think he can be right? (Laughter)

KRISHNAMURTI: Now, let us first understand what we mean by effort and what we mean by concentration. Do we understand anything through effort?—effort being exertion of will, action of will, which is desire. By the action of will to understand, that is, by deliberately making an effort, do we understand? Or is understanding something entirely different, which comes not through effort but through passive alertness?—which is not the action of will. When do you understand? Have you ever examined it? When do you understand? Not when you are battling with something, with some object which you want to understand. Surely, there is no understanding when you are constantly probing, questioning, tearing to pieces, analyzing—in that there is no understanding. It is only when the mind is passively aware and alert—that is, immediately in contact with or experiencing that thing—that there is a possibility of understanding it, surely. Please, to some of you what I am saying may be outrageous or new, but experiment with it, don't reject it right off.

When we are in battle with each other, in conflict with each other, is there an understanding? It is only when you and I sit down quietly, discuss, try to find out, that there is a possibility of understanding. So, effort is obviously detrimental to understanding. That is, you may have a problem, you may go into it, worry over it, tear it to pieces, look at it from different sides. In that process, there is no understanding. It is only when the mind leaves the problem alone, lets it drop, only when the mind becomes quiet in relation to the problem that there is understanding of it. But whether conflict, analysis, is a necessary step in understanding is quite a different question, which we won't go into now.

Then there is concentration. What do you mean by concentration? Fixing the mind on a particular object to the exclusion of other interests, isn't it? That is what we mean by concentration: to fix the mind on an idea, an image, an interest, and exclude all other interests—which is a form of suppression. And the questioner says that it does not do him any harm; though he has dreams, he can easily interpret and put them aside.

Now, what does such concentration do? What does exclusion do? What is the result of exclusion? Obviously, conflict, isn't it? I may have the capacity to concentrate on one thing and exclude others, but the others are still there, wanting to come in. Therefore, there is a conflict going on—whether I am conscious of it or not is not the point, but there is conflict. And, as long as that conflict continues, there is no understanding, surely. I may be able to concentrate, but as long as there is conflict within me between that which attracts my attention and that which I am excluding—as long as there is conflict in me, it must have a wrong effect. Because, suppression of any kind must psychologically tear, making me either physically ill or mentally unbalanced. What is suppressed must eventually come out, and one way is through dreams. The questioner says he can interpret his dreams and thereby get rid of them. Apparently he feels satisfied with this, and he wants to know if he is smug. As long as you are satisfied with the result, obviously you must be smug. Most of us hate to be in discontent; and being discontented inwardly, as most of us are, we find ways and means to cover up that discontent, that burning thing. And one of the escapes, one of the best ways of covering up this discontent, is to learn concentration so that you can successfully conceal your discontent. Then you can fix your mind on an interest and go after it and feel that you have at last conquered, canalized your discontent. But, surely, discontent cannot be canalized by the mind because the mind in its very nature is discontent. That is why mere concentration, which is exclusion, does not bring about freedom from discontent—which is to understand it. Concentration, which is a process of exclusion, does not bring understanding; but, as I was explaining yesterday, if you go after each interest as each interest arises, if you go into it, examine it, understand it—then there is a possibility of coming to a different kind of attention which is not exclusion. We will discuss this presently, in another question.

Question: How can we ever start anew, as you constantly suggest, if the cup of our experience is permanently sullied? How can we really forget that which we are? Will you please explain what is meant by self-forgetfulness. How can I throw away the cup, which I am?

KRISHNAMURTI: Renewal is possible only if there is no continuity. That which continues has no possibility of renewal; that which ends has a possibility of renewal. That which dies has a possibility of being reborn.

And, when you say that you are sullied permanently, which is but a verbal assertion, then, surely, you are merely continuing. When you say you are permanently sullied, is that a fact? And, how is it possible to forget what we are? We cannot forget what we are, but we can examine what we are; we can be aware, without any justification or identification, of what we are. Be aware of it, and you will see there comes a transformation. But the difficulty is to be passively aware without condemnation; only then is there an ending. But if you merely identify, condemn, then you give continuity to that particular character, and that which continues has no reality, has no renewal.

"Will you please explain what is meant by self-forgetfulness." Don't you know? Don't you know those moments when one is happy, when one is peaceful, when one is very quiet? Does not a state come into being in which no effort is involved, in which there is a cessation of the thought process as myself? As long as there is self-consciousness as the 'me', there can be no forgetfulness of the activities of the 'me'. Any action of the will, of desire, obviously must cultivate and strengthen the self; and the self is the bundle of memories, characteristics, idiosyncrasies, which creates conflict. As long as there is conflict, there must be self-consciousness; and if there is conflict, there can never be peace, however deeply concealed, at whatever level that conflict may be.

"How can I throw away the cup which I am?" Why do you want to throw away the cup? You cannot, surely, throw it away. All that you can do is to know it—all the intricacies, the subtleties, the extraordinary depth of oneself. When you know something, you are free of it; but merely to reject it, to suppress it, to sublimate it, to translate it into different verbal expressions, is surely not understanding; and only in understanding something is there freedom from it. You cannot understand something if there is continued identity with it. So there is renewal only when there is no continuity. But most of our intentions, purposes, thoughts, are to continue. In name, in property, in virtue, in everything, we are struggling to establish a permanency and therefore a continuity; and in that there is no renewal, there is no creativeness. Surely, creativeness comes into being only from moment to moment.

Question: Will you please carefully explain what is true meditation. There are so many systems of meditation. Are they really varied basically, or are the variations due to the personal idiosyncracies of their proponents?

KRISHNAMURTI: This is really an important question, and if I may suggest, let us go into it together. Because, meditation has a great deal of significance. It may be the door to real self-knowledge, and it may open the door to reality, and in opening the door and experiencing directly, there is a possibility of understanding life, which is relationship. Meditation, the right kind of meditation, is essential. So, let us find out what is the right kind of meditation, and to find out what is right, we must approach it negatively. Merely to say this or that is right meditation will give you only a pattern, which you will adopt, practice; and that will not be right meditation. So, as I am talking about it, please follow me closely and experience it as we go along together. Because, there are different types of meditation. I do not know if any of you have practiced them or have indulged in them—gone away by yourself in a locked room, sat in a dark corner, and so on, and so on. So, let us examine the whole process of what we call meditation.

First of all, let us take the meditation in which discipline is involved. Any form of discipline only strengthens the self, and the self is a source of contention, conflict. That is, if we discipline ourselves to be something, as so many people do—"This month I am going to be kind, I am going to practice kindliness," and so on—such discipline, such practice, is bound to strengthen the 'me'. You may be outwardly kind, but surely, a man who practices kindliness and is conscious of his kindliness is not kind. So, that practice, which people also call meditation, is obviously not the right kind because, as we discussed yesterday, if you practice something, in that the mind is caught, and so there is no freedom. But, most of us desire a result—that is, we hope to be kind at the end of the month or at the end of a certain period because teachers have said that ultimately we must be kind in order to find God. Since our desire is to find God as the ultimate source of our security and happiness, we buy God through kindliness—which is obviously the strengthening of the 'me' and the 'mine', a self-enclosing process, and anything that encloses, any action that is binding, can never give freedom. Surely, that is obvious. Perhaps we can discuss it another time if it is not clear.

Then, there is this whole process of concentration, which is also called meditation. You sit crosslegged, because that is the fashion from India, or in a chair, in a dark room, in front of a picture or an image, and you try to concentrate on a word, on a phrase, or a mental image, and exclude all other thoughts. I am sure many of you have done this. But the other thoughts keep pouring in, and you push them out; and you keep on with the struggle until you are able to concentrate on one thought to the exclusion of everything else. Then you feel gratified—at last you have learned to fix your mind on a point, which you think is essential. Again, through exclusion, do you find anything? Through exclusion, suppression, denial, can the mind be quiet? Because, as I said, there can be understanding only when the mind is really quiet, not suppressed, not so concentrated on one idea that it becomes exclusive—whether the idea is of a Master or of some virtue or what you will. Through concentration, the mind can never be quiet. Superficially, at the higher levels of consciousness, you may enforce stillness, make your body perfectly still, your mind very quiet; but that, surely, is not the quietness of your whole being. So, again, that is not meditation; that is merely compulsion—when the engine wants to run at full speed, you hold it back, you put on the brake. Whereas, if you are able to examine every interest, every thought that comes into your mind, go into it fully, completely, think every thought out, then there will be no wandering of the mind because the mind has found the value of each thought; therefore, it is no longer attracted, which means there is no distraction. A mind that is capable of being distracted, and which resists distraction, is not capable of meditation. Because, what is distraction? I hope you are experimenting with what I am saying, experiencing as I am talking, to find out the truth of this matter. It is the truth that liberates, not my words or your opinions.

We call distraction any movement away from that in which we think we should be interested. So you choose a particular interest, a so-called noble interest, and fix your mind on it, but any movement away from it is a distraction, so you resist distraction. But why do you choose that one particular interest? Obviously, because it is gratifying, because it gives you a sense of security, a sense of fullness, a sense of otherness. So you say, "I must fix my mind on that," and any movement away from it is a distraction. You spend your life in battle against distractions and fix your mind on something else. Whereas, if you examine every distraction, and not merely fix your mind on a particular attraction, then you will see that the mind is no longer capable of being distracted because it has understood the distractions as well as the attractions, and therefore the mind is capable of extraordinary, extensive awareness without exclusion. So, concentration is not meditation, and disciplining is not meditation.

Then, there are prayers—this whole problem of praying and receiving. That also is called meditation. What do we mean by praying? The gross form is supplication, and there are subtle forms at different levels of prayer. The gross form we all know. "I am in trouble, I am in misery, physically or psychologically, and I want some help." So I beg, I supplicate, and obviously, there is an answer. If there were no answer, people would not pray. Millions pray. You pray only when you are in trouble, not when you are happy, not when there is that extraordinary sense of otherness.

Now, what happens when you pray? You have a formula, haven't you? By repetition of a formula, the superficial mind becomes quiet, doesn't it? Try it, and you will see. By repeating certain phrases or words, gradually you will see your being becomes quiet. That is, your superficial consciousness is calm; and then, in that state, you are able to receive, aren't you, the intimations of something else. So, through calming the mind by a repetitive word, by so-called prayers, you may receive hints and intimations, not only from the subconscious, but from anything around you; but, surely, that is not meditation. Because, what you receive must be gratifying, otherwise you would reject it. So when you pray and thereby quiet the mind, your desire is to solve a particular problem or a confusion or something which gives you pain. Therefore, you are seeking an answer which will be gratifying. And when you see this, you say, "I must not seek gratification, I will be open to something which is painful." The mind is so capable of playing tricks upon itself that one must be aware of the whole content of this question of prayer. One has learned a trick—how to quiet the mind so that it can receive certain answers, pleasurable or not pleasurable. But that is not meditation, is it?

Then, there is this question of devotion to somebody—pouring out your love to God, to an image, to some saint, to some Master. Is that meditation? Why do you pour out your love to God, to that which you cannot possibly know? Why are we so attracted to the unknown, and give our lives, our being, to it? This whole question of devotion—does it not indicate that, being miserable in our own lives, having no vital relationship with other human beings, we try to project ourselves into something, into the unknown, and worship the unknown? You know, people who are devoted to somebody, to some God, to some image, to some Master, are generally cruel, obstinate. They are intolerant of others; they are willing to destroy others because they have so identified themselves with that image, with that Master, with that experience. So, again, the outpouring of devotion to an object, self-created or created by another, is surely not meditation.

So, what is meditation? If none of these things is meditation—discipline, concentration, prayer, devotion—then what is meditation? Those are the forms we know, with which we are familiar. But, to find out that with which we are not familiar, we have first to be free of those things with which we are familiar, haven't we? If they are not true, then they must be set aside. Then only, are you capable of finding out what is right meditation. If we have been accustomed to false values, those false values must cease, must they not, to find out the new value—not because I say so, but because you think it out, feel it out for yourself. And when they have gone, what have you left? What is the residue of your examination of these things?

Do they not reveal the process of your own thinking? If you have indulged in these things and you see that they are false, you find out why you have indulged in them; and therefore, the very examination of all this reveals the way of your own thinking. So, the examination of these things is the beginning of self-knowledge, is it not?

So, meditation is the beginning of self-knowledge. Without self-knowledge, you may sit in a corner, meditate on the Masters, develop virtues—they are all illusions, and they have no meaning for the person who really wants to discover what is right meditation. Because, without self-knowledge, you yourself project an image which you call the Master, and that becomes your object of devotion for which you are willing to sacrifice, to build, to destroy. Therefore, as I have explained, there is a possibility of self-knowledge only as we examine our relationship to these things, which reveals the process of our own thinking; and therefore there is a clarity in our whole being; and this is the beginning of understanding, of self-knowledge. Without self-knowledge, there can be no meditation, and without meditation, there can be no self-knowledge. Shutting yourself up in a corner, sitting in front of a picture, developing virtues month by month—a different virtue each month, green, purple, white, and all the rest of it—going to churches, performing ceremonies: none of those things are meditation, or real spiritual life. Spiritual life arises in the understanding of relationship, which is the beginning of self-knowledge.

Now, when you have gone through that and have abandoned all those processes which only reveal the self and its activity, then there is a possibility that the mind can be not only superficially quiet but inwardly quiet, for then there is a cessation of all demands. There is no pursuit of sensation; there is no sense of becoming—myself becoming something in the future or tomorrow. The Master, the initiate, the pupil, the Buddha, you know, climbing the ladder of success, becoming something—all that has stopped because all that implies the process of becoming. There is a cessation of becoming only when there is the understanding of *what is,* and the understanding of *what is* comes through self-knowledge, which reveals exactly what one is. And when there is the cessation of all desire, which can only come through self-knowledge, the mind is quiet.

The cessation of desire cannot come through compulsion, through prayer, through devotion, through concentration. All these merely emphasize the conflict of desire in the opposites. But when there is the cessation of all these, then the mind is really still—not only superficially, on the higher levels, but inwardly, deeply. Then only is it possible for it to receive that which is immeasurable. The understanding of all this is meditation, not just one part of it. Because, if we do not know how to meditate, we will not know how to act. Action, after all, is self-knowledge in relationship, and merely to shut yourself in a sacred room with incense burning, reading about the other people's meditations and their significance, is utterly useless—it has no meaning. It is a marvelous escape. But to be aware of all this human activity, which is ourselves—the desire to attain, the desire to conquer, the desire to have certain virtues, all emphasizing the 'me' as important in the now or in the future, this becoming of the 'me'—to be aware of all that in its totality is the beginning of self-knowledge and the beginning of meditation. Then you will see, if you are really aware, that there comes a marvelous transformation which is not a verbal expression, which is not verbalization, mere repetition, sensation. But actually, really, vigorously, there takes place a thing which cannot be named, which cannot be termed. And that is not the gift of the few, it is not the gift of the Masters—self-knowledge is possible for everybody if you are willing to experiment, try. You don't have to join any society, read any book, or be at the feet of any Master, for self-knowledge liberates you from all that absurdity, the stupidities of human invention. And then only, through self-knowledge and right meditation, there is freedom. In that freedom there comes reality, but you cannot have reality through mental processes. It must come to you, and it can only come to you when there is freedom from desire.

July 31, 1949

Seventh Talk in The Oak Grove

For the last three weekends, we have been discussing, in different ways, the problem of self-knowledge and how it is necessary to understand the process of our own thinking and feeling. Without understanding oneself clearly and definitely, it is not possible to think rightly. But, unfortunately, it seems to have left an impression among many, or at least among those who are committed to a particular form of prejudice which they call thinking, that this approach is individualistic and utterly selfish and self-centered and does not lead to reality, that there are many paths to reality, and that this particular approach of self-knowledge must invariably lead to inaction, to self-centeredness, and individual ruggedness.

Now, if you go into it very clearly and thoroughly, with intelligence, you see that to truth there can be no path; there is no path as yours and mine—the path of service, the path of knowledge, the path of devotion, and the other innumerable paths that philosophers have invented, depending on their particular idiosyncrasies and neurological responses. Now, if one can think clearly about this matter without prejudice—I mean by prejudice, being committed to a particular action on thought or belief, and being utterly unaware that one particular form of thinking, one particular approach, must inevitably limit, whether it is the path of knowledge, the path of devotion, or the path of action—one will see that any particular path must invariably limit and therefore cannot lead to reality. Because a path of action or a path of knowledge or a path of devotion, in itself, is not sufficient, surely. A man of learning, however erudite, however encyclopedic his knowledge may be, if he has no love, surely his knowledge is worthless; it is merely booklearning. A man of belief, as we discussed, must inevitably shape his life according to the dogma, the tenet, that he holds, and therefore his experience must be limited because one experiences according to one's beliefs, and such experience can never be liberating. On the contrary, it is binding. And, as we said, only in freedom can we discover anything new, anything fundamental.

So, the difficulty with the majority of us is, it seems to me, that we are committed to so many beliefs, dogmas, that they prevent us from looking afresh at anything new; and therefore—as reality, God, or what you will, must be something unimaginable, something immeasurable—the mind cannot possibly understand. Do what it will, it cannot go beyond itself. It can create reality in its own image, but it will not be reality. It will be only its own self-projection. And, therefore, to understand reality, or for that immensity to come into being, one must understand the process of one's own thinking. That is, surely, the obvious approach. It is not my approach or your approach; it is the only intelligent approach. And intelligence is not yours or mine; it is quite beyond all countries and all paths, beyond all religious, social, or political activity. It does not belong to any particular society or group. Intelligence comes into being only with the understanding of oneself—which does not mean, surely, emphasis on the individual. On the contrary. It is the insistence on a path or a belief, on any ideology, that emphasizes the individual, though that individual may belong to a large group, be identified with a large group. Mere identification with the collective does not mean that one is free from the limited individuality.

So, it is important, surely, to understand that reality or God or what you will is not to be found through any particular path. The Hindus have very cleverly divided human beings into various types and established paths for them. And, surely, any path—which is the emphasis of individuality and not the freedom from individuality—cannot lead to reality because it cultivates a particularity; it is not the freedom from selfishness, from prejudice, which is so essential to understanding. Therefore, we have been discussing, for the last three weeks, the importance of self-knowledge—which is not emphasis on individuality, on the personal, at all. If I do not know myself, I have no basis for thinking; whatever I think is merely an imposition, an external acceptance of various influences, circumstantial enforcement. Surely, that is not thinking. Because I have been brought up in a particular society, of the left or of the right, and have accepted a certain ideology from childhood, it does not mean that I am capable of thinking of life anew. I merely function in that particular pattern and reject anything else that is given to me. Whereas, to think rightly, truly, profoundly, one has to begin by questioning the whole environmental process and the influence of the environment from the outside, of which I am a part. Without understanding that process in all its subtlety, surely I have no basis for thinking.

So, it is absolutely essential, is it not, that the process of the mind be thoroughly understood—not only the conscious, the upper level, the superficial level of the mind, but the deeper levels of the mind. Because, it is comparatively easy to understand the superficial mind—to watch its reactions, its responses, to see how instinctively it acts and thinks. But that is only the beginning, is it not? It is much more difficult to go more profoundly, more deeply, into the whole process of our thinking; and without knowing the whole process, the total process, then what you believe, what you don't believe, what you think, whether you believe in Masters or don't believe in Masters, whether you believe in God or don't—all that is really irrelevant, is almost immature.

Now, it is comparatively easy, in listening to another, to see in that relationship a mirror in which we discover ourselves; but our problem is also to go into it much more profoundly, and that is where our difficulty lies. Perhaps a few of us can throw off our superficial prejudices, beliefs, give up a few societies and join new organizations—the many things that one does; but surely it is much more important, isn't it, to go below to the deeper layers of consciousness and find out exactly what is taking place—what are our commitments of which we are so unconscious, our beliefs, our fears of which we are utterly unaware, but which actually guide and shape our action. Because, the inner always overcomes the outer. You may cunningly sift the outer, but the inner eventually breaks down the outer. In any utopian society, you may build a social order very carefully and very cunningly, but without this psychological understanding of man's whole makeup, the outer is always smashed.

How is it possible, then, to go into the deeper layers of consciousness? Because, that is where most of our idiosyncrasies, most of our fears that create beliefs, most of our desires, ambitions, lie hidden. How is it possible to open them up, to expose and understand them? If we can have the capacity to delve into that and really experience these things, not merely verbally, then it is possible to be free of them, isn't it?

Take, for example, anger. Is it possible to experience anger and be aware of anger without giving it a name? I do not know if you have ever tried, if you have ever experienced a state which is not named. If we have an experience, we give it a term, and we term it in order to explore it or to communicate it or to strengthen it. But we never experience a thing without naming it. That is extremely difficult, isn't it, for most of us. Verbalization comes almost before experience. But if we do not name an experience, then perhaps it is possible to go into the deeper layers of consciousness. And that is why we must be aware, even at the superficial level, of our prejudices, fears, ambitions, of our fixations in a particular groove, whether we are young or old, whether of the left or of the right. Therefore, there must be a certain discontent—which is obviously often denied to the older, because they don't want to be discontented. They are fixed, they are going to disappear slowly; therefore, they establish, crystallize in a particular groove and deny everything new. But, surely, discontent is necessary—not the discontent that is easily canalized into a particular groove, a particular action, a particular belief, but discontent that is never satisfied. Because, most of our discontent arises from dissatisfaction. The moment we have found satisfaction, dissatisfaction ceases, discontent comes to an end. So most of our discontent is really a search for satisfaction. Whereas, discontent, surely, is a state in which there is no search for satisfaction. The moment I am easily satisfied, the problem is over. If I accept the left ideology or the right or some particular belief, my dissatisfaction is easily gratified. But discontent is of another quality, surely. Contentment is that state in which *what is* is understood. To understand *what is,* there must be no prejudice. To see things as they are requires enormous alertness of mind. But if we are easily satisfied, that alertness is dulled, made blunt.

So, our problem is, in all this—which is a question of relationship—to be aware of ourselves in action, in what we are thinking, in what we are saying, so that in relationship we discover ourselves, we see ourselves as we are. But to superimpose our beliefs on what we are surely does not help to bring about understanding of what we are. Therefore, it is necessary to be free of this imposition—political, sociological, or religious—which can only be revealed in relationship. And as long as that relationship is not understood, there must be conflict—between two or between many. For the ending of that conflict, there must be self-knowledge, and when the mind is quiet—not made quiet—then only is it possible to understand reality.

Many questions have been given to me, and naturally they cannot all be answered, but I will try to answer as many representative questions as possible, though sometimes the questions may be put in different words, with a change of terms. So, I hope you will not mind.

Question: If I am perfectly honest, I have to admit that I resent, and at times, hate almost everybody. It makes my life very unhappy and painful. I understand intellectually that I am this resentment, this hatred; but I cannot cope with it. Can you show me a way?

KRISHNAMURTI: Now, what do we mean by "intellectually"? When we say that we understand something intellectually, what do we mean by that? Is there such a thing as intellectual understanding? Or is it that the mind merely understands the words because that is our only way of communicating with each other? Do we understand anything verbally? That is the first thing we have to be clear about—whether so-called intellectual understanding is not an impediment to understanding. Surely, understanding is integral, not divided, not partial. Either I understand something, or I don't. To say to oneself, "I understand something intellectually," is surely a barrier to understanding. It is a partial process, and therefore, no understanding at all.

Now, the question is this: How am I, who am resentful, hateful, how am I to be free of, or cope with that problem? How do we cope with a problem? What is a problem? Surely, a problem is something which is disturbing.

Please, may I suggest something? Just follow what I am saying. Don't try to solve your problem of resentment and hate—just follow it. Although it is difficult to go into this so that at the end you are free of it, let us see if we can do it now. It will be rather an interesting experiment to try together.

I am resentful, I am hateful, I hate people, and it causes pain. And I am aware of it. What am I to do? It is a very disturbing factor in my life. What am I to do, how am I to be really free of it—not just momentarily slough it off, but fundamentally be free of it? How am I to do it?

Now, it is a problem to me because it disturbs me. If it were not a disturbing thing, it would not be a problem to me, would it? Because it causes pain, disturbance, anxiety, because I think it is ugly, I want to get rid of it. Therefore, the thing that I am objecting to is the disturbance, isn't it? I give it different names at different times, in different moods; I call it one day this, and one day something else. But the desire is, basically, not to be disturbed. Isn't that it? Because pleasure is not disturbing, I accept it. I don't want to be free from pleasure because there is no disturbance—at least for the time being. But hate, resentment, are very disturbing factors in my life, and I want to get rid of them.

So, my concern is not to be disturbed, and I am trying to find a way in which I shall never be disturbed. And why should I not be disturbed? I must be disturbed to find out, must I not? I must go through tremendous upheavals, turmoil, anxiety, to find out, must I not? Because, if I am not disturbed, I shall go to sleep; and perhaps that is what most of us do want—to be pacified, to be put to sleep, to get away from any disturbance, to find isolation, seclusion, security. So, if I do not mind being disturbed—really, not just superficially—if I don't mind being disturbed because I want to find out, then my attitude toward hate, toward resentment, undergoes a change, doesn't it? If I do not mind being disturbed, then the name is not important, is it? The word *hate* is not important, is it? Or *resentment* against people is not important, is it? Because, then I am directly experiencing the state which I call resentment without verbalizing that experience. I do not know if I am explaining myself.

That is, anger is a very disturbing quality, as hate and resentment are, and very few of us experience anger directly, without verbalizing it. If we do not verbalize it, if we do not call it anger, surely there is a different experience, is there not? Because we term it, we reduce a new experience or fix it in the terms of the old. Whereas, if we do not name it, then there is an experience which is directly understood, and this understanding brings about a transformation in that experiencing. Am I making myself clear? Please, it is not simple.

Take, for example, meanness. Most of us, if we are mean, are unaware of it—mean about money matters, mean about forgiving people, you know, just being mean. I am sure we are familiar with that. Now, being aware of it, how are we going to be free from that quality?—not to become generous, that is not the important point. To be free from meanness implies generosity—you haven't got to become generous. So, obviously, one must be aware of it. You may be very generous in giving a large donation to your society, to your friends, but awfully mean about giving a bigger tip—you know what I mean by "mean." One is unconscious of it. When one becomes aware of it, what happens? We exert our will to be generous; we try to overcome it; we discipline ourselves to be generous, and so on, and so on. But, after all, the exertion of will to be something is still part of meanness in a larger circle. So, if we do not do any of those things but are merely aware of the implications of meanness without giving it a term, then we will see that there takes place a radical transformation. Take anger: if you do not give it a term, but merely experience it—not through verbalization because verbalization is a process of dulling the experience, but if you do not give it a term—then it is acute, it becomes very sharp, and it acts as a shock, and only then is it possible to be free.

Please, experiment with this. First, one must be disturbed, and it is obvious that most of us do not like to be disturbed. We think we have found a pattern of life—the Master, the belief, whatever it is—and there we settle down. It is like having a good bureaucratic job and functioning there for the rest of one's life. With that same mentality we approach various qualities of which we want to be rid. We do not see the importance of being disturbed, of being inwardly insecure, of not being dependent. Surely, it is only in insecurity that you discover, that you see, that you understand. We want to be like a man with plenty of money, at ease; but surely, he will not be disturbed, he doesn't want to be disturbed.

So, disturbance is essential for understanding, and any attempt to find security is a hindrance to understanding, and when we want to get rid of something which is disturbing, it is surely a hindrance. But if we can experience a feeling directly, without naming it, I think we will find a great deal in it; then there is no longer a battle with it because the experiencer and the thing experienced are one, and that is essential. As long as the experiencer verbalizes the feeling, the experience, he separates himself from it and acts upon it; and such action is an artificial, illusory action. But if there is no verbalization, then the experiencer and the thing experienced are one. That integration is necessary and has to be radically faced. I hope this is clear. If not, we will discuss it at other meetings.

Question: I listened to you some years ago, and it did not mean much to me then,[61] *but listening to you now seems to mean a great deal. How is this?*

KRISHNAMURTI: There are various explanations for this: that you have matured, that you have progressed, that life has knocked at your door, that you have suffered a great deal, and so on, and so on—that is, if what we are discussing means something to you. If you think it is all rot, then it is very simple. Now, people who believe in progress will give one kind of explanation: that you have slowly matured, that you must have time, not only a few years but another life, that time is essential for understanding, and that though you have not understood at the beginning, you will understand later through gradual ripening of experience—you know, all the various theories one has. But, surely, there is a much simpler way of looking at it, isn't there? For some unknown reason your friend, perhaps, brings you here, and you listen casually and go away; it doesn't mean much, except there are nice trees, you have had a nice drive, you know, and all the rest of it. And you go away. But, unconsciously, surely, you have taken something in. Haven't you noticed when you are driving, or walking, though your conscious mind may be attending to the driving or seeing a particular thing attentively, the other part of your mind is absorbing unconsciously. Something has taken place, a seed has been sown of which you are unconscious, but later it comes out. It is there. So what at the beginning may not have meant much—because you have listened to something of which you have not been conscious—later reacts on you.

Surely, that is the whole purpose of propaganda, isn't it? Not that I am a propagandist—I have a horror of propaganda. But that is what is happening in the world, isn't it, with the newspapers, magazines, cinemas, the radio, and all the rest of it. You go on really interested in what you are doing, and the radio or the newspaper is giving you propaganda. Your mind is elsewhere, but you are absorbing unconsciously; and later on when that absorption is called forth, it comes out—like the automatic response to war, to nationalism, to the acceptance of certain beliefs, whether of the right or of the left. How do you think children are impregnated with certain ideas? It is the constant impingement of those ideas on the unconscious. And they accept; when they grow up, they are the same, either of the left or of the right, of this religion or that religion, with innumerable beliefs and conditioned minds. The unconscious has been absorbing all the time. And, it can absorb the ugly as well as the beautiful, the true as well as the false. And our difficulty is, is it not, to be free of all these imprints and to look at life anew. Is it possible to be free from the influence of these constant impacts? That is, to be aware of these impacts and not to be influenced by them? Because they are there. Can we be sensitive enough, alert enough, so that we know what is false, what is untrue, so that there is no resistance even? Because, the moment you resist, you strengthen what you are resisting; therefore, you become part of it. But if you understand it, surely, then there is no longer its influence on the conscious or on the unconscious.

So, is it possible to be free from all the conditioning influences in which we have been brought up? From nationalism, class differences, from the innumerable beliefs of religions and political ideologies? Surely, one must be free; otherwise, one cannot find out what lies beyond freedom. But, to be free, one must examine all these things, must one not, and not accept a thing—which is not the cultivation of doubt. Therefore, for that very process one must understand the content of one's own consciousness, of what one is.

Question: Would you talk to us about sin?

KRISHNAMURTI: Every organized religion has unfortunately cultivated, for purposes of civilization, the feeling of guilt. Most of us have it—the more sensitive we are, the more acute the feeling. The more you feel responsible, the more guilty you feel. You see this world mess, the impending wars, and all the chicanery that is going on, and—being sensitive, being alert, being sufficiently interested and intelligent—you feel that you are responsible. And, as one can do so little, one feels guilty. That is one part of it. Then, in order to hold man within civilized limits, this sense of doing wrong has been very carefully, sedulously cultivated, has it not? Otherwise you would go over the border. Because, if we had no standards, if we had no sanctions, if we had no moral code—not that there is much now—it would be worse. So, religion, organized belief, has carefully maintained, cultivated this sense that you must toe the line, that you must not sin, that you must not commit ugly things. It has held us within a pattern, and it is only the very few that can go beyond the pattern because we want to remain in the pattern. We want to be respectable—fear of public opinion and so many things hold us to the pattern. And, being afraid, not depending on our own understanding, most of us rely on another—the priest, the psychologist, the leader, the politician, you know, the innumerable dependencies that one cultivates. All those naturally strengthen our inherent anxiety to do the right thing. From all this, the sense of guilt arises.

And, there is the rigmarole in religion about sin. But, there are certain obvious things, are there not?—for example, that virtue is essential. But virtue which is cultivated is no longer virtue; it is merely the strengthening of oneself with a different name. Virtue comes into being only when there is the freedom from desire to be something, when one is not afraid of being nothing. And, it is the repetition of a particular disturbance, of a particular action that has brought misfortune to others and to oneself, which may be called a sin. Surely, that is the first thing, is it not? To see something very clearly, which is discovered in relationship, and not to repeat it. The repetition, surely, is the mistake, not the first action; and to understand that, the repetitive quality of desire, one has to understand the whole structure of oneself.

So, there is this thing called sin, the feeling of guilt. One may have done something wrong, like worry, like gossip; but to keep on at it, surely, is the worst thing that one can do. If you see that you have done something wrong, observe it, go into it thoroughly, and be rid of it—don't keep on repeating it. Because, surely, this sense of worry about something that one has done in the past or which one may do the next minute, this constant anxiety about it, this fear, only strengthens the restlessness of the mind, does it not? Gossip, worry, indicate the restlessness of the mind. When there is no restlessness, no distraction, but alertness, watchfulness, then the problem disappears, does it not? The feeling of guilt, with the majority of us, holds us in check. But that is only fear; and fear, surely, does not bring about clarity of understanding. In fear there is no communion. And it is that fear that must be eradicated, not the feeling that one is sinning.

Question: There is no possibility of collective action without a coordinated plan which involves the subservience of the individual will to the common purpose. If individuals were selfless, then control and authority would be needless. How can we achieve a common aim without curbing the erratic will of the individual, even if he is now and then well-intentioned?

KRISHNAMURTI: In order to have collective action, we resort to compulsion or authoritarianism, or to a form of fear, threat, or reward, with which we are all familiar. The state, or a group of individuals, establishes a certain aim and then compels, coaxes, or persuades others to cooperate by giving them rewards or punishment—all the various ways to bring about coordinated action which we know. And the questioner wants to know if the emphasis on the individual, which is implied, does not prevent coordinated action. Which means, if there is a common purpose with which we all agree, then must we not submit to that and put aside our own will?

How is cooperation possible—that is really the crux of the matter, isn't it? Cooperation, coordination in action, lies either through fear or through intelligence and love. When a particular nation is at war, then there is cooperation through fear, and apparently fear, hatred, jealousy, bring people together more quickly than intelligence and love. Clever statesmen, politicians, are aware of this and instigate it—with which, again, we are familiar. But is it possible to bring people together intelligently, through affection? That is really the problem, isn't it? Because, we see more and more people coming together through hatred, through fear, through compulsion—mass movements, the use of psychological methods to persuade, propaganda, and all the rest of it. And if that is the way, then what we are discussing is futile. But if you do not cooperate, come together, through greed, is there any other way? And, if there is a way, must you not submit the individual will to a higher purpose?

Say, for example, we all agree that there must be peace in the world. And how is that peace possible? Peace is possible only when there is selflessness, surely, when the 'me' is not important. Because I in myself am peaceful, therefore in my actions I will be peaceful, therefore I will not be antisocial. And anything that makes for antagonism, I will put away from myself. Therefore, I must pay the price for peace, must I not? But it must originate from me. And the more of us there are who are for that, surely, the greater the possibility of peace in the world—which does not mean the subservience of the individual will to the whole, to a purpose, to a plan, to a utopia. Because, I see that there can be no peace until I am peaceful, which means no nationalism, no class, you know, all the things that are involved in being peaceful—which means being completely selfless. And when that is there, then we will cooperate. Then, there is bound to be cooperation. When there is compulsion from the outside to make me cooperate with the state, with a group, I may cooperate, but inwardly I will be fighting, inwardly there is no release. Or I may use the utopia as a means of self-fulfillment, which is also expansion of oneself.

So, as long as there is the submitting of the individual will to a particular idea through greed, through identification, there must be conflict eventually between the individual and the many. So, the emphasis, surely, is not on the individual and the collective as opposed to each other, but on the freedom from the sense of the 'me' and the 'mine'. If that freedom exists, then there is no question of the individual as opposed to the collective. But, as that seems almost impossible, we are persuaded to join the collective to produce a certain action, to sacrifice the individual for the whole; and the sacrifice is urged upon us by others, by the leaders. Whereas, we can look at this whole problem, not as concerning the individual and the collective, but intelligently, and realize that there can be no peace as long as you and I are not peaceful in ourselves, and that peace cannot be bought at any price. You and I have to be free from the causes that are producing conflict in ourselves. And the center of conflict is the self, the 'me'. But most of us do not want to be free from that 'me'. That is the difficulty. Most of us like the pleasures and the pains that the 'me' brings; and as long as we are controlled by the pleasure and the pains of the 'me', there will be conflict between the 'me' and society, between the 'me' and the collective; and the collective will dominate the 'me' and destroy the 'me', if it can. But the 'me' is much stronger than the collective, so it always circumvents it and tries to get a position in it, to expand, to fulfill.

Surely, the freedom from the self and therefore the search for reality, the discovery and the coming into being of reality, is the true function of man. Religions play with it in their rituals and rigmarole—you know, the whole business of it. But, if one becomes aware of this whole process, which we have been discussing for so many years, then there is a possibility for the newly-awakened intelligence to function. In that there is not self-release, not self-fulfillment, but creativeness.

It is this creativeness of reality, which is not of time, that sets one free from all the business of the collective and the individual. Then one is really in a position to help create the new.

August 6, 1949

Eighth Talk in The Oak Grove

I am sure many of you believe in immortality, in the soul, or the atma, and so on. And perhaps some of you have had a passing experience of these things. But, if I may, I would like this morning to approach it from a different point of view; let us go into it very seriously and earnestly and discover the truth of it—not according to any particular pattern of belief or religious dogma, or your own personal experience, however vast, however beautiful and romantic it may be. So, please examine what we are going to discuss intelligently and without any prejudice, with the intention of finding out rather than rejecting or defending it. Because, it is quite a difficult problem to discuss. The implications are many, and if one can think of it anew, perhaps we shall have a different approach to action and to life.

We seem to think that ideas are very important. Our minds are filled with ideas. Our mind is idea—there is no mind without idea, without thought, without verbalization. And ideas play an extraordinarily important part in our life—what we think, what we feel, the beliefs and ideas in which we are conditioned. Ideas have an extraordinary significance with most of us—ideas which seem coherent, intelligent, logical, and also ideas that are romantic, stupid, without much significance. We are crowded with ideas, our whole structure is based on them. And these ideas come into being, obviously, through external influences and environmental conditioning as well as through inward demands. We can see very well how ideas come into being. Ideas are sensations. There is no idea without sensation. As most of us feed on sensation, our whole structure is based on ideas. Being limited and seeking expansion through sensation, ideas become very important—ideas on God, ideas on morality, ideas on various forms of social organization, and so on, and so on.

So, ideas shape our experience, which is an obvious fact. That is, ideas condition our action. Not that action creates ideas, but ideas create action. First, we think it out, then we act, and the action is based on ideas. So, experience is the outcome of ideas, but experience is different from experiencing. In the state of experiencing, if you have noticed, there is no ideation at all. There is merely an experiencing, an acting. Later on comes the ideation of likes and dislikes, derived from that experiencing. We either want that experience to continue or not to continue. If we like it, we go back to the experience in memory, which is a demand for the sensation of that experience—not experiencing anew. Surely, there is a difference between experiencing and experience, and that should be made fairly clear. In experiencing there is not the experiencer and the experience; there is only a state of experiencing. But after experiencing, the sensations of that experiencing are demanded, are longed for, and out of that desire, arises idea.

Say, for example, you have had a pleasurable experience. It is over and you are longing for it. That is, you are longing for the sensation, not the state of experiencing; and sensation creates ideas, based on pleasure and pain, avoidance and acceptance, denial and continuance. Now, ideas are not basically important because one sees that ideas have continuity. You may die, but the ideas that you have had, the bundle of ideas which you are, have a continuance, either partially or wholly, either fully manifested or only a little; but they have a form of continuity, obviously.

So, if ideas are the result of sensation, which they are, and if the mind is filled with ideas, if the mind is idea, then there is a continuance of the mind as a bundle of ideas. But that, surely, is not immortality because ideas are merely the result of sensations, of pleasure and not-pleasure; and immortality must be something which is beyond ideas, upon which the mind cannot possibly speculate because it can only speculate in terms of pleasure and pain, avoidance and acceptance. As the mind can only think in those terms, however extensively, however deeply, it is still based on idea; but thought, idea, has continuity, and that which continues is obviously not immortality. So, to know or to experience immortality, or for the experiencing of that state, there must be no ideation. One cannot think about immortality. If we can be free of ideation, that is, if we do not think in terms of ideas, then there is a state of experiencing only, a state in which ideation has stopped altogether. You can experiment with this yourself and not accept what I am saying. Because, there is a great deal involved in this. The mind must be entirely quiet, without movement backward or forward, neither delving nor soaring. That is, ideation must entirely cease. And that is extremely difficult. That is why we cling to words like *the soul, immortality, continuity, God*—they all have neurological effects, which are sensations. And on these sensations the mind feeds; deprive the mind of these things, it is lost. So, it holds on with great strength to past experiences, which have now become sensations.

Is it possible for the mind to be so quiet—not partially, but in its totality—as to have direct experience of that which is not thinkable, of that which cannot be put into words? That which continues is obviously within the limits of time; and through time, the timeless cannot come into being; therefore God, or what you will, cannot be thought of. If you think of it, there is merely an idea, a sensation; therefore, it is no longer true. It is merely an idea which has a continuance, which is inherited or conditioned; and such an idea is not eternal, immortal, timeless. It is essential to really feel this, see the truth of it as we discuss it—not say, "This is so, that is not so," "I believe in immortality, and you don't," "You are agnostic, and I am godly." All such expressions are immature, thoughtless—they have no significance. We are dealing with something which is not merely a matter of opinion, of like or dislike, of prejudice. We are trying to find out what is immortality—not as do so-called religious people who belong to some particular cult or other, but to experience that thing, to be aware of it—because in that is creation. When once there is the experiencing of that, then the whole problem of life undergoes a significant, revolutionary change; and without that, all the squabbles and petty opinions have really no significance at all.

So, one has to be aware of this total process of how ideas come into being, how action springs from ideas, and how ideas control action and therefore limit action, depending on sensation. It doesn't matter whose ideas they are, whether from the left or from the extreme right. As long as we cling to ideas, we are in a state in which there can be no experiencing at all. Then we are merely living in the field of time—in the past, which gives further sensation, or in the future, which is another form of sensation. It is only when the mind is free from idea that there can be experiencing. Just listen to this, don't reject or accept it. Listen to it as you would listen to the wind in the trees. You don't object to the wind in the trees; it's pleasant. Or, if you dislike it, you go away. Do the same thing here. Don't reject, just find out. Because, so many people have expressed their opinion on this question of immortality; religious teachers speak of it, as does every preacher around the corner. So many saints, so many writers either deny or assert; they say that there is immortality or that man is merely the outcome of environmental influences, and so on, and so on—so many opinions. Opinions are not truth, and truth is something that must be experienced directly, from moment to moment; it is not an experience which you want—which is then merely sensation. And only when one can go beyond the bundle of ideas—which is the 'me', which is the mind, which has a partial or complete continuity—only when one can go beyond that, when thought is completely silent, only then is there a state of experiencing. Then one shall know what truth is.

Question: How is one to know or feel unmistakably the reality, the exact and immutable significance of an experience which is truth? Whenever I have a realization and feel it to be truth, someone to whom I communicate it tells me I am merely self-deluded. Whenever I think I have understood, someone is there to tell me I am in illusion. Is there a way of knowing what is the truth about myself without delusion, self-deception?

KRISHNAMURTI: Any form of identification must lead to illusion. There is the psychiatric illusion and the psychological illusion. The psychiatric illusion we know what to do with. When one thinks one is Napoleon or a great saint, you know what to do. But the psychological identification and illusion is quite different. The political, religious person identifies himself with the country or with God. He is the country, and if he has a talent, then he is a nightmare to the rest of the world, whether peacefully or violently. There are various forms of identification: identification with authority, with a country, with an idea; identification with a belief, which makes one do all kinds of things; with an ideology, for which you are willing to sacrifice everybody and everything, including yourself and your country in order to achieve what you want; identification with a utopia, for which you force others into a particular pattern. Then, there is the identification of the actor, playing different roles. And most of us are in that position of acting, posing, whether consciously or unconsciously.

So, our difficulty is that we identify ourselves with a country, with a political party, with propaganda, with a belief, with an ideology, with a leader—all that is one kind of identification.

Then, there is the identification with our own experiences. I have had an experience, a thrilling thing; and the more I dwell on it, the more intense, the more romantic, the more sentimental, the more blurred it becomes; and to that I give the name God—you know the innumerable ways of self-deception. Surely, illusion arises when I cling to something. If I have had an experience which is over, finished, and I go back to it, I am in illusion. If I want something repeated, if I hold on to the repetition of an experience, it is bound to lead me to illusion. So, the basis of illusion is identification—identification with an image, with an idea of God, with a voice, or with experiences to which we ardently cling. It is not to the experience that we cling but to the sensation of that experience which we had at the moment of experiencing. A man who has built around himself various methods of identification is living in illusion. A man who believes because of a sensation, of an idea to which he clings, is bound to live in illusion, in self-deception. Therefore, any experience about yourself to which you go back or which you reject is bound to lead to illusion. Illusion ceases only when you understand an experience and do not hold on to it. This desire to possess is the basis of illusion, of self-deception. You desire to be something, and this desire to be something must be understood in order to understand the process of illusion, of self-deception. If I think I shall be a great teacher, a great Master, the Buddha, X, Y, Z, in my next life, or if I think that I am that now and hold on to that, surely I must be in illusion because I live on a sensation, which is an idea, and my mind feeds on ideas, whether false or true.

How is one to know if an experience at a given moment is truth? That is part of the question. Why do you want to know if it is truth? A fact is a fact, it is not true or false. It is only when I want to translate a fact according to my sensation, to my ideation, that I enter into delusion. When I am angry, it is a fact; there is no question of self-deception. When I am lustful, when I am greedy, when I am irritated, it is a fact; it is only when I begin to justify it, find explanations for it, translate it according to my prejudice in my favor, or avoid it—only then I have to ask, "What is truth?" That is, the moment we approach a fact emotionally, sentimentally, with ideation, then we enter into the world of illusion and self-deceit. To look at a fact and be free of all this requires an extraordinary watchfulness. Therefore, it is more important to find out for oneself not whether one is in illusion or self-deception but whether one is free from the desire to identify, from the desire to have a sensation, which you call experience, from the desire to repeat, possess, or revert to an experience. After all, from moment to moment you can know yourself as you are, factually, not through the screen of ideation, which is sensation. To know yourself, there is no necessity to know the truth, or what is not the truth. To look at yourself in the mirror and see that you are ugly or beautiful, factually, not romantically, does not demand truth. But the difficulty with most of us is that when we see the image, the expression, we want to do something about it, we want to alter it, give it a different name; if it is pleasurable, we identify with it; if it is painful, we avoid it. In this process, surely, lies self-deception, with which you are somewhat familiar. The politicians do it; the priests do it when they talk of God in the name of religion; and we ourselves do it when we are caught up in the sensation of ideas and hold on to them—that is true, this is false, the Masters exist or don't exist—which is all so absurd and immature and childish. But to find out what is factual, one needs an extraordinary alertness, an awareness in which there is neither condemnation nor justification.

So, one can say that one deceives oneself, and there is illusion, when there is identification with a country, with a belief, with an idea, with a person, and so on; or when there is the desire to repeat an experience, which is the sensation of the experience; or when one goes back to childhood and wants the repetition of the experiences of childhood, the delight, the nearness, the sensitivity; or when one wants to be something. It is extremely difficult not to be deceived, either by oneself or by another, and deception ceases only when there is no desire to be something. Then the mind is capable of looking at things as they are, of seeing the significance of *what is;* then there is no battle between the false and the true; then there is no search for truth apart from the false. So, the important thing is to understand the process of the mind; and that understanding is factual, not theoretical, not sentimental, romantic, going into dark rooms and thinking it all out, having images, visions—all that has nothing to do with reality. And, as most of us are sentimental, romantic, seeking sensation, we are caught by ideas, and ideas are not *what is.* So, the mind that is free of ideas, which are sensations, such a mind is free from illusion.

Question: Experience shows that understanding arises only when argumentation and conflict cease and a kind of tranquillity or intellectual sympathy is realized. This is true even in the understanding of mathematical and technical problems. However, this tranquillity has been experienced only after every effort of analysis, examination, or experimentation has been made. Does this mean that this effort is a necessary, though not sufficient preliminary, to the tranquillity?

KRISHNAMURTI: I hope you have understood the question. The questioner, to put it briefly, asks: Is not effort, digging, analyzing, examining, necessary before there is tranquillity of the mind? Before the mind can understand, is not effort necessary? That is, is not technique necessary before creativeness? If I have a problem, must I not go into it, think it out fully, search it out, analyze it, dissect it, worry over it, and be free of it? Then, when the mind is quiet, the answer is found. This is the process we go through. We have a problem, we think about it, we question it, we talk it over; and then the mind, becoming weary of it, is quiet. Then, the answer is found, unknowingly. With that process we are familiar. And the questioner asks: Is that not necessary, first?

Why do I go through that process? Don't let us put this question wrongly—whether it is necessary or not, but why do I go through that process? I go through that process, obviously, in order to find an answer. My anxiety is to find an answer, isn't it? That fear of not finding an answer makes me do all these things; and then, after going through this process, I am exhausted and say, "I can't answer it." Then the mind becomes quiet, and then there is an answer, sometimes or always.

So, the question is not, is the preliminary process necessary, but why do I go through that process? Obviously, because I am seeking an answer. I am not interested in the problem but in how to get away from the problem. I am not seeking the understanding of the problem but the answer to the problem. Surely, there is a difference, isn't there? Because, the answer is in the problem, not away from the problem. I go through the searching, analyzing, dissecting process in order to escape from the problem. But, if I do not escape from the problem and try to look at the problem without any fear or anxiety, if I merely look at the problem—mathematical, political, religious, or any other—and not look to an answer, then the problem will begin to tell me. Surely, this is what happens. We go through this process and eventually throw it aside because there is no way out of it. So, why can't we start right from the beginning, that is, not seek an answer to a problem?—which is extremely arduous, isn't it? Because, the more I understand the problem, the more significance there is in it. To understand it, I must approach it quietly, not impose on the problem my ideas, my feelings of like and dislike. Then the problem will reveal its significance.

Why is it not possible to have tranquillity of the mind right from the beginning? And there will be tranquillity only when I am not seeking an answer, when I am not afraid of the problem. Our difficulty is the fear involved in the problem. So, if one puts the question whether it is necessary or not to make an effort, one receives a false answer.

Let us look at it differently. A problem demands attention, not distraction through fear; and there is no attention when we are seeking an answer away from the problem, an answer that will suit us, that will be preferable, that will give us satisfaction or avoidance. In other words, if we can approach the problem without any of these, then it is possible to understand the problem.

So, the question is not whether we should go through this process of analyzing, examining, dissecting, whether it is necessary in order to have tranquillity. Tranquillity comes into being when we are not afraid; and because we are afraid of the problem, of the issue of the problem, we are caught in the desires of our own pursuits, the pursuits of our own desires.

Question: I no longer suppress my thoughts, and I am shocked by what sometimes arises. Can I be as bad as that? (Laughter)

KRISHNAMURTI: It is good to be shocked, isn't it? Shock implies sensitivity, doesn't it? But, if you are not shocked, if you merely say there is a certain thing in you which you do not like, and you are going to discipline it, change it, then you are shockproof, are you not? (Laughter) No, please don't laugh it away. Because, most of us want to be shockproof; we do not want to know what we are, and that is why we have learned to suppress, to discipline, to destroy the neighbor and ourselves for our country and for ourselves. We don't want to know ourselves as we are. So, to discover oneself as one is, is a shocking thing, and it should be. Because, we want it to be different; we like to think of ourselves, picture ourselves as being beautiful, noble, this or that—which is all a resistance. Our virtue has become merely resistance, and therefore it is no longer virtue. To be sensitive to what one is requires a certain spontaneity, and in that spontaneity, one discovers. But, if you have suppressed, disciplined your thoughts and feelings so completely that there is no spontaneity, then there is no possibility of discovering anything; and I am not at all sure that is not what most of us want—to become inwardly dead. Because, it is much easier to live that way—to give ourselves to an idea, to a belief, to an organization, to service, to God knows what else—and function automatically. It is much easier. But to be sensitive, to be aware inwardly of all the possibilities is much too dangerous, much too painful; and we use a respectable way of dulling ourselves, an approved form of discipline, suppression, sublimation, denial—you know, the various practices which make us dull, insensitive.

Now, when you discover what you are, which, as the questioner says, is bad, what will you do with it? Previously, you have suppressed and therefore never discovered; now you no longer suppress, and you discover what you are. What is your next response? Surely, that is much more important—how you deal with it, how you approach it. Then what happens, when you discover that you are what you call bad? What do you do? The moment you discover, your mind is already at work on it, isn't it? Haven't you noticed it? I discover that I am mean. It is a shock to me. What do I do? The mind then says, "I must not be mean," so it cultivates generosity. Generosity of the hand is one thing, and generosity of the heart is another. The cultivation of generosity is of the hand, and you cannot cultivate generosity of the heart. If you do cultivate the generosity of the heart, then you fill the heart with the things of the mind. So, what do we do when we discover certain things that are not generous? Watch yourselves, please, don't wait for my answer, my explanation—look at it and experience it as we go along together. Not that this is a psychology class; but surely, in listening to something like this, we must experience and be free as we go along, not continue day after day in the same stupid way.

So, what do we do? The instinctive response is either to justify or to deny, which is to make ourselves insensitive. But to see it as it is, to see that I am mean and then to stop there without giving any explanations—merely to know that one is mean is an extraordinary thing, which means there is no verbalization, no naming even of that feeling which one has. If one really stops there, then one will see there is an extraordinary transformation. Then one is aware extensively of the implications of that feeling; then one doesn't have to do a thing with regard to that feeling. Because, when you don't name a thing, it withers away. Experiment with it and you will find out what an extraordinary quality of awareness comes into being when you are not naming or justifying but merely looking, silently observing the fact that you are not generous, or that you are mean. I am using the words *generous, mean,* only for communication. The word is not the thing, so don't be carried away by the word. But look at this thing. Surely, it is important to discover what one is, to be surprised and shocked to discover what one is when one thought one was so marvelous. It is all romantic and idiotic and stupid to think one is this or that. So, when you put all that aside and merely look at *what is*—which needs an extraordinary alertness, not courage, not virtue—when you no longer suppress it, justify it, condemn it, or give it a name, then you will see there is a transformation.

Question: What is it that determines the duration between the perception of one's thought-feeling and the modification or permanent disappearance of the condition perceived? In other words, why is it that certain undesirable conditions in oneself do not vanish as soon as they are observed?

KRISHNAMURTI: Surely, that depends on right attention, doesn't it? When one perceives an undesirable quality—I am using these words merely to communicate; I am not giving any special significance to "perceiving"—there is an interval of time before there is transformation, and the questioner wants to know why. Surely, the interval between perception and change depends on attention. Is there attention if I am merely resisting that, if I am condemning or justifying it? Surely, there is no attention. I am merely avoiding it. If I am trying to overcome it, discipline it, change it, that is not attention, is it? There is attention only when I am fully interested in the thing itself—not how to transform it, for then I am merely avoiding, being distracted, running away. So, what is important is not what takes place but to have that capacity of right attention when one discovers an undesirable thing; and there is no right attention if there is any form of identification, any feeling of pleasure or displeasure. Surely, that is very clear—the moment I am distracted by my pleasure of wanting it, or not wanting it, there is no attention. If that is very clear, then the problem is simple. Then there is no interval. But we like the interval. We like to go through all this rigmarole of labyrinthine ways to avoid the thing which we have to tackle. And we have cultivated marvelously and sedulously the escapes, and the escapes have become more important than the thing itself. But if one sees the escapes, not verbally, but actually sees that one is escaping, then there is right attention, then one doesn't have to struggle against the escapes. When you see a poisonous thing, you don't have to escape; it is a poisonous thing, you leave it alone. Similarly, right attention is spontaneous when the problem is really great, when the shock is intense. Then there is immediate response. But when the shock, the problem is not great—and we take care not to make any problem too great—then our minds are made dull and weary.

Question: Is the artist, the musician, engaged in a futile thing? I am not speaking of one who takes up art or music, but one who is inherently an artist. Would you go into this?

KRISHNAMURTI: It is a very complicated problem, so let us go into it slowly. As the questioner says, there are two types of people—those who are inherently artists and those who take up art or music. Those who take it up, obviously, do it either for sensation, for upliftment, for various forms of escape, or merely as an amusement, an addiction. You might take it up as another takes up drink or an ism or religious dogma; perhaps it is less harmful because you are by yourself. Then, there is the other type, the artist—if there is such a person. Inherently, for itself, he paints, plays or composes music, and all the rest of it. Now, what happens to that person? You must know such people. What is happening to him as an individual? As a social entity? What is happening to such a person? The danger, for all those people who have a capacity, a gift, is that they think they are superior, first of all. They think they are the salt of the earth. They are people especially chosen from above, and with that feeling of apartness, of being chosen, all the evils come: they are antisocial, they are individualistic, aggressive, extraordinarily self-centered—almost all gifted people are like that. So, gift, capacity, is a danger, is it not? Not that one can avoid the talent or the capacity, but one must be aware of the implications, the dangers of it. Such people may come together in a laboratory or in a gathering of musicians and artists, but they have always this barrier between themselves and others, have they not? You are the layman and I am the specialist—the man who knows more, and the man who knows less, and all the identification that goes with it.

I am not speaking slightingly of anybody because that would be too stupid, but one must be aware of all these things. To point them out is not to abuse or deride somebody. Few of us are inherently artists, first of all. We like to play with it because it is profitable or gives a certain éclat, a certain show, certain verbal expressions which we have learned. It gives us a place, a position. And if we are artists, really, genuinely, surely there is the quality of sensitivity, not of isolation. Art does not belong to any particular country or to any particular person, but the artist soon makes his gift into the personal—he paints, it is his work, his poem, it puffs him up, like the rest of us. And therefore, he becomes antisocial, he is more important. And, as most of us are not in that position, fortunately or unfortunately, we use music or art merely as sensation. We may have a quick experience when we hear something lovely, but the repetition of that thing over and over and over again soon dulls us. It is merely the sensation we indulge in. If we do not indulge in that, then beauty has quite a different significance. Then we approach it anew every time. And it is this fresh approach to something every time, whether ugly or beautiful, that is important, that makes for sensitivity; but you cannot be sensitive if you are captured by your own addiction or capacity, by your own delight, by your own sensation. Surely, the really creative person comes to things anew; he does not merely repeat what the radio announcer has told him or what the critics say.

So, the difficulty in this is to keep that sensitivity all the time, to be alert, whether you are an artist or merely playing with art. And that sensitivity is dulled when you give importance to yourself as the artist. You may have vision, and you may have the capacity to put that vision into paint, into marble, into words; but the moment you identify yourself with it, you are lost, it is finished. You lose that sensitivity. The world loves to praise you, to say what a marvelous artist you are, and you like that. And, for most of us who are not great artists inherently, our difficulty is not to get lost in sensations, because sensations dull; through sensations you cannot experience. Experiencing comes only when there is direct relationship, and there is no direct relationship when there is the screen of sensation, the desire to be, to alter, or to continue. So, our problem is to keep alert and sensitive; and that is denied when we are merely seeking sensation and the repetition of sensation.

August 7, 1949

Ninth Talk in The Oak Grove

I think I will only answer questions this evening and not give the usual preliminary talk; but before answering, I would like to point out one or two things concerning these questions and answers.

First of all, most of us are very inclined to believe. The mind is very clever in persuading us to think differently, to adopt a new point of view, or to believe in things that are not fundamentally true. Now, in answering these questions, I would like to say that I am not persuading you to think along my particular line. We are trying to find the right answer together. I am not answering for you just to accept or deny. We are going to find out together what is true, and that requires an open mind, an intelligent mind, an inquiring mind, an alert mind—not a mind that is so prejudiced that it merely denies or so eager that it accepts. And, in answering these questions, one fundamental thing must be born in mind. It is that they are merely a reflection of the ways of our own thinking, they reveal to us what we think. They should act as a mirror in which we perceive ourselves. After all, these discussions, these talks, have only one purpose, and that is the pursuit of self-knowledge. For, as I said, it is only in knowing ourselves first—deeply, profoundly, not superficially—that we can know truth. And it is extremely arduous to know ourselves deeply, not superficially. It is not a matter of time but a question of intensity; it is direct perception and experience that are important. And these discussions and talks are meant for that; so that each one of us may experience directly whatever is being discussed and not merely understand it on the verbal level. It is important also to bear in mind that each of us must find the truth, each of us must be the Master and the pupil—and that requires a great deal of humility, not mere acceptance of assurance or denial from me.

So, when I answer these questions, please bear all this in mind. Because, all of us have innumerable problems. Life is not very pleasant or simple; it is very complicated, and we can understand it only when we understand the whole, total process; and the total process is in us, not outside of us. Therefore, it is important to understand ourselves. Then we can deal with the things that we face every day, the influences that are constantly impinging upon us.

Question: Gossip has value in self-revelation, especially in revealing others to me. Seriously, why not use gossip as a means of discovering what is? *I do not shiver at the word* gossip *just because it has been condemned for ages.*

KRISHNAMURTI: I wonder why we gossip? Not because it reveals others to us. And why should others be revealed to us? Why do you want to know others? Why this extraordinary concern about others? First of all, sir, why do we gossip? It is a form of restlessness, is it not? Like worry, it is an indication of a restless mind. And why this desire to interfere with others, to know what others are doing, saying? It is a very superficial mind that gossips, isn't it? An inquisitive mind which is wrongly directed. The questioner seems to think that others are revealed to him by his being concerned with them—with their doings, with their thoughts, with their opinions. But, do we know others if we don't know ourselves? Can we judge others if we do not know the way of our own thinking, the way we act, the way we behave? And why this extraordinary concern over others? Is it not an escape, really, this desire to find out what others are thinking and feeling and gossiping about? Doesn't it offer an escape from ourselves? And, is there not in it also the desire to interfere with others' lives? Isn't our own life sufficiently difficult, sufficiently complex, sufficiently painful, without dealing with others, interfering with others? Is there time to think about others in that gossipy, cruel, ugly manner? Why do we do this? You know, everybody does it. Practically everybody gossips about somebody else. Why?

I think, first of all, we gossip about others because we are not sufficiently interested in the process of our own thinking and of our own action. We want to see what others are doing, and perhaps, to put it kindly, to imitate others. Generally when we gossip, it is to condemn others. But, stretching it charitably, it is perhaps to imitate others. Why do we want to imitate others? Doesn't it all indicate an extraordinary shallowness on our own part? It is an extraordinarily dull mind that wants excitement and goes outside of itself to get it. In other words, gossip is a form of sensation, isn't it, in which we indulge. It may be a different kind of sensation, but there is always this desire to find excitement, distraction. And so, if one really goes into this question deeply, one comes back to oneself, which shows that one is really extraordinarily shallow and seeking excitement from outside by talking about others. Catch yourself the next time you are gossiping about somebody, and if you are aware of it, it will indicate an awful lot to you about yourself. Don't cover it up by saying that you are merely inquisitive about others. It indicates restlessness, a sense of excitement, a shallowness, a lack of real, profound interest in people, which has nothing to do with gossip.

Now, the next problem is how to stop gossip. That is the next question, isn't it? When you are aware that you are gossiping, how do you stop gossiping? If it has become a habit, an ugly thing that continues day after day, how do you stop it? Does that question arise? When you know you are gossiping, when you are aware that you are gossiping, aware of all its implications, do you then say to yourself, "How am I to stop it?" Does it not stop of its own accord the moment you are aware that you are gossiping? The "how" does not arise at all. The "how" arises only when you are unaware; and, surely, gossip indicates a lack of awareness. Experiment with this for yourself the next time you are gossiping and see how quickly, how immediately you stop gossiping when you are aware of what you are talking about, aware that your tongue is running away with you. It does not demand the action of will to stop it. All that is necessary is to be aware, to be conscious of what you are saying and to see the implications of it. You don't have to condemn or justify gossip. Be aware of it, and you will see how quickly you stop gossiping because it reveals to oneself one's own ways of action, one's behavior, thought pattern; and in that revelation, one discovers oneself, which is far more important than gossiping about others, about what they are doing, what they are thinking, how they behave.

Most of us who read daily newspapers are filled with gossip, global gossip. It is all an escape from ourselves, from our own pettiness, from our own ugliness. We think that through a superficial interest in world events we are becoming more and more wise, more capable of dealing with our own lives. All these, surely, are ways of escaping from ourselves, are they not? Because, in ourselves we are so empty, shallow; we are so frightened of ourselves. We are so poor in ourselves that gossip acts as a form of rich entertainment and escape from ourselves. We try to fill that emptiness in us with knowledge, with rituals, with gossip, with group meetings—with the innumerable ways of escape. So, the escapes become all-important and not the understanding of *what is*. The understanding of *what is* demands attention; to know that one is empty, that one is in pain, needs immense attention, and not escapes. But most of us like these escapes because they are much more pleasurable, more pleasant. Also, when we know ourselves as we are, it is very difficult to deal with ourselves, and that is one of the problems with which we are faced. We don't know what to do. When I know that I am empty, that I am suffering, that I am in pain, I don't know what to do, how to deal with it. And so we resort to all kinds of escapes.

So, the question is, what to do? Of course, obviously, one cannot escape, for that is most absurd and childish. But when you are faced with yourself as you are, what are you to do? First, is it possible not to deny or justify it, but just to remain with it as you are?—which is extremely arduous because the mind seeks explanation, condemnation, identification. If it does not do any of those things but remains with it, then it is like accepting something. If I accept that I am brown, that is the end of it; but if I am desirous of changing to a lighter color, then the problem arises. So to accept *what is* is most difficult, and one can do that only when there is no escape; and condemnation or justification is a form of escape. So, when one understands the whole process of why one gossips, and when one realizes the absurdity of it, the cruelty and all the things involved in it, then one is left with what one is; and we approach it always either to destroy it or to change it into something else. But, if we don't do either of those things, but approach it with the intention of understanding it, being with it completely, then we will find that it is no longer the thing that we dreaded. Then there is a possibility of transforming that *which is*.

Question: We have a collection of ideals, and the choice is wide. We try to realize them through various methods. This is a long and time-taking way. In listening to you, I feel that the distinction or space between ideal and practice is illusory. Is this so?

KRISHNAMURTI: First of all, are we aware, each one of us, that we have ideals; and that, having these ideals, we are trying to practice them or live up to them or approximate ourselves to them? Take the question of violence. We have the ideal of nonviolence, and we try to practice that ideal in our daily lives. Or take any other ideal that you have. We are trying to live up to it all the time, to practice it, if we are serious and not merely living on the verbal level. And that takes time, a constant application, a series of failures, and so on.

Why do we have ideals? Any collection of them—why do we have them? Do they better our lives? And is virtue to be gained through constant disciplining? Is virtue a result? Or is it something quite different? Take humility. Can you practice humility? Or does humility come into being when the self is not important? Then the 'me' and the 'mine' do not predominate. But if we make that into an ideal—that the self should not predominate—then arises the question, how to come to that state? So, this whole process is very complicated and unreal, is it not? There must be a different approach to this problem, surely. Is not a collection of ideals an escape? Because, it gives us time to play with it. We say, "I am practicing it, I am disciplining myself; one day I will be that; it is necessary to go slowly, to evolve towards it"—you know all the various explanations that we give.

Now, is there a different approach? Because, we can see that the constant disciplining towards an ideal, approximating oneself to an ideal, does not really bring about the solution of the problem. We are no more kindly. We are not less violent. We may be superficially—but not fundamentally. So, how is one, then, to be nongreedy without having the ideal of nongreed? Suppose, for example, I am greedy or I am mean or angry—any of these things. The ordinary process is to have an ideal and try to approximate myself to that ideal all the time through practice, discipline, and so on. Does that free me from greed, from anger, from violence? What will free me from violence is to be free from my desire to be something, from my desire to gain something, to protect something, to achieve a result, and so on. So, our difficulty is, is it not, that having these ideals, there is this constant desire to be something, to become something; and that is really the crux of the matter. After all, greed or anger is one of the expressions of the 'me', the self, the 'I'; and as long as that 'I' remains, anger will continue. Merely to discipline it to function in a certain way does not free it from anger. This process only emphasizes the self, the 'me', does it not?

Now, if I realize that I am angry or greedy, need I go through all the disciplinary process in order to be free from it? Is there not a different approach to it, a different way of tackling it? I can tackle it differently only when I no longer take pleasure in sensation. Anger gives me a sensation of pleasure, doesn't it; though I may dislike it afterwards, at the time there is an excitement involved in it. It is a release. So, the first thing, it seems to me, is to be aware of this process, to see that the ideal does not eradicate anything. It is merely a form of postponement. That is, to understand something, I must give it full attention; and an ideal is merely a distraction which prevents my giving that feeling or that quality full attention at a given time. If I am fully aware, if I give my full attention to the quality I call greed without the distraction of an ideal, then am I not in a position to understand greed and so dissolve it? You see, we are so accustomed to postponement, and ideals help us to postpone; but if we can put away all ideals because we understand the escapes, the postponing quality of an ideal, and face the thing as it is, directly, immediately, give our full attention to it—then, surely, there is a possibility of transforming it.

If I realize that I am violent, if I am aware of it without trying to transform it or become nonviolent, if I am merely aware of it—then, because my attention is fully given to it, it opens up the various implications of violence, and therefore, surely, there is an inward transformation. But if I practice nonviolence or nongreed or what you will, then I am merely postponing, am I not, because I am not giving my attention to *what is,* which is greed or violence. You see, most of us have ideals either as a means of postponing or to be something, to achieve a result. In the very desire to become the ideal, surely there is violence involved. In the very becoming of something, moving myself towards a goal, surely violence is involved, is it not? You see, we all want to be something. We want to be happy, we want to be more beautiful, we want to be more virtuous, we want to be more and more and more. Surely, in the very desire for something more there is violence involved, there is greed involved. But, if we realize that the more we want to be something, the more conflict there is, then we can see that the ideal merely helps us to increase our conflict—which doesn't mean that I am satisfied with what I am. On the contrary. As long as I want to be something more, there must be conflict, there must be pain, there must be anger, violence. If I really feel that, if I am profoundly affected by it, see it, am aware of it, then I am able to deal with the problem immediately, without having a collection of ideals to encourage me to be this or that. Then my action is immediate, my relationship with it is direct.

But there also arises in this another problem, which is that of the experiencer and the experience. With most of us, the experiencer and the experience are two different processes. The ideal and myself are two different states. I want to become that. Therefore, the 'I', the experiencer, the thinker, is different from the thought. Is that so? Is the thinker different from the thought? Or is there only thought, which creates the thinker? So, as long as I am separate from the thought, I can manipulate thought, I can change it, transform it. But is the 'I', who is operating on a thought, different from the thought? Surely, they are a joint phenomenon, are they not? The thinker and the thought are one, not separate. When one is angry, one is angry; there is an integrated feeling which we term anger. Then I say, "I am angry"; therefore, I separate myself from that anger, and then I can operate on it, do something about it. But if I realize that I am anger, that I am that quality itself, that the quality is not separable from me, surely, when I experience that, then there is quite a different action, quite a different approach. Now, we separate ourselves from the thought, from the feeling, from the quality. Therefore, the 'I' is a separate entity from the quality, and therefore the 'I' can operate on the quality. But the quality is not different from the 'I', from the thinker; and when there is that integrated experience in which the thinker and the thought are one, not separate, then, surely, there is quite a different approach, a different response. Again, experiment with this and you will see. Because, at the moment of experiencing there is neither the experiencer nor the experience. It is only as the experiencing fades that there is the experiencer and the experience. Then, the experiencer says, "I like that," or "I don't like it," "I want more of it," or "I want less of it." Then, he wants to cultivate the ideal, to become the ideal. But if the thinker is the thought, and there are not two separate processes, then his whole attitude is transformed, is it not? Then there is quite a different response with regard to thought; then there is no longer approximating thought to an ideal or getting rid of thought; then there is no maker of effort. And I think it is really very important to discover this for oneself, to experience this directly, not because I say so or someone else says so. It is important to come to this experience—that the thinker is the thought. Don't let that become a new jargon, a new set of words which we use. Through verbalization we don't experience. We merely have sensations, and sensations are not experience. And if one can be aware of this joint phenomenon, of this process in which the thinker and the thought are one, then I think the problem will be understood much more profoundly than when we merely have ideals or have none, which is really beside the point.

If I am my thoughts and my thoughts are not different from me, then there is no maker of effort, is there? Then I do not become that; then I am no longer cultivating virtue. Not that I am already virtuous. The moment I am conscious that I am virtuous, I am not virtuous. The moment I am conscious that I am humble, surely humility ceases. So, if I can understand the maker of effort—the 'me' becoming its own self-projected demands, desires, which are the same as myself—then, surely, there is a radical transformation in my whole outlook. That is why it is important to have right meditation, to know what right meditation means. It is not the approximation to an ideal, it is not trying to reach out and get something, it is not to attain, to concentrate, to develop certain qualities, and so on, which we discussed previously. Right meditation is the understanding of this whole process of the 'me', of the self. Because, as I said, right meditation is self-knowledge, and without meditation, one cannot find out what the process of the self is. If there is no meditator to meditate upon something, then meditation is the experiencing of that which is, the total process of the thinker as the thought. Then only is there a possibility that the mind can be really quiet. Then it is possible to discover if there is something beyond the mind, which is not a mere verbal assertion that there is or that there is not, that there is atma, the soul, or what you will—we are not discussing those things. It is going beyond all verbal expression. Then the mind is quiet—not merely on the higher level, the upper level of the mind, but the whole content of the mind, the whole consciousness, is quiet. But there is no quietness if there is a maker of effort, and there will be the maker, the will of action, as long as he thinks he is separate from the thought. And this requires a great deal of going into, of thinking out, not just experiencing it superficially and sensationally. And when one has that direct experience, then becoming the ideal is illusory; it has no meaning at all. Then it is altogether a wrong approach. Then one sees that this whole process of becoming the 'more', the greater, has nothing to do with reality. Reality comes into being only when the mind is completely quiet, when there is no effort. Virtue is that state of freedom in which there is no maker of effort. Therefore, virtue is a state in which effort has completely ceased, but if you make an effort to become virtuous, surely it is no longer virtue, is it?

So, as long as we do not understand, do not experience that the thinker and the thought are one, all these problems will exist. But the moment we experience that, the maker of effort comes to an end. To experience that, one must be completely aware of the process of one's own thinking and feeling, of one's desire to become. And that is why it is important, if one is really seeking reality or God or what you will, to see that this whole mentality of climbing, evolving, growing, achieving, must come to an end. We are much too worldly. With the mentality of the clerk becoming the boss, the foreman becoming the executive—with that mentality we approach reality. We think we will do the same thing, climb the ladder of success. I am afraid it cannot be done that way. If you do, you will live in a world of illusion and therefore of conflict, pain, misery, and strife. But if one discards all such mentality, such thoughts, such points of view, then one becomes really humble. One is, not becomes. Then there is a possibility of having a direct experience of reality, which alone will dissolve all our problems—not our cunning efforts, not our great intellect, not our deep and wide knowledge.

Question: I am free from ambition. Is there something wrong with me? (Laughter)

KRISHNAMURTI: If you are conscious that you are free from ambition, then there is something wrong. (Laughter) Then one becomes smug, respectable, unimaginative, thoughtless. Why should you be free from ambition? And how do you know you are free from ambition? Surely, to have the desire to be free from something is the beginning of illusion, is it not, of ignorance. You see, we find ambition painful; we want to be something, and we have failed. And so now we say, "It is too painful, I will get rid of it." If you succeeded in your ambition, if you fulfilled yourself in the thing which you want to be, then this problem wouldn't arise. But, not succeeding, and seeing there is no fulfillment there, you discard it and condemn ambition. Obviously, ambition is unworthy. A man who is ambitious, surely, cannot find reality. He may become the president of some club or some society or some country. But surely, he is not seeking reality. But the difficulty is, with most of us, if we don't succeed in what we want, we either become bitter, cynical, or we try to become spiritual. So we say, "That is a wrong thing to do," and we discard it. But our mentality is the same. We may not succeed in the world and be a great person there, but "spiritually" we still want to succeed—in a little group, as a leader. Ambition is the same, whether it is in the world or turned towards God. To know consciously that you are free from ambition is surely an illusion, is it not? And if you are really free of it, can there be any question that you are or are not? Surely one knows within oneself when one is ambitious, does one not? And we can see very well all the effects of ambition in the world—the ruthlessness of it, the cruelty of it, the desire for power, position, prestige. But when one is consciously free of something, is there not the danger of becoming very respectable, of being smug, satisfied with oneself?

I assure you, it is a very difficult thing to be alert, to be aware, to walk delicately, sensitively, not to be caught in the opposites. It requires a great deal of alertness and intelligence and watchfulness. And then, even if you are free from ambition, where are you? Are you any more kindly, any more intelligent, any more sensitive to the outward and inward events? Surely, there is a danger in all this, is there not, of becoming stultified, of becoming static, becoming dull, weary; and the more one is sensitive, alert, watchful, the more there is a possibility of really being free—not free from this or that. Freedom requires intelligence, and intelligence is not a thing that you sedulously cultivate. Intelligence is something which can be experienced directly in relationship, not through the screen of what you think the relationship should be. After all, our life is a process of relationship. Life is relationship. And that requires an extraordinary watchfulness, alertness, not speculating whether you are free or not free from ambition. But ambition perverts that relationship. The ambitious man is an isolated man; therefore, he cannot have relationship, either with his wife or with society. Life is relationship, whether with the one or with the many, and that relationship is perverted, is destroyed, is corrupted through ambition; and when one is aware of that corruption, surely, there is no question of being free from it.

So, in all this, our difficulty is to be watchful, to be watchful of what we are thinking, feeling, saying—not in order to transform it into something else, but just to be aware of it. And if we are so aware—in which there is no condemnation, no justification, but mere attention, full cognizance of *what is*—that awareness in itself has an extraordinary effect. But if we are merely trying to become less, or more, then there is dullness, weariness, a smug respectability; and a man who is respectable, surely, can never find reality. Awareness demands a great deal of inward discontent which is not easily canalized through any satisfaction or gratification.

Now, if we see all this, all that we have discussed this evening, not merely on the verbal level, but really experience it, not at odd moments, not when we are pushed into a corner as perhaps some of you are now, but every day, from moment to moment, if we are aware, silently observing—then we become extremely sensitive, not sentimental, which only blurs, distorts. To be sensitive inwardly needs great simplicity—not wearing a loincloth or having few clothes or no car, but the simplicity in which the 'me' and the 'mine' are not important, in which there is no sense of possession—a simplicity in which there is no longer the maker of effort. Then there is a possibility of experiencing that reality, or of that reality coming into being. After all, this is the only thing that can bring about real, lasting happiness. Happiness is not an end in itself. It is a byproduct, and it comes into being only with reality. Not that you go after reality—you cannot. It must come to you. And it can come to you only when there is complete freedom, silence. Not that you become silent. That is a wrong process of meditation. There is a vast difference between being silent and becoming silent. When there is real silence, not put together, then there is something inexplicable, then creation comes into being.

August 13, 1949

Tenth Talk in The Oak Grove

For the last five weeks we have been discussing the importance of self-knowledge, for without knowing oneself—not partially, but fully, integrally—it is not possible to think rightly and therefore act rightly. Without self-knowledge there cannot be complete, integrated action. There can only be partial action if there is no self-knowledge, and as partial action invariably leads to conflict and to misery, it is important for those who would really understand the problems of life completely to understand the problem of relationship—not only with one or two, but with the whole, which is society. To understand this problem of relationship, we must understand ourselves; and to understand ourselves is action, it is not a withdrawal from action. There is action only when we understand relationship—relationship not only with people and ideas, but with things, with nature. So, action is relationship with regard to things, to property, to nature, to people, and to ideas. Without the comprehension of all this process, which we call life, life must be contradictory, painful, and a constant conflict. So, to understand this process of life, which is ourselves, we have to understand the whole significance of our own thoughts and feelings, and that is why we have been discussing the importance of self-knowledge. Perhaps some of us have read a few books on psychology, have some smattering of psychoanalytical phrases, but I am afraid mere superficial knowledge is not sufficient. Verbal expression of an understanding which comes through mere knowledge, mere study, is not sufficient. What is important is to understand ourselves in relationship, and that relationship is not static—it is constantly in motion. Therefore, to follow that relationship there must be no fixation on an idea. Most of us are slaves to ideas. We are ideas. We are a bundle of ideas. Our actions are shaped by ideas, and our whole outlook is conditioned by ideas. Therefore, ideas shape our relationship. That shaping of relationship by an idea prevents the understanding of relationship. To us, idea is very important, extraordinarily significant. You have your ideas, and I have my ideas, and we are in constant conflict over ideas; whether political, religious, or otherwise, each is in opposition to others. Ideas invariably create opposition because ideas are the outcome of sensation, and as long as our relationship is conditioned by sensation, by idea, there is no understanding of that relationship. Hence ideas prevent action. Ideas do not further action—they limit action, which we see in everyday life.

So, is it possible for action to be without idea? Can we act without ideation first? Because, we see how ideas divide people—ideas which are beliefs, prejudices, sensations, political and religious opinions. These are dividing people and tearing the world to pieces at the present time. The cultivation of the intellect has become the predominant factor, and our intellect guides, shapes our action. So, is it possible to act without idea? We do act without idea when the problem is really intense, very profound, demanding all our attention. We may try to conform the act to an idea, but if we go into the problem, if we really try to understand the problem itself, we will begin to discard the idea, the prejudice, the particular point of view, and approach the problem afresh. This is what we do when we have a problem, surely. We try to solve the problem according to a particular idea or depending on a particular result, and so on. When the problem cannot be solved that way, then we push aside all ideas, then we give up our ideas, and therefore approach the problem afresh, with a quiet mind. We do this unconsciously. Surely, this is what happens, isn't it? When you have a problem, you worry over it. You want a particular result from that problem, or you translate that problem according to certain ideas. You go through all that process, and yet the problem is not solved. So, the mind, becoming weary, stops thinking about the problem. Then it is quiet, it is relaxed, it is not worried over the problem. And presently, as often happens, the solution of the problem is immediately perceived; there is a hint with regard to that problem.

So, action, surely, does not lie in conforming to a particular idea. Then it is merely a continuation of thought—it is not action. And, can we not live without conforming action to an idea? Because, ideas continue; and if we conform action to an idea, then we give continuity to action, and therefore, there is an identification with action as the 'me' and the 'mine'. Therefore, the strengthening, through ideation, of the 'me', which is the source of all conflict and misery.

Surely, immortality is not an idea. It is something beyond ideation, beyond thought, beyond the bundle of memories, which are all the 'me'. And there is the experiencing of that state only when ideation stops, when the thinking process stops. The experiencing of that which we call the immortal, the timeless state, is not the product of thought because thought is merely the continuance of memory, the response to memory; and the experiencing of that extraordinary state can only come into being with the understanding of the self—not through trying to reach it because that is merely trying to experience something which is self-projected, therefore unreal. For this reason it is important to understand the whole, total process of our consciousness, which we call the 'me' and the 'mine', which can be understood only in relationship, not in isolation.

That is why it is imperative for those who would really understand truth or reality or God or what you will to fully grasp the significance of relationship; because, that is the only action. If relationship is based on idea, then action is not. If I try to circumscribe my relationship, conform or limit it to an idea, which most of us do, then it is not action; there is no understanding in relationship. But if we see that that is a false process leading to illusion, to limitation, to conflict, to separateness—ideas always separate—then we will begin to understand relationship directly and not impose upon relationship a prejudice, a condition. Then we will see that love is not a thought process. You cannot think about love. But most of us do, and so it is merely sensation. And, if we limit relationship to an idea based on sensation, then we discard love, then we fill our hearts with the things of the mind. Though we may feel the sensation and call it love, it is not love. Surely, love is something beyond the thought process, but it can be discovered only through understanding the thought process in relationship—not through denying the thought process, but through being aware of the whole significance of the ways of our mind and of our action in relationship. If we can proceed more deeply, then we will see that action is not related to idea. Then action is from moment to moment, and in that experience, which is right meditation, there is immortality.

Question: What place has criticism in relationship? What is the difference between destructive and constructive criticism?

KRISHNAMURTI: First of all, why do we criticize? Is it in order to understand? Or is it merely a nagging process? If I criticize you, do I understand you? Does understanding come through judgment? If I want to comprehend, if I want to understand not superficially but deeply the whole significance of my relationship to you, do I begin to criticize you? Or, am I aware of this relationship between you and me, silently observing it—not projecting my opinions, criticisms, judgments, identifications, or condemnations, but silently observing what is happening? And, if I do not criticize, what happens? One is apt to go to sleep, is one not? Which does not mean that we do not go to sleep if we are nagging. Perhaps that becomes a habit, and we put ourselves to sleep through habit. Is there a deeper, wider understanding of relationship through criticism? It doesn't matter whether criticism is constructive or destructive—that is irrelevant, surely. Therefore, the question is: What is the necessary state of mind and heart that will understand relationship? What is the process of understanding? How do we understand something? How do you understand your child, if you are interested in your child? You observe, don't you? You watch him at play; you study him in his different moods; you don't project your opinion onto him. You don't say he should be this or that. You are alertly watchful, aren't you, actively aware. Then, perhaps, you begin to understand the child. But if you are constantly criticizing, constantly injecting your own particular personality, your idiosyncrasies, your opinions, deciding the way he should or should not be, and all the rest of it, obviously you create a barrier in that relationship. But, unfortunately, most of us criticize in order to shape, in order to interfere; and it gives us a certain amount of pleasure, a certain gratification, to shape something—your relationship with your husband, child, or whoever it be. You feel a sense of power in it; you are the boss, and in that there is a tremendous gratification. Surely, through all that process there is no understanding of relationship. There is mere imposition, the desire to mold another to the particular pattern of your idiosyncrasy, your desire, your wish. All these prevent, do they not, the understanding of relationship.

Then, there is self-criticism. To be critical of oneself, to criticize, condemn, or justify oneself—does that bring understanding of oneself? When I begin to criticize myself, do I not limit the process of understanding, of exploring? Does introspection, a form of self-criticism, unfold the self? What makes the unfoldment of the self possible? To be constantly analytical, fearful, critical—surely, that does not help to unfold. What brings about the unfoldment of the self so that you begin to understand it is the constant awareness of it without any condemnation, without any identification. There must be a certain spontaneity; you cannot be constantly analyzing it, disciplining it, shaping it. This spontaneity is essential to understanding. If I merely limit, control, condemn, then I put a stop to the movement of thought and feeling, do I not? It is in the movement of thought and feeling that I discover—not in mere control. And, when one discovers, then it is important to find out how to act about it. Now, if I act according to an idea, according to a standard, according to an ideal, then I force the self into a particular pattern. In that there is no understanding, there is no transcending. But if I can watch the self without any condemnation, without any identification, then it is possible to go beyond it. That is why this whole process of approximating oneself to an ideal is so utterly wrong. Ideals are home-made gods, and to conform to a self-projected image is surely not a release.

So, there can be understanding only when the mind is silently aware, observing—which is arduous because we take delight in being active, in being restless, critical, in condemning, justifying. That is our whole structure of being; and through the screen of ideas, prejudices, points of view, experiences, memories, we try to understand. Is it possible to be free of all these screens and so understand directly? Surely, we do that when the problem is very intense; we do not go through all these methods—we approach it directly. So, the understanding of relationship comes only when this process of self-criticism is understood, and the mind is quiet. If you are listening to me and are trying to follow with not too great an effort what I wish to convey, then there is a possibility of our understanding each other. But if you are all the time criticizing, throwing up your opinions, what you have learned from books, what somebody else has told you, and so on, and so on, then you and I are not related because this screen is between us. But if we are both trying to find out the issues of the problem, which lie in the problem itself, if both of us are eager to go to the bottom of it, find the truth of it, discover what it is—then we are related. Then your mind is both alert and passive, watching to see what is true in this. So, your mind must be extraordinarily swift, not anchored to any idea or ideal, to any judgment, to any opinion that you have consolidated through your particular experiences. Understanding comes, surely, when there is the swift pliability of a mind which is passively aware. Then it is capable of reception, then it is sensitive. A mind is not sensitive when it is crowded with ideas, prejudices, opinions, either for or against.

So, to understand relationship, there must be a passive awareness, which does not destroy relationship. On the contrary, it makes relationship much more vital, much more significant. Then there is in that relationship a possibility of real affection; there is a warmth, a sense of nearness, which is not mere sentiment or sensation. And if we can so approach or be in that relationship to everything, then our problems will be easily solved—the problems of property, the problems of possession. Because, we are that which we possess. The man who possesses money is the money. The man who identifies himself with property is the property or the house or the furniture. Similarly with ideas or with people, and when there is possessiveness, there is no relationship. But most of us possess because we have nothing else if we do not possess. We are empty shells if we do not possess, if we do not fill our life with furniture, with music, with knowledge, with this or that. And that shell makes a lot of noise, and that noise we call living, and with that we are satisfied. And when there is a disruption, a breaking away of that, then there is sorrow because then you suddenly discover yourself as you are—an empty shell without much meaning. So, to be aware of the whole content of relationship is action; and from that action there is a possibility of true relationship a possibility of discovering its great depth, its great significance, and of knowing what love is.

Question: When you speak of timelessness, it seems you must mean something besides a sequence of events. Time, to me, is necessary for action, and I cannot imagine existence without a sequence of events. Do you per-

haps mean that by knowing what part of you is eternal, time no longer becomes a means to an end or a means to progress?

KRISHNAMURTI: First of all, we cannot discuss what the timeless is. A mind that is the product of time cannot think of something which is timeless. Because, after all, my mind, your mind, is a result of the past; it is founded upon the past; its thought is the outcome of the past, which is time. And with that instrument, we try to think of something which is not of time, and that is not possible, surely. We can speculate upon it, we can write books about it, we can imagine it, do all kinds of tricks with it, but it will not be the real. So, do not let us speculate about it. Let us not even talk about it. To speculate what the timeless state is, is utterly useless, it has no meaning. But we can do something else, which is to find out how to make the mind free from its own past, from its own self-projection; we can find out what gives it continuity, a sequence of events as a means of progress, as a means of understanding, or what you will. We can see that a thing which continues must decay. That which has continuance cannot renew itself. Only that which comes to an end can renew. A mind that is merely caught in a habit or in a particular opinion or held in the net of ideals, beliefs, dogmas—for such a mind there can be no renewal, surely. It cannot look at life anew. It is only when those things are put aside and it is free that the mind can look at life anew. There is a renewal, a creative urge, only when the past has come to an end, which means, when there is no longer identification giving continuity as the 'me' and the 'mine'—my property, my home, my wife, my child, my ideal, my gods, my political opinions. It is this constant identification that gives continuity to the sequence of events as the 'me' becoming wider, bigger, nobler, more worthy, cleverer, and so on, and so on.

Is life, existence, a matter of the sequence of events? What do we mean by sequence of events? Do I know that I am alive because I remember yesterday? Do I know that I am alive because I know the way to my house? Or do I know that I am alive because I am going to be somebody? How do I know that I am alive? It is only in the present, surely, that I know I am conscious. Is consciousness merely the result of the sequence of events? With most of us, it is. I know I am alive, I am conscious, because of my past, of my identification with something. Is it possible to know that one is conscious without this process of identification? And, why does one identify? Why do I identify myself as my property, my name, my ambition, my progress? Why? And what would happen if we did not identify? Would it deny all existence? Perhaps, if we did not identify, there might be a wider field for action, a greater depth to feeling and to thought. We identify because it gives us the feeling of being alive as an entity, as a separate entity. So, the feeling that one is separate has become important because through separateness we enjoy the 'more'; and if we deny separateness, we are afraid that we shall not be capable of enjoying, having pleasures. Surely, that is the basis of the desire for continuity, is it not? But there is also a collective process at work. Since separateness involves a great deal of destruction and so on, there is in opposition to that, collectivism, discarding the individual separateness. But the individual becomes the collective through another form of identification and so retains his separateness—as we can see.

As long as there is continuity through identification, there can be no renewal. Only with the cessation of identification is there a possibility of renewal. And most of us are frightened of coming to an end. And most of us are frightened of death. Innumerable books have been written about what is after death. We are more interested in death than in living. Because, with death, there seems to be an end, an end to identification. That which continues, surely, has no rebirth, no renewal. Only in dying is there renewal, and therefore it is important to die every minute—not wait to die of old age and disease. That means dying to all one's accumulations and identifications, one's gathered experiences; and that is real simplicity, not the accumulated continuance of identification.

So, when this process of identification—which revives memory and gives continuance to memory in the present—when that ceases, then there is a possibility of rebirth, renewal, creativeness; and in that renewal there is no continuity. That which renews cannot continue. It is from moment to moment.

The questioner asks also, "Do you perhaps mean that by knowing what part of you is eternal, time no longer becomes a means to an end?" Is there a part of you that is eternal? That which you can think about is still the product of thought and therefore not the eternal. Because, thought is the result of the past, of time. And if you posit something eternal in you, you have already thought about it. I am not cleverly arguing this matter. You can see very well that the eternal is not what you can think about. You cannot progress to the eternal, you cannot evolve to it; if you do, it is merely a projection of thought and therefore still within the net of time. That way leads to illusion, misery, to all the ugliness of deception—which we like because the mind can function only within the known, from safety to safety, from security to security. The eternal is not if it is within the bondage of time, and the moment the mind thinks about it, it is in the bondage of time, and therefore it is not real.

So, when you perceive this whole process of identification, when you see how thought gives continuity to things in order to be secure, how the thinker separates himself from the thought and thereby makes himself secure—when you see all this process of time and understand it, not merely verbally, but deeply feel it, inwardly experience it, then you will find that you no longer think of the timeless. Then the mind is quiet, not only superficially, but profoundly; then it becomes tranquil—is tranquil. Then there is a direct experience of that which is measureless. But merely to speculate upon what is the timeless is a waste of time. You might just as well play poker. All speculation is brushed aside the moment you have a direct experience. And that is what we are discussing—how to have this direct experience without the intervention of the mind. But when once there is this direct experiencing, the mind clings to the sensations of it and then wants a repetition of that experience, which means, really, that the mind is interested in sensation, not in experiencing. Therefore, mind can never experience; it can only know sensations. The experiencing comes only when the mind is not the experiencer. So, the timeless cannot be known or imagined or experienced through the mind. And as that is the only instrument which we have cultivated, at the expense of everything else, we are lost when we look at the process of the mind. We must be lost. We must come to an end—which is not despair, not fear. Know the process of the mind; see what it is, and when you see what it is, it comes to an end without any enforcement. Only then is there a possibility of that renewal which is eternal.

Question: Is there a gulf, an interval of any duration, between my perceiving something and being or realizing it? Does not this interval imply an ideal at one end and its realization at the other, through practice and technique? It is this "how" or the method that we want from you.

KRISHNAMURTI: Is there an interval between perception and action? Most of us would say yes. We say there is an interval: "I see, and later on I will act." "I understand intellectually, but how am I to put it into practice?" "I see what you mean, but I don't know how to carry it out." This gap, this gulf, this interval—is it necessary? Or, are we only deceiving ourselves? When I say, "I see," I really don't see. If I do see, then there is no problem. If I see something, action follows. If I see a poisonous snake, I don't say, "I see, and how am I to act?" I act. But we don't see, and we don't see because we don't want to see, because it is too imminent, too dangerous, too vital. To see would upset our whole process of thinking, living. Therefore, we say, "I see, and please tell me how to act." Therefore you are interested in the method, the "how" to do it, the practice. So we say, "I see the idea, I comprehend, but how am I to act?" Then we try to bridge, to connect the action with the idea, and we get lost. Then we search for methods. You go to various teachers, psychologists, gurus, or what you will, and you join societies that will help you to bridge the action with the idea. That is a very convenient way of living, a happy escape, a very respectable way of avoiding action. And, in that process we are all caught. I realize I must be virtuous, I must not be angry, mean—but please tell me how to do it. And this process of "how to do it" becomes a religious investment, an exploitation, and all the rest of it follows—vast properties, you know, the whole game of it. In other words, we don't see, and we don't want to see. But we don't say that honestly. The moment we admit that, we have to act. Then we know we are deceiving ourselves, and it is very unpleasant. So we say, "Please, I am gradually learning, I am still weak, I am not strong enough, it is a matter of progress, evolution, growth; eventually I will get there." So, we should never say that we see or perceive or understand, because mere verbalization has no significance. There is no gap between seeing and acting. The moment you see, you act. You do that when you are driving a car. If you did not, there would be danger. But we have invented so many ways of avoiding. We have become so clever, so cunning, as not to change radically. But there is no gap between perception and action. When you see a poisonous snake, how quickly you respond—the action is instantaneous. When there is a gap, it indicates sluggishness of the mind, laziness, avoidance. And that avoidance, that laziness, becomes very respectable because all of us are doing it. So, you look for a method to bridge the idea with the action, and so you live in illusion. And perhaps you may like it. But for a man who actually perceives, there is no problem; there is action. We do not perceive because of our innumerable prejudices, our disinclination, our laziness, our hopes that something will alter it.

So, to think in terms of idea separate from action is obviously ignorant. To say, "I will be something"—the Buddha, the Master, what you will—is obviously a wrong process. What is important is to understand what you are now, and that cannot be understood if you are postponing, if you have an interval between the ideal and yourself. And as most of us indulge in that particular form of excitement, obviously you will pay scant attention to all this. Ideas can never free action. On the contrary, ideas limit action; and there is action only when I understand as I go along from moment to moment, not tethered to particular beliefs or to a particular ideal which I am going to realize. That is to die from moment to moment, in which there is renewal. And that renewal will answer the next problem. That renewal gives a new light, a new significance to everything. And there can be renewal only when there is freedom from the gap, from the gulf, from the interval, between idea and action.

Question: You often speak of living, experiencing, and yet being as nothing. What is this state of consciously being as nothing? Has this anything to do with humility, being open to the grace of God?

KRISHNAMURTI: To be consciously anything is not to be free. If I am conscious that I am nongreedy, beyond anger, surely I am not free from greed, anger. Humility is something of which you cannot be conscious. To cultivate humility is to cultivate self-expansion negatively. Therefore, any virtue that is deliberately cultivated, practiced, lived, is obviously not virtue. It is a form of resistance; it is a form of self-expansion, which has its own gratification. But it is no longer virtue. Virtue is merely a freedom in which you discover the real. Without virtue, there can be no freedom. Virtue is not an end in itself. Now, it is not possible by deliberate, conscious effort to be as nothing, because then it is another achievement. Innocence is not the result of careful cultivation. To be as nothing is essential. As a cup is useful only when it is empty, so only when one is as nothing is it possible to receive the grace of God or truth or what you will. Is it possible to be nothing in the sense of arriving at it? Can you achieve it? As you have built a house or gathered money, can you get this also? To sit down and meditate about nothingness, consciously throwing out everything, making yourself receptive, surely, is a form of resistance, isn't it? That is a deliberate action of the will, and will is desire; and when you desire to be nothing, you are something already. Please, see the importance of this: when you desire positive things, you know what it implies—struggle, pain—and so you reject them, and you say to yourself, "Now I will be nothing." The desire is still the same; it is the same process in another direction. The will to be nothing is as the will to be something. So, the problem is not to be nothing, or to be something, but to understand the whole process of desire—craving to be, or not to be. In that process the entity that desires is different from desire. You don't say, "Desire is me," but, "I am desirous of something." Therefore, there is a separation between the experiencer, the thinker, and the experience, the thought. Don't, please, make this metaphysical and difficult. You can look at it very simply—simply in the sense that one can feel one's way into it.

So, as long as there is the desire to be nothing, you are something. And that desire to be something divides you as the experiencer and the experience; and in that condition, there is no possibility of experiencing. Because, in the state of experiencing, there is neither the experiencer nor the experience. When you are experiencing something, you aren't thinking that you are experiencing. When you are really happy, you don't say, "I am happy." The moment you say it, it is gone. So, our problem is not how to be nothing, which is really quite childish, or how to learn a new jargon and try to become that jargon, but how to understand the whole process of desire, craving. And it is so subtle, so complex, that you must approach it very simply—not with all the conflicts of condemnation, justification, what it should be, what it should not be, how it must be destroyed, how it must be sublimated, all of which you have learned from books, from religious organizations. If we can discard all that and merely silently observe the process of desire, which is oneself—which is not, you experience desire, but experienc*ing* desire—then we will see that there is a freedom from this burning, constant urge to be or not to be, to become, to gain, to be the Master, to have virtue, and all the idiocy of desire and its pursuits. Then there can be a direct experiencing, that is, experiencing without the observer. Then only is there a possibility of being completely open, of being as nothing, and then there is the reception of the real.

August 14, 1949

Eleventh Talk in The Oak Grove

We have been discussing, for the past several weeks, the problem of understanding oneself. Because, the more one thinks about the many conflicting and ever-increasing problems of life, private and social, the more one sees that unless there is a fundamental, radical transformation within oneself, obviously it is not possible to deal with those problems that confront each one of us. So, it is essential, is it not, if one is to resolve any of these problems of our life, to tackle them oneself, directly, to be in relationship with them and not merely rely on specialists, experts, religious leaders, or political givers of panaceas. And, as our life, our culture, and civilization are getting more and more complicated, it is becoming correspondingly difficult to deal with the ever-increasing problems directly.

Now, it seems to me that one of the problems, amongst others, which most of us have not very deeply and fundamentally faced is the question of domination and submission. And, if I may, I would like to discuss this double-sided nature of domination rather briefly and succinctly before I answer the questions. Why is it that we dominate, consciously or unconsciously—the man and the woman, the woman and the man, and so on? There is domination in different ways, not only in private life, but the whole tendency of governments is also to dominate. Why is this spirit of domination going on constantly, from period to period? Only very few seem to escape it. Can we think of it in a different sense? That is, can we understand it without going to the opposite? Because, the moment we recognize it, the moment we are aware of this problem of domination, we at once begin to submit, or we think of it in terms of the opposite, submission. Can we not think without the opposite and look at the problem directly? Perhaps we shall then be able to understand this whole complex problem of domination—seeking power over another or submitting oneself to another. After all, submission is another form of domination. To submit oneself to another, whether it be to a man or to a woman, is the negative form of domination. By the very denial of domination, one becomes submissive, and I do not think we shall be able to solve this problem by thinking in terms of the opposite. So, let us go into it and see why it exists.

First of all, one must be aware, must one not, of the obvious, crude form of domination. Most of us are aware of it, if we are at all alert. But there is the unconscious domination, of which most of us are unaware. That is, this unconscious desire to dominate takes the guise or the cloak of service, of love, of being kind, and so on. The unconscious desire to dominate exists under different forms, and I think it is much more important to understand this fact than merely to try to regulate the superficial domination of one by another.

Now, why is it that we unconsciously want to dominate? Probably most of us are unaware that we dominate at different levels—not only in the family, but at the verbal level as well—and also there is this inward desire to seek power, to seek success, which are all indications of domination. Why? Why do we want to dominate another? Or, be subservient to another? If one deliberately, consciously, put that question to oneself, what would be the response? Most of us wouldn't know why we want to dominate. First of all, there is in it the sensation, the unconscious pleasure of dominating somebody. Is that the only motive which makes us want to dominate? Surely, that is part of it, but there is much more to it, a much deeper significance. I wonder if you have ever watched yourself dominating in relationship, either as the man or as the woman? And if you have been conscious of it, what has been your response, your reaction? And why shouldn't we dominate? In relationship, which is life, do we understand through domination? In relationship, if I dominate you or you dominate me, do we understand each other? After all, that is life, isn't it? Relationship is life, relationship is action, and if I merely live in the self-enclosing action of domination, is there any relationship? Is not domination a process of isolation, which denies relationship? Is not domination a process of separation which destroys relationship? And is this really what I am seeking? And can there be relationship between two people if there is any sense of domination or submission? Life is relationship—one cannot live in isolation. But, is not our purpose unconsciously to isolate ourselves within the cloak, within that feeling of aggressive assertiveness which is domination?

So, is not the process of domineering a process of isolation, and isn't this what most of us want? Most of us sedulously cultivate it. Because, to be open in relationship is very painful; it needs extraordinary intelligence and adaptability, quickness, understanding, and when that is not, we try to isolate ourselves. And is not the process of domination a process of isolation? Obviously, it is. It is a process of self-enclosure. And when I am enclosed, encased in my own opinion, my own desires, my own ambitions, my urge to dominate, am I related? And if there is no relationship, how is any real existence possible? Is there not constant friction and therefore sorrow? So, our unconscious desire in relationship is not to be hurt, to seek security, refuge; and when that is thwarted, there is no fulfillment. Then I begin to isolate myself. And one of the processes of isolation is domination. And that fear which leads to isolation takes another form also, does it not? There is not only the desire to assert, to dominate, or be submissive, but there is also in this process of isolation the consciousness of being alone, of being lonely. After all, most of us are lonely—I won't use the word *alone*, for that has a different sense. Most of us are isolated, we live in our own world though we may be related; though we may be married and have children, we live in a world of our own. And that is a very lonely world. It is a sorrowful world with an occasional opening of joy and amusement, happiness, and so on; but it is a solitary world. And, to escape from that, we try to be something, we try to assert, we try to dominate. And hence, in order to escape from what we are, domination becomes a means through which we can take flight from ourselves.

So, does not this whole process of domination take place not only when there is the desire to avoid facing that which we are but also when there is a desire to be isolated? If we can look at this process in ourselves, not in a condemnatory spirit, which is merely taking the opposite side, but to understand why we have this extraordinary desire to dominate or to become very subservient, if we can be aware of it without any sense of taking the opposite side, I think we will really experience that state of isolation from which we are trying to run away, and then we shall be able to solve it. That is, if we understand something, we are free of it. It is only when we do not understand that there is fear.

So, can we look at this problem without condemnation? Can we merely observe, silently watch this process at work within ourselves? It can be observed very easily in all our relationships. Just silently watch the whole phenomenon unfold itself. You will find that when there is no condemnation, no justification for your domination, it begins to unfold, there is no hindrance; then you will begin to see all the implications, not only of personal domination, but also of public domination, the domination of one group by another, of one country by another, of one ideology by another, and so on. Self-knowledge is essential for any kind of understanding. And as our relationship is life—without relationship there can be no existence—if you approach it rightly you begin to see this process of domination expressing itself in so many ways, and when you understand this whole process, conscious as well as unconscious, there is a freedom from it. Surely, there must be freedom, and only then is there a possibility of going beyond. Because, a mind that is merely dominating, asserting, tethered to a particular form of belief, to a particular opinion, cannot go further, cannot take a long journey, cannot soar. And so, is it not essential, in understanding oneself, to understand this most difficult and complex problem of domination? It takes such subtle forms, and when it takes a righteous form, it becomes very obstinate. The desire to serve, with the unconscious desire to dominate, is much more difficult to deal with. Can there be love when there is domination? Can you be in relationship to someone whom you say you love, and yet dominate? Then, surely, you are merely using, and when there is using, there is no relationship, is there?

So, to understand this problem, one has to be sensitive to the whole question of domination. Not that you should not dominate, or be submissive, but there should be awareness of this whole problem. To be aware, one must approach it without any condemnation, not taking sides, and it is a very difficult thing to do because most of us are swayed to condemn. And we condemn because we think we understand. We don't. The moment we condemn, we stop understanding. That is one of the easiest ways of brushing things aside—to condemn somebody. But to understand this whole process requires great alertness of mind, and a mind is not alert when it is condemning or justifying or merely identifying itself with what it feels.

So, self-knowledge is a constant discovery from moment to moment, but that discovery is denied if the past throws up an opinion, a barrier; the cumulative action of the mind prevents immediate understanding.

I have several questions, but before I answer them, may I say that those of you who are taking notes should not do so. I will explain why: I am talking to an individual, to you, not to a group. You and I together are experiencing something. You are not taking notes of what I am saying; you are experiencing. We are going together on a journey, and if you are merely concerned with taking notes, you are not really listening. You take it down in order to think it over, you will say, or in order to tell some of your friends who are not here. But, surely, that is not important, is it? What is important is that you and I understand, and to understand, you must give your full attention. And how can you give your full attention when you are taking notes? Please, see the importance of this, and then you will naturally abstain from taking notes. You don't have to be compelled, you don't have to be told. Because, what is important in these meetings is not so much the words but the content behind, the psychological implications, and you cannot understand those unless you give your full attention, your conscious attention.

Question: Is not the experience of the past a help towards freedom and right action in the present? Cannot knowledge be a liberating factor, and not a hindrance?

KRISHNAMURTI: Do we understand the present through the past? Do we understand something through the accumulation of experiences? What do we mean by knowledge? What do we mean by the accumulation of experiences which you say gives you understanding? What do we mean by all that? And what do we mean by past experience? Let's go into it a little bit because it is very important to find out whether the past, which is the accumulation of your memories of incidents, of experiences, will give you understanding of an experience in the present.

Now, what happens when there is an experience? What is the process of it? What is an experience? A challenge and a response, is it not? That is what we call experience. Now, the challenge must always be new; otherwise, it is not a challenge, and do I meet it adequately, fully, completely, if I respond according to my past conditioning? Do I understand it? After all, life is a process of challenge and response. That is the constant process. And there is friction between challenge and response when the response is inadequate—there is sorrow, pain. When the response is equal to the challenge, then there is harmony, then there is integration between challenge and response. Now, can my response to a challenge, if it is based on the various experiences of the past, can such a response be adequate? Can it meet the challenge on the same level? And what is the response? The response is the outcome of the accumulation of various experiences—the memory, the sensation of various experiences, not the experience itself, but the memory and the sensation of the experience. Therefore, it is sensation which meets the challenge, it is memory which meets the challenge. That is what we call accumulated knowledge, isn't it? Therefore, knowledge is always the known, the past, the conditioned; the conditioned meets the unconditioned, the challenge, and therefore there is no relationship between the two; then you translate the challenge according to the conditioned mind, conditioned responses. And is that not a hindrance?

So, how to meet the challenge adequately is the question. If I meet it with my past experiences, I can see very well that it is not adequate. And my mind is the past; my thought is the result of the past. So, can thought meet the challenge—thought, the outcome of knowledge, the result of various experiences, and so on? Can thought meet the challenge? As thought is conditioned, how can it meet it? It can meet it partially, therefore inadequately—and therefore there is friction, pain, and all the rest of it. So, there is a different way of meeting the challenge, is there not? And what is that way, that process? That is what is implied in this question.

First of all, one must see that the challenge is always new—it must be new—otherwise it is not a challenge. A problem is always a new problem because it is varying from moment to moment, and if it does not, it is not a problem. It is static. So, if the challenge is new, the mind must be new; it must come to it afresh and not burdened by the past. But the mind is the past; therefore, the mind must be silent. We do this instinctively, almost without thought, when the problem is very great; when the problem is really new, the mind is silent. It is no longer chattering, no longer burdened by accumulated knowledge. Then, with that newness it responds, and therefore there is a comprehension of the challenge. Surely, that is how all creativeness takes place. Creation, or that sense of creativeness, is from moment to moment; it has no accumulation. You may have the technique for the expression of that creativeness, but that sense of creativeness comes into being only when the mind is absolutely quiet, no longer burdened by the past, by the innumerable experiences, the sensations it has gathered.

So, the adequacy of the response to the challenge depends not on knowledge, not on previous memories, but on its newness, freshness; and that freshness is denied, that quality of renewal is denied when there is a continuity of accumulated experience. Therefore, there must be an ending to each minute, a death to each minute.

Please, perhaps some of you may feel that it is all very well to talk like this, but if you really experiment with it, you will see how extraordinarily, how quickly one understands the challenge, how profoundly one is related to the challenge and not merely responding to it. Surely, one understands only when the mind is capable of renewing itself, being new, fresh—not "open." Then it is like a sieve. And as the problem is always new—sorrow is always new if it is real sorrow, not merely the memory of something else—you must understand it, approach it afresh, you must have a fresh mind. And therefore, knowledge as the accumulation of experiences, individual or collective—such knowledge is an impediment to understanding.

Question: Is my believing in the now well-authenticated fact of survival after death a hindrance to liberation through self-knowledge? Is it not essential to distinguish between belief based on objective evidence and belief arising from inner psychological states?

KRISHNAMURTI: Surely, what is important is not whether there is or is not continuity after death but why we believe. What is the psychological state that demands belief in something? Please let us be very clear. We are not disputing now whether there is or is not life after death. That is another question, and we shall deal with it afterwards, another time. But the question is: What is the compulsion in me, the psychological necessity, to believe? A fact does not demand a belief on your part, surely. The sun sets, the sun rises—that does not demand a belief. Belief arises only when you want to translate the fact according to your desires, to your psychological states, to suit your particular prejudices, vanities, idiosyncrasies. So, what is important is, how you approach the fact—whether it is the fact of life after death, or any other fact. So, the question is not whether there is survival of the individual after death, after his body dies, but why you believe, what is the psychological urge to believe? Surely, that is clear, is it not? So, let us investigate whether that psychological belief is not a hindrance to understanding.

If one is confronted with a fact, there is nothing more to be said about it. It is a fact—the sun sets. But, the problem is why there is this incessant urge in me to believe in something—to believe in God, to believe in an ideology, to believe in a future utopia, to believe in something or other. Why? Why do we believe? Why is there this psychological urge to believe? What would happen if we did not believe, if we merely looked at facts? Can we? It becomes almost impossible, does it not, because we want to translate facts according to our sensations. So, beliefs become sensations, which intervene between the fact and myself. So, belief becomes a hindrance. Are we different from our beliefs? You believe that you are an American or that you are a Hindu; you believe in this and that, in reincarnation—in dozens of things. You are that, are you not? You are what you believe. And why do you believe? Which doesn't mean that I am being atheistic or denying God, and all that stupidity—we are not discussing that. Reality has nothing to do with belief.

So, the problem is, why do you believe? Why the psychological necessity, the investment in belief? Is it not because without belief you are nothing? Without the passport of belief, what are you? Without labeling yourself as something, what are you? If you do not believe in reincarnation, if you do not call yourself this or that, if you have no labels, what are you? Therefore, belief acts as a label, an identifying card; and remove the card, where are you? Is it not that basic fear, that sense of being lost, which necessitates belief? Please, think it over, don't reject it. Let us experience together the things that we are talking about, not merely listen, then go away and carry on with our usual beliefs and nonbeliefs. We are discussing the whole problem of belief.

So, *belief,* the word, has become important. The label has become important. If I did not call myself a Hindu, with all its implications, I would be lost, I would have no identity. But to identify myself with India, as a Hindu, gives me tremendous prestige; it places me, it fixes me, it gives me value. So, belief becomes a necessity when I am psychologically aware, whether consciously or unconsciously, that without the label, I am lost. Then the label becomes important—not what I am, but the label: Christian, Buddhist, Hindu. And we try then to live according to those beliefs, which are self-projected, therefore unreal. Surely, the man who believes in God—his God is a self-projected God, a homemade God, but the man who does not believe in God is still the same. To understand what that is, that supreme something, one must come to it afresh, anew, not tethered to a belief. And I think that is our difficulty—socially, economically, politically, and in our individual relationships—that is, we approach all these problems with a prejudice; and as the problems are vital, living, they can be met adequately only when the mind is new, not tethered to some self-projected, homemade belief.

So, belief becomes a hindrance, obviously, when the desire for belief is not understood, and when it is understood, there is no question of belief. Then you are able to face facts as they are. But even if there is continuity after death, does it solve the problem of living in the present? If I know that I am going to live after this thing dies, have I understood life?—which is now, not tomorrow. And to understand the present, do I have to believe? Surely, to understand the present, which is living, which is not merely a period of time, I must have a mind that is capable of meeting that present completely, giving it full attention. But if my attention is distracted by a belief, surely there is no meeting of the present completely, fully.

So, belief becomes a hindrance to the understanding of reality. As reality is the unknown and belief is the known, how can the known meet the unknown? But our difficulty is, we want the unknown with the known. We don't want to let go of the known because it is too frightening, there is great insecurity, uncertainty; and that is why, to safeguard ourselves, we hedge ourselves about with beliefs. It is only in the state of uncertainty, insecurity, in which there is no sense of refuge, that you discover. That is why you must be lost in order to find. But we don't want to be lost. And to prevent ourselves from getting lost, we have homemade beliefs and gods to protect us. And when the moment of real crisis comes, these gods and beliefs have no value, and hence beliefs are an impediment to him who really wants to discover *what is.*

Question: Why is it that, in spite of all you have said against authority, certain individuals identify themselves with you or with your state of being, and thereby gain authority for themselves? How can the inexperienced prevent themselves from being caught in the net of these individuals? (Laughter)

KRISHNAMURTI: Sir, this is quite an important question because it brings up the matter of our desire to identify ourselves with something. First of all, why do you want to identify yourself with me or with my state of being, or whatever it is? How do you know it? Because I happen to talk or happen to have a name? Surely, you are identifying yourself with something which you have projected. You are not identifying yourself with something that is alive. You are identifying yourself with something which is self-created, and you give it a label; and that label happens to be well-known, or known to a few, and this identification gives you prestige. And then you can exploit people. You know, by calling yourself a friend of somebody or a disciple of somebody, you gain a reflected glory. You go all the way to India to find your god, or your Master, and then identify yourself with that particular cult or that particular idea, and it gives you a certain boost. And then you can exploit the people around you. It is such a stupid process. It gives you a sense of authority, of power, to think that you are the one person that understands; everybody else doesn't understand; you are the nearest disciple—you know, the various forms which we use in order to exploit the blind.

So, the first thing to understand is the desire to exploit people, which means the desire to have for yourself power, position, prestige. And as everybody wants that, the inexperienced as well as the experienced, everybody is caught mutually in the net. We all want to exploit somebody. We don't put it so brutally, but cover it up with soft words. As all of us depend on others, not only for our physical necessities, but also for our psychological necessities, we all use others. If I used you in order to express myself at these meetings, you would like it much more, and I would feel gratified, and we would be mutually exploiting each other, surely. But such a process denies a search for truth, the search for reality. You cannot prevent the inexperienced from being caught in the net of these individuals who claim they understand, who are the "nearest." Sir, perhaps you yourself may be caught in it, because we do not want to be free from all identification. Surely, truth has nothing to do with any individual; it does not depend upon the interpretation of any individual. You have to experience it directly, not through somebody, and it is not a matter of sensation, not a matter of belief. But if we are caught in sensation and belief, then we will use others. So, if one is really seeking truth, honestly, directly, then there is no question of exploiting anybody. But that requires a great deal of honesty; that entails an aloneness, which can be understood only when one has been through loneliness and has gone into it fully, completely. And as most of us do not want to go through the pain, the sorrow, of facing the complications of our psychological states, we are distracted by these exploiters, and we like to be exploited. It requires a great deal of patient awareness, of freedom from identification with anything, to understand, to grasp the whole significance of reality.

August 20, 1949

Twelfth Talk in The Oak Grove

I do not know with what attitude one listens to these talks. I am afraid one is apt to listen to them with the intention of developing a method, a technique, a way; and I think it is very important to understand that tendency because if we are caught in a technique, in a way, in a method, we shall lose entirely the creative release. That is, through the cultivation of a technique, of a method, we shall lose creativeness. And I would like to discuss this morning what are the implications in the cultivation of a technique, a method, a way, and how it dulls the mind, not only at the verbal level, but at the deeper psychological levels. Because, most of us are uncreative. We may paint a little, write a poem or two occasionally, or on rare occasions enjoy beautiful scenery, but for the most part our minds are so caught in the way, in habit, which is a form of technique, that we do not seem to be able to go beyond. The problems of life do not demand a method because they are so vital, they are so alive, that if we approach any one of them with a fixed pattern, a method, a way, we shall totally misunderstand, we shall not adequately meet that problem. And, most of us want a technique, a method, because the problem, the movement of life, is so alive, so vital, so swift, that our minds are incapable of meeting it rapidly, swiftly, with clarity; and we think that we shall be able to meet it if we know *how* to meet it. So, we try to learn from another the how, the method, the technique, the way, the means.

I am not at all sure that most of us here are not concerned with the means. Don't deny it because it is extremely difficult to be free from the desire for a technique in order to achieve. Because, when we have the means, we emphasize the end, the result. We are more concerned with the result than with the understanding of the problem itself, whatever the outcome may be. Why is it that most of us seek a method for happiness, for the right way of thinking, for peace of mind or peace of soul, or whatever it is?

First of all, we carry over the mentality of industrial technology to meet life. That is, we want to meet life efficiently, and to meet it efficiently, we think we need a method; and most religious societies, most teachers, offer a method: how to be peaceful, how to be happy, how to have a tranquil mind, how to concentrate, and so on, and so on. Now, where there is efficiency, there is ruthlessness; and the more you are efficient, the more intolerant, the more enclosed, the more resistant you are. This gradually develops the sense of pride; and pride, obviously, is isolating; it is destructive to understanding. We admire efficient people, and governments throughout the world are concerned with the cultivation of efficiency and the organization of efficiency—efficiency to produce, to kill, to carry out the ideology of a party, of a church, or of a particular religion. We all want to be efficient, and thereby we cultivate the psychological demand for a pattern to which we will conform in order to achieve efficiency. Efficiency, which means the cultivation of a technique, of a method, implies the constant practice of a habit, psychologically. We know about the industrial habits, but very little about the psychological habit of resistance. And I am not at all sure that is not what most of us are seeking—the cultivation of a habit which will make us efficient to meet life, which is so swift. So, if we can understand, not only at the verbal level, but at the deeper, psychological levels, this whole process of the cultivation of technique, method, means, then we shall be able to understand, I think, what it is to be creative. Because, when there is the creative urge, it will find its own technique or its own means of expression. But if we are consumed, taken up, with the cultivation of a technique, obviously we shall never find the other. And why is it that we want technique, the psychological pattern of action which gives us certainty, efficiency, a continuity, a sustained effort? After all, if you must read religious books, most of them, I am pretty sure—not that I have read any of them—contain the way. The way becomes important because the way points the goal; therefore, the goal is separate from the way. Is that so? Is the means different from the end? If, psychologically, you cultivate a habit, a method, a means, a way, a technique, is not the end already projected, already crystallized? Therefore, the means and the end are not separate. That is, you cannot have peace in the world through violent methods, at whatever level. The means and the end are inseparable, and a mind that cultivates a habit will create the end which is already foreseen, already cultivated, already existent, projected by the mind. And that is what most of us want. The technique is only the cultivation of the known, of security, of certainty; and with the known the mind wants to perceive the unknown; therefore, it can never understand it. So, the means matter, not the end, because the end and the means are one. So, the mind which cultivates habit, way, technique, prevents creativeness, that extraordinary sense of spontaneous discovery.

Our problem, then, is not to cultivate a new technique, a new habit, or to discover a new way, but to be altogether free of the psychological search for a technique. If you have something to say, you will say it—the right words will come out. But if you have nothing to say, and you cultivate a marvelous eloquence—you know, go to schools to learn how to speak—then what you project, what you say, will have very little meaning.

So, why is it that most of us are seeking a method, a technique? Obviously, we want to be sure, to be certain not to go wrong; we do not want to experiment, to discover. The practice of a technique prevents discovery from moment to moment because truth, or what you will, is from moment to moment—it is not a continuous, increasing, growing arc. So, can we be free from the psychological urge to be sure, to cultivate a habit, a practice? These are all resistances, defenses; and with this defensive mechanism, we want to understand something which is vital, swift. Now, if we can see that, see the implications in the cultivation or the search for the means, if we can see its psychological significance—not merely the superficial or industrial significance, which is obvious—if we can understand it fully as I am explaining it and as you and I are experimenting with it, then perhaps we can discover what it means to be free of it. And, is it possible to be free from the desire to be secure psychologically? Technique, means, offers security. You run in a groove, and then there is no going right or wrong; you are merely functioning automatically. Is it possible for a mind which has been trained for centuries to cultivate habit, means—is it possible for such a mind to be free? It is possible only when we realize the whole significance of habit, the total process of its momentum. That is, as I am talking about it, silently observe your own process, be aware of the cumulative effect of all your desires to succeed, to gain, to achieve, which denies understanding. Because, the understanding of life, of this total process, does not come through desire—there must be a spontaneous meeting with it. If one can see this whole psychological process as well as its outward expression—how all the governments, all society, all the various communities demand efficiency with all its ruthlessness—then perhaps the mind will begin to break away from its accustomed habits. Then it will really be free, no longer seeking a means. Then, when the mind is quiet, there comes that creative something, which is creation itself. It will find its own expression; you don't have to choose an expression for it. If you are a painter, you will paint. It is that creative understanding that is vital, that gives grace, that gives happiness—not the technical expression of something which you have learned.

So, reality, or God, or what you will, is something that cannot come through a technique, through a means, through long, determined practice and discipline. It is not a course laid out with a known end. One must enter the uncharted sea. There must be an aloneness. Aloneness implies no means. You are not alone when you have a means. There must be complete nakedness, emptiness of all these accumulated practices, hopes, pleasures, desires for security—which are all consistently maintaining a means, a method, a technique. Then only is there the other, and then the problem is solved. A man who is dying from moment to moment, and therefore renewing, is able to meet life. It is not that he is separate from life; he is life.

Question: How can one be aware of an emotion without naming or labeling it? If I am aware of a feeling, I seem to know what that feeling is almost immediately after it arises. Or, do you mean something different when you say, "Do not name"?

KRISHNAMURTI: This is a very difficult problem, and it requires a great deal of thinking, being aware of the whole content of it; and as I explain it, I hope you will follow, not merely verbally, but through experiencing it. I feel if we can understand this question fully, deeply, we shall have understood a great deal. I shall try to approach it from different directions, if I can in the given time, because it is a very intricate and subtle problem. It requires all your attention because you are experiencing what we are discussing, not merely listening and trying to experience it afterwards. There is no afterwards—either you experience now, always now, or never.

Now, why do we name anything? Why do we give a label to a flower, to a person, to a feeling? Either to communicate one's feeling, to describe the flower, and so on, and so on, or to identify oneself with that feeling. Is it not so? I name something, a feeling, to communicate it. "I am angry." Or, I identify myself with that feeling in order to strengthen it, to dissolve it, or to do something about it. That is, we give a name to something, to a rose, to communicate it to others; or by giving it a name, we think we have understood it. We say, "That is a rose," rapidly look at it, and go on. By giving it a name, we think we have understood it; we have classified it and think that thereby we have understood the whole content and the beauty of that flower.

Now, when not merely to communicate, what happens when we give a name to a flower, to anything? Please follow it, think it out with me. Though I may talk aloud, you also are participating in the talking. By giving a name to something, we have merely put it into a category, and we think we have understood it; we don't look at it more closely. But, if we do not give it a name, we are forced to look at it. That is, we approach the flower, or whatever it is, with a newness, with a new quality of examination; we look at it as though we had never looked at it before. Naming is a very convenient way of disposing of people—by saying they are Germans, they are Japanese, they are Americans, they are Hindus, you know—give them a label, and destroy the label. But if you do not give a label to people, you are forced to look at them, and then it is much more difficult to kill somebody. You can destroy the label with a bomb and feel righteous. But if you do not give a label, and must therefore look at the individual thing—whether it is a man or a flower or an incident or an emotion—then you are forced to consider your relationship with it, and the action following. So, terming, or giving a label, is a very convenient way of disposing of anything, of denying, condemning, or justifying it. That is one side of the question.

Then, what is the core from which you name, what is the center which is always naming, choosing, labeling? We all feel there is a center, a core, do we not, from which we are acting, from which we are judging, from which we are naming. What is that center, that core? Some would like to think it is a spiritual essence, God, or what you will. So, let us find out what is that core, that center, which is naming, terming, judging. Surely, that core is memory, isn't it? A series of sensations, identified and enclosed—the past, given life through the present. That core, that center, feeds on the present through naming, labeling, remembering. I hope you are following this. We will see presently, as we unfold it, that as long as this center, this core exists, there can be no understanding. It is only with the dissipation of this core that there is understanding. Because, after all, that core is memory—memory of various experiences which have been given names, labels, identifications. With those named and labeled experiences, from that center, there is acceptance and rejection, determination to be or not to be, according to the sensations, pleasures, and pains of the memory of experience. So, that center is the word. If you do not name that center, is there a center? That is, if you do not think in terms of words, if you do not use words, can you think? Thinking comes into being through verbalization, or, verbalization begins to respond to thinking. So, the center, the core, is the memory of innumerable experiences of pleasure and pain, verbalized. Watch it in yourself, please, and you will see that words have become much more important, labels have become much more important, than the substance; and we live on words. Please, don't deny it, don't say it is right or wrong. We are exploring. If you merely explore one side of a thing or stay put in one place, you won't understand the whole content of it. Therefore, let us approach it from different angles.

For us, words like *truth*, *God*, have become very important—or the feeling which those words represent. When we say the words *American*, *Christian*, *Hindu*, or the word *anger*, we are the word representing the feeling. But we don't know what that feeling is because the word has become important. When you call yourself a Buddhist, a Christian, what does the word mean, what is the meaning behind that word which you have never examined? Our center, the core, is the word, the label. If the label does not matter, if what matters is that which is behind the label, then you are able to inquire; but if you are identified with the label and stuck with it, you cannot proceed. And we are identified with the label: the house, the form, the name, the furniture, the bank account, our opinions, our stimulants, and so on, and so on. We are all those things—those things being represented by a name. The things have become important, the names, the labels; and therefore the center, the core, is the word.

Now, if there is no word, no label, there is no center, is there? There is a dissolution, there is an emptiness—not the emptiness of fear, which is quite a different thing. There is a sense of being as nothing, and because you have removed all the labels, or rather, because you have understood why you give labels to feelings and ideas, you are completely new, are you not? There is no center from which you are acting. The center, which is the word, has been dissolved. The label has been taken away, and where are you as the center? You are there, but there has been a transformation. And that transformation is a little bit frightening; therefore, you do not proceed with what is still involved in it; you are already beginning to judge it, to decide whether you like or don't like it. You don't proceed with the understanding of what is coming, but you are already judging, which means that you have a center from which you are acting. Therefore, you stay fixed the moment you judge; the words *like* and *dislike* become important. But what happens when you do not name? You look at emotion, at sensation, more directly and therefore have quite a different relationship to it, just as you have to a flower when you do not name it. You are forced to look at it anew. When you do not name a group of people, you are compelled to look at each individual face and not treat them all as the mass. Therefore, you are much more alert, much more observing, more understanding, you have a deeper sense of pity, love; but if you treat them all as the mass, it is over.

If you do not label, you have to regard every feeling as it arises. Now, when you label, is the feeling different from the label? Or, does the label awaken the feeling? Please, think it over. When we label, most of us intensify the feeling. The feeling and the naming are instantaneous. If there were a gap between naming and feeling, then you could find out if the feeling is different from the naming, and then you would be able to deal with the feeling without naming it. Is this all becoming rather too difficult? I'm glad. I'm afraid it should be difficult. (Laughter)

The problem is this, is it not, how to be free from a feeling which we term, such as anger? Not subjugate it, not sublimate it, not suppress it, which are all idiotic and immature; but how to be really free from it? And to be really free from it, we have to discover whether the word is more important than the feeling. The word *anger* has more significance than the feeling itself. And, to find that out, there must be a gap between the feeling and the naming. That is one part.

Then, if I do not name a feeling, that is, if thought is not functioning merely because of words, or if I do not think in terms of words, images, or symbols—which most of us do—then what happens? Surely, the mind, then, is not merely the observer. That is, when the mind is not thinking in terms of words, symbols, images, there is no thinker separate from the thought, which is the word. Then the mind is quiet, is it not?—not made quiet, it *is* quiet. And, when the mind is really quiet, then the feelings that arise can be dealt with immediately. It is only when we give names to feelings and thereby strengthen them that the feelings have continuity; they are stored up in the center from which we give further labels, either to strengthen or to communicate them.

So, when the mind is no longer the center as the thinker made up of words, of past experiences—which are all memories, labels, stored and put in categories, in pigeonholes—when it is not doing any of those things, then, obviously the mind is quiet. It is no longer bound; it has no longer a center as the 'me'—my house, my achievement, my work—which are still words, giving impetus to feeling, and thereby strengthening memory. When none of those things is happening, the mind is very quiet. That state is not negation. On the contrary, to come to that point, you have to go through all this, which is an enormous undertaking; it is not merely learning a few sets of words and repeating them like a schoolboy—not to name, not to name. To follow through all its implications, to experience it, to see how the mind works and thereby come to that point when you are no longer naming, which means that there is no longer a center apart from the thought—surely, this whole process is real meditation. And when the mind is really tranquil, then it is possible for that which is immeasurable to come into being. Any other process, any other search for reality, is merely self-projected, homemade, and therefore unreal. But this process is arduous, and it means that the mind has to be constantly aware of everything that is inwardly happening to it. To come to this point, there can be no judgment or justification from the beginning to the end—not that this is an end. There is no end because there is something extraordinary still going on. There is no promise. It is for you to experiment, to go into yourself deeper and deeper and deeper, so that all the many layers of the center are dissolved, and you can do it rapidly, or lazily. But it is extraordinarily interesting to watch the process of the mind—how it depends on words, how the words stimulate memory, resuscitate the dead experience and give life to it. And, in that process the mind is living, either in the future or in the past. Therefore, words have an enormous significance, neurologically as well as psychologically. And please, don't learn all this from me or from a book. You cannot learn it from another or find it in a book. What you learn or find in a book won't be the real. But you can experience it, you can watch yourself in action, watch yourself thinking, see how you think, how rapidly you are naming the feeling as it arises—and watching this whole process frees the mind from its center. Then the mind, being quiet, can receive that which is eternal.

Question: What is the right relationship, if any, between the individual and the collective, the mass?

KRISHNAMURTI: Do you think there is any relationship between the individual and the mass? Between you and the collective? The state, the government, would like us to be merely the citizen, the collective. But we are man first and afterwards the citizen—not the citizen first and man afterwards. The state would like us not to be the man, the individual, but the mass. Because, the more we are the citizen, the greater our capacity, the greater our efficiency—we become the tool which the bureaucrats, the authoritarian states, the governments, want us to be.

So, we must distinguish between the private individual and the citizen, the man and the mass. The individual, the man, has his private feelings, hopes, failures, disappointments, longings, sensations, pleasures. And there is the point of view which wants to reduce all that to the collective, for it is very simple to deal with the collective. Pass an edict, and it is done. Give a sanction, and it is followed. So, the more organizations there are, and the more efficiently they are organized, the more the individual is denied, whether by the church or by the state—we are then all Christians, all Hindus, not individuals. And with that mentality, in that state, which most of us want, has the individual reality any place? We recognize there must be collective action. But does collective action come into being with the denial of the individual? Is the individual in opposition to the collective? Is the collective not fictitious, the mass not unreal? Seeing the difficulty of dealing with the individual, we create the opposite, the mass, and then try to establish a relationship between the individual and the collective. If the individual is intelligent, he will cooperate. Surely, that is our problem, isn't it? We first create the mass and then try to find the relationship of the individual with the mass. But let us find out if the mass is real. The group of us here can be made into the collective by hypnotism, by propaganda; through various means we can be aroused to act collectively for an ideology, for a state, for a church, for an idea, and so on, and so on. That is, collective action can be externally imposed, directed, or compelled through fear, reward, and all the rest of it. Having produced that condition, we try to establish the relationship of the individual, which is the actual, with that which is produced. Whereas, is it not possible for the individual to lose his sense of separateness through definite understanding of all the implications of separateness, and therefore act cooperatively? But, as that is so difficult, states, governments, churches, organized religions, force or entice the individual to become the corporate. What place has the individual in history? What does it matter what you and I do? There is the historical movement going on. What place has reality with this movement? Probably none at all. You and I don't count at all. This movement is gigantic; it is going on; it has the momentum of centuries, and it will go on. What is your relationship, as an individual, to this movement? Whatever you do, will it affect it? Can you stop a war because you are a pacifist? You are a pacifist, not because there is a war, not because you have found a relationship with it, but because in itself war is wrong and you feel you cannot kill, and there the matter ends. But to try to find a relationship between your understanding, your intelligence, and this monstrous, logical movement of war seems to me utterly futile. I can be an individual and yet see what creates antisocial feelings in me and so be free of separative actions. I may have a little property; surely, that doesn't make me a separative entity. But it is the whole psychological state to be separate, to be isolated, to be something—it is that which is calamitous, which is so destructive. And, in order to overcome that, we have all the external sanctions and impositions and edicts.

Question: What is the significance of pain and suffering?

KRISHNAMURTI: When you suffer, when you have pain, what is the significance of it? Physical pain has one significance, but probably we mean psychological pain and suffering, which has quite a different significance at different levels. What is the significance of suffering? Why do you want to find the significance of suffering? Not that it has no significance—we are going to find out. But why do you want to find it? Why do you want to find out why you suffer? When you put that question to yourself, "Why do I suffer?" and are looking for the cause of suffering, are you not escaping from suffering? When I seek the significance of suffering, am I not avoiding, evading it, running away from it? The fact is, I am suffering; but the moment I bring the mind to operate upon it and say, "Now, why?" I have already diluted the intensity of suffering. In other words, we want suffering to be diluted, alleviated, put away, explained away. Surely, that doesn't give an understanding of suffering. So, if I am free from that desire to run away from it, then I begin to understand what is the content of suffering.

Now, what is suffering? A disturbance, isn't it, at different levels—at the physical and at the different levels of the subconscious. It is an acute form of disturbance, which I don't like. My son is dead, I have built around him all my hopes—or around my daughter, my husband, what you will. I have enshrined him with all the things I wanted him to be. And I have kept him as my companion—you know, all that—and suddenly he is gone. So, there is a disturbance, isn't there? That disturbance I call suffering. Please, I am not being harsh; we are examining, trying to understand it. If I don't like that suffering, then I say, "Why am I suffering?" "I loved him so much." "He was this." "I had that." And I try to escape in words, in labels, in beliefs, as most of us do. They act as a narcotic. But, if I do not do that, what happens? I am simply aware of suffering. I don't condemn it, I don't justify it—I am suffering. Then I can follow its movement, can't I? Then I can follow the whole content of what it means—"I follow" in the sense of trying to understand something.

So, what does it mean? What is it that is suffering? Not why there is suffering, not what is the cause of suffering, but what is actually happening? I do not know if you see the difference. Then I am simply aware of suffering, not as apart from me, not as an observer watching suffering—it is part of me—that is, the whole of me is suffering. Then I am able to follow its movement, see where it leads. Surely, if I do that, then it opens up, does it not? Then I see that I have laid emphasis on the 'me'—not on the person whom I love. He only acted to cover me from my misery, from my loneliness, from my misfortune. As I am not something, I hoped he would be that. So, that has gone; I am left, I am lost, I am lonely. Without him, I am nothing. So I cry. It is not that he is gone, but that I am left. I am alone. To come to that point is very difficult, isn't it? It is difficult to really recognize it and not merely say, "I am alone, and how am I to get rid of that loneliness?" which is another form of escape, but to be conscious of it, to remain with it, to see its movement. I am only taking this as an example. So, gradually, if I allow it to unfold, to open up, I see that I am suffering because I am lost; I am being called to give my attention to something which I am not willing to look at; something is being forced upon me which I am reluctant to see and to understand. And there are innumerable people to help me to escape—thousands of so-called religious people with their beliefs and dogmas, hopes and fantasies—"It is karma, it is God's will," you know, all giving me a way out. But if I can stay with it and not put it away from me, not try to circumscribe or deny it, then what happens? What is the state of my mind when it is thus following the movement of suffering? Now, please follow this, continuing what we discussed previously.

Is *suffering* merely a word or an actuality? If it is an actuality, and not just a word, then the word has no meaning now. So, there is merely the feeling of intense pain. With regard to what? With regard to an image, to an experience, to something which you have or have not. If you have it, you call it pleasure; if you haven't, it is pain. So, pain, sorrow, is in relationship to something. Is that something merely a verbalization or an actuality? I don't know if you are following all this. That is, when sorrow exists, it exists only in relationship to something. It cannot exist by itself—as fear cannot exist by itself, but in relationship to something: to an individual, to an incident, to a feeling. Now, you are fully aware of the suffering. Is that suffering apart from you, and therefore you are merely the observer who perceives the suffering, or, is that suffering part of you? Surely, we are trying to understand what suffering, pain, is; we are trying to go into it fully, not just superficially.

Now, when there is no observer who is suffering, is the suffering different from you? You are the suffering, are you not? You are not apart from the pain—you are the pain. Now, what happens? Please, follow it up. There is no labeling, there is no giving it a name and thereby brushing it aside—you are merely that pain, that feeling, that sense of agony. Then, when you are that, what happens? When you do not name it, when there is no fear with regard to it, is the center related to it? If the center is related to it, then it is afraid of it. Then it must act and do something about it. But if the center is that, then what do you do? There is nothing to be done, is there? Please, it is not mere acceptance. Follow it, and you will see. If you are that, and you are not accepting it, not labeling it, not pushing it aside—if you are that thing, what happens? Do you say you suffer then? Surely, a fundamental transformation has taken place. Then there is no longer "I suffer," because there is no center to suffer; and the center suffers because we have never examined what the center is. We just live from word to word, from reaction to reaction. We never say, "Let me see what that thing is that suffers." And you cannot see by enforcement, by discipline. You must look with interest, with spontaneous comprehension. Then you will see that the thing we call suffering, pain, the thing that we avoid, and the discipline, all have gone. As long as I have no relationship to the thing as outside of me, the problem is not, but the moment I establish a relationship with it outside me, the problem is. As long as I treat suffering as something outside—I suffer because I lost my brother, because I have no money, because of this or that—I establish a relationship to it, and that relationship is fictitious. But if I am that thing, if I see the fact, then the whole thing is transformed, it all has a different meaning. Then there is full attention, integrated attention; and that which is completely regarded is understood and dissolved, and so there is no fear; and therefore the word *sorrow* is nonexistent.

August 21, 1949

Thirteenth Talk in The Oak Grove

For the past few weeks we have been discussing the importance of self-knowledge and how it is essential, before there can be any action, before there can be right thinking, that one should know oneself—not only the superficial, conscious mind, but also the hidden, the unconscious. And those of you who have tried and experimented with what we have been discussing must have come upon a very curious thing in experimenting: that through self-knowledge one accentuates self-consciousness. That is, one becomes more concerned about oneself. Most of us are caught in that, and one doesn't seem able to go beyond. And I would like to discuss this evening why it is that most of us contain ourselves, limit ourselves in self-consciousness and are not capable of going beyond. Because, there is a great deal in it which needs further explanation and discussion, but, before I go into that, I would like to point out one or two things.

First of all, please don't bother to take photographs. You know, all this, what one is talking about, is very serious, at least for me. This is not meant for autograph hunters. You wouldn't be thinking of taking pictures and asking for autographs if you were really very, very serious. Also, if I may say so, it is so infantile, immature. And the other thing I would like to point out is that, as I have already said before, you and I are trying to experiment together here, to feel our way into the problems that confront us. And that is impossible if you are anxiously interested in taking notes of what I am saying. You should be able to deal directly with the problem, not think it over afterwards, because when you are really experiencing something, you don't take notes. You take notes when you are not experiencing, when you are not really thinking, feeling, experimenting. But if you are really experiencing, going along with what is being said, then there is no time or occasion to take notes. Surely, experiencing does not come through words. That is only furthering sensation, but there is an experiencing if we can go more and more deeply and immediately into what is being said. So, it would be good if each one of us were serious enough to experiment with what is being said and not merely postpone or be distracted from the central issue.

As I was saying, in the search of self-knowledge, in the exploration of it, one gets caught in self-consciousness, one accentuates, emphasizes the 'me' more and more; and how is it that that happens? As we have said during all these talks, what is important is the freedom from the 'me', the 'mine', the self, because, obviously, a man who does not know the whole process and content of the self is incapable of right thinking—which is axiomatic. But yet we shun, we avoid the understanding of the self, and we think that by avoiding it, we shall be able to deal with the self or forget it more easily. Whereas, if we are capable of looking at it more intensely, more attentively, there is the danger of becoming more and more self-conscious. And is it possible to go beyond?

Now, to understand that, we have to go into the problem of sincerity. Simplicity is not sincerity. One who is sincere can never be simple because the one who is trying to be sincere has always the desire to fashion or to approximate himself to an idea. And one needs extraordinary simplicity to understand oneself—the simplicity which comes when there is no desire to attain, to achieve, to gain something; and the moment we desire to gain something through self-knowledge, there is self-consciousness in which we get caught, which is a fact. If you do not merely examine what the various psychologists and saints have said but experiment with yourself, you will come to a point when you will see that unless there is not sincerity but complete simplicity, you cannot proceed. Self-consciousness arises only when there is a desire to achieve something—happiness, reality, or even understanding—through self-knowledge. That is, when there is a desire for achievement through self-knowledge, there is self-consciousness, which prevents going further into the problem. And as most of us, especially so-called religious people, try to be sincere, we have to understand this question, this word *sincerity*. Because sincerity develops will, and will is essentially desire. You have to be sincere in order to approximate yourself to an idea, and hence the pattern and the carrying out of that pattern become most important. To carry out a pattern, you must have will, which denies simplicity. Simplicity comes into being only when there is freedom from the desire to achieve and when you are willing to go into self-knowledge without any end in view. And I think that that is really important to think over. What is required is not sincerity, not the exertion of will to be or not to be something, but to understand oneself from moment to moment, spontaneously, as things arise. How can you be spontaneous when you are approximating yourself to something?

When do you discover anything in yourself? Only at unexpected moments, when you are not consciously, deliberately, shaping your mind, your thoughts, and feelings; only when there is a spontaneous response to the incidents of life. Then, according to those responses, you find out. But a man who is trying to be sincere to an idea can never be simple, and therefore there can never be full, complete self-knowledge. And self-knowledge can be discovered more fully, more deeply and widely, only when there is passive awareness, which is not an exertion of will. Will and sincerity go together; simplicity and passive awareness are companions. Because, when one is passively aware, deeply, then there is a possibility of immediate understanding. As we discussed, when you want to understand something, if you are all the time consumed with the desire to understand it, making an effort to understand it, naturally there is no understanding. But if there is a passive, alert awareness, then there is a possibility of understanding. Similarly, to understand oneself ever more deeply and widely, there must be passive awareness, which is extremely difficult, for most of us either condemn or justify. We never look at anything passively. We project ourselves upon the subject—a painting, a poem, or anything else—especially where we are concerned. We are incapable of looking at ourselves without any condemnation or justification, and that is essential, surely, if we are to understand more and more widely and deeply. As most of us, in the search of self-knowledge, get caught in self-consciousness, the danger is that, being caught, we make that in which we are caught the most important thing. To go beyond self-consciousness, there must be freedom from the desire to achieve a result. Because, after all, the attainment of a result is what the mind wants; it wants to be secure, to be safe, and therefore projects, out of its own momentum, an image, an idea, in which it takes shelter. And to avoid all the illusions that the mind creates, to avoid being caught in them, is possible only when there is no desire for a result, only when one is living from moment to moment.

Question: Would you please explain what you mean by dying daily?

KRISHNAMURTI: Why is it that we are so frightened of death? Because death is the unknown. We don't know what is going to happen tomorrow; actually, we don't know what is going to happen. Though we build for tomorrow, actually, realistically, we don't know; and so there is always the fear of tomorrow. So, fear is the guiding factor, which is the incapacity to meet the unknown, and therefore we continue taking today over into tomorrow. That is what we are doing, is it not? We give continuity to our idiosyncrasies, to our jealousies, to our stupidities, to our memories; wherever we are, we carry them over from day to day. Don't we do that? And so there is no dying, there is only an assurance of continuity. That is a fact. Our names, our actions, the things that we do, our property, the desire to be—all these give a continuity. Now, that which continues obviously cannot renew. There can be renewal only when there is an ending. If you are the same tomorrow as you are today, how can there be renewal? That is, if you are attached to an idea, to an experience which you have had yesterday and which you desire to continue tomorrow, there is no renewal; there is a continuity of the memory of the sensation of that experience, but the experience itself is dead. There is only the memory of the sensation of that experience, and it is that sensation you want to continue. And where there is continuity, obviously there is no renewal. And yet it is what most of us want—we want to continue. We want to continue with our worries, with our pleasures, with our memories; and so most of us are actually uncreative. There is no possibility of a rebirth, a renewal. Whereas, if each day we died, finished at the end of the day all our worries, all our jealousies, all our idiocies and vanities, our cruel gossip—you know, the whole business—if each day we came to an end and did not carry all that over into tomorrow, then there would be a possibility of renewal, would there not?

So, why do we accumulate? And what is it that we accumulate, apart from furniture and a few other things? What is it that we accumulate? Ideas, words, and memories, do we not? And with these we live—we are those things. With those things we want to live, we want to continue. But if we did not continue, there would be a possibility of a new understanding, a new opening. This is not metaphysical, this is not something fantastic. Experiment with it yourself and you will see that an extraordinary thing takes place. How the mind worries over a problem, over and over and over again, day after day! Such a mind is incapable, obviously, of seeing something new, is it not? We are caught in our beliefs—religious, sociological, or any other form of belief—and those beliefs are oneself. Beliefs are words, and the word becomes important, and so we live in a sensation which we want to continue, and therefore there is no renewal. But if one does not continue, if one does not give continuity to a worry, but thinks it out, goes into it fully and dissolves it, then one's mind is fresh to meet something else anew. But the difficulty is that most of us want to live in the past, in past memories, or in the future, future hopes, future longings—which indicates that the present is not significant, and therefore we live yesterday and tomorrow, and give continuity to both. If one actually experiments with this thing, really dying each day, each minute, to everything that one has accumulated, then there is a possibility of immortality. Immortality is not continuity, which is merely time; there is continuity only to memory, to ideas, to words. But, when there is freedom from continuity, then there is a state of timelessness, which cannot be understood if you are merely the result of continuity. Therefore, it is important to die every minute and to be reborn again—not as you were yesterday. This is really very important, if you would go into it seriously. Because, in this there is a possibility of creation, of transformation. And most of our lives are so unhappy because we don't know how to renew; we are worn out, we are destroyed by yesterday, by yesterday's memories, misfortunes, unhappiness, incidents, failures. Yesterday burdens our minds and hearts, and with that burden we want to understand something which cannot be understood within the limits of time. And that is why it is essential, if one would be creative in the deep sense of that word, that there be death to all the accumulations of every minute. This is not fantastic, this is not some mystical experience. One can experience this directly, simply, when one understands the whole significance of how time as continuity prevents creativeness.

Question: How does a truth, as you have said, when repeated, become a lie? What really is a lie? Why is it wrong to lie? Is this not a profound and subtle problem on all the levels of our existence?

KRISHNAMURTI: There are two questions in this, so let us examine the first, which is: When a truth is repeated, how does it become a lie? What is it that we repeat? Can you repeat an understanding? I understand something. Can I repeat that? I can verbalize it, I can communicate it; but the experience is not what is repeated, surely. But we get caught in the word and miss the significance of the experience. If you had an experience, can you repeat it? You may want to repeat it, you may have the desire for its repetition, for its sensation, but once you have an experience, it is over, it cannot be repeated. What can be repeated is the sensation and the corresponding word that gives life to that sensation. And as, unfortunately, most of us are propagandists, we are caught in the repetition of the word. So, we live on words, and the truth is denied.

Take, for example, the feeling of love. Can you repeat it? When you hear, "Love your neighbor," is that a truth to you? It is truth, only when you love your neighbor, and that love cannot be repeated, but only the word. Yet most of us are happy, content, with the repetition, "Love your neighbor," or "Don't be greedy." So, the truth of another or an actual experience which you have had merely through repetition does not become a reality. On the contrary, repetition prevents reality. Merely repeating certain ideas is not reality.

Now, the difficulty in this is to understand the question without thinking in terms of the opposite. A lie is not something opposed to truth. One can see the truth of what is being said, not in opposition, or in contrast, as a lie or a truth; but just see that most of us repeat without understanding. For instance, we have been discussing "not naming." Many of you will repeat it, I am sure of it, thinking that it is the "truth." You will never repeat an experience if it is a direct experience. You may communicate it, but when it is a real experience, the sensations behind it are gone, the emotional content behind the words is entirely dissipated.

Take, for example, the question, which we discussed a few weeks ago, that the thinker and the thought are one. It may be a truth to you because you have directly experienced it. But if I repeated it, it would not be true, would it?—true, not as opposed to the false, please. It wouldn't be actual, it would be merely repetitive, and therefore would have no significance. But you see, by repetition, we create a dogma, we build a church, and in that we take refuge. The word, and not truth, becomes the "truth." The word is not the thing. But to us, the thing is the word, and that is why one has to be so extremely careful not to repeat something which one does not really understand. If you understand something, you can communicate it, but the words and the memory have lost their emotional significance. Thereby, in ordinary conversation, one's outlook, one's vocabulary, changes.

So, as we are seeking truth through self-knowledge and are not mere propagandists, it is important to understand this. Because, through repetition one mesmerizes oneself by words or by sensations. One gets caught in illusions. And, to be free of that, it is imperative to experience directly; and to experience directly, one must be aware of oneself in the process of repetition, of habits, of words, of sensations. That awareness gives one an extraordinary freedom so that there can be a renewal, a constant experiencing, a newness.

The other question is, "What really is a lie? Why is it wrong to lie? Is this not a profound and subtle problem on all the levels of our existence?" What is a lie? A contradiction, isn't it, a self-contradiction. One can consciously contradict, or unconsciously; it can either be deliberate, or unconscious; the contradiction can be either very, very subtle, or obvious. And when the cleavage in contradiction is very great, then either one becomes unbalanced, or one realizes the cleavage and sets about to mend it. Now, to understand this problem, what is a lie and why we lie, one has to go into it without thinking in terms of an opposite. Can we look at this problem of contradiction in ourselves without trying not to be contradictory? I don't know if I am making myself clear. Our difficulty in examining this question is, isn't it, that we so readily condemn a lie, but to understand it, can we think of it not in terms of truth and falsehood but of what is contradiction? Why do we contradict? Why is there contradiction in ourselves? Is there not an attempt to live up to a standard, up to a pattern—a constant approximation of ourselves to a pattern, a constant effort to be something, either in the eyes of another or in our own eyes? There is a desire, is there not, to conform to a pattern, and when one is not living up to that pattern, there is a contradiction.

Now, why do we have a pattern, a standard, an approximation, an idea which we are trying to live up to? Why? Obviously, to be secure, to be safe, to be popular, to have a good opinion of ourselves, and so on, and so on. There is the seed of contradiction. As long as we are approximating ourselves to something, trying to be something, there must be contradiction; therefore, there must be this cleavage between the false and the true. I think this is important, if you will quietly go into it. Not that there is not the false and the true, but why the contradiction in ourselves? Is it not because we are attempting to be something—to be noble, to be good, to be virtuous, to be creative, to be happy, and so on, and so on? And, in the very desire to be something, there is a contradiction not to be something else. And it is this contradiction that is so destructive. If one is capable of complete identification with something, with this or with that, then contradiction ceases; but when we do identify ourselves completely with something, there is self-enclosure, there is a resistance, which brings about unbalance—which is an obvious thing.

So, why is there contradiction in ourselves? I have done something, and I don't want it to be discovered; I have thought something which doesn't come up to the mark, which puts me in a state of contradiction, and I don't like it. So, where there is an approximation, there must be fear, and it is this fear that contradicts. Whereas, if there is no becoming, no attempting to be something, then there is no sense of fear, then there is no contradiction, then there is no lie in us at any level, consciously or unconsciously—something to be suppressed, something to be shown. And as most of our lives are a matter of moods and poses, depending on our moods, we pose—which is a contradiction. When the mood disappears, we are what we are. It is this contradiction that is really important, not whether you tell a polite white lie or not. As long as this contradiction exists, there must be a superficial existence and therefore superficial fears which have to be guarded—and then white lies, you know, all the rest of it follows. We can look at this question, not asking what is a lie and what is truth, but without taking the opposites, go into the problem of contradiction in ourselves—which is extremely difficult. Because, as we depend so much on our sensations, most of our lives are contradictory. We depend on memories, on opinions; we have so many fears which we want to cover up—all these create contradiction in ourselves, and when that contradiction becomes unbearable, one goes off one's head. One wants peace, and everything that one does creates war, not only in the family, but outside. And, instead of understanding what creates conflict, we only try to become more and more one thing or the other, the opposite, thereby creating greater cleavage.

So, is it possible to understand why there is contradiction in ourselves—not only superficially, but much more deeply, psychologically? First of all, is one aware that one lives a contradictory life? We want peace, and we are nationalists; we want to avoid social misery, and yet each one of us is so individualistic, limited, self-enclosed. So we are constantly living in contradiction. Why? Is it not because we are slaves to sensation? This is neither to be denied or accepted. It requires a great deal of understanding of the implications of sensation, which are desires. We want so many things all in contradiction with one another. We are so many conflicting masks; we take on a mask when it suits us and deny it when something else is more profitable, more pleasurable. It is this state of contradiction that creates the lie. And, in opposition to that, we create "truth." But, surely, truth is not the opposite of lie. That which has an opposite is not truth. The opposite contains its own opposite; therefore, it is not truth, and to understand this problem very profoundly, one must be aware of all the contradictions in which we live. When I say, "I love you," with it goes jealousy, envy, anxiety, fear—which is a contradiction. And it is this contradiction that must be understood, and one can understand it only when one is aware of it, aware without any condemnation or justification—merely looking at it. And to look at it passively, one has to understand all the processes of justification and condemnation. So, it is not an easy problem to look passively at something, but in understanding that, one begins to understand the whole process of the ways of one's feeling and thinking. And, when one is aware of the full significance of contradiction in oneself, it does bring an extraordinary change; you are yourself then, not something which you are trying to be. You are no longer following an ideal, seeking happiness. You are what you are, and from there you can proceed. Then there is no possibility of contradiction.

Question: I feel sincerely that I desire to help people, and I think I can help; but whatever I say or do to another is interpreted as interference and as the desire to domineer. So I am thwarted by others and feel myself frustrated. Why does this happen to me?

KRISHNAMURTI: When we say we want to help another, what do we mean by that word? Like the word *service*—what does it mean? You go to the gas station, the attendant serves you, and you pay him, but he uses the word *serve*, like all the business people. All the commercial people use that word. Now those who wish to serve—have they not also the same spirit? They want to help if you also give them something; that is, they want to help you in order to fulfill themselves. And when you resist, you begin to criticize, they feel frustrated. In other words, they are not really helping you. Through help, through service, they are fulfilling themselves. In other words, they are seeking self-fulfillment under the guise of help and service—which, when thwarted, gets angry, begins to gossip, begins to tear you to pieces. This is an obvious fact, is it not? And can you not help and serve another without asking anything?—which is most difficult, which is not easy; you cannot just say, "It can be done." When you give something to somebody, a few hundred dollars, haven't you something with which you are tied; don't you tie yourself with that hundred dollars; hasn't it a tail? Can you give and forget? This giving from the heart is real generosity. But the generosity of the hand has always something to be held, and it holds. Similarly, those who want to help, when they are prevented for various reasons, feel frustrated, feel lost; they won't stand criticism; it is misrepresented, mistranslated, misinterpreted, because through their anxiety to help you, they are fulfilling themselves.

So, the problem is, is it not, is there self-fulfillment? That is the next question. Is there self-fulfillment? Is not that word *self-fulfillment* a contradiction? When you want to fulfill yourself in something, what is that something in which you are fulfilling? Is it not self-projection? Say, I want to help you. I use the word *help*, which covers my desire for self-fulfillment. What happens when I have such a desire? I neither help you nor fulfill. Because, to fulfill means, for most of us, to have pleasure in doing something which gives us gratification. In other words, self-fulfillment is gratification, is it not? I am seeking gratification, superficial or permanent, which I call self-fulfillment. But can gratification be permanent? Obviously not. Surely, when we talk about self-fulfillment, we mean a gratification that is deeper, more profound, than the superficial; but can gratification ever be permanent? As it can never be permanent, we change our self-fulfillment—at one period it is this, and later it is that, and ultimately we say, "My fulfillment must be in God, in reality." Which means, we make of reality a permanent gratification. So, in other words, we are seeking gratification when we talk of self-fulfillment. And, instead of saying, "I want to help you in order to gratify myself," which would be too crude and we are too subtle for that, we say, "I want to serve you, I want to help you." And when we are prevented, we feel lost, we feel frustrated, angry, irritated. Under the guise of help and service we do a lot of monstrous things—deceptions, illusions. Therefore, words like *self-fulfillment*, like *help*, like *service*, need examination. And when we really understand them, not just verbally, but deeply, profoundly, then we will help without asking anything in return. Such help will never be misrepresented—and even if it is, it doesn't matter. Then there is no sense of frustration, no sense of anger, criticism, gossip.

Question: What is aloneness? Is it a mystical state? Does it imply freeing oneself from relationship? Is aloneness a way to understanding, or is it an escape from outward conflicts and inward pressures?

KRISHNAMURTI: Are not most of us trying to isolate ourselves in relationship? We try to possess people, we try to dominate people—which is a form of isolation, is it not? Our beliefs, our ideas, are a form of isolation. When we withdraw, when we renounce, it is a form of isolation, is it not? The inward pressures and outward conflicts force us to protect ourselves, to enclose ourselves. That is a form of isolation, is it not? And through isolation, can there be any understanding? Do I understand you if I resist you, if I enclose myself within my ideas, my prejudices, my criticism of you, and so on, and so on? I can understand you only when I am not isolated, when there is no barrier between us, neither a verbal barrier nor the barrier of psychological states, of moods and idiosyncrasies. But to understand, I must be alone, must I not? Alone in the sense of unenclosed, uninfluenced. Most of us are put together; we are made up of memories, of idiosyncrasies, of prejudices, of innumerable influences. And through all that we try to understand something. How can there be understanding when we are produced, brought together, made up? And when there is a freedom from that, there is an aloneness which is not an escape. On the contrary, it is the understanding of all these things that brings about an aloneness with which you meet life directly. If we are a mass of opinions, beliefs, if we are merely put together, we think that we are an integrated being, or we try to seek integration with all these burdens. Surely, there can be integration not merely at the superficial level but completely, right through, only when there is a freedom, through understanding, from all the influences that are constantly impinging upon one—beliefs, memories, idiosyncrasies, and so on; one cannot merely throw them aside. Then, as one begins to understand these, there is an aloneness which is not contradiction, which is not an opposite of the collective or the individual. When you would understand something, aren't you alone? Aren't you completely integrated at that moment? Is not your attention completely given? And through withdrawal, can there be any understanding? Through resistance, can there be any understanding? When you renounce something, does that bring understanding? Surely, understanding comes not through resistance, not through withdrawal, not through renunciation. Only when you understand the full significance of a problem, then the problem disappears. You don't have to renounce it. You don't have to renounce wealth, certain obvious greeds. But when you are capable of looking at them directly, without any criticism, being passively aware of them, they drop away from you. And in that state of passive awareness, is there not complete attention?—not as an opposite, or exclusive concentration. It is an awareness in which there is no contradiction, and therefore loneliness disappears. Most of us are lonely, most of us are solitary—there is no depth, we come to an end very quickly. And it is this loneliness that creates the withdrawals, the escapes, the covering up; and if we would understand that loneliness, we must discard all these coverings and be with it. It is that being that is alone. Then you are uninfluenced, then you are not caught in moods, and it is essential to be alone—which most of us dread. We hardly ever go out by ourselves; we always have the radio, magazines, newspapers, books, or if we haven't those, we are occupied with our own thoughts. The mind is never quiet. It is this quietness that is alone. That aloneness is not induced, is not made up. When there is a lot of noise and you are silent, you are alone, are you not? You must be alone. If you are a success, then there is something obviously wrong. Most of us seek success, and that is why we are never alone; we are lonely, but we are never alone. Only when there is aloneness, then you can meet that which is true, which has no comparison. And, as most of us are afraid to be alone, we build various refuges, various safeties, and give them big-sounding names, and they offer marvelous escapes. But they are all illusions, they have no significance. It is only when we see that they have no significance—actually, not verbally—only then are we alone. Then only can we really understand, which means that we have to strip ourselves of all past experiences, of memories, of sensations, which we have built so sedulously and guard so carefully. Surely, only an unconditioned mind can understand that which is unconditioned, reality; and to uncondition the mind, one must not only face loneliness, but go beyond; one must not hold on to memories that are crowding in. For memories are mere words, words that have sensations. It is only when the mind is utterly quiet, uninfluenced, that it can realize that which is.

August 27, 1949

Fourteenth Talk in The Oak Grove

This morning I shall answer some of the questions first and then wind up with a talk. Many questions have been sent in, and, unfortunately, it has not been possible to answer all of them. So, I have chosen those which are representative and have tried to answer as many of them as possible. And also, in answering questions, naturally one cannot go into full details because that would take too long; and so one can only deal with the fundamentals; the details will have to be filled in by yourself. Those of you who have been coming here regularly will find that if you carry away not merely a memory of the words and the pleasant sensations of listening under trees, of being distracted by birds, cameras, notes, and the various things that divert the mind—if you live not merely in words but are really living, actually experiencing those things that we have discussed, then you will find that, having understood the outline from the answers which have been somewhat brief and succinct, you can fill in the details.

Question: Ideas do separate, but ideas also bring people together. Is this not the expression of love which makes communal life possible?

KRISHNAMURTI: I wonder, when you ask such a question, whether you do realize that ideas, beliefs, opinions, separate people; that ideologies break up; that ideas inevitably disrupt? Ideas do not hold people together—though you may try to bring together people belonging to differing and opposed ideologies. Ideas can never bring people together, which is obvious. Because, ideas can always be opposed and destroyed through conflict. After all, ideas are images, sensations, words. Can words, sensations, thoughts, bring people together? Or does one require quite a different thing to bring people together? One sees that hate, fear, and nationalism bring people together. Fear brings people together. A common hatred sometimes brings together people opposed to one another, as nationalism brings together people of opposing groups. Surely, these are ideas. And is love an idea? Can you think above love? You are able to think about the person whom you love or the group of people whom you love. But is that love? When there is thought about love, is that love? Is thought love? And, surely, only love can bring people together, not thought—not one group in opposition to another group. Where love is, there is no group, no class, no nationality. So, one has to find out what we mean by love.

We know what we mean by ideas, opinions, beliefs, which we have sufficiently discussed during the past several weeks. So, what do we mean by love? Is it a thing of the mind? It is a thing of the mind when the things of the mind fill the heart. And with most of us, it is so. We have filled our heart with the things of the mind, which are opinions, ideas, sensations, beliefs; and around that and in that we live and love. But is that love? Can we think about love? When you love, is thought functioning? Love and thought are not in opposition; do not let us divide them as opposites. When one loves, is there a sense of separateness, of bringing people together, or disbanding them, pushing them away? Surely, that state of love can be experienced only when the process of thought is not functioning—which does not mean that one must become crazy, unbalanced. On the contrary. It requires the highest form of thought to go beyond.

So, love is not a thing of the mind. It is only when the mind is really quiet, when it is no longer expecting, asking, demanding, seeking, possessing, being jealous, fearful, anxious—when the mind is really silent, only then is there a possibility of love. When the mind is no longer projecting itself, pursuing its particular sensations, demands, urges, hidden fears, seeking self-fulfillment, held in bondage to belief—only then is there a possibility of love. But most of us think love can go with jealousy, with ambition, with the pursuit of personal desires and ambitions. Surely, when these things exist, love is not. So, we must be concerned not with love, which comes into being spontaneously, without our particularly seeking it, but we must be concerned with the things that are hindering love, with the things of the mind which project themselves and create a barrier. And that is why it is important, before we can know what love is, to know what is the process of the mind, which is the seat of the self. And that is why it is important to go ever more deeply into the question of self-knowledge—not merely say, "I must love," or "Love brings people together," or "Ideas disrupt," which would be a mere repetition of what you have heard, therefore utterly useless. Words entangle. But, if one can understand the whole significance of the ways of one's thought, the ways of our desires and their pursuits and ambitions, then there is a possibility of having or understanding that which is love. But that requires an extraordinary understanding of oneself. When there is self-abnegation, when there is self-forgetfulness—not intentionally but spontaneously, that self-forgetfulness, self-denial, which is not the outcome of a series of practices, disciplines, which only limit—then there is a possibility of love. That self-denial comes into being when the whole process of the self is understood, consciously as well as unconsciously, in the waking hours as well as in dreaming. Then, the total process of the mind is understood as it is actually taking place in relationship, in every incident, in every response to every challenge that one has. In understanding that, and therefore freeing the mind from its own self-erecting, self-limiting process, there is a possibility of love. Love is not sentiment, not romanticism, not dependent on something, and that state is extremely arduous and difficult to understand or to be in. Because, our minds are always interfering, limiting, encroaching upon its functioning, and therefore it is important to understand first the mind and its ways; otherwise, we shall be caught in illusions, caught in words and sensations that have very little significance. And as, for most people, ideas merely act as a refuge, as an escape—ideas which have become beliefs—naturally they prevent complete living, complete action, right thinking. It is possible to think rightly, to live freely and intelligently only when there is ever-deeper and wider self-knowledge.

Question: Would you kindly explain the distinction you make between factual and psychological memory?

KRISHNAMURTI: Do not let us bother for the moment with the distinction between factual and psychological memory. Let us consider memory. Why do we live in memories? Are memories separate from us? Are you different from memory? What do we mean by memory? It is the residue of certain incidents, experiences, sensations, is it not? You have had an experience yesterday; it has left a certain mark, a certain sensation. That sensation we call memory, verbalized or not, and we are the sum total of all these memories, all these residues. Surely, you are not different from your memory. There are conscious memories, as there are the unconscious. The conscious memories respond easily, spontaneously; and the unconscious memories are very deep, hidden, quiet, waiting, watchful. All of that, surely, is you and me: the racial, the group, the particular—all that, all those memories, are you and me. You are not different from your memories. Remove your memories, where are you? If you remove them, you will end up in an asylum. But, why does the mind—which is the result of memories, of the past—why does the mind cling to the past? That is the question, is it not? Why does the mind—which is the result of the past, which is the outcome of yesterday, of many yesterdays—why does the thinker cling to yesterday? Memories without any emotional content have their significance; but we give to them emotional content, as like and dislike: "This I will keep, that I won't keep." "This I will think about, and that I will ponder over in my old age or continue in my future." Why do we do that? Surely, that is the problem, is it not? Not that we must forget factual or psychological memories. Because, all the impressions, all the responses, everything is there, unconsciously: every incident, every thought, every sensation which you have lived through is there—hidden, covered up, but still there. And as we grow older, we return to those memories and live in the past, or in the future, according to our conditioning. We remember the pleasant times we had when we were youthful, or we think of the future—what we are going to be.

So, we live in these memories. Why? We live as though we were different from those memories. Surely, that is the problem, is it not? We mean, by memories, words, don't we? Images, symbols, which are merely a series of sensations—and on those sensations we live. Therefore, we separate ourselves from the sensations and say, "I want those sensations." Which means that the 'I', having separated itself from memories, gives to itself permanency. But it is not permanent. It is a fictitious permanency.

Now, this whole process of the 'I' separating itself from memory and giving life to that memory in response to the present—this total process obviously hinders our meeting the present, does it not? If I would understand something not theoretically, verbally, abstractly, but actually, I must give my full attention to it. I cannot give my full attention to it if I am distracted by my memories, by my beliefs, by my opinions, my experiences of yesterday. Therefore, I must respond fully, adequately, to the challenge. But that 'I', which has separated itself from memory, thus giving itself permanency, that 'I' regards the present, looks at the incident, the experience, and draws from it according to its past condition—which is all very simple and obvious, if you examine it. It is the memory of yesterday—of possessions, of jealousies, of anger, of contradiction, of ambition, of what one ought or ought not to be—it is all these things that make up the 'I'; and the 'I' is not different from memory. The quality cannot be separated from the thing, from the self.

So, memory is the self. Memory is the word, the word which symbolizes sensation, physical as well as psychological sensation, and it is to that we cling. It is to the sensations we cling, not to the experience, because in the moment of experience, there is neither the experiencer nor the experience—there is only experiencing. It is when we are not experiencing that we cling to memory, like so many people do, especially as they grow older. Watch yourself and you will see. We live in the past or in the future and use the present merely as a passage from the past to the future; therefore, the present has no significance. All the politicians indulge in this, all the ideologists, all the idealists—they always look to the future, or to the past.

So, if one understands the whole significance of memory, one does not put away memories or destroy them or try to be free of them, but one understands how the mind is attached to memory and thereby strengthens the 'me'. The 'me', after all, is sensation, a bundle of sensations, a bundle of memories. It is the known, and from the known we want to understand the unknown. But the known must be an impediment to the unknown because to understand reality, there must be a newness of the mind, a freshness—not the burden of the known. God, or reality, or what you will, cannot be imagined, cannot be described, cannot be put into words; and if you do, that which you put into words is not reality; it is merely the sensation of a memory, the reaction to a condition, and therefore it is not real. Therefore, if one would understand that which is eternal, timeless, the mind as memories must come to an end. Mind must no longer cling to the known; therefore, it must be capable of receiving the unknown. You cannot receive the unknown if the mind is burdened with memories, with the known, with the past. Therefore, the mind must be entirely silent—which is very difficult. Because, the mind is always projecting, always wandering, always creating, breeding; and it is this process that must be understood in relationship to memory. Then the distinction between psychological and factual memory is obvious and simple. So, in understanding memory, one understands the process of thinking, which is, after all, self-knowledge. To go beyond the limits of the mind, there must be freedom from the desire to be, to achieve, to gain.

Question: Is not life true creation? Are we not really seeking happiness, and is there not serenity in life, that true being of which you speak?

KRISHNAMURTI: In answering this question, to understand it fully and significantly, should we not perhaps understand first this idea of seeking? Why are we seeking happiness? Why this incessant pursuit to be happy, to be joyous, to be something? Why is there this search, this immense effort made to find? If we can understand that and go into it fully, which I will do presently, perhaps we shall know what happiness is without seeking it. Because, after all, happiness is a byproduct, of secondary importance. It is not an end in itself; it has no meaning if it is an end in itself. What does it mean to be happy? The man who takes a drink is happy. The man who drops a bomb over a great number of people feels elated and says he is happy or that God is with him. Momentary sensations, which disappear, give that sense of being happy. Surely, there is some other quality that is essential for happiness. For happiness is not an end, any more than virtue. Virtue is not an end in itself; it gives freedom, and in that freedom there is discovery. Therefore, virtue is essential. Whereas, an unvirtuous person is slavish, is disorderly, is all over the place, lost, confused. But to treat virtue as an end in itself or happiness as an end in itself has very little meaning. So, happiness is not an end. It is a secondary issue, a byproduct which will come into being if we understand something else. It is this understanding of something else, and not merely the search for happiness, that is important.

Now, why do we seek? What does it mean to make an effort? We are making an effort. Why are we making an effort? What is the significance of effort? We say we are making an effort in order to find, in order to change, in order to be something. If we did not make an effort, we should disintegrate, or retard, go back. Is that so? Please, this is very important to go into fully, and I will try as much as I can this morning to go into it. If we did not make an effort, what would happen? Would we stagnate? But we are making an effort. And why? Effort to change, effort to be different in ourselves, to be more happy, to be more beautiful, to be more virtuous—this constant strife and constant effort. If we can understand that, then perhaps we will understand more deeply, other issues.

Why do you seek? Is the search prompted by disease, by ill health, by moods? Do you make an effort because you are unhappy and you want to be happy? Do you seek because you are going to die, and therefore you want to find? Do you seek because you have not fulfilled yourself in the world; therefore, you want to fulfill here? Do you seek because you are unhappy, and, hoping for happiness, you seek, you search, you try to find out? So, one must understand the motive for one's search, must one not? What is the motive for your eternal search?—if you are really searching, which I question. What you want is substitution: "As this is not profitable, perhaps that will be." "As this hasn't given me happiness, perhaps that will." So one is really seeking, not truth, not happiness, but a substitution that will give one happiness, a thing that will be profitable, that will be safe, that will give one gratification. Surely, that is what we are seeking, if we were very honest and clear in ourselves, but we clothe our gratification with words like God, love, and so on.

Now, why do we not approach this question differently? Why don't we understand *what is?* Why are we not capable of looking at the thing exactly "as is?" Which means that if we are in pain, let us live with it, look at it, and not try to transform it into something else. If I am in misery, not only physically but especially psychologically, how am I to understand it? By not wishing it to be different, surely. First, I must look at it, I must live with it, I must go into it; I mustn't condemn it, I mustn't compare it, wish it to be something else; I must be entirely with that thing, must I not?—which is extremely arduous because the mind refuses to look at it. It wants to go off at a tangent; it says, "Let me seek an answer, a solution, there must be one." In other words, it is escaping from *what is.* And this escape, with most of us, is what we call search—search for the Master, search for truth, search for love, search for God: you know the various terms we use to escape from what exactly is taking place. And, do we have to make an effort to understand what is taking place? We have to make an effort to escape when we don't want it. But when it is there, to understand it, do we have to make an effort? Obviously, we have made an effort to escape, to avoid, to cover up *what is;* and with that same mentality, which is to make an effort in order to avoid, in order to escape, we approach *what is.* Do you understand *what is* with an effort? Or, must there be no effort to understand *what is?* So, that is one of the problems, is it not? This constant effort to avoid the understanding of *what is* has become habitual with most of us, and with that same mentality of making an effort in order to escape, we say, "All right, I'll drop all escapes and make an effort to understand *what is.*" Do we understand anything really, significantly, deeply; do we understand anything that has a meaning through effort? To understand something, must there not obviously be a passivity of the mind, an alertness which is yet passive? Please, you cannot arrive at that passivity of the mind which is alert through effort, can you? If you make an effort to be passive, you are no longer passive. If one really understands that, the significance of that, and sees the truth of it, then one will be passive. One doesn't have to make an effort.

So, when we seek, we are seeking either with the motive of escape or of trying to be something more than *what is,* or else one says, "I am all these things, I must run away"—which is unbalance, insanity. Surely, the search for truth, for the Master, is a state of insanity when the thing is there which must be understood before you can go further. That breeds illusion, ignorance. So, first one must find out what one is seeking, and why. Most of us know what we are seeking, and therefore it is a projection, therefore unreal; it is merely a homemade thing. Therefore, it is not truth, it is not the real. And, in understanding this process of search, this constant making effort to be, to discipline, to deny, to assert, one must inquire into the question of what is the thinker. Is the one who makes the effort separate from the thing which he wants to be? Sorry, it may be a little difficult to pursue this, but I hope you don't mind. You have asked the question, and I am going to try to answer it.

Is the maker of effort different from the object toward which he is making effort? This is really very important because if we can find the truth of this, we will see that there comes immediate transformation, which is essential for understanding—which is understanding, rather. Because, as long as there is a separate entity which makes the effort, as long as there is a separate entity as the experiencer, the thinker, different from the thought, from the object, from the experience, there will always be this problem of seeking, disciplining, bridging the gulf between the thought and the thinker, and so on. Whereas, if we can find the truth of this matter—whether the thinker is separate from the thought—and see the real truth of it, then there will be quite a different process at work. Therefore, you have to find out before you seek, before you find the object of your search—whether it is a Master or a cinema or any other excitement, they are all on the same level—whether the seeker is different from the object of his search, and why he is different. Why is the maker of effort different from the thing which he wants to be? And is he different? To put it another way: you have thoughts, and you are also the thinker. You say, "I think." "I am this, and I must be that." "I am greedy or mean or envious or angry." "I have certain habits, and I must break away from them." Now, is the thinker different from the thought? If he is different, then the whole process must exist of making an effort to bridge, of the thinker trying to alert his thought, the thinker trying to concentrate, to avoid, resist the encroachments of other thoughts. But if he is not different, then there is complete transformation of the way one lives. So, we will have to go into that very carefully and discover—not at the verbal level at all, but experience it directly, if we can, as we go along this morning. Which is not to be mesmerized by what I am saying, or accept it, because that has no meaning, but actually to experience for oneself whether this division is true and why it exists.

Surely, memories are not different from the 'me' which thinks about them. I am those memories. The memory of the way to the place where I live, the memory of my youth, the memories of both inexperienced and fulfilled desires, the memories of injuries, resentments, ambitions—all that is me; I am not separate from it. Surely, that is an obvious fact, isn't it? The 'me' is not separate, even though you may believe that it is. Since you can think about it, it is still part of thought, and thought is the result of the past. Therefore, it is still within the net of thought, which is memory.

So, the division between the maker of effort, the seeker, the thinker, and the thought is artificial, fictitious; and the division has been made because we see that thoughts are transient—they come and go. They have no substance in themselves, and so the thinker separates himself to give himself permanency—he exists while thoughts vary. It is a false security, and if one sees the falseness of it, actually experiences it, then there are only thoughts, and not the thinker and the thought. Then you will see—if it is an actual experience, not merely a verbal assertion nor just an amusement, a hobby—then you will find, if it is a real experiencing, that there is a complete revolution in your thinking. Then there is a real transformation because then there is no longer a seeking for quietude or aloneness. Then there is only the concern with what is thinking, what is thought. Then you will see, if this transformation takes place, that there is no longer an effort but an extraordinary, alert passivity in which there is understanding of every relationship, of every incident as it arises; therefore, the mind is always fresh to meet things anew. And hence that silence, which is so essential, is not a thing to be cultivated but comes into being naturally when you understand this fundamental thing—that the thinker is the thought, and therefore the 'I' is transient. Therefore, the 'I' has no permanency, the 'I' is not a spiritual entity. If you are able to think that the 'I' is gone or is something spiritual, everlasting, it is still the product of thought, and therefore of the known, therefore not true.

Therefore, it is really important, essential to understanding, to have this sense of complete integration—which cannot be forced—between the thinker and the thought. It is like a deep experience which cannot be invited; you cannot lie awake thinking about it. It must be seen immediately, and we do not see it because we are clinging to past beliefs, conditioning, what we have learned—that the 'I' is something spiritual, more than all the thoughts. Surely, it is so obvious that whatever you think is the product of the past, of your memories, of words, sensations, of your conditioning. You cannot think about the unknown, surely; you cannot know the unknown; therefore, you cannot think about it. What you can think about is the known. Therefore, it is a projection from the past. And, one must see the significance of all this, and then there will be the experiencing of that integration between the thought and the thinker. The division has been artificially created for self-protection and is therefore unreal. When once there is the experiencing of that integration, then there is a complete transformation with regard to our thinking, feeling, and outlook on life. Then there is only a state of experiencing, and not the experiencer apart from the experienced, which has to be altered, modified, changed. There is only a state of constant experiencing—not the core experiencing, not the center, the 'me', the memory experiencing, but only a state of experiencing. We do this occasionally when we are completely absent, when the self is absent.

I do not know if you have noticed that when there is a deep experiencing of anything, there is neither the sensation of the experiencer nor the experience, but only a state of experiencing, a complete integration. When you are violently angry, you are not conscious of yourself as the experiencer.

Later on, as that experience of anger fades, you become conscious of yourself being angry. Then you do something about that anger to deny it, to justify it, to condone it—you know, various forms of trying to pass it away. But if there is not the entity who is angry, but only that state of experiencing, then there is a complete transformation.

If you will experiment with this, you will see that there is this radical experiencing, this radical transformation, which is a revolution. Then the mind is quiet—not made quiet, not compelled, disciplined—such quietness is death, is stagnation. A mind that is made quiet through discipline, through compulsion, through fear, is a dead mind. But, when there is the experiencing of that which is vital, which is essential, which is real, which is the beginning of transformation, then the mind is quiet without any compulsion. And, when the mind is quiet, then it is capable of receiving because you are not spending your efforts in resisting, in building barriers between yourself and reality, whatever that reality may be. All that you have read about reality is not reality. Reality cannot be described, and if it is described, it is not the real. And, for the mind to be new, for the mind to be capable of receiving the unknown, it must be empty. The mind can be empty only when the whole content of the mind is understood. To understand the content of the mind, one must be watchful, aware of every movement, of every incident, of every sensation. Therefore, self-knowledge is essential. But, if one is seeking achievement through self-knowledge, then again self-knowledge leads to self-consciousness, and there one is stuck; and it is extraordinarily difficult to withdraw from that net when once you are caught. Not to be caught in it, we must understand the process of desire, the craving to be something—not the desire for food, clothes, and shelter, which is quite different, but the psychological craving to be something, to achieve a result, to have a name, to have a position, to be powerful, or to be humble. Surely, only when the mind is empty, then only can it be useful. But a mind crowded with fears, with memories of what it has been in the past, with the sensations of past experiences—such a mind is utterly useless, is it not? Such a mind is incapable of knowing what is creation.

Surely, we must all have had experiences of those moments when the mind is absent, and suddenly there is a flash of joy, a flash of an idea, a light, a great bliss. How does that happen? It happens when the self is absent, when the process of thought, worry, memories, pursuits, is still. Therefore, creation can take place only when the mind, through self-knowledge, has come to that state when it is completely naked. All this means arduous attention, not merely indulging in verbal sensations, seeking, going from one guru to another, from teacher to teacher, doing absurd and vain rituals, repeating words, seeking Masters—all these are illusions; they have no meaning. They are hobbies. But to go into this question of self-knowledge and not be caught in self-consciousness, to go ever more deeply, more profoundly so that the mind is completely quiet—that is true religion. Then the mind is capable of receiving that which is eternal.

August 28, 1949

London, England, 1949

First Talk in London

This is the first talk of the series, and as most of the people will not be able to come to all the talks, I will try to make each talk complete in itself, if I can.

For most of us who have problems, the difficulty lies in that we try to solve each problem on its own plane. We do not try to solve the problem integrally, as a whole, but try to solve it from a particular point of view; or we try to differentiate or separate the problem from the total process which is life. If we have an economic problem, we try to solve it on that plane alone, disregarding the total process of life; and each problem, when so tackled, obviously must fail to be solved because our life is not in watertight compartments. Our life is a total process, psychologically as well as physiologically, and when we try to solve the psychological problems without understanding the physiological problems, we give wrong emphasis and therefore further complicate the problem. What we have to do, it seems to me, is to take each problem and not deal with it as a separate issue but as part of a whole. So, what are our problems in life? Because, it seems to me that if we can understand how to approach each problem rightly, we shall be able to understand not only that problem but the whole significance of existence. And that is our difficulty, is it not?—how to approach a problem integrally, as a whole, and not keep it on a separate level, not try to look at it from one particular point of view, but to regard it as part of a whole.

How is it possible to approach a problem integrally? What is it that we mean by a problem? Because, all of us have various problems, acute or superficial, immediate or which can be postponed. We are driven by innumerable problems, subtle or obvious, and how can we really approach them rightly, and what do we mean by a problem? And are we aware that we have problems, and how do we approach them? What is our attitude towards the problem?

What do we mean by a problem? Surely, we mean a state in which there is conflict. As long as there is a conflict in us, we regard that conflict as a problem, as something to be dissolved, to be understood, to be solved, or from which we wish to escape. So, we approach a problem, a conflict, do we not, either with a desire to escape from it or to find an answer for it, to find a solution for it.

Now, is the solution different from the problem, or does the solution lie in understanding the problem itself, and not away from it? Obviously, those of us who want to escape from a problem have innumerable ways—drink, amusement, religious or psychological illusions, and so on. It is comparatively easy to find an escape from our problems and shut our eyes to them, which most of us do because we do not know how to tackle them. We always have a ready-made answer according to our beliefs, our prejudices, according to what a teacher, a psychologist, or someone else has told us; and with that ready-made answer we try to solve, to approach the problem. Surely, that doesn't solve it. That is but another form of escape.

So it seems to me that to understand a problem requires not a ready-made answer, not trying to seek a solution for the problem, but a direct consideration of the problem itself, which is to approach it without the desire to find an answer, if one may so put it. Then you are directly in relationship with the problem, then you are the problem; the problem is no longer separate from yourself. And I think that is the first thing one must realize—that the problem of existence, with all its complexities, is not different from ourselves. We are the problem, and as long as we regard the problem as something away from us, or apart from us, our approach must inevitably result in failure. Whereas, if we can regard the problem as our own, as part of us, not separate from us, then perhaps we shall be able to understand it significantly—which means essentially, does it not, that a problem exists because there is no self-knowledge. If I do not understand myself, the whole complexity of myself, I have no basis for thinking. 'Myself' is not at any one particular level, surely. 'Myself' is at all levels, at whatever level I may place it. So, as long as I have no comprehension of myself, as long as I do not understand myself fully, significantly—the conscious as well as the unconscious, the superficial as well as the hidden—obviously I have no means of approaching the problem, whether it be economic, social, psychological, or any other problem.

Self-knowledge is the beginning of the understanding of the problem. Belief, ideas, knowledge, have really no significance at all without self-knowledge. Without self-knowledge they lead to illusion, to all kinds of complications and stupidities into which we can so subtly escape—and most of us do. That is why we join so many societies, so many groups, so many exclusive organizations and secret bodies. Is it not the nature of stupidity to be exclusive? The more one is stupid, the more one is exclusive, religiously or socially; and each exclusiveness creates its own problems.

So, it seems to me, our difficulty in understanding the many problems that confront us, both the subtle and the obvious, comes about through ignorance of ourselves. It is we who create the problem, we who are part of the environment—as well as something more, which we shall discover if we can understand ourselves. Merely to assert that we are something more, something divine, spiritual, that there is something eternal, some spiritual essence in us—all that, it seems to me, is obviously an illusion because it is mere verbalization of something which you do not know. You may have a feeling, a sensation, but that is not factual. What is a fact must be discovered, must be experienced. But, to experience something deeply, fundamentally, there must be no belief because what you experience then is merely conditioned by your belief. Belief creates its own experience; therefore, such an experience is not true. It is merely the conditioned response to a challenge.

So, to understand the innumerable problems that each one of us has, is it not essential that there be self-knowledge? And that is one of the most difficult things—to be self-aware, which does not mean an isolation, a withdrawal. Obviously, to know oneself is essential, but to know oneself does not imply a withdrawal from relationship. And it would be a mistake, surely, to think that one can know oneself significantly, completely, and fully, through isolation, through exclusion, or by going to some psychologist or to some priest, or that one can learn self-knowledge through a book. Self-knowledge is obviously a process, not an end in itself, and to know oneself, one must be aware of oneself in action, which is relationship. You discover yourself not in isolation, not in withdrawal, but in relationship—in relationship to society, to your wife, your husband, your brother, to man; but to discover how you react, what your responses are, requires an extraordinary alertness of mind, a keenness of perception.

So, as any problem is the result of a total process and not an exclusive, isolated result, to understand it we must understand the total process of ourselves; and to understand ourselves—not only superficially, in one or two layers of the upper mind, but through the whole content of consciousness, the whole content of our being—to understand that fully, significantly, it must be perceived and experienced in relationship. We can either make that relationship exclusive, narrow, limited, and thereby hinder our self-knowledge, or we can look at, be aware of that relationship as a whole, as the means of self-discovery. Surely, only in relationship the process of what I am unfolds, does it not? Relationship is a mirror in which I see myself as I am; but as most of us do not like what we are, we begin to discipline, either positively or negatively, what we perceive in the mirror of relationship. That is, I discover something in relationship, in the action of relationship, and I do not like it. So, I begin to modify what I do not like, what I perceive as being unpleasant. I want to change it—which means I already have a pattern of what I should be. The moment there is a pattern of what I should be, there is no comprehension of what I am. The moment I have a picture of what I want to be, or what I should be, or what I ought not to be—a standard according to which I want to change myself—then, surely, there is no comprehension of what I am at the moment of relationship.

I think it is really important to understand this, for I think this is where most of us go astray. We do not want to know what we actually are at a given moment in relationship. If we are concerned merely with self-improvement, there is no comprehension of ourselves, of *what is*. You are merely concerned with achieving results, and to achieve a result is in the end an awful bore because it leads nowhere. But to know what I am, not what I should be, is extremely arduous because the mind is so subtle, so eager to avoid anything which is. And so it has developed various standards, patterns, assumptions, which deny *what is*. So, to understand oneself, which is not a dead thing but a living thing, your approach must be actively new, and therefore it cannot have the positive or the negative assertion of a standard.

So, to understand oneself—which can be done only in relationship, not outside relationship—there must be no condemnation. If I condemn something, I do not understand it; or if I accept something, I do not understand it. Acceptance is merely identification with the problem, and denial or condemnation is another form of identification. But, if we can look at the problem without condemnation or justification—that is, the problem of myself as I am in relationship, which is action—then there is a possibility of understanding *what is*, and therefore unfolding *what is*.

So, as our problems are the result of the total process of ourselves, which is action in relationship, whether with things, ideas, or people, it is essential, is it not, that there should be understanding of ourselves. Without knowing myself, I have no real basis for thinking. I can think, or at least I think I can think. I may have opinions, I may have innumerable beliefs, I may belong to this society, to that organization or church, have immense knowledge. Surely, all that is not a basis for right thinking. It leads to illusion. It leads to further conflict, further confusion. So, to think rightly, it is essential, is it not, that there be self-knowledge—which is to know yourself as you are from moment to moment, to be aware of everything that is going on, of all the inward responses to every outward challenge, to every experience. But you cannot know yourself fully, completely, deeply, extensively, if there is any form of belief, any form of adherence to an experience of yesterday. To understand something, you need a fresh mind—not a mind that is prejudiced, not a mind that is clogged with experience, because to understand yourself, there must be self-discovery. Obviously, discovery can only be from moment to moment; therefore, there must be spontaneity—not merely thought which is conditioned to a particular pattern, however noble or however absurd and stupid.

So, it is not very easy to be aware of the whole significance of a particular experience, which is relationship. It requires an extraordinarily alert, keen mind; but a mind is made dull by clinging to an experience of yesterday; a mind is made dull by belief. As I said, experience according to belief merely conditions the mind; and such an experience, though very satisfactory, gratifying, obviously limits the extraordinary, extensive self-knowledge which comes through awareness of the response in relationship. Because, if you have an experience and you cling to that experience, which is memory, and with that conditioned thought, with that memory, you approach a new challenge, obviously there is no comprehension of that challenge. And relationship, surely, is challenge, is it not? Relationship is not a static thing. And, because we are not capable of meeting that challenge adequately, fully, we have problems. Because we are nationalists, Catholics, Protestants, Buddhists, or God knows what else, or because we belong to this society or that group, which are all limiting, we are incapable of meeting a challenge which is constantly arising; for to meet a challenge, there must be complete self-knowledge. And to rely on memory, on a past experience, as a means of discovering ourselves obviously limits our thinking, our perception. Because, after all, what is it that most of us are seeking? Though we have our problems, though we are worried economically, though there is immense insecurity, wars, the nuisance of nationalism, the exclusiveness of innumerable cults, religions, and our own desire to be exclusive—in spite of all these stupidities, what is it that we are actually seeking? If we can know that, perhaps we shall be able to understand. Because, we seek according to our age, according to the period and circumstances of our lives.

Do we not seek, through all this confusion, something permanent, something lasting, something which we call real, God, truth, what you like—the name doesn't matter, the word is not the thing, surely. So don't let us be caught in words. Leave that to the professional lecturers. There is surely a search for something permanent, is there not, in most of us—something we can cling to, something which will give us assurance, a hope, a lasting enthusiasm, a lasting certainty, because in ourselves we are so uncertain. We do not know ourselves. We know a lot about facts, what the books have said, but we do not know for ourselves; we do not have a direct experience.

And what is it that we call permanent? What is it that we are seeking, which will or which we hope will give us permanency? Are we not seeking lasting happiness, lasting gratification, lasting certainty? We want something that will endure everlastingly, which will gratify us. If we strip ourselves of all the words and phrases and actually look at it, this is what we want. We want permanent pleasure, permanent gratification—which we call truth, God, or what you will.

So, we want pleasure. Perhaps that may be putting it very crudely, but that is actually what we want—knowledge that will give us pleasure, experience that will give us pleasure, a gratification that will not wither away by tomorrow. And we have experimented with various gratifications, and they have all faded away, and we hope now to find permanent gratification in reality, in God. Surely, that is what we are all seeking—the clever ones and the stupid ones, the theorist and the factual person who is striving after something. And is there permanent gratification? Is there something which will endure?

Now, if you seek permanent gratification, calling it God or truth or what you will—the name does not matter—surely you must understand, must you not, the thing you are seeking. When you say, "I am seeking permanent happiness"—God or truth or what you like—must you not also understand the thing that is searching, the searcher, the seeker? Because, there may be no such thing as permanent security, permanent happiness. Truth may be something entirely different, and I think it is utterly different from what you can see, conceive, formulate. So, before we seek something permanent, is it not obviously necessary to understand the seeker? Is the seeker different from the thing he seeks? When you say, "I am seeking happiness," is the seeker different from the object of his search? Is the thinker different from the thought? Are they not a joint phenomenon rather than separate processes? Therefore, it is essential, is it not, to understand the seeker before you try to find out what it is he is seeking.

And that is why it seems to me so essential, so important, to understand oneself—because in oneself is the whole problem and the whole issue. To stipulate, to formulate, that you are the end, that you are the absolute, that you are God, this or that, is obviously a verbalization which gives you an escape, and through which you do escape. To say that you are, or you are not, the real or the false has no meaning because you have no basis for any such thinking, and you can think rightly only when you know yourself. To know yourself, you must be completely aware of every movement of thought; then, in that awareness, you will find out whether the thinker is different from his thought. If he is different, then we have the many complex problems of how to control the thought, and then begin all the stupidities of disciplining—the meditations, the approximation of the thinker to the thought. But is there a thinker different from his thoughts? Is not the thinker the thought? They are not separate but a unitary process. Therefore we are thought, not the thinker thinking thoughts. And this must be a direct experience, this realization that the thinker is the thought; and when there is such an experience, then we will see that there is a possibility of going beyond thought.

Because, after all, thought is merely the response of memory, and what memory creates, fabricates, projects, is not the real. God is not the result of memory, of education, of belonging to this society or that society, or believing in this or in that dogma. Those are all merely the results of thought, which is the response of memory, of experience. But to find out if there is reality, if there is such a thing as God, obviously it is essential to understand oneself first, and not to speculate if there is God or if there is not, for all speculation is a waste of time.

So, to understand the problems which confront each one of us, however complex, however subtle, surely one must understand that they are not something outside of us, outside of our thinking—but that these problems are the process or the result of ourselves. The world is us, not separated from us. The world's problem is my problem, your problem, not something to be dealt with, apart. And to resolve these problems—not superficially, not temporarily, but fundamentally, lastingly—there must be comprehension of oneself, and to understand oneself, there must be choiceless awareness in relationship. Then, one perceives oneself as one is, and then one can go into it more fully, deeply. But if you cover up what you are by condemnation or by approximation, identification, then there is no understanding, then the process of self-knowledge is limited. Only in understanding oneself completely and fully, both the conscious as well as the unconscious, only when the mind is still, not made still—only then is there a possibility of discovering or experiencing or knowing the real.

That is why meditation is important, but not the meditation that most of us indulge in which is merely compulsion or approximation to an idea or disciplining in order to make the mind still—which is infantile because the mind cannot be made still. Who is it that makes the mind still? Such effort leads to illusion, which we will deal with another time. But when the mind is still, not through compulsion, not through any form of approximation; when it is not compelled, not forced, not made to conform; when the mind is really still through understanding its own process—then only is there a possibility of discovering that which is eternal. Then you don't have to seek truth; to seek truth is to deny truth because truth cannot be sought after—it must come to you. And it can come only when the mind is quiet—not made quiet, but is quiet. And there is quietness, there is tranquillity, there is stillness, only through self-knowledge.

I have been given a few questions, and I will try to answer some of them.

Question: Is there going to be another war, and how soon?

KRISHNAMURTI: You want a prediction from me! So you may safeguard your investments! Now why do we ask such a question? Don't you know if there is going to be a war or not? Not from the newspapers, not from your political leaders—for, after all, you choose your leaders according to your confusion: the more you are confused, the more leaders you have; the less confused you are and the clearer you are in yourself, which is not through your learning, the fewer leaders you need. So, don't you know for yourself if there is going to be a war or not?

What do we mean by war? War is not only the dramatic, spectacular bloodshed—that is the ultimate. But aren't we continuously at war with ourselves, and therefore with our environment, with our neighbors? Surely, you don't have to be told that we are at war. What we are, that we make the world to be. War is inevitable so long as we are nationalistic; so long as you are English and I am Hindu, there is sure to be war. As long as there are frontiers, sovereign governments, separate armies, there is bound to be war. As long as there are social, economic divisions, the exclusiveness of different castes and classes, there is bound to be war.

We all know this. Perhaps you may read one or two history books and have a superficial knowledge of history. These are the obvious causes of war: when one nation wants to be superior to another nation, one group feels inferior to another group, when there is prejudice—the white and the black and the brown and the purple, or whatever it is. How do you think all this comes about? Obviously, what we are, we project. The world is the result of ourselves, of our self-projection.

So, there will be war as long as you are nationalistic, as long as you are exclusive in your beliefs, though you may be "tolerant." Tolerance is a thing of the mind, invented by the clever people; when you love, you do not "tolerate." Only when you and I are no longer bound to castes, to classes; only when we are not bound to any form of religion, organized belief, whether it is small or large; only when we are no longer greedy for power, for position, for authority, for comfort—only then will there be peace. Peace is not a result of legislation; peace isn't going to be brought about by the United Nations. How can outside law make you peaceful? How can an outside compulsion make you love? And if you rely on an outside authority to make you peaceful, to make you kind, nongreedy, then you are looking to something which will never come into being. So, war—whether on the physical or on a different level of consciousness, it is all the same—conflict is inevitable as long as you and I are striving after our own particular security through nationalism, through belief, through illusions. We are merely perpetuating conflict in ourselves, and so outwardly.

You see, we all know these things. Every preacher on the corner talks about them. But we are not peaceful; we haven't stopped being greedy. Though we may not be greedy for money, we are greedy for more things, more power, more self-expansion, wishing to be something, now, or at some future date. This whole sense of hierarchical, social development, or inward development—all this obviously indicates a process which will eventually result in conflict, in war, in destruction and misery. We all know these things, but yet we don't ask why they continue to exist. Surely, that is much more important—to find out why we don't live the things which we feel. Probably we don't feel them. Probably we are merely living on the verbal level, saying, "There must be no war. We will all believe in brotherhood, join various organizations that believe in brotherhood." But inwardly we are as corrupt as the person who sits in an office and plans war—because, we want to be somebody in the family, in a group, in society, in the nation. We want power. We are not content to be as nothing because we are so carried away by the desire for outward stimulants, outward show, because inwardly we are empty—and of that we are so frightened. Therefore, we pile up possessions, either of ideas or of things. And it is only when we are content to be as nothing—which is not fundamentally the contentment of satisfaction, of sluggishness, lethargy, stupidity—only when we are content with *what is,* which requires an extraordinary understanding of all the escapes, only then will there be peace.

Question: What is prejudice? How can one really overcome it? What is the state of mind free from all prejudices?

KRISHNAMURTI: Can you overcome a prejudice? To overcome something is to reconquer it again and again. Can you really overcome a prejudice? Or is this overcoming merely a substitution of one prejudice for another? Surely, our problem is not how to overcome prejudice because then we are merely seeking a substitution; it is to understand the whole process of prejudice, what are the implications of prejudice, not merely verbally, on the verbal level of the mind, but fundamentally, deeply. Then there is a possibility of being free from prejudice. But if you are striving to overcome one prejudice, or various prejudices, then you are merely seeking to overcome a pain which you call prejudice, a hindrance which you call prejudice.

Now, what do we mean by prejudice? When is there freedom from prejudice? How does prejudice come into being? One way, obviously, is through so-called education. History books are full of prejudice. All religious literature is full of it—the instilled belief; and that belief, which is created, manufactured from childhood, grows into prejudice. You are this, and I am that. You are Protestant, and I am Hindu. Therefore, my belief and your belief come into conflict. You try to proselytize me, convert me, and I am going to try to do the same. Or we are "tolerant"—you hold to your belief, I hold to mine, and we try to be friendly. That is, I live in my fortress of prejudice, and you live in yours, and we look over it and try to be friends, which is called "tolerance," but it is really intolerance. It is really the most absurd form of trying to be friends. How can we be friends, how can we have real affection, if I am living in my prejudice and you are living in yours?

So, we know the various causes of prejudice—ignorance, purposely cultivated, creates prejudices through education, through environmental influences, through religion, and so on; and there is our own desire to be exclusive, to be protected in our beliefs. Surely, it is very obvious how prejudices come into being. And also we like to think in terms of races or nationalities because it requires less effort than treating people as individual human beings. It's easier to deal with people when you are prejudiced. When you call them Germans, Hindus, Russians, Negroes, or whatever it is, you think you have solved the problem. But to look at each individual person requires a great deal of thought, of exertion; and as we do not want to do that, we say, "Well, we'll call them by some name," and thereby we think we have understood them.

So, we know why prejudices come into being, how they are produced for our own self-protection, which is a process of isolation. It is much easier to hate, to be prejudiced, to be limited, and that is what most of us are. You belong to this or that society, which is a form of prejudice. You believe that your experience is superior to mine, or is as good as mine, and are therefore held in your experience. All this indicates, does it not, forms of prejudice, forms of exclusion, self-protective guards which you have so carefully cultivated. How can you overcome them? When you do, you will find substitutions for them, for if you have no prejudice, you are extremely vulnerable, sensitive, and you suffer much more. And therefore, to guard ourselves, we throw up walls, either self-projected or created for us by others, which we accept. And to try to overcome prejudices is to find other protections which will be more pleasurable, more instructive, more cultured. But they are still prejudices.

So, to be free of prejudice is to live in a state of uncertainty, is to live in a state of insecurity. Now, we must understand what we mean by insecurity. Obviously, there must be reasonable physical security; otherwise, it is impossible to live at all. But that physical security is denied when you are seeking psychological security, and that is what we are doing. When we want to be psychologically secure through nationalism, through belief, through a particular form of society, left or right—it is this psychological desire, this inward desire to be certain, to be secure, to be dependent, that creates outward insecurity. And it is only when the mind is free from self-protective reactions, inward self-protective reactions—only then is there a possibility of being free from prejudice.

"What is the state of the mind which is free from prejudice?" is the next question. Why do you want to know? I think you want to know in order to experience it, and therefore make that into a standard, into something which is to be achieved; or you want to understand what it is to be free, what it means for a mind to be free from self-protective reactions.

To find that out, you must experience it directly, must you not—not merely listen to my words, or those of another. That is, you have to be aware of your own process of thinking and feeling, haven't you, not only when you happen to like it, but all the time; which means, surely, that to be free from prejudice—which is a self-protective reaction, whether cultivated or instinctively brought into being—there must be an awareness of the total process of yourself. But to speculate on what is the state of mind which is free from prejudice is surely vain, is it not? So, all that we can do is not to wonder what is the state of mind when it is free but to understand ourselves. And to understand ourselves, there must be an awareness in which there is no compulsion, in which there is no justification or condemnation—one must be aware easily, without any form of fear. In that awareness there is the unfoldment of the movement of thought and feeling. And then, when the mind is still—not made still—there is a possibility of discovering that which is timeless.

October 2, 1949

Second Talk in London

Probably most of us have definite views, or we have come to definite conclusions from which it is very difficult to deviate or to look at another point of view because most of us have lived quite painfully, have suffered, and we have come to certain points of view which we find difficult to change. And if we listen to another at all, we listen through the screen of our own conclusions or of our own experiences, of our own knowledge, and so it is extremely difficult to understand another fully and completely. And, if I may suggest, we should, for the time being or at least for this morning, put aside our particular conclusions and points of view and try to consider together the problems that confront us. Our difficulty is going to be that we want conclusions, we want answers to the various problems. But, if we can examine each problem that arises sufficiently, intelligently, which means without being bound by conclusions, without definite opinions, then perhaps we shall be able to understand the problem fully, integrally.

One of the problems in our life is, is it not, that of the individual and his relationship to the state. Perhaps, if we can understand the whole process of the individual, then we shall be able to understand our relationship, not only to the one or two, but to the many, to the mass, to the country, to the people as a whole. So, this division between the state and the individual seems to me to be erroneous because, after all, what we are, we make the state to be. We project that which each one of us is. This may seem to be a very simple philosophy, a very simple idea, and not worthwhile examining because our minds are so complicated, we have read so much, we are so intelligent, so clever, that we cannot think of a problem simply. But, it seems to me, we must think of this highly complex problem very directly and simply because, after all, a complex problem can be understood fully only when we approach it negatively. And in understanding the individual and his process, we shall perhaps understand the relationship of the individual to the state or to the mass or to another individual.

So, to me, the problem of the relationship of the individual to the state can be understood only when we understand the process of the individual because without the individual, the state is not. There is no such thing as the mass. It is a political implement convenient for various purposes, for exploitation, and so on. And also, for most of us, when we talk about the mass, it is a convenient way of disposing of people because, to look at an individual, to look at another, requires a great deal of attention, thought, consideration, which we are unwilling to give, and therefore we call them the mass—and the mass is ourselves, you and me.

To understand the whole projection which we call society, with all its complexities, surely we have to understand ourselves. But most of us are unwilling to understand ourselves because that is a tedious job, unexciting, and we think it has not much significance, that the understanding of oneself will lead nowhere. Whereas, if we can work, help to bring about certain reformations, certain alterations in society, that perhaps will be worthwhile. And also, there is the impression that in understanding ourselves we will inevitably be self-centered, self-enclosed.

Surely, fully to understand oneself and the whole process of what the individual is requires not isolation, not a withdrawal, but the understanding of relationship because, after all, all action is relationship—there is no action without relationship. And, if in my relationship with another there is antagonism, greed, envy, if there are all the various causes that bring about conflict, surely I will create a society which will be the result of that relationship. So, the understanding of myself is not an egocentric process; on the contrary, it requires an awareness of relationship. Therefore, relationship is the mirror in which I discover myself, I see myself—whether it be the relationship with the one or with the many, with society. And if I want a radical transformation in society, I must obviously understand myself.

This may sound rather childish and infantile, without much significance, but I do not think it is so easy, nor so easily brushed off.

You may say, "What can the individual do to affect history?" Can he do anything by his life? I don't think you are going to stop wars immediately or bring about a better understanding between the various peoples. But, at least in the world I live in, in the world of my immediate relationship—whether it is with my boss, with my wife, with my children, or with a neighbor—there, at least, I can bring about a certain reformation, a certain transformation, a certain understanding. I may not be able to bring about understanding with the Russians or the Germans or the Hindus, but at least in the world I am living in, there can be a certain peace, a certain happiness, a certain love, affection, and all the rest of it. And I think, though it may not widely affect the world at large, at least I can be a nucleus, a center of different value, of different understanding and significance, and perhaps that may gradually bring about a transformation in the world.

But, surely, we are not principally concerned with the transformation of the world because what I do, what you do, will have little effect. But, if I can stop being greedy—not superficially but profoundly—if I can stop being ambitious, then perhaps I shall be able to bring a new breath, a new understanding to life. And surely, that is the most effective and direct action, is it not?—to bring about transformation, a radical change in oneself, for after all, that is how all great movements are started: with the individual, with oneself. So, my relationship—or your relationship, the relationship of the individual—to the state can be understood, and a change in that relationship brought about only when I understand the total process of myself.

Do not, please, brush this aside, saying, "This is infantile, stupid; it has no effect in the world." What has a fundamental effect in the world? A mass movement? Or, is that fundamental effect brought about by a few creative people who are not self-centered, egotistic, self-enclosed, who do not project their interests and ambitions, a few who are really free of their egotism?

So, to understand this, one must know the process, one must be aware of oneself in action, which is relationship. In understanding what we are, we shall find the solution to the many problems that confront us, understanding not only what we are superficially, on the upper levels of the mind, but knowing the whole content of oneself, the hidden as well as the open, the superficial as well as the many layers of our consciousness, of which at present we are unaware. Perhaps we are aware of them at rare moments, but to bring all the hidden into the conscious and so dissolve the personal, egotistic, narrow intentions and pursuits—thereby establishing right relationship—seems to me of the utmost importance. That is the only thing which I feel is worthwhile discussing, talking about, and living—how to be free of greed, not only superficially, but inwardly. Because, that is one of the causes of conflict, is it not?—greed, not only for things, possessions, but greed for power, greed for knowledge, greed for prestige. And to understand greed requires, surely, a great deal of attention—not to find out who is greedy or to imitate the pattern of a person who is not greedy, but to be aware of oneself as being greedy, and to follow and understand every implication of that greed. Because, obviously, greed has a social effect: individuals being greedy, seeking power, bring about a group or a nation that is equally greedy for power, position, prestige, which creates wars.

Is it possible to be free from greed and live in a society which is nothing but the result of greed, of violence? I think that question can be answered only through direct experience—not verbally trying to be free from greed, but when we know the experience, the true experience, of nongreed. After all, greed expresses itself in so many ways—the greed for truth, the greed for position, the greed for happiness, and the greed for things, for security. Is outward, physical security denied when there is no inward, psychological security? Is it not possible to live in this world without each one seeking his own security? After all, each one of us is seeking psychological security much more than physical security. We use possessions, things, outward security, as a means of psychological security. When the physical needs become a psychological necessity, then that psychological necessity destroys outward security. We can think this out—it is so obvious. As long as I am using things, possessions, property, as a means of self-expression, as a means of aggressive, self-projecting existence, then the needs become all-important, then things, property, become all-dominant because I am using things, property, for my inward psychological security.

And why do we want to be inwardly secure? It is essential to be outwardly, materially secure; otherwise, we cannot live; you and I could not be here if I hadn't my normal food and you hadn't yours. We must have outward security. But I feel that our security is denied, is destroyed, when we use the outward security as a means of inward expansion, of inward pursuit of greed, because then we use things, not as necessities, but we give to them psychological significance. Property then becomes for us a means of psychological survival. After all, the titles, positions, degrees, wealth are used as a means, are they not, of psychological survival, psychological certainty, security; and as long as we seek psychological security through things, there must be contention about things.

Is it possible to live in relationship without being inwardly secure, psychologically certain? After all, that is what we mean by the words *certain, secure.* Most of us are seeking psychological security, are we not, apart from physical security. We must have physical security, much or little, depending on our environment, and so on. But need there be psychological security? Do we want it? Though we are seeking it, though our eternal pursuit is to be secure inwardly, is that not a wrong process, a wrong approach to life? Is there inward security? You and I may want it—but is there such a thing as inward security? When I want to be certain in relationship—whether it be with an idea, with a person, or with a thing—do I find security in that relationship, inward certainty in that relationship?

And, if I am secure in my relationship, is it a relationship? If I am sure of you as my wife or my boss or my friend—sure in the sense of using you as a means of my inward security—is there a relationship between us? Is there any relationship between you and me when I use you? As long as I am using you as a means of my inward security, what is our relationship? You are only a useful instrument for me. I am not related to you. You are a piece of furniture, to be used. That is, inwardly, psychologically, I am poor, empty, insufficient, so I use you as a means of covering myself up, as a means of escape from myself. And such usage we call love, or what you will.

This escape we call relationship, whether it is relationship with property, with people, or with ideas. And, surely, such a relationship must inevitably create conflict, sorrow, and disaster. And that is the state we live in—using people, things, as a means of covering up our own inward poverty. Therefore, the things that we use become all-important; the person, the possession, the idea, the belief become all-important because without them we are lost; therefore, more knowledge, more people, more things. And yet, that which we are, we have never understood. And it seems to me, as long as we are seeking psychological security, we shall never understand ourselves. But, when we are aware that we are using people, things, ideas for our own escape from ourselves, being aware of that escape surely brings about a different relationship. Then the person, the idea, or the thing is no longer important in itself. Therefore, we are not so attached to things, to people; then there is an intelligent approach to the question of property. But I cannot approach it intelligently as long as I am using property as a means of covering up my inward poverty because as long as we are attached to things, we are those things. As long as you are attached to property, you are the property, you are not a spiritual entity—that is just a lot of phony talk. As long as you are attached to a belief, you are that belief. As long as you are attached to a person, you are that person. And we are attached so desperately because in ourselves we are empty, in ourselves we are nothing; being afraid of that emptiness, we hold onto outward things, to ideas, to ideals which are self-projected.

So, this question of relationship cannot be understood superficially or verbally or read about in books, but the whole significance of it, with its intricacies and its extraordinary depth, can be understood only when we are aware of our relationship with each other. And what that relationship is, society is. Merely to talk about brotherhood has no meaning without understanding oneself. You may join societies, form groups for brotherhood, but as long as you are using a society or people or things as a means of your inward security, you are bound to create more conflict, more illusion, more pain in the world, which is what is happening, just as nationalism, used as a means of covering up one's own poverty and of identifying oneself with a particular country, leads to war.

What is important is to understand oneself and to come face to face with oneself, with that poverty which we are avoiding, that emptiness which we all shun. And when we understand that, really experience it, without condemnation, when we are fully related to that emptiness, then only is there a possibility of going beyond and discovering what is truth, or what is God.

There are several questions, and I will try to answer some of them.

Question: I have tried very hard, but cannot stop drinking. What should I do?

KRISHNAMURTI: You know, each one of us has various escapes. You take a drink, and I follow a Master. You are addicted to knowledge, and I to amusement. All escapes are similar, are they not, whether one takes to drink, follows a Master, or is addicted to knowledge. They are all the same, surely, because the intention, the purpose, is to escape. Perhaps drinking may have a social value, or may be more harmful, but I am not at all sure that ideational escapes are not worse. They are much more subtle, more hidden, and more difficult to be aware of. A man addicted to rituals, ceremonies, is no different from the man addicted to drink because both are trying to escape through stimulants.

And I think it is possible to stop escapes only when you are aware that you are escaping, that you are using all these things—drink, Masters, ceremonies, knowledge, love of country, what you will—as stimulants, sensations, to get away from yourself. After all, there are various ways to stop drinking. But if you merely stop drinking, you will take up something else. You may become a nationalist, or pursue some teacher on the other side of the world, or become ideationally fanciful.

Surely, the reason for escape is obvious—we are dissatisfied with ourselves, with our state, outwardly and inwardly. And so we have many escapes, and we think we shall understand, dissolve the escape, the drinking, when we discover the cause. When we know the cause of escape, do we stop escaping? When I know that I am drinking because I am quarreling with my wife or because I have a rotten job—when I know the cause, do I stop drinking? Surely not. I stop drinking only when I establish right relationship with my wife, with another, and remove the conflict which is causing pain.

That is, to put it differently, as long as I am seeking self-fulfillment in which there is frustration, there must be an escape. As long as I am frustrated, I must find an escape. When I want to be something—a politician, a leader, the pupil of a Master, anything—as long as I want to be something, I am inviting frustration; and as being frustrated is painful, I seek an escape from it, whether it is a drink or a Master or a ceremony or becoming a politician, it doesn't matter what it is, they are all the same.

So, then, the question arises, is there self-fulfillment? Can the self, the 'me', be something, become something? And what is the 'me' which wants to become something? The 'me' is a bundle of memories, a chain of memories in reaction with the present; I am the result of the past in conjunction with the present. And that 'me' wants to perpetuate itself through family, through a name, through property, through ideas. The 'me' is merely an idea, an idea which is satisfying, giving sensations, and to that the mind clings—the mind is that. And as long as the mind is seeking fulfillment as the 'me', obviously there must be frustration; as long as I give importance to myself as being something, there must be frustration; as long as I am the center of everything, of my thoughts, my reactions, as long as I give myself importance, there must be frustration. Therefore, there must be pain, and from that pain we try to escape through innumerable ways. And the means of escape are similar.

So, don't let us worry over the means of escape—whether yours is superior to mine. What is important is to realize that as long as one is seeking fulfillment in the self, there must be misery, strife; and this misery cannot be avoided as long as the self is important, the 'me' is important.

So, you will say, "What has drinking got to do with all this? You haven't answered my question, how to stop drinking." I think the problem of drinking, as any other problem, can be understood and put an end to only when I understand the process of myself, when there is self-knowledge. And that understanding of oneself requires constant watchfulness—not a conclusion, not something you can hold on to, but constant awareness of every movement of thought and feeling. And, to be so aware is tiresome, and so we say, "Oh, it isn't worth it." We push it aside, and therefore increase the sorrow, the pain. But surely, only in understanding oneself as a total process do we solve the innumerable problems that we have.

Question: I find it impossible to believe in God. I am a scientist, and yet my science gives me no satisfaction. I cannot bring myself to believe in anything. Is this merely a matter of conditioning? If so, is faith in God more real? How can I come to that faith?

KRISHNAMURTI: Why do we believe? What is the necessity of believing? Which doesn't mean that you must not believe—that is not the problem. Why do we believe? And believing can only condition experience. Surely, what I believe, that I experience. If I believe in God, that I will experience. But such experience is not reality; it is only a self-projected experience.

So, it is important, is it not, to find out why we believe; and through belief, can we find anything? Can we discover something? Or, is a mind capable of discovering only when it is not held, tethered to a belief, to a conclusion? But why do we believe in God? Obviously, it is because we see that everything about us is transient, everything about us is changing, being destroyed, coming to an end—our thoughts, our feelings, our existence; and we want something permanent, lasting, enduring. Either we create that permanency in ourselves, calling it the soul, the atma, or what you like, or we project that demand for permanency into an idea which we call God.

Ideas can never be permanent. I may like an idea to be permanent, but in itself it is not permanent. I may want permanency, but as long as I am wanting it, I am creating a permanency which is nonexistent. And belief, faith in God, is merely the reaction, the response, of a person who is seeking permanency. Therefore, his belief conditions his experience. He says, "I know there is God. I have experienced that extraordinary feeling." But surely, such experience based on the desire for permanency is a self-projected experience and therefore not an experience of reality. And, what is real can be found only when there is no longer any question of seeking security, permanency, that is, when the mind is utterly still and free from all want.

So, as long as we believe, we can never find. Therefore, to find what is real, what is God—whatever name you like to call it—there must be freedom: freedom from fear, freedom from the desire to be inwardly secure, freedom from that fear of the unknown. And only then, surely, is it possible to experience whatever that something is, to know if there is such a thing as God. But a man who believes in God or a man who does not believe in God, if he holds on to that conclusion, is obviously caught in an illusion. I can know that something, understand it, experience it directly, only when I am not self-enclosed, when I am not conditioned by belief, by fear, by greed, by envy, and so on.

Belief, then, obviously destroys the experiencing of reality. And it is very difficult to think that way because most of us are so conditioned in belief—the scientist as well as you and I because we all find satisfaction in belief. And if I do not find satisfaction in things, in people, in ideas, then I create a super-idea, which is God. And to that I cling because that is much more satisfying, more gratifying. So, the search for gratification must inevitably create barriers, and to these barriers we cling. You are a believer or a nonbeliever; but if you and I really want to understand if there is reality, if there is God, if there is something not fabricated by the mind, not the result of sensation or the search for sensation—if we want to find such a thing, then we must understand the process of sensation. Because, belief gives us sensation, as does drink, and to these sensations we cling, and these sensations are self-projected. We make from our minds the image of God, and to that we cling.

But, if you and I really experience that thing which is not nameable, which is not of time, we cannot cling to beliefs, which are self-projected images, because anything which is named is not the real; it is the outcome of memory, of our conditioning; and if it is of time, then it is still part of the mind, for the mind is the result of the past, of the various influences, social, environmental, educational, and so on. So, if we understand the process of time, of naming, if we understand the conditions which exist in us, the influences in which we are caught, that understanding brings about a tranquillity of the mind. As I said, the mind is not made still. When you make the mind still, then it is a dead mind. When you discipline the mind to be quiet, though it may be superficially quiet, it is still in a state of agitation, like a child being put in a corner. But when we understand the whole process of belief, the stimulants, the desire to be secure, the search for permanency; when we understand the truth of all these things, fully, not just superficially or verbally, but actually experience it—then the mind is quiet, you don't have to make the mind quiet. It is no use to make the mind quiet. You are the mind; you are the thinker as well as the thought. But if the thinker separates himself and tries to control his thought, that leads to illusion.

So, then, you see all this, understand it, experience it directly—then the mind is quiet. And in that quietness you will know if there is God, reality, or if there isn't; in that stillness, in that silence, you will know. Before that, to speculate on God or no God, on whether you are following the right Master or not—all that seems to me so childish, immature. But the experiencing of reality is not a thing that can be imagined, that can be speculated upon. It is only in the state of experiencing that you will find the real; but to seek faith as a means of stimulation, as an escape from our daily existence of relationship, must inevitably lead to illusion, at whatever level you may like to place that illusion.

So, obviously, to discover, there must be freedom, freedom from greed; and whether you are a scientist and I a layman, or whether I am ignorant and you full of knowledge, we can find that reality only when we understand ourselves. And in the understanding of ourselves comes tranquillity, for self-knowledge brings wisdom. And it is only in wisdom that there is tranquillity—not in knowledge, not in intellectual amusement and ideations. There is no tranquillity in ideas. And that tranquillity comes into being only when the mind is no longer pursuing its own projections. The experiencing of reality is not a thing to be handed to one—no Master, no savior, can give it to you. It comes into being only with the depth of our own understanding of ourselves.

Question: If what you talk about is so rare and apparently only for a few once in a while, what is the purpose of your talking to us? Can you really help us, the mass?

KRISHNAMURTI: I think the purpose of my talking is very clear—at least, to me. First, I am not talking in order to exploit you. I am not getting a kick out of it, nor do I feel lost if I do not talk. It isn't that. I talk for a simple reason: because I feel that you and I can help each other to understand our problems—and not because I feel that I am a superior person who has achieved something or other. By talking over the innumerable problems that we have—the problems of relationship, for there are no other problems—we can understand them. We can talk them over quietly, free of any bias, or, being biased, prejudiced, we can be aware of that bias and prejudice.

After all, we are trying to establish a relationship between us, you and I. If I am using you, or you are using me, we have no relationship. Then you exploit me and I exploit you. But if each one of us is trying to understand the problem which is oneself, then we shall establish right relationship. Then, perhaps, when we discuss—not intellectually, not verbally—we can explore ourselves, we can see ourselves as we are because, after all, relationship is a mirror in which I see myself as I am—that is, if I want to see myself. But, as most of us dislike to see *what is,* we make relationship a farce. Relationship then becomes an escape.

If you do not want to escape through me, or I through you, then it is possible in understanding the various problems together to see ourselves as we are, whether we are one or many. To me, there is no such thing as the mass. The mass is you and me. We think we understand people when we call them Germans, Russians, English, or Hindus. It is a lazy mind that does that, a slack mind that says, "Oh, you are a Hindu," or "You are English." Because, it is so much easier, isn't it, to call someone by a name, and then to think, "I understand him." But if I do not call you by a name, I have to look at you much more closely; I have to see your face, to study your individual movements of thought. I have to be aware of you as an individual. But if I treat you as the mass, then I can bomb you very easily, destroy you.

So, to help another, I must see the other, not as being this or that, belonging to this nationality or to that, but to see him as he is. I cannot see him as he is if I am myself caught in my own petty nationalism, in my own societies, beliefs, and ridiculous superstitions, my own nonsense. So, to understand each other we must look at each other very clearly—that is, to understand you, I must know myself; I must see myself very clearly in my relationship with you. And then only is there a possibility of our helping each other.

October 9, 1949

Third Talk in London

I think it is fairly obvious that to understand a complex, and especially a psychological problem, requires a very quiet mind, a mind that is still, but not with an enforced stillness, a mind that is peaceful, silent, so that it is capable of understanding directly the complex problem and its answer.

What prevents this quietness of mind is obviously conflict. Most of us are in such turmoil, worried about so many things, anxious about life, death, security, and our relationship. There is constant agitation, and it is extremely difficult, naturally, for a mind that is so agitated to understand the ever-increasing social as well as psychological problems. And it is essential, is it not, that to understand a problem completely there should be a silent mind, a mind that is not biased, a mind that is capable of being free, still, and allowing the problem to reveal itself, unfold itself. And such a quiet mind is not possible when there is conflict.

Now, what makes for conflict? Why are we in such conflict, each one of us, and so society, and so the state and the whole world? Why? From what does conflict arise? When conflict ceases, obviously there can be a peaceful mind, but a mind that is caught in conflict cannot be tranquil. And, desiring tranquillity, a certain sense of peace, we try to escape from conflict through every kind of means—social service, losing ourselves in some ritual, or in some kind of activity, mental and otherwise. But, obviously, escapes lead to illusion and to further conflict. Escapes only lead to isolation and therefore to greater resistance. And, if one did not escape, or if one were aware of the escapes, and therefore were capable of understanding directly the process of conflict, then perhaps there would be a quietness of the mind.

And I think it is essential to see that a tranquil mind is necessary—but not a tranquillity that is forced, that remains in isolation, enclosed; not a tranquillity that is attached to one particular idea and therefore is enclosed, held in that idea, or in a belief. Such tranquillity is not reality; it is death because there is no creative process in its self-enclosed isolation.

So, if we could understand the process of conflict and how it arises, then perhaps there would be a possibility of the mind being free, quiet. But, the difficulty in understanding conflict is that most of us are so eager to get away from it, to go beyond conflict, to find a way out of it, to find the cause of it; and I do not think that merely looking for the cause or discovering the cause of conflict is going to resolve conflict. But, if one can understand the total process of conflict, see conflict from every point of view, psychological as well as physiological; if one can have patience to investigate silently, without any condemnation or justification—then perhaps it will be possible to understand conflict.

After all, conflict arises, does it not, through the desire to be something, to be other than *what is*. This constant desire to be something other than *what is* is one of the ways of conflict, which does not mean that we should be content with *what is*—one never is. But to understand *what is,* we must understand this desire to be something other than *what is.* I am something—ugly, greedy, envious—and I want to be something else, the opposite to *what is.* Surely, that is one of the causes of conflict—these opposing and contradictory desires of which we are made up.

I think that merely looking at conflict, being aware of its process, is in itself freeing. That is, if we are aware without any friction, without any choice, merely aware of *what is,* and if we are also aware of the desire to run away from *what is* into the self-projected ideal—and all ideals are home-made, and therefore fictitious, unreal—if we are merely aware of all that, then that very awareness will bring about a tranquillity of the mind. And then you can proceed with *what is;* then there is a possibility of understanding *what is.*

But, surely, conflict is much more significant than the mere friction between opposites. Conflict arises, does it not, through approximation of action to an idea. We are always trying to approximate action to a belief, to an ideal, to an idea. I have an idea of what I should be, of what the state should be, and I'm trying to live up to that ideal. Therefore, conflict arises when there is the attempt to bridge idea and action. But, is it possible to bridge idea and action? Action is real, is actual, isn't it? Without action I cannot live. But why should I try to conform action to an idea? Is idea more real than action? Has idea more substance than action? Is idea truer than action? And yet, if we watch ourselves, all our action is based on idea. We have the idea first, and then there is action. Only rarely is there action which is spontaneous, free, without the idea encompassing it.

So, why is there this division between idea and action? If we can understand that, perhaps we may be able radically to put an end to conflict because conflict is obviously not the way to understanding. If I quarrel with you, if I am in conflict with you, with my wife, with society, with my neighbors, close by or far away, there can be no understanding. Does understanding come through the struggle between thesis and antithesis, between the opposites? Does synthesis come through conflict? Or, is there understanding when there is no conflict? That understanding we try to translate through action, from which again arises conflict. To put it differently, when there is creativeness, when we have that creative feeling, there is no struggle, there is absence of struggle, which means that the self, the 'me', with all its prejudices, its conditioning, is not there. In that state when the self is not, there is creativeness; and that creative feeling, that creative state, we try to express in action—through music, painting, or what you will. Then the struggle begins—the desire for recognition, and so on.

Surely, the creative state does not demand struggle; on the contrary, when there is struggle, there is no creative state. When the self, the 'me', is totally absent, there is a possibility for that creative state to come into being. And as long as idea predominates, there must be struggle, there must be conflict. That is, to shape action according to idea must further conflict. So, if we can understand why idea predominates in our minds, then perhaps we shall be able to approach action differently.

Most of us are concerned with how to live according to an idea. We have the idea first—how to be noble, how to be good, how to be spiritual, and all the rest of it—and then try to live according to it. Why do we do this? We first establish a mental pattern which we call the idea, or the ideal, and according to that we try to live. Why? Is not the whole process of ideation brought about through the 'me', the 'I', the self? Is not the self, the 'me', an idea? There is no 'me' apart from the idea of the 'me'. The 'me' creates the pattern. The 'me' is an idea, and according to that idea we live, we try to act.

So, the idea is primarily, is it not, the outcome of the importance of the self. And, having established the importance of the 'me' and 'mine', the pattern of behavior, we try to live according to that. Therefore, idea controls action, idea impedes action. Take for instance, generosity, complete generosity—not the generosity of mind, but of heart. If one lived according to that, it would be very dangerous, wouldn't it? If one were to act completely generously, it would lead to all kinds of friction with existing standards. So, the idea intervenes, controls generosity. And it is safer to live according to the idea of generosity than according to the generosity of the heart.

So, when idea predominates, it is obvious that we are seeking security, safety, comfort, exclusion, isolation—and are therefore creating more friction. Because, nothing can live in isolation—to be is to be related. Idea brings isolation, and action does not. And our conflict is always between idea and action. And I think that if we can understand this process of ideation, if we can understand ourselves not superficially but the whole process of ourselves, the conscious as well as the unconscious, then perhaps we shall understand this conflict. After all, conflict arises because the 'me' is important—the 'me' which is identified with the country, with the particular belief, with the particular name or family. That is the source of all conflict, is it not?—because the 'me' is ever seeking isolation, exclusion. Action based on the idea of exclusion must inevitably create conflict from which we try to escape, consciously or unconsciously, and therefore conflict is increased.

So, to understand conflict it is important, it seems to me, to know the whole process of one's thinking and to be aware of how actually, in daily life, we are trying to approximate action to an idea. And, can one live without idea? Can one live without the self? Really and basically it comes to that—can one live in this monstrously ugly, conflicting world without the thought of 'me'? I think this can be answered actually, not theoretically, only when one understands the process of the 'me', what makes up the 'me'. One sees that these tortuous ways, the contradictions, the denials, the approximations, all belong to the self-projected pattern of an idea. So, in knowing oneself totally—not at any one level of consciousness, but as a total process that is going on constantly—in being aware of that, there does come about a freedom from the self, and only then is it possible for the mind to be silent.

Only when the self is absent is there a possibility for the mind to be quiet and therefore be able to understand, able to receive that which is eternal. But to make a picture of eternity, to conceive an idea of it, or to hold to a belief about it is really self-projection; it is merely an illusion, it has no reality. But, for the timeless to be, the workings, the fabrications, the projections of the self must, obviously, entirely cease. And the cessation of that self-projection is the beginning of meditation, is it not?—because understanding oneself is the beginning of meditation, and without meditation there is no possibility of understanding the self. Without understanding the process of the self, there is no basis for thought, there is no basis for right thinking. Merely to approximate action to an idea or to an ideal is utterly vain. Whereas, if we can understand ourselves in action, which is relationship in daily life—relationship with one's wife, one's husband, the way one talks to one's servant, the snobbishness, the nationalism, the prejudices, the greeds and the envies of everyday life, not the self placed at a higher level, which is still within the field of thought and therefore still part of self—to be aware of all this action in relationship is the beginning of meditation. And in understanding this action of the self, surely, there is tranquillity. Only when the mind is really quiet, not made quiet; only when it is not compelled, not conforming, but is quiet—only then is there a possibility of discovering that which is eternal.

Question: Would you tell us what, according to you, is the truth which will free us? What is meant by your statement, "Truth must come to you; you cannot seek it"?

KRISHNAMURTI: Surely, by understanding what is false, what is illusion, what is ignorance, truth comes into being, does it not? You don't have to seek it because thought is the instrument with which you are seeking. If I am greedy, envious, prejudiced, and I try to seek truth, obviously my truth will be the result of greed, envy, prejudice—therefore it is not truth. All that I can do is to see what is false, to be aware that I am conditioned, that I am greedy, that I am envious. That is all I can do—to be aware of it choicelessly. Then, when I am so aware, and therefore free from greed, truth comes into being. But if we seek truth, the result obviously will be illusion. How can you seek truth? Truth must be something unknown to a mind that is caught in the false—and we are because we are conditioned, psychologically as well as physiologically, and a conditioned mind, do what it will, cannot possibly measure the immeasurable.

These are not just words. You can see the truth of it if you are really willing to listen rightly. How can I, when I am conditioned by belief, by fear, by my nationalism, by my prejudices, and in innumerable ways by greed and envy—how can I see the truth? If I do, it will be a self-projection. What the self seeks is obviously its own creation, therefore untrue. And seeing the truth of this, the truth of what I have just now said, is already a liberating process, is it not?—merely to see it, to be aware that greed cannot find, envy cannot find, that which is true. Merely to observe it, to see it, to silently be aware of it will bring about not only release from greed, but the realization of what is true.

So, those who are trying to seek truth will obviously be caught in illusion, and therefore, truth must come to you, you cannot go after it, you cannot chase it. Because, after all, what is it we all want? We want gratification, we want comfort, we want inward security, peace—and that is what we are seeking. We call it truth, we give it a name. Therefore, what we are seeking in different forms, at different levels, is gratification, not truth. Truth can come into being only when the desire for gratification, for security, has come to an end—which is extremely arduous, and as most of us are lazy, sluggish, we pretend to seek truth and form societies and organizations around it.

So, all that we can do is to be aware of our own appetites, desires, and vanities—it does not matter at what level you may place them—to be aware of all that and to be free of it, which means to be free of the self, the 'me'. Then, you do not have to seek truth; then truth will come to you because the field is there—a mind that is quiet, undisturbed by its own agitations. Such a mind is capable of receiving. It must be negatively aware, passively aware, which again is very, very arduous because the mind wants to be something; it wants a result, an achievement. And if it has failed in one direction, it will seek success in another. That success it calls the search for truth. Whereas, truth is the unknown; it must be discovered from moment to moment, not in some abstraction, not in some isolated action, but in every moment of our daily existence. To see the false as the false is the beginning of the truth—the false in our speech, the false in our relationships, the little appetites, the little vanities, the barbarities which we indulge in. To see the truth of the falseness of all that is the beginning of the perception of what is true.

But you see, most of us do not want to be so aware. It is tiresome. We'd rather escape into some illusion, into some belief, in which we can find isolation and consolation—it's so much easier, and in that isolation we say that we seek truth. It is not possible to find truth in isolation. It is not possible, being psychologically secure, certain, for the great uncertainty of truth to come into being. So, all that we can do if we are really serious, earnestly interested, is to give truth an opportunity to come into being by understanding our relationship with things, with people, with ideas. Then, understanding brings freedom, and in that freedom alone can there be the real.

Question: Your teachings some years ago were understandable and inspiring. You then spoke earnestly about evolution, the path, discipleship, and the Masters. Now it is all different. I am utterly bewildered. I readily believed you then and would like to believe you now. I am confused. Which is the truth—what you said then or what you say now?

KRISHNAMURTI: This really needs serious consideration and I hope those of you who are bored with this kind of stuff will listen patiently.

First of all, it's not a question of belief. You don't have to believe what I say—far from it. If you believe what I say, then it is your misery, not mine; then you will use me as another authority and therefore take shelter, comfort. But what I am saying is merely that without self-knowledge, without knowing yourself, there can be no understanding of life. That does not demand belief. It demands watchfulness on your part—not belief in what I say. So, let us be very clear on that point because I think that to believe is a hindrance to the understanding of truth—which does not mean that you must become an atheist, which is another form of belief. But to understand the total process of believing, of why you believe, is the beginning of wisdom.

We believe because we want to hold on to something, because we want security; we are so uncertain in ourselves, we are so discontented, we are so inwardly poor that we want something rich to hold on to. As the worldly man holds on to property, so the so-called believer holds on to his belief—there is not much difference between the two. Both want security, both want comfort, both want certainty. And these beliefs are self-projected and therefore do not lead to reality.

Now, the questioner wants to know why I have changed. At one time, some years ago, I talked of Masters, discipleship, progress, spiritual growth, and all that kind of thing. And now I do not. Why? Where has the change come, and what has produced it?—isn't that the basis of the question? And he wants to know which to believe—those things which I said previously or what I am saying now.

What was said previously demanded belief. After all, you need a belief about the Masters. You can rationalize that belief, but still it is a belief. And it's very convenient to have such a belief, especially when the Master is somewhere far away because then you can play with that idea. But if you have a guru, a teacher directly in relationship with you physically, then it's much more difficult, isn't it, because he will criticize you, he will watch over you, he will tell you off—which is much more painful. Whereas, to have a Master in India or in the Himalayas or on some mountain far away from all our daily life is very convenient, very encouraging. And such a thing needs belief. It is a self-projected idea. And that gives you comfort because then you can postpone action, then you can say, "Well, I'll be like him in my next life. It will take me a long time to be free from greed"—and that you call evolution. Surely, greed is not a thing to be postponed—either you are free from greed now or you will never be. To say that you will become free from greed some day is the continuation of greed. And the idea that someone is looking after you, patting you on the back, encouraging you, showing special interest in you, while you discipline yourself according to him, according to his ideals laid down by him—all this is obviously puffing up the self. Naturally, it gives you encouragement, it gives you inspiration to think that someone is looking after you, that you have all eternity in front of you to be something, that the path is a thing to tread slowly, taking your time, and that one day you will arrive.

All such thoughts and beliefs are very encouraging and inspiring. That's why societies are formed for people who want to be encouraged. Such a process, to me, is the way of exploitation because you like to be exploited by the Master, or by the representative of the Master, and you choose the representative according to your desires and gratifications. When you are being gratified, it's very inspiring—at least, you call it inspiring; it's really another form of sensation.

Now, when you see all that as being false, utterly without any basis, when you see that nothing can lead you to the truth except your own understanding of yourself, that no Master can give you the light save yourself—then it's not so inspiring, not so encouraging, because to know oneself demands watchfulness, alertness, constant vigilance; and it is rather boring, tiresome, depressing, to know that one is ugly. But to be told there is something in you which is eternal, marvelous—that you like. And so you follow the Master and accept all the illusions that go with it. Then it gives you satisfaction, and that is, after all, what most of us are seeking—not truth, not to understand what is false, but to be gratified. And as you seek certainty, security, in the physical world, so you carry that over into the psychological, spiritual world. But there is no security in the psychological world. If you seek security, then there is illusion, for it is only in great uncertainty that you find.

Now, when you see all that, obviously you put those things away from you. You no longer play with them. And what I say now is not the other side of the coin—it has nothing to do with those things, which are false. To understand oneself is the beginning of wisdom. When you see that which is false, you are already beginning to see that which is true. Obviously, this whole structure of self-expansion, with spiritual degrees of discipleship, the ladder of hierarchical achievement, is utterly false because that which is true has no divisions. But we like divisions; we like exclusions; socially we like to be called by a title. And you carry the same snobbishness into the other world. But when one sees this whole process as being self-expansive, giving importance to the 'me', to the 'mine', giving prestige to myself, then, surely, it fades away; you don't have to struggle against it. It's like seeing something poisonous—it has no attraction, it is no longer true; therefore, you no longer belong to that way of thinking.

You see, all this implies that one must stand alone. But most of us are afraid to be alone—not alone in the sense of isolation, but alone in the sense of seeing something as it is, seeing the false as the false and the true as the true. To see the false as the false, when everybody is seeing what is false as the true, needs certain choiceless awareness. And, as most of us dread to be alone, quiet, free from all self-projected illusions, we cling to things made by the mind. Without understanding yourself, do what you will—invent any theory, any Master, follow any discipline—it will not lead to happiness. You may deceive yourself; you may deceive yourself by saying, "What you say and what I believe are the same. They're the two sides of the coin." You may say what you like, but that is mere self-deception. But to go into this whole problem of the self, to see all its ways, its deceptions and illusions, its comforts—to know oneself so completely brings tranquillity of the mind, which another can not give you. Then, in that tranquillity, that which is eternal can be.

Question: How is one to be free of the constant fear of death?

KRISHNAMURTI: What is it that creates fear? Why is one afraid of death? If you don't mind, let us experiment with this—not only with what I have said previously, but with this also. You see, while most of us are afraid of death, we also know why. Obviously, we don't want to come to an end. We know the body is going to perish, be destroyed like any other thing which is used constantly. But, psychologically, we don't want to come to an end. Why?

Because we don't want to come to an end, we have rationalized innumerable theories: that we will continue in the hereafter, that there is reincarnation, that some kind of self continues, and so on. But still, in spite of all these rationalized beliefs, convictions, and determinations, there is fear. Why? Is it not because we want certainty of the unknown? We don't know what is after death. We would like to continue with all our qualities, with all our achievements, with all our identifications. We seek permanency, which we call immortality. We seek permanency in this world through name, property, possessions, family, and so on—which is an obvious thing we are doing all the time. And we also want to continue in another realm of thought, of feeling—in the psychological world, the spiritual world.

What is it that continues? Idea, thought, is it not? The idea of yourself as a name, as a particular identified individual—which is still an idea, which is memory, which means the word. So, thought, mind, identifying itself as memory, as the word, as the name, wants to continue. Surely, most of us are clinging to that, aren't we, in different ways. As I grow older, I look back upon life, or I look forward with fear to death. So, we want to continue in some form or other. And, being uncertain of that continuity, we are afraid. You are not afraid of leaving your family, your children; that is just an excuse. Actually, you're afraid to come to an end.

Now, that which continues, that which has continuity—can that be creative? Is there a renewal in that which continues? Surely, there is renewal only in that which comes to an end. Where there is an ending, there is a rebirth—but not in that which continues. If I continue as I am, as I have been in this life, with all my ignorance, prejudices, stupidities, illusions, memories, and attachments—what have I? And yet it is to that we cling so tenaciously.

Surely, in ending there is renewal, is there not? It's only in death that a new thing comes into being. I am not giving you comfort. This is not something to be believed or thought about or intellectually examined and accepted, for then you will make it into another comfort, as you now believe in reincarnation or continuity in the hereafter, and so on. But the actual fact is that that which continues has no rebirth, no renewal. Therefore, in dying every day there is renewal, there is a rebirth. That is immortality. In death there is immortality—not the death of which you are afraid, but the death of previous conclusions, memories, experiences, with which you are identified as the 'me'. In the dying of the 'me' every minute there is eternity, there is immortality, there is a thing to be experienced—not to be speculated upon or lectured about as you do about reincarnation and all that kind of stuff. Only when you come to an end as the 'me', when you cease to be attached to your family, to your properties, to your ideas—only then is there immortality, which does not mean that you become indifferent, callous, or irresponsible.

When you are no longer afraid, because every minute there is an ending and therefore a renewal, then you are open to the unknown. Reality is the unknown. Death is also the unknown. But to call death beautiful, to say how marvelous it is because we shall continue in the hereafter and all that nonsense has no reality. What has reality is seeing death as it is—an ending, an ending in which there is renewal, a rebirth, not a continuity. For, that which continues, decays; and that which has the power to renew itself, is eternal. But a mind that is attached, possessed, can never renew itself. Therefore, such a mind is afraid of the unknown, of the future. Fear ceases only when there is constant renewal, which means constant death. But most of us do not want to die that way. We like to be attached to our furniture and properties, to our beliefs, to our so-called loved ones. We want to continue in that state, with our conflicts, with our experiences, with our attachments. And, when all that is threatened, we are frightened. And so there are innumerable books written about death. You're more interested in death than in living; whereas, in understanding living—that is, yourself in constant relationship, in seeing the false as the false, and therefore dying every minute, not in theory, but actually, to the things to which you are attached, to beliefs, to memories—only then is there renewal in which there is no death.

October 16, 1949

Fourth Talk in London

For the past few weeks we have been discussing the problem of self-awareness and self-knowledge. It is so obviously essential to know oneself completely. And to know oneself is not a withdrawal from life but rather the understanding of relationship—relationship with things, with people, with ideas. And, experience can be understood only through self-knowledge; experience is not apart from self-knowledge.

Unfortunately, most of us do not seek self-knowledge but cling to experience. And we use experience as a measure to discover truth, to discover reality, or God, or what you will. So experience, with most of us, has become the standard of valuation.

But does experience reveal truth, or whatever name you like to call it? Surely, experience is a distraction, a process away from oneself. That is, most of us are so unaware of the total process of our existence, we do not see that we are running away from ourselves. In ourselves, whether we admit it or not, consciously or unconsciously, there is a state of poverty, an emptiness, which we try to cover up, from which we try to run away. And in the process of covering it up, we have various experiences; we cling to various points of view, beliefs. And these distractions, which are obviously away from ourselves, are experiences. That is, one is aware, consciously or unconsciously, of a sense of emptiness in oneself, a sense of being nothing, a sense of being insufficient. Most of us are aware of it, but we are not willing to face it, not willing to understand what it is; we try to run away from that state of emptiness, that state of nothingness, either through holding on to property, through name, through position or family, through people, or through knowledge. This flight from ourselves is called experience, and to these escapes we cling, and therefore the means of escape becomes much more important than the understanding of ourselves. The means of escape from our own state offer happiness, and therefore experience becomes a hindrance to the understanding of *what is.*

That is, to put it differently, most of us are aware that we are lonely, and to escape from that loneliness, we turn on the radio or read a book or cling to a person or become addicted to knowledge. This escape from *what is* gives us various experiences, and to these experiences we cling. Then property, name, position, prestige, become extraordinarily important. Similarly, the person becomes important, whether the one or the many, the individual or the group, the society. And likewise knowledge, as a means of escape from ourselves, becomes extraordinarily important.

So, we cover up that emptiness, that loneliness, through knowledge, through relationship, and through possessions; therefore, possessions, relationships, and knowledge become extraordinarily important because without them we should be lost. Without them we are face to face with ourselves as we are, and to escape from that, we resort to all these means and are caught in the experiences of these escapes. We use those experiences as a standard, as a measure, to discover reality. But reality, or God, is the unknown; it cannot be measured by our experience, by our conditioning; and to come to it, we must put aside all escapes and face *what is*—which is our loneliness, our extraordinary sense of being nothing. Because, we are empty, though we do not like to acknowledge it, and we have therefore surrounded ourselves with things through which we escape from ourselves.

So, experience is not a measure, is not the way to reality because, after all, we experience according to our belief, according to our conditioning, and that belief is obviously an escape from ourselves. To know myself, I need not have any belief; I only have to watch myself, clearly and choicelessly—watch myself in relationship, watch myself in escape, watch myself in attachment. And one has to watch oneself without any prejudice, without any conclusion, without any determination. In that passive awareness one discovers this extraordinary sense of aloneness. I am sure most of you have felt this—the sense of complete emptiness which nothing can fill. It is only in abiding in that state, when all values have utterly ceased, it is only when we are capable of being alone and facing that aloneness without any sense of escape—only then does reality come into being. Because, values are merely the result of our conditioning; like experience, they are based on a belief and are a hindrance to the understanding of reality.

But, that is an arduous task, which most of us are unwilling to go through. So we cling to experiences—mystical, superstitious, the experiences of relationship, of so-called love, and the experiences of possession. These become very significant because it is of these that we are made. We are made of beliefs, of conditionings, of environmental influences—that is our background. And from that background, we judge, we value. And when one goes through, understands, the whole process of this background, then one comes to a point where one is utterly alone. One must be alone to find reality—which does not mean escape, withdrawal from life. On the contrary, it is the complete intensification of life because then there is freedom from the background, from the memory of the experiences of escape. In that aloneness, in that loneliness, there is no choice, there is no fear of *what is*. Fear arises only when we are unwilling to acknowledge or see *what is*.

Therefore, it is essential for reality to come into being, to set aside the innumerable escapes that one has established, in which one is caught up. After all, if you observe, you will see how we use people—how we use our husbands and wives or groups or nationalities—to escape from ourselves. We seek comfort in relationship. Such a search for comfort in relationship brings certain experiences, and to those experiences we cling. Also, to escape from ourselves, knowledge becomes extraordinarily important, but knowledge is obviously not the way to reality. Mind must be completely empty and still for reality to come into being. But a mind that is rattling around with knowledge, addicted to ideas and beliefs, ever chattering, is incapable of receiving that which is. Similarly, if we seek comfort in relationship, then relationship is an avoidance of ourselves. After all, in relationship we want comfort, we want something to lean on, we want support, we want to be loved, we want to be possessed—which all indicates the poverty of our own being. Similarly, our desire for property, for name, for titles, for possessions, indicates that inward insufficiency.

When one realizes that this is not the way to reality, then one comes to that state when the mind is no longer seeking comfort, when the mind is completely content with *what is*—which does not mean stagnation. In the flight from *what is,* there is death; in the recognition and awareness of *what is,* there is life. So, experience based on conditioning, the experience of a belief, which is the result of escape from ourselves, and the experience of relationship—these become a hindrance, a block; they cover up our insufficiencies. And it is only when we recognize that these things are an escape and therefore see their true value—only then is there a possibility of remaining quiet, still, in that emptiness, in that loneliness. And when the mind is very quiet, neither accepting nor rejecting, being passively aware of that which is—then there is a possibility for that immeasurable reality to be.

Question: Is there, or is there not, a divine plan? What is the sense of our striving if there is not one?

KRISHNAMURTI: Why do we strive? And what are we striving for? What would happen if we did not strive? Would we stagnate and decay? What is this constant striving to be something? What does this strife, this effort, indicate? And, does understanding come through effort, through striving? One is constantly striving to become better, to change oneself, to fit oneself to a certain pattern, to become something—from the clerk to the manager, from the manager to the divine. And, does this striving bring understanding?

I think the question of effort should really be understood. What is it that is making the effort, and what do we mean by "the will to be"? We make an effort, do we not, in order to achieve a result, in order to become better, in order to be more virtuous, or less of something else. There is this constant battle going on in us between positive and negative desires, one superseding the other, one desire controlling the other—only we call it the higher and the lower self. But, obviously, it is still desire. You can place it at any level and give it a different name—it is still desire, a craving to be something. There is also the constant strife within oneself and with others, with society.

Now, does this conflict of desires bring understanding? Does the conflict of opposites, the want and the nonwant, bring clarification? And is there understanding in the struggle to approximate ourselves to an idea? So, the problem is not the strife, the struggle, or what would happen if we did not struggle, if we did not make an effort, if we did not strive to be something, psychologically as well as outwardly; the problem is, how does understanding come into being? Because, when once there is understanding, there is no strife. What you understand, of that you are free.

How does understanding come into being? I do not know if you have ever noticed that the more you struggle to understand, the less you understand any problem. But, the moment you cease to struggle and let the problem tell you the whole story, give all its significance—then there is understanding, which means, obviously, that to understand, the mind must be quiet. The mind must be choicelessly, passively, aware; and in that state, there is understanding of the many problems of our life.

The questioner wants to know if there is or if there is not a divine plan. I do not know what you mean by a "divine plan." But we do know, do we not, that we are in sorrow, that we are in confusion, that confusion and sorrow are ever on the increase, socially, psychologically, individually, and collectively. It is what we have made of this world. Whether this is a divine plan or not is not important at all. But what is important is to understand the confusion in which we live, outwardly as well as inwardly. And to understand that confusion, we must begin, obviously, with ourselves—because we *are* confusion; it is we who have produced this outward confusion in the world. And to clear up that confusion, we must begin with ourselves; because, what we are, the world is.

Now, you will say, "Well, it will take a very long time in this way to bring about order in the world." I'm not at all sure that you are right because, after all, it's one or two who are very clear, who understand, that bring about a revolution, a change. But we are lazy, you see; that is the difficulty. We want others to change, we want circumstances to change, we want the government to order our lives or some miracle to take place that will transform us. And so, we abide with confusion.

So, what is really important is not to inquire if there is or if there is not a divine plan, because over that you will waste speculative hours, proving that there is or there is not. That becomes a game for the propagandists. But what is important is really to free oneself from confusion, and that does not take a long period of time. What is essential is to see that one is confused, that all activity, all action which springs from confusion, must be confused also. It's like a confused person seeking a leader—his leader must also be confused. So, what is essential is to see that one is confused and not try to escape from it, not try to find explanations for it; be passively, choicelessly, aware. And then you will see that quite a different action springs from that passive awareness, because if you make an effort to clarify the state of confusion, what you create will still be confused. But, if you are aware of yourself, choicelessly, passively aware, then that confusion unfolds and fades away.

You will see, if you will experiment with this—and it will not take a long period of time because time is not involved in it at all—that clarification comes into being. But you must give your whole attention, your whole interest, to it. And I am not at all sure that most of us do not like to be confused because in the state of confusion you need not act. And so we are satisfied with the confusion because to understand confusion demands action which is not the pursuit of an ideal or an ideation.

So, the question whether there is or whether there is not a divine plan is irrelevant. We have to understand ourselves and the world we have created—the misery, the confusion, the conflict, the wars, the divisions, the exploitations. All that is the result of ourselves in relationship with others. And if we can understand ourselves in relationship with others, if we can see how we use others, how we try to escape from ourselves through people, through property, through knowledge, and therefore give immense significance to relationship, to property, to knowledge—if we can see all that, be aware of it passively, then we shall be free from that background which we are. Then only is there a possibility of finding out *what is.* But, to spend hours speculating whether there is a divine plan or not, striving to find out about it, lecturing about it, seems to me so infantile. For, peace does not come into being through conformity to any plan, whether the plan is left, right, or divine. Conformity is mere suppression, and in suppression there is fear. Only in understanding can there be peace and tranquillity, and in that tranquillity, reality comes into being.

Question: Does understanding come to one suddenly, unrelated to past effort and experience?

KRISHNAMURTI: What do we mean by past experience? How do you experience a challenge? After all, life is a process of challenge and response, is it not?—the challenge always being new; otherwise, it is not a challenge. And our response is inevitably the outcome of the background, of our conditioning. So, the response, if it is not adequate, full, complete with regard to the challenge, must create friction, must create conflict. It is this conflict between the challenge and the response that we call experience. I do not know if you have ever noticed that if your response to the challenge is complete, there is only a state of experiencing, not the remembrance of an experience. But, when the response is not adequate to the challenge, then we cling to the memory of the experience.

It is not so difficult; don't be so puzzled. Let us explore it a little more, and you will see. As I said, life is a process of challenge and response—at all levels, not at one particular level—and as long as that response is not adequate to the challenge, there must be conflict. Surely, that is obvious. And conflict invariably prevents understanding. Through conflict, one cannot understand any problem, can one? If I am constantly quarreling with my neighbor, with my wife, with my associates, it is not possible to understand that relationship. It is possible to understand only when there is no conflict.

And does understanding come suddenly? That is, can conflict cease suddenly? Or, must one go through innumerable conflicts, understanding each conflict, and then be free of all conflict? That is, to put the problem differently, behind this question I'm sure there is another question: "Since you have been through the various fogs, confusions, conflicts, belief in Masters, in reincarnation, the various societies, and so on, and so on, must I not also go through them? Since you have been through certain phases, must I not also go through those phases in order to be free?" That is, must we not all experience confusion in order to be free of confusion?

So, the problem is, is it not, does understanding come through following or accepting certain patterns and living through these patterns in order to be free? Say, for example, at one time you believed in certain ideas, but now you have pushed them aside, you are free and have understanding. And I come along and see that you have lived through certain beliefs and have pushed them aside and gained understanding. So, I say to myself, "I will also follow those beliefs, or accept those beliefs, and eventually, I will come to understanding." Surely, that is a wrong process, is it not? What is important is to understand. Is understanding a matter of time? Surely not. If you are interested in something, there is no question of time. Your whole being is there, concentrated, completely absorbed in that thing. And it is only when you want to gain a result that the question of time comes in. So, if you treat understanding as an end to be gained, then you require time, then you talk about "immediate" or "postponed." But, understanding, surely, is not an end process. Understanding comes when you are quiet, when the mind is still. And if you see the necessity of the mind being still, then immediately there is understanding.

Question: What, according to you, is true meditation?

KRISHNAMURTI: Now, what is the purpose of meditation? And what do we mean by meditation? I do not know if you have meditated, so, let us experiment together to find out what is true meditation. Don't listen merely to my expression of it, but together we'll find out and experience what is true meditation. Because, meditation is important, isn't it? If you do not know what is right meditation, there is no self-knowledge, and without knowing yourself, meditation has no meaning. To sit in a corner or walk about in the garden or in the street and try to meditate has no meaning. That only leads to a peculiar concentration, which is exclusion. I'm sure some of you have tried all those methods. That is, you try to concentrate on a particular object, try to force the mind, when it is wandering all over the place, to be concentrated; and when that fails, you pray.

So, if one really wants to understand what is right meditation, one must find out what are the false things which we have called meditation. Obviously, concentration is not meditation because, if you observe, in the process of concentration there is exclusion, and therefore there is distraction. You are trying to concentrate on something, and your mind is wandering off towards something else, and there is this constant battle going on to be fixed on one point while the mind refuses and wanders off. And so we spend years trying to concentrate, to learn concentration, which is mistakenly called meditation.

Then there is the question of prayer. Prayer obviously produces results; otherwise, millions wouldn't pray. And in praying, obviously the mind is made quiet; by constant repetition of certain phrases, the mind does become quiet. And in that quietness there is a certain intimation, certain perceptions, certain responses. But, that is still a part of the trick of the mind because, after all, through a form of mesmerism you can make the mind very quiet. And in that quietness there are certain hidden responses arising from the unconscious and from outside the consciousness. But, it is still a state in which there is no understanding.

And, meditation is not devotion—devotion to an idea, to a picture, to a principle—because the things of the mind are still idolatrous. One may not worship a statue, considering it idolatrous and silly, superstitious; but one does worship, as most people do, the things in the mind—and that is also idolatrous. And, to be devoted to a picture or an idea, to a Master, is not meditation. Obviously, it's a form of escape from oneself. It's a very comforting escape, but it's still an escape.

And this constant striving to become virtuous, to acquire virtue through discipline, through careful examination of oneself, and so on, is obviously not meditation either. Most of us are caught in these processes, and since they do not give understanding of ourselves, they are not the way of right meditation. After all, without understanding yourself, what basis have you for right thinking? All that you will do without that understanding of yourself is to conform to the background, to the response of your conditioning. And such response to the conditioning is not meditation. But to be aware of those responses, that is, to be aware of the movements of thought and feeling without any sense of condemnation so that the movements of the self, the ways of the self, are completely understood—that way is the way of right meditation.

Meditation is not a withdrawal from life. Meditation is a process of understanding oneself. And when one begins to understand oneself, not only the conscious, but all the hidden parts of oneself as well, then there comes tranquillity. A mind that is made still through meditation, through compulsion, through conformity, is not still. It is a stagnant mind. It is not a mind that is alert, passive, capable of creative receptivity. Meditation demands constant watchfulness, constant awareness of every word, every thought and feeling which reveals the state of our own being, the hidden as well as the superficial; and as that is arduous, we escape into every kind of comforting, deceptive thing and call it meditation.

If one can see that self-knowledge is the beginning of meditation, then the problem becomes extraordinarily interesting and vital. Because, after all, if there is no self-knowledge, you may practice what you call meditation and still be attached to your principles, to your family, to your property; or, giving up your property, you may be attached to an idea and be so concentrated on it that you create more and more of that idea. Surely, that is not meditation. So, self-knowledge is the beginning of meditation; without self-knowledge there is no meditation. And as one goes deeper into the question of self-knowledge, not only does the upper mind become tranquil, quiet, but the different layers of the hidden are revealed. When the superficial mind is quiet, then the unconscious, the hidden layers of consciousness project themselves; they reveal their content; they give their intimations so that the whole process of one's being is completely understood.

So, the mind becomes extremely quiet—is quiet. It is not made quiet, it is not compelled to be quiet by a reward, by fear. Then there is a silence in which reality comes into being. But that silence is not Christian silence or Hindu silence or Buddhist silence. That silence is silence, not named. Therefore, if you follow the path of Christian silence, or Hindu or Buddhist, you will never be silent. Therefore, a man who would find reality must abandon his conditioning completely—whether Christian, Hindu, Buddhist, or of any other group. Merely to strengthen the background through meditation, through conformity, brings about stagnation of the mind, dullness of the mind; and I'm not at all sure that's not what most of us want, because it's so much easier to create a pattern and follow it. But to be free of the background demands constant watchfulness in relationship.

And, when once that silence is, then there is an extraordinary, creative state—not that you must write poems, paint pictures; you may or you may not. But that silence is not to be pursued, copied, imitated—then it ceases to be silence. You cannot come to it through any path. It comes into being only when the ways of the self are understood, and the self, with all its activities and mischief, comes to an end. That is, when the mind ceases to create, then there is creation. Therefore, the mind must become simple, must become quiet, must be quiet—the "must" is wrong: to say the mind must be quiet, implies compulsion. And the mind is quiet only when the whole process of the self has come to an end. When all the ways of the self are understood, and therefore the activities of the self have come to an end—then only is there silence. That silence is true meditation, and in that silence the eternal comes into being.

October 23, 1949

Fifth Talk in London

It must seem very difficult for most of us to bring about a real transformation within ourselves. We see the necessity of real, deep, radical revolution, both inwardly and in outward things; and it is obvious that this transformation should be not momentary but constant. We want to bring about changes in the world—economic changes, social changes, and so on, but it seems to me that one cannot really bring about a significant outward change, unless there is a radical psychological revolution, transformation. For the inner, surely, always overcomes the outer. What one is, that one creates outwardly. And unless this transformation takes place, mere outward reforms, outward changes, however carefully worked out, will inevitably fail because the thing that is missing is this inward revolution, this inward transformation.

And how is this inner transformation to be brought about? If we can really discuss it this morning, we may see that it is not so impossible, that it is not just for the few, but for those who are really serious and earnest. And what do we mean by this revolution, by this transformation within? Because, if there is no inner transformation, one can see that whatever one may do outwardly, whatever social reforms one may bring about will inevitably fail. Unless the inner motives, desires, impulses are understood, they overpower the outward structure.

So, it is essential to begin within oneself, to bring about the transformation in one's own attitude, actions, and direction. That transformation, surely, must begin with self-knowledge, because without self-knowledge, there can be no radical revolution. Revolution is not according to an idea, according to a pattern; then it is not a revolution—it is merely a modified continuity. But, if one can understand the psychological process of oneself, the inward demands, pursuits, fears, ambitions, hopes; and if one can go through the whole process of them—then it is possible to bring about a transformation. And therefore it is necessary, surely, to understand oneself before one can bring about a transformation, outwardly or inwardly.

Now, this study of oneself cannot take place without understanding relationship. And as I've been saying over and over again, it is only in relationship that one begins to see the ways of the self—the self at whatever level one may place it—because relationship is the fundamental issue, is it not? Without understanding relationship, the relationship between yourself and another, and without bringing about a radical transformation there, mere attempts at social revolution will inevitably fail because our whole existence is based on relationship—the relationship between yourself and your wife, between yourself and your neighbor, and therefore the relationships of society as a whole. It is there that there must be transformation. And, there cannot be transformation in relationship if the self is not fully investigated and understood, because the self is obviously the source of all conflict. One may give full expression to that self, thinking that it is the only thing one has, but it will invariably bring conflict and confusion in relationship. And it is only in understanding relationship that there can be transformation. So, transformation must surely begin with relationship and not merely with the trimming of outward circumstances.

So, the problem of transformation, that is, of complete inward revolution, is not so difficult. It comes about only in understanding relationship because relationship is the mirror in which I discover myself in action. And without understanding the total process of myself, there can be no radical revolution. So, in the unfolding of relationship, I begin to discover myself—not only at the superficial level, but at the deeper levels as well. Surely, one can begin there, can one not? One can begin to watch oneself constantly, to observe the sense of possessiveness, the sense of domination, which expresses itself outwardly in your office and at home.

And why is there this sense of possession in relationship? Obviously, if we did not possess the person whom we say we love, we would feel frustrated, we would be at a loss, we would be faced with ourselves and our own emptiness, our own loneliness. So, we begin to possess, we begin to dominate, and are thereby caught in jealousy. So, in relationship we begin to discover ourselves, but in possessing, in dominating another, that relationship does not unfold itself, does not uncover the process of ourselves.

Most of us do not want to know ourselves. But that is the first necessity, is it not, if we are to understand ourselves. Most of us are afraid to know, afraid to discover, what we are—the ugly and the beautiful—whatever it is. So, we run away from it and use relationship as a means of comfort, as a means of security, and therefore we never understand ourselves. The self is a closed door when we seek comfort in relationship. And it is this desire for comfort from which arise all the complications of relationship—domination, jealousy, differentiation, loving one more than another, trying to make love impersonal, trying to be detached, and so on. There can be transformation only in the understanding of oneself. Only then is it possible to have a still mind—a mind that is not made still, but is still, through comprehension.

So, what is important is the intention to discover in relationship *what is,* what exactly is. And in understanding *what is* without condemnation, without justification, one can go beyond it. It is this capacity to look clearly at *what is*—jealousy, ambition, greed, or whatever is discovered through relationship—it is this capacity to look at it, to be with it, without any sense of condemnation or suppression, without any sense of escape, that makes it possible to go beyond *what is.* And it is only then that there can be radical transformation.

Therefore, virtue is that state which comes into being when *what is* is transcended. But the transcending, the going beyond *what is,* cannot take place if there is effort to be something. After all, that is what we are all trying to do, is it not? We all want to be something—more virtuous, more religious—we want to come nearer to the truth, or we are ambitious, worldly, and so on. We want to be something. We want to have greater understanding, greater happiness, greater wisdom. The very wanting to be something is the denial of that which is. If I want to be something, I'm not understanding what I am. To understand what I am, this desire to be something, this desire to become, must be understood. Why do we want to be other than we are? If I do not make an effort to be something, will that lead to contentment, that false, respectable stagnation? Is that the reason why we want to be something? Or, is it because we do not face what we are?—therefore, it is a process of escape from *what is.* This constant desire to be something, with all its turmoil, confusion, struggle, effort, is an escape from *what is,* an escape from ourselves. And as long as we do not understand ourselves and merely escape from *what is,* we only create greater conflict, greater misery. And if we can see that, see the futility of becoming something, of trying to achieve something psychologically, then there comes a contentment with *what is.* It is only then that there is no struggle with *what is,* trying to make it into something else—then it is possible to understand it. But, as long as we are trying to modify, to change *what is,* then there is no going beyond it. To discover *what is,* to be content with *what is,* is not stagnation; on the contrary, to be content with *what is* is the most effective action; it does not bring confusion, it does not create enmity. There is so much enmity and confusion in the world, so much misery; and if we desire to bring about a radical transformation there, we must begin with ourselves, begin to understand *what is,* live with it, look at it without any sense of trying to sublimate, to change, to modify it. And that is not possible when we merely discard *what is* by giving it a name, because the very naming of it is a process of condemnation or acceptance. But, when we do not name *what is,* it is transformed; and with that transformation there comes contentment—not the contentment of acquisition, not the contentment of having or possessing or achieving a result, but the contentment that comes when there is no conflict, because it is conflict that creates discontent. And conflict is not creative, it cannot bring understanding. Conflict is unnecessary in life, and conflict comes to an end only when we can understand *what is.*

The understanding of *what is* comes with freedom from the whole background of condemnation, justification, or identification. And as we discussed the other day, condemnation arises only when there is the analyzer, the examiner, the observer. But, the observer and the observed are a joint phenomenon;

and that unification, that integration between the observer and the observed takes place only when there is no sense of condemnation, justification, or identification—that is, when there is freedom from the background, which is the 'I', the 'me', the 'mine'. It is only when there is that freedom from the background that there is a possibility of responding to the challenge anew. Life is a process of challenge and response, and whenever the response is inadequate, there is conflict; and the inadequacy of the response can be removed only through understanding the process of relationship. And as we understand more and more the process of relationship, which is the process of myself in action, there is a possibility of the mind being still. A mind that is not still—whether it is pursuing knowledge or greed or becoming something now or in the hereafter—such a mind is incapable, obviously, of discovering because there must be freedom to discover. And as long as the mind is trying to be something, there can be no discovery. It is only in freedom that there can be discovery, and freedom is virtue, because virtue gives freedom. But, to strive to be virtuous is not freedom; it is another form of becoming, which is self-expansion.

So, virtue is the denial of becoming, and that denial takes place only with the understanding of *what is*. And when there is this radical transformation through self-knowledge, then there is a possibility of creative living. For, truth is not something to be achieved; it is not an end; it is not something to be gained. It comes into being from moment to moment. It is not a result of accumulated, stored-up knowledge, which is merely memory, conditioning, experience. But truth comes into being from moment to moment when the mind is capable of being free from all accumulations. For, the accumulator is the self—the self that gathers in order to assert, to dominate, to expand, to self-fulfill. Only with the freedom of the self does truth come into being—not as a continuous process, but to be discovered from moment to moment. Therefore, to discover, the mind must be fresh, alert, and still.

Question: In what way can I help you in your work?

KRISHNAMURTI: Is it my work, or your work? If it is my work, then you will become propagandists. And those who do propaganda are incapable of telling the truth because they are merely repetitive machines, not knowing what they are saying. They may know the clever expressions, the slogans, the clichés, but they can never discover what is true. And most of us are directed by the propagandists, because we live mostly by words, without much content. We accept words so easily—words like democracy, peace, communist, God, or soul. We never look into these things. We never go beyond the transitory sensations these words evoke. And so, if you are merely a propagandist, or live by propaganda, then you cannot find that which is eternal. And without discovery of truth, life becomes tedious, painful.

So, you are not doing my work, you are not helping me. But, what you are doing in all this is discovering yourself as you are, understanding yourself, because without understanding yourself, there is no basis for action, there is no basis for right thinking. So, you are not helping me in my work, but understanding yourself. And whatever you understand of yourself, that, for the time being, is the truth. And that can be discovered only in daily relationship—and in the relationship between you and me, as I talk and you listen, and how you listen. If you listen with prejudice, if you listen with your own background, with all your condemnations, prejudices, for or against, then you are not listening; you and I have no relationship. But if you listen to find out about yourself, to discover yourself in relationship, then it's your work and not my work. Then, since you are seeking truth, you will not be a mere propagandist. Then you are not concerned with convincing another, trying to convert another to your particular form of belief, trying to reform another, trying to bring another to your particular group, to your particular society. Then you, with your belief, are not important. But, the man with the belief—he is important because the belief with which he is identified gives him importance. The man who is seeking real self-knowledge is not enclosed by belief; he is not hedged about by any society, any organization, by any religion. Therefore, there is no question of your work and my work. What is important is to discover truth, and the discovery of truth is not yours or mine.

So, since it is not my work but your own, it is important how you deal with it, how you approach the whole structure of your life. That is what we are discussing—to see it, to see the structure of your being, and thereby bring about a transformation. The very perception of *what is* brings a radical transformation. But if you are listening in order to conform to what I am saying, then you will be a mere propagandist, then you will be a believer—you will create enmity and contention. And, God knows, there are enough groups, beliefs, in the world, all contending with each other, fighting with each other for money, for membership, and all that nonsense. But the man who is seeking self-knowledge will not create enmity because he is honest, he is true to himself, he is true to *what is.*

But, what is important in this question is to cease to be a propagandist and to experience directly—not through a book, not through another, not through your own particular illusions and deceptions, but to experience the truth directly for yourself from moment to moment. And such perception of truth is the liberating process. It brings joy to life, it brings clarity, an intensity that does not depend on moods. Therefore, it is your work, and that work begins with self-knowledge.

Question: Is all activity an escape? Is the service of humanity in its greatest need also an escape? Is not individual creative expression a true way of resolving conflict within oneself?

KRISHNAMURTI: What do we mean by activity and escape? Surely, those of us who are at all aware know that we are extraordinarily dull, extraordinarily empty. We have plenty of knowledge of what others say, of what others have written. We read, we listen, we try to copy, to imitate. But in ourselves we are as nothing. We are empty, insufficient, poor, lonely, driven like a leaf. And to escape from that, that sense of enormous fear, that gnawing anxiety of loneliness, we do all kinds of things, we indulge in all kinds of activities, religious, political, scientific, and so on. And this escape from ourselves is called activity. Is it activity? It is movement, it is agitation, it is something to do, because if you are left to yourself, you will be aware of that loneliness. So, you turn on the radio, or you pick up a book, or you run after somebody, or cry when that somebody leaves, or dies, because you are left with yourself.

So, without understanding that emptiness, going through with it, understanding it fully, completely, how can you help humanity? What is humanity? Yourself and another, is it not? You and your wife, you and your neighbor, the immediate world in which you live—not the Russian world or the Indian world, but the world you live in. If there is no understanding there, if there is conflict, misery, strife, jealousy, envy there, how can you help humanity at large? It has no meaning, has it? It is merely a phrase of the exploiter, of the lecturer.

So, without understanding yourself, without observing all your activities—the escapes, the process of covering up your own ugliness, your own poverty, your own strife, the pursuit of the Master, the pursuit of virtue—any of these activities must lead to confusion and enmity. So, all activity becomes an escape, without understanding yourself. But, the understanding of yourself does not come through isolation, through cessation of activity. Activity is obviously relationship; action is relationship, and if whatever you discover in that action is shunned, put away, suppressed, avoided, then such activity is bound to create mischief and misery. But if in action, which is relationship, you discover what you are—the pettiness, the shallowness, the snobbishness, the sense of domination, and so on—and be with what you are, then out of that comes action which is entirely different from the activity of escape. Then, that action is releasing, creative. That action is not the outcome of a self-enclosing movement.

And the questioner wants to know if individual creative expression is not a way of resolving the individual conflict. That is, if you have a conflict, go and paint and forget it, release yourself through color, through action, write a poem, go out for a walk, listen to a concert, pick up a book, go to church, think of the Master, serve humanity—do something. Will that put an end to conflict? Will that resolve the struggle, the pain? You may, as a scientist, be creative in your room, in your laboratory. Or you may paint creatively. But will that resolve your conflict? You may, at that moment of creative expression, escape from or put aside your conflict. But, the moment your work is finished, you are back again where you were, are you not? You may be a scientist, but the moment you leave your laboratory, you are an ordinary human being, are you not, with your prejudices, with your nationalism, with your pettiness, your ambition, and all the rest of it. Similarly, you may have moments of creative understanding, creative expression—and then you paint. But the moment you stop painting, you are back with yourself.

Surely, no action will help to put an end to conflict, no activity of any kind will resolve conflict. What resolves conflict is to be the conflict, completely; and you cannot be directly in relationship with conflict if you are trying to escape from it. And one of the many ways of escaping is to condemn it, to justify it, to suppress it, to sublimate it, to find a substitute for it. But, if we do not do any of these things but merely live with it, be passively aware, choicelessly aware of conflict, then the conflict itself will unfold its meaning; it will reveal its content, and only when the content of conflict is revealed is there freedom from conflict.

Therefore, a mind that is escaping is incapable of looking at *what is* with tranquillity. You may place that escape at any level—whether it be drink, a temple, knowledge, or sensation. As long as activity is merely an escape from *what is*, it must breed contention and enmity. But, if there is the understanding of *what is*, then there is liberation which brings its own action, and that action is entirely different from the activity of escape.

Question: No matter what you say, there are and there have to be leaders, guides, Masters, teachers. You yourself are one of them. What is your purpose in denying this obvious fact and creating a new conflict in us?

KRISHNAMURTI: Whether there are leaders, guides, Masters, and teachers is not important, but what is important is why you need them. If we begin to discuss whether there are or there are not Masters, guides, and teachers, we shall be lost in opinion and in so-called experience—which is really a self-projected reaction. But it is important, is it not, to find out why you demand leaders, why you follow teachers, why you worship Masters, why you obey gurus or guides. So, if you can find out why you want them, why you need them, then the problem can be tackled.

You need them, you'll say, because you are confused—you do not know in what direction to go. You need a refuge, a comfort, a crutch, somebody to lean on; you need the glorified father, the glorified mother; you want somebody to tell you what to do, give you a pattern for action, a code, someone to encourage you, to tell you how wonderful you are or that you are making progress. This all resolves itself into a very simple fact: that you are in conflict and confusion, you are in misery and strife, in hopeless unhappiness, caught in the everyday routine of boring relationship. So, either you create a romantic world of Masters, teachers, a romantic world of superknowledge, or, because you are confused, you want someone to help you to clear up the confusion.

So, in other words, you are confused, miserable, and you want help from someone to clarify that confusion. And what do you do? When, out of your confusion, you choose a leader, a guru, or a Master, that leader, that guru, that Master, must also be confused. Do you choose when there is clarity? If you are clear, there is no choice, there is no question of demanding, asking, looking for a guide. It is only when you are confused that you look for a guide, for a teacher—not when you are happy, not when you are joyous, not when you have completely forgotten yourself. It is only when you are with yourself, with your miseries, conflicts, and want to escape—only then do you look for a guide, and out of your confusion, you choose. Therefore, what you have chosen must also be confused. Therefore, your leaders are confused, whether political or religious.

So, you want someone to help you out of your confusion. In other words, you want to run away from your confusion. And those who give you the means of escape, you worship, you make leaders of. And what you have made, the confusion that you have created, is the outcome of yourself, the outcome of your environment, of your background, of your education, of your social and environmental influences. So, since you are yourself the cause of all this confusion, it is no good going away, seeking somebody to help you. You have to clear it up yourself. And as that is a painful task, you want to be romantic, sentimental. So you chase the gurus, the Masters, and create contention between the believer and the nonbeliever. Whereas, to be aware of your confusion, see all its intricacies, its subtleties, its structure, to understand who creates the confusion—confusion with regard to things, to property, to possessions; confusion with regard to people, to relationships; confusion with regard to ideas, what to believe and what not to believe, what is true and what is false—to be aware of all this process, not only at the superficial level of the mind, but also in the hidden depths, demands great alertness, great watchfulness. It does not demand any teacher, including myself. On the contrary, any teacher whom you choose will deceive you because you want to be deceived. But what *is* important is to watch this process of confusion, to be aware of it in your relationships. In the very awareness of *what is,* in the very awareness of this process of confusion, there is freedom.

Since it is our problem, yours and mine, you and I must clear it up, and not another. We have to be a light unto ourselves, not seek light from another. We are not candles to be lit by any savior. We have created this confusion in the world, which is the outcome of our own confusion, and we cannot clear it up, save through understanding ourselves. To understand ourselves, we do not need a Master. The Master will lead you astray, because the Master whom you choose is self-projected. To clear up this confusion, you have to observe yourself in relationship, which is action; you have to be aware of yourself in relationship, in action, from moment to moment, watching every word, every thought, every feeling, without any distortion, without any condemnation, looking at it simply, as you look at a child you love and wish to understand. Then there is freedom. Then you are no longer creating confusion. Confusion arises only as long as there is a center—the center of 'me' and 'mine', of accumulated memories, experiences, frustrations, and fears. And when that center does not exist, what need is there for a teacher, a Master, a guide?

What is important is not who is the teacher and who is the guide but to understand ourselves, for that brings about happiness, that brings creative joy. And that joy, that bliss, is not a thing that you can learn from a Master. You can learn the words, you can learn the technique, but the technique is not the thing, the word is not the real. Through a technique you cannot experience. Experiencing is a state in which the 'me' is nonexistent. The 'me' is the technique; the 'me' is the way through which we achieve a result, a gain, or through which we deny, and the 'me' can never be in that state of experiencing. After all, when you are experiencing something, there is no consciousness of the 'me'. But the 'me' exists as long as there is the consciousness of the center, demanding, denying, and creating confusion. That consciousness is a state of experience in which there is naming and recording. But if there is no recorder as the 'me', there is only the state of experiencing, and that experiencing of the real cannot take place without self-knowledge. Without knowing yourself, to follow another—it does not matter who it is, whether a political or a religious leader—leads to illusion, to destruction, to misery.

So, what is important is not to find out why you have created the leaders, the Masters, whether they exist or do not exist, whether their existence is factual or not, but why you follow them, why you listen, why you worship. You deny idolatry, and yet this is a form of idolatry. You deny the idols made by the hand, the carven image, but the image carved by the mind, you worship. They are all escapes from your own poverty, your own insufficiency, your own misery; and you can understand that conflict only when you confront yourself in relationship, which is action.

Question: What is true simplicity?

KRISHNAMURTI: To understand a question of this kind, we must not only consider it at the verbal level but also experience it directly. Perhaps we can experiment, at least for a few minutes, with this question. Though I shall be talking about it verbally, giving it an expression in order to communicate, we can still find out what is true simplicity, and experience it. It is the experiencing that is of vital importance, not the mere listening to words.

So, what is true simplicity? Obviously, to find out we must approach it negatively because our minds are stuffed with positive conceptions of what it is according to the dictionary, to the Bible, to the religious books, and so on. But, that is merely imitation, merely approximation. That is not simplicity. There is one obvious fact—that a mind that is crowded with conclusions is not a simple mind. Therefore, we can understand it only through the negative process.

So, simplicity does not begin with the loincloth. Possessing only a few essential things obviously does not indicate simplicity. Renunciation and its effect, which is pride, is not simplicity. There is no simplicity as long as the mind is trying to achieve a result, as long as the mind is becoming something, as long as the mind is caught in effort negatively or positively—to be or not to be. We seem to think simplicity consists mostly in having few possessions. Few possessions are convenient, that is all; if you want to travel, you have to travel lightly. But it's not a virtue; it doesn't make you simple.

Simplicity is for the mind to be free from belief, to be free from the struggle of becoming, to remain with *what is.* And a mind that is crowded with beliefs, struggles, effort, pursuing virtue, is not a simple mind. But unfortunately, we worship the outward expression of simplicity; because we have so crowded our life with things, with properties, with furniture, books, clothes, we worship anybody who denies all that; we think he is a marvelously simple person, a saint. Surely, that is not simplicity. Simplicity comes when the self is absent. And the self is when there is the desire to be, positively or negatively; and the desire to be creates complexity, confusion. So, out of fear, we deny this confusion, this complexity and pain, by worshipping the simple expression of having few things. Surely, the man who has given up the world but who lives in the world of ideas and beliefs, of hidden pursuits and secret ambitions, who is burning with his own desires, is not a simple person; he is not a saint. There is simplicity only when there is no desire to be something, positively or negatively; then the 'me' is absent; it is not identified with anything—with a nation, with a group, with a particular ideology or religious dogma. When that 'me' is totally absent, then there is simplicity, which expresses itself in the world of action. But to copy, to imitate, to try to have few things, and be crowded in our minds with ideas, beliefs, desires, passions—such a life is not the simpl life.

So, simplicity comes into being only with the process of understanding the complex 'me', the structure of myself. The more I understand *what is,* and the wider and deeper that understanding, the greater the freedom from conflict, from misery. And it is this freedom that brings simplicity. Then the mind is quiet; the mind is no longer crowded, pursuing. And as the pool is tranquil, so the mind is quiet when the whole process of effort is understood. And with the quietness of the mind, the timeless comes into being. That which is causeless is simple, and the causeless is the true. It cannot be invented by you because your inventions, your fabrications of the true have causation. But that which is true has no causation. God has no cause: it *is.* And for that state to be, the mind must be extraordinarily simple—not regimented, not disciplined, which is not simplicity, which is merely bondage. When the mind is simple, that which is a blessing comes into being.

October 30, 1949

Questions

Bangalore, 1948

Poona, 1948

New Delhi, 1948

Banaras, 1949

Ojai, 1949

London, 1949

Index

www.ingramcontent.com/pod-product-compliance
Lightning Source LLC
Jackson TN
JSHW060340310525
85040JS00003B/11
9781934989388